3D Graphics Rendering Cookbook

A comprehensive guide to exploring rendering algorithms in modern OpenGL and Vulkan

Sergey Kosarevsky

Viktor Latypov

BIRMINGHAM—MUMBAI

3D Graphics Rendering Cookbook

Copyright © 2021 Packt Publishing

Associate Group Product Manager: Pavan Ramchandani

Publishing Product Manager: Ashitosh Gupta

Senior Editor: Mark Dsouza

Content Development Editor: Divya Vijayan

Technical Editor: Joseph Aloocaran

Copy Editor: Safis Editing

Project Coordinator: Manthan Patel

Proofreader: Safis Editing

Indexer: Manju Arasan

Production Designer: Nilesh Mohite

First published: July 2021

Production reference: 1290721

Published by Packt Publishing Ltd.

Livery Place

35 Livery Street

Birmingham

B3 2PB, UK.

ISBN 978-1-83898-619-3

www.packt.com

To my mom, Irina Leonidovna Kosarevskaya, for your sacrifices;
to my granny, Ludmila Fedorovna Sitorkina,
for always cheering me on regardless of the hobbies I pursued;
to the memory of my grandpa, Leonid Mikhailovich Sirotkin
(1936-2013), for bringing me my first computer at the age of nine.

– Sergey Kosarevsky

To my daughter, Polina.

To my wife, Maria.

To my parents, Nikolai and Galina.

– Viktor Latypov

Contributors

About the authors

Sergey Kosarevsky is a rendering lead at Ubisoft RedLynx. He worked in the mobile industry at SPB Software, Yandex, Layar and Blippar, TWNKLS, and DAQRI, where he designed and implemented real-time rendering technology. He has more than 18 years of software development experience and more than 10 years of mobile and embedded 3D graphics experience. In his Ph.D. thesis, Sergey employed computer vision to solve mechanical engineering problems. He has co-authored several books on mobile software development in C++.

I wish to thank our reviewers and my friends, Alexander Pavlov, Anton Gerdelan, and Chris Forbes, for putting their time and effort into making this book happen. Thank you for your massive support, guys!

Viktor Latypov is a software engineer specializing in embedded C/C++, 3D graphics, and computer vision. With more than 15 years of software development experience and a Ph.D. in applied mathematics, he has implemented a number of real-time renderers for medical and automotive applications over the last 10 years.

Together with Sergey, he has co-authored two books on mobile software development in C++.

I would like to thank our reviewers for all their time, effort, and invaluable comments to make this book much better. Without you, we wouldn't have made it through the crazy year of 2020.

About the reviewers

Alexander Pavlov is a Senior Software Engineer with Google. He has more than 20 years of experience in various areas of industrial software development. His primary areas of interest are large-scale system design, compiler theory, and 3D graphics. Alexander is also an informal technical reviewer and proofreader behind the Android NDK Game Development Cookbook, published by Packt.

Chris Forbes works as a software developer for Google, working on Vulkan validation support and other ecosystem components. Previously, he has been involved in implementing OpenGL 3 and 4 support in open source graphics drivers for Linux [www.mesa3d.org], as well as rebuilding classic strategy games to run on modern systems [www.openra.net].

Anton Gerdelan is a computer graphics programmer and is most well known for writing an introductory book for graphics students, titled *Anton's OpenGL 4 Tutorials*, and recently, *Professional Programming Tools for C and C++*. Anton taught computer graphics and programming at Trinity College Dublin in Ireland, and at Blekinge Tekniska Högskola in Sweden. Anton is the Director of Engineering at Volograms.

Table of Contents

Preface

1

Establishing a Build Environment

2

Using Essential Libraries

3
Getting Started with OpenGL and Vulkan

4
Adding User Interaction and Productivity Tools

5

Working with Geometry Data

6

Physically Based Rendering Using the glTF2 Shading Model

7
Graphics Rendering Pipeline

8

Image-Based Techniques

9

Working with Scene Graphs

10
Advanced Rendering Techniques and Optimizations

Other Books You May Enjoy

Index

Preface

The *3D Graphics Rendering Cookbook* is your one-stop-shop practical guide to learning modern graphics rendering algorithms and techniques using the C++ programming language and APIs such as OpenGL and Vulkan. Starting with the configuration of your OpenGL and Vulkan development environment, you will immerse yourself in various common graphics development aspects, including shader development and handling geometrical data, among others. Going further, the book delves into building a 3D rendering engine, guiding you step by step through a number of small yet self-contained recipes. After each recipe, you will be able to incrementally add features to your code base while learning how to integrate numerous possible 3D graphics methods and algorithms into one big project. The book dives deep into the discussion of the relevant graphics techniques, such as physically-based rendering, image-based rendering, and CPU/GPU geometry culling, to name a few. You will be introduced to common techniques and solutions when dealing with large datasets for 2D and 3D rendering and will apply optimization techniques to build high-performance and feature-rich graphics applications. By the end of this book, you will be able to create fast and versatile 3D rendering frameworks, and have a solid understanding of best practices in modern graphics API programming.

This book is about rendering and will be focusing on modern, real-time, GPU-accelerated rendering techniques rather than on just one specific graphics API. Nonetheless, we will use the latest version of OpenGL, a programming interface for creating real-time 3D graphics, with a flavor of the *Approaching Zero Driver Overheads* philosophy. Some parallels with Vulkan will be drawn to demonstrate the differences between these two APIs and how all the rendering concepts and techniques discussed in the book can be implemented using both programming interfaces.

Who this book is for

We expect our readers to have a good grasp of real-time 3D graphics. The opening chapters explain what you need to get started with OpenGL and Vulkan. However, we will not focus for long on the basics and will quickly move forward to cover more sophisticated content instead. If you are familiar with OpenGL 3 or OpenGL ES 2 and want to learn more about modern rendering approaches and migration paths toward present-day rendering APIs, this book is probably a good fit for you.

Even though graphics programming might seem an easy and fun way to get into software development, it actually requires the mastery of numerous advanced programming concepts. The reader is expected to have a thorough understanding of modern C++ and some math skills, such as basic linear algebra and computational geometry.

What this book covers

This book is divided into distinct chapters. Each chapter covers specific aspects of 3D rendering and contributes more material to build a versatile 3D graphics demo by the end of the book, starting from the basics, then exposing more complicated approaches, and finally adding some advanced rendering techniques to the code:

Chapter 1, Establishing a Build Environment, explains the current state of OpenGL, its place in the computer world, and how it compares to Vulkan. The reader will learn which tools and dependencies are necessary to work with the source code of this book, as well as how to set them up.

Chapter 2, Using Essential Libraries, contains a set of recipes for the rapid building of minimalistic graphical applications in pure OpenGL and Vulkan from scratch using popular open source libraries, such as GLFW, GLM, STB, ImGui, EasyProfiler, Optick, AssImp, Etc2Comp, TaskFlow, and MeshOptimizer.

Chapter 3, Getting Started with OpenGL and Vulkan, covers basic aspects of rendering APIs, such as intercepting API calls, working with buffers and textures, converting between different texture formats, implementing programmable vertex pulling, and compiling Vulkan shaders to SPIR-V at runtime.

Chapter 4, Adding User Interaction and Productivity Tools, focuses primarily on debugging, profiling, and user interaction mechanisms. The reader will learn how to debug and profile graphical applications in different ways, starting with onscreen counters and graphs, then going into open source instrumenting profilers, and finishing with useful helper classes to allow interactive application debugging.

Chapter 5, Working with Geometry Data, teaches you how to deal with geometry data in a modern 3D rendering pipeline and also how to get comfortable with advanced topics such as geometry **Level of Detail** (**LOD**) and tessellation. Besides that, some GL shading language techniques will be discussed to show how various utility functions for geometry rendering can be implemented.

Chapter 6, Physically Based Rendering Using the glTF2 Shading Model, presents the glTF2 physically-based shading model and the ways to render it using the GL shading language in OpenGL and Vulkan. Different aspects of data preprocessing techniques will be covered, including the precalculation of **Bidirectional Reflectance Distribution Function** (**BRDF**) look-up tables and irradiance maps.

Chapter 7, Graphics Rendering Pipeline, goes into the representation of complex 3D scene data with multiple internal dependencies and cross-references. You will learn how to apply performance-oriented techniques such as data-oriented design to build a high-performance 3D rendering system. This is where the real OpenGL and Vulkan stuff begins to happen.

Chapter 8, Image-Based Techniques, contains a series of recipes on how to improve graphics rendering realism by using image-based techniques, such as screen space ambient occlusion, high dynamic range rendering with light adaptation, and projective shadow mapping.

Chapter 9, Working with Scene Graph, extends the series of scene graph-related recipes by showing how to modify scene data and extend it with components showing potential ways of scaling this approach to build a real-world graphics engine. This is followed by a short discussion on how to use a physics engine with a rendering engine.

Chapter 10, Advanced Rendering Techniques and Optimization, dives deeper into approaches to the construction of GPU-driven rendering pipelines, multithreaded rendering, and other advanced techniques for feature-rich graphics applications. Here, we conclude the book by combining numerous recipes and techniques into a single application.

To get the most out of this book

You will need a machine supporting OpenGL 4.6 and Vulkan 1.2 with the latest GPU drivers. All code examples in this book have been tested using Visual Studio 2019 on Windows 10 and GCC 8 on Linux. macOS users will be able to run only the very first demos from this book due to the lack of API support. To run our Bootstrap dependency downloader script, Python 3.x is required. CMake is used to build the source code.

Software/hardware covered in the book	OS requirements
Visual Studio 2019	Windows
GCC 8	Linux
Python 3.x	Windows, Linux
Vulkan SDK	Windows, Linux

We advise you to download the source code from the GitHub repository
(`https://github.com/PacktPublishing/3D-Graphics-Rendering-Cookbook`). **Doing so will help you avoid any potential errors related to the copying and pasting of code.**

Download the example code files

You can download the example code files for this book from GitHub at `https://github.com/PacktPublishing/3D-Graphics-Rendering-Cookbook`. If there's an update to the code, it will be updated in the GitHub repository.

We also have other code bundles from our rich catalog of books and videos available at `https://github.com/PacktPublishing/`. Check them out!

Download the color images

We also provide a PDF file that has color images of the screenshots/diagrams used in this book. You can download it here: `https://static.packt-cdn.com/downloads/9781838986193_ColorImages.pdf`.

Conventions used

There are a number of text conventions used throughout this book.

`Code in text`: Indicates code words in text, database table names, folder names, filenames, file extensions, pathnames, dummy URLs, user input, and Twitter handles. Here is an example: "After setting the project name, this macro uses the `GLOB_RECURSE` function to collect all source and header files into the `SRC_FILES` and `HEADER_FILES` variables."

A block of code is set as follows:

```
macro(SETUP_GROUPS src_files)
  foreach(FILE ${src_files})
    get_filename_component(PARENT_DIR "${FILE}" PATH)
```

When we wish to draw your attention to a particular part of a code block, the relevant lines or items are set in bold:

```
macro(SETUP_APP projname)
  set(PROJ_NAME ${projname})
  project(${PROJ_NAME})
```

Any command-line input or output is written as follows:

```
sudo apt-get update
```

Bold: Indicates a new term, an important word, or words that you see on screen. For example, words in menus or dialog boxes appear in the text like this. Here is an example: "Choose **Custom Installation** and make sure that the pip box is checked."

> **Tips or important notes**
> Appear like this.

Sections

In this book, you will find several headings that appear frequently (*Getting ready*, *How to do it...*, *How it works...*, *There's more...*, and *See also*).

To give clear instructions on how to complete a recipe, use these sections as follows:

Getting ready

This section tells you what to expect in the recipe and describes how to set up any software or any preliminary settings required for the recipe.

How to do it...

This section contains the steps required to follow the recipe.

How it works...

This section usually consists of a detailed explanation of what happened in the previous section.

There's more...

This section consists of additional information about the recipe in order to make you more knowledgeable about the recipe.

See also

This section provides helpful links to other useful information for the recipe.

Get in touch

Feedback from our readers is always welcome.

General feedback: If you have questions about any aspect of this book, mention the book title in the subject of your message and email us at customercare@packtpub.com.

Errata: Although we have taken every care to ensure the accuracy of our content, mistakes do happen. If you have found a mistake in this book, we would be grateful if you would report this to us. Please visit www.packtpub.com/support/errata and fill in the form.

Piracy: If you come across any illegal copies of our works in any form on the Internet, we would be grateful if you would provide us with the location address or website name. Please contact us at copyright@packt.com with a link to the material.

If you are interested in becoming an author: If there is a topic that you have expertise in and you are interested in either writing or contributing to a book, please visit authors.packtpub.com.

Share Your Thoughts

Once you've read *3D Graphics Rendering Cookbook*, we'd love to hear your thoughts! Scan the QR code below to go straight to the Amazon review page for this book and share your feedback.

https://packt.link/r/< 1838986197>

Your review is important to us and the tech community and will help us make sure we're delivering excellent quality content.

1
Establishing a Build Environment

In this chapter, we will learn how to set up 3D graphics development environment on your computer for Windows and Linux operating systems. We will cover the following recipes:

- OpenGL 4.6 with AZDO and Vulkan
- Setting up our development environment on Windows
- Setting up our development environment on Linux
- Installing the Vulkan SDK for Windows and Linux
- Managing dependencies
- Getting the demo data
- Creating utilities for CMake projects

Technical requirements

You can find the code files present in this chapter on GitHub at `https://github.com/PacktPublishing/3D-Graphics-Rendering-Cookbook/tree/master/Chapter1`

OpenGL 4.6 with AZDO and Vulkan

Approaching Zero Driver Overhead (**AZDO**) is not a single specific OpenGL feature. It is more of a set of techniques, a software development approach with OpenGL, and a way of structuring data access and API usage to make it faster by batching a lot of draw calls together. It was originally presented by Cass Everitt, Tim Foley, John McDonald, and Graham Sellers. Many things possible with Vulkan are also possible with OpenGL/AZDO. However, Vulkan is very different to OpenGL because it can precompile the pipeline state, while in modern OpenGL, a comparable level of performance can be achieved through a completely different set of methods; for example, bindless textures and buffers, programmable vertex pulling, and combining multiple draw calls into a single one.

There is a vendor-specific OpenGL extension, **NV_command_list**, from NVIDIA, which can compile OpenGL commands into a command list for efficient reuse. We will not be covering it here because it is not part of standard OpenGL. For those who are interested, here is the specification to read: `https://www.khronos.org/registry/OpenGL/extensions/NV/NV_command_list.txt`.

What is the essence of modern OpenGL?

First, let's focus on some of the modern OpenGL extensions that have made it into OpenGL Core and form the basis of AZDO, making the porting of OpenGL renderers to Vulkan easier, as well as helping to improve their performance in OpenGL:

- OpenGL 4.2:

  ARB_texture_storage introduces immutable textures whose metadata should be provided up front. For example, the classic `glTexImage()` function does not have any information on how many MIP levels would be required for a texture. The new `glTexStorage/glTextureStorage` API is more versatile and allows more driver-side optimizations.

- OpenGL 4.3:

  ARB_multi_draw_indirect (MDI) is batching "on steroids" and, compared to the classic *instancing*, can render a number of different geometries at once in a single draw call. This feature plays best when object data, such as geometry and material properties, is stored in large buffers. When combined with persistent mapped buffers, MDI buffers can be filled with commands from different threads. Pointers to the buffers can be passed to threads and do not require any OpenGL context to be available. The buffer content does not have to be regenerated every frame so it can be reused and even changed by the GPU directly. This allows for various GPU-based culling techniques and automatic level-of-detail implemented via compute shaders.

- OpenGL 4.4:

  ARB_buffer_storage gives better usage hints than `glBufferData()` and allows applications to pass additional information about the requested allocation to the implementation, which may use this information for further optimizations. Furthermore, this extension introduces the concept of persistent mapped buffers, which allow applications to retain mapped buffer pointers. To implement a buffer update workflow identical to Vulkan, OpenGL app developers should use persistent mapped buffers for all buffers that are expected to be used for read or write access on the CPU. Persistent mapped buffers allow multiple threads to write them without using OpenGL at all. This opens the possibility to do straightforward multi-threaded command buffer generation for MDI buffers.

  ARB_enhanced_layouts allows, among other things, the use of compile-time constant expressions in layout qualifiers and specifying explicit byte offsets within a uniform or shader storage block. These features are added on top of the explicit GLSL attribute locations functionality introduced in OpenGL 3.3, which allows us to explicitly specify our binding points. Vulkan uses hardcoded SPIR-V bindings as well and does not allow querying binding information at all.

- OpenGL 4.5:

  ARB_direct_state_access (DSA) provides a set of API functions to manipulate OpenGL objects, such as textures and buffers, directly rather than by means of the classic *bind-to-edit* approach. Using DSA allows one to modify an object state without affecting the global OpenGL state shared among all parts of the application. It also makes the API more Vulkan-like, enabling handle-based object access.

- OpenGL 4.6:

  GL_ARB_indirect_parameters allows us to store some parameters like draw count to MDI drawing commands inside buffers. This approach introduces even more possibilities to create novel GPU-driven rendering pipelines.

  GL_ARB_shader_draw_parameters adds new built-in variables to GLSL vertex shader inputs, `gl_BaseVertexARB` and `gl_BaseInstanceARB`, which contain the values passed in the `baseVertex` and `baseInstance` parameters of the draw call. Besides the two previously mentioned input variables, this extension adds the `gl_DrawID` variable to store the index of the draw call that is currently being processed by the MDI drawing commands.

  ARB_gl_spirv allows a SPIR-V module to be used as a shader stage in OpenGL. This extension is not directly related to the runtime performance or driver overhead per se. However, it allows the usage of the GL shading language compiler to produce binary modules consumable by both OpenGL and Vulkan, which makes porting to Vulkan more straightforward.

Besides the preceding core features of OpenGL, there are a few ARB OpenGL extensions that are considered to be a part of AZDO.

ARB_bindless_texture reinvents the binding of textures by using 64-bit handles instead of texture objects. Texture handles stored in buffers work fairly similarly to Vulkan's **DescriptorSets** and provide functionality comparable to **VK_EXT_descriptor_indexing**.

A very important thing to remember when switching from OpenGL/AZDO to Vulkan is that it is not necessarily going to give you any significant performance boost. The GPU hardware is the same and all the graphics rendering functionality exposed by Vulkan is almost identical to that found in OpenGL. One of the major Vulkan design goals is to considerably reduce the CPU time spent in the driver, therefore if your application is limited by the GPU rendering performance, it is highly unlikely that Vulkan will give you better performance.

Furthermore, there is a *Vulkan & OpenGL Threaded CAD Scene* sample from NVIDIA that compares various rendering code paths using modern OpenGL and Vulkan `https://developer.nvidia.com/vulkan-opengl-threaded-cad-scene-sample`. The result of this demo is that **NV_command_list** can deliver better performance than Vulkan on the CPU side, as it benefits from having the API designed directly with the hardware in mind.

Setting up our development environment on Windows

In this recipe, we will get started by setting up our development environment on Windows. We will go through the installation of each of the required tools individually and in detail.

Getting ready

In order to start working with the examples from this book in the Microsoft Windows environment, you will need some essential tools to be installed in your system.

The most important one is Microsoft Visual Studio 2019. Additional tools include the Git version control system, the CMake build tool, and the Python programming language. Throughout this book, we use these tools on the command line only, so no GUI add-ons will be required.

How to do it...

Let's install each of the required tools individually.

Microsoft Visual Studio 2019

Follow these steps to install Microsoft Visual Studio 2019:

1. Open `https://visualstudio.microsoft.com` and download the Visual Studio 2019 Community Edition installer.
2. Start the installer and follow the onscreen instructions. For the purposes of this book, you need to have a native C++ compiler for the 64-bit Intel platform. Other components of the Visual Studio development environment are not required to run the sample code.

Git

Follow these steps to install Git:

1. Download the Git installer from `https://git-scm.com/downloads`, run it, and follow the on-screen instructions.

2. We assume that Git is added to the system PATH variable. Enable the option shown in the following screenshot during installation:

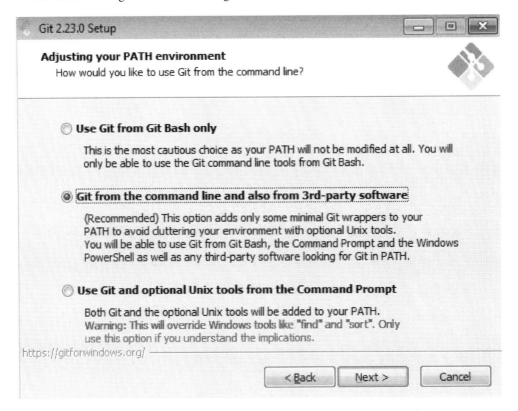

Figure 1.1 – Git from the command line and also from third-party software

3. Also, select **Use Windows' default console window** as shown in the next screenshot. This way, you will be able to run the build scripts from the book seamlessly from any directory on your computer:

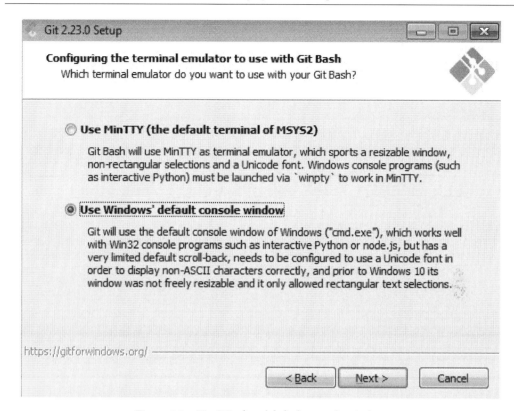

Figure 1.2 – Use Windows' default console window

> **Important note**
>
> Git is complex software and a huge topic in itself. We recommend the book *Mastering GIT, Jakub Narębski, Packt Publishing,* `https://www.packtpub.com/application-development/mastering-git`, along with the downloadable e-book *ProGit, Scott Chacon & Ben Straub, APress* at `https://git-scm.com/book/en/v2`.

CMake

To install CMake, please follow these steps:

1. Download the latest 64-bit CMake installer from `https://cmake.org/download/`.

2. Run it and follow the on-screen instructions. If you already have an earlier version of CMake installed, it is best to uninstall it first.

3. Select the **Add CMake to system PATH for all users** option, as shown here:

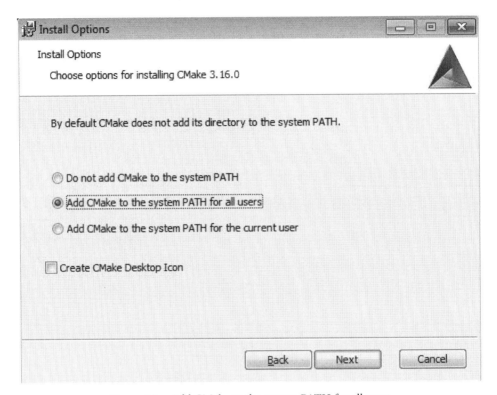

Figure 1.3 – Add CMake to the system PATH for all users

Python

To install Python, please follow these steps:

1. Download the Python 3 installer for 64-bit systems from https://www.python.org/downloads/.

2. Run it and follow the onscreen instructions.

3. During the installation, you also need to install the `pip` feature. Choose **Custom Installation** and make sure that the **pip** box is checked:

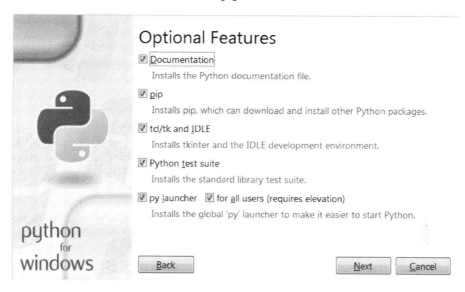

Figure 1.4 – Custom Installation options

4. Once the installation is complete, make sure to add the folder containing `python.exe` to the PATH environment variable.

There's more...

Besides Git, there are other popular version control systems, such as SVN and Mercurial. While developing large software systems, you will inevitably need to download some libraries from a non-Git repository. We recommend getting familiar with Mercurial.

While working in the command-line environment, it is useful to have some tools from the Unix environment, such as `wget`, `grep`, and `find`. The **GnuWin32** project provides precompiled binaries of these tools, which can be downloaded from `http://gnuwin32.sourceforge.net`.

Furthermore, in the Windows environment, orthodox file managers make file manipulation a lot easier. We definitely recommend giving the open source Far Manager a try. You can download it from `https://farmanager.com/index.php?l=en`. It is shown in the following screenshot:

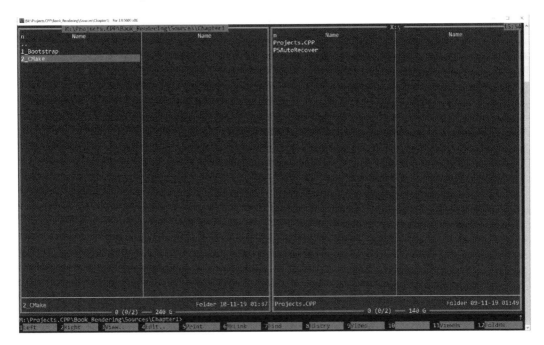

Figure 1.5 – The look and feel of Far Manager

Setting up our development environment on Linux

Linux is becoming more and more attractive for 3D graphics development, including gaming technology. Let's go through the list of the tools required to start working with this book on Linux.

Getting ready

We assume our reader has a desktop computer with a Debian-based GNU/Linux operating system installed. We also assume the reader is familiar with the apt package manager.

To start developing modern graphics programs on Linux, you need to have up-to-date video card drivers installed that support OpenGL 4.6 and Vulkan 1.2. To build the examples from this book, a C++ compiler with C++20 support is required. We use the GNU Compiler Collection.

How to do it...

On a Debian-based system, the installation process is straightforward. However, before installing any of the required packages, we recommend running the following command to ensure your system is up to date:

```
sudo apt-get update
```

Let's go through the list of essential software and install whatever is missing:

1. GCC Compiler

    Assuming you have a properly configured **apt** package manager, run the following command to install the GCC compiler and related tools:

    ```
    sudo apt-get install build-essential
    ```

2. CMake

    The CMake build tool is also available in the standard repositories. To install CMake, run the following command:

    ```
    sudo apt-get install cmake
    ```

    CMake 3.15 or above is sufficient for the code examples in this book.

3. Git

    To install the Git version control system, run the following command:

    ```
    sudo apt-get install git
    ```

4. Python 3

    To install the Python 3 package, run the following command:

    ```
    sudo apt-get install python3.7
    ```

    The exact version of Python may vary between distributions. Any version of Python 3 will suffice for the scripts in this book.

Now we are done with the basic packages, and we can install graphics-related software. Let's jump into the next recipe to learn how to deal with the Vulkan SDK.

Installing the Vulkan SDK for Windows and Linux

In this recipe, we will learn how to get started with the Vulkan SDK. We will describe the requirements and procedure for installing the LunarG Vulkan SDK for Windows and Linux.

In principle, it is possible to write Vulkan applications without the Vulkan SDK using only C/C++ header files provided by Khronos. You can get these header files by cloning the Git repository at `https://github.com/KhronosGroup/Vulkan-Headers`. However, it is advised to install the complete Vulkan SDK in order to use Vulkan Validation Layers and a standalone GLSL compiler.

Getting ready

Make sure you have the latest video card drivers for your operating system.

How to do it...

To install Vulkan 1.2 on Linux, follow these steps:

1. Open the `https://www.lunarg.com/vulkan-sdk/` page in a browser and download the appropriate Vulkan SDK for Windows or Linux.

2. After the download has finished, run the Windows installer file and follow the onscreen instructions. If you have Ubuntu 20.04 installed, use the following commands provided by LunarG's website:

    ```
    wget -qO - http://packages.lunarg.com/lunarg-signing-key-
    pub.asc | \
    sudo apt-key add -
    sudo wget -qO /etc/apt/sources.list.d/lunarg-vulkan-
    1.2.176-focal.list https://packages.lunarg.com/
    vulkan/1.2.176/lunarg-vulkan-1.2.176-focal.list
    sudo apt-get update
    sudo apt-get install vulkan-sdk
    ```

3. Alternatively, you may need to download the `.tar.gz` SDK archive and unpack it manually.

There's more...

We do not explicitly describe the development process on macOS because it seems to be a rather turbulent environment with frequent breaking changes in the development infrastructure. However, some general guidance is given along the way.

The installation of well-known frameworks mentioned in the following chapters is similar to Linux. Instead of Synaptic (apt), the installation is performed using the Brew or MacPorts package managers.

The OpenGL support is now deprecated for newer applications in favor of the Metal API, on top of which Vulkan is implemented in the **MoltenVK** library. The LunarG site `https://vulkan.lunarg.com` provides the macOS version of the Vulkan SDK, which is the MoltenVK package. Its installation guide can be found at `https://vulkan.lunarg.com/doc/sdk/latest/mac/getting_started.html`. Make sure you are using CMake version 3.15 or later so that the `find_package(Vulkan)` macro yields the correct results. Here are the steps required to install the Vulkan SDK on Linux:

1. Let's download and unpack the Vulkan SDK with the following commands:

    ```
    cd ~/
    wget https://sdk.lunarg.com/sdk/download/1.2.176.1/mac/
    vulkansdk-macos-1.2.176.1.dmg
    hdiutil mount vulkansdk-macos-1.2.176.1.dmg
    ```

2. Then we have to set a few environment variables. To make these settings permanent, add the following lines to `$HOME/.bash_profile`:

    ```
    export VULKAN_ROOT_LOCATION="$HOME/"
    export VULKAN_SDK_VERSION="1.2.176.1"
    export VULKAN_SDK="$VULKAN_ROOT_LOCATION/vulkansdk-macos-
    $VULKAN_SDK_VERSION/macOS"
    export VK_ICD_FILENAMES="$VULKAN_SDK/etc/vulkan/icd.d/
    MoltenVK_icd.json"
    export VK_LAYER_PATH="$VULKAN_SDK/etc/vulkan/explicit_
    layers.d"
    export PATH="$VULKAN_SDK/bin:$PATH"
    ```

This way you can install a new version of the SDK and only change the VULKAN_SDK_ VERSION value.

To check that your installation is correct, run `Applications/vkcube.app` from the SDK. To check whether you can build your Vulkan applications on macOS with CMake, create the following `CMakeLists.txt` file:

```
cmake_minimum_required(VERSION 3.15)
project("VulkanTest" CXX C)
find_package(Vulkan)
if (NOT Vulkan_FOUND)
message( FATAL_ERROR "Vulkan not found" )
endif()
```

If the output of `cmake -G "Unix Makefiles"` does not contain *Vulkan not found*, you are ready to use Vulkan in your macOS applications.

> **Important Note**
>
> When developing cross-platform applications, it is good to use similar tools for each platform. Since both macOS and Linux support GCC and Clang compilers, using GCC on Windows ensures that you avoid the most common portability issues. A complete package of C and C++ compilers can be downloaded from `http://www.equation.com/servlet/equation.cmd?fa=fortran`.
>
> An alternative way to use GCC on Windows is to install the MSys2 environment from `https://www.msys2.org`. It features the package management system used in Arch Linux, **Pacman**.

Managing dependencies

This book's examples use multiple open source libraries. To manage these dependencies, we use a free and open source tool called **Bootstrap**. The tool is similar to Google's **repo** tool and works both on Windows and Linux, as well as on macOS for that matter.

In this section, we learn how to use **Bootstrap** to download libraries using the Vulkan Headers repository as an example.

Getting ready

Make sure you have Git and Python installed, as described in the previous recipes. After that, clone the **source code bundle** repository from GitHub:

```
git clone https://github.com/PacktPublishing/3D-Graphics-
Rendering-Cookbook
```

How to do it...

Let's look into the source code bundle and run the `bootstrap.py` script:

```
bootstrap.py
```

The script will start downloading all the third-party libraries required to compile and run the source code bundle for this book. The tail of the output should look as follows:

```
Cloning into 'M:\Projects.CPP\Book_Rendering\Sources\deps\src\
assimp'...
remote: Enumerating objects: 25, done.
remote: Counting objects: 100% (25/25), done.
remote: Compressing objects: 100% (24/24), done.
remote: Total 51414 (delta 2), reused 10 (delta 1), pack-reused
51389
Receiving objects: 100% (51414/51414), 148.46 MiB | 3.95 MiB/s,
done.
Resolving deltas: 100% (36665/36665), done.
Checking out files: 100% (2163/2163), done.
```

Once the download process is complete, we are ready to build the project.

How it works...

Bootstrap takes a JSON file as input, opening `bootstrap.json` from the current directory by default. It contains metadata of libraries we want to download; for example, their names, where to retrieve them from, a specific version to download, and so on. Besides that, each used library can have some additional instructions on how to build it. They can be patches, unpacking instructions, SHA hashes to check archive integrity, and many others.

Source code location for each library can be represented by either a URL of a version control system repository or by an archive file with the library source files.

A typical JSON file entry corresponding to one library looks like in the following snippet. The `type` field can have one of the following values: `archive`, `git`, `hg`, or `svn`. The first value corresponds to an archive file, such as `.zip`, `.tar.gz`, `.tar.bz2`, while the last three types describe different version control system repositories. The `url` field contains a URL of the archive file to be downloaded or a URL of the repository. The `revision` field can specify a particular revision, tag, or branch to check out:

```
[
{
    "name": "vulkan",
    "source": {
        "type": "git",
        "url": "https://github.com/KhronosGroup/Vulkan-
            Headers.git",
```

```
        "revision": "v1.2.178"
    }
  }
]
```

The complete JSON file is a comma-separated list of such entries. For this recipe, we have got only one library to download. We will add more libraries in the next chapters. The accompanying source code bundle contains a JSON file with all the libraries used in this book.

There's more...

There is comprehensive documentation for this tool that describes other command-line options and JSON fields in great detail. It can be downloaded from `https://github.com/corporateshark/bootstrapping`.

The **Bootstrap** tool does not differentiate between source code and binary assets. All the textures, 3D models, and other resources for your application can also be downloaded, organized, and kept up to date automatically.

Getting the demo data

This book makes use of free 3D graphics datasets as much as possible. The comprehensive list of large 3D datasets is maintained by Morgan McGuire, Computer Graphics Archive, July 2017 (`https://casual-effects.com/data`). We will use some large 3D models from his archive for demonstration purposes in this book. Let's download and patch one of them.

How to do it

To download the entire dataset, follow these simple steps:

1. Open the `https://casual-effects.com/data/` page in a browser and find the **Amazon Lumberyard Bistro** dataset.

2. Click on the **Download** link and allow the browser to download all the data files. The following is a screenshot of Morgan McGuire's site with the download link:

Amazon Lumberyard Bistro

Created by Amazon Lumberyard for a 2017 GDC demo. Released publicly in the NVIDIA ORCA collection. The exterior contains 2,837,181 triangles and 2,910,304 vertices. The interior contains 1,020,907 triangles and 762,263 vertices.

This version has some manually remastered materials by Morgan McGuire to correct for limitations of the original OBJ export from Lumberyard, and it was split across multiple zipfiles to make downloading easier.Unzip each file into a directory of the same name or load the compressed files directly using the G3D Innovation Engine.

Download 2.4 GB

Cite this model as:

Triangles: 3858088
Vertices: 3672567
Updated: 2019-05-07
License: CC-BY 4.0
© 2017 Amazon Lumberyard

```
@misc{ORCAAmazonBistro,
    title = {Amazon Lumberyard Bistro, Open Research Content Archive (ORCA)},
    author = {Amazon Lumberyard},
    year = {2017},
    month = {July},
    note = {\small \texttt{http://developer.nvidia.com/orca/amazon-lumberyard-bistro}},
    url = {http://developer.nvidia.com/orca/amazon-lumberyard-bistro}
}
```

Figure 1.6 – Amazon Lumberyard Bistro as pictured on casualeffects.com as a 2.4-GB download

There's more...

Some of the material properties in the downloaded dataset should be updated. Use the interior.mtl and exterior.mtl files from the https://github.com/corporateshark/bistro_materials repository to replace the corresponding ones from the downloaded dataset.

Creating utilities for CMake projects

In this recipe, we will see how CMake is used to configure all the code examples in this book and learn some small tricks along the way.

> **Note**
>
> For those who are just starting with CMake, we recommend reading the books *CMake Cookbook* (*Radovan Bast and Roberto Di Remigio*), *Packt Publishing* and *Mastering CMake* (*Ken Martin and Bill Hoffman*), *Kitware*.

Getting ready

For a starter, let's create a minimalistic C++ application with a trivial main() function and build it using CMake:

```
int main()
{
    return 0;
}
```

How to do it...

Let's introduce two helper macros for CMake. You can find them in the CMake/CommonMacros.txt file of our source code bundle:

1. The SETUP_GROUPS macro iterates over a space-delimited list of C and C++ files, whether it is a header or source file, and assigns each file into a separate group. The group name is constructed based on the path of each individual file. This way we end up with a nice folder-like directory structure in the Visual Studio Solution Explorer window, as we can see on the right in the following screenshot:

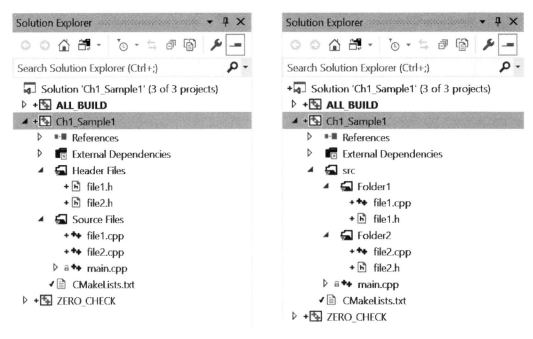

Figure 1.7 – Without groups (left) and with groups (right)

2. The macro starts by iterating over a list of files passed in the `src_files` parameter:

```
macro(SETUP_GROUPS src_files)
  foreach(FILE ${src_files})
    get_filename_component(PARENT_DIR "${FILE}" PATH)
```

3. We store the parent directory name as a default group name and replace all the backslash characters with forward slashes:

```
    set(GROUP "${PARENT_DIR}")
    string(REPLACE "/" "\\" GROUP "${GROUP}")
```

4. Then, we can tell CMake to assign the current file into a source group with this name:

```
    source_group("${GROUP}" FILES "${FILE}")
  endforeach()
endmacro()
```

5. The second macro, `SETUP_APP` is used as a shortcut to create a new CMake project with all the standard properties we want it to have. It is very convenient when you have a number of very similar subprojects, like in this book:

```
macro(SETUP_APP projname)
  set(PROJ_NAME ${projname})
  project(${PROJ_NAME})
```

6. After setting the project name, this macro uses the `GLOB_RECURSE` function to collect all source and header files into the `SRC_FILES` and `HEADER_FILES` variables:

```
  file(GLOB_RECURSE SRC_FILES LIST_DIRECTORIES
    false RELATIVE
    ${CMAKE_CURRENT_SOURCE_DIR} src/*.c??)
  file(GLOB_RECURSE HEADER_FILES LIST_DIRECTORIES
    false RELATIVE
    ${CMAKE_CURRENT_SOURCE_DIR} src/*.h)
```

7. In all our code samples, we use the `src` directory containing the source files as an `include` directory as well:

```
  include_directories(src)
```

8. All enumerated source and header files are added to an executable inside the current project:

```
  add_executable(${PROJ_NAME} ${SRC_FILES}
                 ${HEADER_FILES})
```

9. We use the previously mentioned SETUP_GROUP macro to place each source and header file into an appropriate group inside the project:

```
SETUP_GROUPS("${SRC_FILES}")
SETUP_GROUPS("${HEADER_FILES}")
```

10. The next three properties set different executable filenames for each supported build configuration. These lines are optional, yet they are really useful when using CMake with the Visual Studio IDE. The reason is that Visual Studio can change build configurations (or build types, as they are called in CMake) dynamically directly from the IDE, and each build configuration can have its own output filename. We add prefixes to these filenames so that they can co-exist in a single output folder:

```
set_target_properties(${PROJ_NAME}
   PROPERTIES OUTPUT_NAME_DEBUG ${PROJ_NAME}_Debug)
set_target_properties(${PROJ_NAME}
   PROPERTIES OUTPUT_NAME_RELEASE
${PROJ_NAME}_Release)
set_target_properties(${PROJ_NAME}
   PROPERTIES OUTPUT_NAME_RELWITHDEBINFO
${PROJ_NAME}_ReleaseDebInfo)
```

11. Since we use C++20 throughout this book, we require CMake to enable it.

```
set_property(TARGET ${PROJ_NAME} PROPERTY
CXX_STANDARD 20)
set_property(TARGET ${PROJ_NAME} PROPERTY
CXX_STANDARD_REQUIRED ON)
```

12. To make debugging with Visual Studio easier, we enable console the output by changing the application type to Console. We also set the local debugger working directory to CMAKE_SOURCE_DIR, which will make finding assets a lot more straightforward and consistent:

```
if(MSVC)
  add_definitions(-D_CONSOLE)
  set_property(TARGET ${PROJ_NAME} PROPERTY
              VS_DEBUGGER_WORKING_DIRECTORY
              "${CMAKE_SOURCE_DIR}")
  endif()
endmacro()
```

13. Finally, the top-level `CMakeLists.txt` file of our first project will look like this:

```
cmake_minimum_required(VERSION 3.12)
project(Chapter1)
include(../../CMake/CommonMacros.txt)
SETUP_APP(Ch1_Sample2_CMake "Chapter 01")
```

You may notice that the `project(Chapter1)` line is overridden by a call to `project()` inside the `SETUP_APP` macro. This is due to the following CMake warning, which will be emitted if we do not declare a new project right from the get-go:

```
CMake Warning (dev) in CMakeLists.txt:
No project() command is present. The top-level
CMakeLists.txt file must contain a literal, direct
call to the project() command. Add a line of
project(ProjectName) near the top of the file, but after
cmake_minimum_required().
```

14. To build and test the executable, create the `build` subfolder, change the working directory to `build`, and run CMake as follows:

- For Windows and Visual Studio 2019, run the following command to configure our project for the 64-bit target platform architecture:

```
cmake .. -G "Visual Studio 16 2019" -A x64
```

- For Linux, we can use the `Unix Makefiles` CMake generator as follows:

```
cmake .. -G "Unix Makefiles"
```

- To build an executable for the **release** build type, you can use the following command on any platform:

```
cmake --build . --config Release
```

All the demo applications from the source code bundle should be run from the folder where the `data/` subfolder is located.

There's more...

Alternatively, you can use the cross-platform build system **Ninja** along with CMake. It is possible to do so simply by changing the CMake project generator name:

```
cmake .. -G "Ninja"
```

Invoke Ninja from the command line to compile the project:

```
ninja
[2/2] Linking CXX executable Ch1_Sample1.exe
```

Notice how quickly everything gets built now, compared to the classic cmake --build command. See https://ninja-build.org for more details.

2
Using Essential Libraries

There are many production-quality open source C++ libraries and frameworks out there. One of the traits of an experienced graphics developer is their comprehensive knowledge of available open source libraries that are suitable for getting the job done.

In this chapter, we will learn about essential open source libraries and tools that can bring a great productivity boost for you as a developer of graphical applications.

In this chapter, we will cover the following recipes:

- Using the GLFW library
- Doing math with GLM
- Loading images with STB
- Rendering a basic UI with Dear ImGui
- Integrating EasyProfiler
- Integrating Optick
- Using the Assimp library
- Getting started with Etc2Comp
- Multithreading with Taskflow
- Introducing MeshOptimizer

Technical requirements

You can find the code files present in this chapter on GitHub at `https://github.com/PacktPublishing/3D-Graphics-Rendering-Cookbook/tree/master/Chapter2`

Using the GLFW library

The GLFW library hides all the complexity of creating windows, graphics contexts, and surfaces, and getting input events from the operating system. In this recipe, we build a minimalistic application with GLFW and OpenGL to get some basic 3D graphics out onto the screen.

Getting ready

We are building our examples with GLFW 3.3.4. Here is a JSON snippet for the Bootstrap script so that you can download the proper library version:

```json
{
  "name": "glfw",
  "source": {
    "type": "git",
    "url": "https://github.com/glfw/glfw.git",
    "revision": "3.3.4"
  }
}
```

The complete source code for this recipe can be found in the source code bundle under the name of `Chapter2/01_GLFW`.

How to do it...

Let's write a minimal application that creates a window and waits for an exit command from the user. Perform the following steps:

1. First, we set the GLFW error callback via a simple lambda to catch potential errors:

    ```cpp
    #include <GLFW/glfw3.h>
    ...
    int main() {
      glfwSetErrorCallback(
    ```

```
[] ( int error, const char* description ) {
    fprintf( stderr, "Error: %s\n", description );
});
```

2. Now, we can go forward to try to initialize GLFW:

```
if ( !glfwInit() )
    exit(EXIT_FAILURE);
```

3. The next step is to tell GLFW which version of OpenGL we want to use. Throughout this book, we will use OpenGL 4.6 Core Profile. You can set it up as follows:

```
glfwWindowHint(GLFW_CONTEXT_VERSION_MAJOR, 4);
glfwWindowHint(GLFW_CONTEXT_VERSION_MINOR, 6);
glfwWindowHint(
    GLFW_OPENGL_PROFILE, GLFW_OPENGL_CORE_PROFILE);
GLFWwindow* window = glfwCreateWindow(
    1024, 768, "Simple example", nullptr, nullptr);
if (!window) {
    glfwTerminate();
    exit( EXIT_FAILURE );
}
```

4. There is one more thing we need to do before we can focus on the OpenGL initialization and the main loop. Let's set a callback for key events. Again, a simple lambda will do for now:

```
glfwSetKeyCallback(window,
    [](GLFWwindow* window,
        int key, int scancode, int action, int mods) {
        if ( key == GLFW_KEY_ESCAPE && action ==
            GLFW_PRESS )
                glfwSetWindowShouldClose(
                    window, GLFW_TRUE );
    });
```

5. We should prepare the OpenGL context. Here, we use the GLAD library to import all OpenGL entry points and extensions:

```
glfwMakeContextCurrent( window );
gladLoadGL( glfwGetProcAddress );
glfwSwapInterval( 1 );
```

Now we are ready to use OpenGL to get some basic graphics out. Let's draw a colored triangle. To do that, we need a vertex shader and a fragment shader, which are both linked to a shader program, and a **vertex array object** (**VAO**). Follow these steps:

1. First, let's create a VAO. For this example, we will use the vertex shader to generate all vertex data, so an empty VAO will be sufficient:

    ```
    GLuint VAO;
    glCreateVertexArrays( 1, &VAO );
    glBindVertexArray( VAO );
    ```

2. To generate vertex data for a colored triangle, our vertex shader should look as follows. Those familiar with previous versions of OpenGL 2.x will notice the layout qualifier with the explicit location value for vec3 color. This value should match the corresponding location value in the fragment shader, as shown in the following code:

    ```
    static const char* shaderCodeVertex = R"(
    #version 460 core
    layout (location=0) out vec3 color;
    const vec2 pos[3] = vec2[3](
      vec2(-0.6, -0.4),
      vec2(0.6, -0.4),
      vec2(0.0, 0.6)
    );
    const vec3 col[3] = vec3[3](
      vec3(1.0, 0.0, 0.0),
      vec3(0.0, 1.0, 0.0),
      vec3(0.0, 0.0, 1.0)
    );
    void main() {
      gl_Position = vec4(pos[gl_VertexID], 0.0, 1.0);
      color = col[gl_VertexID];
    }
    )";
    ```

> **Important note**
>
> More details on **OpenGL Shading Language** (**GLSL**) layouts can be found in the official Khronos documentation at https://www.khronos.org/opengl/wiki/Layout_Qualifier_(GLSL).

We use the GLSL built-in `gl_VertexID` input variable to index into the `pos []` and `col []` arrays to generate the vertex positions and colors programmatically. In this case, no user-defined inputs to the vertex shader are required.

3. For the purpose of this recipe, the fragment shader is trivial. The location value of 0 of the `vec3 color` variable should match the corresponding location in the vertex shader:

```
static const char* shaderCodeFragment = R"(
#version 460 core
layout (location=0) in vec3 color;
layout (location=0) out vec4 out_FragColor;
void main() {
  out_FragColor = vec4(color, 1.0);
};
)";
```

4. Both shaders should be compiled and linked to a shader program. Here is how we do it:

```
const GLuint shaderVertex =
  glCreateShader(GL_VERTEX_SHADER);
glShaderSource(
  shaderVertex, 1, &shaderCodeVertex, nullptr);
glCompileShader(shaderVertex);
const GLuint shaderFragment =
  glCreateShader(GL_FRAGMENT_SHADER);
glShaderSource(shaderFragment, 1,
  &shaderCodeFragment, nullptr);
glCompileShader(shaderFragment);
const GLuint program = glCreateProgram();
glAttachShader(program, shaderVertex);
glAttachShader(program, shaderFragment);
glLinkProgram(program);
glUseProgram(program);
```

For the sake of brevity, all error checking is omitted in this chapter. We will come back to it in the next *Chapter 3, Getting Started with OpenGL and Vulkan*.

Now, when all of the preparations are complete, we can jump into the GLFW main loop and examine how our triangle is being rendered.

Let's explore how a typical GLFW application works. Perform the following steps:

1. The main loop starts by checking whether the window should be closed:

```
while ( !glfwWindowShouldClose(window) ) {
```

2. Implement a resizable window by reading the current width and height from GLFW and updating the OpenGL viewport accordingly:

```
int width, height;
glfwGetFramebufferSize(
   window, &width, &height);
glViewport(0, 0, width, height);
```

> **Important note**
>
> Another approach is to set a GLFW window resize callback via `glfwSetWindowSizeCallback()`. We will use this later on for more complicated examples.

3. Clear the screen and render the triangle. The `glDrawArrays()` function can be invoked with the empty VAO that we bound earlier:

```
glClearColor(1.0f, 1.0f, 1.0f, 1.0f);
glClear(GL_COLOR_BUFFER_BIT);
glDrawArrays(GL_TRIANGLES, 0, 3);
```

4. The fragment shader output was rendered into the back buffer. Let's swap the front and back buffers to make the triangle visible. To conclude the main loop, do not forget to poll the events with `glfwPollEvents()`:

```
glfwSwapBuffers(window);
glfwPollEvents();
}
```

5. To make things nice and clean at the end, let's delete the OpenGL objects that we created and terminate GLFW:

```
glDeleteProgram(program);
glDeleteShader(shaderFragment);
glDeleteShader(shaderVertex);
glDeleteVertexArrays(1, &VAO);
```

```
glfwDestroyWindow(window);
glfwTerminate();
return 0;
}
```

Here is a screenshot of our tiny application:

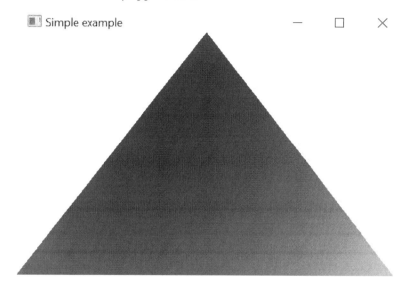

Figure 2.1 – Our first triangle is on the screen

There's more...

The GLFW setup for macOS is quite similar to the Windows operating system. In the CMakeLists.txt file, you should add the following line to the list of used libraries: -framework OpenGL -framework Cocoa -framework CoreView -framework IOKit.

Further details about how to use GLFW can be found at https://www.glfw.org/documentation.html.

Doing math with GLM

Every 3D graphics application needs some sort of math utility functions, such as basic linear algebra or computational geometry. This book uses the **OpenGL Mathematics** (**GLM**) header-only C++ mathematics library for graphics, which is based on the GLSL specification. The official documentation (`https://glm.g-truc.net`) describes GLM as follows:

> *GLM provides classes and functions designed and implemented with the same naming conventions and functionalities as GLSL so that anyone who knows GLSL, can use GLM as well as C++.*

Getting ready

Get the latest version of GLM using the Bootstrap script. We use version 0.9.9.8:

```
{
  "name": "glm",
  "source": {
    "type": "git",
    "url": "https://github.com/g-truc/glm.git",
    "revision": "0.9.9.8"
  }
}
```

Let's make use of some linear algebra and create a more complicated 3D graphics example. There are no lonely triangles this time. The full source code for this recipe can be found in `Chapter2/02_GLM`.

How to do it...

Let's augment the example from the previous recipe using a simple animation and a 3D cube. The model and projection matrices can be calculated inside the main loop based on the window aspect ratio, as follows:

1. To rotate the cube, the model matrix is calculated as a rotation around the diagonal `(1, 1, 1)` axis, and the angle of rotation is based on the current system time returned by `glfwGetTime()`:

```
const float ratio = width / (float)height;
const mat4 m = glm::rotate(
  glm::translate(mat4(1.0f), vec3(0.0f, 0.0f, -3.5f)),
  (float)glfwGetTime(), vec3(1.0f, 1.0f, 1.0f));
```

```
const mat4 p = glm::perspective(
   45.0f, ratio, 0.1f, 1000.0f);
```

2. Now we should pass the matrices into shaders. We use a **uniform** buffer to do that. First, we need to declare a C++ structure to hold our data:

```
struct PerFrameData {
   mat4 mvp;
   int isWireframe;
};
```

The first field, mvp, will store the premultiplied model-view-projection matrix. The isWireframe field will be used to set the color of the wireframe rendering to make the example more interesting.

3. The buffer object to hold the data can be allocated as follows. We use the **Direct-State-Access (DSA)** functions from OpenGL 4.6 instead of the classic bind-to-edit approach:

```
const GLsizeiptr kBufferSize = sizeof(PerFrameData);
GLuint perFrameDataBuf;
glCreateBuffers(1, &perFrameDataBuf);
glNamedBufferStorage(perFrameDataBuf, kBufferSize,
   nullptr, GL_DYNAMIC_STORAGE_BIT);
glBindBufferRange(GL_UNIFORM_BUFFER, 0,
   perFrameDataBuf, 0, kBufferSize);
```

The GL_DYNAMIC_STORAGE_BIT parameter tells the OpenGL implementation that the content of the data store might be updated after creation through calls to glBufferSubData(). The glBindBufferRange() function binds a range within a buffer object to an indexed buffer target. The buffer is bound to the indexed target of 0. This value should be used in the shader code to read data from the buffer.

4. In this recipe, we are going to render a 3D cube, so a depth test is required to render the image correctly. Before we jump into the shaders' code and our main loop, we need to enable the depth test and set the polygon offset parameters:

```
glEnable(GL_DEPTH_TEST);
glEnable(GL_POLYGON_OFFSET_LINE);
glPolygonOffset(-1.0f, -1.0f);
```

Polygon offset is needed to render a wireframe image of the cube on top of the solid image without Z-fighting. The values of -1.0 will move the wireframe rendering slightly toward the camera.

Let's write the GLSL shaders that are needed for this recipe:

1. The vertex shader for this recipe will generate cube vertices in a procedural way. This is similar to what we did in the previous triangle recipe. Notice how the `PerFrameData` input structure in the following vertex shader reflects the `PerFrameData` structure in the C++ code that was written earlier:

```
static const char* shaderCodeVertex = R"(
#version 460 core
layout(std140, binding = 0) uniform PerFrameData {
  uniform mat4 MVP;
  uniform int isWireframe;
};
layout (location=0) out vec3 color;
```

2. The positions and colors of cube vertices should be stored in two arrays. We do not use normal vectors here, which means we can perfectly share 8 vertices among all the 6 adjacent faces of the cube:

```
const vec3 pos[8] = vec3[8](
  vec3(-1.0,-1.0, 1.0), vec3( 1.0,-1.0, 1.0),
  vec3(1.0, 1.0, 1.0), vec3(-1.0, 1.0, 1.0),

  vec3(-1.0,-1.0,-1.0), vec3(1.0,-1.0,-1.0),
  vec3( 1.0, 1.0,-1.0), vec3(-1.0, 1.0,-1.0)
);
const vec3 col[8] = vec3[8](
  vec3(1.0, 0.0, 0.0), vec3(0.0, 1.0, 0.0),
  vec3(0.0, 0.0, 1.0), vec3(1.0, 1.0, 0.0),

  vec3(1.0, 1.0, 0.0), vec3(0.0, 0.0, 1.0),
  vec3(0.0, 1.0, 0.0), vec3(1.0, 0.0, 0.0)
);
```

3. Let's use indices to construct the actual cube faces. Each face consists of two triangles:

```
const int indices[36] = int[36](
  // front
  0, 1, 2, 2, 3, 0,
  // right
  1, 5, 6, 6, 2, 1,
```

```
// back
7, 6, 5, 5, 4, 7,
// left
4, 0, 3, 3, 7, 4,
// bottom
4, 5, 1, 1, 0, 4,
// top
3, 2, 6, 6, 7, 3
);
```

4. The `main()` function of the vertex shader looks similar to the following code block. The `gl_VertexID` input variable is used to retrieve an index from `indices[]`, which is used to get corresponding values for the position and color. If we are rendering a wireframe pass, set the vertex color to black:

```
void main() {
    int idx = indices[gl_VertexID];
    gl_Position = MVP * vec4(pos[idx], 1.0);
    color = isWireframe > 0 ? vec3(0.0) : col[idx];
}
)";
```

5. The fragment shader is trivial and simply applies the interpolated color:

```
static const char* shaderCodeFragment = R"(
#version 460 core
layout (location=0) in vec3 color;
layout (location=0) out vec4 out_FragColor;
void main()
{
    out_FragColor = vec4(color, 1.0);
};
)";
```

The only thing we are missing now is how we update the uniform buffer and submit actual draw calls. We update the buffer twice per frame, that is, once per each draw call:

1. First, we render the solid cube with the polygon mode set to `GL_FILL`:

```
PerFrameData perFrameData = {
    .mvp = p * m,
    .isWireframe = false
};
```

```
glNamedBufferSubData(
  perFrameDataBuf, 0, kBufferSize, &perFrameData);
glPolygonMode(GL_FRONT_AND_BACK, GL_FILL);
glDrawArrays(GL_TRIANGLES, 0, 36);
```

2. Then, we update the buffer and render the wireframe cube using the GL_
    LINE polygon mode and the -1.0 polygon offset that we set up earlier with
    glPolygonOffset():

```
perFrameData.isWireframe = true;
glNamedBufferSubData(
  perFrameDataBuf, 0, kBufferSize, &perFrameData);
glPolygonMode(GL_FRONT_AND_BACK, GL_LINE);
glDrawArrays(GL_TRIANGLES, 0, 36);
```

The resulting image should look similar to the following screenshot:

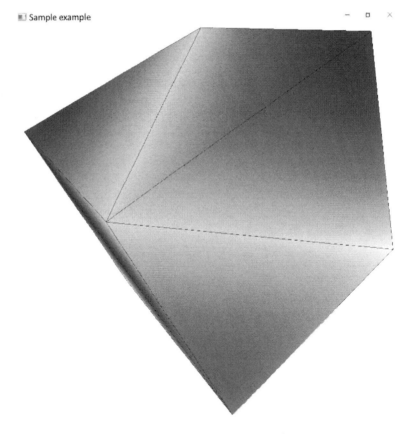

Figure 2.2 – The rotating 3D cube with wireframe contours

There's more...

As you might have noticed in the preceding code, the `glBindBufferRange()` function takes an offset into the buffer as one of its input parameters. That means we can make the buffer twice as large and store two different copies of `PerFrameData` in it. One with `isWireframe` set to `true` and another one set to `false`. Then, we can update the entire buffer with just one call to `glNamedBufferSubData()`, instead of updating the buffer twice, and use the offset parameter of `glBindBufferRange()` to feed the correct instance of `PerFrameData` into the shader. This is the correct and most attractive approach, too.

The reason we decided not to use it in this recipe is that the OpenGL implementation might impose alignment restrictions on the value of `offset`. For example, many implementations require `offset` to be a multiple of `256`. Then, the actual required alignment can be queued as follows:

```
GLint alignment;
glGetIntegerv(
   GL_UNIFORM_BUFFER_OFFSET_ALIGNMENT, &alignment);
```

The alignment requirement would make the simple and straightforward code of this recipe more complicated and difficult to follow without providing any meaningful performance improvements. In more complicated real-world use cases, particularly as the number of different values in the buffer goes up, this approach becomes more useful.

Loading images with STB

Almost every graphics application requires texture images to be loaded from files in some image file formats. Let's take a look at the STB image loader and discuss how we can use it to support popular formats, such as `.jpeg`, `.png`, and a floating point format `.hdr` for high dynamic range texture data.

Getting ready

The STB project consists of multiple header-only libraries. The entire up-to-date package can be downloaded from `https://github.com/nothings/stb`:

```
{
   "name": "stb",
   "source": {
     "type": "git",
     "url": "https://github.com/nothings/stb.git",
```

```
    "revision": "c9064e317699d2e495f36ba4f9ac037e88ee371a"
  }
}
```

The demo source code for this recipe can be found in `Chapter2/03_STB`.

How to do it...

Let's add texture mapping to the previous recipe. Perform the following steps:

1. The STB library has separate headers for loading and saving images. Both can be included within your project, as follows:

```
#define STB_IMAGE_IMPLEMENTATION
#include <stb/stb_image.h>
#define STB_IMAGE_WRITE_IMPLEMENTATION
#include <stb/stb_image_write.h>
```

2. To load an image as a 3-channel RGB image from any supported graphics file format, use this short code snippet:

```
int w, h, comp;
const uint8_t* img = stbi_load(
  "data/ch2_sample3_STB.jpg", &w, &h, &comp, 3);
```

3. Besides that, we can save images into various image file formats. Here is a snippet that enables you to save a screenshot from an OpenGL GLFW application:

```
int width, height;
glfwGetFramebufferSize(window, &width, &height);
uint8_t* ptr = (uint8_t*)malloc(width * height * 4);
glReadPixels(0, 0, width, height, GL_RGBA,
  GL_UNSIGNED_BYTE, ptr);
stbi_write_png(
  "screenshot.png", width, height, 4, ptr, 0);
free(ptr);
```

Please check `stb_image.h` and `stb_image_write.h` for a list of supported file formats.

4. The loaded `img` image can be used as an OpenGL texture in a DSA fashion, as follows:

```
GLuint texture;
glCreateTextures(GL_TEXTURE_2D, 1, &texture);
glTextureParameteri(texture, GL_TEXTURE_MAX_LEVEL, 0);
glTextureParameteri(
    texture, GL_TEXTURE_MIN_FILTER, GL_LINEAR);
glTextureParameteri(
    texture, GL_TEXTURE_MAG_FILTER, GL_LINEAR);
glTextureStorage2D(texture, 1, GL_RGB8, w, h);
glPixelStorei(GL_UNPACK_ALIGNMENT, 1);
glTextureSubImage2D(texture, 0, 0, 0, w, h, GL_RGB,
    GL_UNSIGNED_BYTE, img);
glBindTextures(0, 1, &texture);
```

Please refer to the source code in `Chapter2/03_STB` for a complete working example and the GLSL shader changes that are necessary to apply the texture to our cube.

There's more...

STB supports the loading of high-dynamic-range images in Radiance `.HDR` file format. Use the `stbi_loadf()` function to load files as floating-point images. This will preserve the full dynamic range of the image and will be useful to load high-dynamic-range light probes for physically-based lighting in the *Chapter 6, Physically Based Rendering Using the glTF2 Shading Model*.

Rendering a basic UI with Dear ImGui

Graphical applications require some sort of UI. The interactive UI can be used to debug real-time applications and create powerful productivity and visualization tools. Dear ImGui is a fast, portable, API-agnostic immediate-mode GUI library for C++ developed by Omar Cornut (`https://github.com/ocornut/imgui`):

> *Dear ImGui is designed to enable fast iterations and to empower programmers to create content creation tools and visualization/debug tools (as opposed to UI for the average end user). It favors simplicity and productivity toward this goal and lacks certain features normally found in more high-level libraries. Dear ImGui is particularly suited to integration in game engines (for tooling), real-time 3D applications, full-screen applications, embedded applications, or any applications on gaming consoles where operating system features can be non-standard.*

The ImGui library provides numerous comprehensive examples that explain how to make a GUI renderer for different APIs, including a 700-line code example using OpenGL 3 and GLFW (`imgui/examples/imgui_impl_opengl3.cpp`). In this recipe, we will demonstrate how to make a minimalistic ImGui renderer in 200 lines of code using OpenGL 4.6. This is not feature-complete, but it can serve as a good starting point for those who want to integrate ImGui into their own modern graphical applications.

Getting ready

Our example is based on ImGui version v1.83. Here is a JSON snippet for our Bootstrap script so that you can download the library:

```
{
  "name": "imgui",
  "source": {
    "type": "git",
    "url": "https://github.com/ocornut/imgui.git",
    "revision" : "v1.83"
  }
}
```

The full source code can be found in `Chapter2/04_ImGui`.

How to do it...

Let's start by setting up the vertex arrays, buffers, and shaders that are necessary to render our UI. Perform the following steps:

1. To render geometry data coming from ImGui, we need a VAO with vertex and index buffers. We will use an upper limit of 256 kilobytes for the indices and vertices data:

```
GLuint VAO;
glCreateVertexArrays(1, &VAO);
GLuint handleVBO;
glCreateBuffers(1, &handleVBO);
glNamedBufferStorage(handleVBO, 256 * 1024, nullptr,
  GL_DYNAMIC_STORAGE_BIT);
GLuint handleElements;
glCreateBuffers(1, &handleElements);
glNamedBufferStorage(handleElements, 256 * 1024,
  nullptr, GL_DYNAMIC_STORAGE_BIT);
```

2. The geometry data consist of 2D vertex positions, texture coordinates, and RGBA colors, so we should configure the vertex attributes as follows:

```
glVertexArrayElementBuffer(VAO, handleElements);
glVertexArrayVertexBuffer(
   VAO, 0, handleVBO, 0, sizeof(ImDrawVert));
glEnableVertexArrayAttrib(VAO, 0);
glEnableVertexArrayAttrib(VAO, 1);
glEnableVertexArrayAttrib(VAO, 2);
```

The `ImDrawVert` structure is a part of ImGui, which is declared as follows:

```
struct ImDrawVert {
   ImVec2 pos;
   ImVec2 uv;
   ImU32  col;
};
```

3. Vertex attributes corresponding to the positions, texture coordinates, and colors are stored in an interleaved format and should be set up like this:

```
glVertexArrayAttribFormat(
   VAO, 0, 2, GL_FLOAT, GL_FALSE,
   IM_OFFSETOF(ImDrawVert, pos));
glVertexArrayAttribFormat(
   VAO, 1, 2, GL_FLOAT, GL_FALSE,
   IM_OFFSETOF(ImDrawVert, uv));
glVertexArrayAttribFormat(
   VAO, 2, 4, GL_UNSIGNED_BYTE, GL_TRUE,
   IM_OFFSETOF(ImDrawVert, col));
```

The `IM_OFFSETOF()` macro is a part of ImGui, too. It is used to calculate the offset of member fields inside the `ImDrawVert` structure. The macro definition itself is quite verbose and platform-dependent. Please refer to `imgui/imgui.h` for implementation details.

4. The final touch to the VAO is to tell OpenGL that every vertex stream should be read from the same buffer bound to the binding point with an index of `0`:

```
glVertexArrayAttribBinding(VAO, 0, 0);
glVertexArrayAttribBinding(VAO, 1, 0);
glVertexArrayAttribBinding(VAO, 2, 0);
glBindVertexArray(VAO);
```

5. Now, let's take a quick look at the shaders that are used to render our UI. The vertex
    shader looks similar to the following code block. The `PerFrameData` structure in
    the shader corresponds to the similar structure of the C++ code:

```
const GLchar* shaderCodeVertex = R"(
  #version 460 core
  layout (location = 0) in vec2 Position;
  layout (location = 1) in vec2 UV;
  layout (location = 2) in vec4 Color;
  layout (std140, binding = 0) uniform PerFrameData
  {
      uniform mat4 MVP;
  };
  out vec2 Frag_UV;
  out vec4 Frag_Color;
  void main()
  {
      Frag_UV = UV;
      Frag_Color = Color;
      gl_Position = MVP * vec4(Position.xy,0,1);
  }
)";
```

6. The fragment shader simply modulates the vertex color with a texture. It should
    appear as follows:

```
const GLchar* shaderCodeFragment = R"(
  #version 460 core
  in vec2 Frag_UV;
  in vec4 Frag_Color;
  layout (binding = 0) uniform sampler2D Texture;
  layout (location = 0) out vec4 out_Color;
  void main()
{
      out_Color = Frag_Color * texture(
        Texture, Frag_UV.st);
  }
)";
```

7. The vertex and fragment shaders are compiled and linked in a similar way to the *Using the GLFW library* recipe, so some parts of the code here have been skipped for the sake of brevity. Please refer to the source code bundle for the complete example:

```
const GLuint handleVertex =
  glCreateShader(GL_VERTEX_SHADER);...
const GLuint handleFragment =
  glCreateShader(GL_FRAGMENT_SHADER);...
const GLuint program = glCreateProgram();...
glUseProgram(program);
```

These were the necessary steps to set up vertex arrays, buffers, and shaders for UI rendering. There are still some initialization steps that need to be done for ImGui itself before we can render anything. Follow these steps:

1. Let's set up the data structures that are needed to sustain an ImGui context:

```
ImGui::CreateContext();
ImGuiIO& io = ImGui::GetIO();
```

2. Since we are using `glDrawElementsBaseVertex()` for rendering, which has a vertex offset parameter of `baseVertex`, we can tell ImGui to output meshes with more than 65535 vertices that can be indexed with 16-bit indices. This is generally good for performance, as it allows you to render the UI with fewer buffer updates:

```
io.BackendFlags |=
  ImGuiBackendFlags_RendererHasVtxOffset;
```

3. Now, let's build a texture atlas that will be used for font rendering. ImGui will take care of the `.ttf` font loading and create a font atlas bitmap, which we can use as an OpenGL texture:

```
ImFontConfig cfg = ImFontConfig();
```

4. Tell ImGui that we are going to manage the memory ourselves:

```
cfg.FontDataOwnedByAtlas = false;
```

5. Brighten up the font a little bit (the default value is `1.0f`). Brightening up small fonts is a good trick you can use to make them more readable:

```
Cfg.RasterizerMultiply = 1.5f;
```

6. Calculate the pixel height of the font. We take our default window height of `768` and divide it by the desired number of text lines to be fit in the window:

```
cfg.SizePixels = 768.0f / 32.0f;
```

7. Align every glyph to the pixel boundary and rasterize them at a higher quality for sub-pixel positioning. This will improve the appearance of the text on the screen:

```
cfg.PixelSnapH = true;
cfg.OversampleH = 4;
cfg.OversampleV = 4;
```

8. And, finally, load a `.ttf` font from a file:

```
ImFont* Font = io.Fonts->AddFontFromFileTTF(
    "data/OpenSans-Light.ttf", cfg.SizePixels, &cfg);
```

Now, when the ImGui context initialization is complete, we should take the font atlas bitmap created by ImGui and use it to create an OpenGL texture:

1. First, let's take the font atlas bitmap data from ImGui in 32-bit RGBA format and upload it to OpenGL:

```
unsigned char* pixels = nullptr;
int width, height;
io.Fonts->GetTexDataAsRGBA32(
    &pixels, &width, &height);
```

2. The texture creation code should appear as follows:

```
GLuint texture;
glCreateTextures(GL_TEXTURE_2D, 1, &texture);
glTextureParameteri(texture, GL_TEXTURE_MAX_LEVEL, 0);
glTextureParameteri(
    texture, GL_TEXTURE_MIN_FILTER, GL_LINEAR);
glTextureParameteri(
    texture, GL_TEXTURE_MAG_FILTER, GL_LINEAR);
glTextureStorage2D(
    texture, 1, GL_RGBA8, width, height);
```

3. Scanlines in the ImGui bitmap are not padded. Disable the pixel unpack alignment in OpenGL by setting its value to 1 byte to handle this correctly:

```
glPixelStorei(GL_UNPACK_ALIGNMENT, 1);
glTextureSubImage2D(texture, 0, 0, 0,
```

```
        width, height, GL_RGBA, GL_UNSIGNED_BYTE, pixels);
    glBindTextures(0, 1, &texture);
```

4. We should pass the texture handle to ImGui so that we can use it in subsequent draw calls when required:

```
    io.Fonts->TexID = (ImTextureID)(intptr_t)texture;
    io.FontDefault = Font;
    io.DisplayFramebufferScale = ImVec2(1, 1);
```

Now we are ready to proceed with the OpenGL state setup for rendering. All ImGui graphics should be rendered with blending and the scissor test turned on and the depth test and backface culling disabled. Here is the code snippet to set this state:

```
glEnable(GL_BLEND);
glBlendEquation(GL_FUNC_ADD);
glBlendFunc(GL_SRC_ALPHA, GL_ONE_MINUS_SRC_ALPHA);
glDisable(GL_CULL_FACE);
glDisable(GL_DEPTH_TEST);
glEnable(GL_SCISSOR_TEST);
```

Let's go into the main loop and explore, step by step, how to organize the UI rendering workflow:

1. The main loop starts in a typical GLFW manner, as follows:

```
while ( !glfwWindowShouldClose(window) ) {
    int width, height;
    glfwGetFramebufferSize(window, &width, &height);
    glViewport(0, 0, width, height);
    glClear(GL_COLOR_BUFFER_BIT);
```

2. Tell ImGui our current window dimensions, start a new frame, and render a demo UI window with ShowDemoWindow():

```
    ImGuiIO& io = ImGui::GetIO();
    io.DisplaySize =
      ImVec2( (float)width, (float)height );
    ImGui::NewFrame();
    ImGui::ShowDemoWindow();
```

3. The geometry data is generated in the `ImGui::Render()` function and can be retrieved via `ImGui::GetDrawData()`:

```
ImGui::Render();
const ImDrawData* draw_data = ImGui::GetDrawData();
```

4. Let's construct a proper orthographic projection matrix based on the left, right, top, and bottom clipping planes provided by ImGui:

```
Const float L = draw_data->DisplayPos.x;
const float R = draw_data->DisplayPos.x +
                draw_data->DisplaySize.x;
const float T = draw_data->DisplayPos.y;
const float B = draw_data->DisplayPos.y +
                draw_data->DisplaySize.y;
const mat4 orthoProj = glm::ortho(L, R, B, T);
glNamedBufferSubData( perFrameDataBuffer, 0,
   sizeof(mat4), glm::value_ptr(orthoProj) );
```

5. Now we should go through all of the ImGui command lists, update the content of the index and vertex buffers, and invoke the rendering commands:

```
for (int n = 0; n < draw_data->CmdListsCount; n++) {
    const ImDrawList* cmd_list =
    draw_data->CmdLists[n];
```

6. Each ImGui command list has vertex and index data associated with it. Use this data to update the appropriate OpenGL buffers:

```
glNamedBufferSubData(handleVBO, 0,
   (GLsizeiptr)cmd_list->VtxBuffer.Size *
   sizeof(ImDrawVert), cmd_list->VtxBuffer.Data);
glNamedBufferSubData(handleElements, 0,
   (GLsizeiptr)cmd_list->IdxBuffer.Size *
   sizeof(ImDrawIdx), cmd_list->IdxBuffer.Data);
```

7. Rendering commands are stored inside the command buffer. Iterate over them and render the actual geometry:

```
for (int cmd_i = 0; cmd_i < cmd_list->
    CmdBuffer.Size; cmd_i++ )
{
    const ImDrawCmd* pcmd =
      &cmd_list->CmdBuffer[cmd_i];
    const ImVec4 cr = pcmd->ClipRect;
```

```
    glScissor(
        (int)cr.x, (int)(height - cr.w),
        (int)(cr.z - cr.x), (int)(cr.w - cr.y) );

    glBindTextureUnit(
        0, (GLuint)(intptr_t)pcmd->TextureId);

    glDrawElementsBaseVertex(GL_TRIANGLES,
        (GLsizei)pcmd->ElemCount, GL_UNSIGNED_SHORT,
        (void*)(intptr_t)(pcmd->IdxOffset *
        sizeof(ImDrawIdx)), (GLint)pcmd->VtxOffset);

    }

}
```

8. After the UI rendering is complete, reset the scissor rectangle and do the usual
    GLFW stuff to swap the buffers and poll user events:

```
    glScissor(0, 0, width, height);
    glfwSwapBuffers(window);
    glfwPollEvents();
}
```

Once we exit the main loop, we should destroy the ImGui context with
`ImGui::DestroyContext()`. OpenGL object deletion is similar to some of the
previous recipes and will be omitted here for the sake of brevity.

The preceding code will render the UI. To enable user interaction, we need to pass user
input events from GLWF to ImGui. Let's demonstrate how to deal with the mouse input to
make our minimalistic UI interactive:

1. First, let's install a cursor position callback for GLFW:

```
glfwSetCursorPosCallback(window,
    []( auto* window, double x, double y ) {
        ImGui::GetIO().MousePos = ImVec2(x, y );
    });
```

2. The final thing we need to bring our UI to life is to set the mouse button callback
    and route the mouse button events into ImGui:

```
glfwSetMouseButtonCallback(window,
    [](auto* window, int button, int action, int mods) {
        auto& io = ImGui::GetIO();
        int idx = button == GLFW_MOUSE_BUTTON_LEFT ?
            0 : button == GLFW_MOUSE_BUTTON_RIGHT ? 2 : 1;
        io.MouseDown[idx] = action == GLFW_PRESS;
    });
```

Now we can run our demo application. The application for this recipe renders a Dear ImGui demo window. If everything has been done correctly, the resulting output should look similar to the following screenshot. It is possible to interact with the UI using a mouse:

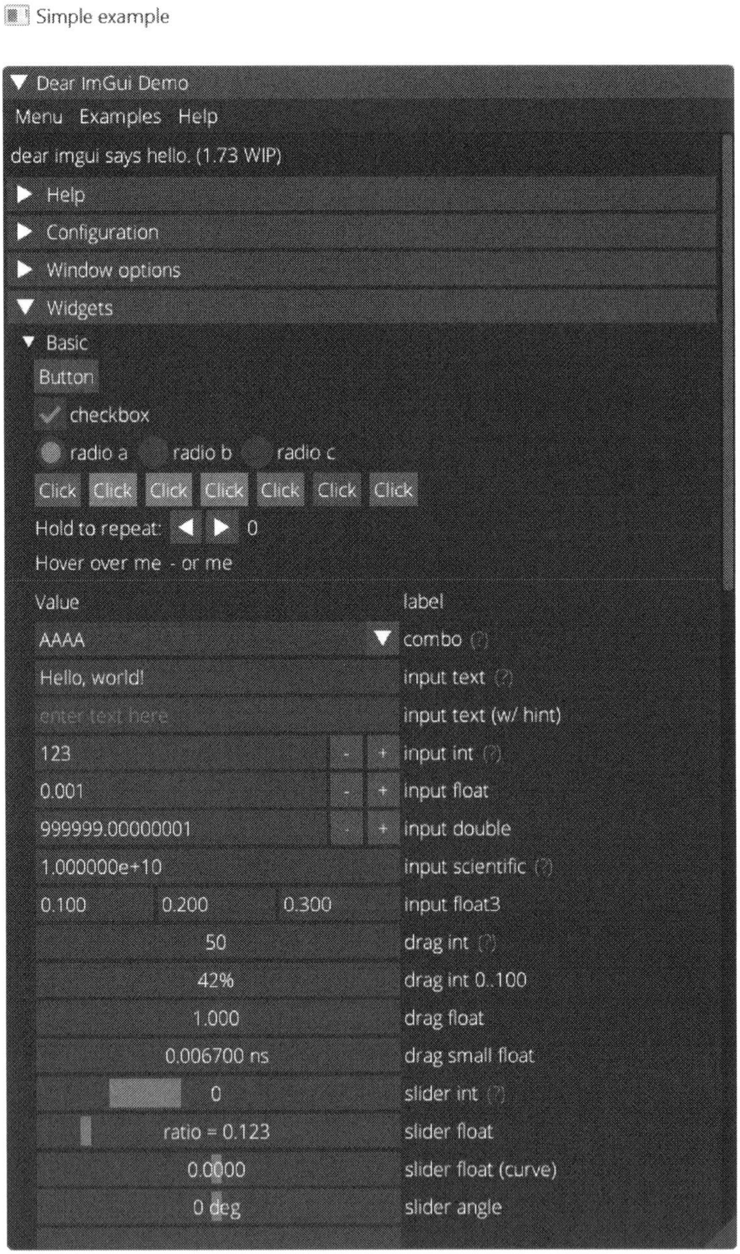

Figure 2.3 – The Dear ImGui demo window

There's more...

Our minimalistic implementation skipped some features that were needed to handle all ImGui rendering possibilities. For example, we did not implement user-defined rendering callbacks or the handling of flipped clipping rectangles. Please refer to `imgui/examples/imgui_impl_opengl3.cpp` for more details.

Another important part is to pass all of the necessary GLFW events into ImGui, including numerous keyboard events, cursor shapes, scrolling, and more. The complete reference implementation can be found in `imgui/examples/imgui_impl_glfw.cpp`.

Integrating EasyProfiler

Profiling enables developers to get vital measurement data and feedback in order to optimize the performance of their applications. EasyProfiler is a lightweight cross-platform profiler library for C++, which can be used to profile multithreaded graphical applications (`https://github.com/yse/easy_profiler`).

Getting ready

Our example is based on EasyProfiler version 2.1. The JSON snippet for Bootstrap to download it looks like this:

```json
{
  "name": "easy_profiler",
  "source": {
    "type": "archive",
    "url": "https://github.com/yse/easy_profiler/
            releases/download/v2.1.0/
            easy_profiler-v2.1.0-msvc15-win64.zip",
    "sha1": "d7b99c2b0e18e4c6f963724c0ff3a852a34b1b07"
  }
}
```

There are two CMake options to set up in `CMakeLists.txt` so that we can build EasyProfiler without the GUI and demo samples:

```
set(EASY_PROFILER_NO_GUI ON CACHE BOOL "")
set(EASY_PROFILER_NO_SAMPLES ON CACHE BOOL "")
```

Now we are good to go and can use it in our application. The full source code for this recipe can be found in `Chapter2/05_EasyProfiler`.

How to do it...

Let's build a small application that integrates EasyProfiler and outputs a profiling report. Perform the following steps:

1. First, let's initialize EasyProfiler at the beginning of our `main()` function:

```
#include <easy/profiler.h>
...
int main() {
  EASY_MAIN_THREAD;
  EASY_PROFILER_ENABLE;
  ...
```

2. Now we can manually mark up blocks of code to be reported by the profiler:

```
EASY_BLOCK("Create resources");
const GLuint shaderVertex =
  glCreateShader(GL_VERTEX_SHADER);
...
const GLuint shaderFragment =
  glCreateShader(GL_FRAGMENT_SHADER);
...
GLuint perFrameDataBuffer;
glCreateBuffers(1, &perFrameDataBuffer);
...
EASY_END_BLOCK;
```

Blocks can be automatically scoped. So, once we exit a C++ scope via `}`, the block will be automatically ended even if there is no explicit call to `EASY_END_BLOCK`, as shown in the following snippet:

```
{
    EASY_BLOCK("Set state");
    glClearColor(1.0f, 1.0f, 1.0f, 1.0f);
    glEnable(GL_DEPTH_TEST);
    glEnable(GL_POLYGON_OFFSET_LINE);
    glPolygonOffset(-1.0f, -1.0f);
}
```

3. Let's create some nested blocks inside the main loop. We use `std::this_ thread::sleep_for( std::chrono::milliseconds(2) )` to simulate some heavy computations inside blocks:

```cpp
while ( !glfwWindowShouldClose(window) ) {
    EASY_BLOCK("MainLoop");
    ...
    {
        EASY_BLOCK("Pass1");
        std::this_thread::sleep_for(
        std::chrono::milliseconds(2) );
        ...
    }
    {
        EASY_BLOCK("Pass2");
        std::this_thread::sleep_for(
        std::chrono::milliseconds(2) );
        ...
    }
    {
        EASY_BLOCK("glfwSwapBuffers()");
        glfwSwapBuffers(window);
    }
    {
        EASY_BLOCK("glfwPollEvents()");
        std::this_thread::sleep_for(
        std::chrono::milliseconds(2) );
        glfwPollEvents();
    }
}
```

4. At the end of the main loop, we save the profiling data to a file like this:

```cpp
profiler::dumpBlocksToFile( "profiler_dump.prof" );
```

Now we can use the GUI tool to inspect the results.

How it works...

On Windows, we use the precompiled version of `profiler_gui.exe`, which comes with EasyProfiler:

```
profiler_gui.exe profiler_dump.prof
```

The output should look similar to the following screenshot:

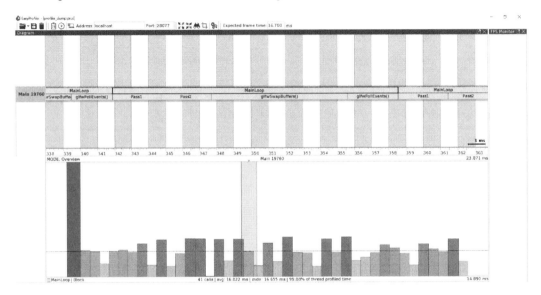

Figure 2.4 – The EasyProfiler GUI

There's more...

Blocks can have different colors, for example, `EASY_BLOCK("Block1", profiler::colors::Magenta)`. Besides that, there is an `EASY_FUNCTION()` macro that will automatically create a block using the current function name as the block name. Custom ARGB colors can be used in the hexadecimal notation; for example, take a look at the following:

```
void bar() {
  EASY_FUNCTION(0xfff080aa);
}
```

Integrating Optick

There are numerous profiling libraries for C++ that are useful for 3D graphics development. Some of them are truly generic, such as the one in the previous recipe, while others have specific functionality for profiling graphics applications. There is yet another popular, super-lightweight C++ open source profiler for games, called Optick (`https://github.com/bombomby/optick`). Besides Windows, Linux, and macOS, it supports Xbox and PlayStation 4 (for certified developers), as well as GPU counters in Direct3D 12 and Vulkan.

Getting ready

We use Optick version 1.3.1, which can be downloaded with the following Bootstrap script:

```
{
  "name": "optick",
  "source": {
    "type": "git",
    "url": "https://github.com/bombomby/optick.git",
    "revision": "1.3.1.0"
  }
}
```

If you want to compile the Optick GUI for Linux or macOS, please refer to the official documentation at `https://github.com/bombomby/optick/wiki/How-to-start%3F-(Programmers-Setup)`. The source code for this recipe can be found in `Chapter2/06_Optick`.

How to do it...

Integration with Optick is similar to EasyProfiler. Let's go through it step by step:

1. To start the capture, use the following two macros near the beginning of the `main()` function:

```
OPTICK_THREAD("MainThread");
OPTICK_START_CAPTURE();
```

2. To mark up blocks for profiling, use the `OPTICK_PUSH()` and `OPTICK_POP()` macros, as follows:

```
{
  OPTICK_PUSH( "Pass1" );
  std::this_thread::sleep_for(
  std::chrono::milliseconds(2) );
  . . .
  OPTICK_POP();
}
{
  OPTICK_PUSH( "Pass2" );
  std::this_thread::sleep_for(
  std::chrono::milliseconds(2) );
  . . .
  OPTICK_POP();
}
```

Blocks defined with `OPTICK_PUSH()` do not close automatically at the scope exit; therefore, an explicit call to `OPTICK_POP()` is required.

3. At the end of the main loop, we save the profiling data to a file like this:

```
OPTICK_STOP_CAPTURE();
OPTICK_SAVE_CAPTURE("profiler_dump");
```

Now we can compile and run the demo application. The capture data will be saved inside a `.opt` file with the appended date and time: `profiler_dump(2019-11-30.07-34-53).opt`. Let's examine what the profiling results look like next.

How it works...

After the demo application exits, run the Optick GUI with the following command to inspect the profiling report:

```
Optick.exe "profiler_dump(2019-11-30.07-34-53).opt"
```

The output should be similar to the following screenshot. Each CPU frame can be inspected by clicking on it in the flame graph:

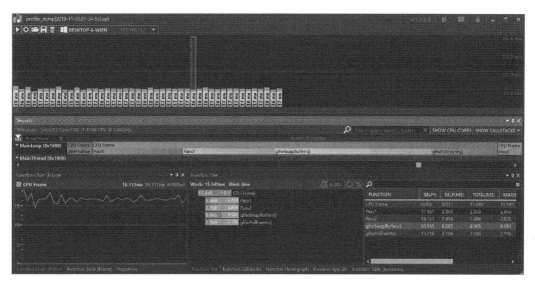

Figure 2.5 – The Optick GUI

> **Note**
>
> Building the Optick GUI for Linux or macOS is not possible since it is written in C# and requires at least the MS VS 2010 CMake generator.

There's more...

Optick provides integration plugins for Unreal Engine 4. For more details, please refer to the documentation at `https://github.com/bombomby/optick/wiki/UE4-Optick-Plugin`.

At the time of writing this book, building the Optick GUI was only possible on Windows. Therefore, Linux and OS X can only be used for data collection.

Using the Assimp library

Open Asset Import Library, which can be shortened to Assimp, is a portable open source C++ library that can be used to load various popular 3D model formats in a uniform manner.

Getting ready

We will use Assimp version 5.0 for this recipe. Here is the Bootstrap JSON snippet that you can use to download it:

```json
{
  "name": "assimp",
  "source": {
    "type": "git",
    "url": "https://github.com/assimp/assimp.git",
    "revision": "a9f82dbe0b8a658003f93c7b5108ee4521458a18"
  }
}
```

Before we can link to Assimp, let's disable the unnecessary functionality in `CMakeLists.txt`. We will only be using the `.obj` and `.gltf` 3D format importers throughout this book:

```
set(ASSIMP_NO_EXPORT ON CACHE BOOL "")
set(ASSIMP_BUILD_ASSIMP_TOOLS OFF CACHE BOOL "")
set(ASSIMP_BUILD_TESTS OFF CACHE BOOL "")
set(ASSIMP_INSTALL_PDB OFF CACHE BOOL "")
set(
  ASSIMP_BUILD_ALL_IMPORTERS_BY_DEFAULT OFF CACHE BOOL "")
set(ASSIMP_BUILD_OBJ_IMPORTER ON CACHE BOOL "")
set(ASSIMP_BUILD_GLTF_IMPORTER ON CACHE BOOL "")
```

The full source code can be found in `Chapter2/07_Assimp`.

How to do it...

Let's load a 3D model from a `.glft2` file via Assimp. The simplest code to do this will look like this:

1. First, we request the library to convert any geometric primitives it might encounter into triangles:

```
const aiScene* scene = aiImportFile(
   "data/rubber_duck/scene.gltf",
   aiProcess_Triangulate);
```

2. Additionally, we do some basic error checking, as follows:

```
if ( !scene || !scene->HasMeshes() ) {
   printf("Unable to load file\n");
   exit( 255 );
}
```

3. Now we can convert the loaded 3D scene into a data format that we can use to upload the model into OpenGL. For this recipe, we will only use vertex positions in `vec3` format without indices:

```
std::vector<vec3> positions;
const aiMesh* mesh = scene->mMeshes[0];
for (unsigned int i = 0; i != mesh->mNumFaces; i++) {
   const aiFace& face = mesh->mFaces[i];
   const unsigned int idx[3] = { face.mIndices[0],
      face.mIndices[1], face.mIndices[2] };
```

4. To keep this example as simple as possible, we can flatten all of the indices and store only the vertex positions. Swap the `y` and `z` coordinates to orient the model:

```
for (int j = 0; j != 3; j++) {
      const aiVector3D v = mesh->mVertices[idx[j]];
      positions.push_back( vec3(v.x, v.z, v.y) );
   }
}
```

5. Now we can deallocate the `scene` pointer with `aiReleaseImport(scene)` and upload the content of `positions[]` into an OpenGL buffer:

```
GLuint VAO;
glCreateVertexArrays(1, &VAO);
glBindVertexArray(VAO);
GLuint meshData;
glCreateBuffers(1, &meshData);
glNamedBufferStorage(meshData,
  sizeof(vec3) * positions.size(),
  positions.data(), 0);
glVertexArrayVertexBuffer(
  VAO, 0, meshData, 0, sizeof(vec3) );
glEnableVertexArrayAttrib(VAO, 0 );
glVertexArrayAttribFormat(
  VAO, 0, 3, GL_FLOAT, GL_FALSE, 0);
glVertexArrayAttribBinding(VAO, 0, 0);
```

6. Save the number of vertices to be used by `glDrawArrays()` in the main loop and render the 3D model:

```
const int numVertices =
  static_cast<int>(positions.size());
```

Here, we use the same two-pass technique from the *Doing math with GLM* recipe to render a wireframe 3D model on top of a solid image:

```
while ( !glfwWindowShouldClose(window) ) {
  ...
  glPolygonMode(GL_FRONT_AND_BACK, GL_FILL);
  glDrawArrays(GL_TRIANGLES, 0, numVertices);
  ...
  glPolygonMode(GL_FRONT_AND_BACK, GL_LINE);
  glDrawArrays(GL_TRIANGLES, 0, numVertices);
  glfwSwapBuffers(window);
  glfwPollEvents();
}
```

The output graphics should look similar to the following screenshot:

Simple example

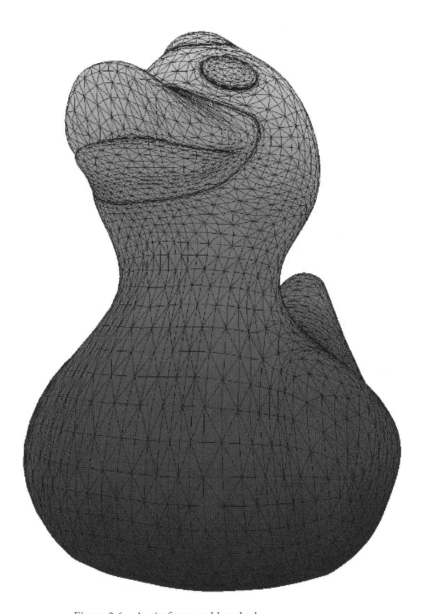

Figure 2.6 – A wireframe rubber duck

Getting started with Etc2Comp

One significant drawback of high-resolution textured data is that it requires a lot of GPU memory to store and process. All modern, real-time rendering APIs provide some sort of texture compression, allowing us to store textures in compressed formats on the GPU. One such format is **ETC2**. This is a standard texture compression format for OpenGL and Vulkan.

Etc2Comp is an open source tool that converts bitmaps into **ETC2** format. The tool is built with a focus on encoding performance to reduce the amount of time required to package asset-heavy applications and reduce the overall application size. In this recipe, you will learn how to integrate this tool within your own applications to construct tools for your custom graphics preparation pipelines.

Getting ready

The project can be downloaded using this Bootstrap snippet:

```
{
  "name": "etc2comp",
  "source": {
    "type": "git",
    "url": "https://github.com/google/etc2comp",
    "revision": "9cd0f9cae0f32338943699bb418107db61bb66f2"
  }
}
```

Etc2Comp was released by Google "as-is" with the intention of being used as a command-line tool. Therefore, we will need to include some additional `.cpp` files within the CMake target to use it as a library that is linked to our application. The `Chapter2/08_ETC2Comp/CMakeLists.txt` file contains the following lines to do this:

```
target_sources(Ch2_Sample08_ETC2Comp PUBLIC
               ${CMAKE_CURRENT_BINARY_DIR}/../../../
               deps/src/etc2comp/EtcTool/EtcFile.cpp)
target_sources(Ch2_Sample08_ETC2Comp PUBLIC
               ${CMAKE_CURRENT_BINARY_DIR}/../../../
               deps/src/etc2comp/EtcTool/EtcFileHeader.cpp)
```

The complete source code is located at `Chapter2/08_ETC2Comp`.

How to do it...

Let's build an application that loads a `.jpg` image via the STB library, converts it into an ETC2 image, and saves it within the `.ktx` file format:

1. First, it is necessary to include some header files:

```
#include "etc2comp/EtcLib/Etc/Etc.h"
#include "etc2comp/EtcLib/Etc/EtcImage.h"
#include "etc2comp/EtcLib/Etc/EtcFilter.h"
#include "etc2comp/EtcTool/EtcFile.h"
#define STB_IMAGE_IMPLEMENTATION
#include <stb/stb_image.h>
```

2. Let's load an image as a 4-component RGBA bitmap:

```
int main() {
  int w, h, comp;
  const uint8_t* img = stbi_load(
    "data/ch2_sample3_STB.jpg", &w, &h, &comp, 4);
```

3. Etc2Comp takes floating-point RGBA bitmaps as input, so we have to convert our data, as follows:

```
std::vector<float> rgbaf;
for (int i = 0; i != w * h * 4; i+=4) {
  rgbaf.push_back(img[i+0] / 255.0f);
  rgbaf.push_back(img[i+1] / 255.0f);
  rgbaf.push_back(img[i+2] / 255.0f);
  rgbaf.push_back(img[i+3] / 255.0f);
}
```

> **Note**
>
> Besides manual conversion, as mentioned earlier, STB can load 8-bit-per-channel images as floating-point images directly via the `stbi_loadf()` API. However, it will do an automatic gamma correction. Use `stbi_ldr_to_hdr_scale(1.0f)` and `stbi_ldr_to_hdr_gamma(2.2f)` if you want to control the amount of gamma correction.

4. Now we can encode the floating-point image into ETC2 format using Etc2Comp.
    Because we don't use alpha transparency, our target format should be RGB8. We will
    use the default BT.709 error metric minimization schema:

```
const auto etcFormat = Etc::Image::Format::RGB8;
const auto errorMetric = Etc::ErrorMetric::BT709;
Etc::Image image(rgbaf.data(), w, h, errorMetric);
```

The encoder takes the number of threads as input. Let's use the value returned
by thread::hardware_concurrency() and 1024 as the number of
concurrent jobs:

```
image.Encode(etcFormat, errorMetric,
    ETCCOMP_DEFAULT_EFFORT_LEVEL,
    std::thread::hardware_concurrency(), 1024);
```

5. Once the image is converted, we can save it into the .ktx file format, which can
    store compressed texture data that is directly consumable by OpenGL. Etc2Comp
    provides the Etc::File helper class to do this:

```
Etc::File etcFile("image.ktx",
    Etc::File::Format::KTX,
    etcFormat,
    image.GetEncodingBits(),
    image.GetEncodingBitsBytes(),
    image.GetSourceWidth(),
    image.GetSourceHeight(),
    image.GetExtendedWidth(),
    image.GetExtendedHeight());
etcFile.Write();
return 0;
}
```

The bitmap is saved within the image.ktx file. It can be loaded into an OpenGL or
Vulkan texture, which we will do in subsequent chapters.

There's more...

Pico Pixel is a great tool that you can use to view .ktx files and other texture formats
(https://pixelandpolygon.com). It is freeware but not open source. There is an
issues tracker that is publicly available on GitHub. You can find it at https://github.
com/inalogic/pico-pixel-public/issues.

For those who want to jump into the latest state-of-the-art texture compression
techniques, please refer to the Basis project from Binomial at https://github.com/
BinomialLLC/basis_universal.

Multithreading with Taskflow

Modern graphical applications require us to harness the power of multiple CPUs to be performant. **Taskflow** is a fast C++ header-only library that can help you write parallel programs with complex task dependencies quickly. This library is extremely useful as it allows you to jump into the development of multithreaded graphical applications that make use of advanced rendering concepts, such as frame graphs and multithreaded command buffers generation.

Getting ready

Here, we use Taskflow version 3.1.0. You can download it using the following Bootstrap snippet:

```
{
  "name": "taskflow",
  "source": {
    "type": "git",
    "url": "https://github.com/taskflow/taskflow.git",
    "revision": "v3.1.0"
  }
}
```

To debug dependency graphs produced by Taskflow, it is recommended that you install the **GraphViz** tool from https://www.graphviz.org.

The complete source code for this recipe can be found in Chapter2/09_Taskflow.

How to do it...

Let's create and run a set of concurrent dependent tasks via the for_each() algorithm. Each task will print a single value from an array in a concurrent fashion. The processing order can vary between different runs of the program:

1. Include the taskflow.hpp header file:

    ```
    #include <taskflow/taskflow.hpp>
    using namespace std;
    int main() {
    ```

2. The `tf::Taskflow` class is the main place to create a task dependency graph. Declare an instance and a data vector to process:

```
tf::Taskflow taskflow;
std::vector<int> items{ 1, 2, 3, 4, 5, 6, 7, 8 };
```

3. The `for_each()` member function returns a task that implements a parallel-for loop algorithm. The task can be used for synchronization purposes:

```
auto task = taskflow.for_each(
    items.begin(), items.end(),
    [](int item) { std::cout << item; }
);
```

4. Let's attach some work before and after the parallel-for task so that we can view `Start` and `End` messages in the output. Let's call the new `S` and `T` tasks accordingly:

```
taskflow.emplace(
    []() {
        std::cout << "\nS - Start\n";
    }).name("S").precede(task);
taskflow.emplace(
    []() {
        std::cout << "\nT - End\n";
    }).name("T").succeed(task);
```

5. Save the generated tasks dependency graph in `.dot` format so that we can process it later with the GraphViz `dot` tool:

```
std::ofstream os("taskflow.dot");
taskflow.dump(os);
```

6. Now we can create an `executor` object and run the constructed taskflow graph:

```
Tf::Executor executor;
executor.run(taskflow).wait();
return 0;
}
```

One important part to mention here is that the dependency graph can only be constructed once. Then, it can be reused in every frame to run concurrent tasks efficiently.

The output from the preceding program should look similar to the following listing:

```
S - Start
39172 runs 6
46424 runs 5
17900 runs 2
26932 runs 1
26932 runs 8
23888 runs 3
45464 runs 7
32064 runs 4
T - End
```

Here, we can see our S and T tasks. Between them, there are multiple threads with different IDs processing different elements of the items[] vector in parallel.

There's more...

The application saved the dependency graph inside the taskflow.dot file. It can be converted into a visual representation by GraphViz using the following command:

```
dot -Tpng taskflow.dot > output.png
```

The resulting .png image should look similar to the following screenshot:

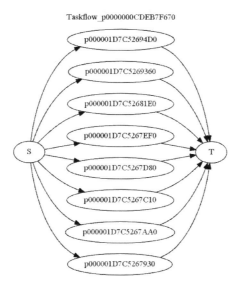

Figure 2.7 – The Taskflow dependency graph for for_each()

This functionality is extremely useful when you are debugging complex dependency graphs (and producing complex-looking images for your books and papers).

The Taskflow library functionality is vast and provides implementations for numerous parallel algorithms and profiling capabilities. Please refer to the official documentation for in-depth coverage at `https://taskflow.github.io/taskflow/index.html`.

Introducing MeshOptimizer

For GPUs to render a mesh efficiently, all vertices in the vertex buffer should be unique and without duplicates. Solving this problem efficiently can be a complicated and computationally intensive task in any modern 3D content pipeline.

MeshOptimizer is an open source C++ library developed by Arseny Kapoulkine, which provides algorithms to help optimize meshes for modern GPU vertex and index processing pipelines. It can reindex an existing index buffer or generate an entirely new set of indices from an unindexed vertex buffer.

Getting ready

We use MeshOptimizer version 0.16. Here is the Bootstrap snippet that you can use to download this version:

```
{
  "name": "meshoptimizer",
  "source": {
    "type": "git",
    "url": "https://github.com/zeux/meshoptimizer",
    "revision": "v0.16"
  }
}
```

The complete source code for this recipe can be found in `Chapter2/10_MeshOptimizer`.

How to do it...

Let's use MeshOptimizer to optimize the vertex and index buffer layouts of a mesh loaded by the Assimp library. Then, we can generate a simplified model of the mesh:

1. First, we load our mesh via Assimp, as shown in the following code snippet. We preserve the existing vertices and indices exactly as they were loaded by Assimp:

```cpp
const aiScene* scene = aiImportFile(
  "data/rubber_duck/scene.gltf",
  aiProcess_Triangulate);
const aiMesh* mesh = scene->mMeshes[0];
std::vector<vec3> positions;
std::vector<unsigned int> indices;
for (unsigned i = 0; i != mesh->mNumVertices; i++) {
  const aiVector3D v = mesh->mVertices[i];
  positions.push_back( vec3(v.x, v.z, v.y) );
}
for (unsigned i = 0; i != mesh->mNumFaces; i++) {
  for ( unsigned j = 0; j != 3; j++ )
    indices.push_back(mesh->mFaces[i].mIndices[j]);
}
aiReleaseImport(scene);
```

2. Now we should generate a remap table for our existing vertex and index data:

```cpp
std::vector<unsigned int> remap( indices.size() );
const size_t vertexCount =
  meshopt_generateVertexRemap( remap.data(),
    indices.data(), indices.size(), positions.data(),
    indices.size(), sizeof(vec3) );
```

The MeshOptimizer documentation (https://github.com/zeux/meshoptimizer) tells us the following:

> *The remap table is generated based on binary equivalence of the input vertices, so the resulting mesh will be rendered in the same way.*

3. The returned `vertexCount` value corresponds to the number of unique vertices that have remained after remapping. Let's allocate space and generate new vertex and index buffers:

```cpp
std::vector<unsigned int> remappedIndices(
  indices.size() );
std::vector<vec3> remappedVertices( vertexCount );
```

```
meshopt_remapIndexBuffer( remappedIndices.data(),
    indices.data(), indices.size(), remap.data() );
meshopt_remapVertexBuffer( remappedVertices.data(),
    positions.data(), positions.size(), sizeof(vec3),
    remap.data() );
```

Now we can use other MeshOptimizer algorithms to optimize these buffers even further. The official documentation is pretty straightforward. We will adapt the example it provides for the purposes of our demo application.

4. When we want to render a mesh, the GPU has to transform each vertex via a vertex shader. GPUs can reuse transformed vertices by means of a small built-in cache, usually storing between 16 and 32 vertices inside it. In order to use this small cache effectively, we need to reorder the triangles to maximize the locality of vertex references. How to do this with MeshOptimizer in place is shown next. Pay attention to how only the indices data is being touched here:

```
meshopt_optimizeVertexCache( remappedIndices.data(),
    remappedIndices.data(), indices.size(), vertexCount );
```

5. Transformed vertices form triangles that are sent for rasterization to generate fragments. Usually, each fragment is run through a depth test first, and fragments that pass the depth test get the fragment shader executed to compute the final color. As fragment shaders get more and more expensive, it becomes increasingly important to reduce the number of fragment shader invocations. This can be achieved by reducing pixel overdraw in a mesh, and, in general, it requires the use of view-dependent algorithms. However, MeshOptimizer implements heuristics to reorder the triangles and minimize overdraw from all directions. We can use it as follows:

```
meshopt_optimizeOverdraw( remappedIndices.data(),
    remappedIndices.data(),
    indices.size(),
    glm::value_ptr(remappedVertices[0]),
    vertexCount,
    sizeof(vec3),
    1.05f );
```

The last parameter, 1.05, is the threshold that determines how much the algorithm can compromise the vertex cache hit ratio. We use the recommended default value from the documentation.

6. Once we have optimized the mesh to reduce pixel overdraw, the vertex buffer access pattern can still be optimized for memory efficiency. The GPU has to fetch specified vertex attributes from the vertex buffer and pass this data into the vertex shader. To speed up this fetch, a memory cache is used, which means optimizing the locality of vertex buffer access is very important. We can use MeshOptimizer to optimize our index and vertex buffers for vertex fetch efficiency, as follows:

```
meshopt_optimizeVertexFetch(
    remappedVertices.data(),
    remappedIndices.data(),
    indices.size(),
    remappedVertices.data(),
    vertexCount,
    sizeof(vec3) );
```

This function will reorder vertices in the vertex buffer and regenerate indices to match the new contents of the vertex buffer.

7. The last thing we will do in this recipe is simplify the mesh. MeshOptimizer can generate a new index buffer that uses existing vertices from the vertex buffer with a reduced number of triangles. This new index buffer can be used to render **Level-of-Detail (LOD)** meshes. The following code snippet shows you how to do this using the default threshold and target error values:

```
const float threshold = 0.2f;
const size_t target_index_count = size_t(
    remappedIndices.size() * threshold);
const float target_error = 1e-2f;
std::vector<unsigned int> indicesLod(
    remappedIndices.size() );
indicesLod.resize( meshopt_simplify(
    &indicesLod[0],
    remappedIndices.data(), remappedIndices.size(),
    &remappedVertices[0].x, vertexCount, sizeof(vec3),
    target_index_count, target_error) );
```

Multiple LOD meshes can be generated this way by changing the `threshold` value.

Let's render the optimized and LOD meshes that we created earlier:

1. For the simplicity of this demo, we copy the remapped data back into the original vectors as follows:

```
indices = remappedIndices;
positions = remappedVertices;
```

2. With modern OpenGL, we can store vertex and index data inside a single buffer. You can do this as follows:

```
const size_t sizeIndices =
  sizeof(unsigned int) * indices.size();
const size_t sizeIndicesLod =
  sizeof(unsigned int) * indicesLod.size();
const size_t sizeVertices =
  sizeof(vec3) * positions.size();
glNamedBufferStorage(meshData,
  sizeIndices + sizeIndicesLod + sizeVertices,
  nullptr, GL_DYNAMIC_STORAGE_BIT);
glNamedBufferSubData(
  meshData, 0, sizeIndices, indices.data());
glNamedBufferSubData(meshData, sizeIndices,
  sizeIndicesLod, indicesLod.data());
glNamedBufferSubData(meshData, sizeIndices +
  sizeIndicesLod, sizeVertices, positions.data());
```

3. Now we should tell OpenGL where to read the vertex and index data from. The starting offset to the vertex data is `sizeIndices + sizeIndicesLod`:

```
glVertexArrayElementBuffer(VAO, meshData);
glVertexArrayVertexBuffer(VAO, 0, meshData,
  sizeIndices + sizeIndicesLod, sizeof(vec3));
glEnableVertexArrayAttrib(VAO, 0);
glVertexArrayAttribFormat(
  VAO, 0, 3, GL_FLOAT, GL_FALSE, 0);
glVertexArrayAttribBinding(VAO, 0, 0);
```

4. To render the optimized mesh, we can call `glDrawElements()`, as follows:

```
glDrawElements(GL_TRIANGLES, indices.size(),
  GL_UNSIGNED_INT, nullptr);
```

5. To render the simplified LOD mesh, we use the number of indices in the LOD and use an offset to where its indices start in the index buffer. We need to skip `sizeIndices` bytes to do it:

```
glDrawElements(GL_TRIANGLES, indicesLod.size(),
  GL_UNSIGNED_INT, (void*)sizeIndices);
```

The resulting image should look similar to the following screenshot:

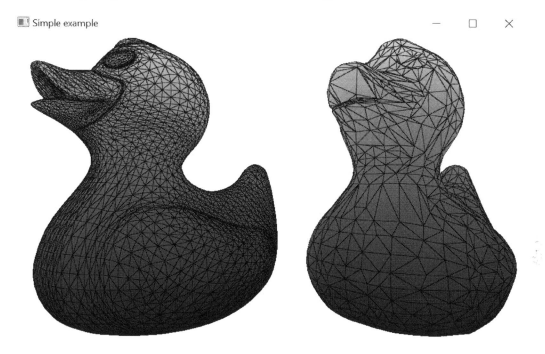

Figure 2.8 – LOD mesh rendering

There's more...

This recipe uses a slightly different technique for the wireframe rendering. Instead of rendering a mesh twice, we use barycentric coordinates to identify the proximity of the triangle edge inside each triangle and change the color accordingly. Here is the geometry shader to generate barycentric coordinates for a triangular mesh:

```glsl
#version 460 core
layout( triangles ) in;
layout( triangle_strip, max_vertices = 3 ) out;
layout (location=0) in vec3 color[];
layout (location=0) out vec3 colors;
layout (location=1) out vec3 barycoords;
void main()
{
```

Next, store the values of the barycentric coordinates for each vertex of the triangle:

```
const vec3 bc[3] = vec3[] (
  vec3(1.0, 0.0, 0.0),
  vec3(0.0, 1.0, 0.0),
  vec3(0.0, 0.0, 1.0)
);
for ( int i = 0; i < 3; i++ )
{
    gl_Position = gl_in[i].gl_Position;
    colors = color[i];
    barycoords = bc[i];
    EmitVertex();
}
EndPrimitive();
}
```

Barycentric coordinates can be used inside the fragment shader to discriminate colors in the following way:

```
#version 460 core
layout (location=0) in vec3 colors;
layout (location=1) in vec3 barycoords;
layout (location=0) out vec4 out_FragColor;
float edgeFactor(float thickness)
{
  vec3 a3 = smoothstep( vec3(0.0), fwidth(barycoords) *
    thickness,barycoords );
  return min( min(a3.x, a3.y), a3.z );
}
void main()
{
  out_FragColor =
    vec4(mix(vec3(0.0), colors, edgeFactor(1.0)), 1.0);
};
```

The fwidth() function calculates the sum of the absolute values of the derivatives in the x and y screen coordinates and is used to determine the thickness of the lines. The smoothstep() function is used for antialiasing.

3

Getting Started with OpenGL and Vulkan

In this chapter, we will cover the basic steps of modern OpenGL and Vulkan. We will also learn how to deal with textures, buffers, shaders, and pipelines. The recipes in this chapter will not focus solely on the graphics APIs that are available, but on various tips and tricks that are necessary for improving graphical application development and various 3D graphics algorithms. On the Vulkan side, we will cover the basics so that we can get it up and running.

In this chapter, we will cover the following recipes:

- Intercepting OpenGL API calls
- Working with Direct State Access (DSA)
- Loading and compiling shaders in OpenGL
- Implementing programmable vertex pulling (PVP) in OpenGL
- Working with cube map textures
- Compiling Vulkan shaders at runtime
- Initializing Vulkan instances and graphical devices
- Initializing the Vulkan swap chain

- Setting up Vulkan's debugging capabilities
- Tracking and cleaning up Vulkan objects
- Using Vulkan command buffers
- Dealing with buffers in Vulkan
- Using texture data in Vulkan
- Using mesh geometry data in Vulkan
- Using Vulkan descriptor sets
- Initializing Vulkan shader modules
- Initializing the Vulkan pipeline
- Putting it all together into a Vulkan application

Technical requirements

To complete the recipes in this chapter, you must have a computer with a video card that can support OpenGL 4.6 and Vulkan 1.1. Read *Chapter 1, Establishing a Build Environment*, if you want to learn how to configure your computer properly.

You can find the code files present in this chapter on GitHub at `https://github.com/PacktPublishing/3D-Graphics-Rendering-Cookbook/tree/master/Chapter3`

Intercepting OpenGL API calls

Sometimes, it is very desirable to intercept OpenGL API calls for debugging purposes or, for example, to manipulate the underlying OpenGL state before passing API calls into the real OpenGL system. You can do this to simulate mobile OpenGL on top of a desktop OpenGL implementation or vice versa. Manually writing wrappers for each and every API function is a tedious and thankless job. In this recipe, you will learn how to quickly make custom OpenGL hooks and use them in your applications.

Getting ready

This recipe uses a Python script to parse `glcorearb.h` and generate all the necessary scaffolding code for the wrapper functions. The complete source code for this recipe can be found in this book's source code bundle, under the name `Chapter3/GL01_APIWrapping`.

How to do it...

Let's write a small OpenGL application that prints all the GL API functions that have been used, along with their parameters, in the console window while the application is running:

1. First, let's run the supplementary Python script with the following command:

```
python GetGLAPI.py > GLAPITrace.h
```

This script reads input from `funcs_list.txt`, which contains the list of OpenGL functions that we want to wrap, in the following format:

```
glActiveTexture
glAttachShader
glBeginQuery
glBindAttribLocation
glBindBuffer
...
```

This script creates two files called `GLAPI.h` and `GLAPITrace.h`.

2. Now, we can declare the `GL4API` struct, including the first generated file, as follows:

```
struct GL4API {
#   include "GLAPI.h"
};
```

This structure contains pointers to all the required OpenGL functions.

3. Next, declare a function type and two function prototypes:

```
using PFNGETGLPROC = void* (const char*);
void GetAPI4(GL4API* api, PFNGETGLPROC GetGLProc);
void InjectAPITracer4(GL4API* api);
```

Their implementations can be found in `GLAPITrace.h`.

Now, we can use these functions in our application.

4. Define a `GL4API` instance, fill it with OpenGL function pointers, and inject the wrapping code. Use `glfwGetProcAddress()` to retrieve the pointers to OpenGL functions:

```
GL4API api;
GetAPI4(&api, [] (const char* func) -> void*
{ return (void *)glfwGetProcAddress(func); });
InjectAPITracer4(&api);
```

5. Invoke all subsequent OpenGL commands using the `api.` structure:

```
const GLuint shaderVertex =
  api.glCreateShader(GL_VERTEX_SHADER);
api.glShaderSource(
  shaderVertex, 1, &shaderCodeVertex, nullptr);
api.glCompileShader(shaderVertex);
...
```

The console output of the running program should look as follows:

```
glViewport(0, 0, 1024, 768)
glClear(16384)
glUseProgram(3)
glNamedBufferSubData(1, 0, 64, 000000F5508FF6B0)
glDrawArrays(GL_TRIANGLES, 0, 3)
glViewport(0, 0, 1024, 768)
glClear(16384)
glUseProgram(3)
glNamedBufferSubData(1, 0, 64, 000000F5508FF6B0)
glDrawArrays(GL_TRIANGLES, 0, 3)
```

This approach can be used for logging and debugging, and it can even be extended to record sequences of OpenGL commands or similar purposes. By changing the Python script, it is easy to customize the generated wrappers to your own needs.

How it works...

The first generated file, `GLAPI.h`, contains a list of declarations in the following form:

```
PFNGLACTIVETEXTUREPROC        glActiveTexture;
PFNGLATTACHSHADERPROC         glAttachShader;
PFNGLBEGINQUERYPROC           glBeginQuery;
PFNGLBINDATTRIBLOCATIONPROC   glBindAttribLocation;
PFNGLBINDBUFFERPROC           glBindBuffer;
...
```

The second generated file, GLAPITrace.h, contains a long list of actual wrappers for every specified OpenGL function call. Each wrapper prints parameters in the console, invokes the actual function through a pointer, which, in turn, might be a wrapper as well, and checks for GL errors once the function returns. Let's take a look at a couple of functions from this file:

```
void GLTracer_glCullFace(GLenum mode) {
  printf("glCullFace(" "%s)\n", E2S(mode));
  apiHook.glCullFace(mode);
  assert(apiHook.glGetError() == GL_NO_ERROR);
}
void GLTracer_glPolygonMode(GLenum face, GLenum mode) {
  printf(
    "glPolygonMode(" "%s, %s)\n", E2S(face), E2S(mode));
  apiHook.glPolygonMode(face, mode);
  assert(apiHook.glGetError() == GL_NO_ERROR);
}
...
```

The Enum2String() helper function, which is used inside the wrappers via the E2S() macro, converts a GLenum value into an appropriate string representation. This is just a hardcoded list of values; there's nothing really fancy here. For values not in the list, the function will return a numerical representation of the enum via std::to_string():

```
#define W( en ) if ( e == en ) return #en;
std::string Enum2String(GLenum e) {
  W(GL_POINTS);
  W(GL_LINES);
  W(GL_LINE_LOOP);
  W(GL_LINE_STRIP);
  W(GL_TRIANGLES);
  ...
  return std::to_string(e);
}
```

Besides that, there are two more function definitions that are generated here. The first one loads OpenGL function pointers into the `GL4API` structure using the supplied lambda, like so:

```
#define LOAD_GL_FUNC(f) api->func =
  (decltype(api->f))GetGLProc(#f);
void GetAPI4(GL4API* api, PFNGETGLPROC GetGLProc) {
  LOAD_GL_FUNC(glActiveTexture);
  LOAD_GL_FUNC(glAttachShader);
  LOAD_GL_FUNC(glBeginQuery);
  LOAD_GL_FUNC(glBindAttribLocation);
  ...
```

The second one, called `InjectAPITracer4()`, is defined as follows:

```
#define INJECT(S) api->S = &GLTracer_##S;
void InjectAPITracer4(GL4API* api) {
  apiHook = *api;
  INJECT(glActiveTexture);
  INJECT(glAttachShader);
  INJECT(glBeginQuery);
  INJECT(glBindAttribLocation);
  ...
```

This function saves the previous value of `GL4API` into a static global variable and replaces the function pointers with pointers to the custom wrapper functions.

Working with Direct State Access (DSA)

Starting with version 4.5, OpenGL Core Profile allows us to modify the state of objects without enforcing the bind-to-edit model that was used in previous versions of OpenGL. Let's take a closer look at the new functions that provide a straightforward, object-oriented interface and do not affect the global state.

Getting ready

The OpenGL examples provided in this book use the DSA programming model, which you were exposed to in *Chapter 2, Using Essential Libraries*. If you are not familiar with DSA yet, it is recommended that you go through the source code for all the applications covered in *Chapter 2, Using Essential Libraries*, to get a solid grasp of this approach to small, self-contained examples.

All DSA functions can be separated into the following object families:

- Texture
- Framebuffer
- Buffer
- Transform feedback
- Vertex array
- Sampler
- Query
- Program

Let's go through a couple of these object families to understand how the new API works.

How to do it...

The first family of functions is related to texture objects. Let's take a look:

1. Create a set of texture objects with the following command, which specifies a texture target right from the get-go:

   ```
   void glCreateTextures(
      GLenum target, GLsizei n, GLuint* textures);
   ```

2. All texture parameters should be set directly with this group function, based on the parameter type. It is the DSA equivalent of glTexParameter...() functions:

   ```
   void glTextureParameter...(
      GLuint texture, GLenum pname, ...);
   ```

3. Using glActiveTexture() and glBindTexture() is no longer required. Instead, a single command should be used:

   ```
   void glBindTextureUnit(GLuint unit, GLuint texture);
   ```

> **Note**
>
> Typically, we would use the following pair of functions:
>
> ```
> glActiveTexture(GL_TEXTURE0 + 2);
> glBindTexture(GL_TEXTURE_2D, texId);
> ```
>
> Instead of this, you can use the one-liner shown here. The texture target will be inferred from the texture object itself, which means using GL_TEXTURE0 is no longer required:
>
> ```
> glBindTextureUnit(2, texId);
> ```

Alternatively, if you want to bind a few textures to a sequence of texture units at the same time, use the following command:

```
void glBindTextures(GLuint first, GLsizei count,
  const GLuint* textures);
```

4. Generating texture mipmaps can now be done directly. Like all the DSA functions, this one takes the OpenGL `GLuint` name instead of a texture target:

```
void glGenerateTextureMipmap(GLuint texture);
```

5. Uploading data into textures should be done in the following way. First, we should tell OpenGL how much and what kind of storage should be allocated for a texture using one of the following functions:

```
void glTextureStorage...();
```

6. The actual pixels can be uploaded, compressed, or decompressed with one of the following calls:

```
void glTextureSubImage...();
void glCompressedTextureSubImage...();
```

Let's take a look at how a 2D texture can be uploaded in one of the examples from the previous chapter; that is, `Chapter2\03_STB\src\main.cpp`:

```
GLuint t;
glCreateTextures(GL_TEXTURE_2D, 1, &t);
glTextureParameteri(t, GL_TEXTURE_MAX_LEVEL, 0);
glTextureParameteri(t, GL_TEXTURE_MIN_FILTER, GL_LINEAR);
glTextureParameteri(t, GL_TEXTURE_MAG_FILTER, GL_LINEAR);
glTextureStorage2D(t, 1, GL_RGB8, w, h);
```

```
glTextureSubImage2D(
    t, 0, 0, 0, w, h, GL_RGB, GL_UNSIGNED_BYTE, img);
```

This API prevents many situations where a texture object might remain in an incomplete state due to a wrong sequence of legacy `glTexImage...()` calls.

Let's look at another family of functions related to buffers. It all starts with a call to `glCreateBuffers()`, which will create a set of buffers. It does not require a specific buffer target, which means that buffers can be created and reused for specific purposes later, making them completely interchangeable. For example, a shader storage buffer can be filled on a GPU via a compute shader and be reused as an indirect buffer for draw commands. We will touch on this mechanic in the subsequent chapters. For now, let's focus on how to create and set up buffer objects using the new DSA functions. Check out `Chapter2\07_Assimp\src\main.cpp` for the full source code:

1. A uniform buffer object can be created in the following way:

```
const GLsizeiptr kBufSize = sizeof(PerFrameData);
GLuint buf;
glCreateBuffers(1, &buf);
```

2. Now, we should specify the storage for our uniform buffer. The `GL_DYNAMIC_STORAGE_BIT` flag tells the OpenGL implementation that the contents of the buffer may be updated later through calls to `glBufferSubData()`:

```
glNamedBufferStorage(
    buf, kBufSize, nullptr, GL_DYNAMIC_STORAGE_BIT);
```

3. To make the entire buffer accessible from GLSL shaders at binding point 0, we should use the following function call:

```
glBindBufferRange(
    GL_UNIFORM_BUFFER, 0, buf, 0, kBufSize);
```

Other types of buffers can be created in a similar fashion. We will discuss them on an as-needed basis in subsequent chapters.

There is one more important thing to mention, which is how to set up the vertex attributes format for **vertex array objects** (**VAOs**). Let's take a closer look at how to store vertex positions in `vec3` format inside a buffer and render from it:

1. First, we should create a buffer to store vertex data in. The flag should be set to 0 as the contents of this buffer will be immutable:

    ```
    GLuint buf;
    glCreateBuffers(1, &buf);
    glNamedBufferStorage(
        buf, sizeof(vec3) * pos.size(), pos.data(), 0);
    ```

2. Now, let's use this buffer to set up a vertex array object:

    ```
    GLuint vao;
    glCreateVertexArrays(1, &vao);
    ```

3. The data for GLSL attribute stream (location) 0, which we use for vertex 3D positions, should be sourced from the `buf` buffer, start from an offset of 0, and use a stride equal to the size of `vec3`. This means that positions are tightly packed inside the buffer, without any interleaving with other data, such as normal vectors or texture coordinates:

    ```
    glVertexArrayVertexBuffer(
        vao, 0, buf, 0, sizeof(vec3));
    glEnableVertexArrayAttrib(vao, 0 );
    ```

4. Now, we should describe what the format our data will be in for attribute stream number 0. Each value contains 3 components of the GL_FLOAT type. No normalization is required. The relative offset, which is the distance between the elements within a buffer, should be zero in the case of tightly packed values. Here is how to set it up:

    ```
    glVertexArrayAttribFormat(
        vao, 0, 3, GL_FLOAT, GL_FALSE, 0);
    ```

5. The following call connects a vertex buffer binding point of 0 within the vertex attribute format we described as number 0:

    ```
    glVertexArrayAttribBinding(vao, 0, 0);
    ```

This might sound confusing at first, but imagine that we have one big buffer containing interleaving positions, texture coordinates, and colors, as in the Chapter2\04_ImGui example. Let's look at a complete code fragment for how this VAO should be set up:

1. Create a VAO, like so:

```
GLuint vao;
glCreateVertexArrays(1, &vao);
```

2. Bind a buffer containing indices to this VAO:

```
glVertexArrayElementBuffer(vao, handleElements);
```

3. Bind a buffer containing the interleaved vertex data to this VAO's buffer binding point; that is, 0:

```
glVertexArrayVertexBuffer(
    vao, 0, handleVBO, 0, sizeof(ImDrawVert));
```

4. Enable all three vertex attributes streams:

```
glEnableVertexArrayAttrib(vao, 0);
glEnableVertexArrayAttrib(vao, 1);
glEnableVertexArrayAttrib(vao, 2);
```

5. Specify a data format for each attribute stream. The streams have their indices set to 0, 1, and 2, which correspond to the location binding points in the GLSL shaders:

```
glVertexArrayAttribFormat(vao, 0, 2, GL_FLOAT,
    GL_FALSE, IM_OFFSETOF(ImDrawVert, pos));
glVertexArrayAttribFormat(vao, 1, 2, GL_FLOAT,
    GL_FALSE, IM_OFFSETOF(ImDrawVert, uv));
glVertexArrayAttribFormat(vao, 2, 4, GL_UNSIGNED_BYTE,
    GL_TRUE, IM_OFFSETOF(ImDrawVert, col));
```

6. Now, tell OpenGL to read the data for streams 0, 1, and 2 from the buffer, which is attached to buffer binding point 0:

```
glVertexArrayAttribBinding(vao, 0, 0);
glVertexArrayAttribBinding(vao, 1, 0);
glVertexArrayAttribBinding(vao, 2, 0);
```

There's more...

The VAO setup is probably the most complicated part of the new DSA API. Other objects are much simpler to set up; we will discuss how to work with them in subsequent chapters.

Loading and compiling shaders in OpenGL

In *Chapter 2, Using Essential Libraries*, our tiny OpenGL examples loaded all the GLSL shaders directly from the const char* variables defined inside our source code. While this approach is acceptable in the territory of 100-line demos, it does not scale well beyond that. In this recipe, we will learn how to load, compile, and link shaders and shader programs. This approach will be used throughout the rest of the examples in this book.

Getting ready

Before we can proceed with the actual shader loading, we need two graphics API-agnostic functions. The first one loads a text file as std::string:

```
std::string readShaderFile(const char* fileName) {
  FILE* file = fopen(fileName, "r");
  if (!file) {
    printf("I/O error. Cannot open '%s'\n", fileName);
    return std::string();
  }
  fseek(file, 0L, SEEK_END);
  const auto bytesinfile = ftell(file);
  fseek(file, 0L, SEEK_SET);
  char* buffer = (char*)alloca(bytesinfile + 1);
  const size_t bytesread = fread(
    buffer, 1, bytesinfile, file);
  fclose(file);
  buffer[bytesread] = 0;
```

The important thing to mention here is that we parse and eliminate the UTF byte-order marker. If present, it might not be handled properly by some legacy GLSL compilers, especially on Android:

```
static constexpr unsigned char BOM[] =
  { 0xEF, 0xBB, 0xBF };
if (bytesread > 3)
```

```
    if (!memcmp(buffer, BOM, 3))
        memset(buffer, ' ', 3);
std::string code(buffer);
```

We should also handle #include directives inside the shader source code. This code is not robust enough to be shipped, but it is good enough for our purposes:

```
while (code.find("#include ") != code.npos) {
    const auto pos = code.find("#include ");
    const auto p1 = code.find('<', pos);
    const auto p2 = code.find('>', pos);
    if (p1 == code.npos ||
        p2 == code.npos || p2 <= p1) {
        printf("Error while loading shader program: %s\n",
            code.c_str());
        return std::string();
    }
    const std::string name =
        code.substr(p1 + 1, p2 - p1 - 1);
    const std::string include =
        readShaderFile(name.c_str());
    code.replace(pos, p2-pos+1, include.c_str());
}
return code;
}
```

The second helper function prints shader source code in the console. Each source code line is annotated with a line number, making it extremely easy to debug shader compilation using the error line number generated by the GLSL compiler's output:

```
static void printShaderSource(const char* text) {
    int line = 1;
    printf("\n(%3i) ", line);
    while (text && *text++) {
        if (*text == '\n') printf("\n(%3i) ", ++line);
        else if (*text == '\r') {}
        else printf("%c", *text);
    }
    printf("\n");
}
```

The source code for these functions can be found in the `shared/Utils.cpp` and `shared/GLShader.cpp` files.

How to do it...

Let's create some C++ **resource acquisition is initialization** (**RAII**) wrappers on top of our OpenGL shaders and programs:

1. First, we need to convert a shader file name into an OpenGL shader type based on the file's extension:

    ```
    GLenum GLShaderTypeFromFileName(const char* fileName)
    {
      if (endsWith(fileName, ".vert"))
        return GL_VERTEX_SHADER;
      if (endsWith(fileName, ".frag"))
        return GL_FRAGMENT_SHADER;
      if (endsWith(fileName, ".geom"))
        return GL_GEOMETRY_SHADER;
      if (endsWith(fileName, ".tesc"))
        return GL_TESS_CONTROL_SHADER;
      if (endsWith(fileName, ".tese"))
        return GL_TESS_EVALUATION_SHADER;
      if (endsWith(fileName, ".comp"))
        return GL_COMPUTE_SHADER;
      assert(false);
      return 0;
    }
    ```

2. The `endsWith()` helper function is basically a one-liner and checks if a string ends with a specified substring:

    ```
    int endsWith(const char* s, const char* part) {
      return (strstr(s, part) - s) ==
        (strlen(s) - strlen(part));
    }
    ```

3. The shader wrapper interface looks as follows. Constructors take either a filename or a shader type and source code as input:

    ```
    class GLShader {
    public:
    ```

```
explicit GLShader(const char* fileName);
GLShader(GLenum type, const char* text);
~GLShader();
```

4. The shader type will be required later, once we want to link our shaders to a shader program:

```
GLenum getType() const { return type_; }
GLuint getHandle() const { return handle_; }
private:
GLenum type_;
GLuint handle_;
};
```

5. The two-parameter constructor does all the heavy lifting, as shown here:

```
GLShader::GLShader(GLenum type, const char* text)
: type_(type)
, handle_(glCreateShader(type))
{
glShaderSource(handle_, 1, &text, nullptr);
glCompileShader(handle_);
```

Once the shader has been compiled, we can retrieve its compilation status via glGetShaderInfoLog(). If the message buffer is not empty, which means there were some issues during the shader's compilation, we must print the annotated shader's source code:

```
char buffer[8192];
GLsizei length = 0;
glGetShaderInfoLog(
  handle_, sizeof(buffer), &length, buffer);
if (length) {
  printf("%s\n", buffer);
  printShaderSource(text);
  assert(false);
}
}
```

6. Let's define the explicit constructor, which takes a filename as input and delegates all the work to the first constructor we mentioned previously:

```
GLShader::GLShader(const char* fileName)
 : GLShader(GLShaderTypeFromFileName(fileName),
    readShaderFile(fileName).c_str())
{}
```

7. Deallocate the shader object in the destructor:

```
GLShader::~GLShader() {
  glDeleteShader(handle_);
}
```

8. Finally, we should load some shaders from files using GLShader, like so:

```
GLShader shaderVertex(
  "data/shaders/chapter03/GL02.vert");
GLShader shaderGeometry(
  "data/shaders/chapter03/GL02.geom");
GLShader shaderFragment(
  "data/shaders/chapter03/GL02.frag");
```

If we compile the shader source code and make a mistake, the output from our helper class will look similar to the following listing. The compiler error message, which mentions that line 12 contains an error, can now be directly matched to the shader source code:

```
0(12) : error C1503: undefined variable "texture12"
(  1) //
(  2) #version 460 core
(  3)
(  4) layout (location=0) in vec3 dir;
(  5)
(  6) layout (location=0) out vec4 out_FragColor;
(  7)
(  8) layout (binding=1) uniform samplerCube texture1;
(  9)
( 10) void main()
( 11) {
( 12)   out_FragColor = texture(texture12, dir);
( 13) };
```

```
( 14)
Assertion failed: false, file Sources\shared\GLShader.
cpp, line 53
```

We can use compiled shaders in OpenGL by linking them to a shader program. In a similar fashion, let's write a RAII wrapper for that purpose:

1. First, let's declare a helper class called GLProgram. Constructors that take multiple GLShader arguments are declared to make the class's use more convenient. Normally, we use GLProgram with just a pair of shaders; that is, a vertex and a fragment shader. However, sometimes, other shaders will be linked together:

```cpp
class GLProgram {
public:
  GLProgram(const GLShader& a, const GLShader& b);
  GLProgram(const GLShader& a, const GLShader& b,
            const GLShader& c);
  ...
  ~GLProgram();
  void useProgram() const;
  GLuint getHandle() const { return handle_; }
private:
  GLuint handle_;
};
```

2. Let's add yet another constructor that takes two shaders. The other constructors look identical and have been skipped here for the sake of brevity:

```cpp
GLProgram::GLProgram(
    const GLShader& a, const GLShader& b)
  : handle_(glCreateProgram())
{
  glAttachShader(handle_, a.getHandle());
  glAttachShader(handle_, b.getHandle());
  glLinkProgram(handle_);
  printProgramInfoLog(handle_);
}
```

3. Now, let's write a function that handles the program linking information.
    The `printProgramInfoLog()` function is reused across all `GLProgram`
    constructors and prints the messages reported by the OpenGL implementation:

```cpp
void printProgramInfoLog(GLuint handle) {
  char buffer[8192];
  GLsizei length = 0;
  glGetProgramInfoLog(
    handle, sizeof(buffer), &length, buffer);
  if (length) {
    printf("%s\n", buffer);
    assert(false);
  }
}
```

4. The destructor deletes the shader program in a RAII way:

```cpp
GLProgram::~GLProgram() {
  glDeleteProgram(handle_);
}
```

5. To install a program object as part of the current rendering state, use the
    following method:

```cpp
void GLProgram::useProgram() const {
  glUseProgram(handle_);
}
```

Once the shaders have compiled, the shader program can be linked and used like so:

```cpp
GLProgram program(
  shaderVertex, shaderGeometry, shaderFragment);
program.useProgram();
```

The helper classes we implemented in this recipe will make our OpenGL programming
less verbose and will let us focus on the actual graphics algorithms.

There's more...

There is yet another way to use GLSL shaders in modern OpenGL. It is possible to link a single shader to a separate, standalone shader program and combine those programs into a program pipeline, like so:

```
const char* vtx = ...
const char* frg = ...
const GLuint vs = glCreateShaderProgramv(
  GL_VERTEX_SHADER, 1, &vtx);
const GLuint fs = glCreateShaderProgramv(
  GL_FRAGMENT_SHADER, 1, &frg);
GLuint pipeline;
glCreateProgramPipelines(1, &pipeline);
glUseProgramStages(pipeline, GL_VERTEX_SHADER_BIT, vs);
glUseProgramStages(pipeline, GL_FRAGMENT_SHADER_BIT, fs);
glBindProgramPipeline(pipeline);
```

This approach allows you to mix and match shaders where, for example, a single vertex shader can be reused with many different fragment shaders. This provides much better flexibility and reduces shader combinations exploding exponentially. We recommend using this approach if you decide to stick with modern OpenGL.

Implementing programmable vertex pulling (PVP) in OpenGL

The concept of **programmable vertex pulling** (**PVP**) was proposed in 2012 by Daniel Rákos in the amazing book *OpenGL Insights*. This article goes deep into the architecture of the GPUs of that time and why it was beneficial to use this data storage approach. Initially, the idea of vertex pulling was to store vertex data inside one-dimensional buffer textures and, instead of setting up standard OpenGL vertex attributes, read the data using `texelFetch()` and a GLSL `samplerBuffer` in the vertex shader. The built-in GLSL `gl_VertexID` variable was used as an index to calculate texture coordinates for texel fetching. The reason this trick was implemented was because developers were hitting CPU limits with many draw calls. Due to this, it was beneficial to combine multiple meshes inside a single buffer and render them in a single draw call, without rebinding any vertex arrays or buffer objects to improve draw calls batching.

This technique opens possibilities for merge instancing, where many small meshes can be merged into a bigger one, to be handled as part of the same batch. We will use this technique extensively in our examples, starting from *Chapter 7, Graphics Rendering Pipeline*.

In this recipe, we will use shader storage buffer objects to implement a similar technique with modern OpenGL.

Getting ready

The complete source code for this recipe can be found in this book's source code bundle, under the name `Chapter3/GL02_VtxPulling`.

How to do it...

Let's render the 3D rubber duck model from *Chapter 2, Using Essential Libraries*. However, this time, we will be using the programmable vertex pulling technique. The idea is to allocate two buffer objects – one for the indices and another for the vertex data – and access them in GLSL shaders as shader storage buffers. Let's get started:

1. First, we must load the 3D model via Assimp:

```
const aiScene* scene = aiImportFile(
  "data/rubber_duck/scene.gltf",
  aiProcess_Triangulate);
```

2. Next, convert the per-vertex data into a format suitable for our GLSL shaders. Here, we are going to use `vec3` for our positions and `vec2` for our texture coordinates:

```
struct VertexData {
  vec3 pos;
  vec2 tc;
};
const aiMesh* mesh = scene->mMeshes[0];
std::vector<VertexData> vertices;
for (unsigned i = 0; i != mesh->mNumVertices; i++) {
  const aiVector3D v = mesh->mVertices[i];
  const aiVector3D t = mesh->mTextureCoords[0][i];
  vertices.push_back({
    .pos = vec3(v.x, v.z, v.y),
    .tc = vec2(t.x, t.y) });
}
```

3. For simplicity, we will store the indices as unsigned 32-bit integers. In real-world applications, consider using 16-bit indices for small meshes and ensure you can switch between them:

```
std::vector<unsigned int> indices;
for (unsigned i = 0; i != mesh->mNumFaces; i++) {
  for (unsigned j = 0; j != 3; j++)
     indices.push_back(mesh->mFaces[i].mIndices[j]);
}
```

4. Once the index and vertex data is ready, we can upload it into the OpenGL buffers. We should create two buffers – one for the vertices and one for the indices:

```
const size_t kSizeIndices =
  sizeof(unsigned int) * indices.size();
const size_t kSizeVertices =
  sizeof(VertexData) * vertices.size();
GLuint dataIndices;
glCreateBuffers(1, &dataIndices);
glNamedBufferStorage(
  dataIndices, kSizeIndices, indices.data(), 0);
GLuint dataVertices;
glCreateBuffers(1, &dataVertices);
glNamedBufferStorage(
  dataVertices, kSizeVertices, vertices.data(), 0);
```

5. Now, we should create a vertex array object. In this example, we will make OpenGL read indices from the VAO and use them to access vertex data in a shader storage buffer:

```
GLuint vao;
glCreateVertexArrays(1, &vao);
glBindVertexArray(vao);
glVertexArrayElementBuffer(vao, dataIndices);
```

> **Important Note**
>
> Please note that it is completely possible to store indices inside a shader storage buffer as well, and then read that data manually in the vertex shader. We will leave this as an exercise for you.

6. Before we proceed with the actual rendering, we should bind our vertex data shader storage buffer to binding point 1. Here, we are using sequential binding point indices for uniforms and storage buffers for the sake of simplicity:

```
glBindBufferBase(
  GL_SHADER_STORAGE_BUFFER, 1, dataVertices);
```

7. Let's load and set up the texture for this model:

```
int w, h, comp;
const uint8_t* img = stbi_load(
  "data/rubber_duck/textures/Duck_baseColor.png",
  &w, &h, &comp, 3);
GLuint tx;
glCreateTextures(GL_TEXTURE_2D, 1, &tx);
glTextureParameteri(
  tx, GL_TEXTURE_MIN_FILTER, GL_LINEAR);
glTextureParameteri(
  tx, GL_TEXTURE_MAG_FILTER, GL_LINEAR);
glTextureStorage2D(tx, 1, GL_RGB8, w, h);
glPixelStorei(GL_UNPACK_ALIGNMENT, 1);
glTextureSubImage2D(tx, 0, 0, 0, w, h, GL_RGB,
  GL_UNSIGNED_BYTE, img);
glBindTextures(0, 1, &tx);
```

This is the complete initialization code for C++. Now, let's look at the GLSL vertex shader to understand how to read the vertex data from buffers. The source code for this shader can be found in data\shaders\chapter03\GL02.vert.

How it works...

The declaration of our PerFrameData remains the same and just stores the combined model-view-projection matrix:

```
#version 460 core
layout(std140, binding = 0) uniform PerFrameData {
  uniform mat4 MVP;
};
```

The Vertex structure here should match the VertexData structure in C++ that we used previously to fill in the data for our buffers. Here, we are using arrays of float instead of vec3 and vec2 because GLSL has alignment requirements and will pad vec3 to vec4. We don't want that:

```
struct Vertex {
    float p[3]; float tc[2];
};
```

The actual buffer is attached to binding point 1 and is declared as readonly. The buffer holds an unbounded array of Vertex[] elements. Each element corresponds to exactly one vertex:

> **Note**
>
> The binding points for uniforms and buffers are separate entities, so it is perfectly fine to use 0 for both PerFrameData and Vertices. However, we are using different numbers here to avoid confusion.

```
layout(std430, binding = 1) readonly buffer Vertices {
    Vertex in_Vertices[];
};
```

The accessor functions are required to extract the vec3 position data and the vec2 texture coordinates data from the buffer. Three consecutive floats are used in getPosition(), while two are used in getTexCoord():

```
vec3 getPosition(int i) {
    return vec3( in_Vertices[i].p[0], in_Vertices[i].p[1],
      in_Vertices[i].p[2]);
}
vec2 getTexCoord(int i) {
    return vec2(in_Vertices[i].tc[0], in_Vertices[i].tc[1]);
}
```

The vertex shader only outputs texture coordinates as vec2:

```
layout (location=0) out vec2 uv;
```

Now, we can read the data from the buffer by using the built-in GLSL `gl_VertexID` variable as an index. Because we used VAO with a buffer containing indices to set up our rendering code, the values of `gl_VertexID` will follow the values of the provided indices. Hence, we can use this value directly as an index into the buffer:

```glsl
void main() {
    vec3 pos = getPosition(gl_VertexID);
    gl_Position = MVP * vec4(pos, 1.0);
    uv = getTexCoord(gl_VertexID);
}
```

That's it for the programmable vertex pulling part. The fragment shader applies the texture and uses the barycentric coordinates trick for wireframe rendering, as we described in the previous chapter. The resulting output from the program should look as follows:

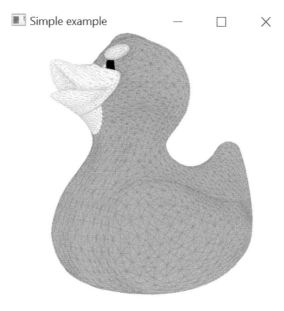

Figure 3.1 – Textured mesh rendered using programmable vertex pulling

There's more...

Programmable vertex pulling is a complex topic and has different performance implications. There is an open source project that does an in-depth analysis of this and provides runtime metrics of PVP performance based on different vertex data layouts and access methods, such as storing data as array of structures or structure of arrays, reading data as multiple floats or a single vector type, and so on.

Check it out at `https://github.com/nlguillemot/ProgrammablePulling`. It should be one of your go-to tools when you're designing PVP pipelines in your OpenGL applications.

Working with cube map textures

A cube map is a texture that contains six individual 2D textures, comprising six sides of a cube. A useful property of cube maps is that they can be sampled using a direction vector. This comes in handy when you're representing light coming into a scene from different directions. For example, we can store the diffuse part of a physically-based lighting equation in an irradiance cube map.

Loading six faces of a cube map into OpenGL is a fairly straightforward operation. However, instead of just six faces, cube maps are often stored as equirectangular projections or as vertical or horizontal crosses. In this recipe, we will learn how to convert this cube map representation into six faces and load them into OpenGL.

Getting ready

There are many websites that offer high-dynamic range environment textures under various licenses. Check out `https://hdrihaven.com` and `https://hdrmaps.com` for useful content.

The complete source code for this recipe can be found in this book's source code bundle, under the name `Chapter3/GL03_CubeMap`.

Before we start working with cube maps, let's introduce a simple helper class for working with bitmap images in 8-bit and 32-bit floating-point formats:

1. Let's declare the interface part of the `Bitmap` class, as follows:

```
class Bitmap {
public:
  Bitmap() = default;
  Bitmap(int w, int h, int comp, eBitmapFormat fmt);
  Bitmap(
    int w, int h, int d, int comp, eBitmapFormat fmt);
  Bitmap(int w, int h, int comp, eBitmapFormat fmt,
    const void* ptr);
```

2. Declare the width, height, depth, and number of components per pixel:

```
int w_ = 0;
int h_ = 0;
int d_ = 1;
int comp_ = 3;
```

3. Set the type of a single component, either `unsigned byte` or `float`. The type of this bitmap should be a 2D texture or a cube map. We will store the actual bytes of this bitmap in an `std::vector` container for simplicity:

```
eBitmapFormat fmt_ = eBitmapFormat_UnsignedByte;
eBitmapType type_ = eBitmapType_2D;
std::vector<uint8_t> data_;
```

4. The following helper function gets the number of bytes necessary for storing one component of a specified format:

```
static int getBytesPerComponent(eBitmapFormat fmt);
```

5. Finally, we need a getter and a setter for our two-dimensional image. We will come back to this later:

```
void setPixel(int x, int y, const glm::vec4& c);
glm::vec4 getPixel(int x, int y) const;
};
```

This implementation is located in `shared/Bitmap.h`. Now, let's use this class to build more high-level cube map conversion functions.

How to do it...

We have a cube map called `data/piazza_bologni_1k.hdr` that was originally downloaded from `https://hdrihaven.com/hdri/?h=piazza_bologni`. The environment map image is provided as an equirectangular projection and looks like this:

Figure 3.2 – Equirectangular projection

Let's convert this project into a vertical cross. In vertical cross format, each cube map's face is represented as a rectangle inside the entire image, as follows:

Figure 3.3 – Vertical cross

If we naively convert the equirectangular projection into cube map faces by iterating over its pixels, calculating the Cartesian coordinates for each pixel, and saving the pixel into a cube map face using these Cartesian coordinates, we will end up with a texture that's been heavily damaged by a Moiré pattern. Here, it's best to do things the other way around; that is, iterate over each pixel of the resulting cube map faces, calculate the source floating-point equirectangular coordinates corresponding to each pixel, and sample the equirectangular texture using bilinear interpolation. This way, the final cube map will be free of artifacts. Let's take a look at this:

1. The first step is to introduce a helper function that maps integer coordinates inside a specified cube map face as floating-point normalized coordinates. This helper is handy because all the faces of the vertical cross cube map have different vertical orientations:

```
vec3 faceCoordsToXYZ(
    int i, int j, int faceID, int faceSize) {
    const float A = 2.0f * float(i) / faceSize;
    const float B = 2.0f * float(j) / faceSize;
    if (faceID == 0)
        return vec3(-1.0f, A - 1.0f, B - 1.0f);
    if (faceID == 1)
        return vec3(A - 1.0f, -1.0f, 1.0f - B);
    if (faceID == 2)
        return vec3(1.0f, A - 1.0f, 1.0f - B);
    if (faceID == 3)
        return vec3(1.0f - A, 1.0f, 1.0f - B);
    if (faceID == 4)
        return vec3(B - 1.0f, A - 1.0f, 1.0f);
    if (faceID == 5)
        return vec3(1.0f - B, A - 1.0f, -1.0f);
    return vec3();
}
```

2. The conversion function starts as follows and calculates the required faceSize, width, and height of the resulting bitmap:

```
Bitmap convertEquirectangularMapToVerticalCross(
    const Bitmap& b) {
    if (b.type_ != eBitmapType_2D) return Bitmap();
    const int faceSize = b.w_ / 4;
    const int w = faceSize * 3;
    const int h = faceSize * 4;
    Bitmap result(w, h, 3);
```

3. The following points define the locations of individual faces inside the cross:

```
const ivec2 kFaceOffsets[] = {
    ivec2(faceSize, faceSize * 3),
    ivec2(0, faceSize),
    ivec2(faceSize, faceSize),
    ivec2(faceSize * 2, faceSize),
    ivec2(faceSize, 0),
    ivec2(faceSize, faceSize * 2)
};
```

4. Two constants will be necessary to clamp the texture lookup:

```
const int clampW = b.w_ - 1;
const int clampH = b.h_ - 1;
```

5. Now, we can start iterating over the six cube map faces and each pixel inside each face:

```
for (int face = 0; face != 6; face++) {
    for (int i = 0; i != faceSize; i++) {
        for (int j = 0; j != faceSize; j++) {
```

6. Use trigonometry functions to calculate the latitude and longitude coordinates of the Cartesian cube map coordinates:

```
const vec3 P = faceCoordsToXYZ(
    i, j, face, faceSize);
const float R = hypot(P.x, P.y);
const float theta = atan2(P.y, P.x);
const float phi = atan2(P.z, R);
```

7. Now, we can map the latitude and longitude of the floating-point coordinates inside the equirectangular image:

```
const float Uf = float(2.0f * faceSize *
    (theta + M_PI) / M_PI);
const float Vf = float(2.0f * faceSize *
    (M_PI / 2.0f - phi) / M_PI);
```

8. Based on these floating-point coordinates, we will get two pairs of integer UV coordinates. We will use these to sample four texels for bilinear interpolation:

```
const int U1 =
    clamp(int(floor(Uf)), 0, clampW);
const int V1 =
    clamp(int(floor(Vf)), 0, clampH);
const int U2 = clamp(U1 + 1, 0, clampW);
const int V2 = clamp(V1 + 1, 0, clampH);
```

9. Get the fractional part for bilinear interpolation:

```
const float s = Uf - U1;
const float t = Vf - V1;
```

10. Fetch four samples from the equirectangular map:

```
const vec4 A = b.getPixel(U1, V1);
const vec4 B = b.getPixel(U2, V1);
const vec4 C = b.getPixel(U1, V2);
const vec4 D = b.getPixel(U2, V2);
```

11. Perform bilinear interpolation and set the resulting pixel value in the vertical cross cube map:

```
const vec4 color = A * (1 - s) * (1 - t) +
    B * (s) * (1 - t) +
    C * (1 - s) * t + D * (s) * (t);
result.setPixel(
    i + kFaceOffsets[face].x, j +
    kFaceOffsets[face].y, color);
        }
      }
    }
  return result;
}
```

The Bitmap class takes care of the pixel format inside the image data.

Now, we can write some code to cut the vertical cross into tightly packed rectangular cube map faces. Here's how to do it:

1. First, let's review the layout of the vertical cross image that corresponds to the OpenGL cube map faces layout:

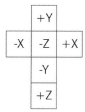

Figure 3.4 – Layout of the vertical cross image

2. The layout is 3x4 faces, which makes it possible to calculate the dimensions of the resulting cube map as follows:

```
Bitmap convertVerticalCrossToCubeMapFaces(
   const Bitmap& b) {
   const int faceWidth = b.w_ / 3;
   const int faceHeight = b.h_ / 4;
   Bitmap cubemap(
      faceWidth, faceHeight, 6, b.comp_, b.fmt_);
```

3. Let's set up some pointers to read and write the data. This function is pixel-format agnostic, so it needs to know the size of each pixel in bytes to be able to memcpy() pixels around:

```
const uint8_t* src = b.data_.data();
uint8_t* dst = cubemap.data_.data();
const int pixelSize = cubemap.comp_ *
   Bitmap::getBytesPerComponent(cubemap.fmt_);
```

4. Iterate over the faces and over every pixel of each face. The order of the cube map faces here corresponds to the order of the OpenGL cube map faces, as defined by the GL_TEXTURE_CUBE_MAP_* constants:

```
for (int face = 0; face != 6; ++face) {
   for (int j = 0; j != faceHeight; ++j) {
      for (int i = 0; i != faceWidth; ++i) {
         int x = 0;
         int y = 0;
```

5. Calculate the source pixel position in the vertical cross layout based on the destination cube map face index:

```
switch (face) {
// GL_TEXTURE_CUBE_MAP_POSITIVE_X
case 0: x = i;
        y = faceHeight + j;
        break;
// GL_TEXTURE_CUBE_MAP_NEGATIVE_X
case 1: x = 2 * faceWidth + i;
        y = 1 * faceHeight + j;
        break;
// GL_TEXTURE_CUBE_MAP_POSITIVE_Y
case 2: x = 2 * faceWidth - (i + 1);
        y = 1 * faceHeight - (j + 1);
        break;
// GL_TEXTURE_CUBE_MAP_NEGATIVE_Y
case 3: x = 2 * faceWidth - (i + 1);
        y = 3 * faceHeight - (j + 1);
        break;
// GL_TEXTURE_CUBE_MAP_POSITIVE_Z
case 4: x = 2 * faceWidth - (i + 1);
        y = b.h_ - (j + 1);
        break;
// GL_TEXTURE_CUBE_MAP_NEGATIVE_Z
case 5: x = faceWidth + i;
        y = faceHeight + j;
        break;
}
```

6. Copy the pixel and advance to the next one:

```
          memcpy(dst, src + (y * b.w_ + x) *
            pixelSize, pixelSize);
          dst += pixelSize;
        }
      }
    }
  return cubemap;
}
```

The resulting cube map contains a stack of six images. Let's write some more C++ code to load and convert the actual texture data and upload it to OpenGL.

7. Use the `STB_image` floating-point API to load a high dynamic range image from a `.hdr` file:

```
int w, h, comp;
const float* img = stbi_loadf(
  "data/piazza_bologni_1k.hdr", &w, &h, &comp, 3);
Bitmap in(w, h, comp, eBitmapFormat_Float, img);
stbi_image_free((void*)img);
```

8. Convert an equirectangular map into a vertical cross and save the resulting image in a `.hdr` file for further inspection:

```
Bitmap out =
  convertEquirectangularMapToVerticalCross(in);
stbi_write_hdr("screenshot.hdr",
  out.w_, out.h_, out.comp_,
  reinterpret_cast<const float*>(out.data_.data()));
```

9. Convert the vertical cross into the actual cube map faces:

```
Bitmap cm = convertVerticalCrossToCubeMapFaces(out);
```

10. Now, uploading to OpenGL is straightforward. All we need to do is create a texture, set the texture parameters, allocate storage for an RGB floating-point texture, and upload the individual faces one by one. Note how the `glTextureSubImage3D()` function is used to upload individual cube map faces. The `zoffset` parameter of the function is used to specify the `i` index of the face:

```
glCreateTextures(GL_TEXTURE_CUBE_MAP, 1, &tex);
glTextureParameteri(
  tex, GL_TEXTURE_WRAP_S, GL_CLAMP_TO_BORDER);
glTextureParameteri(
  tex, GL_TEXTURE_WRAP_T, GL_CLAMP_TO_BORDER);
glTextureParameteri(
  tex, GL_TEXTURE_WRAP_R, GL_CLAMP_TO_BORDER);
glTextureParameteri(
  tex, GL_TEXTURE_MIN_FILTER, GL_LINEAR);
glTextureParameteri(
  tex, GL_TEXTURE_MAG_FILTER, GL_LINEAR);
glTextureStorage2D(tex, 1, GL_RGB32F, cm.w_, cm.h_);
const uint8_t* data = cm.data_.data();
for (unsigned i = 0; i != 6; ++i) {
```

```
    glTextureSubImage3D(tex, 0, 0, 0, i, cm.w_, cm.h_,
      1, GL_RGB, GL_FLOAT, data);
  data += cm.w_ * cm.h_ * cm.comp_ *
    Bitmap::getBytesPerComponent(cm.fmt_);
}
```

Now, let's learn how to write the GLSL shaders for this example:

1. Let's make the vertex shader take a separate model matrix and a world space camera position as its inputs:

    ```
    layout(std140, binding = 0) uniform PerFrameData {
      uniform mat4 model;
      uniform mat4 MVP;
      uniform vec4 cameraPos;
    };
    ```

2. The per-vertex output should be calculated as follows. Positions, normal vectors, and texture coordinates are read from the SSBO buffer using the PVP technique we discussed in the previous recipe. Normal vectors are transformed with a matrix calculated as the inverse transpose of the model matrix:

    ```
    struct PerVertex {
      vec2 uv;
      vec3 normal;
      vec3 worldPos;
    };
    layout (location=0) out PerVertex vtx;
    void main() {
      vec3 pos = getPosition(gl_VertexID);
      gl_Position = MVP * vec4(pos, 1.0);
      mat3 normalMatrix = mat3(transpose(inverse(model)));
      vtx.uv = getTexCoord(gl_VertexID);
      vtx.normal = getNormal(gl_VertexID) * normalMatrix;
      vtx.worldPos = (model * vec4(pos, 1.0)).xyz;
    }
    ```

3. The fragment shader uses `samplerCube` to sample the cube map. Reflected and refracted direction vectors are calculated using GLSL's built-in `reflect()` and `refract()` functions, respectively:

```
layout (binding = 0) uniform sampler2D texture0;
layout (binding = 1) uniform samplerCube texture1;
void main() {
  vec3 n = normalize(vtx.normal);
  vec3 v = normalize(cameraPos.xyz - vtx.worldPos);
  vec3 reflection = -normalize(reflect(v, n));
```

4. To add some more complicated visual appearances, use the index of refraction of ice and calculate the specular reflection coefficient using Schlick's approximation (https://en.wikipedia.org/wiki/Schlick%27s_approximation):

```
float eta = 1.00 / 1.31;
vec3 refraction = -normalize(refract(v, n, eta));
const float R0 = ((1.0-eta) * (1.0-eta)) /
                 ((1.0+eta) * (1.0+eta));
const float Rtheta =
   R0 + (1.0 - R0) * pow((1.0 - dot(-v, n)), 5.0);
vec4 color = texture(texture0, vtx.uv);
```

5. Sample the cube map using the calculated direction vectors:

```
vec4 colorRefl = texture(texture1, reflection);
vec4 colorRefr = texture(texture1, refraction);
```

6. The combined reflection and refraction color is modulated here with the diffuse texture to produce a clean looking image. It doesn't attempt to physically correct the process:

```
color = color * mix(colorRefl, colorRefr, Rtheta);
out_FragColor = color;
};
```

The resulting output from the application looks as follows. Note the blown out white areas of the sky due to how a high dynamic range image is being displayed directly on a low dynamic range framebuffer. We will come back to this issue in *Chapter 8, Image-Based Techniques*, and implement a simple tone mapping operator:

Figure 3.5 – Reflective rubber duck

There's more...

Modern rendering APIs can filter cube maps seamlessly across all faces. To enable this feature for all cube map textures in the current OpenGL context, use `glEnable()`:

```
glEnable(GL_TEXTURE_CUBE_MAP_SEAMLESS);
```

Besides that, seamless cube map filtering can be enabled on a per-texture basis using the `ARB_seamless_cubemap_per_texture` extension, as follows:

```
glTextureParameteri(tex, GL_TEXTURE_CUBE_MAP_SEAMLESS,
                    GL_TRUE);
```

Make sure you use this OpenGL functionality since seamless cube map filtering is almost always what you want from a cube map.

In Vulkan, all cube map texture fetches are seamless (see *Cube Map Edge Handling* in the Vulkan specification), except the ones with `VK_FILTER_NEAREST` enabled on them, which are clamped to the face edge.

Compiling Vulkan shaders at runtime

In the previous recipes, we only covered OpenGL, while Vulkan was only mentioned a few times now and again. In the rest of this chapter, we will show you how to create a Vulkan rendering application with functionality similar to what we've done with OpenGL so far. The code from this and the subsequent recipes will be reused later to build more complex Vulkan demos.

Before we start using Vulkan, we must learn how to significantly speed up the iterative process of writing shaders. Vulkan consumes shaders in their final compiled binary form, called SPIR-V, and it uses a standalone shader compiler to precompile shaders offline. While being perfect for a released product, this approach slows down early stages of graphics application development and rapid prototyping, where shaders are changed a lot and should be recompiled on each application run. In this recipe, we will show you how to compile Vulkan shaders at runtime using Kronos' reference shader compiler, known as `glslang`.

Getting ready

Our application is statically linked to the `glslang` shader compiler. The compiler version we used in this recipe was downloaded using the following Bootstrap snippet:

```
{
  "name": "glslang",
  "source": {
    "type": "git",
    "url": "https://github.com/KhronosGroup/glslang.git",
    "revision": "6fe560f74f472726027e4059692c6eb1e7d972dc"
  }
}
```

The complete source code for this recipe can be found in this book's source code bundle, under the name `Chapter3/VK01_GLSLang`.

How to do it...

Let's learn how to compile a shader using `glslang`:

1. First, we should declare storage for our compiled binary SPIR-V shaders:

    ```
    struct ShaderModule {
      std::vector<unsigned int> SPIRV;
      VkShaderModule shaderModule;
    };
    ```

2. Use the following helper function to compile a shader from its source code for a specified Vulkan pipeline stage; then, save the binary SPIR-V result in the `ShaderModule` structure:

```
size_t compileShader(glslang_stage_t stage,
  const char* shaderSource,
  ShaderModule& shaderModule) {
```

3. The compiler's input structure initialization is pretty verbose. We should specify the source shader language as `GLSLANG_SOURCE_GLSL` and use proper targets to generate SPIR-V 1.3 for Vulkan version 1.1. Using the new C++20 feature known as designated initializers for this task is a breeze. The same applies to low-level Vulkan development in general, since the most frequent thing a developer will do is fill in structure members with values:

```
const glslang_input_t input = {
    .language = GLSLANG_SOURCE_GLSL,
    .stage = stage,
    .client = GLSLANG_CLIENT_VULKAN,
    .client_version = GLSLANG_TARGET_VULKAN_1_1,
    .target_language = GLSLANG_TARGET_SPV,
    .target_language_version =GLSLANG_TARGET_SPV_1_3,
    .code = shaderSource,
    .default_version = 100,
    .default_profile = GLSLANG_NO_PROFILE,
    .force_default_version_and_profile = false,
    .forward_compatible = false,
    .messages = GLSLANG_MSG_DEFAULT_BIT,
    .resource = (const glslang_resource_t*)
      &glslang::DefaultTBuiltInResource,
};
```

4. Let's create a shader using the constructed input:

```
glslang_shader_t* shd =
  glslang_shader_create(&input);
```

5. First, the shader needs to be preprocessed by the compiler. This function returns `true` if all the extensions, pragmas, and version strings mentioned in the shader source code are valid:

```
if ( !glslang_shader_preprocess(shd, &input) ) {
    fprintf(stderr, "GLSL preprocessing failed\n" );
    fprintf(stderr, "\n%s",
      glslang_shader_get_info_log(shd));
    fprintf(stderr, "\n%s",
```

```
        glslang_shader_get_info_debug_log(shd));
      fprintf(stderr, "code:\n%s", input.code );
      return 0;
    }
```

6. Then, the shader gets parsed in an internal parse tree representation inside the compiler:

```
if ( !glslang_shader_parse(shd, &input) ) {
  fprintf(stderr, "GLSL parsing failed\n");
  fprintf(stderr, "\n%s",
    glslang_shader_get_info_log(shd) );
  fprintf(stderr, "\n%s",
    glslang_shader_get_info_debug_log(shd));
  fprintf(stderr, "%s",
    glslang_shader_get_preprocessed_code(shd));
  return 0;
}
```

7. If everything went well during the previous stages, we can link the shader to a program and proceed with the binary code generation stage:

```
glslang_program_t* prog = glslang_program_create();
glslang_program_add_shader(prog, shd);
int msgs = GLSLANG_MSG_SPV_RULES_BIT |
  GLSLANG_MSG_VULKAN_RULES_BIT;
if ( !glslang_program_link(prog, msgs) ) {
  fprintf(stderr, "GLSL linking failed\n");
  fprintf(stderr, "\n%s",
    glslang_program_get_info_log(prog));
  fprintf(stderr, "\n%s",
    glslang_program_get_info_debug_log(prog));
  return 0;
}
```

8. Generate some binary SPIR-V code and store it inside the shaderModule output variable:

```
glslang_program_SPIRV_generate(prog, stage);
shaderModule.SPIRV.resize(
  glslang_program_SPIRV_get_size(prog));
glslang_program_SPIRV_get(
  prog, shaderModule.SPIRV.data());
```

9.   Some messages may be produced by the code generator. Check and print them if there are any:

```
const char* spirv_messages =
    glslang_program_SPIRV_get_messages(prog);
if (spirv_messages)
    fprintf(stderr, "%s", spirv_messages);
```

10.   Clean up and return the number of uint32_t values in the generated binary blob. This is how Vulkan requires the size to be specified:

```
glslang_program_delete(program);
glslang_shader_delete(shader);
return shaderModule.SPIRV.size();
}
```

How it works...

The demo application is straightforward: it loads the shader source code from a text file and uses the compileShader() function we just wrote to compile it into SPIR-V:

```
size_t compileShaderFile(
  const char* file, ShaderModule& shaderModule)
{
  if (auto shaderSource = readShaderFile(file);
      !shaderSource.empty())
    return compileShader(
      glslangShaderStageFromFileName(file),
      shaderSource.c_str(), shaderModule);
  return 0;
}
```

Each generated SPIR-V binary blob is saved in a file for further inspection:

```
void testShaderCompilation(
  const char* sourceFilename, const char* destFilename)
{
  ShaderModule;
  if (compileShaderFile(sourceFilename, shaderModule) < 1)
    return;
  saveSPIRVBinaryFile(destFilename,
    shaderModule.SPIRV.data(), shaderModule.SPIRV.size());
}
```

The main() function, which drives the demo application, initializes the glslang compiler and runs the necessary tests:

```
int main() {
  glslang_initialize_process();
  testShaderCompilation(
    "data/shaders/chapter03/VK01.vert", "VK01.vrt.bin");
  testShaderCompilation(
    "data/shaders/chapter03/VK01.frag", "VK01.frg.bin");
  glslang_finalize_process();
  return 0;
}
```

The aforementioned program produces the same SPIR-V output as the following commands:

```
glslangValidator -V110 --target-env spirv1.3 VK01.vert -o VK01.vrt.bin
glslangValidator -V110 --target-env spirv1.3 VK01.frag -o VK01.frg.bin
```

There's more...

While being convenient during application development phases, shipping a big compiler alongside a release version of your application is a questionable practice. Unless compiling shaders at runtime is a feature of your application, you should prefer shipping precompiled SPIR-V shader binaries in the release version. One transparent way to do this is to implement a shader caching mechanism in your application. Once a shader is required, the application checks if a compiled shader is present. If there are none, it can load the glslang compiler from .dll or .so at runtime and compile the shader. This way, you can ensure that you always have compiled shaders for the release version of your app and that you do not need to ship shared libraries of the compiler.

If you want to learn how to load compiled shaders from .bin files produced by glslangValidator, take a look at this tutorial: https://vulkan-tutorial.com/Drawing_a_triangle/Graphics_pipeline_basics/Shader_modules.

Initializing Vulkan instances and graphical devices

The new Vulkan API is much more verbose, so we must split creating a graphical demo into separate, smaller recipes. In this recipe, we will learn how to create a Vulkan instance, enumerate all the physical devices in the system that are capable of 3D graphics rendering, and initialize one of these devices to create a window with an attached surface.

Getting ready

Teaching Vulkan from scratch is not the goal of this book, so we recommend starting with the book *Vulkan Cookbook*, published by Packt, and *Vulkan Programming Guide: The Official Guide to Learning Vulkan*, by Addison-Wesley Professional.

The hardest part of transitioning from OpenGL to Vulkan, or any other similar modern graphics API, is getting used to the amount of explicit code necessary to set up the rendering process, which, thankfully, only needs to be done once. It is also useful to get a grasp of Vulkan's object model. As a good starting point, we recommend reading `https://gpuopen.com/understanding-vulkan-objects/` as a reference. For the remaining recipes in this chapter, we aim to start rendering 3D scenes with the bare minimum amount of setup.

All our Vulkan recipes use the Volk meta loader for the Vulkan API, which can be downloaded from `https://github.com/zeux/volk` using the following Bootstrap snippet. The meta loader allows you to dynamically load the entry points required to use Vulkan, without having to statically link any Vulkan loaders:

```
{
  "name": "volk",
  "source": {
    "type": "git",
    "url": "https://github.com/zeux/volk.git",
    "revision": "1.2.170"
  }
}
```

The complete Vulkan example for this recipe can be found in `Chapter3/VK02_DemoApp`.

How to do it...

Let's start with some error checking facilities:

1. Any function call from a complex API may fail. To handle failure, or to at least let the developer know the exact location of the failure, we can wrap most of the Vulkan calls in the `VK_CHECK()` and `VK_CHECK_RET()` macros, which internally call the following `VK_ASSERT()` function:

```
static void VK_ASSERT(bool check) {
    if (!check) exit(EXIT_FAILURE);
}
```

2. The `VK_CHECK()` and `VK_CHECK_RET()` macros compare the result of a Vulkan call with the success value and return either a Boolean flag or a result value. If the comparison fails, the program should exit immediately:

```
#define VK_CHECK(value) \
    if ( value != VK_SUCCESS ) \
      { VK_ASSERT(false); return false; }
#define VK_CHECK_RET(value) \
    if ( value != VK_SUCCESS ) \
      { VK_ASSERT(false); return value; }
```

Now, we can start creating our first Vulkan object. The `VkInstance` object serves as an interface to the Vulkan API:

1. The `createInstance()` routine is called at the beginning of the initialization process. Using the Vulkan instance, we can acquire a list of physical devices with the required properties:

```
void createInstance(VkInstance* instance) {
```

2. First, we will declare a list of so-called layers, which will allow us to enable debugging output for every Vulkan call. The only layer we will be using is the debugging layer:

```
const std::vector<const char*> layers = {
    "VK_LAYER_KHRONOS_validation"
};
```

3. Next, we must declare the array with a list of extensions. The minimum number of extensions to allow rendering to take place is two. We need VK_KHR_surface and another platform-specific extension that takes an OS window handle and attaches a rendering surface to it. Amazingly, the following code is the only part of this example that explicitly requires us to use macros to detect the OS and assign the extension name:

```
const std::vector<const char*> exts = {
    "VK_KHR_surface",
#if defined (WIN32)
    "VK_KHR_win32_surface",
#endif
```

4. macOS is supported via the MoltenVK implementation. However, most of the examples in this book are based on Vulkan 1.2, which is not supported by MoltenVK yet:

```
#if defined (__APPLE__)
    "VK_MVK_macos_surface",
#endif
```

5. On Linux, only libXCB-based window creation is supported. Similarly, the Wayland protocol is also supported, but that is outside the scope of this book:

```
#if defined (__linux__)
    "VK_KHR_xcb_surface",
#endif
    VK_EXT_DEBUG_UTILS_EXTENSION_NAME,
    VK_EXT_DEBUG_REPORT_EXTENSION_NAME
};
```

6. After constructing the list of surface-related extensions, we should fill in some mandatory information about our application:

```
const VkApplicationInfo appInfo = {
    .sType = VK_STRUCTURE_TYPE_APPLICATION_INFO,
    .pNext = nullptr,
    .pApplicationName = "Vulkan",
    .applicationVersion = VK_MAKE_VERSION(1, 0, 0),
    .pEngineName = "No Engine",
    .engineVersion = VK_MAKE_VERSION(1, 0, 0),
    .apiVersion = VK_API_VERSION_1_1
};
```

7. To create a `VkInstance` object, we should fill in the `VkInstanceCreateInfo` structure. Use a pointer to the aforementioned `appInfo` constant and the list of extensions in the member fields of `createInfo`:

```
const VkInstanceCreateInfo createInfo = {
  .sType = VK_STRUCTURE_TYPE_INSTANCE_CREATE_INFO,
  .pNext = nullptr,
  .flags = 0,
  .pApplicationInfo = &appInfo,
  .enabledLayerCount =
    static_cast<uint32_t>(layers.size()),
  .ppEnabledLayerNames = layers.data(),
  .enabledExtensionCount =
    static_cast<uint32_t>(exts.size()),
  .ppEnabledExtensionNames = exts.data()
};
VK_ASSERT(vkCreateInstance(
  &createInfo, nullptr, instance) == VK_SUCCESS);
```

8. Finally, we must ask the Volk library to retrieve all the Vulkan API function pointers for all the extensions that are available for the created `VkInstance`:

```
  volkLoadInstance(*instance);
}
```

Once we have a Vulkan instance ready and the graphics queue index set up with the selected physical device, we can create a logical representation of a GPU. Vulkan treats all devices as a collection of queues and memory heaps. To use a device for rendering, we need to specify a queue that can execute graphics-related commands, and a physical device that has such a queue. Let's get started:

1. The `createDevice()` function accepts a list of required device features (for example, geometry shader support), a graphics queue index, a physical device, and an output handle for the logical device as input:

```
VkResult createDevice(
  VkPhysicalDevice physicalDevice,
  VkPhysicalDeviceFeatures deviceFeatures,
  uint32_t graphicsFamily,
  VkDevice* device)
{
```

2. Let's declare a list of extensions that our logical device must support. For our early demos, we need the device to support the swap chain object, which allows us to present rendered frames on the screen. This list is going to be extended in subsequent chapters:

```
const std::vector<const char*> extensions = {
  VK_KHR_SWAPCHAIN_EXTENSION_NAME
};
```

3. We will only use a single graphics queue that has maximum priority:

```
const float queuePriority = 1.0f;
const VkDeviceQueueCreateInfo qci = {
  .sType =VK_STRUCTURE_TYPE_DEVICE_QUEUE_CREATE_INFO,
  .pNext = nullptr,
  .flags = 0,
  .queueFamilyIndex = graphicsFamily,
  .queueCount = 1,
  .pQueuePriorities = &queuePriority
};
```

4. To create something in Vulkan, we should fill in a ...CreateInfo structure and pass all the required object properties to an appropriate vkCreate...() function. Here, we will define a VkDeviceCreateInfo constant with a reference to a single queue:

```
const VkDeviceCreateInfo ci = {
  .sType = VK_STRUCTURE_TYPE_DEVICE_CREATE_INFO,
  .pNext = nullptr,
  .flags = 0,
  .queueCreateInfoCount = 1,
  .pQueueCreateInfos = &qci,
  .enabledLayerCount = 0,
  .ppEnabledLayerNames = nullptr,
  .enabledExtensionCount =
    static_cast<uint32_t>(extensions.size()),
  .ppEnabledExtensionNames = extensions.data(),
  .pEnabledFeatures = &deviceFeatures
};
return vkCreateDevice(
  physicalDevice, &ci, nullptr, device );
}
```

5. The `createDevice()` function expects a reference to a physical graphics-capable device. The following function finds such a device:

```
VkResult findSuitablePhysicalDevice(
  VkInstance instance,
  std::function<bool(VkPhysicalDevice)> selector,
  VkPhysicalDevice* physicalDevice)
{
  uint32_t deviceCount = 0;
  VK_CHECK_RET(vkEnumeratePhysicalDevices(instance,
    &deviceCount, nullptr));
  if (!deviceCount)
    return VK_ERROR_INITIALIZATION_FAILED;
  std::vector<VkPhysicalDevice> devices(deviceCount);
  VK_CHECK_RET(vkEnumeratePhysicalDevices(
    instance, &deviceCount, devices.data()));
  for (const auto& device : devices)
    if (selector(device)) {
      *physicalDevice = device;
      return VK_SUCCESS;
    }
  return VK_ERROR_INITIALIZATION_FAILED;
}
```

6. Once we have a physical device reference, we will get a list of its queues. Here, we must check for the one with our desired capability flags:

```
uint32_t findQueueFamilies(
  VkPhysicalDevice device, VkQueueFlags desiredFlags)
{
  uint32_t familyCount;
  vkGetPhysicalDeviceQueueFamilyProperties(
    device, &familyCount, nullptr);
  std::vector<VkQueueFamilyProperties>
    families(familyCount);
  vkGetPhysicalDeviceQueueFamilyProperties(
    device, &familyCount, families.data());
  for (uint32_t i = 0; i != families.size(); i++)
    if ( families[i].queueCount &&
         (families[i].queueFlags & desiredFlags) )
           return i;
```

```
        return 0;
    }
```

At this point, we have selected a suitable physical device, but we are far from finished with rendering the Vulkan pipeline. The next thing we will do is create a swap chain object. Let's move on to the next recipe to learn how to do this.

Initializing the Vulkan swap chain

Normally, each frame is rendered as an offscreen image. Once the rendering process is complete, the offscreen image should be made visible. An object that holds a collection of available offscreen images – or, more specifically, a queue of rendered images waiting to be presented to the screen – is called a swap chain. In OpenGL, presenting an offscreen buffer to the visible area of a window is performed using system-dependent functions, namely `wglSwapBuffers()` on Windows, `eglSwapBuffers()` on OpenGL ES embedded systems, `glXSwapBuffers()` on Linux, and automatically on macOS. Using Vulkan, we need to select a sequencing algorithm for the swap chain images. Also, the operation that presents an image to the display is no different from any other operation, such as rendering a collection of triangles. The Vulkan API object model treats each graphics device as a collection of command queues where rendering, computation, or transfer operations can be enqueued.

In this recipe, we will show you how to create a Vulkan swap chain object using the Vulkan instance and graphical device we initialized in the previous recipe.

Getting ready

Revisit the previous recipe, which discusses Vulkan instance creation and enabling the validation layer.

How to do it...

Before we can create a swap chain object, we need some helper functions:

1. First, let's write a function that retrieves swap chain support details based on the specified physical device and the Vulkan surface. The result is returned inside the `SwapchainSupportDetails` structure:

```
struct SwapchainSupportDetails {
    VkSurfaceCapabilitiesKHR capabilities = {};
    std::vector<VkSurfaceFormatKHR> formats;
    std::vector<VkPresentModeKHR> presentModes;
```

```
    };
    SwapchainSupportDetails querySwapchainSupport(
      VkPhysicalDevice device, VkSurfaceKHR surface) {
```

2. Query the basic capabilities of a surface:

```
    SwapchainSupportDetails details;
    vkGetPhysicalDeviceSurfaceCapabilitiesKHR(
      device, surface, &details.capabilities);
```

3. Get the number of available surface formats. Allocate the storage to hold them:

```
    uint32_t formatCount;
    vkGetPhysicalDeviceSurfaceFormatsKHR(
      device, surface, &formatCount, nullptr);
    if (formatCount) {
      details.formats.resize(formatCount);
      vkGetPhysicalDeviceSurfaceFormatsKHR(
        device, surface, &formatCount,
        details.formats.data());
    }
```

4. Retrieve the supported presentation modes in a similar way:

```
    uint32_t presentModeCnt;
    vkGetPhysicalDeviceSurfacePresentModesKHR(
      device, surface, &presentModeCnt, nullptr);
    if (presentModeCnt) {
      details.presentModes.resize(presentModeCnt);
      vkGetPhysicalDeviceSurfacePresentModesKHR(
        device, surface, &presentModeCnt,
        details.presentModes.data());
    }
    return details;
  }
```

5. Let's write a helper function for choosing the required surface format. We will use a hardcoded value here for the RGBA 8-bit per channel format with the sRGB color space:

```
    VkSurfaceFormatKHR chooseSwapSurfaceFormat(
      const std::vector<VkSurfaceFormatKHR>&
      availableFormats) {
```

```
    return
      { VK_FORMAT_B8G8R8A8_UNORM,VK_COLOR_SPACE_SRGB_
        NONLINEAR_KHR};
}
```

6. Now, we should select presentation mode. The preferred presentation mode is
    VK_PRESENT_MODE_MAILBOX_KHR, which specifies that the Vulkan presentation
    system should wait for the next vertical blanking period to update the current
    image. Visual tearing will not be observed in this case. However, it's not guaranteed
    that this presentation mode will be supported. In this situation, we can always fall
    back to VK_PRESENT_MODE_FIFO_KHR. The differences between all possible
    presentation modes are described in the Vulkan specification at https://www.
    khronos.org/registry/vulkan/specs/1.1-extensions/man/html/
    VkPresentModeKHR.html:

```
VkPresentModeKHR chooseSwapPresentMode(
  const std::vector<VkPresentModeKHR>&
    availablePresentModes) {
  for (const auto mode : availablePresentModes)
    if (mode == VK_PRESENT_MODE_MAILBOX_KHR)
      return mode;
  return VK_PRESENT_MODE_FIFO_KHR;
}
```

7. The last helper function we need will choose the number of images in the swap
    chain object. It is based on the surface capabilities we retrieved earlier. Instead of
    using minImageCount directly, we will request one additional image to make sure
    we are not waiting on the GPU to complete any operations:

```
uint32_t chooseSwapImageCount(
  const VkSurfaceCapabilitiesKHR& caps)
{
  const uint32_t imageCount = caps.minImageCount + 1;
  const bool imageCountExceeded =
    caps.maxImageCount &&
    imageCount > caps.maxImageCount;
  return imageCountExceeded ?
    caps.maxImageCount : imageCount;
}
```

8. Once we have all of our helper functions in place, the `createSwapchain()` wrapper function becomes rather short and mostly consists of filling in the `VkSwapchainCreateInfoKHR` structure:

```
VkResult createSwapchain(
  VkDevice device, VkPhysicalDevice physicalDevice,
  VkSurfaceKHR surface,
  uint32_t graphicsFamily,
  uint32_t width, uint32_t height,
  VkSwapchainKHR* swapchain)
{
  auto swapchainSupport = querySwapchainSupport(
    physicalDevice, surface);
  auto surfaceFormat = chooseSwapSurfaceFormat(
    swapchainSupport.formats);
  auto presentMode = chooseSwapPresentMode(
    swapchainSupport.presentModes);
```

9. Let's fill in the `VkSwapchainCreateInfoKHR` structure. Our initial example will not use a depth buffer, so only `VK_IMAGE_USAGE_COLOR_ATTACHMENT_BIT` will be used. The `VK_IMAGE_USAGE_TRANSFER_DST_BIT` flag specifies that the image can be used as the destination of a transfer command:

```
const VkSwapchainCreateInfoKHR ci = {
  .sType =
    VK_STRUCTURE_TYPE_SWAPCHAIN_CREATE_INFO_KHR,
  .flags = 0,
  .surface = surface,
  .minImageCount = chooseSwapImageCount(
    swapchainSupport.capabilities),
  .imageFormat = surfaceFormat.format,
  .imageColorSpace = surfaceFormat.colorSpace,
  .imageExtent =
    {.width = width, .height = height },
  .imageArrayLayers = 1,
  .imageUsage =
    VK_IMAGE_USAGE_COLOR_ATTACHMENT_BIT |
    VK_IMAGE_USAGE_TRANSFER_DST_BIT,
  .imageSharingMode = VK_SHARING_MODE_EXCLUSIVE,
  .queueFamilyIndexCount = 1,
  .pQueueFamilyIndices = &graphicsFamily,
  .preTransform =
    swapchainSupport.capabilities.currentTransform,
  .compositeAlpha =
    VK_COMPOSITE_ALPHA_OPAQUE_BIT_KHR,
  .presentMode = presentMode,
```

```
      .clipped = VK_TRUE,
      .oldSwapchain = VK_NULL_HANDLE
  };
  return vkCreateSwapchainKHR(
    device, &ci, nullptr, swapchain);
}
```

10. Once the swapchain object has been created, we should retrieve the actual images from the swapchain. Use the following function to do so:

```
size_t createSwapchainImages(
  VkDevice device, VkSwapchainKHR swapchain,
  std::vector<VkImage>& swapchainImages,
  std::vector<VkImageView>& swapchainImageViews)
{
  uint32_t imageCount = 0;
  VK_ASSERT(vkGetSwapchainImagesKHR(device, swapchain,
    &imageCount, nullptr) == VK_SUCCESS);
  swapchainImages.resize(imageCount);
  swapchainImageViews.resize(imageCount);
  VK_ASSERT(vkGetSwapchainImagesKHR(device, swapchain,
    &imageCount, swapchainImages.data()) ==
    VK_SUCCESS);
  for (unsigned i = 0; i < imageCount; i++)
    if (!createImageView(device, swapchainImages[i],
        VK_FORMAT_B8G8R8A8_UNORM,
        VK_IMAGE_ASPECT_COLOR_BIT,
        &swapchainImageViews[i]))
      exit(EXIT_FAILURE);
  return imageCount;
}
```

11. One last thing to mention is the helper function that creates an image view for us:

```
bool createImageView(VkDevice device, VkImage image,
  VkFormat format, VkImageAspectFlags aspectFlags,
  VkImageView* imageView)
{
  const VkImageViewCreateInfo viewInfo = {
    .sType =
      VK_STRUCTURE_TYPE_IMAGE_VIEW_CREATE_INFO,
    .pNext = nullptr,
    .flags = 0,
    .image = image,
```

```
      .viewType = VK_IMAGE_VIEW_TYPE_2D,
      .format = format,
      .subresourceRange = {
        .aspectMask = aspectFlags,
        .baseMipLevel = 0,
        .levelCount = 1,
        .baseArrayLayer = 0,
        .layerCount = 1
      }
    };
    VK_CHECK(vkCreateImageView(device, &viewInfo,
      nullptr, imageView));
    return true;
}
```

Now, we can start the Vulkan initialization process. In the next recipe, we will show you how to catch errors that are encountered during the initialization phase.

Setting up Vulkan's debugging capabilities

Once we have created a Vulkan instance, we can start tracking all possible errors and warnings that may be produced by the validation layer. To do so, we should create a couple of callback functions and register them with the Vulkan instance. In this recipe, we will learn how to set up and use them.

How to do it...

There are two callback functions that catch the debug output from Vulkan: vulkanDebugCallback() and vulkanDebugReportCallback(). Let's get started:

1. The first function, vulkanDebugCallback() prints all messages coming into the system console:

```
static VKAPI_ATTR VkBool32 VKAPI_CALL
vulkanDebugCallback(
  VkDebugUtilsMessageSeverityFlagBitsEXT Severity,
  VkDebugUtilsMessageTypeFlagsEXT Type,
  const VkDebugUtilsMessengerCallbackDataEXT*
    CallbackData, void* UserData)
{
  printf("Validation layer: %s\n",
    CallbackData->pMessage);
  return VK_FALSE;
}
```

2. `vulkanDebugReportCallback()` is more elaborate and provides information about an object that's causing an error or a warning. Some performance warnings are silenced to make the debug output more readable:

```
static VKAPI_ATTR VkBool32 VKAPI_CALL
vulkanDebugReportCallback(
  VkDebugReportFlagsEXT flags,
  VkDebugReportObjectTypeEXT objectType,
  uint64_t object, size_t location,
  int32_t messageCode,
  const char* pLayerPrefix,
  const char* pMessage, void* UserData)
{
  if (flags &
      VK_DEBUG_REPORT_PERFORMANCE_WARNING_BIT_EXT)
    return VK_FALSE;
  printf("Debug callback (%s): %s\n",
    pLayerPrefix, pMessage);
  return VK_FALSE;
}
```

3. To associate these callbacks with a Vulkan instance, we should create two more objects, `messenger` and `reportCallback`, in the following function. They will be destroyed at the end of the application:

```
bool setupDebugCallbacks(
  VkInstance instance,
  VkDebugUtilsMessengerEXT* messenger,
  VkDebugReportCallbackEXT* reportCallback)
{
  const VkDebugUtilsMessengerCreateInfoEXT ci1 = {
    .sType = VK_STRUCTURE_TYPE_DEBUG_UTILS_MESSENGER
             _CREATE_INFO_EXT,
    .messageSeverity =
      VK_DEBUG_UTILS_MESSAGE_SEVERITY
        _WARNING_BIT_EXT |
      VK_DEBUG_UTILS_MESSAGE_SEVERITY_ERROR_BIT_EXT,
    .messageType =
      VK_DEBUG_UTILS_MESSAGE_TYPE_GENERAL_BIT_EXT|
      VK_DEBUG_UTILS_MESSAGE_TYPE_VALIDATION_BIT_EXT|
      VK_DEBUG_UTILS_MESSAGE_TYPE
        _PERFORMANCE_BIT_EXT,
    .pfnUserCallback = &VulkanDebugCallback,
    .pUserData = nullptr
  };
```

```
    VK_CHECK(vkCreateDebugUtilsMessengerEXT(
      instance, &ci1, nullptr, messenger));
    const VkDebugReportCallbackCreateInfoEXT ci2 = {
      .sType = VK_STRUCTURE_TYPE_DEBUG_REPORT
      _CALLBACK_CREATE_INFO_EXT,
      .pNext = nullptr,
      .flags =
        VK_DEBUG_REPORT_WARNING_BIT_EXT |
        VK_DEBUG_REPORT_PERFORMANCE_WARNING_BIT_EXT |
        VK_DEBUG_REPORT_ERROR_BIT_EXT |
        VK_DEBUG_REPORT_DEBUG_BIT_EXT,
      .pfnCallback = &VulkanDebugReportCallback,
      .pUserData = nullptr
    };
    VK_CHECK(vkCreateDebugReportCallbackEXT(instance,
      &ci, nullptr,reportCallback));
    return true;
}
```

This code is sufficient to get you started with reading the validation layer messages and debugging your Vulkan applications.

There's more...

To make our validation layers even more useful, we can add symbolic names to Vulkan objects. This is useful for debugging Vulkan applications in situations where the validation layer reports object handles. Use the following code snippet to do this:

```
bool setVkObjectName(VulkanRenderDevice& vkDev,
    void object,
    VkObjectType objType, const char name) {
    VkDebugUtilsObjectNameInfoEXT nameInfo = {
      .sType = VK_STRUCTURE_TYPE_DEBUG_UTILS
        _OBJECT_NAME_INFO_EXT,
      .pNext = nullptr,
      .objectType = objType,
      .objectHandle = (uint64_t)object,
      .pObjectName = name
    };
    return (vkSetDebugUtilsObjectNameEXT(vkDev.device,
      &nameInfo) == VK_SUCCESS);
}
```

Also, please note that you should destroy the validation layer callbacks right before the Vulkan instance is destroyed. Check the full source code for details.

Tracking and cleaning up Vulkan objects

To keep things under control, we must carefully collect and recycle all our previously allocated Vulkan objects. In this recipe, we will learn how to keep track of allocated Vulkan objects and deallocate them properly at the end of our application.

Getting ready

Since Vulkan is an asynchronous interface, there must be a way to synchronize operations and ensure they complete. One of these synchronization objects is a semaphore. Here, we are declaring a helper function to create a semaphore:

```
VkResult createSemaphore(
  VkDevice device, VkSemaphore* outSemaphore) {
  const VkSemaphoreCreateInfo ci = {
    .sType = VK_STRUCTURE_TYPE_SEMAPHORE_CREATE_INFO };
  return vkCreateSemaphore(
    device, &ci, nullptr, outSemaphore);
}
```

Now, we can go ahead and use this function in this recipe.

How to do it...

Let's make the ad hoc approach to Vulkan initialization we used in the previous recipes more organized:

1. First, we should combine all our related VkInstance objects into the following structure:

    ```
    struct VulkanInstance {
      VkInstance instance;
      VkSurfaceKHR surface;
      VkDebugUtilsMessengerEXT messenger;
      VkDebugReportCallbackEXT reportCallback;
    };
    ```

2. In a similar way, all our related `VkDevice` objects should be combined into
    the `VulkanRenderDevice` structure. The new `VkCommandPool` and
    `VkCommandBuffers` objects will be discussed later. We will extend this structure
    with the Vulkan functionality in *Chapter 6, Physically Based Rendering Using the
    glTF2 Shading Model*:

```
struct VulkanRenderDevice {
  VkDevice device;
  VkQueue graphicsQueue;
  VkPhysicalDevice physicalDevice;
  uint32_t graphicsFamily;
  VkSemaphore semaphore;
  VkSemaphore renderSemaphore;
  VkSwapchainKHR swapchain;
  std::vector<VkImage> swapchainImages;
  std::vector<VkImageView> swapchainImageViews;
  VkCommandPool commandPool;
  std::vector<VkCommandBuffer> commandBuffers;
};
```

3. Now, we can proceed with the complete initialization routine of the Vulkan
    render device:

```
bool initVulkanRenderDevice(
  VulkanInstance& vk, VulkanRenderDevice& vkDev,
  uint32_t width, uint32_t height,
  std::function<bool(VkPhysicalDevice)> selector,
  VkPhysicalDeviceFeatures deviceFeatures)
{
  VK_CHECK(findSuitablePhysicalDevice(
    vk.instance, selector, &vkDev.physicalDevice));
  vkDev.graphicsFamily =
    findQueueFamilies(vkDev.physicalDevice,
    VK_QUEUE_GRAPHICS_BIT);
  VK_CHECK(createDevice(vkDev.physicalDevice,
    deviceFeatures, vkDev.graphicsFamily,
    &vkDev.device));
  vkGetDeviceQueue(
    vkDev.device, vkDev.graphicsFamily, 0,
    &vkDev.graphicsQueue);
  if (vkDev.graphicsQueue == nullptr)
    exit(EXIT_FAILURE);
```

```
VkBool32 presentSupported = 0;
vkGetPhysicalDeviceSurfaceSupportKHR(
  vkDev.physicalDevice, vkDev.graphicsFamily,
  vk.surface, &presentSupported);
if (!presentSupported) exit(EXIT_FAILURE);
VK_CHECK(createSwapchain(vkDev.device,
  vkDev.physicalDevice, vk.surface,
  vkDev.graphicsFamily,
  width, height, &vkDev.swapchain));
const size_t imageCount = createSwapchainImages(
  vkDev.device, vkDev.swapchain,
  vkDev.swapchainImages, vkDev.swapchainImageViews);
 vkDev.commandBuffers.resize(imageCount);
```

4. There are two semaphores that are necessary for rendering. We will use the first one, called vkDev.semaphore, to ensure that the rendering process waits for the swap chain image to become available; the second one, called vkDev.renderSemaphore, will ensure that the presentation process waits for rendering to have completed:

```
VK_CHECK(createSemaphore(vkDev.device,
  &vkDev.semaphore));
VK_CHECK(createSemaphore(vkDev.device,
  &vkDev.renderSemaphore));
```

5. A command pool is necessary to allocate command buffers:

```
const VkCommandPoolCreateInfo cpi = {
  .sType =
    VK_STRUCTURE_TYPE_COMMAND_POOL_CREATE_INFO,
  .flags = 0,
  .queueFamilyIndex = vkDev.graphicsFamily
};
VK_CHECK(vkCreateCommandPool(vkDev.device, &cpi,
  nullptr, &vkDev.commandPool));
```

6. Allocate one command buffer per swap chain image:

```
const VkCommandBufferAllocateInfo ai = {
  .sType =
    VK_STRUCTURE_TYPE_COMMAND_BUFFER_ALLOCATE_INFO,
  .pNext = nullptr,
  .commandPool = vkDev.commandPool,
  .level = VK_COMMAND_BUFFER_LEVEL_PRIMARY,
  .commandBufferCount =
    (uint32_t)(vkDev.swapchainImages.size())
};
```

```
    VK_CHECK(vkAllocateCommandBuffers(
      vkDev.device, &ai, &vkDev.commandBuffers[0]));
  return true;
}
```

7. Deinitialization is straightforward. First, we should destroy everything stored inside the `VulkanRenderDevice` structure:

```
void destroyVulkanRenderDevice(
  VulkanRenderDevice& vkDev)
{
  for (size_t i = 0; i < vkDev.swapchainImages.size();
      i++)
    vkDestroyImageView(vkDev.device,
      vkDev.swapchainImageViews[i], nullptr);
  vkDestroySwapchainKHR(
    vkDev.device, vkDev.swapchain, nullptr);
  vkDestroyCommandPool(vkDev.device,
    vkDev.commandPool, nullptr);
  vkDestroySemaphore(vkDev.device, vkDev.semaphore,
    nullptr);
  vkDestroySemaphore(vkDev.device,
  vkDev.renderSemaphore, nullptr);
  vkDestroyDevice(vkDev.device, nullptr);
}
```

8. Now, the swap chain and Vulkan instance can be destroyed:

```
void destroyVulkanInstance(VulkanInstance& vk)
{
  vkDestroySurfaceKHR(
    vk.instance, vk.surface, nullptr);
  vkDestroyDebugReportCallbackEXT(vk.instance,
    vk.reportCallback, nullptr);
  vkDestroyDebugUtilsMessengerEXT(vk.instance,
    vk.messenger, nullptr);
  vkDestroyInstance(vk.instance, nullptr);
}
```

At this point, we have well-structured Vulkan initialization and deinitialization code, and we've also created the command pool and command buffers. In the next recipe, we will fill our first command buffers with drawing commands.

Using Vulkan command buffers

In the previous recipes, we learned how to create a Vulkan instance, a device for rendering, and a swap chain object with images and image views. In this recipe, we will learn how to fill command buffers and submit them using queues, which will bring us a bit closer to rendering our first image with Vulkan.

How to do it...

Let's prepare a command buffer that will begin a new render pass, clear the color and depth attachments, bind pipelines and descriptor sets, and render a mesh:

1. First, we need to fill in a structure describing a command buffer:

```
bool fillCommandBuffers(size_t i) {
   const VkCommandBufferBeginInfo bi = {
      .sType =
         VK_STRUCTURE_TYPE_COMMAND_BUFFER_BEGIN_INFO,
      .pNext = nullptr,
      .flags =
         VK_COMMAND_BUFFER_USAGE_SIMULTANEOUS_USE_BIT,
      .pInheritanceInfo = nullptr
   };
```

2. Now, we need an array of values to clear the framebuffer and `VkRect2D` to hold its dimensions:

```
   const std::array<VkClearValue, 2> clearValues = {
      VkClearValue { .color = clearValueColor },
      VkClearValue { .depthStencil = { 1.0f, 0 } }
   };
   const VkRect2D screenRect = {
      .offset = { 0, 0 },
      .extent = { .width = kScreenWidth,
                  .height = kScreenHeight }
   };
```

3. Each command buffer corresponds to a separate image in the swap chain. Let's fill in the current one:

```
   VK_CHECK(vkBeginCommandBuffer(
      vkDev.commandBuffers[i], &bi));
   const VkRenderPassBeginInfo renderPassInfo = {
      .sType =
         VK_STRUCTURE_TYPE_RENDER_PASS_BEGIN_INFO,
      .pNext = nullptr,
```

```
    .renderPass = vkState.renderPass,
    .framebuffer = vkState.swapchainFramebuffers[i],
    .renderArea = screenRect,
    .clearValueCount =
      static_cast<uint32_t>(clearValues.size()),
    .pClearValues = clearValues.data()
  };
  vkCmdBeginRenderPass(vkDev.commandBuffers[i],
    &renderPassInfo, VK_SUBPASS_CONTENTS_INLINE);
```

4. Bind the pipeline and descriptor sets. In the subsequent recipes, we will show you how to set up pipelines, buffers, and descriptor sets to render a mesh:

```
  vkCmdBindPipeline(vkDev.commandBuffers[i],
    VK_PIPELINE_BIND_POINT_GRAPHICS,
    vkState.graphicsPipeline);
  vkCmdBindDescriptorSets(vkDev.commandBuffers[i],
    VK_PIPELINE_BIND_POINT_GRAPHICS,
    vkState.pipelineLayout, 0, 1,
    &vkState.descriptorSets[i], 0, nullptr);
  vkCmdDraw( vkDev.commandBuffers[i],
    static_cast<uint32_t>(indexBufferSize /
    sizeof(uint32_t)), 1, 0, 0 );
  vkCmdEndRenderPass(vkDev.commandBuffers[i]);
  VK_CHECK(vkEndCommandBuffer(
    vkDev.commandBuffers[i]));
  return true;
}
```

Now, we have a bunch of command buffers filled with commands that are ready to be submitted into a rendering queue. In the next recipe, we will learn how to use command buffers to transfer data.

See also

We recommend referring to *Vulkan Cookbook*, by Packt, for in-depth coverage of swap chain creation and command queue management.

Dealing with buffers in Vulkan

Buffers in Vulkan are regions of memory that store data that can be rendered on the GPU. To render a 3D scene using the Vulkan API, we must transform the scene data into a format that's suitable for the GPU. In this recipe, we will describe how to create a GPU buffer and upload vertex data into it.

Getting ready

Uploading data into GPU buffers is an operation that is executed, just like any other Vulkan operation, using command buffers. This means we need to have a command queue that's capable of performing transfer operations. We learned how to create and use command buffers earlier in this chapter, in the *Using Vulkan command buffers* recipe.

How to do it...

Let's create some helper functions for dealing with different buffers:

1. First, we need the `findMemoryType()` function, which selects an appropriate heap type on the GPU, based on the required properties and a filter:

```
uint32_t findMemoryType(
  VkPhysicalDevice device,
  uint32_t typeFilter,
  VkMemoryPropertyFlags properties)
{
  VkPhysicalDeviceMemoryProperties memProperties;
  vkGetPhysicalDeviceMemoryProperties(
      device, &memProperties );
  for (uint32_t i = 0; i <
       memProperties.memoryTypeCount; i++) {
    if ((typeFilter & (1 << i)) &&
        memProperties.memoryTypes[i].propertyFlags
        & properties) == properties)
        return i;
      }
  return 0xFFFFFFFF;
}
```

2. Now, we can write a function that will create a buffer object and an associated device memory region. We will use this function to create uniform, shader storage, and other types of buffers. The exact buffer usage is specified by the `usage` parameter. The access permissions for the memory block are specified by `properties` flags:

```cpp
bool createBuffer(
  VkDevice device, VkPhysicalDevice physicalDevice,
  VkDeviceSize size, VkBufferUsageFlags usage,
  VkMemoryPropertyFlags properties,
  VkBuffer& buffer, VkDeviceMemory& bufferMemory)
{
  const VkBufferCreateInfo bufferInfo = {
    .sType = VK_STRUCTURE_TYPE_BUFFER_CREATE_INFO,
    .pNext = nullptr,
    .flags = 0,
    .size = size,
    .usage = usage,
    .sharingMode = VK_SHARING_MODE_EXCLUSIVE,
    .queueFamilyIndexCount = 0,
    .pQueueFamilyIndices = nullptr
  };
  VK_CHECK(vkCreateBuffer(
    device, &bufferInfo, nullptr, &buffer));
  VkMemoryRequirements memRequirements;
  vkGetBufferMemoryRequirements(device, buffer,
    &memRequirements);
  const VkMemoryAllocateInfo ai = {
    .sType = VK_STRUCTURE_TYPE_MEMORY_ALLOCATE_INFO,
    .pNext = nullptr,
    .allocationSize = memRequirements.size,
    .memoryTypeIndex = findMemoryType(physicalDevice,
      memRequirements.memoryTypeBits, properties)
  };
  VK_CHECK(vkAllocateMemory(
    device, &ai, nullptr, &bufferMemory));
  vkBindBufferMemory(device, buffer, bufferMemory, 0);
  return true;
}
```

3. Once the buffer has been created, we can upload some data into a GPU buffer using the following routine:

```
void copyBuffer(
  VkDevice device, VkCommandPool commandPool,
  VkQueue graphicsQueue, VkBuffer srcBuffer,
  VkBuffer dstBuffer, VkDeviceSize size)
{
  VkCommandBuffer commandBuffer =
    beginSingleTimeCommands(device, commandPool,
      graphicsQueue);
  const VkBufferCopy copyParam = {
    .srcOffset = 0,
    .dstOffset = 0,
    .size = size
  };
  vkCmdCopyBuffer(commandBuffer, srcBuffer, dstBuffer,
    1,&copyParam);
  endSingleTimeCommands(device, commandPool,
    graphicsQueue, commandBuffer);
}
```

4. The `copyBuffer()` routine needs two helper functions to work. The first one is called `beginSingleTimeCommands()` and creates a temporary command buffer that contains transfer commands:

```
VkCommandBuffer beginSingleTimeCommands(
  VulkanRenderDevice& vkDev)
{
  VkCommandBuffer commandBuffer;
  const VkCommandBufferAllocateInfo allocInfo = {
    .sType =
      VK_STRUCTURE_TYPE_COMMAND_BUFFER_ALLOCATE_INFO,
    .pNext = nullptr,
    .commandPool = vkDev.commandPool,
    .level = VK_COMMAND_BUFFER_LEVEL_PRIMARY,
    .commandBufferCount = 1
  };
  vkAllocateCommandBuffers(
    vkDev.device, &allocInfo, &commandBuffer);
  const VkCommandBufferBeginInfo beginInfo = {
    .sType =
      VK_STRUCTURE_TYPE_COMMAND_BUFFER_BEGIN_INFO,
    .pNext = nullptr,
    .flags =
```

```
      VK_COMMAND_BUFFER_USAGE_ONE_TIME_SUBMIT_BIT,
    .pInheritanceInfo = nullptr
  };
  vkBeginCommandBuffer(commandBuffer, &beginInfo);
  return commandBuffer;
}
```

The second one is called `endSingleTimeCommands()` and submits the command buffer to the graphics queue and waits for the entire operation to complete:

```
void endSingleTimeCommands(
  VulkanRenderDevice& vkDev,
  VkCommandBuffer commandBuffer)
{
  vkEndCommandBuffer(commandBuffer);
  const VkSubmitInfo submitInfo = {
    .sType = VK_STRUCTURE_TYPE_SUBMIT_INFO,
    .pNext = nullptr,
    .waitSemaphoreCount = 0,
    .pWaitSemaphores = nullptr,
    .pWaitDstStageMask = nullptr,
    .commandBufferCount = 1,
    .pCommandBuffers = &commandBuffer,
    .signalSemaphoreCount = 0,
    .pSignalSemaphores = nullptr
  };
  vkQueueSubmit(vkDev.graphicsQueue, 1, &submitInfo,
    VK_NULL_HANDLE);
  vkQueueWaitIdle(vkDev.graphicsQueue);
  vkFreeCommandBuffers(vkDev.device,
    vkDev.commandPool, 1, &commandBuffer);
}
```

These functions will be used in the subsequent recipes to transfer geometry and image data to Vulkan buffers, as well as to convert data into different formats.

How it works...

Using this recipe, we can create a uniform buffer object for storing our combined model-view-projection matrix:

```
struct UniformBuffer {
  mat4 mvp;
} ubo;
```

Let's look at the functions for creating a uniform buffer object and filling it with data. The first one creates a buffer that will store the `UniformBuffer` structure:

```
bool createUniformBuffers() {
  VkDeviceSize bufferSize = sizeof(UniformBuffer);
  vkState.uniformBuffers.resize(
    vkDev.swapchainImages.size());
  vkState.uniformBuffersMemory.resize(
    vkDev.swapchainImages.size());
  for (size_t i = 0; i<vkDev.swapchainImages.size(); i++) {
    if (!createBuffer(vkDev.device, vkDev.physicalDevice,
            bufferSize,
            VK_BUFFER_USAGE_UNIFORM_BUFFER_BIT,
            VK_MEMORY_PROPERTY_HOST_VISIBLE_BIT |
            VK_MEMORY_PROPERTY_HOST_COHERENT_BIT,
            vkState.uniformBuffers[i],
            vkState.uniformBuffersMemory[i])) {
      printf("Fail: buffers\n");
      return false;
    }
  }
  return true;
}
```

The second one is called every frame to update our data in the buffer:

```
void updateUniformBuffer(
  uint32_t currentImage, const UniformBuffer& ubo)
{
  void* data = nullptr;
  vkMapMemory(vkDev.device,
    vkState.uniformBuffersMemory[currentImage], 0,
    sizeof(ubo), 0, &data);
    memcpy(data, &ubo, sizeof(ubo));
  vkUnmapMemory(vkDev.device,
    vkState.uniformBuffersMemory[currentImage]);
}
```

We will use these in the final recipe of this chapter; that is, *Putting it all together into a Vulkan application*.

Using texture data in Vulkan

Before we can write a meaningful 3D rendering application with Vulkan, we need to learn how to deal with textures. This recipe will show you how to implement several functions for creating, destroying, and modifying texture objects on the GPU using the Vulkan API.

Getting ready

Uploading texture data to a GPU requires a staging buffer. Read the previous recipe, *Dealing with buffers in Vulkan*, before you proceed further.

The complete source code for these functions can be found in the `shared/UtilsVulkan.cpp` source file.

How to do it...

The first thing we will do is create an image. A Vulkan image is another type of buffer that's designed to store a 1D, 2D, or 3D image, or even an array of these images. Those of you who are familiar with OpenGL are probably wondering about cube maps. Cube maps are special entities in Vulkan that are represented as an array of six 2D images, and they can be constructed by setting the `VK_IMAGE_CREATE_CUBE_COMPATIBLE_BIT` flag inside the `VkImageCreateInfo` structure. We will come back to this later. For now, let's investigate a basic use case with just a 2D image:

1. The `createImage()` function is similar to `createBuffer()` from the *Dealing with buffers in Vulkan* recipe. The difference is that `vkBindImageMemory()` is used instead of `vkBindBufferMemory()`:

```cpp
bool createImage(
   VkDevice device, VkPhysicalDevice physicalDevice,
   uint32_t width, uint32_t height, VkFormat format,
   VkImageTiling tiling, VkImageUsageFlags usage,
   VkMemoryPropertyFlags properties, VkImage& image,
   VkDeviceMemory& imageMemory )
{
   const VkImageCreateInfo imageInfo = {
      .sType = VK_STRUCTURE_TYPE_IMAGE_CREATE_INFO,
      .pNext = nullptr,
      .flags = 0,
      .imageType = VK_IMAGE_TYPE_2D,
      .format = format,
      .extent = VkExtent3D
            { .width = width, .height = height,.depth = 1},
      .mipLevels = 1,
      .arrayLayers = 1,
```

```
      .samples = VK_SAMPLE_COUNT_1_BIT,
      .tiling = tiling,
      .usage = usage,
      .sharingMode = VK_SHARING_MODE_EXCLUSIVE,
      .queueFamilyIndexCount = 0,
      .pQueueFamilyIndices = nullptr,
      .initialLayout = VK_IMAGE_LAYOUT_UNDEFINED
   };
   VK_CHECK(vkCreateImage(
      device, &imageInfo, nullptr, &image));
   VkMemoryRequirements memRequirements;
   vkGetImageMemoryRequirements(
      device, image, &memRequirements);
   const VkMemoryAllocateInfo ai = {
      .sType = VK_STRUCTURE_TYPE_MEMORY_ALLOCATE_INFO,
      .pNext = nullptr,
      .allocationSize = memRequirements.size,
      .memoryTypeIndex = findMemoryType(
        physicalDevice,
        memRequirements.memoryTypeBits, properties)
   };
   VK_CHECK(vkAllocateMemory(
      device, &ai, nullptr, &imageMemory));
   vkBindImageMemory(device, image, imageMemory, 0);
   return true;
}
```

2. An image is just a region in memory. Its internal structure, such as the number of layers for a cube map or the number of mipmap levels is has, is specified in the `VkImageView` object. The `createImageView()` function, which was shown in the *Initializing the Vulkan swapchain* recipe, creates an image view that's suitable for 2D textures.

3. Having the texture data in GPU memory is not enough. We must create a sampler that allows our fragment shaders to fetch texels from the image. This simple wrapper on top of the `vkCreateSampler()` function is all we need to access 2D textures for now:

```
bool createTextureSampler(
   VkDevice device, VkSampler* sampler)
{
   const VkSamplerCreateInfo samplerInfo = {
      .sType = VK_STRUCTURE_TYPE_SAMPLER_CREATE_INFO,
      .pNext = nullptr, .flags = 0,
```

```
      .magFilter = VK_FILTER_LINEAR,
      .minFilter = VK_FILTER_LINEAR,
      .mipmapMode = VK_SAMPLER_MIPMAP_MODE_LINEAR,
      .addressModeU = VK_SAMPLER_ADDRESS_MODE_REPEAT,
      .addressModeV = VK_SAMPLER_ADDRESS_MODE_REPEAT,
      .addressModeW = VK_SAMPLER_ADDRESS_MODE_REPEAT,
      .mipLodBias = 0.0f,
      .anisotropyEnable = VK_FALSE,
      .maxAnisotropy = 1,
      .compareEnable = VK_FALSE,
      .compareOp = VK_COMPARE_OP_ALWAYS,
      .minLod = 0.0f,  .maxLod = 0.0f,
      .borderColor = VK_BORDER_COLOR_INT_OPAQUE_BLACK,
      .unnormalizedCoordinates = VK_FALSE
    };
    VK_CHECK(vkCreateSampler(
      device, &samplerInfo, nullptr, sampler));
    return true;
  }
```

4. Finally, to upload the data to an image, we should implement a function similar to `copyBuffer()` from the previous recipe. The `copyBufferToImage()` function uses ...`SingleTimeCommands()` helpers to copy the data:

```
  void copyBufferToImage(VulkanRenderDevice& vkDev,
    VkBuffer buffer, VkImage image,
    uint32_t width, uint32_t height)
  {

    VkCommandBuffer commandBuffer =
      beginSingleTimeCommands(vkDev);
    const VkBufferImageCopy region = {
      .bufferOffset = 0,
      .bufferRowLength = 0,
      .bufferImageHeight = 0,
      .imageSubresource = VkImageSubresourceLayers {
        .aspectMask = VK_IMAGE_ASPECT_COLOR_BIT,
        .mipLevel = 0,
        .baseArrayLayer = 0,
        .layerCount = 1
      },
      .imageOffset = VkOffset3D{ .x = 0,.y = 0,.z = 0 },
      .imageExtent = VkExtent3D{
        .width=width, .height=height, .depth=1 }
    };
```

```
   vkCmdCopyBufferToImage(commandBuffer, buffer, image,
     VK_IMAGE_LAYOUT_TRANSFER_DST_OPTIMAL, 1, &region);
   endSingleTimeCommands(vkDev, commandBuffer);
}
```

5. Since we're using an image, an image view, and an associated device memory block, we should declare a structure that will hold all three objects:

```
struct VulkanTexture {
  VkImage image;
  VkDeviceMemory imageMemory;
  VkImageView imageView;
};
```

6. The texture destruction process is straightforward and simply calls the appropriate `vkDestroy...()` functions:

```
void destroyVulkanTexture(VkDevice device,
  VulkanTexture& texture) {
  vkDestroyImageView(
    device, texture.imageView, nullptr);
  vkDestroyImage(device, texture.image, nullptr);
  vkFreeMemory(device, texture.imageMemory, nullptr);
}
```

7. The GPU may need to reorganize texture data internally for faster access. This reorganization happens when we insert a pipeline barrier operation into the graphics command queue. The following lengthy function handles the necessary format transitions for 2D textures and depth buffers. This function is necessary if you want to resolve all the validation layer warnings for swap chain images. We will quote the entire function here because it is not readily available in any online tutorials. This will also serve as a good starting point for cleaning up validation layer warnings:

```
void transitionImageLayout(
  VulkanRenderDevice& vkDev, VkImage image,
  VkFormat format, VkImageLayout oldLayout,
  VkImageLayout newLayout, uint32_t layerCount, uint32_t
mipLevels)
{
  VkCommandBuffer commandBuffer =
    beginSingleTimeCommands(vkDev);
  transitionImageLayoutCmd(commandBuffer, image,
    format,oldLayout, newLayout,
```

```
      layerCount, mipLevels);
    endSingleTimeCommands(vkDev, commandBuffer);
}
```

8. The bulk of the `transitionImageLayout()` method consists of filling out the `VkImageMemoryBarrier` structure. Here, we are presenting all the use cases for the image transitions that are necessary for this chapter. Later, in *Chapter 8, Image-Based Techniques*, for image-based effects, we will add plenty of additional image and depth buffer transitions to this function:

```
void transitionImageLayoutCmd(
  VkCommandBuffer commandBuffer, VkImage image,
  VkFormat format,
  VkImageLayout oldLayout, VkImageLayout newLayout,
  uint32_t layerCount, uint32_t mipLevels)
{
  VkImageMemoryBarrier barrier = {
    .sType = VK_STRUCTURE_TYPE_IMAGE_MEMORY_BARRIER,
    .pNext = nullptr,
    .srcAccessMask = 0,
    .dstAccessMask = 0,
    .oldLayout = oldLayout,
    .newLayout = newLayout,
    .srcQueueFamilyIndex = VK_QUEUE_FAMILY_IGNORED,
    .dstQueueFamilyIndex = VK_QUEUE_FAMILY_IGNORED,
    .image = image,
    .subresourceRange = VkImageSubresourceRange {
      .aspectMask = VK_IMAGE_ASPECT_COLOR_BIT,
      .baseMipLevel = 0,
      .levelCount = 1,
      .baseArrayLayer = 0,
      .layerCount = 1
    }
  };
  VkPipelineStageFlags sourceStage, destinationStage;
  if (newLayout ==
   VK_IMAGE_LAYOUT_DEPTH_STENCIL_ATTACHMENT_OPTIMAL) {
      barrier.subresourceRange.aspectMask =
        VK_IMAGE_ASPECT_DEPTH_BIT;
    if (hasStencilComponent(format))
        barrier.subresourceRange.aspectMask |=
          VK_IMAGE_ASPECT_STENCIL_BIT;
  }
  else {
```

```
          barrier.subresourceRange.aspectMask =
            VK_IMAGE_ASPECT_COLOR_BIT;
  }
  if (oldLayout == VK_IMAGE_LAYOUT_UNDEFINED &&
      newLayout ==
        VK_IMAGE_LAYOUT_TRANSFER_DST_OPTIMAL) {
    barrier.srcAccessMask = 0;
    barrier.dstAccessMask =
      VK_ACCESS_TRANSFER_WRITE_BIT;
    sourceStage = VK_PIPELINE_STAGE_TOP_OF_PIPE_BIT;
    destinationStage =
      VK_PIPELINE_STAGE_TRANSFER_BIT;
  }
  else if (oldLayout ==
           VK_IMAGE_LAYOUT_TRANSFER_DST_OPTIMAL &&
           newLayout ==
             VK_IMAGE_LAYOUT_SHADER_READ_ONLY_OPTIMAL)
  {
    barrier.srcAccessMask =
      VK_ACCESS_TRANSFER_WRITE_BIT;
    barrier.dstAccessMask =
      VK_ACCESS_SHADER_READ_BIT;
    sourceStage = VK_PIPELINE_STAGE_TRANSFER_BIT;
    destinationStage =
      VK_PIPELINE_STAGE_FRAGMENT_SHADER_BIT;
  }
  else if (oldLayout ==
    VK_IMAGE_LAYOUT_UNDEFINED &&
    newLayout ==
    VK_IMAGE_LAYOUT_DEPTH_STENCIL_ATTACHMENT_OPTIMAL)
  {
    barrier.srcAccessMask = 0;
    barrier.dstAccessMask =
      VK_ACCESS_DEPTH_STENCIL_ATTACHMENT_READ_BIT |
      VK_ACCESS_DEPTH_STENCIL_ATTACHMENT_WRITE_BIT;
    sourceStage = VK_PIPELINE_STAGE_TOP_OF_PIPE_BIT;
    destinationStage =
      VK_PIPELINE_STAGE_EARLY_FRAGMENT_TESTS_BIT;
  }
  vkCmdPipelineBarrier(
    commandBuffer, sourceStage, destinationStage,
    0, 0, nullptr, 0, nullptr, 1, &barrier );
}
```

9. To support depth buffering in the subsequent examples in this book, we will implement a function that will create a depth buffer image object. However, before we can do that, we need three helper functions to find the appropriate image formats. The first function accepts the required format features and tiling options and returns the first suitable format that satisfies these requirements:

```
VkFormat findSupportedFormat(VkPhysicalDevice device,
  const std::vector<VkFormat>& candidates,
  VkImageTiling tiling,
  VkFormatFeatureFlags features)
{
  const bool isLin = tiling == VK_IMAGE_TILING_LINEAR;
  const bool isOpt =
    tiling == VK_IMAGE_TILING_OPTIMAL;
  for (VkFormat format : candidates) {
    VkFormatProperties props;
    vkGetPhysicalDeviceFormatProperties(
      device, format, &props);
    if (isLin && (props.linearTilingFeatures &
        features) == features)
      return format;
    else
    if (isOpt && (props.optimalTilingFeatures &
        features) == features)
      return format;
  }
  printf("Failed to find supported format!\n");
  exit(0);
}
```

10. The other two functions find the requested depth format and check if it has a suitable stencil component:

```
VkFormat findDepthFormat(VkPhysicalDevice device) {
  return findSupportedFormat(device,
    { VK_FORMAT_D32_SFLOAT,
      VK_FORMAT_D32_SFLOAT_S8_UINT,
      VK_FORMAT_D24_UNORM_S8_UINT },
    VK_IMAGE_TILING_OPTIMAL,
    VK_FORMAT_FEATURE_DEPTH_STENCIL_ATTACHMENT_BIT);
}
bool hasStencilComponent(VkFormat format) {
  return format == VK_FORMAT_D32_SFLOAT_S8_UINT ||
```

```
          format == VK_FORMAT_D24_UNORM_S8_UINT;
}
```

11. Now, we can create a depth image:

```
void createDepthResources(VulkanRenderDevice& vkDev,
  uint32_t width, uint32_t height,
  VulkanTexture& depth)
{
  VkFormat depthFormat = findDepthFormat(
    vkDev.physicalDevice );
  createImage(vkDev.device, vkDev.physicalDevice,
    width, height, depthFormat,
    VK_IMAGE_TILING_OPTIMAL,
    VK_IMAGE_USAGE_DEPTH_STENCIL_ATTACHMENT_BIT,
    VK_MEMORY_PROPERTY_DEVICE_LOCAL_BIT,
    depth.image, depth.imageMemory);
  createImageView(vkDev.device, depth.image,
    depthFormat, VK_IMAGE_ASPECT_DEPTH_BIT,
    &depth.imageView);
  transitionImageLayout(vkDev.device,
    vkDev.commandPool,
    vkDev.graphicsQueue, depth.image, depthFormat,
    VK_IMAGE_LAYOUT_UNDEFINED,
    VK_IMAGE_LAYOUT_DEPTH_STENCIL_ATTACHMENT_OPTIMAL);
}
```

12. Finally, let's implement a simple function that will load a 2D texture from an image file to a Vulkan image. This function uses a staging buffer in a similar way to the vertex buffer creation function from the previous recipe:

```
bool createTextureImage(VulkanRenderDevice& vkDev,
  const char* filename, VkImage& textureImage,
  VkDeviceMemory& textureImageMemory)
{
  int texWidth, texHeight, texChannels;
  stbi_uc* pixels = stbi_load(filename, &texWidth,
    &texHeight, &texChannels, STBI_rgb_alpha);
  VkDeviceSize imageSize = texWidth * texHeight * 4;
  if (!pixels) {
    printf("Failed to load [%s] texture\n",
      filename);
    return false;
  }
```

13. A staging buffer is necessary to upload texture data into the GPU via memory mapping. This buffer should be declared as VK_MEMORY_PROPERTY_HOST_ VISIBLE_BIT:

```
VkBuffer stagingBuffer;
VkDeviceMemory stagingMemory;
createBuffer(vkDev.device, vkDev.physicalDevice,
  imageSize, VK_BUFFER_USAGE_TRANSFER_SRC_BIT,
  VK_MEMORY_PROPERTY_HOST_VISIBLE_BIT |
  VK_MEMORY_PROPERTY_HOST_COHERENT_BIT,
  stagingBuffer, stagingMemory);
void* data;
vkMapMemory(vkDev.device, stagingMemory, 0,
  imageSize, 0, &data);
memcpy(
  data, pixels, static_cast<size_t>(imageSize));
vkUnmapMemory(vkDev.device, stagingMemory);
```

14. The actual image is located in the device memory and can't be accessed directly from the host:

```
createImage(vkDev.device, vkDev.physicalDevice,
  texWidth, texHeight, VK_FORMAT_R8G8B8A8_UNORM,
  VK_IMAGE_TILING_OPTIMAL,
  VK_IMAGE_USAGE_TRANSFER_DST_BIT |
  VK_IMAGE_USAGE_SAMPLED_BIT,
  VK_MEMORY_PROPERTY_DEVICE_LOCAL_BIT,
  textureImage, textureImageMemory);
transitionImageLayout(vkDev.device,
  vkDev.commandPool,
  vkDev.graphicsQueue, textureImage,
  VK_FORMAT_R8G8B8A8_UNORM,
  VK_IMAGE_LAYOUT_UNDEFINED,
  VK_IMAGE_LAYOUT_TRANSFER_DST_OPTIMAL);
copyBufferToImage(vkDev, stagingBuffer,
  textureImage,
  static_cast<uint32_t>(texWidth),
  static_cast<uint32_t>(texHeight));
transitionImageLayout(vkDev.device,
  vkDev.commandPool,
  vkDev.graphicsQueue, textureImage,
  VK_FORMAT_R8G8B8A8_UNORM,
  VK_IMAGE_LAYOUT_TRANSFER_DST_OPTIMAL,
  VK_IMAGE_LAYOUT_SHADER_READ_ONLY_OPTIMAL);
```

```
    vkDestroyBuffer(
      vkDev.device, stagingBuffer, nullptr);
    vkFreeMemory(vkDev.device, stagingMemory, nullptr);
    stbi_image_free(pixels);
    return true;
}
```

This code is sufficient for providing basic texturing capabilities for our first Vulkan demo. Now, let's learn how to deal with mesh geometry data.

Using mesh geometry data in Vulkan

No graphical application can survive without working with at least some geometry data. In this recipe, we will learn how to load meshes into Vulkan buffers using Assimp. We will use **shader storage buffer objects** (**SSBOs**) and implement the **programmable vertex pulling** (**PVP**) technique, similar to what we did in the *Implementing programmable vertex pulling (PVP) in OpenGL* recipe.

Getting ready

The implementation of programmable vertex pulling for Vulkan is quite similar to OpenGL's. Please revisit the *Implementing programmable vertex pulling (PVP) in OpenGL* recipe for more information. The complete source code for all the Vulkan recipes in this chapter can be found in `Chapter3/VK02_DemoApp`.

How to do it...

Let's load an indexed mesh with vertex and texture coordinates. The data format for the texture mesh is the same as it was in the OpenGL recipes:

1. The following function loads a mesh via Assimp from a file into a Vulkan shader storage buffer. The loading part is identical to OpenGL:

```
bool createTexturedVertexBuffer(
  VulkanRenderDevice& vkDev, const char* filename,
  VkBuffer* storageBuffer,
  VkDeviceMemory* storageBufferMemory,
  size_t* vertexBufferSize, size_t* indexBufferSize)
{
  const aiScene* scene = aiImportFile(
    filename, aiProcess_Triangulate);
```

```
if (!scene || !scene->HasMeshes()) {
    printf("Unable to load %s\n", filename);
    exit( 255 );
}
const aiMesh* mesh = scene->mMeshes[0];
struct VertexData {
    vec3 pos;
    vec2 tc;
};
std::vector<VertexData> vertices;
for (unsigned i = 0; i != mesh->mNumVertices; i++) {
    const aiVector3D v = mesh->mVertices[i];
    const aiVector3D t = mesh->mTextureCoords[0][i];
    vertices.push_back(
       { vec3(v.x, v.z, v.y), vec2(t.x, t.y) });
}
std::vector<unsigned int> indices;
for ( unsigned i = 0; i != mesh->mNumFaces; i++ )
    for ( unsigned j = 0; j != 3; j++ )
        indices.push_back(
            mesh->mFaces[i].mIndices[j]);
aiReleaseImport(scene);
```

2. We need a staging buffer to upload the data into the GPU memory:

```
*vertexBufferSize =
  sizeof(VertexData) * vertices.size();
*indexBufferSize =
  sizeof(unsigned int) * indices.size();
VkDeviceSize bufferSize =
  *vertexBufferSize + *indexBufferSize;
VkBuffer stagingBuffer;
VkDeviceMemory stagingMemory;
createBuffer(vkDev.device, vkDev.physicalDevice,
  bufferSize,
  VK_BUFFER_USAGE_TRANSFER_SRC_BIT,
  VK_MEMORY_PROPERTY_HOST_VISIBLE_BIT |
  VK_MEMORY_PROPERTY_HOST_COHERENT_BIT,
  stagingBuffer, stagingMemory);
void* data;
```

```
vkMapMemory(vkDev.device, staginMemory, 0,
   bufferSize, 0, &data);
memcpy(data, vertices.data(), *vertexBufferSize);
memcpy((unsigned char *)data + *vertexBufferSize,
   indices.data(), *indexBufferSize);
vkUnmapMemory(vkDev.device, stagingMemory);
createBuffer(vkDev.device, vkDev.physicalDevice,
   bufferSize,
   VK_BUFFER_USAGE_TRANSFER_DST_BIT |
   VK_BUFFER_USAGE_STORAGE_BUFFER_BIT,
   VK_MEMORY_PROPERTY_DEVICE_LOCAL_BIT,
   *storageBuffer, *storageBufferMemory);
```

3. The `copyBuffer()` function from the *Dealing with buffers in Vulkan* recipe comes in handy here:

```
copyBuffer(vkDev.device, vkDev.commandPool,
   vkDev.graphicsQueue, stagingBuffer,
   *storageBuffer, bufferSize);
vkDestroyBuffer(
   vkDev.device, stagingBuffer, nullptr);
 vkFreeMemory(vkDev.device, stagingMemory, nullptr);
return true;
}
```

4. At this point, we have our geometry data, along with our indices and vertices, loaded into a single shader storage buffer object. To render such a model, we must use an ad hoc vertex shader. This fetches indices and vertices data from the shader storage buffers attached to two binding points:

```
#version 460
layout(location = 0) out vec3 fragColor;
layout(location = 1) out vec2 uv;
layout(binding = 0) uniform UniformBuffer {
  mat4 mvp;
} ubo;
struct VertexData {
  float x, y, z;
  float u, v;
};
layout(binding=1)
  readonly buffer Vertices { VertexData data[]; }
```

```
  in_Vertices;
layout(binding=2)
  readonly buffer Indices { uint data[]; } in_Indices;
void main() {
  uint idx = in_Indices.data[gl_VertexIndex];
  VertexData vtx = in_Vertices.data[idx];
  vec3 pos = vec3(vtx.x, vtx.y, vtx.z);
  gl_Position = ubo.mvp * vec4(pos, 1.0);
  fragColor = pos;
  uv = vec2(vtx.u, vtx.v);
}
```

5. This geometry shader is used to render a wireframe 3D model, similar to how it
    worked with OpenGL. It constructs a triangle strip consisting of a single triangle
    and assigns the appropriate barycentric coordinates to each vertex:

```
#version 460
layout(triangles) in;
layout(triangle_strip, max_vertices = 3) out;
layout (location=0) in vec3 color[];
layout (location=1) in vec2 uvs[];
layout (location=0) out vec3 fragColor;
layout (location=1) out vec3 barycoords;
layout (location=2) out vec2 uv;
void main() {
  const vec3 bc[3] = vec3[] (
    vec3(1.0, 0.0, 0.0),
    vec3(0.0, 1.0, 0.0),
    vec3(0.0, 0.0, 1.0)
  );
  for ( int i = 0; i < 3; i++ ) {
    gl_Position = gl_in[i].gl_Position;
    fragColor = color[i];
    barycoords = bc[i];
    uv = uvs[i];
    EmitVertex();
  }
  EndPrimitive();
}
```

6. The fragment shader should look as follows:

```glsl
#version 460
layout(location = 0) in vec3 fragColor;
layout(location = 1) in vec3 barycoords;
layout(location = 2) in vec2 uv;
layout(location = 0) out vec4 outColor;
layout(binding = 3) uniform sampler2D texSampler;
float edgeFactor(float thickness) {
  vec3 a3 = smoothstep(vec3(0.0), fwidth(barycoords) *
            thickness, barycoords);
  return min(min(a3.x, a3.y), a3.z);
}
void main() {
  outColor = vec4(
    mix(vec3(0.0), texture(texSampler, uv).xyz,
    edgeFactor(1.0)), 1.0);
}
```

In terms of GLSL, everything is now ready to render our first Vulkan 3D graphics. However, a few more things must be done on the C++ side before we can see anything. In the next recipe, we will discuss how to set up Vulkan descriptor sets.

Using Vulkan descriptor sets

A descriptor set object is an object that holds a set of descriptors. Think of each descriptor as a handle or a pointer to a resource. We can think of a descriptor set as everything that is "external" to the graphics pipeline or as a resource set. Also, the descriptor set is the only way to specify which textures and buffers can be used by the shader modules in the pipeline. The Vulkan API does not allow you to bind individual resources in shaders; they must be grouped into sets, and only a limited number of descriptor sets can be bound to a given pipeline. This design decision was mostly due to the limitations of some legacy hardware, which must be able to run Vulkan applications. In the next few chapters, we will learn how to partially overcome this constraint on modern hardware with Vulkan 1.2.

Now, let's learn how to work with descriptor sets in Vulkan.

How to do it...

Descriptor sets cannot be created directly. They must come from a descriptor pool, which is similar to the command pool we allocated in the *Tracking and cleaning up Vulkan objects* recipe. Let's get started:

1. First, let's implement a function to create a descriptor pool. The allocated descriptor pool must contain enough items for each texture sample and buffer that's used. We must also multiply these numbers by the number of swap chain images since, later in this recipe, we will allocate one descriptor set to each swap chain image:

```cpp
bool createDescriptorPool(
  VkDevice device, uint32_t imageCount,
  uint32_t uniformBufferCount,
  uint32_t storageBufferCount,
  uint32_t samplerCount, VkDescriptorPool* descPool)
{
  std::vector<VkDescriptorPoolSize> poolSizes;
  if (uniformBufferCount) poolSizes.push_back(
      VkDescriptorPoolSize{
        .type = VK_DESCRIPTOR_TYPE_UNIFORM_BUFFER,
        .descriptorCount =
          imageCount * uniformBufferCount
    });
  if (storageBufferCount) poolSizes.push_back(
      VkDescriptorPoolSize{
        .type = VK_DESCRIPTOR_TYPE_STORAGE_BUFFER,
        .descriptorCount =
          imageCount * storageBufferCount
    });
  if (samplerCount) poolSizes.push_back(
      VkDescriptorPoolSize{
        .type =
          VK_DESCRIPTOR_TYPE_COMBINED_IMAGE_SAMPLER,
        .descriptorCount = imageCount * samplerCount
    });
  const VkDescriptorPoolCreateInfo pi = {
    .sType =
      VK_STRUCTURE_TYPE_DESCRIPTOR_POOL_CREATE_INFO,
    .pNext = nullptr, .flags = 0,
    .maxSets = static_cast<uint32_t>(imageCount),
    .poolSizeCount =
      static_cast<uint32_t>(poolSizes.size()),
    .pPoolSizes = poolSizes.empty() ?
      nullptr : poolSizes.data()
  };
```

```
    VK_CHECK(vkCreateDescriptorPool(
      device, &pi, nullptr, descPool));
    return true;
}
```

2. Now, we can use the descriptor pool to create the required descriptor set for
    our demo application. However, the descriptor set must have a fixed layout that
    describes the number and usage type of all the texture samples and buffers. This
    layout is also a Vulkan object. Let's create this now:

```
bool createDescriptorSet()
{
```

3. Now, we must declare a list of buffer and sampler descriptions. Each entry in this list
    defines which shader unit this entity is bound to, the exact data type of this entity,
    and which shader stage (or multiple stages) can access this item:

```
const std::array<VkDescriptorSetLayoutBinding, 4>
bindings = {
   descriptorSetLayoutBinding(0,
       VK_DESCRIPTOR_TYPE_UNIFORM_BUFFER,
       VK_SHADER_STAGE_VERTEX_BIT),
   descriptorSetLayoutBinding(1,
       VK_DESCRIPTOR_TYPE_STORAGE_BUFFER,
       VK_SHADER_STAGE_VERTEX_BIT ),
   descriptorSetLayoutBinding(2,
       VK_DESCRIPTOR_TYPE_STORAGE_BUFFER,
       VK_SHADER_STAGE_VERTEX_BIT ),
   descriptorSetLayoutBinding(3,
       VK_DESCRIPTOR_TYPE_COMBINED_IMAGE_SAMPLER,
       VK_SHADER_STAGE_FRAGMENT_BIT )
};
const VkDescriptorSetLayoutCreateInfo li = {
   .sType =
VK_STRUCTURE_TYPE_DESCRIPTOR_SET_LAYOUT_CREATE_INFO,
   .pNext = nullptr,
   .flags = 0,
   .bindingCount =
     static_cast<uint32_t>(bindings.size()),
   .pBindings = bindings.data()
};
VK_CHECK(vkCreateDescriptorSetLayout(
   vkDev.device, &li, nullptr,
   &vkState.descriptorSetLayout));
```

4. Next, we must allocate a number of descriptor set layouts, one for each swap chain image, just like we did with the uniform and command buffers:

```cpp
std::vector<VkDescriptorSetLayout> layouts(
   vkDev.swapchainImages.size(),
   vkState.descriptorSetLayout
);
VkDescriptorSetAllocateInfo ai = {
   .sType =
     VK_STRUCTURE_TYPE_DESCRIPTOR_SET_ALLOCATE_INFO,
   .pNext = nullptr,
   .descriptorPool = vkState.descriptorPool,
   .descriptorSetCount = static_cast<uint32_t>(
     vkDev.swapchainImages.size()),
   .pSetLayouts = layouts.data()
};
vkState.descriptorSets.resize(
   vkDev.swapchainImages.size());
VK_CHECK(vkAllocateDescriptorSets(vkDev.device, &ai,
   vkState.descriptorSets.data());
```

5. Once we have allocated the descriptor sets with the specified layout, we must update these descriptor sets with concrete buffer and texture handles. This operation can be viewed as an analogue of texture and buffer binding in OpenGL. The crucial difference is that we do not do this at every frame since binding is prebaked into the pipeline. The minor downside of this approach is that we cannot simply change the texture from frame to frame.

6. For this example, we will use one uniform buffer, one index buffer, one vertex buffer, and one texture:

```cpp
for (size_t i = 0; i < vkDev.swapchainImages.size();
     i++) {
  VkDescriptorBufferInfo bufferInfo = {
    .buffer = vkState.uniformBuffers[i],
    .offset = 0,
    .range = sizeof(UniformBuffer)
  };
  VkDescriptorBufferInfo bufferInfo2 = {
    .buffer = vkState.storageBuffer,
    .offset = 0,
    .range = vertexBufferSize
  };
```

```
VkDescriptorBufferInfo bufferInfo3 = {
    .buffer = vkState.storageBuffer,
    .offset = vertexBufferSize,
    .range = indexBufferSize
};
VkDescriptorImageInfo imageInfo = {
    .sampler = vkState.textureSampler,
    .imageView = vkState.texture.imageView,
    .imageLayout =
      VK_IMAGE_LAYOUT_SHADER_READ_ONLY_OPTIMAL
};
```

7. The `VkWriteDescriptorSet` operation array contains all the "bindings" for the buffers we declared previously:

```
std::array<VkWriteDescriptorSet, 4> descriptorWrites
= {
    VkWriteDescriptorSet {
        .sType =
          VK_STRUCTURE_TYPE_WRITE_DESCRIPTOR_SET,
        .dstSet = vkState.descriptorSets[i],
        .dstBinding = 0,
        .dstArrayElement = 0,
        .descriptorCount = 1,
        .descriptorType =
          VK_DESCRIPTOR_TYPE_UNIFORM_BUFFER,
        .pBufferInfo = &bufferInfo
    },
    VkWriteDescriptorSet {
        .sType =
          VK_STRUCTURE_TYPE_WRITE_DESCRIPTOR_SET,
        .dstSet = vkState.descriptorSets[i],
        .dstBinding = 1,
        .dstArrayElement = 0,
        .descriptorCount = 1,
        .descriptorType =
          VK_DESCRIPTOR_TYPE_STORAGE_BUFFER,
        .pBufferInfo = &bufferInfo2
    },
    VkWriteDescriptorSet {
        .sType =
          VK_STRUCTURE_TYPE_WRITE_DESCRIPTOR_SET,
        .dstSet = vkState.descriptorSets[i],
        .dstBinding = 2,
        .dstArrayElement = 0,
        .descriptorCount = 1,
        .descriptorType =
```

```
            VK_DESCRIPTOR_TYPE_STORAGE_BUFFER,
        .pBufferInfo = &bufferInfo3
    },
    VkWriteDescriptorSet {
        .sType =
            VK_STRUCTURE_TYPE_WRITE_DESCRIPTOR_SET,
        .dstSet = vkState.descriptorSets[i],
        .dstBinding = 3,
        .dstArrayElement = 0,
        .descriptorCount = 1,
        .descriptorType =
            VK_DESCRIPTOR_TYPE_COMBINED_IMAGE_SAMPLER,
        .pImageInfo = &imageInfo
    },
};
```

8. Finally, we must update the descriptor by applying the necessary descriptor
    write operations:

```
vkUpdateDescriptorSets(vkDev.device,
    static_cast<uint32_t>(descriptorWrites.size()),
    descriptorWrites.data(), 0, nullptr);
}
return true;
}
```

With the descriptor set in place, we are getting one big step closer to being able to render
a 3D scene with Vulkan. The next important step is loading the shaders into Vulkan. We'll
learn how to do this in the next recipe.

There's more...

The vast topic of efficient resource management and allowing dynamic texture change is
outside the scope of this recipe. We will return to descriptor set management later when
we discuss 3D scene data management and rendering material definitions.

Initializing Vulkan shader modules

The Vulkan API consumes shaders in the form of compiled SPIR-V binaries. In the
Compiling Vulkan shaders at runtime recipe, we learned how to compile shaders from
source code to SPIR-V using the open source **glslang** compiler from Khronos. In this
recipe, we will learn how to use these binaries in Vulkan.

Getting ready

We recommend reading the *Compiling Vulkan shaders at runtime* recipe before proceeding.

How to do it...

1. Let's declare a structure that will hold a SPIR-V binary and its corresponding shader module object:

```
struct ShaderModule {
  std::vector<unsigned int> SPIRV;
  VkShaderModule shaderModule;
};
```

2. The following function will compile a shader that's been loaded from a file using `glslang` and upload the resulting SPIR-V binary to Vulkan:

```
VkResult createShaderModule(
  VkDevice device, ShaderModule* sm,
  const char* fileName)
{
  if (!compileShaderFile(fileName, *sm))
    return VK_NOT_READY;
  const VkShaderModuleCreateInfo createInfo = {
    .sType =
      VK_STRUCTURE_TYPE_SHADER_MODULE_CREATE_INFO,
    .codeSize = shader->SPIRV.size() *
      sizeof(unsigned int),
    .pCode = shader->SPIRV.data()
  };
  return vkCreateShaderModule(
    device, &createInfo, nullptr, &sm->shaderModule);
}
```

3. We can use these functions to create shader modules via the following code:

```
VK_CHECK(createShaderModule(vkDev.device,
         &vkState.vertShader,
         "data/shaders/chapter03/VK02.vert"));
VK_CHECK(createShaderModule(vkDev.device,
         &vkState.fragShader,
         "data/shaders/chapter03/VK02.frag"));
VK_CHECK(createShaderModule(vkDev.device,
         &vkState.geomShader,
         "data/shaders/chapter03/VK02.geom"));
```

Now, our shader modules are ready to be used inside the Vulkan pipeline. We'll learn how to initialize them in the next recipe.

Initializing the Vulkan pipeline

A Vulkan pipeline is an implementation of an abstract graphics pipeline, which is a sequence of operations used to transform vertices and rasterize the resulting image. This is similar to a single snapshot of a "frozen" OpenGL state. Vulkan pipelines are almost completely immutable, which means multiple pipelines should be created to allow different data paths to be made through the graphics pipeline. In this recipe, we will learn how to create a Vulkan pipeline that's suitable for our texture's 3D mesh rendering demo by using the programmable vertex pulling approach.

Getting ready...

To learn about the basics of Vulkan pipelines, we recommend reading *Vulkan Cookbook*, by Pawel Lapinski, which was published by Packt, or the *Vulkan Tutorial* series, by Alexander Overvoorde: `https://vulkan-tutorial.com/Drawing_a_triangle/Graphics_pipeline_basics/Introduction`.

For additional information on descriptor set layouts, check out `https://vulkan-tutorial.com/Uniform_buffers/Descriptor_layout_and_buffer`.

How to do it...

Let's dive deep into how to create and configure a Vulkan pipeline that's suitable for our application. Due to the extreme verbosity of the Vulkan API, this recipe will be the longest. In the following chapters, we will introduce a few simple wrappers that help somewhat conceal the API's verbosity and make our job much easier:

1. First, we must create a Vulkan pipeline layout, as follows:

```
bool createPipelineLayout(VkDevice device,
  VkDescriptorSetLayout dsLayout,
  VkPipelineLayout* pipelineLayout)
{
  const VkPipelineLayoutCreateInfo pipelineLayoutInfo=
  {
    .sType =
      VK_STRUCTURE_TYPE_PIPELINE_LAYOUT_CREATE_INFO,
    .pNext = nullptr,
    .flags = 0,
    .setLayoutCount = 1,
```

```
      .pSetLayouts = &dsLayout,
      .pushConstantRangeCount = 0,
      .pPushConstantRanges = nullptr
   };
   return vkCreatePipelineLayout(device,
      &pipelineLayoutInfo,
      nullptr, pipelineLayout) == VK_SUCCESS;
}
```

2. Now, we need to create one render pass that uses color and depth buffers. This
    render pass will clear the color and depth attachments up-front using the values
    provided later. The RenderPassCreateInfo structure is used to simplify the
    creation process. The VulkanRenderDerive structure was described earlier in
    this chapter in the *Tracking and cleaning up Vulkan objects* recipe:

```
struct RenderPassCreateInfo final {
  bool clearColor_ = false;
  bool clearDepth_ = false;
  uint8_t flags_ = 0;
};
enum eRenderPassBit : uint8_t {
  // clear the attachment
  eRenderPassBit_First    = 0x01,
  // transition to VK_IMAGE_LAYOUT_PRESENT_SRC_KHR
  eRenderPassBit_Last     = 0x02,
  // transition to
  //         VK_IMAGE_LAYOUT_SHADER_READ_ONLY_OPTIMAL
  eRenderPassBit_Offscreen = 0x04,
  // keep VK_IMAGE_LAYOUT_*_ATTACHMENT_OPTIMAL
  eRenderPassBit_OffscreenInternal = 0x08,
};
bool createColorAndDepthRenderPass(
  VulkanRenderDevice& device, bool useDepth,
  VkRenderPass* renderPass,
  const RenderPassCreateInfo& ci,
  VkFormat colorFormat = VK_FORMAT_B8G8R8A8_UNORM);
{
  const bool offscreenInt =
    ci.flags_ & eRenderPassBit_OffscreenInternal;
  const bool first = ci.flags_ & eRenderPassBit_First;
  const bool last  = ci.flags_ & eRenderPassBit_Last;
  VkAttachmentDescription colorAttachment = {
    .flags = 0,
    .format = colorFormat,
    .samples = VK_SAMPLE_COUNT_1_BIT,
```

3. If the `loadOp` field is changed to `VK_ATTACHMENT_LOAD_OP_DONT_CARE`, the framebuffer will not be cleared at the beginning of the render pass. This can be desirable if the frame has been composed with the output of another rendering pass:

```
  .loadOp = offscreenInt ?
   VK_ATTACHMENT_LOAD_OP_LOAD :
    (ci.clearColor_ ? VK_ATTACHMENT_LOAD_OP_CLEAR :
     VK_ATTACHMENT_LOAD_OP_LOAD),
  .storeOp = VK_ATTACHMENT_STORE_OP_STORE,
  .stencilLoadOp = VK_ATTACHMENT_LOAD_OP_DONT_CARE,
  .stencilStoreOp =
   VK_ATTACHMENT_STORE_OP_DONT_CARE,
  .initialLayout = first ? VK_IMAGE_LAYOUT_UNDEFINED
   : (offscreenInt ?
     VK_IMAGE_LAYOUT_SHADER_READ_ONLY_OPTIMAL :
     VK_IMAGE_LAYOUT_COLOR_ATTACHMENT_OPTIMAL),
  .finalLayout = last ?
   VK_IMAGE_LAYOUT_PRESENT_SRC_KHR :
   VK_IMAGE_LAYOUT_COLOR_ATTACHMENT_OPTIMAL
}
const VkAttachmentReference colorAttachmentRef = {
  .attachment = 0,
  .layout =
   VK_IMAGE_LAYOUT_COLOR_ATTACHMENT_OPTIMAL
};
```

4. The depth attachment is handled in a similar way:

```
VkAttachmentDescription depthAttachment = {
  .flags = 0,
  .format = useDepth ?
   findDepthFormat(vkDev.physicalDevice) :
   VK_FORMAT_D32_SFLOAT,
  .samples = VK_SAMPLE_COUNT_1_BIT,
  .loadOp = offscreenInt ?
   VK_ATTACHMENT_LOAD_OP_LOAD :
    (ci.clearDepth_ ? VK_ATTACHMENT_LOAD_OP_CLEAR :
   VK_ATTACHMENT_LOAD_OP_LOAD),
  .storeOp = VK_ATTACHMENT_STORE_OP_STORE,
  .stencilLoadOp = VK_ATTACHMENT_LOAD_OP_DONT_CARE,
  .stencilStoreOp =
   VK_ATTACHMENT_STORE_OP_DONT_CARE,
  .initialLayout = ci.clearDepth_ ?
   VK_IMAGE_LAYOUT_UNDEFINED : (offscreenInt ?
   VK_IMAGE_LAYOUT_SHADER_READ_ONLY_OPTIMAL :
   VK_IMAGE_LAYOUT_DEPTH_STENCIL_ATTACHMENT_
   OPTIMAL),
  .finalLayout =
```

```
        VK_IMAGE_LAYOUT_DEPTH_STENCIL_ATTACHMENT_OPTIMAL
};
const VkAttachmentReference depthAttachmentRef = {
    .attachment = 1,
    .layout =
        VK_IMAGE_LAYOUT_DEPTH_STENCIL_ATTACHMENT_OPTIMAL
};
```

5. The subpasses in a render pass automatically take care of image layout transitions.
    This render pass also specifies one subpass dependency, which instructs Vulkan to
    prevent the transition from happening until it is actually necessary and allowed.
    This dependency only makes sense for color buffer writes. In case of an offscreen
    render pass, we use subpass dependencies for layout transitions. We do not mention
    them here for the sake of brevity. Take a look at `shared/UtilsVulkan.cpp` for
    the full list of dependencies:

```
if (ci.flags_ & eRenderPassBit_Offscreen)
    colorAttachment.finalLayout =
    VK_IMAGE_LAYOUT_SHADER_READ_ONLY_OPTIMAL;
const VkSubpassDependency dependency = {
    .srcSubpass = VK_SUBPASS_EXTERNAL,
    .dstSubpass = 0,
    .srcStageMask =
        VK_PIPELINE_STAGE_COLOR_ATTACHMENT_OUTPUT_BIT,
    .dstStageMask =
        VK_PIPELINE_STAGE_COLOR_ATTACHMENT_OUTPUT_BIT,
    .srcAccessMask = 0,
    .dstAccessMask =
        VK_ACCESS_COLOR_ATTACHMENT_READ_BIT |
        VK_ACCESS_COLOR_ATTACHMENT_WRITE_BIT,
    .dependencyFlags = 0
};
```

6. Let's add two explicit dependencies which ensure all rendering operations are
    completed before this render pass and before the color attachment can be used in
    subsequent passes:

```
if (ci.flags_ & eRenderPassBit_Offscreen) {
    colorAttachment.finalLayout =
    VK_IMAGE_LAYOUT_SHADER_READ_ONLY_OPTIMAL;
    depthAttachment.finalLayout =
    VK_IMAGE_LAYOUT_SHADER_READ_ONLY_OPTIMAL;
    dependencies.resize(2);
    dependencies[0] = {
        .srcSubpass = VK_SUBPASS_EXTERNAL,
```

```
    .dstSubpass = 0,
    .srcStageMask =
      VK_PIPELINE_STAGE_FRAGMENT_SHADER_BIT,
    .dstStageMask =
      VK_PIPELINE_STAGE_COLOR_ATTACHMENT_OUTPUT_BIT,
    .srcAccessMask = VK_ACCESS_SHADER_READ_BIT,
    .dstAccessMask =
      VK_ACCESS_COLOR_ATTACHMENT_WRITE_BIT,
    .dependencyFlags = VK_DEPENDENCY_BY_REGION_BIT
  };
  dependencies[1] = {
    .srcSubpass = 0,
    .dstSubpass = VK_SUBPASS_EXTERNAL,
    .srcStageMask =
      VK_PIPELINE_STAGE_COLOR_ATTACHMENT_OUTPUT_BIT,
    .dstStageMask =
      VK_PIPELINE_STAGE_FRAGMENT_SHADER_BIT,
    .srcAccessMask =
      VK_ACCESS_COLOR_ATTACHMENT_WRITE_BIT,
    .dstAccessMask = VK_ACCESS_SHADER_READ_BIT,
    .dependencyFlags = VK_DEPENDENCY_BY_REGION_BIT
  };
}
```

7. The rendering pass consists of a single subpass that only uses color and
    depth buffers:

```
const VkSubpassDescription subpass = {
  .flags = 0,
  .pipelineBindPoint =
    VK_PIPELINE_BIND_POINT_GRAPHICS,
  .inputAttachmentCount = 0,
  .pInputAttachments = nullptr,
  .colorAttachmentCount = 1,
  .pColorAttachments = &colorAttachmentRef,
  .pResolveAttachments = nullptr,
  .pDepthStencilAttachment =
    useDepth ? &depthAttachmentRef : nullptr,
  .preserveAttachmentCount = 0,
  .pPreserveAttachments = nullptr
};
```

8. Now, use the two attachments we defined earlier:

```
std::array<VkAttachmentDescription, 2> attachments =
  { colorAttachment, depthAttachment };
const VkRenderPassCreateInfo renderPassInfo = {
```

```
      .sType =
        VK_STRUCTURE_TYPE_RENDER_PASS_CREATE_INFO,
      .attachmentCount =
        static_cast<uint32_t>(useDepth ? 2 : 1),
      .pAttachments = attachments.data(),
      .subpassCount = 1,
      .pSubpasses = &subpass,
      .dependencyCount = 1,
      .pDependencies = &dependency
   };
   return (vkCreateRenderPass(device, &renderPassInfo,
     nullptr, renderPass) == VK_SUCCESS);
}
```

9. Now, we should create the graphics pipeline:

```
bool createGraphicsPipeline(
  VkDevice device, uint32_t width, uint32_t height,
  VkRenderPass renderPass,
  VkPipelineLayout pipelineLayout,
  const std::vector<VkPipelineShaderStageCreateInfo>&
    shaderStages, VkPipeline *pipeline)
{
  const VkPipelineVertexInputStateCreateInfo
    vertexInputInfo = {
    .sType = VK_STRUCTURE_TYPE_PIPELINE_
      VERTEX_INPUT_STATE_CREATE_INFO
  };
```

10. Since we are using programmable vertex pulling, the only thing we need to specify for the input assembly is the primitive topology type. We must disable the primitive restart capabilities that we won't be using:

```
const VkPipelineInputAssemblyStateCreateInfo
  inputAssembly = {
    .sType = VK_STRUCTURE_TYPE_PIPELINE_
      INPUT_ASSEMBLY_STATE_CREATE_INFO,
    .topology = VK_PRIMITIVE_TOPOLOGY_TRIANGLE_LIST,
    .primitiveRestartEnable = VK_FALSE
};
```

11. The VkViewport structure is defined as follows:

```
const VkViewport viewport = {
    .x = 0.0f,
    .y = 0.0f,
    .width = static_cast<float>(width),
```

```
        .height = static_cast<float>(height),
        .minDepth = 0.0f,
        .maxDepth = 1.0f
};
```

12. `scissor` covers the entire viewport:

```
const VkRect2D scissor = {
    .offset = { 0, 0 },
    .extent = { width, height }
};
```

13. Let's combine the viewport and scissor declarations in the required viewport state:

```
const VkPipelineViewportStateCreateInfo
  viewportState = {
    .sType = VK_STRUCTURE_TYPE_PIPELINE_
            VIEWPORT_STATE_CREATE_INFO,
    .viewportCount = 1,
    .pViewports = &viewport,
    .scissorCount = 1,
    .pScissors = &scissor
};
```

14. We must provide one more declaration to configure the rasterization state of our graphics pipeline. We will not be using backface culling yet:

```
const VkPipelineRasterizationStateCreateInfo
  rasterizer = {
    .sType = VK_STRUCTURE_TYPE_PIPELINE_
      RASTERIZATION_STATE_CREATE_INFO,
    .polygonMode = VK_POLYGON_MODE_FILL,
    .cullMode = VK_CULL_MODE_NONE,
    .frontFace = VK_FRONT_FACE_CLOCKWISE,
    .lineWidth = 1.0f
};
```

15. Multisampling should be disabled:

```
const VkPipelineMultisampleStateCreateInfo
  multisampling = {
    .sType = VK_STRUCTURE_TYPE_PIPELINE_
            MULTISAMPLE_STATE_CREATE_INFO,
    .rasterizationSamples = VK_SAMPLE_COUNT_1_BIT,
    .sampleShadingEnable = VK_FALSE,
    .minSampleShading = 1.0f
};
```

16. All the blending operations should be disabled as well. A color mask is required if we want to see any pixels that have been rendered:

```
const VkPipelineColorBlendAttachmentState
  colorBlendAttachment = {
    .blendEnable = VK_FALSE,
    .colorWriteMask = VK_COLOR_COMPONENT_R_BIT |
                      VK_COLOR_COMPONENT_G_BIT |
                      VK_COLOR_COMPONENT_B_BIT |
                      VK_COLOR_COMPONENT_A_BIT
};
```

17. Disable any logic operations:

```
const VkPipelineColorBlendStateCreateInfo
  colorBlending = {
    .sType = VK_STRUCTURE_TYPE_PIPELINE_
      COLOR_BLEND_STATE_CREATE_INFO,
    .logicOpEnable = VK_FALSE,
    .logicOp = VK_LOGIC_OP_COPY,
    .attachmentCount = 1,
    .pAttachments = &colorBlendAttachment,
    .blendConstants = { 0.0f, 0.0f, 0.0f, 0.0f }
};
```

18. Enable depth test using the VK_COMPARE_OP_LESS operator:

```
const VkPipelineDepthStencilStateCreateInfo
  depthStencil = {
    .sType =
      VK_STRUCTURE_TYPE_PIPELINE_DEPTH_STENCIL_STATE
      _CREATE_INFO,
    .depthTestEnable = VK_TRUE,
    .depthWriteEnable = VK_TRUE,
    .depthCompareOp = VK_COMPARE_OP_LESS,
    .depthBoundsTestEnable = VK_FALSE,
    .minDepthBounds = 0.0f,
    .maxDepthBounds = 1.0f
};
```

19. Now, it is time to bring all the previously defined rendering states and attachments into the VkGraphicsPipelineCreateInfo structure. Then, we can call the vkCreateGraphicsPipelines() function to create an actual Vulkan graphics pipeline:

```
const VkGraphicsPipelineCreateInfo pipelineInfo = {
  .sType = VK_STRUCTURE_TYPE_GRAPHICS_
    PIPELINE_CREATE_INFO,
```

```
      .stageCount =
        static_cast<uint32_t>(shaderStages.size()),
      .pStages = shaderStages.data(),
      .pVertexInputState = &vertexInputInfo,
      .pInputAssemblyState = &inputAssembly,
      .pTessellationState = nullptr,
      .pViewportState = &viewportState,
      .pRasterizationState = &rasterizer,
      .pMultisampleState = &multisampling,
      .pDepthStencilState = &depthStencil,
      .pColorBlendState = &colorBlending,
      .layout = pipelineLayout,
      .renderPass = renderPass,
      .subpass = 0,
      .basePipelineHandle = VK_NULL_HANDLE,
      .basePipelineIndex = -1
    };
  VK_CHECK(vkCreateGraphicsPipelines(
    device, VK_NULL_HANDLE, 1, &pipelineInfo,
    nullptr, pipeline));
  return true;
}
```

With that, we have initialized everything we need to start rendering the scene with Vulkan. Let's check out the main loop and how the preceding code can be used in an actual application.

There's more...

As we mentioned at the beginning of this recipe, the pipeline is a "frozen" rendering API state. There are, however, occasions where you will need to tweak some parameters, such as the viewport's size or the scissor clipping rectangle. For these purposes, we can specify the pDynamicState field of the VkGraphicsPipelineCreateInfo structure. This is an array of state identifiers that can change. The most commonly used values are VK_DYNAMIC_STATE_SCISSOR and VK_DYNAMIC_STATE_VIEWPORT. When a graphics pipeline is created with these options enabled, we can use the vkCmdSetScissor() and vkCmdSetViewport() functions to record frame-dependent values into Vulkan command buffers.

See also

The *Managing Vulkan resources* recipe in the *Chapter 7, Graphics Rendering Pipeline*, will touch on some additional details of the Vulkan pipeline creation process.

Putting it all together into a Vulkan application

In the previous recipes, we discussed various sides of the Vulkan initialization process, without rendering anything on screen. Now, let's render our rubber duck 3D model using the Vulkan API.

Getting ready

The final Vulkan demo application for this chapter is located in `Chapter3/VK02_DemoApp`.

How to do it...

The main routine is similar to any of the previous OpenGL samples in that it initializes the GLFW library, sets the keyboard callback, initializes any Vulkan-related objects, enters the main loop, and calls the deinitialization routine:

```
int main()
{
```

1. Initialize the `glslang` compiler, the Volk library, and GLFW:

    ```
    glslang_initialize_process();
    volkInitialize();
    if (!glfwInit())
        exit( EXIT_FAILURE );
    if (!glfwVulkanSupported())
        exit( EXIT_FAILURE );
    ```

2. Since GLFW was originally an OpenGL helper library, we should set the option to disable any GL context creation. The process of setting up GLFW callbacks is identical to the previous OpenGL demos, so this will be skipped here for the sake of brevity. Yes, brevity is the most desired thing while working with the Vulkan API:

    ```
    const uint32_t kScreenWidth = 1280;
    const uint32_t kScreenHeight = 720;
    glfwWindowHint(GLFW_CLIENT_API, GLFW_NO_API);
    glfwWindowHint(GLFW_RESIZABLE, GL_FALSE);
    window = glfwCreateWindow(kScreenWidth,
      ScreenHeight, "VulkanApp", nullptr, nullptr);
    ...
    ```

3. The `initVulkan()` function calls all the long setup code we wrote in the previous recipes. We will look at it here in a moment. The main loop and the termination stage of the application are very simple and look as follows:

```
initVulkan();
while ( !glfwWindowShouldClose(window) ){
    drawOverlay();
    glfwPollEvents();
}
terminateVulkan();
glfwTerminate();
glslang_finalize_process();
return 0;
}
```

Now, let's look at the `initVulkan()` function:

1. First, it creates a Vulkan instance (*Initializing Vulkan instances and graphical devices*) and then sets up any Vulkan debugging callbacks (*Setting up Vulkan's debugging capabilities*):

```
bool initVulkan() {
    createInstance(&vk.instance);
    if (!setupDebugCallbacks(
        vk.instance, &vk.messenger, &vk.reportCallback))
      exit(EXIT_FAILURE);
```

2. Then, it creates a window surface attached to the GLFW window and our Vulkan instance:

```
    if (glfwCreateWindowSurface(
        vk.instance, window, nullptr, &vk.surface))
      exit(EXIT_FAILURE);
```

3. Now, we should initialize our Vulkan objects (*Tracking and cleaning up Vulkan objects*):

```
    if (!initVulkanRenderDevice(vk, vkDev, kScreenWidth,
        kScreenHeight, isDeviceSuitable,
        { .geometryShader = VK_TRUE } ))
      exit(EXIT_FAILURE);
```

4. We must also create shader modules for our vertex, fragment, and geometry shaders (*Initializing Vulkan shader modules*):

```
VK_CHECK(createShaderModule(vkDev.device,
   &vkState.vertShader,
   "data/shaders/chapter03/VK02.vert"));
VK_CHECK(createShaderModule(vkDev.device,
   &vkState.fragShader,
   "data/shaders/chapter03/VK02.frag"));
VK_CHECK(createShaderModule(vkDev.device,
   &vkState.geomShader,
   "data/shaders/chapter03/VK02.geom"));
```

5. Load the rubber duck 3D model into a shader storage buffer (*Using mesh geometry in Vulkan*):

```
if (!createTexturedVertexBuffer(vkDev,
      "data/rubber_duck/scene.gltf",
      &vkState.storageBuffer,
      &vkState.storageBufferMemory,
      &vertexBufferSize, &indexBufferSize)
   || !createUniformBuffers()) {
   printf("Cannot create data buffers\n");
   exit(EXIT_FAILURE);
}
```

6. Initialize the pipeline shader stages using the shader modules we created:

```
const std::vector<VkPipelineShaderStageCreateInfo>
shaderStages = {
   shaderStageInfo(
      VK_SHADER_STAGE_VERTEX_BIT,
      vkState.vertShader, "main"),
   shaderStageInfo(
      VK_SHADER_STAGE_FRAGMENT_BIT,
      vkState.fragShader, "main"),
   shaderStageInfo(
      VK_SHADER_STAGE_GEOMETRY_BIT,
      vkState.geomShader, "main")
};
```

7. Load a texture from file and create an image view with a sampler (*Using texture data in Vulkan*):

```
createTextureImage(vkDev,
  "data/rubber_duck/textures/Duck_baseColor.png",
  vkState.texture.image,
  vkState.texture.imageMemory);
createImageView(vkDev.device, vkState.texture.image,
  VK_FORMAT_R8G8B8A8_UNORM,
  VK_IMAGE_ASPECT_COLOR_BIT,
  &vkState.texture.imageView);
createTextureSampler(vkDev.device,
  &vkState.textureSampler);
```

8. Create a depth buffer (*Using texture data in Vulkan*):

```
createDepthResources(vkDev, kScreenWidth,
  kScreenHeight, vkState.depthTexture);
```

9. Initialize the descriptor pool, sets, passes, and the graphics pipeline (*Initializing the Vulkan pipeline*):

```
const bool isInitialized = createDescriptorPool(
    vkDev.device, static_cast<uint32_t>(
    vkDev.swapchainImages.size()),
    1, 2, 1, &vkState.descriptorPool) &&
  createDescriptorSet() &&
  createColorAndDepthRenderPass(vkDev, true,
    &vkState.renderPass, RenderPassCreateInfo{
      .clearColor_ = true,
      .clearDepth_ = true,
      .flags_ =
      eRenderPassBit_First|eRenderPassBit_Last }) &&
  createPipelineLayout(vkDev.device,
    vkState.descriptorSetLayout,
    &vkState.pipelineLayout) &&
  createGraphicsPipeline(vkDev.device, kScreenWidth,
    kScreenHeight, vkState.renderPass,
    vkState.pipelineLayout, shaderStages,
    &vkState.graphicsPipeline);
if (!isInitialized) {
  printf("Failed to create pipeline\n");
  exit(EXIT_FAILURE);
}
```

```
  createColorAndDepthFramebuffers(vkDev,
    vkState.renderPass,
    vkState.depthTexture.imageView, kScreenWidth,
    kScreenHeight,
    vkState.swapchainFramebuffers);
  return VK_SUCCESS;
}
```

The `drawOverlay()` function does the bulk of the rendering job. Let's take a look:

1. First, we should acquire the next available image from the swap chain and reset the command pool:

```
bool drawOverlay() {
  uint32_t imageIndex = 0;
  VK_CHECK(vkAcquireNextImageKHR( vkDev.device,
    vkDev.swapchain, 0,
    vkDev.semaphore, VK_NULL_HANDLE, &imageIndex);
  VK_CHECK(vkResetCommandPool(vkDev.device,
    vkDev.commandPool, 0));
```

2. Fill in the uniform buffer with data (*Dealing with buffers in Vulkan*). Rotate the model around the vertical axis, similar to what we did in the OpenGL examples in the previous chapter:

```
int width, height;
glfwGetFramebufferSize(window, &width, &height);
const float ratio = width / (float)height;
const mat4 m1 = glm::rotate(glm::translate(
    mat4(1.0f), vec3(0.f, 0.5f, -1.5f)) *
  glm::rotate(mat4(1.f),
    glm::pi<float>(), vec3(1, 0, 0)),
    (float)glfwGetTime(), vec3(0.0f, 1.0f, 0.0f));
const mat4 p = glm::perspective(
  45.0f, ratio, 0.1f, 1000.0f);
const UniformBuffer ubo{ .mvp = p * m1 };
updateUniformBuffer(imageIndex, ubo);
```

3. Now, fill in the command buffers (*Using Vulkan command buffers*). In this recipe, we are doing this each frame, which is not really required since the commands are identical. We are only doing this to show you where the command buffers can be updated:

```
fillCommandBuffers();
```

4. Submit the command buffer to the graphics queue:

```
const VkPipelineStageFlags waitStages[] =
  { VK_PIPELINE_STAGE_COLOR_ATTACHMENT_OUTPUT_BIT };
const VkSubmitInfo si = {
  .sType = VK_STRUCTURE_TYPE_SUBMIT_INFO,
  .pNext = nullptr,
  .waitSemaphoreCount = 1,
  .pWaitSemaphores = &vkDev.semaphore,
  .pWaitDstStageMask = waitStages,
  .commandBufferCount = 1,
  .pCommandBuffers =
    &vkDev.commandBuffers[imageIndex],
  .signalSemaphoreCount = 1,
  .pSignalSemaphores = &vkDev.renderSemaphore
};
VK_CHECK(vkQueueSubmit(
  vkDev.graphicsQueue, 1, &si, nullptr ));
```

5. Present the rendered image on screen:

```
const VkPresentInfoKHR pi = {
  .sType = VK_STRUCTURE_TYPE_PRESENT_INFO_KHR,
  .pNext = nullptr,
  .waitSemaphoreCount = 1,
  .pWaitSemaphores = &vkDev.renderSemaphore,
  .swapchainCount = 1,
  .pSwapchains = &vkDev.swapchain,
  .pImageIndices = &imageIndex
};
VK_CHECK(
  vkQueuePresentKHR(vkDev.graphicsQueue, &pi));
VK_CHECK(vkDeviceWaitIdle(vkDev.device));
return true;
}
```

Now, if you run this example application, it should display the following rotating duck 3D model. It should have a texture and a wireframe overlay:

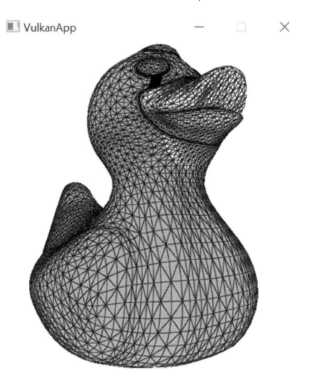

Figure 3.6 – The rendered image on the screen

4

Adding User Interaction and Productivity Tools

In this chapter, we will learn how to implement basic helpers to drastically simplify the debugging of graphical applications. There are a couple of demos implemented in OpenGL. However, a significant part of our code in this chapter is Vulkan-based. In *Chapter 3*, *Getting Started with OpenGL and Vulkan*, we demonstrated how to implement numerous helper functions to create and maintain basic Vulkan states and objects. In this chapter, we will show how to start organizing Vulkan frame rendering in a way that is easily extensible and adaptable for different applications.

We will cover the following recipes:

- Organizing Vulkan frame rendering code
- Organizing mesh rendering in Vulkan
- Implementing an immediate mode drawing canvas
- Rendering a Dear ImGui user interface with Vulkan

- Working with a 3D camera and basic user interaction

- Adding a frames-per-second counter

- Adding camera animations and motion

- Integrating EasyProfiler and Optick into C++ applications

- Using cube map textures in Vulkan

- Rendering onscreen charts

- Putting it all together into a Vulkan application

Technical requirements

Here is what it takes to run the code from this chapter on your Linux or Windows PC. You will need a GPU with recent drivers supporting OpenGL 4.6 and Vulkan 1.1. The source code can be downloaded from `https://github.com/PacktPublishing/3D-Graphics-Rendering-Cookbook`.

Organizing Vulkan frame rendering code

As we learned from the previous chapter, the Vulkan API is pretty verbose. We need something to conceal the API's verbosity and organize our frame rendering code in a manageable way. Let's assume that each frame is composed of multiple *layers*, just like an image in a graphics editor. The first, and rather formal, layer is the solid background color. The next layer might be a 3D scene with models and lights. On top of a beautifully rendered 3D scene, we could optionally add some wireframe meshes to draw useful debugging information. These wireframe objects belong in another layer. Next, we add a 2D user interface, for example, using the ImGui library. There might be some additional layers, such as fullscreen charts with performance statistics or **frames-per-second** (**FPS**) counters. Finally, the finishing layer transitions the swapchain image to the `VK_LAYOUT_PRESENT_SRC_KHR` layout.

In this recipe, we define an interface to render a single layer and implement this interface for screen-clearing and finishing layers.

Getting ready

The source code for this recipe is a part of the utility code located in `shared/vkRenderers/`. Take a look at these files: `VulkanModelRenderer.h`, `VulkanMultiRenderer.h`, and `VulkanQuadRenderer.h`.

How to do it...

In terms of programming, each layer is an object that contains a Vulkan pipeline object, framebuffers, a Vulkan rendering pass, all descriptor sets, and all kinds of buffers necessary for rendering. This object provides an interface that can fill Vulkan command buffers for the current frame and update GPU buffers with CPU data, for example, per-frame uniforms such as the camera transformation.

Let's look at how to define the base class for our layer rendering interface, `RendererBase`:

1. The first function this interface provides is `fillCommandBuffer()`. This function injects a stream of Vulkan commands into the passed command buffer. The second parameter to this function, `currentImage`, is required to use appropriate uniform and data buffers associated with one of the swapchain images:

```cpp
class RendererBase {
public:
  explicit RendererBase(
    const VulkanRenderDevice& vkDev,
    VulkanImage depthTexture)
  : device_(vkDev.device)
  , framebufferWidth_(vkDev.framebufferWidth)
  , framebufferHeight_(vkDev.framebufferHeight)
  , depthTexture_(depthTexture)
  {}
  virtual ~RendererBase();
  virtual void fillCommandBuffer(
    VkCommandBuffer commandBuffer,
    size_t currentImage) = 0;
```

2. The `getDepthTexture()` method gives access to the internally managed depth buffer, which can be shared between layers:

```
inline VulkanImage getDepthTexture() const
{ return depthTexture_; }
```

3. The state of the object consists of the fields, most of which we have already seen in the `VulkanState` class from the Chapter 3 demo application. Two member functions, commonly used by the derived classes, are the render pass starter and the uniform buffer allocator. The first one emits the `vkCmdBeginRenderPass`, `vkCmdBindPipeline`, and `vkCmdBindDescriptorSet` commands to begin rendering. The second function allocates a list of GPU buffers that contain uniform data, with one buffer per swapchain image:

```
protected:
    void beginRenderPass(VkCommandBuffer commandBuffer,
        size_t currentImage);
    bool createUniformBuffers(VulkanRenderDevice& vkDev,
        size_t uniformDataSize);
```

4. Each layer renderer internally uses the size of the framebuffer to start a rendering pass:

```
uint32_t framebufferWidth_;
uint32_t framebufferHeight_;
```

5. All textures and buffers are bound to the shader modules by descriptor sets. We maintain one descriptor set per swapchain image. To define these descriptor sets, we also need the descriptor set layout and the descriptor pool:

```
VkDescriptorSetLayout descriptorSetLayout_;
VkDescriptorPool descriptorPool_;
std::vector<VkDescriptorSet> descriptorSets_;
```

6. Each command buffer operates on a dedicated framebuffer object:

```
std::vector<VkFramebuffer> swapchainFramebuffers_;
```

7. We store the depth buffer reference, which is passed here during the initialization phase. The render pass, pipeline layout, and the pipeline itself are also taken from the `VulkanState` object:

```
VulkanImage depthTexture_;
VkRenderPass renderPass_;
```

```
VkPipelineLayout pipelineLayout_;
VkPipeline graphicsPipeline_;
```

8. Each swapchain image has an associated uniform buffer. We declare these buffers here:

```
std::vector<VkBuffer> uniformBuffers;
std::vector<VkDeviceMemory> uniformBuffersMemory;
};
```

Let's look into the implementation code of the previously mentioned `RenderBase` interface, which is reused by all its subclasses:

1. The implementation of `createUniformBuffers()` is a simple loop over all swapchain images that calls `createUniformBuffer()` for each of them:

```
bool RendererBase::createUniformBuffers(
  VulkanRenderDevice& vkDev, size_t uniformDataSize)
{
  uniformBuffers_.resize(
    vkDev.swapchainImages.size());
  uniformBuffersMemory_.resize(
    vkDev.swapchainImages.size());
  for (size_t i = 0;
       i < vkDev.swapchainImages.size(); i++) {
    if (!createUniformBuffer(vkDev,
          uniformBuffers_[i],
          uniformBuffersMemory_[i],
          uniformDataSize)) {
      printf("Cannot create uniform buffer\n");
      return false;
    }
  }
  return true;
}
```

2. The `beginRenderPass()` routine marks the start of a rendering pass and does graphics pipeline binding and descriptor set binding for the current image in the swapchain:

```
void RendererBase::beginRenderPass(
  VkCommandBuffer commandBuffer, size_t currentImage)
{
  const VkRect2D screenRect = {
```

```
    .offset = { 0, 0 },
    .extent = {
      .width = framebufferWidth_,
      .height = framebufferHeight_
    }
  };
  const VkRenderPassBeginInfo renderPassInfo = {
    .sType = VK_STRUCTURE_TYPE_RENDER_PASS_BEGIN_INFO,
    .pNext = nullptr,
    .renderPass = renderPass_,
    .framebuffer =
      swapchainFramebuffers_[currentImage],
    .renderArea = screenRect
  };
  vkCmdBeginRenderPass(commandBuffer,
    &renderPassInfo,
    VK_SUBPASS_CONTENTS_INLINE);
  vkCmdBindPipeline(commandBuffer,
    VK_PIPELINE_BIND_POINT_GRAPHICS,
    graphicsPipeline_);
  vkCmdBindDescriptorSets(commandBuffer,
    VK_PIPELINE_BIND_POINT_GRAPHICS, pipelineLayout_,
    0, 1, &descriptorSets_[currentImage], 0, nullptr);
}
```

3. Finally, the destructor cleans up each allocated object. In a bigger application, you might want to write an RAII wrapper for each of these resources to ensure automatic deallocation:

```
RendererBase::~RendererBase() {
  for (auto buf : uniformBuffers_)
    vkDestroyBuffer(device_, buf, nullptr);
  for (auto mem : uniformBuffersMemory_)
    vkFreeMemory(device_, mem, nullptr);
  vkDestroyDescriptorSetLayout(
    device_, descriptorSetLayout_, nullptr);
  vkDestroyDescriptorPool(
    device_, descriptorPool_, nullptr);
  for (auto framebuffer : swapchainFramebuffers_)
    vkDestroyFramebuffer(
      device_, framebuffer, nullptr);
  vkDestroyRenderPass(device_, renderPass_, nullptr);
```

```
    vkDestroyPipelineLayout(
        device_, pipelineLayout_, nullptr);
    vkDestroyPipeline(
        device_, graphicsPipeline_, nullptr);
}
```

Note that this assumes all these objects were actually allocated in the initialization routines of the derived classes.

Now that we have our basic layer rendering interface, we can define the first layer. The `VulkanClear` object initializes and starts an empty rendering pass whose only purpose is to clear the color and depth buffers. Let's look at the steps:

1. The initialization routine takes a reference to our rendering device object and a possibly empty depth buffer handle:

```
class VulkanClear: public RendererBase {
public:
    VulkanClear(VulkanRenderDevice& vkDev,
        VulkanImage depthTexture);
```

2. The only function we implement here starts and finishes our single rendering pass. The private part of the class contains a Boolean flag that tells it to clear the depth buffer:

```
    virtual void fillCommandBuffer(
        VkCommandBuffer commandBuffer,
        size_t currentImage) override;
private:
    bool shouldClearDepth;
};
```

3. The constructor creates framebuffers, the rendering pass, and the graphics pipeline:

```
VulkanClear::VulkanClear(
    VulkanRenderDevice& vkDev, VulkanImage depthTexture)
: RendererBase(vkDev, depthTexture)
, shouldClearDepth(
    depthTexture.image != VK_NULL_HANDLE)
{
```

4. The `RenderPassCreateInfo` structure defines how this rendering pass should be created. We introduce a set of flags to simplify this process. The `eRenderPassBit_First` flag defines a rendering pass as the first pass. What this means for Vulkan is that before this rendering pass, our swapchain image should be in the `VK_LAYOUT_UNDEFINED` state and, after this pass, it is not yet suitable for presentation but only for rendering:

```
if (!createColorAndDepthRenderPass(
        vkDev, shouldClearDepth, &renderPass_,
        RenderPassCreateInfo {
            .clearColor_ = true, .clearDepth_ = true,
            .flags_ = eRenderPassBit_First})) {
    printf(
      "VulkanClear: failed to create render pass\n");
    exit(EXIT_FAILURE);
}
createColorAndDepthFramebuffers(vkDev, renderPass_,
    depthTexture.imageView, swapchainFramebuffers_);
}
```

5. The `fillCommandBuffer()` function starts and finishes the render pass, also filling the `clearValues` member field in the `VkBeginRenderPassInfo` structure:

```
void VulkanClear::fillCommandBuffer(
  VkCommandBuffer commandBuffer,
  size_t swapFramebuffer)
{
  const VkClearValue clearValues[2] = {
    VkClearValue {.color = {1.0f, 1.0f, 1.0f, 1.0f} },
    VkClearValue {.depthStencil = { 1.0f, 0.0f } }
  };
  const VkRect2D screenRect = {
    .offset = { 0, 0 },
    .extent = { .width  = framebufferWidth_,
                .height = framebufferHeight_ }
  };
```

6. If we need to clear the depth buffer in this render pass, we should use both clear values from the `clearValues` array. Otherwise, use only the first value to clear the color buffer:

```
const VkRenderPassBeginInfo renderPassInfo = {
  .sType = VK_STRUCTURE_TYPE_RENDER_PASS_BEGIN_INFO,
  .renderPass = renderPass_,
  .framebuffer =
    swapchainFramebuffers_[swapFramebuffer],
  .renderArea = screenRect,
  .clearValueCount = shouldClearDepth ? 2u : 1u,
  .pClearValues = &clearValues[0]
};
vkCmdBeginRenderPass(commandBuffer, &renderPassInfo,
  VK_SUBPASS_CONTENTS_INLINE);
vkCmdEndRenderPass(commandBuffer);
}
```

Now we are able to start rendering our frame, but it is equally important to finish the frame. The following `VulkanFinish` object helps us to create another empty rendering pass that transitions the swapchain image to the `VK_IMAGE_LAYOUT_PRESENT_SRC_KHR` format:

1. Let's take a look at the `VulkanFinish` class declaration:

```
class VulkanFinish: public RendererBase {
public:
  VulkanFinish(VulkanRenderDevice& vkDev,
    VulkanImage depthTexture);
  virtual void fillCommandBuffer(
    VkCommandBuffer commandBuffer,
    size_t currentImage) override;
};
```

There are no additional members introduced and all resource management is done in the base class.

2. The class constructor creates one empty rendering pass:

```
VulkanFinish::VulkanFinish(
  VulkanRenderDevice& vkDev, VulkanImage depthTexture)
  : RendererBase(vkDev, depthTexture)
{
  if (!createColorAndDepthRenderPass(
      vkDev, (depthTexture.image != VK_NULL_HANDLE),
      &renderPass_,
```

```
            RenderPassCreateInfo{
                .clearColor_ = false,
                .clearDepth_ = false,
                .flags_ = eRenderPassBit_Last
          })) {
        printf(
          "VulkanFinish: failed to create render pass\n");
        exit(EXIT_FAILURE);
      }
      createColorAndDepthFramebuffers(vkDev,
        renderPass_, depthTexture.imageView,
        swapchainFramebuffers_);
  }
```

This rendering pass is the last one and should not clear any buffers.

3. Starting and finishing the rendering pass is rather similar to the functionality of
    VulkanClear described previously, except that here we do not clear any buffers:

```
void VulkanFinish::fillCommandBuffer(
  VkCommandBuffer commandBuffer, size_t currentImage)
{
  const VkRect2D screenRect = {
    .offset = { 0, 0 },
    .extent = { .width = screenWidth,
                .height = screenHeight }
  };
  const VkRenderPassBeginInfo renderPassInfo = {
    .sType = VK_STRUCTURE_TYPE_RENDER_PASS_BEGIN_INFO,
    .renderPass = renderPass,
    .framebuffer = swapchainFramebuffers[currentImage],
    .renderArea = screenRect
  };
  vkCmdBeginRenderPass(commandBuffer, &renderPassInfo,
    VK_SUBPASS_CONTENTS_INLINE);
  vkCmdEndRenderPass(commandBuffer);
}
```

This class essentially hides all the hassle necessary to finalize frame rendering in Vulkan.
We will use it in our demos together with VulkanClear.

There's more...

We have only started our frame rendering reorganization. The complete Vulkan usage example, which will put together the functionality of all the recipes of this chapter, is postponed until we go through and discuss all the recipes here. The next recipe will show how to simplify static 3D mesh rendering with Vulkan.

Organizing mesh rendering in Vulkan

In *Chapter 3*, *Getting Started with OpenGL and Vulkan*, we learned how to render a textured 3D model on the screen using Vulkan in a direct and pretty ad hoc way. Now we will show how to move one step closer to creating a more scalable 3D model renderer with Vulkan. In the subsequent chapters, we will further generalize the rendering approach so that we can build a minimalistic Vulkan rendering engine from scratch, step by step.

Getting ready

Revisit the *Organizing Vulkan frame rendering code* recipe and recall how the RendererBase interface works. The code we will discuss in this recipe can be found in shared/vkRenderers/VulkanModelRenderer.cpp and the corresponding header file.

How to do it...

Let's declare the ModelRenderer class, which contains a texture and combined vertex and index buffers:

1. The declaration looks as follows:

```
class ModelRenderer: public RendererBase {
public:
  ModelRenderer(VulkanRenderDevice& vkDev,
    const char* modelFile,
    const char* textureFile,
    uint32_t uniformDataSize);
  virtual ~ModelRenderer();
  virtual void fillCommandBuffer(
    VkCommandBuffer commandBuffer,
    size_t currentImage) override;
  void updateUniformBuffer(VulkanRenderDevice& vkDev,
    uint32_t currentImage,
    const void* data, size_t dataSize);
```

We add a new function to the interface, which allows us to modify per-frame uniform constants. In this case, we pass only the premultiplied model-view matrix to the shaders. The `fillCommandBuffer()` function emits the appropriate `vkCmdDraw` command into a Vulkan command buffer.

2. The storage buffer holds index and vertex data combined. Besides that, we should store the sizes of vertex and index data separately:

```
private:
   size_t vertexBufferSize_;
   size_t indexBufferSize_;
   VkBuffer storageBuffer_;
   VkDeviceMemory storageBufferMemory_;
```

3. Add a single texture sampler and a texture:

```
   VkSampler textureSampler_;
   VulkanImage texture_;
   bool createDescriptorSet(
      VulkanRenderDevice& vkDev,
      uint32_t uniformDataSize);
};
```

In this recipe, we limit our 3D model to containing only one texture. This is a pretty strong constraint but it will help us to keep our code structure for this chapter reasonably simple without adding too much complexity here at once. Materials will be covered in *Chapter 7, Graphics Rendering Pipeline*.

Now, let's switch to the implementation part of this class:

1. Everything starts with loading a texture and a mesh. To that end, we reuse the mesh loading code from *Chapter 3, Getting Started with OpenGL and Vulkan*, like so:

```
ModelRenderer::ModelRenderer(
  VulkanRenderDevice& vkDev,
  const char* modelFile, const char* textureFile,
  uint32_t uniformDataSize)
: RendererBase(vkDev, VulkanImage()) {
  if (!createTexturedVertexBuffer(vkDev, modelFile,
        &storageBuffer_, &storageBufferMemory_,
        &vertexBufferSize_, &indexBufferSize_)) {
    printf("ModelRenderer:
      createTexturedVertexBuffer failed\n");
```

```
     exit(EXIT_FAILURE);
  }
```

2. The same applies to the texture image, image view, and sampler:

```
createTextureImage(
  vkDev, textureFile, texture_.image,
  texture_.imageMemory);
createImageView(vkDev.device, texture_.image,
  VK_FORMAT_R8G8B8A8_UNORM,
  VK_IMAGE_ASPECT_COLOR_BIT,
  &texture_.imageView);
createTextureSampler(vkDev.device, &textureSampler_);
  ...
}
```

They are created using the code from *Chapter 3*, *Getting Started with OpenGL and Vulkan*. The pipeline creation code contains only calls to various `create*()` functions and it is skipped here for the sake of brevity. Take a look at `UtilsVulkanModelRenderer.cpp` for all the details.

The longest member function is `createDescriptorSet()` whose code is mostly similar to the demo application from *Chapter 3*, *Getting Started with OpenGL and Vulkan*. This code differs only in the number and type of used Vulkan buffers. We will go through its content here once because in the remaining part of this chapter, similar code is reused to create descriptor sets for different rendering purposes:

1. The first part of this method declares usage types, binding points, and accessibility flags for buffers used in all shader stages:

```
bool ModelRenderer::createDescriptorSet(
  VulkanRenderDevice& vkDev, uint32_t uniformDataSize)
{
  const std::array<VkDescriptorSetLayoutBinding, 4>
    bindings = {
    descriptorSetLayoutBinding(0,
      VK_DESCRIPTOR_TYPE_UNIFORM_BUFFER,
      VK_SHADER_STAGE_VERTEX_BIT),
    descriptorSetLayoutBinding(1,
      VK_DESCRIPTOR_TYPE_STORAGE_BUFFER,
      VK_SHADER_STAGE_VERTEX_BIT),
    descriptorSetLayoutBinding(2,
      VK_DESCRIPTOR_TYPE_STORAGE_BUFFER,
      VK_SHADER_STAGE_VERTEX_BIT),
```

```
    descriptorSetLayoutBinding(3,
      VK_DESCRIPTOR_TYPE_COMBINED_IMAGE_SAMPLER,
      VK_SHADER_STAGE_FRAGMENT_BIT)
};
```

2. This `LayoutBinding` description is used to create an immutable descriptor set layout that does not change later:

```
const VkDescriptorSetLayoutCreateInfo layoutInfo = {
  .sType = VK_STRUCTURE_TYPE_DESCRIPTOR_SET
           _LAYOUT_CREATE_INFO,
  .pNext = nullptr,
  .flags = 0,
  .bindingCount =
    static_cast<uint32_t>(bindings.size()),
  .pBindings = bindings.data()
};
VK_CHECK(vkCreateDescriptorSetLayout(vkDev.device,
  &layoutInfo, nullptr, &descriptorSetLayout_));
```

3. Once we have `descriptorSetLayout`, we should proceed with the actual `descriptorSet` creation:

```
std::vector<VkDescriptorSetLayout>
layouts(vkDev.swapchainImages.size(),
  descriptorSetLayout_);
const VkDescriptorSetAllocateInfo allocInfo = {
  .sType = VK_STRUCTURE_TYPE_DESCRIPTOR_
           SET_ALLOCATE_INFO,
  .pNext = nullptr,
  .descriptorPool = descriptorPool_,
  .descriptorSetCount = static_cast<uint32_t>(
    vkDev.swapchainImages.size()),
  .pSetLayouts = layouts.data()
};
descriptorSets_.resize(
  vkDev.swapchainImages.size());
VK_CHECK(vkAllocateDescriptorSets(vkDev.device,
  &allocInfo, descriptorSets_.data()));
```

4. Finally, for each `swapchainImage`, we update the corresponding
    `descriptorSet` with specific buffer handles. We use one uniform buffer and one
    shader storage buffer to store combined vertices and indices for the programmable
    vertex pulling technique:

```
for (size_t i = 0; i < vkDev.swapchainImages.size();
    i++)
{
  VkDescriptorSet ds = descriptorSets_[i];
  const VkDescriptorBufferInfo bufferInfo =
    { uniformBuffers_[i], 0, uniformDataSize };
  const VkDescriptorBufferInfo bufferInfo2 =
    { storageBuffer_, 0, vertexBufferSize_ };
  const VkDescriptorBufferInfo bufferInfo3 =
    { storageBuffer_, vertexBufferSize_,
      indexBufferSize_ };
  const VkDescriptorImageInfo  imageInfo =
    { textureSampler_, texture_.imageView,
      VK_IMAGE_LAYOUT_SHADER_READ_ONLY_OPTIMAL };
  const std::array<VkWriteDescriptorSet, 4>
    descriptorWrites = {
    bufferWriteDescriptorSet(ds, &bufferInfo,  0,
      VK_DESCRIPTOR_TYPE_UNIFORM_BUFFER),
    bufferWriteDescriptorSet(ds, &bufferInfo2, 1,
      VK_DESCRIPTOR_TYPE_STORAGE_BUFFER),
    bufferWriteDescriptorSet(ds, &bufferInfo3, 2,
      VK_DESCRIPTOR_TYPE_STORAGE_BUFFER),
    imageWriteDescriptorSet(ds, &imageInfo, 3)
  };
  vkUpdateDescriptorSets(vkDev.device,
    static_cast<uint32_t>(descriptorWrites.size()),
    descriptorWrites.data(), 0, nullptr);
}
  return true;
}
```

Because all the mesh data is immutable, this function is invoked only once from the
`ModelRenderer` constructor.

There are two more functions that are required to render our 3D model:

1. The first one should be called every frame to update the uniform buffer with the model-view matrix. All it does is delegate the call to the `uploadBufferData()` function we implemented in the previous chapter, using the Vulkan buffer corresponding to the current swapchain image:

```
void ModelRenderer::updateUniformBuffer(
    VulkanRenderDevice& vkDev, uint32_t currentImage,
    const void* data, const size_t dataSize)
{
    uploadBufferData(
        vkDev, uniformBuffersMemory_[currentImage],
        0, data, dataSize);
}
```

2. The second one, `fillCommandBuffer()`, does the actual rendering by starting a `RenderPass` and emitting a single `vkCmdDraw` command into the Vulkan command buffer:

```
void ModelRenderer::fillCommandBuffer(
    VkCommandBuffer commandBuffer, size_t currentImage)
{
    beginRenderPass(commandBuffer, currentImage);
    vkCmdDraw(
        commandBuffer, indexBufferSize_/(sizeof(uint32_t),
        1, 0, 0);
    vkCmdEndRenderPass(commandBuffer);
}
```

This recipe could indeed be called a somewhat generalized version of the rendering routines from the previous chapter. With this code, we can use Vulkan to render multiple 3D models in a single scene, which is a considerable step forward. However, the efficiency of rendering multiple meshes using the approach described in this recipe is somewhat debatable and should be avoided in cases where a lot of meshes need to be rendered. We will return to the question of efficiency in the next chapter.

Implementing an immediate mode drawing canvas

Chapter 3, Getting Started with OpenGL and Vulkan, only scratched the surface of the topic of graphical application debugging. The validation layers provided by the Vulkan API are invaluable but they do not allow you to debug logical and calculation-related errors. To see what is happening in our virtual world, we need to be able to render auxiliary graphical information such as object bounding boxes, plot time-varying charts of different values, or just plain straight lines. The Vulkan API and modern OpenGL do not provide or, rather, explicitly prohibit any immediate mode rendering facilities. To overcome this difficulty and add an immediate mode rendering canvas to our frame composition mechanism, we have to write some additional code. Let's learn how to do that in this recipe.

Getting ready

We will need to revisit the `RendererBase` and `ModelRenderer` classes discussed in the two previous recipes. Check the `shared/UtilsVulkanCanvas.cpp` file for a working implementation of this recipe.

How to do it...

The `VulkanCanvas` object contains a CPU-accessible list of 3D lines defined by two points and a color. For each frame, the user can call the `line()` method to draw a new line that should be rendered in the current frame. To render these lines into the framebuffer, we pre-allocate a reasonably large GPU buffer to store line geometry data, which we will update every frame:

1. The `VulkanCanvas` class is derived from `RendererBase` and is similar to the previously discussed `ModelRenderer` class:

```
class VulkanCanvas: public RendererBase {
public:
  explicit VulkanCanvas(
    VulkanRenderDevice& vkDev, VulkanImage depth);
  virtual ~VulkanCanvas();
  virtual void fillCommandBuffer(
    VkCommandBuffer commandBuffer,
    size_t currentImage) override;
  void updateBuffer(
    VulkanRenderDevice& vkDev, size_t currentImage);
```

```
void updateUniformBuffer(
  VulkanRenderDevice& vkDev,
  const glm::mat4& m, float time,
  uint32_t currentImage);
```

2. The actual drawing functionality consists of three functions. We want to be able to clear the canvas, render one line, and render a wireframe representation of a 3D plane. Further utility functions can easily be built on top of the functionality provided by `line()`:

```
void clear();
void line(const vec3& p1, const vec3& p2,
  const vec4& color);
void plane3d(
  const vec3& orig, const vec3& v1, const vec3& v2,
  int n1, int n2, float s1, float s2,
  const vec4& color, const vec4& outlineColor);
```

3. Our internal data representation stores a pair of vertices for each and every line, whereas each vertex consists of a 3D position and a color. A uniform buffer holds the combined model-view-projection matrix and the current time:

```
private:
  struct VertexData {
    vec3 position;
    vec4 color;
  };
  struct UniformBuffer {
    glm::mat4 mvp;
    float time;
  };
  std::vector<VertexData> lines;
  std::vector<VkBuffer> storageBuffer;
  std::vector<VkDeviceMemory> storageBufferMemory;
```

4. The longest method of this class, just as is the case with `ModelRenderer`, is `createDescriptorSet()`. It is almost the same as in the previous recipe, with the obvious changes to omit textures and the unused index buffer. We omit citing its implementation here, which can be found in the `UtilsVulkanCanvas.cpp` file:

```
bool createDescriptorSet(VulkanRenderDevice& vkDev);
```

5. We need to define the maximum number of lines we may want to render. This is necessary to be able to pre-allocate GPU storage for our geometry data:

```
static constexpr unsigned kMaxLinesCount = 65536;
static constexpr unsigned kMaxLinesDataSize = 2 *
    kMaxLinesCount * sizeof(VulkanCanvas::VertexData);
};
```

Now, let's deal with the non-Vulkan part of the code:

1. The `plane3d()` method uses `line()` internally to create the 3D representation of a plane spanned by the `v1` and `v2` vectors:

```
void VulkanCanvas::plane3d(const vec3& o,
    const vec3& v1, const vec3& v2,
    int n1, int n2, float s1, float s2,
    const vec4& color, const vec4& outlineColor)
{
```

2. Draw the four outer lines representing a plane segment:

```
line(o - s1 / 2.0f * v1 - s2 / 2.0f * v2,
     o - s1 / 2.0f * v1 + s2 / 2.0f * v2,
     outlineColor);
line(o + s1 / 2.0f * v1 - s2 / 2.0f * v2,
     o + s1 / 2.0f * v1 + s2 / 2.0f * v2,
     outlineColor);
line(o - s1 / 2.0f * v1 + s2 / 2.0f * v2,
     o + s1 / 2.0f * v1 + s2 / 2.0f * v2,
     outlineColor);
line(o - s1 / 2.0f * v1 - s2 / 2.0f * v2,
     o + s1 / 2.0f * v1 - s2 / 2.0f * v2,
     outlineColor);
```

3. Draw `n1` "horizontal" lines and `n2` "vertical" lines:

```
for(int ii = 1 ; ii < n1 ; ii++) {
  const float t =
    ((float)ii - (float)n1 / 2.0f) * s1 / (float)n1;
  const vec3 o1 = o + t * v1;
  line(o1 - s2 / 2.0f * v2, o1 + s2 / 2.0f * v2,
    color);
}
for(int ii = 1 ; ii < n2 ; ii++) {
```

```
    const float t =
        ((float)ii - (float)n2 / 2.0f) * s2 / (float)n2;
    const vec3 o2 = o + t * v2;
    line(o2 - s1 / 2.0f * v1, o2 + s1 / 2.0f * v1,
        color);
    }
}
```

4. The `line()` member function itself just adds two points to the collection:

```
void VulkanCanvas::line(
    const vec3& p1, const vec3& p2, const vec4& color)
{
    lines.push_back({ .position = p1, .color = color });
    lines.push_back({ .position = p2, .color = color });
}
```

5. The `clear()` method is fairly trivial:

```
void VulkanCanvas::clear() {
    lines.clear();
}
```

Now, let's go back to the Vulkan code necessary to render the lines:

1. In the constructor, we will allocate one geometry data buffer for each swapchain image:

```
VulkanCanvas::VulkanCanvas(
    VulkanRenderDevice& vkDev, VulkanImage depth)
: RendererBase(vkDev, depth) {
    const size_t imgCount =
        vkDev.swapchainImages.size();
    storageBuffer.resize(imgCount);
    storageBufferMemory.resize(imgCount);
    for(size_t i = 0 ; i < imgCount ; i++) {
        if (!createBuffer(vkDev.device,
            vkDev.physicalDevice,
            kMaxLinesDataSize,
            VK_BUFFER_USAGE_STORAGE_BUFFER_BIT,
            VK_MEMORY_PROPERTY_HOST_VISIBLE_BIT |
            VK_MEMORY_PROPERTY_HOST_COHERENT_BIT,
            storageBuffer[i], storageBufferMemory[i]))
        {
```

```
        printf("VulkanCanvas: createBuffer() failed\n");
        exit(EXIT_FAILURE);
      }
    }
    // ... pipeline creation code skipped here ...
}
```

We will skip the Vulkan pipeline creation boilerplate code again for the sake of brevity. Check the `UtilsVulkanCanvas.cpp` file for all the details.

2. The `updateBuffer()` routine checks that our lines list is not empty and then calls the `uploadBufferData()` function to upload the lines' geometry data into the GPU buffer:

```
void VulkanCanvas::updateBuffer(
  VulkanRenderDevice& vkDev, size_t i)
{
  if (lines.empty()) return;
  VkDeviceSize bufferSize =
    lines.size() * sizeof(VertexData);
  uploadBufferData(vkDev, storageBufferMemory[i], 0,
    lines.data(), bufferSize);
}
```

3. `updateUniformBuffer()` packs two per-frame parameters in a structure and calls the usual `uploadBufferData()` for the current swapchain image:

```
void VulkanCanvas::updateUniformBuffer(
  VulkanRenderDevice& vkDev,
  const glm::mat4& modelViewProj,
  float time,
  uint32_t currentImage)
{
  const UniformBuffer ubo = {
    .mvp = modelViewProj,
    .time = time
  };
  uploadBufferData(vkDev,
    uniformBuffersMemory_[currentImage],
    0, &ubo, sizeof(ubo));
}
```

4. `fillCommandBuffer()` checks the lines' presence and emits `vkCmdDraw` to render all the lines in one draw call:

```
void VulkanCanvas::fillCommandBuffer(
  VkCommandBuffer commandBuffer, size_t currentImage)
{
  if (lines.empty()) return;
  beginRenderPass(commandBuffer, currentImage);
  vkCmdDraw(commandBuffer, lines.size(), 1, 0, 0);
  vkCmdEndRenderPass(commandBuffer);
}
```

For a comprehensive example showing how to use this canvas, check the last recipe in this chapter *Putting it all together into a Vulkan application*.

The next recipe will conclude Vulkan auxiliary rendering by showing how to render user interfaces with the ImGui library.

Rendering a Dear ImGui user interface with Vulkan

In *Chapter 3, Getting Started with OpenGL and Vulkan*, we demonstrated how to render the Dear ImGui user interface using OpenGL in 200 lines of C++ code. Here we try to transfer this knowledge to Vulkan and complement our existing frame composition routines. Even though fitting the entire Vulkan ImGui renderer into a few hundred lines of code is definitely not possible, we will do our best to keep the implementation reasonably compact for it to serve as a good teaching example.

Getting ready

It is recommended to revisit the *Rendering a basic UI with Dear ImGui* recipe from *Chapter 2, Using Essential Libraries*, and also recall our Vulkan frame composition scheme described in the first two recipes of this chapter.

This recipe covers the source code of `shared/vkRenderers/VulkanImGui.cpp`.

How to do it...

Let's take a look at the minimalistic ImGui Vulkan renderer implementation, which takes the `ImDrawData` data structure as the input and fills Vulkan command buffers with appropriate drawing commands:

1. The `ImGuiRenderer` class is derived from `RendererBase` and contains the four usual member functions:

```cpp
class ImGuiRenderer: public RendererBase {
public:
  explicit ImGuiRenderer(VulkanRenderDevice& vkDev);
  virtual ~ImGuiRenderer();
  virtual void fillCommandBuffer(
    VkCommandBuffer commandBuffer, size_t
    currentImage) override;
  void updateBuffers(
    VulkanRenderDevice& vkDev, uint32_t currentImage,
    const ImDrawData* imguiDrawData);
```

2. Let's store a pointer to `ImDrawData` that holds all the ImGui-rendered widgets:

```cpp
private:
  const ImDrawData* drawData = nullptr;
  bool createDescriptorSet(VulkanRenderDevice& vkDev);
```

3. We allocate one geometry buffer for each swapchain image to avoid any kind of synchronization, just like in the case with `VulkanCanvas`:

```cpp
  VkDeviceSize bufferSize;
  std::vector<VkBuffer> storageBuffer;
  std::vector<VkDeviceMemory> storageBufferMemory;
  VkSampler fontSampler;
  VulkanImage font;
};
```

The descriptor set creation function is also present. It is almost entirely identical to `ModelRenderer::createDescriptorSet()`, with one minor difference. Each geometry buffer from the `storageBuffer` container is bound to its corresponding descriptor set and there is one descriptor set per swapchain image.

Let's quickly go through the initialization code:

1. First, we define constants to hold the maximum size of the vertex and index buffers. 65536 elements are enough for the default ImGui rendering mode:

```
const uint32_t ImGuiVtxBufferSize =
   64 * 1024 * sizeof(ImDrawVert);
const uint32_t ImGuiIdxBufferSize =
   64 * 1024 * sizeof(int);
```

2. The constructor loads all the necessary resources, a TTF font file, and a font texture generated by ImGui; it creates a sampler and a texture view, allocates buffers for geometry, and creates a Vulkan pipeline:

```
ImGuiRenderer::ImGuiRenderer(
   VulkanRenderDevice& vkDev)
: RendererBase(vkDev, VulkanImage())
{
   ImGuiIO& io = ImGui::GetIO();
   createFontTexture(io, "data/OpenSans-Light.ttf",
      vkDev, font_.image, font_.imageMemory);
   createImageView(vkDev.device, font_.image,
      VK_FORMAT_R8G8B8A8_UNORM,
      VK_IMAGE_ASPECT_COLOR_BIT, &font_.imageView);
   createTextureSampler(vkDev.device, &fontSampler_);
   const size_t imgCount =
      vkDev.swapchainImages.size();
   storageBuffer_.resize(imgCount);
   storageBufferMemory_.resize(imgCount);
   bufferSize = ImGuiVtxBufferSize +
                ImGuiIdxBufferSize;
```

3. The code for buffer creation is essentially boilerplate code similar to the previous recipe and can be safely skipped here:

```
for(size_t i = 0 ; i < imgCount ; i++) {
   ... buffers creation code skipped here ...
}
// ... pipeline creation code is skipped again ...
}
```

Let's quickly review the `createFontTexture()` function:

1. Similar to how `createTextureFromFile()` works, `createFontTexture()` uses the `createTextureFromData()` helper function internally:

```
bool createFontTexture(ImGuiIO& io,
    const char* fontFile,
    VulkanRenderDevice& vkDev, VkImage& textureImage,
    VkDeviceMemory& textureImageMemory)
{
    ImFontConfig cfg = ImFontConfig();
    cfg.FontDataOwnedByAtlas = false;
    cfg.RasterizerMultiply = 1.5f;
    cfg.SizePixels = 768.0f / 32.0f;
    cfg.PixelSnapH = true;
    cfg.OversampleH = 4;
    cfg.OversampleV = 4;
```

2. We will use ImGui to rasterize the TrueType font file into a bitmap:

```
    ImFont* Font = io.Fonts->AddFontFromFileTTF(
        fontFile, cfg.SizePixels, &cfg);
    unsigned char* pixels = nullptr;
    int texWidth, texHeight;
    io.Fonts->GetTexDataAsRGBA32(
        &pixels, &texWidth, &texHeight);
```

3. Then we will call `createTextureImageFromData()` to build a Vulkan texture from bitmap data:

```
    if (!pixels || !createTextureImageFromData(vkDev,
          textureImage, textureImageMemory,
          pixels, texWidth, texHeight,
          VK_FORMAT_R8G8B8A8_UNORM)) {
      printf("Failed to load texture\n");
      return false;
    }
```

4. At the end, we will store the ImGui font handle inside the `ImGuiIO` structure, similar to how it was done in OpenGL:

```
io.Fonts->TexID = (ImTextureID)0;
io.FontDefault = Font;
io.DisplayFramebufferScale = ImVec2(1, 1);
return true;
}
```

The actual rendering code that populates a Vulkan command buffer consists of two functions:

- The first one starts a rendering pass, iterates the entire collection of ImGui command lists, invokes `addImGuiItem()` for each of them, and calls `vkCmdEndRenderPass()` at the end:

```
void ImGuiRenderer::fillCommandBuffer(
  VkCommandBuffer commandBuffer, size_t currentImage)
{
  beginRenderPass(commandBuffer, currentImage);
  ImVec2 clipOff = drawData->DisplayPos;
  ImVec2 clipScale = drawData->FramebufferScale;
  int vtxOffset = 0;
  int idxOffset = 0;
  for (int n = 0; n < drawData->CmdListsCount; n++) {
    const ImDrawList* cmdList = drawData->CmdLists[n];
    for (int cmd = 0; cmd < cmdList->CmdBuffer.Size;
        cmd++) {
      const ImDrawCmd* pcmd =
        &cmdList->CmdBuffer[cmd];
      addImGuiItem(
        framebufferWidth_, framebufferHeight_,
        commandBuffer, pcmd, clipOff, clipScale,
        idxOffset, vtxOffset);
    }
    idxOffset += cmdList->IdxBuffer.Size;
    vtxOffset += cmdList->VtxBuffer.Size;
  }
  vkCmdEndRenderPass(commandBuffer);
}
```

- The second helper function handles the generation of Vulkan commands for a single ImGui item:

```
void addImGuiItem(uint32_t width, uint32_t height,
  VkCommandBuffer commandBuffer,
  const ImDrawCmd* pcmd,
  ImVec2 clipOff, ImVec2 clipScale,
  int idxOffset, int vtxOffset)
{
  if (pcmd->UserCallback) return;
  ImVec4 clipRect;
  clipRect.x =
    (pcmd->ClipRect.x - clipOff.x) * clipScale.x;
  clipRect.y =
    (pcmd->ClipRect.y - clipOff.y) * clipScale.y;
  clipRect.z =
    (pcmd->ClipRect.z - clipOff.x) * clipScale.x;
  clipRect.w =
    (pcmd->ClipRect.w - clipOff.y) * clipScale.y;
  if (clipRect.x < width && clipRect.y < height &&
      clipRect.z >= 0.0f && clipRect.w >= 0.0f)
  {
    if (clipRect.x < 0.0f) clipRect.x = 0.0f;
    if (clipRect.y < 0.0f) clipRect.y = 0.0f;
```

5. Apply the clipping rectangle provided by ImGui to construct a Vulkan scissor. The ImGui rectangle is stored as `vec4`:

```
    const VkRect2D scissor = {
      .offset = {
        .x = (int32_t)(clipRect.x),
        .y = (int32_t)(clipRect.y) },
      .extent = {
        .width = (uint32_t)(clipRect.z - clipRect.x),
        .height = (uint32_t)(clipRect.w - clipRect.y) }
    };
    vkCmdSetScissor(commandBuffer, 0, 1, &scissor);
    … Chapter 6 will add descriptor indexing here
        using vkCmdPushConstants() …
    vkCmdDraw(commandBuffer, pcmd->ElemCount, 1,
      pcmd->IdxOffset + idxOffset,
      pcmd->VtxOffset + vtxOffset);
  }
}
```

6. One more important point to mention is how to update GPU buffers with vertex and index data and with the projection matrix. Here is a function to do that:

```
void ImGuiRenderer::updateBuffers(
  VulkanRenderDevice& vkDev,
  uint32_t currentImage,
  const ImDrawData* imguiDrawData)
{
  drawData = imguiDrawData;
  const float L = drawData->DisplayPos.x;
  const float R =
    drawData->DisplayPos.x+drawData->DisplaySize.x;
  const float T = drawData->DisplayPos.y;
  const float B =
    drawData->DisplayPos.y+drawData->DisplaySize.y;
  const mat4 inMtx = glm::ortho(L, R, T, B);
  uploadBufferData(vkDev,
    uniformBuffersMemory_[currentImage],
    0, glm::value_ptr(inMtx), sizeof(mat4));
  void* data = nullptr;
  vkMapMemory(vkDev.device,
    storageBufferMemory_[currentImage],
    0, bufferSize_, 0, &data);
  ImDrawVert* vtx = (ImDrawVert*)data;
  for (int n = 0; n < drawData->CmdListsCount; n++) {
    const ImDrawList* cmdList = drawData->CmdLists[n];
    memcpy(vtx, cmdList->VtxBuffer.Data,
      cmdList->VtxBuffer.Size * sizeof(ImDrawVert));
    vtx += cmdList->VtxBuffer.Size;
  }
  const uint32_t* idx = (const uint32_t*)(
    (uint8_t*)data + ImGuiVtxBufferSize);
  for (int n = 0; n < drawData->CmdListsCount; n++) {
    const ImDrawList* cmdList = drawData->CmdLists[n];
    const uint16_t* src =
      (const uint16_t*)cmdList->IdxBuffer.Data;
    for (int j = 0; j < cmdList->IdxBuffer.Size; j++)
      *idx++ = (uint32_t)*src++;
  }
  vkUnmapMemory(vkDev.device,
    storageBufferMemory_[currentImage]);
}
```

Now we have all the frame composition routines for this chapter's Vulkan demo application. Feel free to jump directly to the last recipe to see how the frame composition works. However, it is useful to get familiar with other user interface and productivity helpers discussed in the next recipes, such as the 3D camera control implementation, FPS counters, rendering charts, and profiling.

Working with a 3D camera and basic user interaction

To debug a graphical application, it is very helpful to be able to navigate and move around within a 3D scene using a keyboard or mouse. Graphics APIs by themselves are not familiar with the concepts of camera and user interaction, so we have to implement a camera model that will convert user input into a view matrix usable by OpenGL or Vulkan. In this recipe, we will learn how to create a very simple yet extensible camera implementation and use it to enhance the functionality of examples from the previous chapter.

Getting ready

The source code for this recipe can be found in `Chapter4/GL01_Camera`.

How to do it...

Our camera implementation will calculate a view matrix and a 3D position point based on the selected dynamic model. Let's look at the steps:

1. First, let's implement the `Camera` class, which will represent our main API to work with the 3D camera. The class stores a reference to an instance of the `CameraPositionerInterface` class, which will represent a polymorphic implementation of the underlying camera model:

```cpp
class Camera final {
public:
  explicit Camera(
    CameraPositionerInterface& positioner)
  : positioner_(positioner) {}
  glm::mat4 getViewMatrix() const {
    return positioner_.getViewMatrix();
  }
  glm::vec3 getPosition() const {
    return positioner_.getPosition(); }
```

```
    private:
        CameraPositionerInterface& positioner_;
};
```

The interface of `CameraPositionerInterface` contains only pure virtual methods and the default virtual destructor:

```
class CameraPositionerInterface {
public:
  virtual ~CameraPositionerInterface() = default;
  virtual glm::mat4 getViewMatrix() const = 0;
  virtual glm::vec3 getPosition() const = 0;
};
```

2. Now we can implement an actual camera model. We will start with a quaternion-based first-person camera that can be freely moved in space in any direction.

   Let's look at the `CameraPositioner_FirstPerson` class. The inner `Movement` structure contains Boolean flags that define the current motion state of our camera. This is useful to decouple keyboard input from the camera logic:

```
class CameraPositioner_FirstPerson final:
  public CameraPositionerInterface
{
public:
  struct Movement {
    bool forward_ = false;
    bool backward_ = false;
    bool left_ = false;
    bool right_ = false;
    bool up_ = false;
    bool down_ = false;
    bool fastSpeed_ = false;
  } movement_;
```

3. Various numeric parameters define how responsive the camera will be to acceleration and damping. These parameters can be tweaked as you see fit:

```
    float mouseSpeed_ = 4.0f;
    float acceleration_ = 150.0f;
    float damping_ = 0.2f;
    float maxSpeed_ = 10.0f;
    float fastCoef_ = 10.0f;
```

4. Some private data members are necessary to control the camera state, such as the previous mouse position, current camera position and orientation, and current movement speed:

```
private:
  glm::vec2 mousePos_ = glm::vec2(0);
  glm::vec3 cameraPosition_ =
    glm::vec3(0.0f, 10.0f, 10.0f);
  glm::quat cameraOrientation_ =
    glm::quat(glm::vec3(0));
  glm::vec3 moveSpeed_ = glm::vec3(0.0f);
```

5. The non-default constructor takes the camera's initial position, a target position, and a vector pointing upward. This input is similar to what you might normally use to construct a *look-at* viewing matrix. Indeed, we use the glm::lookAt() function to initialize the camera:

```
public:
  CameraPositioner_FirstPerson() = default;
  CameraPositioner_FirstPerson(const glm::vec3& pos,
      const glm::vec3& target, const glm::vec3& up)
  : cameraPosition_(pos)
  , cameraOrientation_(glm::lookAt(pos, target, up))
  {}
```

6. Now, we want to add some dynamics to our camera model:

```
void update(double deltaSeconds,
    const glm::vec2& mousePos, bool mousePressed) {
  if (mousePressed) {
    const glm::vec2 delta = mousePos - mousePos_;
    const glm::quat deltaQuat = glm::quat(glm::vec3(
      mouseSpeed_ * delta.y,
      mouseSpeed_ * delta.x, 0.0f));
    cameraOrientation_ = glm::normalize(
      deltaQuat * cameraOrientation_);
  }
  mousePos_ = mousePos;
```

The update() method should be called at every frame and take the time elapsed since the previous frame, as well as the mouse position and a mouse button pressed flag. In cases when the mouse button is pressed, we calculate a delta vector versus the previous mouse position and use it to construct a rotation quaternion. This quaternion is used to rotate the camera. Once the camera rotation is applied, we should update the mouse position state.

7. Now we should establish the camera's coordinate system to calculate the camera movement. Let's extract the forward, right, and up vectors from the 4x4 view matrix:

```
const glm::mat4 v =
  glm::mat4_cast(cameraOrientation_);
const glm::vec3 forward =
  -glm::vec3(v[0][2], v[1][2], v[2][2]);
const glm::vec3 right =
  glm::vec3(v[0][0], v[1][0], v[2][0]);
const glm::vec3 up = glm::cross(right, forward);
```

The *forward* vector corresponds to the camera's direction, that is, the direction the camera is pointing. The *right* vector corresponds to the positive *x* axis of the camera space. The *up* vector is the positive *y* axis of the camera space, which is perpendicular to the first two vectors and can be calculated as their cross product.

8. The camera coordinate system has been established. Now we can apply our input state from the Movement structure to control the movement of our camera:

```
glm::vec3 accel(0.0f);
if (movement_.forward_) accel += forward;
if (movement_.backward_) accel -= forward;
if (movement_.left_) accel -= right;
if (movement_.right_) accel += right;
if (movement_.up_) accel += up;
if (movement_.down_) accel -= up;
if (movement_.fastSpeed_) accel *= fastCoef_;
```

Instead of controlling the camera speed or position directly, we let the user input control only the acceleration vector directly. This way, the camera's behavior is much more natural and non-jerky.

9. If, based on the input state, the calculated camera acceleration is 0, we should decelerate the camera's motion speed gradually, according to the `damping_` parameter. Otherwise, we should integrate the camera motion using simple Euler integration. The maximum possible speed value is clamped according to the `maxSpeed_` parameter:

```cpp
if (accel == glm::vec3(0)) {
  moveSpeed_ -= moveSpeed_ * std::min(
    (1.0f / damping_) *
    static_cast<float>(deltaSeconds), 1.0f);
}
else {
  moveSpeed_ += accel * acceleration_ *
    static_cast<float>(deltaSeconds);
  const float maxSpeed = movement_.fastSpeed_ ?
    maxSpeed_ * fastCoef_ : maxSpeed_;
  if (glm::length(moveSpeed_) > maxSpeed)
    moveSpeed_ =
      glm::normalize(moveSpeed_) * maxSpeed;
}
cameraPosition_ +=
  moveSpeed_ * static_cast<float>(deltaSeconds);
}
```

10. The view matrix can be calculated from the camera orientation quaternion and camera position in the following way:

```cpp
virtual glm::mat4 getViewMatrix() const override {
  const glm::mat4 t = glm::translate(
    glm::mat4(1.0f), -cameraPosition_);
  const glm::mat4 r =
    glm::mat4_cast(cameraOrientation_);
  return r * t;
}
```

The translational part is inferred from the `cameraPosition_` vector and the rotational part is calculated directly from the orientation quaternion.

11. Helpful getters and setters are trivial, except for the `setUpVector()` method, which has to recalculate the camera orientation using the existing camera position and direction as follows:

```
virtual glm::vec3 getPosition() const override {
  return cameraPosition_;
}
void setPosition(const glm::vec3& pos) {
  cameraPosition_ = pos;
}
void setUpVector(const glm::vec3& up)
{
  const glm::mat4 view = getViewMatrix();
  const glm::vec3 dir =
    -glm::vec3(view[0][2], view[1][2], view[2][2]);
  cameraOrientation_ = glm::lookAt(
    cameraPosition_, cameraPosition_ + dir, up);
}
```

12. One additional helper function is necessary to reset the previous mouse position to prevent jerky rotation movements:

```
void resetMousePosition(const glm::vec2& p) {
  mousePos_ = p;
};
};
```

The preceding class can be used in an application to move the viewer around. Let's see how it works.

How it works...

The demo application for this recipe is based on the cube map OpenGL example from the previous chapter:

1. First, we need to add a mouse state and define `CameraPositioner` and `Camera`. Let them be global variables:

```
struct MouseState {
  glm::vec2 pos = glm::vec2(0.0f);
  bool pressedLeft = false;
} mouseState;
```

```
CameraPositioner_FirstPerson positioner( vec3(0.0f),
   vec3(0.0f, 0.0f, -1.0f), vec3(0.0f, 1.0f, 0.0f) );
Camera camera(positioner);
```

2. Now, the GLFW cursor position callback should update `mouseState` in the following way:

```
glfwSetCursorPosCallback(
   window, [](auto* window, double x, double y) {
      int width, height;
      glfwGetFramebufferSize(window, &width, &height);
      mouseState.pos.x = static_cast<float>(x / width);
      mouseState.pos.y = static_cast<float>(y / height);
   }
);
```

Here, we convert window pixel coordinates into normalized 0...1 coordinates.

3. The GLFW mouse button callback raises the `pressedLeft` flag when the left mouse button is pressed:

```
glfwSetMouseButtonCallback(window,
   [](auto* window, int button, int action, int mods)
{
   if (button == GLFW_MOUSE_BUTTON_LEFT)
      mouseState.pressedLeft = action == GLFW_PRESS;
});
```

4. To handle keyboard input for camera movement, let's write the following GLFW keyboard callback:

```
glfwSetKeyCallback(window,
   [](GLFWwindow* window,
      int key, int scancode, int action, int mods)
   {
      const bool press = action != GLFW_RELEASE;
      if (key == GLFW_KEY_ESCAPE)
         glfwSetWindowShouldClose(window, GLFW_TRUE);
      if (key == GLFW_KEY_W)
         positioner.movement_.forward_ = press;
      if (key == GLFW_KEY_S)
         positioner.movement_.backward_ = press;
      if (key == GLFW_KEY_A)
         positioner.movement_.left_ = press;
```

```
    if (key == GLFW_KEY_D)
      positioner.movement_.right_ = press;
    if (key == GLFW_KEY_1)
      positioner.movement_.up_ = press;
    if (key == GLFW_KEY_2)
      positioner.movement_.down_ = press;
    if (mods & GLFW_MOD_SHIFT)
      positioner.movement_.fastSpeed_ = press;
    if (key == GLFW_KEY_SPACE)
      positioner.setUpVector(vec3(0.0f, 1.0f, 0.0f));
});
```

The *WSAD* keys are used to move the camera around and the *Spacebar* is used to reorient the camera up vector to the world (0, 1, 0) vector. The *Shift* key is used to move the camera faster.

5. Now we can update the camera positioner from the main loop using the following statement:

```
positioner.update(deltaSeconds, mouseState.pos,
  mouseState.pressedLeft);
```

6. Here's a code fragment to upload matrices into the OpenGL uniform buffer object, similar to how it was done with fixed values in the previous chapters:

```
const mat4 p = glm::perspective(
  45.0f, ratio, 0.1f, 1000.0f);
const mat4 view = camera.getViewMatrix();
const PerFrameData perFrameData = {
  .view = view,
  .proj = p,
  .cameraPos = glm::vec4(camera.getPosition(), 1.0f) };
glNamedBufferSubData(perFrameDataBuffer, 0,
  kUniformBufferSize, &perFrameData);
```

Run the demo from Chapter4/GL01_Camera to play around with the keyboard and mouse.

There's more...

This camera design approach can be extended to accommodate different motion behaviors. In later recipes, we will learn how to implement some other useful camera positioners.

Adding a frames-per-second counter

The **frames per second (FPS)** counter is the cornerstone of all graphical application profiling and performance measurements. In this recipe, we will learn how to implement a simple FPS counter class and use it to roughly measure the performance of a running application.

Getting ready

The source code for this recipe can be found in Chapter4/GL02_FPS.

How to do it...

Let's implement the FramesPerSecondCounter class containing all the machinery required to calculate the average FPS rate for a given time interval:

1. First, we need some member fields to store the duration of a sliding window, the number of frames rendered in the current interval, and the accumulated time of this interval:

```
class FramesPerSecondCounter {
private:
  const float avgIntervalSec_ = 0.5f;
  unsigned int numFrames_ = 0;
  double accumulatedTime_ = 0;
  float currentFPS_ = 0.0f;
```

2. The single constructor can override the averaging's interval default duration:

```
public:
  explicit FramesPerSecondCounter(
    float avgIntervalSec = 0.5f)
  : avgIntervalSec_(avgIntervalSec)
  { assert(avgIntervalSec > 0.0f); }
```

3. The tick() method should be called from the main loop. It accepts the time elapsed since the previous call and a Boolean flag that should be set to true if a new frame has been rendered during this iteration. This flag is a convenience feature to handle situations when frame rendering can be skipped in the main loop for various reasons. The time is accumulated until it reaches the value of avgInterval_:

```
bool tick(
  float deltaSeconds, bool frameRendered = true)
```

```
{
  if (frameRendered) numFrames_++;
  accumulatedTime_ += deltaSeconds;
```

4. Once enough time has accumulated, we can do averaging, update the current FPS value, and print debug info to the console. We should reset the number of frames and accumulated time here:

```
  if (accumulatedTime_ < avgIntervalSec_)
    return false;
  currentFPS_ = static_cast<float>(
    numFrames_ / accumulatedTime_);
  printf("FPS: %.1f\n", currentFPS_);
  numFrames_ = 0;
  accumulatedTime_ = 0;
  return true;
}
```

5. Let's add a helper method to retrieve the current FPS value:

```
  inline float getFPS() const { return currentFPS_; }
};
```

Now, let's take a look at how to use this class in our main loop. Let's augment the main loop of our OpenGL demo applications to display an FPS counter in the console:

1. First, let's define a `FramesPerSecondCounter` object and a couple of variables to store the current time and the current delta since the last rendered frame. We used a 0.5-second averaging interval; feel free to try out different values:

```
double timeStamp = glfwGetTime();
float deltaSeconds = 0.0f;
FramesPerSecondCounter fpsCounter(0.5f);
```

2. Inside the main loop, update the current timestamp and calculate the frame duration as a delta between the two timestamps:

```
while (!glfwWindowShouldClose(window))
{
  const double newTimeStamp = glfwGetTime();
  deltaSeconds = static_cast<float>(
    newTimeStamp - timeStamp);
  timeStamp = newTimeStamp;
```

3. Pass the calculated delta to the `tick()` method:

```
        fpsCounter.tick(deltaSeconds);
        // ...do the rest of rendering here...
    }
```

The console output of the running application should look similar to the following lines:

```
FPS: 3238.1
FPS: 3101.3
FPS: 1787.5
FPS: 3609.4
FPS: 3927.0
FPS: 3775.0
FPS: 4119.0
```

Vertical sync is turned off.

There's more...

The `frameRendered` parameter in `float tick(float deltaSeconds, bool frameRendered = true)` will be used in the subsequent recipes to allow Vulkan applications to skip frames when a swapchain image is not available.

Adding camera animations and motion

Besides having a user-controlled free camera, it is convenient to be able to position and move the camera programmatically inside a 3D scene. In this recipe, we will show how to do this using a 3D camera framework from the *Working with a 3D camera and basic user interaction* recipe. We will draw a combo box using ImGui to select between two camera modes: a first-person free camera and a fixed camera moving to a user-specified point settable from the user interface.

Getting ready

The full source code for this recipe can be found in `Chapter4/VK01_DemoApp`. Implementations of camera-related functionality are located in `shared/Camera.h`.

How to do it...

Let's look at how to programmatically control our 3D camera using a simple ImGui-based user interface:

1. First, we need to define the camera positioners attached to the camera – just a bunch of global variables:

```
glm::vec3 cameraPos(0.0f, 0.0f, 0.0f);
glm::vec3 cameraAngles(-45.0f, 0.0f, 0.0f);
CameraPositioner_FirstPerson positioner_firstPerson(
  cameraPos, vec3(0.0f, 0.0f, -1.0f),
  vec3(0.0f, 1.0f, 0.0f));
CameraPositioner_MoveTopositioner_moveTo(
  cameraPos, cameraAngles);
Camera camera = Camera(positioner_firstPerson);
```

2. Inside the main loop, we should update both camera positioners:

```
positioner_firstPerson.update(deltaSeconds,
  mouseState.pos, mouseState.pressedLeft);
positioner_moveTo.update(deltaSeconds,
  mouseState.pos, mouseState.pressedLeft);
```

Now, let's draw an ImGui combo box to select which camera positioner should be used to provide data to the camera:

1. First, a few more global variables will come in handy to store the current camera type, items of the combo box user interface, and the new value selected in the combo box:

```
const char* cameraType = "FirstPerson";
const char* comboBoxItems[] =
  { "FirstPerson", "MoveTo" };
const char* currentComboBoxItem = cameraType;
```

2. To render the camera control user interface with a combo box, let's write the following code. A new ImGui window starts with a call to `ImGui::Begin()`:

```
ImGui::Begin("Camera Control", nullptr);
{
```

3. The combo box itself is rendered via `ImGui::BeginCombo()`. The second parameter is the previewed label name to show before opening the combo box. This function will return `true` if the user has clicked on a label:

```
if (ImGui::BeginCombo("##combo",
      currentComboBoxItem))
{
  for (int n = 0; n < IM_ARRAYSIZE(comboBoxItems);
      n++)
  {
    const bool isSelected =
      (currentComboBoxItem == comboBoxItems[n]);
    if (ImGui::Selectable(comboBoxItems[n],
        isSelected))
      currentComboBoxItem = comboBoxItems[n];
```

4. You may set the initial focus when opening the combo. This is useful if you want to support scrolling or keyboard navigation inside the combo box:

```
    if (isSelected) ImGui::SetItemDefaultFocus();
  }
```

5. Finalize the ImGui combo box rendering:

```
  ImGui::EndCombo();
}
```

6. If the `MoveTo` camera type is selected, render `vec3` input sliders to get the camera position and **Euler angles** from the user:

```
if (!strcmp(cameraType, "MoveTo")) {
  if (ImGui::SliderFloat3("Position",
      glm::value_ptr(cameraPos), -10.0f, +10.0f))
    positioner_moveTo.setDesiredPosition(cameraPos);
  if (ImGui::SliderFloat3("Pitch/Pan/Roll",
      glm::value_ptr(cameraAngles), -90.0f, +90.0f))
    positioner_moveTo.setDesiredAngles(cameraAngles);
}
```

7. If the new selected combo box item is different from the current camera type, print a debug message and change the active camera mode:

```
if (currentComboBoxItem &&
    strcmp(currentComboBoxItem, cameraType)) {
  printf("New camera type selected %s\n",
    currentComboBoxItem);
  cameraType = currentComboBoxItem;
  reinitCamera();
  }
}
```

The resulting combo box should look as in the following screenshot:

Figure 4.1 – Camera controls

The previously mentioned code is called from the main loop on every frame. Check out `renderGUI()` in `Chapter4/VK01_DemoApp/src/main.cpp` for the complete source code.

How it works...

Let's take a look at the implementation of the `CameraPositioner_MoveTo` class. Contrary to the first-person camera, this implementation uses a simple Euler angles approach to store the camera orientation, which makes it more intuitive for the user to control:

1. First, we want to have some user-configurable parameters for linear and angular damping coefficients:

```
class CameraPositioner_MoveTo final:
  public CameraPositionerInterface
{
public:
  float dampingLinear_ = 10.0f;
  glm::vec3 dampingEulerAngles_ =
    glm::vec3(5.0f, 5.0f, 5.0f);
```

2. We store the current and desired positions of the camera as well as two sets of pitch, pan, and roll Euler angles in `vec3` member fields. The current camera transformation is updated at every frame and saved in the `mat4` field:

```
private:
  glm::vec3 positionCurrent_ = glm::vec3(0.0f);
  glm::vec3 positionDesired_ = glm::vec3(0.0f);
  glm::vec3 anglesCurrent_ = glm::vec3(0.0f); //
pitch, pan, roll
  glm::vec3 anglesDesired_ = glm::vec3(0.0f);
  glm::mat4 currentTransform_ = glm::mat4(1.0f);
```

A single constructor initializes both the current and desired datasets of the camera:

```
public:
  CameraPositioner_MoveTo(
    const glm::vec3& pos, const glm::vec3& angles)
  : positionCurrent_(pos)
  , positionDesired_(pos)
  , anglesCurrent_(angles)
  , anglesDesired_(angles)
  {}
```

3. The most interesting part happens in the `update()` function. The current camera position is changed to move toward the desired camera position. The movement speed is proportional to the distance between these two positions and is scaled using the linear damping coefficient:

```
void update(float deltaSeconds,
    const glm::vec2& mousePos, bool mousePressed)
{
    positionCurrent_ += dampingLinear_ * deltaSeconds *
      (positionDesired_ - positionCurrent_);
```

4. Now, let's deal with Euler angles. We should make sure that they remain inside the `0...360` degree range and clip them accordingly:

```
    anglesCurrent_ = clipAngles(anglesCurrent_);
    anglesDesired_ = clipAngles(anglesDesired_);
```

5. Similar to how we dealt with the camera position, the Euler angles are updated based on the distance between the desired and current set of angles. Before calculating the camera transformation matrix, clip the updated angles again and convert from degrees to radians. Note how the pitch, pan, and roll angles are swizzled before they are forwarded into `glm::yawPitchRoll()`:

```
anglesCurrent_ -= deltaSeconds *
  angleDelta(anglesCurrent_, anglesDesired_) *
  dampingEulerAngles_;
anglesCurrent_ = clipAngles(anglesCurrent_);
const glm::vec3 ang =
  glm::radians(anglesCurrent_);
currentTransform_ = glm::translate(
    glm::yawPitchRoll(ang.y, ang.x, ang.z),
    -positionCurrent_);
}
```

6. The functions for the angle clipping are straightforward and look as follows:

```
private:
  static inline float clipAngle(float d) {
    if (d < -180.0f) return d + 360.0f;
    if (d > +180.0f) return d - 360.f;
    return d;
  }
  static inline glm::vec3 clipAngles(
    const glm::vec3& angles) {
    return glm::vec3(
      std::fmod(angles.x, 360.0f),
      std::fmod(angles.y, 360.0f),
      std::fmod(angles.z, 360.0f)
    );
  }
```

7. The delta between two sets of angles can be calculated in the following way:

```
static inline glm::vec3 angleDelta(
  const glm::vec3& anglesCurrent,
  const glm::vec3& anglesDesired)
{
  const glm::vec3 d = clipAngles(anglesCurrent) -
    clipAngles(anglesDesired);
  return glm::vec3(
    clipAngle(d.x), clipAngle(d.y), clipAngle(d.z));
}
};
```

Try running the demo application, switch to the MoveTo camera, and change position and orientation from the user interface.

There's more...

Further camera functionality can be built on top of this example implementation. One more useful extension might be a camera that follows a spline curve defined using a set of key points. We will leave it as an exercise for you.

Integrating EasyProfiler and Optick into C++ applications

In *Chapter 2*, *Using Essential Libraries*, we learned how to link our projects with EasyProfiler and Optick, and covered the basic functionality of these profiling libraries. In real-world applications, it is often beneficial to be able to quickly change profiling backends at will due to changes in requirements or to use unique features of different profiling libraries. In this recipe, we will show how to make a minimalistic wrapper on top of EasyProfiler and Optick to allow seamless switching between them using only CMake build options.

Getting ready

The complete source code of the demo application for this recipe is located in Chapter4/VK01_DemoApp.

How to do it...

The demo application, as well as some parts of our Vulkan rendering code, is augmented with calls to profiling functions. Instead of calling EasyProfiler or Optick directly, we have created a set of macros, one of which is picked based on compiler options provided by CMake:

1. First, let's take a look at the root CMakeLists.txt CMake configuration file to see how these options are added. In the beginning, we should add two declarations:

```
option(BUILD_WITH_EASY_PROFILER
  "Enable EasyProfiler usage" ON)
option(BUILD_WITH_OPTICK "Enable Optick usage" OFF)
```

2. A few pages later in the same file, we will convert the CMake options into the C++ compiler definitions and print info messages to the system console:

```
if(BUILD_WITH_EASY_PROFILER)
  message("Enabled EasyProfiler")
  add_definitions(-DBUILD_WITH_EASY_PROFILER=1)
  include_directories(deps/src/easy_profiler/include)
endif()
if(BUILD_WITH_OPTICK)
  message("Enabled Optick")
  add_definitions(-DBUILD_WITH_OPTICK=1)
  set_property(TARGET OptickCore PROPERTY FOLDER
               "ThirdPartyLibraries")
endif()
```

3. Then, let's check the shared/CMakeLists.txt file, which defines linking options for our shared utility code. Based on the enabled CMake options, we will link our utilities library with EasyProfiler and Optick:

```
if(BUILD_WITH_EASY_PROFILER)
  target_link_libraries(SharedUtils PUBLIC
                        easy_profiler)
endif()
if(BUILD_WITH_OPTICK)
  target_link_libraries(SharedUtils PUBLIC OptickCore)
endif()
```

4. CMake code similar to the following is used in the `Chapter4/VK01_DemoApp/CMakeLists.txt` file:

```
if(BUILD_WITH_EASY_PROFILER)
  target_link_libraries(
    Ch4_SampleVK01_DemoApp PRIVATE easy_profiler)
endif()
if(BUILD_WITH_OPTICK)
  target_link_libraries(Ch4_SampleVK01_DemoApp PRIVATE
                        OptickCore)
endif()
```

5. The C++ source code uses only redefined macros for profiling, for example, like in the following block:

```
{
  EASY_BLOCK(
    "vkQueueSubmit", profiler::colors::Magenta);
  VK_CHECK(vkQueueSubmit(
    vkDev.graphicsQueue, 1, &si, nullptr));
  EASY_END_BLOCK;
}
```

This way, we can choose EasyProfiler and Optick at project generation time with the following commands. This one will enable EasyProfiler, which is the default option:

```
cmake .. -G "Visual Studio 16 2019" -A x64
  -DBUILD_WITH_EASY_PROFILER=ON -DBUILD_WITH_OPTICK=OFF
```

This one will switch to Optick:

```
cmake .. -G "Visual Studio 16 2019" -A x64
  -DBUILD_WITH_EASY_PROFILER=OFF -DBUILD_WITH_OPTICK=ON
```

How it works...

The actual wrapping code is located in the `shared/EasyProfilerWrapper.h` file. We decided to unify the profiling API we use so that it looks like the original EasyProfiler API. This way, we don't have to redefine complex EasyProfiler macros and can just use them as is in a pass-through fashion. Let's go through it step by step and see how to do it:

1. First, we should check that only one profiler is actually enabled:

```
#if BUILD_WITH_EASY_PROFILER && BUILD_WITH_OPTICK
#error Cannot enable both profilers at once. Just
 pick one.
#endif // BUILD_WITH_EASY_PROFILER &&
         BUILD_WITH_OPTICK
```

2. If there is no profiler enabled, just declare a bunch of empty macros to skip all the profiling code generation. These macros match the EasyProfiler API:

```
#if !BUILD_WITH_EASY_PROFILER && !BUILD_WITH_OPTICK
#  define EASY_FUNCTION(...)
#  define EASY_BLOCK(...)
#  define EASY_END_BLOCK
#  define EASY_THREAD_SCOPE(...)
#  define EASY_PROFILER_ENABLE
#  define EASY_MAIN_THREAD
#  define PROFILER_FRAME(...)
#  define PROFILER_DUMP(fileName)
#endif // !BUILD_WITH_EASY_PROFILER &&
         !BUILD_WITH_OPTICK
```

3. If EasyProfiler is enabled, just include its header file to use the original API and add two more macros to handle the frame rendering marker, which is supported by Optick and not supported by EasyProfiler. The `PROFILER_DUMP()` macro is used to save the final profiling results into a file:

```
#if BUILD_WITH_EASY_PROFILER
#  include "easy/profiler.h"
#  define PROFILER_FRAME(...)
#  define PROFILER_DUMP(fileName)
     profiler::dumpBlocksToFile(fileName);
#endif // BUILD_WITH_EASY_PROFILER
```

4. If Optick is enabled, convert EasyProfiler API calls into the corresponding Optick function calls and macros:

```
#if BUILD_WITH_OPTICK
#   include "optick.h"
#   define EASY_FUNCTION(...) OPTICK_EVENT()
#   define EASY_BLOCK(name, ...)\
      { OptickScopeWrapper Wrapper(name);
#   define EASY_END_BLOCK };
#   define EASY_THREAD_SCOPE(...)
    OPTICK_START_THREAD(__VA_ARGS__)
#   define EASY_PROFILER_ENABLE OPTICK_START_CAPTURE()
#   define EASY_MAIN_THREAD OPTICK_THREAD("MainThread")
#   define PROFILER_FRAME(name) OPTICK_FRAME(name)
#   define PROFILER_DUMP(fileName)\
      OPTICK_STOP_CAPTURE();\
      OPTICK_SAVE_CAPTURE(fileName);
```

5. One major difference between the EasyProfiler and Optick APIs is that EasyProfiler blocks are based on C++ RAII and are automatically closed when the current scope is exited. For Optick, we have to use OPTICK_PUSH() and OPTICK_POP(), which we wrap into a simple RAII class:

```
class OptickScopeWrapper {
public:
  OptickScopeWrapper(const char* name) {
    OPTICK_PUSH(name);
  }
  ~OptickScopeWrapper() {
    OPTICK_POP();
  }
};
```

6. Yet another thing necessary to use Optick and EasyProfiler interchangeably is
    handling the way they deal with block colors. Both use constants with different
    names. There are many possible solutions to this kind of wrapping; we decided to
    declare constants the following way so that the EasyProfiler API can be emulated by
    adding all necessary colors:

```cpp
namespace profiler {
  namespace colors {
    const int32_t Magenta = Optick::Color::Magenta;
    const int32_t Green = Optick::Color::Green;
    const int32_t Red = Optick::Color::Red;
  } // namespace colors
} // namespace profiler
#endif // BUILD_WITH_OPTICK
```

Let's compare how profiling information of the same demo application looks in
EasyProfiler and Optick. Here is a screenshot from the EasyProfiler user interface showing
a flamegraph of our app:

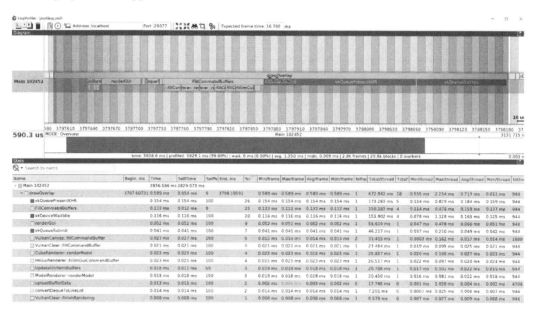

Figure 4.2 – EasyProfiler user interface

Here is the output from the Optick user interface. Conceptually, these two profilers are very similar:

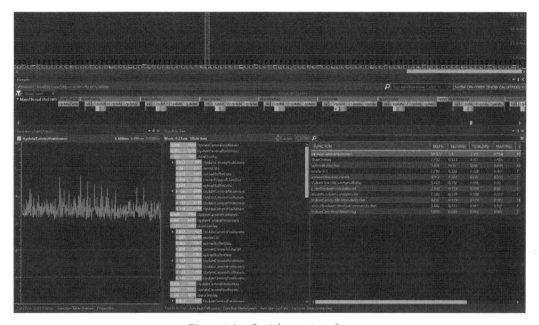

Figure 4.3 – Optick user interface

This approach enables fully transparent switching between EasyProfiler and Optick at build time. Adding other profilers that provide similar APIs is mostly trivial and can be easily implemented.

Using cube map textures in Vulkan

This recipe shows how to implement a feature with Vulkan that was already done using OpenGL in *Chapter 3*, *Getting Started with OpenGL and Vulkan*. The `VulkanCubeRenderer` class implements a simple cube map renderer used to draw a skybox.

Getting ready

Before proceeding with this recipe, it is recommended to revisit the Vulkan texture and texture sampler creation code from *Chapter 3*, *Getting Started with OpenGL and Vulkan*.

How to do it...

As in the previous recipes, we derive our `VulkanCubeRenderer` class from
`RendererBase`. We need a texture sampler and a cube texture. The actual 3D cube
geometry is generated using the programmable vertex pulling technique in the vertex
shader, as shown in the previous chapters:

```
class CubeRenderer: public RendererBase {
public:
  CubeRenderer(VulkanRenderDevice& vkDev,
    VulkanImage inDepthTexture, const char* textureFile);
  virtual ~CubeRenderer();
  virtual void fillCommandBuffer(
    VkCommandBuffer commandBuffer,
    size_t currentImage) override;
  void updateUniformBuffer(
    VulkanRenderDevice& vkDev,
    uint32_t currentImage, const mat4& m);
private:
  VkSampler textureSampler;
  VulkanImage texture;
  bool createDescriptorSet(VulkanRenderDevice& vkDev);
};
```

Let's go through the steps necessary to implement the `CubeRenderer` class:

1. First, the class constructor loads a cube map texture from a file and creates a
   corresponding cube map sampler:

   ```
   CubeRenderer::CubeRenderer(
     VulkanRenderDevice& vkDev,
     VulkanImage inDepthTexture,
     const char* textureFile)
   : RendererBase(vkDev, inDepthTexture)
   {
     createCubeTextureImage(vkDev, textureFile,
       texture.image, texture.imageMemory);
     createImageView(vkDev.device, texture.image,
       VK_FORMAT_R32G32B32A32_SFLOAT,
       VK_IMAGE_ASPECT_COLOR_BIT,
       &texture.imageView, VK_IMAGE_VIEW_TYPE_CUBE, 6);
     createTextureSampler(vkDev.device, &textureSampler);
   ```

2. This time, we will show the full code fragment to create all the necessary Vulkan objects and the pipeline. Check the `shared/UtilsVulkanImGui.cpp` file for further details:

```
if (!createColorAndDepthRenderPass(vkDev, true,
    &renderPass_, RenderPassCreateInfo()) ||
  !createUniformBuffers(vkDev, sizeof(mat4)) ||
  !createColorAndDepthFramebuffers(vkDev,
    renderPass_, depthTexture_.imageView,
    swapchainFramebuffers_) ||
  !createDescriptorPool(vkDev, 1, 0, 1,
    &descriptorPool_) ||
  !createDescriptorSet(vkDev) ||
  !createPipelineLayout(vkDev.device,
    descriptorSetLayout_, &pipelineLayout_) ||
  !createGraphicsPipeline(vkDev, renderPass_,
    pipelineLayout_,
    { "data/shaders/chapter04/VKCube.vert",
      "data/shaders/chapter04/VKCube.frag" },
    &graphicsPipeline_)) {
  printf(
    "CubeRenderer: failed to create pipeline\n");
  exit(EXIT_FAILURE);
  }
}
```

3. The `updateUniformBuffer()` routine uploads the current camera matrix into a GPU buffer:

```
void CubeRenderer::updateUniformBuffer(
  VulkanRenderDevice& vkDev,
  uint32_t currentImg, const mat4& m)
{
  uploadBufferData(vkDev,
    uniformBuffersMemory_[currentImg], 0,
    glm::value_ptr(m), sizeof(mat4));
}
```

4. The `fillCommandBuffer()` member function emits `vkCmdDraw` into the Vulkan command buffer to render 12 triangles representing 6 cube faces:

```
void CubeRenderer::fillCommandBuffer(
  VkCommandBuffer commandBuffer, size_t currentImage)
{
  beginRenderPass(commandBuffer, currentImage);
  vkCmdDraw(commandBuffer, 36, 1, 0, 0);
  vkCmdEndRenderPass(commandBuffer);
}
```

5. The `createDescriptorSet()` function closely mimics a similar function from `ModelRenderer`. Here is how it begins:

```
bool CubeRenderer::createDescriptorSet(
  VulkanRenderDevice& vkDev)
{
  const std::array<VkDescriptorSetLayoutBinding, 2>
    bindings = {
      descriptorSetLayoutBinding(0,
        VK_DESCRIPTOR_TYPE_UNIFORM_BUFFER,
        VK_SHADER_STAGE_VERTEX_BIT),
      descriptorSetLayoutBinding(1,
        VK_DESCRIPTOR_TYPE_COMBINED_IMAGE_SAMPLER,
        VK_SHADER_STAGE_FRAGMENT_BIT)
    };
  ...
```

The rest of the routine is the same, with an obvious omission of the unused buffers in the `vkUpdateDescriptorSet()` call.

Rendering onscreen charts

In the *Implementing an immediate mode drawing canvas* recipe, we learned how to create immediate mode drawing facilities in Vulkan with basic drawing functionality. In this recipe, we will continue adding useful utilities built on top of a 2D line drawing.

Getting ready

We recommend revisiting the *Implementing an immediate mode drawing canvas* recipe to get a better grasp of how a simple Vulkan drawing canvas can be implemented.

How to do it...

What we need at this point essentially boils down to decomposing a 2D chart or graph into a set of lines. Let's go through the code to see how to do it:

1. We introduce the `LinearGraph` class to render a graph of floating-point values. It stores a collection of values and the maximum number of points that should be visible on the screen. A deque is used here for the sake of simplicity:

```
class LinearGraph {
  std::deque<float> graph_;
  const size_t maxPoints_;
public:
  explicit LinearGraph(size_t maxGraphPoints = 256)
  : maxPoints_(maxGraphPoints)
  {}
```

2. When adding a new point to the graph, we check and maintain the maximum number of points:

```
void addPoint(float value) {
  graph_.push_back(value);
  if (graph_.size() > maxPoints_)
    graph_.pop_front();
}
```

3. Rendering is done through the `VulkanCanvas` class introduced in the *Implementing an immediate mode drawing canvas* recipe. The idea is first to find minimum and maximum values to normalize the graph into the `0...1` range:

```
void renderGraph(VulkanCanvas& c,
  const glm::vec4& color = vec4(1.0)) const
{
  float minfps = std::numeric_limits<float>::max();
  float maxfps = std::numeric_limits<float>::min();
  for (float f : graph_) {
    if (f < minfps) minfps = f;
    if (f > maxfps) maxfps = f;
  }
  const float range = maxfps - minfps;
```

4. At this point, we need to iterate all the points once again and draw them from left to right near the bottom part of the screen. The vertical scaling can be tweaked by changing the `scalingFactor` variable:

```
float x = 0.0;
vec3 p1 = vec3(0, 0, 0);
const float scalingFactor = 0.15f;
for (float f : graph_) {
  const float val = (f - minfps) / range;
  const vec3 p2 = vec3(x, val * scalingFactor, 0);
  x += 1.0f / maxPoints_;
  c.line(p1, p2, color);
  p1 = p2;
}
}
};
```

As we add more points to the graph, the old points are popped out, making the graph look like it is scrolling on the screen from right to left. This is helpful to observe local fluctuations in values such as FPS counters, and so on.

How it works...

If we take a look at the `Chapter4/VK01_DemoApp` example, it makes use of LinearGraph to render an FPS graph, and a simple sine graph for reference. Here is how it works:

1. In the main loop, we add points to the graph this way:

```
if (fpsCounter.tick(deltaSeconds, frameRendered))
  fpsGraph.addPoint(fpsCounter.getFPS());
sineGraph.addPoint(
  (float)sin(glfwGetTime() * 10.0));
```

2. Then we render both charts using VulkanCanvas like this, using the current swapchain image:

```
void update2D(uint32_t imageIndex) {
  canvas2d->clear();
  sineGraph.renderGraph(*canvas2d.get(),
    vec4(0.0f, 1.0f, 0.0f, 1.0f));
```

```
fpsGraph.renderGraph(*canvas2d.get(),
    vec4(1.0f, 0.0f, 0.0f, 1.0f));
canvas2d->updateBuffer(vkDev, imageIndex);
}
```

The resulting charts look as in the following screenshot:

Figure 4.4 – FPS and sine wave charts

Putting it all together into a Vulkan application

In this recipe, we use all the material from previous recipes of this chapter to build a Vulkan demo application.

Getting ready

It might be useful to revisit the first recipe, *Organizing Vulkan frame rendering code*, to get to grips with the frame composition approach we use in our applications.

The full source code for this recipe can be found in `Chapter4/VK01_DemoApp`.

How to do it...

Let's skim through the source code to see how we can integrate the functionality from all the recipes together into a single application:

1. Just like in the previous demo, we declare a Vulkan instance and render device objects:

    ```
    VulkanInstance vk;
    VulkanRenderDevice vkDev;
    ```

2. We should declare all our "layer" renderers:

```
std::unique_ptr<ImGuiRenderer> imgui;
std::unique_ptr<ModelRenderer> modelRenderer;
std::unique_ptr<CubeRenderer> cubeRenderer;
std::unique_ptr<VulkanCanvas> canvas;
std::unique_ptr<VulkanCanvas> canvas2d;
std::unique_ptr<VulkanClear> clear;
std::unique_ptr<VulkanFinish> finish;
```

3. Let's create an FPS counter and charts (graphs), like in the *Rendering onscreen charts* recipe:

```
FramesPerSecondCounter fpsCounter(0.02f);
LinearGraph fpsGraph;
LinearGraph sineGraph(4096);
```

4. All camera-related objects should be defined here as well, similar to what we did in the *Working with a 3D camera and basic user interaction* and *Adding camera animations and motion* recipes:

```
glm::vec3 cameraPos(0.0f, 0.0f, 0.0f);
glm::vec3 cameraAngles(-45.0f, 0.0f, 0.0f);
CameraPositioner_FirstPerson positioner_firstPerson(
  cameraPos, vec3(0.0f, 0.0f, -1.0f),
  vec3(0.0f, 1.0f, 0.0f));
CameraPositioner_MoveTo positioner_moveTo(
  cameraPos, cameraAngles);
Camera camera = Camera(positioner_firstPerson);
```

5. Vulkan initialization code does a construction of all the "layer" renderers. Note how we insert profiling markers at the beginning of all heavy functions:

```
bool initVulkan() {
  EASY_FUNCTION();
  createInstance(&vk.instance);
  ...
  imgui = std::make_unique<ImGuiRenderer>(vkDev);
```

6. `modelRenderer` is initialized before other layers, since it contains a depth buffer. The `clear`, `finish`, and `canvas` layers use the depth buffer from `modelRenderer` as well. The `canvas2d` object, which renders fullscreen graphs, takes an empty depth texture to disable depth testing:

```
modelRenderer = std::make_unique<ModelRenderer>(
  vkDev,
  "data/rubber_duck/scene.gltf",
  "data/ch2_sample3_STB.jpg",
  (uint32_t)sizeof(glm::mat4));
cubeRenderer = std::make_unique<CubeRenderer>(vkDev,
  modelRenderer->getDepthTexture(),
  "data/piazza_bologni_1k.hdr");
clear = std::make_unique<VulkanClear>(vkDev,
  modelRenderer->getDepthTexture());
finish = std::make_unique<VulkanFinish>(vkDev,
  modelRenderer->getDepthTexture());
canvas2d = std::make_unique<VulkanCanvas>(vkDev,
  VulkanImage { .image= VK_NULL_HANDLE,
               .imageView= VK_NULL_HANDLE }
);
canvas = std::make_unique<VulkanCanvas>(vkDev,
  modelRenderer->getDepthTexture());
return true;
}
```

7. The current 3D camera selection code is found in `reinitCamera()`, which is called from `renderGUI()` when the user changes the camera mode:

```
void reinitCamera() {
  if (!strcmp(cameraType, "FirstPerson")) {
    camera = Camera(positioner_firstPerson);
  }
  else if (!strcmp(cameraType, "MoveTo")) {
    positioner_moveTo.setDesiredPosition(cameraPos);
    positioner_moveTo.setDesiredAngles(
      cameraAngles.x, cameraAngles.y, cameraAngles.z);
    camera = Camera(positioner_moveTo);
  }
}
```

Check the *Adding camera animations and motion* recipe for more details.

8. All the Dear ImGui user interface rendering for the specified swapchain image is done in the following way:

```
void renderGUI(uint32_t imageIndex) {
  int width, height;
  glfwGetFramebufferSize(window, &width, &height);
  ImGuiIO& io = ImGui::GetIO();
  io.DisplaySize =
    ImVec2((float)width, (float)height);
  ImGui::NewFrame();
```

9. Render the FPS counter in a borderless ImGui window so that just the text is rendered on the screen:

```
const ImGuiWindowFlags flags =
  ImGuiWindowFlags_NoTitleBar |
  ImGuiWindowFlags_NoResize |
  ImGuiWindowFlags_NoMove |
  ImGuiWindowFlags_NoScrollbar |
  ImGuiWindowFlags_NoSavedSettings |
  ImGuiWindowFlags_NoInputs |
  ImGuiWindowFlags_NoBackground;
ImGui::SetNextWindowPos(ImVec2(0, 0));
ImGui::Begin("Statistics", nullptr, flags);
ImGui::Text("FPS: %.2f", fpsCounter.getFPS());
ImGui::End();
```

10. Render the camera controls window. It contains a combo box to select the current camera mode and a couple of sliders to tweak the camera position and orientation:

```
ImGui::Begin("Camera Control", nullptr);
if (ImGui::BeginCombo("##combo",
    currentComboBoxItem)) {
  for (int n = 0; n < IM_ARRAYSIZE(comboBoxItems);
      n++) {
    const bool isSelected =
      (currentComboBoxItem == comboBoxItems[n]);
    if (ImGui::Selectable(comboBoxItems[n],
        isSelected))
      currentComboBoxItem = comboBoxItems[n];
    if (isSelected) ImGui::SetItemDefaultFocus();
```

```
    }
    ImGui::EndCombo();
}
```

11. If the `MoveTo` camera mode is selected, draw the ImGui sliders to select the camera position coordinates and orientation angles:

```
if (!strcmp(cameraType, "MoveTo")) {
    if (ImGui::SliderFloat3("Position",
            glm::value_ptr(cameraPos), -10.0f, +10.0f))
        positioner_moveTo.setDesiredPosition(cameraPos);
    if (ImGui::SliderFloat3("Pitch/Pan/Roll",
            glm::value_ptr(cameraAngles), -90.0f, +90.0f))
        positioner_moveTo.setDesiredAngles(cameraAngles);
}
```

12. Reinitialize the camera if the camera mode has changed. Finalize the ImGui rendering and update the Vulkan buffers before issuing any Vulkan drawing commands:

```
if (currentComboBoxItem &&
        strcmp(currentComboBoxItem, cameraType)) {
    printf("New camera type selected %s\n",
        currentComboBoxItem);
    cameraType = currentComboBoxItem;
    reinitCamera();
}
ImGui::End();
ImGui::Render();
imgui->updateBuffers(
    vkDev, imageIndex, ImGui::GetDrawData());
}
```

13. The `update3D()` function calculates the appropriate view and projection matrices for all objects and updates uniform buffers:

```
void update3D(uint32_t imageIndex)
{
    int width, height;
    glfwGetFramebufferSize(window, &width, &height);
    const float ratio = width / (float)height;
    const mat4 t = glm::translate(mat4(1.0f),
        vec3(0.0f, 0.5f, - 1.5f));
```

```
const float angle = (float)glfwGetTime();
const mat4 m1 = glm::rotate( t * glm::rotate(
    mat4(1.f), glm::pi<float>(), vec3(1, 0, 0)),
  angle, vec3(0.0f, 1.0f, 0.0f) );
const mat4 p = glm::perspective(
  45.0f, ratio, 0.1f, 1000.0f);
const mat4 view = camera.getViewMatrix();
const mat4 mtx = p * view * m1;
EASY_BLOCK("UpdateUniformBuffers");
modelRenderer->updateUniformBuffer(vkDev,
  imageIndex, glm::value_ptr(mtx), sizeof(mat4));
canvas->updateUniformBuffer(
  vkDev, p * view, 0.0f, imageIndex);
canvas2d->updateUniformBuffer(
  vkDev, glm::ortho(0, 1, 1, 0), 0.0f, imageIndex);
cubeRenderer->updateUniformBuffer(
  vkDev, imageIndex, p * view * m1);
EASY_END_BLOCK;
}
```

14. The `update2D()` function does the same thing for the user interface and onscreen graphs as described in the *Rendering onscreen charts* recipe:

```
void update2D(uint32_t imageIndex) {
  canvas2d->clear();
  sineGraph.renderGraph(
    *canvas2d.get(),vec4(0.f, 1.f, 0.f, 1.f));
  fpsGraph.renderGraph(*canvas2d.get());
  canvas2d->updateBuffer(vkDev, imageIndex);
}
```

With all the necessary helper functions defined previously, the frame composition works as follows:

1. First, all the 2D, 3D, and user interface rendering data is updated:

```
void composeFrame(
  uint32_t imageIndex,
  const std::vector<RendererBase*>& renderers)
{
  update3D(imageIndex);
  renderGUI(imageIndex);
  update2D(imageIndex);
```

2. Then we begin to fill a new command buffer by iterating all the layer renderers and calling their `fillCommandBuffer()` virtual function:

```
EASY_BLOCK("FillCommandBuffers");
VkCommandBuffer commandBuffer =
  vkDev.commandBuffers[imageIndex];
const VkCommandBufferBeginInfo bi = {
  .sType =
    VK_STRUCTURE_TYPE_COMMAND_BUFFER_BEGIN_INFO,
  .pNext = nullptr,
  .flags =
    VK_COMMAND_BUFFER_USAGE_SIMULTANEOUS_USE_BIT,
  .pInheritanceInfo = nullptr
};
VK_CHECK(vkBeginCommandBuffer(commandBuffer, &bi));
for (auto& r : renderers)
  r->fillCommandBuffer(commandBuffer, imageIndex);
VK_CHECK(vkEndCommandBuffer(commandBuffer));
EASY_END_BLOCK;
}
```

3. Once our frame composition is done, we can proceed with the frame rendering:

```
bool drawFrame(
  const std::vector<RendererBase*>& renderers)
{
  EASY_FUNCTION();
  uint32_t imageIndex = 0;
  VkResult result = vkAcquireNextImageKHR(
    vkDev.device, vkDev.swapchain, 0,
    vkDev.semaphore, VK_NULL_HANDLE, &imageIndex);
  VK_CHECK(vkResetCommandPool(
    vkDev.device, vkDev.commandPool, 0));
```

4. Here, if the next swapchain image is not yet available, we should return and skip this frame. It might just be that our GPU is rendering frames slower than we are filling in the command buffers:

```
if (result != VK_SUCCESS) return false;
composeFrame(imageIndex, renderers);
const VkPipelineStageFlags waitStages[] =
  { VK_PIPELINE_STAGE_COLOR_ATTACHMENT_OUTPUT_BIT };
```

5. Submit the command buffer into the Vulkan graphics queue:

```
const VkSubmitInfo si = {
  .sType = VK_STRUCTURE_TYPE_SUBMIT_INFO,
  .pNext = nullptr,
  .waitSemaphoreCount = 1,
  .pWaitSemaphores = &vkDev.semaphore,
  .pWaitDstStageMask = waitStages,
  .commandBufferCount = 1,
  .pCommandBuffers =
    &vkDev.commandBuffers[imageIndex],
  .signalSemaphoreCount = 1,
  .pSignalSemaphores = &vkDev.renderSemaphore
};
EASY_BLOCK(
  "vkQueueSubmit", profiler::colors::Magenta);
VK_CHECK(vkQueueSubmit(
  vkDev.graphicsQueue, 1, &si, nullptr));
EASY_END_BLOCK;
```

6. Present the results on the screen:

```
const VkPresentInfoKHR pi = {
  .sType = VK_STRUCTURE_TYPE_PRESENT_INFO_KHR,
  .pNext = nullptr,
  .waitSemaphoreCount = 1,
  .pWaitSemaphores = &vkDev.renderSemaphore,
  .swapchainCount = 1,
  .pSwapchains = &vkDev.swapchain,
  .pImageIndices = &imageIndex
};
EASY_BLOCK(
  "vkQueuePresentKHR", profiler::colors::Magenta);
VK_CHECK(vkQueuePresentKHR(
  vkDev.graphicsQueue, &pi));
EASY_END_BLOCK;
```

7. Wait for the GPU to finish rendering:

```
EASY_BLOCK(
  "vkDeviceWaitIdle", profiler::colors::Red);
VK_CHECK(vkDeviceWaitIdle(vkDev.device));
EASY_END_BLOCK;
return true;
}
```

8. The `drawFrame()` function is invoked from the main loop using the following list of layer renderers:

```
const std::vector<RendererBase*> renderers = {
   clear.get(),
   cubeRenderer.get(),
   modelRenderer.get(),
   canvas.get(),
   canvas2d.get(),
   imgui.get(),
   finish.get()
};
```

The last component of the demo application is the main loop. Conceptually, it remains unchanged. However, it includes some additional elements, such as profiling, initializing the ImGui library, and the 3D camera keyboard controls. Here is a screenshot from the running application:

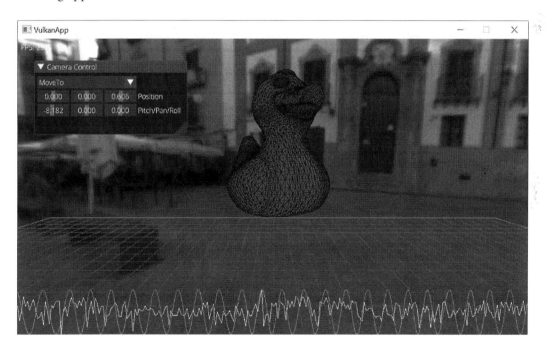

Figure 4.5 – Demo application

This chapter focused on combining multiple rendering aspects into one working Vulkan application. The graphical side still lacks some essential features, such as advanced lighting and materials, but we have almost everything in place to start rendering complex scenes. The next couple of chapters will cover more complicated mesh rendering techniques and physically-based lighting calculations.

5
Working with Geometry Data

Previously, we tried different ad hoc approaches to store and handle 3D geometry data in our graphical applications. The mesh data layout for vertex and index buffers was hardcoded into each of our demo apps. By doing so, it was easier to focus on other important parts of the graphics pipeline. As we move into the territory of more complex graphics applications, we will require additional control over the storage of different 3D meshes within system memory and GPU buffers. However, our focus remains on guiding you through the main principles and practices rather than on pure efficiency.

In this chapter, you will learn how to store and handle mesh geometry data in a more organized way. We will cover the following recipes:

- Organizing the storage of mesh data
- Implementing a geometry conversion tool
- Indirect rendering in Vulkan
- Implementing an infinite grid GLSL shader
- Rendering multiple meshes with OpenGL
- Generating **Levels of Detail** (**LODs**) using MeshOptimizer
- Integrating tessellation into the OpenGL graphics pipeline

Technical requirements

Here is what it takes to run the code from this chapter on your Linux or Windows PC. You will need a GPU with recent drivers supporting OpenGL 4.6 and Vulkan 1.1. The source code can be downloaded from `https://github.com/PacktPublishing/3D-Graphics-Rendering-Cookbook`.

To run the demo applications of this chapter, you are advised to download and unpack the entire Amazon Lumberyard Bistro dataset from the McGuire Computer Graphics Archive. You can find this at `http://casual-effects.com/data/index.html`. Of course, you can use smaller meshes if you cannot download the 2.4 GB package.

Organizing the storage of mesh data

In *Chapter 3*, *Getting Started with OpenGL and Vulkan* and *Chapter 4*, *Adding User Interaction and Productivity Tools*, we used fixed formats for our meshes, which changed between demos and also implicitly included a description of the material; for example, a hardcoded texture was used to provide color information. Let's define a unified mesh storage format that covers all use cases for the remainder of this book.

A triangle mesh is defined by indices and vertices. Each vertex is defined as a set of floating-point attributes. All of the auxiliary physical properties of an object, such as collision detection data, mass, and moments of inertia, can be represented by a mesh. In comparison, other information, such as surface material properties, can be stored outside of the mesh as external metadata.

Getting ready

This recipe describes the basic data structures that we will use to store mesh data for the remainder of this book. The full corresponding source code is located in the `shared/scene/VtxData.h` header.

How to do it...

A vector of homogenous **vertex attributes** stored contiguously is called a **vertex stream**. Examples of such attributes include vertex positions, texture coordinates, and normal vectors, with each of the three representing one attribute. Each attribute can consist of one or multiple floating-point components. Vertex positions have three components, texture coordinates usually have two components, and so on.

LOD is an index buffer of reduced size that uses existing vertices and, therefore, can be used directly for rendering with the original vertex buffer.

We define a **mesh** as a collection of all vertex data streams and a collection of all index buffers – one for each LOD. The length of all vertex data streams is the same and is called the "vertex count." Put simply, we always use 32-bit offsets for our data.

All of the vertex data streams and LOD index buffers are packed into a single blob. This allows us to load data in a single `fread()` call or even use memory mapping to allow direct data access. This simple vertex data representation also enables us to directly upload the mesh to a GPU. The most interesting aspect is the ability to combine the data for multiple meshes in a single file (or, equivalently, into two large buffers – one for indices and the other for vertex attributes). This will come in very handy later when we learn how to implement a LOD switching technique on GPU.

In this recipe, we will only deal with geometrical data. The LOD creation process is covered in the *Generating LODs using MeshOptimizer* recipe, and the material data export process is covered in subsequent chapters. Let's get started by declaring the main data structure for our mesh:

1. First, we need two constants to define the limits on how many LODs and vertex streams we can have in a single mesh:

```
constexpr const uint32_t kMaxLODs    = 8;
constexpr const uint32_t kMaxStreams = 8;
```

2. Next, we define an individual mesh description. We deliberately avoid using pointers that hide memory allocations and prohibit the simple saving and loading of data. We store offsets to individual data streams and LOD index buffers. They are equivalent to pointers but are more flexible and, most importantly, GPU-friendlier. All the offsets in the `Mesh` structure are given relative to the beginning of the data block.

3. Let's declare our main data structure for the mesh. It contains the number of LODs and vertex data streams. The LOD count, where the original mesh counts as one of the LODs, must be strictly less than `kMaxLODs`. This is because we do not store LOD index buffer sizes but calculate them from offsets. To calculate these sizes, we store one additional empty LOD level at the end. The number of vertex data streams is stored directly with no modifications:

```
struct Mesh final {
  uint32_t lodCount;
  uint32_t streamCount;
```

4. We will postpone the question of material data storage for the *Chapter 7, Graphics Rendering Pipeline*. To do this elegantly, let's introduce a level of indirection. The `materialID` field contains an abstract identifier that allows us to reference any material data that is stored elsewhere:

    ```
    uint32_t materialID;
    ```

5. The size of the mesh can be used as a simple substitute for a checksum to control that nothing has been lost on the way without checking whether the mesh data is, in fact, intact. The `meshSize` field must be equal to the sum of all LOD index array sizes and the sum of all individuals stream sizes. The `vertexCount` field contains the total number of vertices in this mesh. This number can be greater than the number of vertices on any individual LOD:

    ```
    uint32_t meshSize;
    uint32_t vertexCount;
    ```

6. Each mesh can potentially be displayed at different LODs. The file contains all the indices for all the LODs, and offsets to the beginning of each LOD are stored in the `lodOffset` array. This array contains one extra item at the end, which serves as a marker to calculate the size of the last LOD:

    ```
    uint32_t lodOffset[kMaxLODs];
    ```

7. Instead of storing the sizes of each LOD, we define a little helper function to calculate their sizes:

    ```
    inline uint64_t lodSize(uint32_t lod) {
      return lodOffset[lod+1] - lodOffset[lod];
    }
    ```

8. Just as the `lodOffset` field contains offsets inside the index buffer where each LOD starts, the `streamOffset` field stores offsets to all of the individual vertex data streams. Next, we need to specify how each data stream is used. Usage semantics is defined by the stream element size. For example, the vertex-only stream has an element size, which is counted in floats, of 3. The stream with vertices and texture coordinates has an element size of 6, and so on. In the demo from the *Rendering multiple meshes with OpenGL* recipe, we use a vertex-only format, which sets `streamElementSize` to 3.

> **Important note**
>
> Besides the element size, we might want to store the element type, such as byte, short integer, or float. This information is important for performance reasons in real-world applications. To simplify the code in this book, we will not do it here.

```
uint64_t streamOffset[kMaxStreams];
uint32_t streamElementSize[kMaxStreams];
};
```

> **Note**
>
> For this book, we assume tightly-packed (Interleaved) vertex attribute streams only. However, it is not difficult to extend the proposed schema to support non-interleaved data storage. One major drawback is that such data reorganization would require us to change all the vertex-pulling code of the vertex shaders. If you are developing production code, measure which storage format works faster on your target hardware before committing to one particular approach.

Our mesh data file begins with a simple header to allow for the rapid fetching of the mesh list. Let's take a look at how it is declared:

1. To ensure data integrity and to check the validity of the header, a magic hexadecimal value of $0x12345678$ is stored in the first 4 bytes of the header:

    ```
    struct MeshFileHeader {
      uint32_t magicValue;
    ```

2. The number of different meshes in this file is stored in the `meshCount` field:

    ```
    uint32_t meshCount;
    ```

3. For convenience, we store an offset to the beginning of the mesh data:

    ```
    uint32_t dataBlockStartOffset;
    ```

4. The last two member fields store the sizes of index and vertex data in bytes, respectively. These values come in handy when you are checking the integrity of a mesh file:

    ```
    uint32_t indexDataSize;
    uint32_t vertexDataSize;
    };
    ```

The file continues with the list of `Mesh` structures. After the header and a list of individual mesh descriptors, we store a large index and vertex data block that can be loaded all at once.

How it works...

Let's go through all of the remaining data structures that are required to store our meshes. To use a mesh file in a rendering application, we need to have an array of mesh descriptions and two arrays with index and vertex data:

```
std::vector<Mesh> meshes;
std::vector<uint8_t> indexData;
std::vector<uint8_t> vertexData;
```

The pseudocode for loading such a file is just four `fread()` calls. They appear as follows:

1. First, we read the file header with the mesh count. In this book, error checks have been skipped, but they are present in the bundled source code:

    ```
    FILE *f = fopen("data/meshes/test.meshes", "rb");
    MeshFileHeader header;
    fread(&header, 1, sizeof(header), f);
    ```

2. Having read the header, we resize the mesh descriptors array and read in all the `Mesh` descriptions:

    ```
    fread(
      meshes.data(), header.meshCount, sizeof(Mesh), f);
    ```

3. Then, we read the main geometry data blocks for this mesh, which contain the actual index and vertex data:

    ```
    indexData.resize(header.indexDataSize);
    vertexData.resize(header.vertexDataSize);
    fread(indexData.data(), 1, header.indexDataSize, f);
    fread(vertexData.data(), 1, header.vertexDataSize, f);
    ```

Alternatively, index and vertex buffers can be combined into a single large byte buffer. We will leave it as an exercise for the reader.

Later, the `indexData` and `vertexData` containers can be uploaded into the GPU directly and accessed as data buffers from shaders to implement programmable vertex pulling, as described in *Chapter 2, Using Essential Libraries*. We will return to this in later recipes.

There's more...

This geometry data format is pretty straightforward for the purpose of storing static mesh data. If the meshes can be changed, reloaded, or loaded asynchronously, we can store separate meshes into dedicated files.

Since it is impossible to predict all use cases, and since this book is all about rendering and not some general-purpose gaming engine creation, it is up to the reader to make decisions about adding extra features such as mesh skinning. One simple example of such a decision is the addition of material data directly inside the mesh file. Technically, all we need to do is add a `materialCount` field to the `MeshFileHeader` structure and store a list of material descriptions right after the list of meshes. Even doing such a simple thing immediately raises more questions. Should we pack texture data in the same file? If yes, then how complex should the texture format be? What material model should we use? And so forth. For now, we will just leave the mesh geometry data separated from the material descriptions. We will come back to materials in the *Chapter 7, Graphics Rendering Pipeline*.

Implementing a geometry conversion tool

In the previous chapters, we learned how to use the Assimp library to load and render 3D models stored in different file formats. In real-world graphics applications, the loading of a 3D model can be a tedious and multistage process. Besides just loading, we might want to preprocess a mesh in a specific way, such as optimizing geometry data or computing LODs for meshes. This process might become slow for sizable meshes, so it makes perfect sense to preprocess meshes offline, before an application starts, and load them later in the app, as described in the *Organizing the storage of mesh data* recipe. Let's learn how to implement a skeleton for a simple offline mesh conversion tool.

Getting ready

The source code for the geometry conversion tool described in this chapter can be found in the `Chapter5/MeshConvert` folder. The entire project is covered in several recipes, including *Implementing a geometry conversion tool* and *Generating LODs using MeshOptimizer*.

How to do it...

Let's examine how the Assimp library is used to export mesh data and save it inside a binary file using the data structures defined in the *Organizing the storage of mesh data* recipe:

1. We start by including some mandatory header files:

    ```
    #include <vector>
    #include <assimp/scene.h>
    #include <assimp/postprocess.h>
    #include <assimp/cimport.h>
    #include "shared/VtxData.h"
    ```

2. A global Boolean flag determines whether we should output textual messages during the conversion process. This comes in handy for debugging purposes:

    ```
    bool verbose = true;
    ```

3. The actual mesh descriptions and mesh geometry data are stored in the following three arrays. We cannot output converted meshes one by one, at least not in a single-pass tool, because we do not know the total size of the data in advance. So, we allocate in-memory storage for all the data and then write these data blobs into the output file:

    ```
    std::vector<Mesh> meshes;
    std::vector<uint32_t> indexData;
    std::vector<float> vertexData;
    ```

4. To fill the `indexData` and `vertexData` fields, we require two counters to track offsets of index and vertex mesh data inside the file. Two flags control whether we need to export texture coordinates and normal vectors:

    ```
    uint32_t indexOffset  = 0;
    uint32_t vertexOffset = 0;
    bool exportTextures = false;
    bool exportNormals  = false;
    ```

5. By default, we only export vertex coordinates into the output file; therefore, 3 elements are specified here. To override this, we parse command-line arguments and check whether texture coordinates or normal vectors are also needed:

    ```
    uint32_t numElementsToStore = 3;
    ```

The main mesh conversion logic of this tool is implemented in the `convertAIMesh()` function, which takes in an Assimp mesh and converts it into our mesh representation. Let's take a look at how it is implemented:

1. First, we check whether a set of texture coordinates is present in the original Assimp mesh:

```
Mesh convertAIMesh(const aiMesh* m)
{
    const bool hasTexCoords = m->HasTextureCoords(0);
```

2. For this recipe, we assume there is a single LOD and all the vertex data is stored as a continuous data stream. In other words, we have data stored in an interleaved manner. Also, for now, we ignore all the material information and deal exclusively with the index and vertex data:

```
const uint32_t numIndices = m->mNumFaces * 3;
const uint32_t numElements = numElementsToStore;
```

3. The size of the stream element in bytes is directly calculated from the number of elements per vertex. Earlier, we agreed to store each component as a floating-point value, so no branching logic is required to do that:

```
const uint32_t streamElementSize =
    static_cast<uint32_t>(
      numElements * sizeof(float));
```

4. The total data size for this mesh is the size of the vertex stream plus the size of the index data:

```
const uint32_t meshSize = static_cast<uint32_t>(
    m->mNumVertices * streamElementSize +
    numIndices * sizeof(uint32_t) );
```

5. The mesh descriptor for the `aiMesh` input object here has its `lodCount` and `streamCount` fields set to `1`:

```
const Mesh result = {
    .lodCount    = 1,
    .streamCount = 1,
```

6. Since we are not yet exporting materials, we set `materialID` to the default value of zero:

```
    .materialID  = 0,
```

7. The mesh data size and the total vertex count for this mesh are also stored in the mesh description:

```
.meshSize     = meshSize,
.vertexCount  = m->mNumVertices,
```

8. Since we have only one LOD, the lodOffset array contains two items. The first one stores the indexOffset counter multiplied by a single index size to determine the byte offset in the indexData array. The second element contains the last item of the indexData, which is used by this mesh:

```
.lodOffset = { indexOffset * sizeof(uint32_t),
               (indexOffset + numIndices) *
                 sizeof(uint32_t) },
.streamOffset =
   { vertexOffset * streamElementSize },
.streamElementSize = { streamElementSize }
};
```

9. For each of the vertices, we extract their data from the aiMesh object and always store vertex coordinates in the vertexData output stream:

```
for (size_t i = 0; i != m->mNumVertices; i++) {
  const aiVector3D& v = m->mVertices[i];
  const aiVector3D& n = m->mNormals[i];
  const aiVector3D& t = hasTexCoords ?
    m->mTextureCoords[0][i] : aiVector3D();
  vertexData.push_back(v.x);
  vertexData.push_back(v.y);
  vertexData.push_back(v.z);
```

10. If the export of texture coordinates or normal vectors is required, we append them to the vertex stream:

```
  if (exportTextures) {
    vertexData.push_back(t.x);
    vertexData.push_back(t.y);
  }
  if (exportNormals) {
    vertexData.push_back(n.x);
    vertexData.push_back(n.y);
    vertexData.push_back(n.z);
  }
}
```

11. The `vertexOffset` variable contains the starting vertex index for the current mesh. We add the `vertexOffset` value to each of the indices imported from the input file:

```
for (size_t i = 0; i != m->mNumFaces; i++) {
  const aiFace& F = m->mFaces[i];
  indexData.push_back(F.mIndices[0] + vertexOffset);
  indexData.push_back(F.mIndices[1] + vertexOffset);
  indexData.push_back(F.mIndices[2] + vertexOffset);
}
```

12. After processing the input mesh, we increment offset counters for the indices and current starting vertex:

```
indexOffset   += numIndices;
vertexOffset += m->mNumVertices;
return result;
}
```

Processing the file comprises loading the scene and converting each mesh into an internal format. Let's take a look at the `loadFile()` function to learn how to do it:

1. The list of flags for the `aiImportFile()` function includes options that allow further usage of imported data without any processing. For example, all the transformation hierarchies are flattened and the resulting transformation matrices are applied to mesh vertices:

```
bool loadFile(const char* fileName) {
  if (verbose) printf("Loading '%s'...\n", fileName);
  const unsigned int flags =
      aiProcess_JoinIdenticalVertices
      aiProcess_Triangulate
      aiProcess_GenSmoothNormals
      aiProcess_PreTransformVertices
      aiProcess_RemoveRedundantMaterials
      aiProcess_FindDegenerates
      aiProcess_FindInvalidData
      aiProcess_FindInstances
      aiProcess_OptimizeMeshes;
```

2. Just as we did in the previous chapters, we use `aiImportFile()` to load all the mesh data from a file:

```
const aiScene* scene =
    aiImportFile(fileName, flags);
if (!scene || !scene->HasMeshes()) {
```

```
      printf("Unable to load '%s'\n", fileName);
      return false;
   }
```

3. After importing the scene, we resize the mesh descriptor container accordingly and call `convertAIMesh()` for each mesh in the scene:

```
   meshes.reserve(scene->mNumMeshes);
   for (size_t i = 0; i != scene->mNumMeshes; i++)
     meshes.push_back(
       convertAIMesh(scene->mMeshes[i]));
   return true;
}
```

Saving converted meshes inside our file format is the reverse process of reading meshes from the file described in the *Organizing the storage of mesh data* recipe:

1. First, we fill the file header structure using the mesh number and offsets:

```
inline void saveMeshesToFile(FILE* f) {
  const MeshFileHeader header = {
    .magicValue = 0x12345678,
    .meshCount = (uint32_t)meshes.size(),
    .dataBlockStartOffset =
      (uint32_t)(sizeof(MeshFileHeader) +
      meshes.size()*sizeof(Mesh)),
```

2. We calculate the byte sizes of the index and vertex data buffers:

```
    .indexDataSize =
      indexData.size() * sizeof(uint32_t),
    .vertexDataSize =
      vertexData.size() * sizeof(float)
  };
```

3. Once all the sizes are known, we save the header and the list of mesh descriptions:

```
   fwrite(&header, 1, sizeof(header), f);
   fwrite(
    meshes.data(), header.meshCount, sizeof(Mesh), f);
```

4. After the header and descriptors, two blocks with index and vertex data are stored:

```
   fwrite(
     indexData.data(), 1, header.indexDataSize, f);
   fwrite(
     vertexData.data(), 1, header.vertexDataSize, f);
}
```

Let's put all of this code into a functioning mesh converter app:

1. The converter's main function checks for command-line parameters and calls the `loadFile()` and `saveMeshesToFile()` functions. Command-line arguments determine whether we should export texture coordinates and normal vectors:

```
int main(int argc, char** argv) {
    bool exportTextures = false;
    bool exportNormals  = false;
```

2. The first and second arguments must contain input and output filenames. If the argument count is low, a short instruction is printed:

```
if (argc < 3) {
    printf("Usage: meshconvert <input> <output>
      --export-texcoords | -t]
      [--export-normals | -n]\n");
    printf("Options: \n");
    printf("\t--export-texcoords | -t: export texture
      coordinates\n");
    printf("\t--export-normals    | -n: export
      normals\n");
    exit(255);
}
```

3. The remaining optional command-line arguments specify whether we want to export texture coordinates and normal vectors:

> **Note**
>
> This sort of manual command-line parsing is tedious and error-prone. It is used for simplicity in this book. In real-world applications, normally, you would use a command-line parsing library. We recommend that you try **Argh!** from `https://github.com/adishavit/argh`.

```
for (int i = 3 ; i < argc ; i++) {
    exportTextures |=
      !strcmp(argv[i], "--export-texcoords") ||
      !strcmp(argv[i], "-t");
    exportNormals |=
      !strcmp(argv[i], "--export-normals") ||
      !strcmp(argv[i], "-n");
    const bool exportAll =
      !strcmp(argv[i], "-tn") ||
      !strcmp(argv[i], "-nt");
```

```
        exportTextures |= exportAll;
        exportNormals |= exportAll;
    }
```

4. Once we know the export parameters, we calculate the amount of per-vertex data counted in floating-point numbers. For example, a mesh with vertex coordinates only stores three floating-point numbers per vertex. Here, we use hardcoded values for simplicity:

```
    if (exportTextures) numElementsToStore += 2;
    if (exportNormals ) numElementsToStore += 3;
```

5. Having determined all the export parameters, we call the `loadFile()` function to load the scene with all of the meshes:

```
    if ( !loadFile(argv[1]) ) exit(255);
```

After loading and converting all of the meshes, we save the output file:

```
  FILE *f = fopen(argv[2], "wb");
  saveMeshesToFile(f);
  fclose(f);
  return 0;
}
```

How it works...

To use the mesh conversion tool, let's invoke it to convert one of the Lumberyard Bistro meshes into our mesh format. That can be done with the following command:

```
Ch5_Tool05_MeshConvert_Release
  exterior.obj exterior.mesh -tn
```

The output mesh is saved inside the `exterior.mesh` file. Let's go through the rest of this chapter to learn how to render this mesh with Vulkan.

There's more...

The complete source code of the converter can be found in the `Chapter5/MeshConvert` folder. The final version of the tool contains LOD-generation functionality, which will be discussed later in the *Generating LODs using MeshOptimizer* recipe.

Indirect rendering in Vulkan

Indirect rendering is the process of issuing drawing commands to the graphics API, where most of the parameters to those commands come from GPU buffers. It is a part of many modern GPU usage paradigms, and it exists in all contemporary rendering APIs in some form. For example, we can do indirect rendering with OpenGL using the `glDraw*Indirect*()` family of functions. Instead of dealing with OpenGL here, let's get more technical and learn how to combine indirect rendering in Vulkan with the mesh data format that we introduced in the *Organizing the storage of mesh data* recipe.

Getting ready

Once we have defined the mesh data structures, we also need to render them. To do this, we allocate GPU buffers for the vertex and index data using the previously described functions, upload all the data to GPU, and, finally, fill the command buffers to render these buffers at each frame.

The whole point of the previously defined `Mesh` data structure is the ability to render multiple meshes in a single Vulkan command. Since version 1.0 of the API, Vulkan supports the technique of indirect rendering. This means we do not need to issue the `vkCmdDraw()` command for each and every mesh. Instead, we create a GPU buffer and fill it with an array of `VkDrawIndirectCommand` structures, fill these structures with appropriate offsets into our index and vertex data buffers, and, finally, emit a single `vkCmdDrawIndirect()` call.

How to do it...

Before we proceed with rendering, let's introduce a data structure to represent an individual mesh instance in our 3D world. We will use it to specify which meshes we want to render, how to transform them, and which material and LOD level should be used:

```
struct InstanceData {
  float    transform[16];
  uint32_t meshIndex;
  uint32_t materialIndex;
  uint32_t LOD;
  uint32_t indexOffset;
};
```

As mentioned in the previous *Chapter 4, Adding User Interaction and Productivity Tools*, we implement another layer for our frame composition system:

1. The `MultiMeshRenderer` class constructor takes in the names of the shader files to render the meshes and filenames with input data. To render multiple meshes, we need the instance data for each mesh, the material description, and the mesh geometry itself:

```
class MultiMeshRenderer: public RendererBase {
public:
  MultiMeshRenderer(
    VulkanRenderDevice& vkDev,
    const char* meshFile,
    const char* instanceFile,
    const char* materialFile,
    const char* vtxShaderFile,
    const char* fragShaderFile);
```

2. We'll return to the constructor later. For now, let's take a look at the private data part. Here, we have containers to store all of the loaded data:

```
private:
  std::vector<InstanceData> instances;
  std::vector<Mesh> meshes;
  std::vector<uint32_t> indexData;
  std::vector<float> vertexData;
```

3. The reference to a Vulkan render device is used all over the code:

```
  VulkanRenderDevice& vkDev;
```

4. This renderer contains all the index and vertex data in a single, large GPU buffer. Its contents are loaded from the `indexData` and `vertexData` containers mentioned earlier:

```
  VkBuffer storageBuffer_;
  VkDeviceMemory storageBufferMemory_;
```

5. Some buffer sizes are used multiple times after allocation, so they are cached in the following variables:

```
  uint32_t maxVertexBufferSize_, maxIndexBufferSize_;
  uint32_t maxInstances_;
  uint32_t maxInstanceSize_, maxMaterialSize_;
```

6. In this recipe, we do not use any material data, but we declare an empty GPU buffer
    for it to be used later:

```
VkBuffer materialBuffer_;
VkDeviceMemory materialBufferMemory_;
```

7. For each of the swapchain images, we declare a copy of indirect rendering data.
    Additionally, we declare buffers for the instance data:

```
std::vector<VkBuffer> indirectBuffers_;
std::vector<VkDeviceMemory> indirectBuffersMemory_;
std::vector<VkBuffer> instanceBuffers_;
std::vector<VkDeviceMemory> instanceBuffersMemory_;
```

8. The routine to create the descriptor set is identical to the routines described in the
    previous examples. Hopefully, its content can be easily derived from the vertex
    shader source found at the end of this recipe or in data/shaders/chapter05/
    VK01.vert:

```
bool createDescriptorSet(VulkanRenderDevice& vkDev);
```

9. The routines to update the uniform and instance buffers simply redirect to the
    uploadBufferData() function:

```
void updateUniformBuffer(VulkanRenderDevice& vkDev,
  size_t currentImage, const mat4&m)
{
  uploadBufferData(vkDev,
    uniformBuffersMemory_[currentImage], 0,
    glm::value_ptr(m), sizeof(mat4));
}
void updateInstanceBuffer(VulkanRenderDevice& vkDev,
  size_t currentImage,
  uint32_t instanceSize, const void* instanceData)
{
  uploadBufferData(vkDev,
    instanceBuffersMemory_[currentImage], 0,
    instanceData, instanceSize);
}
```

10. The geometry data is uploaded into the GPU in two parts. Technically, this can be simplified to a single upload operation if the indices and vertices are stored in a single contiguous buffer:

```
void updateGeometryBuffers(
  VulkanRenderDevice& vkDev,
  uint32_t vertexCount,
  uint32_t indexCount,
  const void* vertices,
  const void* indices)
{
  uploadBufferData(vkDev, storageBufferMemory_, 0,
    vertices, vertexCount);
  uploadBufferData(vkDev, storageBufferMemory_,
    maxVertexBufferSize_, indices, indexCount);
}
```

11. A buffer required for indirect rendering is filled according to the loaded instances list. After mapping a region of GPU-visible memory into a CPU-accessible pointer, we iterate the instance array. For each loaded mesh instance, we fetch the vertex count and vertex offset within the data buffer:

```
void updateIndirectBuffers(
  VulkanRenderDevice& vkDev,
  size_t currentImage)
{
  VkDrawIndirectCommand* data = nullptr;
  vkMapMemory(vkDev.device,
    indirectBuffersMemory_[currentImage], 0,
    2 * sizeof(VkDrawIndirectCommand), 0,
    (void **)&data);
  for (uint32_t i = 0 ; i < maxInstances_ ; i++) {
    const uint32_t j = instances[i].meshIndex;
    data[i] = {
      .vertexCount = static_cast<uint32_t>(
        meshes[j].lodSize(
          instances[i].LOD) / sizeof(uint32_t)),
```

12. For this recipe, the instance count is one. However, if we make a few necessary modifications to the instance buffer layout with transformation matrices, we can render multiple instances of a single mesh at once:

```
      .instanceCount = 1,
```

13. The vertex offset has to be recalculated into a float value count. As we have one instance, we just set the first and only `firstInstance` value to `i`:

```
      .firstVertex = static_cast<uint32_t>(
        meshes[j].streamOffset[0] /
        meshes[j].streamElementSize[0]),
      .firstInstance = i
    };
  }
  vkUnmapMemory(vkDev.device,
    indirectBuffersMemory_[currentImage]);
}
```

14. The code to fill the command buffer is extremely simple. Once we have the indirect rendering data inside a GPU buffer, we call the `vkCmdDrawIndirect()` function:

```
virtual void fillCommandBuffer(
  VkCommandBuffer commandBuffer,
  size_t currentImage) override
{
  beginRenderPass(commandBuffer, currentImage);
  vkCmdDrawIndirect(commandBuffer,
    indirectBuffers_[currentImage],
    0, maxInstances_,
    sizeof(VkDrawIndirectCommand));
  vkCmdEndRenderPass(commandBuffer);
}
```

15. The destructor deallocates all GPU buffers and Vulkan objects:

```
virtual ~MultiMeshRenderer() {
  VkDevice device = vkDev.device;
  vkDestroyBuffer(device, storageBuffer_, nullptr);
  vkFreeMemory(
    device, storageBufferMemory_, nullptr);
  for (size_t i = 0;
      i < swapchainFramebuffers_.size(); i++)
  {
    vkDestroyBuffer(
      device, instanceBuffers_[i], nullptr);
    vkFreeMemory(
      device, instanceBuffersMemory_[i], nullptr);
    vkDestroyBuffer(
      device, indirectBuffers_[i], nullptr);
    vkFreeMemory(
      device, indirectBuffersMemory_[i], nullptr);
  }
```

```
  vkDestroyBuffer(device, materialBuffer_, nullptr);
  vkFreeMemory(
    device, materialBufferMemory_, nullptr);
  destroyVulkanImage(device, depthTexture_);
}
```

The longest part of the code is the constructor. To describe the initialization process, we need to define two helper functions:

1. The first one loads a list of transformations for each mesh:

```
void MultiMeshRenderer::loadInstanceData(
  const char* instanceFile)
{
  FILE* f = fopen(instanceFile, "rb");
  fseek(f, 0, SEEK_END);
  size_t fsize = ftell(f);
  fseek(f, 0, SEEK_SET);
```

After determining the size of the input file, we should calculate the number of instances in this file:

```
  maxInstances_ = static_cast<uint32_t>(
    fsize / sizeof(InstanceData));
  instances.resize(maxInstances_);
```

A single `fread()` call gets the instance data loading job done:

```
  if (fread(instances.data(), sizeof(InstanceData),
        maxInstances_, f) != maxInstances_)
  {
    printf("Unable to read instance data\n");
    exit(255);
  }
  fclose(f);
}
```

2. The second helper function loads the mesh data:

```
MeshFileHeader MultiMeshRenderer::loadMeshData(
  const char* meshFile)
{
  MeshFileHeader header;
  FILE* f = fopen(meshFile, "rb");
```

The loading process is the same as in the pseudocode from the *Implementing a geometry conversion tool* recipe:

```
if (fread(&header, 1, sizeof(header), f)
      != sizeof(header)) {
  printf("Unable to read mesh file header\n");
  exit(255);
}
meshes.resize(header.meshCount);
```

After reading the file header, we read individual mesh descriptions:

```
if (fread(meshes.data(), sizeof(Mesh),
      header.meshCount, f) != header.meshCount) {
  printf("Could not read mesh descriptors\n");
  exit(255);
}
```

Two more `fread()` calls read the mesh indices and vertex data:

```
indexData.resize(
  header.indexDataSize / sizeof(uint32_t));
vertexData.resize(
  header.vertexDataSize / sizeof(float));
if ((fread(indexData.data(), 1,header.indexDataSize,
      f) != header.indexDataSize) ||
    (fread(vertexData.data(),1,header.vertexDataSize,
      f) != header.vertexDataSize))
{
  printf("Unable to read index/vertex data\n");
  exit(255);
}
fclose(f);
```

To ensure the correct initialization within the constructor, we return the initialized `MeshFileHeader` object:

```
  return header;
}
```

We are ready to describe the initialization procedure of the `MultiMeshRenderer` class:

1. Let's take a look at the constructor again:

```
MultiMeshRenderer::MultiMeshRenderer(
  VulkanRenderDevice& vkDev,
  const char* meshFile,
  const char* instanceFile,
  const char* materialFile,
  const char* vtxShaderFile,
  const char* fragShaderFile)
: vkDev(vkDev), RendererBase(vkDev, VulkanImage())
{
```

In the same way as our other **renderers**, we create a render pass object:

```
if (!createColorAndDepthRenderPass(vkDev, false,
      &renderPass_, RenderPassCreateInfo()))
{
  printf("Failed to create render pass\n");
  exit(EXIT_FAILURE);
}
```

2. As always, we start the rendering pass by saving the frame buffer dimensions:

```
framebufferWidth_  = vkDev.framebufferWidth;
framebufferHeight_ = vkDev.framebufferHeight;
```

3. To ensure correct 3D rendering, we allocate a depth buffer:

```
createDepthResources(vkDev, framebufferWidth_,
  framebufferHeight_, depthTexture_);
```

4. To proceed with the GPU buffer allocation, we need to read the mesh and instance data:

```
loadInstanceData(instanceFile);
MeshFileHeader header = loadMesh(meshFile);
const uint32_t indirectDataSize =
  maxInstances_ * sizeof(VkDrawIndirectCommand);
maxInstanceSize_ =
  maxInstances_ * sizeof(InstanceData);
maxMaterialSize_ = 1024;
```

5. We require a copy of the instance and indirect rendering data for each of the
    swapchain images:

```
instanceBuffers_.resize(
    vkDev.swapchainImages.size());
instanceBuffersMemory_.resize(
    vkDev.swapchainImages.size());
indirectBuffers_.resize(
    vkDev.swapchainImages.size());
indirectBuffersMemory_.resize(
    vkDev.swapchainImages.size());
```

For this recipe, we do not need materials or textures. So, we will just allocate the
buffer for the material data and avoid using it for now:

```
if (!createBuffer(vkDev.device,
        vkDev.physicalDevice, materialDataSize,
        VK_BUFFER_USAGE_STORAGE_BUFFER_BIT,
        VK_MEMORY_PROPERTY_HOST_VISIBLE_BIT |
        VK_MEMORY_PROPERTY_HOST_COHERENT_BIT,
        materialBuffer_, materialBufferMemory_))
{
    printf("Cannot create material buffer\n");
    exit(EXIT_FAILURE);
}
```

6. To allocate a descriptor set, we need to save the sizes of the index and vertex buffers:

```
maxVertexBufferSize_ = header.vertexDataSize;
maxIndexBufferSize_  = header.indexDataSize;
```

In the previous chapters, we were lucky that the size of our vertex data was a multiple
of 16 bytes. Now, we want to store arbitrary arrays of mesh vertices and face indices,
so this forces us to support arbitrary offsets of GPU sub-buffers. Our descriptor set for
MultiMeshRenderer has two logical storage buffers for index and vertex data. In the
following snippet, we pad the vertex data with zeros so that its size has the necessary
alignment properties:

1. We fetch the device properties structure to find out the minimal storage buffer
    alignment value:

```
VkPhysicalDeviceProperties devProps;
vkGetPhysicalDeviceProperties(
    vkDev.physicalDevice, &devProps);
const uint32_t offsetAlignment =
    devProps.limits.minStorageBufferOffsetAlignment;
```

2. After that, if the vertex data size does not meet the alignment requirements, we add the necessary zeros to the end of the vertex data array:

```
if ((maxVertexBufferSize_&(offsetAlignment-1)) != 0)
{
  int floats = (offsetAlignment -
    (maxVertexBufferSize_&(offsetAlignment-1))) /
    sizeof(float);
  for (int ii = 0; ii < floats; ii++)
    vertexData.push_back(0);
```

3. We update the vertex buffer size for the buffer allocation as follows:

```
  maxVertexBufferSize_ =
    (maxVertexBufferSize_ +offsetAlignment) &
    ~(offsetAlignment - 1);
}
```

4. Once we have calculated the index and vertex buffer size, we allocate the GPU buffer itself:

```
if (!createBuffer(vkDev.device,
    vkDev.physicalDevice,
    maxVertexBufferSize_ + maxIndexBufferSize_,
    VK_BUFFER_USAGE_STORAGE_BUFFER_BIT,
    VK_MEMORY_PROPERTY_HOST_VISIBLE_BIT |
    VK_MEMORY_PROPERTY_HOST_COHERENT_BIT,
    storageBuffer_, storageBufferMemory_))
{
  printf("Cannot create vertex/index buffer\n");
  exit(EXIT_FAILURE);
}
```

5. In this recipe, we only update the geometry data once, during the initialization stage:

```
  updateGeometryBuffers(vkDev, header.vertexDataSize,
    header.indexDataSize, vertexData.data(),
    indexData.data());
```

6. The remaining GPU buffers are allocated similarly to the uniform buffers in the previous chapters. One swapchain image corresponds to one instance buffer or indirect draw data buffer:

```
  for (size_t i = 0; i < vkDev.swapchainImages.size();
    i++)
  {
```

```
if (!createBuffer(vkDev.device,
    vkDev.physicalDevice, indirectDataSize,
    VK_BUFFER_USAGE_INDIRECT_BUFFER_BIT,
```

7. For the sake of debugging and code simplification, we allocate indirect draw data buffers as host-visible. If the instances are not changed by the CPU, for example, for static geometry, such buffers could be allocated on the GPU for better performance. However, this requires you to allocate a staging buffer. An example of staging buffer allocation can be found in *Chapter 3, Getting Started with OpenGL and Vulkan*, where we dealt with texture images in the *Using texture data in Vulkan* recipe:

```
VK_MEMORY_PROPERTY_HOST_VISIBLE_BIT |
VK_MEMORY_PROPERTY_HOST_COHERENT_BIT,
indirectBuffers_[i], indirectBuffersMemory_[i]))
{
    printf("Cannot create indirect buffer\n");
    exit(EXIT_FAILURE);
}
```

8. Upon allocation, we fill the indirect draw buffers with the required values:

```
updateIndirectBuffers(vkDev, i);
```

In the demo application code snippet at the end of this recipe, we do not update this buffer during runtime. However, it might be necessary to do so if we want to set the LOD for the meshes when the camera position changes.

9. In this example, the instance data also stays immutable after initialization:

```
if (!createBuffer(vkDev.device,
    vkDev.physicalDevice, instanceDataSize,
    VK_BUFFER_USAGE_STORAGE_BUFFER_BIT,
    VK_MEMORY_PROPERTY_HOST_VISIBLE_BIT |
    VK_MEMORY_PROPERTY_HOST_COHERENT_BIT,
    instanceBuffers_[i], instanceBuffersMemory_[i]))
{
    printf("Cannot create instance buffer\n");
    exit(EXIT_FAILURE);
}
```

10. After allocation, we upload local instance data to the GPU buffer:

```
updateInstanceBuffer(
    vkDev, i, instanceDataSize, instances.data());
}
```

This completes the description of our initialization process. Now, let's turn to the shader source code:

1. The `data/shaders/chapter05/VK01.vert` vertex shader uses a whole bunch of buffers to calculate the onscreen vertex position. Each GPU buffer used in rendering is structured. We only use meshes with vertex coordinates. The `InstanceData` buffer contains a transformation matrix, a mesh, a material ID, and a LOD value:

```
#version 460
layout(location = 0) out vec3 uvw;
struct ImDrawVert {
  float x, y, z;
};
struct InstanceData {
  mat4 xfrm;
  uint mesh;
  uint matID;
  uint lod;
};
```

2. Material data has not yet been used in this chapter. So, for the sake of brevity, we will just assume there is a single texture index:

```
struct MaterialData {
  uint tex2D;
};
```

3. All the buffer indices correspond to the ones used in the descriptor set layout creation code in C++ mentioned earlier:

```
layout(binding = 0) uniform  UniformBuffer
  { mat4 inMtx; } ubo;
layout(binding = 1) readonly buffer SBO
  {ImDrawVert data[];} sbo;
layout(binding = 2) readonly buffer IBO
  {uint data[];} ibo;
layout(binding = 3) readonly buffer InstBO
  {InstanceData data[];} instanceBuffer;
```

4. The first four instances of these meshes are colored using the values from the following array:

```
vec3 colors[4] = vec3[] (
   vec3(1.0, 0.0, 0.0),
   vec3(0.0, 1.0, 0.0),
   vec3(0.0, 0.0, 1.0),
   vec3(0.0, 0.0, 0.0)
);
```

5. In the shader program, we use a programmable vertex-pulling technique to read the vertex coordinates. Here, we fetch indices manually to simplify our C++ implementation. While this handling results in a shorter code, it defeats any hardware vertex reuse and should not be used in most real-world applications:

```
void main() {
   uint idx = ibo.data[gl_VertexIndex];
   ImDrawVert v = sbo.data[idx];
```

6. Then, we use the gl_BaseInstance counter to determine where we should fetch the output color from:

```
   uvw = (gl_BaseInstance >= 4) ?
      vec3(1,1,0): colors[gl_BaseInstance];
```

7. Due to the subtleties of the buffer management implementation in Vulkan, we cannot declare our transformation as a mat4 field in the InstanceData structure. Locally, we declare the mat4 object and manually convert a floating-point array into a 4x4 matrix:

```
   mat4 xfrm = transpose(
      instanceBuffer.data[gl_BaseInstance].xfrm);
```

8. Last but not least, we apply the view-projection matrix from the uniform buffer and the xfrm instance model-to-world transform to the input vertex coordinates:

```
   gl_Position =
      ubo.inMtx * xfrm * vec4(v.x, v.y, v.z, 1.0);
}
```

The `data/shaders/chapter05/VK01.frag` fragment shader simply outputs the color passed in the uvw variable from the vertex shader. In the subsequent *Chapter 7, Graphics Rendering Pipeline*, we will use the material information buffer and read material parameters from there. For now, a solid color is enough to run our multi-mesh rendering code:

```
#version 460
layout(location = 0) in vec3 uvw;
layout(location = 0) out vec4 outColor;
void main()
{
  outColor = vec4(uvw, 0.5);
}
```

The `vkCmdDrawIndirect()` function is an extension to the Vulkan API, and it must be explicitly enabled during the Vulkan render device initialization phase:

1. The `initVulkan()` routine is very similar to the initialization routines that we have already implemented. Mandatory instance creation and **GLFW** surface initialization happens before the creation of a Vulkan device:

    ```
    void initVulkan()
    {
      createInstance(&vk.instance);
      if (!setupDebugCallbacks(
          vk.instance, &vk.messenger, &vk.reportCallback))
      {
        exit(EXIT_FAILURE);
      }
      if (glfwCreateWindowSurface(
          vk.instance, window, nullptr, &vk.surface))
      {
        exit(EXIT_FAILURE);
      }
    }
    ```

2. In the `initVulkanRenderDevice()` function, the `deviceFeatures` parameter contains two flags that allow us to use indirect rendering and instance offsets:

    ```
    if (!initVulkanRenderDevice(vk, vkDev, kScreenWidth,
          kScreenHeight,
          isDeviceSuitable,
          { .multiDrawIndirect = VK_TRUE,
            .drawIndirectFirstInstance = VK_TRUE }))
    ```

```
{
    exit(EXIT_FAILURE);
}
```

3. Along with the multi-mesh renderer, we also initialize two auxiliary objects to clear the frame buffer and finalize the rendering pass:

```
clear = std::make_unique<VulkanClear>(
    vkDev, VulkanImage());
finish = std::make_unique<VulkanFinish>(
    vkDev, VulkanImage());
```

4. The `MultiMeshRenderer` class is initialized using the mesh file, the instance list file, an empty string for the material file's name, and names of two shaders which render all the meshes:

```
multiRenderer = std::make_unique<MultiMeshRenderer>(
    vkDev, "data/meshes/test.cubes",
    "data/meshes/test.grid", "",
    "data/shaders/chapter05/VK01.vert",
    "data/shaders/chapter05/VK01.frag");
}
```

5. To save space, we do not comment the entire `drawOverlay()` routine which is invoked every frame. The two new things we do in `drawOverlay()` include a call to `updateUniformBuffer()` to update the uniform buffer with the new model-view-projection matrix, `mtx`, and filling a Vulkan command buffer:

```
multiRenderer->updateUniformBuffer(
    vkDev, imageIndex, mtx);
multiRenderer->fillCommandBuffer(
    commandBuffer, imageIndex);
```

There's more...

It might be challenging to write a modern Vulkan renderer from scratch. For those who are interested, we would like to recommend an open source project, `https://github.com/zeux/niagara`, by Arseny Kapoulkine, which tries to achieve exactly that. Many advanced Vulkan topics are covered in his YouTube streaming sessions.

Implementing an infinite grid GLSL shader

In the previous recipes of this chapter, we learned how to organize geometry storage in a more systematic way. To debug our applications, it is useful to have a visible representation of the coordinate system so that a viewer can quickly infer the camera orientation and position just by looking at a rendered image. A natural way to represent a coordinate system in an image is to render an infinite grid where the grid plane is aligned with one of the coordinate planes. Let's learn how to implement a decent-looking grid in GLSL.

Getting ready

The full C++ source code for this recipe can be found in `Chapter5/GL01_Grid`. The corresponding GLSL shaders are located in the `data/shaders/chapter05/GL01_grid.frag` and `data/shaders/chapter05/GL01_grid.vert` files.

How to do it...

To parametrize our grid, we should introduce some parameters. They can be found and tweaked in the `data/shaders/chapter05/GridParameters.h` GLSL include file:

1. First of all, we need to define the size of our grid extents in the world coordinates, that is, how far from the camera the grid will be visible:

   ```
   float gridSize = 100.0;
   ```

2. The size of one grid cell is specified in the same units as the grid size:

   ```
   float gridCellSize = 0.025;
   ```

3. Let's define the colors of the grid lines. We will use two different colors: one for regular thin lines and the other for thick lines, which are rendered every tenth line. Since we render everything against a white background, we are good with black and 50% gray:

   ```
   vec4 gridColorThin = vec4(0.5, 0.5, 0.5, 1.0);
   vec4 gridColorThick = vec4(0.0, 0.0, 0.0, 1.0);
   ```

4. Our grid implementation will change the number of rendered lines based on the grid LOD. We will switch the LOD when the number of pixels between two adjacent cell lines drops below this value:

   ```
   const float gridMinPixelsBetweenCells = 2.0;
   ```

5. Let's take a look at a simple vertex shader that we can use to generate and transform grid vertices. It takes no input except the `gl_VertexID` parameter and scales the `[-1..+1]` rectangle by grid size:

```
layout (location=0) out vec2 uv;
const vec3 pos[4] = vec3[4](
  vec3(-1.0, 0.0, -1.0),
  vec3( 1.0, 0.0, -1.0),
  vec3( 1.0, 0.0,  1.0),
  vec3(-1.0, 0.0,  1.0)
);
const int indices[6] = int[6](0, 1, 2, 2, 3, 0);
```

6. An additional custom output that it produces is the XZ world coordinates of the vertex inside the `uv` parameter:

```
void main() {
  vec3 vpos = pos[indices[gl_VertexID]] * gridSize;
  gl_Position = proj * view * vec4(vpos, 1.0);
  uv = vpos.xz;
}
```

The fragment shader is somewhat more complex. It will calculate a programmatic texture that looks like a grid. The grid lines are rendered based on how fast the `uv` coordinates change in the image space to avoid the Moiré pattern. Therefore, we are going to need screen space derivatives:

1. First, we introduce a bunch of GLSL helper functions to aid our calculations:

```
float log10(float x) {
  return log(x) / log(10.0);
}
float satf(float x) {
  return clamp(x, 0.0, 1.0);
}
vec2 satv(vec2 x) {
  return clamp(x, vec2(0.0), vec2(1.0));
}
float max2(vec2 v) {
  return max(v.x, v.y);
}
```

2. Let's take a look at the main() function and start by calculating the screen space length of the derivatives of the uv coordinates that we previously generated in the vertex shader. We will use the built-in dFdx() and dFdy() functions to calculate the required derivatives:

```
vec2 dudv = vec2(
  length(vec2(dFdx(uv.x), dFdy(uv.x))),
  length(vec2(dFdx(uv.y), dFdy(uv.y)))
);
```

3. By knowing the derivatives, the current LOD of our grid can be calculated in the following way. The gridMinPixelsBetweenCells value controls how fast we want our LOD level to increase. In this case, it is the minimum number of pixels between two adjacent cell lines of the grid:

```
float lodLevel = max(0.0, log10((length(dudv) *
  gridMinPixelsBetweenCells) / gridCellSize) + 1.0);
float lodFade = fract(lodLevel);
```

Besides the LOD value itself, we are going to need a fading factor to render smooth transitions between the adjacent levels. This can be obtained by taking a fractional part of the floating-point LOD level. A logarithm base of 10 is used to ensure each next LOD covers at least pow(10, lodLevel) more cells of the previous LOD.

4. The LOD levels are blended between each other. To render them, we have to calculate the cell size for each LOD. Here, instead of calculating pow() three times, which is purely done for the sake of explanation, we can calculate it for lod0 only, and multiply each subsequent LOD cell size by 10.0:

```
float lod0 =
  gridCellSize * pow(10.0, floor(lodLevel+0));
float lod1 =
  gridCellSize * pow(10.0, floor(lodLevel+1));
float lod2 =
  gridCellSize * pow(10.0, floor(lodLevel+2));
```

5. To be able to draw antialiased lines using alpha transparency, we need to increase the screen coverage of our lines. Let's make sure each line covers up to 4 pixels:

```
dudv *= 4.0;
```

6. Now we should get a coverage alpha value that corresponds to each calculated LOD level of the grid. To do that, we calculate the absolute distances to the cell line centers for each LOD and pick the maximum coordinate:

```
float lod0a = max2( vec2(1.0) -
    abs(satv(mod(uv, lod0) / dudv) * 2.0 - vec2(1.0)) );
float lod1a = max2(vec2(1.0) -
    abs(satv(mod(uv, lod1) / dudv) * 2.0 - vec2(1.0)) );
float lod2a = max2(vec2(1.0) -
    abs(satv(mod(uv, lod2) / dudv) * 2.0 - vec2(1.0)) );
```

7. Nonzero alpha values represent non-empty transition areas of the grid. Let's blend between them using two colors to handle the LOD transitions:

```
vec4 c = lod2a > 0.0 ? gridColorThick : lod1a > 0.0 ?
    mix(gridColorThick, gridColorThin, lodFade) :
    gridColorThin;
```

8. Last but not least, make the grid disappear when it is far away from the camera. Use the `gridSize` value to calculate the opacity falloff:

```
float opacityFalloff =
    (1.0 - satf(length(uv) / gridSize));
```

9. Now we can blend between the LOD level alpha values and scale the result with the opacity falloff factor. The resulting pixel color value can be stored in the framebuffer:

```
c.a *= lod2a > 0.0 ? lod2a : lod1a > 0.0 ?
    lod1a : (lod0a * (1.0-lodFade));
c.a *= opacityFalloff;
out_FragColor = c;
```

10. The preceding shaders should be rendered using the following OpenGL state:

```
glClearColor(1.0f, 1.0f, 1.0f, 1.0f);
glEnable(GL_BLEND);
glBlendFunc(GL_SRC_ALPHA, GL_ONE_MINUS_SRC_ALPHA);

...

const PerFrameData = {
    .view = view,
    .proj = p,
    .cameraPos = glm::vec4(camera.getPosition(), 1.0f)
};
glNamedBufferSubData(perFrameDataBuffer, 0,
    kUniformBufferSize, &perFrameData);
glDrawArraysInstancedBaseInstance(
    GL_TRIANGLES, 0, 6, 1, 0);
```

View the complete example at `Chapter5/GL01_Grid` for a self-contained demo app. The camera can be controlled with the WSAD keys and a mouse. The resulting image should appear similar to the following screenshot:

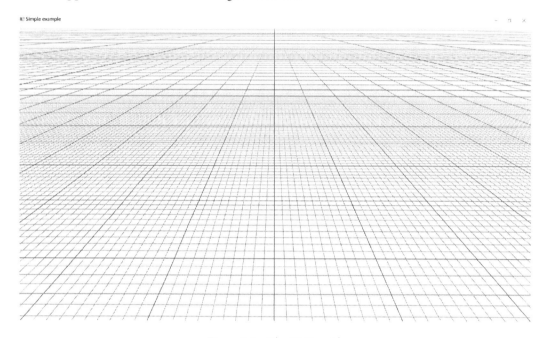

Figure 5.1 – The GLSL grid

There's more...

Besides only considering the distance to the camera to calculate the antialiasing falloff factor, we can use the angle between the viewing vector and the grid line. This will make the overall look and feel of the grid more visually pleasing and can be an interesting improvement if you want to implement a grid not only as an internal debugging tool but also as a part of a customer-facing product, such as an editor. Please refer to the *Our Machinery* blog for additional details about how to implement a more complicated grid (`https://ourmachinery.com/post/borderland-between-rendering-and-editor-part-1`).

Rendering multiple meshes with OpenGL

In the previous recipes, we learned how to build a mesh preprocessing pipeline and convert 3D meshes from data exchange formats, such as `.obj` or `.gltf2`, into our runtime mesh data format and render it via the Vulkan API. Let's switch gears and examine how to render this converted data using OpenGL.

Getting ready

The full source code for this recipe is located in `Chapter5/GL03_MeshRenderer`. It is recommended that you revisit the *Implementing a geometry conversion tool* recipe before continuing further.

How to do it...

Let's implement a simple `GLMesh` helper class to render our mesh using OpenGL:

1. The constructor accepts pointers to the indices and vertices data buffers. The data buffers are used as-is, and they are uploaded directly into the respective OpenGL buffers. The number of indices is inferred from the indices buffer size, assuming the indices are stored as 32-bit unsigned integers:

```
class GLMesh final {
public:
  GLMesh(const uint32_t* indices,
    uint32_t indicesSizeBytes,
    const float* vertexData,
    uint32_t verticesSizeBytes)
  : numIndices_(indicesSizeBytes / sizeof(uint32_t))
  , bufferIndices_(indicesSizeBytes, indices, 0)
  , bufferVertices_(verticesSizeBytes, vertexData, 0)
  {
    glCreateVertexArrays(1, &vao_);
    glVertexArrayElementBuffer(
      vao_, bufferIndices_.getHandle());
    glVertexArrayVertexBuffer(vao_, 0,
      bufferVertices_.getHandle(), 0, sizeof(vec3));
```

2. The vertex data format for this recipe only contains vertices that are represented as `vec3`:

```
    glEnableVertexArrayAttrib(vao_, 0);
    glVertexArrayAttribFormat(
      vao_, 0, 3, GL_FLOAT, GL_FALSE, 0);
    glVertexArrayAttribBinding(vao_, 0, 0);
  }
```

3. The `draw()` method binds the associated OpenGL vertex array object and renders the entire mesh:

```
  void draw() const {
    glBindVertexArray(vao_);
```

```
        glDrawElements(GL_TRIANGLES,
          static_cast<GLsizei>(numIndices_),
          GL_UNSIGNED_INT, nullptr);
      }
```

4. The destructor takes care of removing the **vertex array object** (**VAO**), and that is pretty much it:

```
      ~GLMesh() {
        glDeleteVertexArrays(1, &vao_);
      }
    private:
      GLuint vao_;
      uint32_t numIndices_;
      GLBuffer bufferIndices_;
      GLBuffer bufferVertices_;
    };
```

Now we should read the converted mesh data from our file and load it into a new GLMesh object. Let's discuss how to do this next. Perform the following steps:

1. First, we open the mesh file and read the MeshFileHeader structure, which was described in the *Implementing a geometry conversion tool* recipe:

```
FILE* f = fopen("data/meshes/test.meshes", "rb");
if (!f) {
  printf("Unable to open mesh file\n");
  exit(255);
}
MeshFileHeader header;
if (fread(&header, 1, sizeof(header), f) !=
      sizeof(header)) {
  printf("Unable to read mesh file header\n");
  exit(255);
}
```

2. Once the header has been retrieved, we use the number of meshes from the header to allocate space for the mesh descriptions. We store all of the Mesh structures inside a contiguous container so that all their data can be read from the file in one syscall. Rudimentary error checking will ensure that we read the number of elements that are equal to the number of meshes:

```
std::vector<Mesh> meshes1;
const auto meshCount = header.meshCount;
```

```
meshes1.resize(meshCount);
if (fread(meshes1.data(), sizeof(Mesh), meshCount, f)
        != meshCount) {
  printf("Could not read meshes\n");
  exit(255);
}
```

3. After loading the descriptions of each mesh, we should load the actual geometry into two containers, one for the indices and one for vertices. This code uses a shortcut, that is, the `indexDataSize` and `vertexDataSize` fields from the header:

```
std::vector<uint32_t> indexData;
std::vector<float> vertexData;
const auto idxDataSize = header.indexDataSize;
const auto vtxDataSize = header.vertexDataSize;
indexData.resize(idxDataSize / sizeof(uint32_t));
vertexData.resize(vtxDataSize / sizeof(float));
if ((fread(indexData.data(), 1, idxDataSize, f)
        != idxDataSize) ||
      (fread(vertexData.data(), 1, vtxDataSize, f)
        != vtxDataSize)) {
  printf("Unable to read index/vertex data\n");
  exit(255);
}
fclose(f);
```

4. The resulting index and vertex buffers can be used to invoke the `GLMesh` constructor and prepare our geometry data for rendering:

```
GLMesh mesh(indexData.data(), idxDataSize,
  vertexData.data(), vtxDataSize);
```

Now we can go ahead and configure the OpenGL for rendering. To do that, we follow these simple steps:

1. We should load all the necessary GLSL shaders for this demo app and link them into a shader program. One set of shaders is needed for grid rendering, as described in the *Implementing an infinite grid GLSL shader* recipe:

```
GLShader shdGridVertex(
  "data/shaders/chapter05/GL01_grid.vert");
GLShader shdGridFragment(
  "data/shaders/chapter05/GL01_grid.frag");
GLProgram progGrid(shdGridVertex, shdGridFragment);
```

2. Another set of shaders is needed to render the mesh itself. These shaders are mostly trivial and do not use the programmable vertex-pulling approach for the sake of brevity. So, we will omit their text here:

```
GLShader shaderVertex(
   "data/shaders/chapter05/GL03_mesh_inst.vert");
GLShader shaderGeometry(
   "data/shaders/chapter05/GL03_mesh_inst.geom");
GLShader shaderFragment(
   "data/shaders/chapter05/GL03_mesh_inst.frag");
GLProgram program(
   shaderVertex, shaderGeometry, shaderFragment);
```

3. Since everything in this example is packed into a single mesh, we can allocate a buffer with model-to-world matrices. In this case, it contains only one matrix:

```
const mat4 m(1.0f);
GLBuffer modelMatrices(
   sizeof(mat4), value_ptr(m), GL_DYNAMIC_STORAGE_BIT);
glBindBufferBase(GL_SHADER_STORAGE_BUFFER, 2,
   modelMatrices.getHandle());
```

4. The `modelMatrices` buffer binding slot number 2 corresponds to this description in the `GL03_mesh_inst.vert` shader:

```
layout(std430, binding = 2)
   restrict readonly buffer Matrices
{
   mat4 in_Model[];
}
```

5. We need to set up blending for grid rendering. The depth buffer is needed to correctly render a mesh:

```
glClearColor(1.0f, 1.0f, 1.0f, 1.0f);
glEnable(GL_BLEND);
glBlendFunc(GL_SRC_ALPHA, GL_ONE_MINUS_SRC_ALPHA);
glEnable(GL_DEPTH_TEST);
```

6. The mesh and the grid are rendered as follows:

```
glEnable(GL_DEPTH_TEST);
glDisable(GL_BLEND);
program.useProgram();
mesh.draw();
glDisable(GL_DEPTH_TEST);
```

```
glEnable(GL_BLEND);
progGrid.useProgram();
glDrawArraysInstancedBaseInstance
  (GL_TRIANGLES, 0, 6, 1, 0);
```

The running application will render an image of the Lumberyard Bistro mesh that looks similar to the following screenshot:

Figure 5.2 – The Amazon Lumberyard Bistro mesh geometry loaded and rendered

Generating LODs using MeshOptimizer

Earlier in this chapter, in the *Implementing a geometry conversion tool* recipe, we talked about preprocessing a mesh so that we can store it in a runtime efficient data format. One important part of the preprocessing pipeline is **optimizing geometry** and generating simplified meshes for real-time discrete LOD algorithms that we might want to use later. Let's learn how to generate simplified meshes using the MeshOptimizer library.

Getting ready

It is recommended that you revisit the *Introducing MeshOptimizer* recipe from *Chapter 2, Using Essential Libraries*. The complete source code for this recipe can be found in `Chapter5/MeshConvert`.

How to do it...

We are going to add a `processLODs()` function to our MeshConverter tool so that we can generate all of the necessary LOD meshes for a specified set of indices and vertices. Let's go through this function step by step to learn how to do it:

1. The LOD meshes are represented as a collection of indices that construct a new simplified mesh from the same vertices that are used for the original mesh. This way, we only have to store one set of vertices and can render the corresponding LODs by simply switching the index buffer data. As we did earlier, for simplicity, we store all of the indices as unsigned 32-bit integers:

   ```
   void processLODs(
     std::vector<uint32_t> indices,
     const std::vector<float>& vertices,
     std::vector<std::vector<uint32_t>>& outLods)
   {
   ```

2. Each vertex is constructed from 3 float values, hence the hardcoded value here:

   ```
   size_t verticesCountIn = vertices.size() / 3;
   size_t targetIndicesCount = indices.size();
   ```

3. The first "zero" LOD corresponds to the original mesh indices. Push it as-is into the resulting container and print some debug information:

   ```
   uint8_t LOD = 1;
   printf("\n   LOD0: %i indices",
     int(indices.size()));
   outLods.push_back(indices);
   ```

4. Let's iterate until the number of indices in the last LOD drops below `1024` or the total number of generated LODs reaches 8. Each subsequent LOD is supposed to have half of the number of indices from the previous LOD. The MeshOptimizer library implements two simplification algorithms. The first one, implemented in the `meshopt_simplify()` function, tries to follow the topology of the original mesh. This is so that the attribute seams, borders, and overall appearance can be preserved. The target error value of `0.02` corresponds to the 2% deviation from the original mesh:

   ```
   while ( targetIndicesCount > 1024 && LOD < 8 ) {
     targetIndicesCount = indices.size()/2;
   ```

```
bool sloppy = false;
size_t numOptIndices = meshopt_simplify(
   indices.data(),
   indices.data(), (uint32_t)indices.size(),
   vertices.data(), verticesCountIn,
   sizeof( float ) * 3,
   targetIndicesCount, 0.02f );
```

5. The second simplification algorithm implemented in `meshopt_simplifySloppy()` does not follow the topology of the original mesh. This means it can be more aggressive by collapsing internal mesh details that are too small to matter because they are topologically disjointed but spatially close. We will switch to this aggressive algorithm in case the first algorithm is unable to achieve a significant reduction of the index count by at least 10%. If the aggressive version of the algorithm cannot improve the situation, we should just give up and terminate the sequence:

```
if (static_cast<size_t>(numOptIndices * 1.1f) >
      indices.size()) {
   if (LOD > 1) {
      numOptIndices = meshopt_simplifySloppy(
         indices.data(),
         indices.data(), indices.size(),
         vertices.data(), verticesCountIn,
         sizeof(float) * 3,
         targetIndicesCount);
      sloppy = true;
      if ( numOptIndices == indices.size() ) break;
   }
   else break;
}
```

6. A new set of indices is generated, and we can truncate the total number to match the output of the simplification process. Let's optimize each LOD for the vertex cache, as described in the *Introducing MeshOptimizer* recipe from *Chapter 2, Using Essential Libraries*. The resulting set of indices is ready to be stored as the next LOD:

```
indices.resize( numOptIndices );
meshopt_optimizeVertexCache(
   indices.data(), indices.data(),
   indices.size(), verticesCountIn );
printf("\n   LOD%i: %i indices %s",
   int(LOD), int(numOptIndices),
   sloppy ? "[sloppy]" : "");
```

```
      LOD++;
      outLods.push_back(indices);
    }
  }
```

This code will generate up to eight LOD meshes for a given set of indices and vertices, and it will store them inside our runtime mesh format data structures. We will learn how to make use of these LODs in *Chapter 10, Advanced Rendering Techniques and Optimizations*.

There's more...

The MeshOptimizer library contains many other useful algorithms, such as triangle strip generation, index and vertex buffer compression, mesh animation data compression, and more. All of these might be very useful for your geometry preprocessing stage, depending on the kind of graphics software you are writing. Please refer to the official documentation and releases page to view the latest features. You can find this at `https://github.com/zeux/meshoptimizer`.

Integrating tessellation into the OpenGL graphics pipeline

Now, let's switch gears and learn how to integrate hardware tessellation functionality into the OpenGL 4.6 graphics rendering pipeline.

Hardware tessellation is a feature that was introduced in OpenGL 4.0. It is implemented as a set of two new shader stages types in the graphics pipeline. The first shader stage is called the **tessellation control shader**, and the second stage is called the **tessellation evaluation shader**. The tessellation control shader operates on a set of vertices, which are called control points and define a geometric surface called a patch. The shader can manipulate the control points and calculate the required tessellation level. The tessellation evaluation shader can access the barycentric coordinates of the tessellated triangles and can use them to interpolate any per-vertex attributes that are required, such as texture coordinates, colors, and more. Let's go through the code to examine how these OpenGL pipeline stages can be used to triangulate a mesh depending on the distance from the camera.

Getting ready

The complete source code for this recipe is located in `Chapter5/GL02_Tessellation`.

How to do it...

Before we can tackle the actual GLSL shaders, we should augment our OpenGL shader loading code with a new shader type:

1. To do that, we should change the `GLShaderTypeFromFileName()` helper function in the following way:

```
GLenum GLShaderTypeFromFileName(const char* fileName)
{
  if (endsWith(fileName, ".vert"))
    return GL_VERTEX_SHADER;
  if (endsWith(fileName, ".frag"))
    return GL_FRAGMENT_SHADER;
  if (endsWith(fileName, ".geom"))
    return GL_GEOMETRY_SHADER;
  if (endsWith(fileName, ".tesc"))
    return GL_TESS_CONTROL_SHADER;
  if (endsWith(fileName, ".tese"))
    return GL_TESS_EVALUATION_SHADER;
  if (endsWith(fileName, ".comp"))
    return GL_COMPUTE_SHADER;
  assert(false);
  return 0;
}
```

2. The additional constructor for `GLProgram` can now swallow five different shaders at once. This should be sufficient to simultaneously accommodate vertex, tessellation control, tessellation evaluation, geometry, and fragment shaders in a single OpenGL shader program:

```
GLProgram(const GLShader& a, const GLShader& b,
    const GLShader& c, const GLShader& d,
    const GLShader& e);
```

3. This implementation is similar to other constructors and simply attaches all of the shaders, one by one, to the program object:

```
GLProgram::GLProgram(
  const GLShader& a, const GLShader& b,
  const GLShader& c, const GLShader& d,
  const GLShader& e)
: handle_(glCreateProgram())
{
  glAttachShader(handle_, a.getHandle());
  glAttachShader(handle_, b.getHandle());
```

```
glAttachShader(handle_, c.getHandle());
glAttachShader(handle_, d.getHandle());
glAttachShader(handle_, e.getHandle());
glLinkProgram(handle_);
printProgramInfoLog(handle_);
}
```

What we want to do now is write shaders that will calculate per-vertex tessellation levels based on the distance to the camera. In this way, we can render more geometrical details in the areas that are closer to the viewer. To do that, we should start with a vertex shader, such as data\shaders\chapter05\.

GL02_duck.vert, which will compute the world positions of the vertices and pass them down to the tessellation control shader:

1. Our per-frame data consists of the usual view and projection matrices, together with the current camera position in the world space, and the tessellation scaling factor, which is user-controlled and comes from an ImGui widget:

```
#version 460 core
layout(std140, binding = 0) uniform PerFrameData {
  mat4 view;
  mat4 proj;
  vec4 cameraPos;
  float tessellationScale;
};
```

2. Geometry is accessed using the programmable vertex-pulling technique and stored in the following format, using vec3 for the vertex positions and vec2 for the texture coordinates:

```
struct Vertex {
  float p[3];
  float tc[2];
};
layout(std430, binding = 1)
  restrict readonly buffer Vertices
{
  Vertex in_Vertices[];
};
```

3. The model-to-world matrices are stored in a single shader storage buffer object:

```
layout(std430, binding = 2)
   restrict readonly buffer Matrices
   {
   mat4 in_Model[];
};
```

4. Let's write some helper functions to access the vertex positions and texture coordinates using traditional GLSL data types:

```
vec3 getPosition(int i) {
   return vec3(
      in_Vertices[i].p[0], in_Vertices[i].p[1],
      in_Vertices[i].p[2]);
}
vec2 getTexCoord(int i) {
   return vec2(
      in_Vertices[i].tc[0], in_Vertices[i].tc[1]);
}
```

5. The vertex shader outputs UV texture coordinates and per-vertex world positions. The actual calculation is done as follows. Note that the `gl_DrawID` variable is used to index the matrices buffer:

```
layout (location=0) out vec2 uv_in;
layout (location=1) out vec3 worldPos_in;
void main() {
   mat4 MVP = proj * view * in_Model[gl_DrawID];
   vec3 pos = getPosition(gl_VertexID);
   gl_Position = MVP * vec4(pos, 1.0);
   uv_in = getTexCoord(gl_VertexID);
   worldPos_in =
      ( in_Model[gl_DrawID] * vec4(pos, 1.0) ).xyz;
}
```

Now we can move on to the next shader stage and view the tessellation control shader, data/shaders/chapter05/GL02_duck.tesc:

1. The shader operates on a group of 3 vertices, which correspond to a single triangle in the input data. The uv_in and worldPos_in variables correspond to the ones in the vertex shader. Here, notice how we have arrays instead of single solitary values:

```glsl
#version 460 core
layout (vertices = 3) out;
layout (location = 0) in vec2 uv_in[];
layout (location = 1) in vec3 worldPos_in[];
```

2. The PerFrameData structure should be exactly the same for all of the shader stages in this example:

```glsl
layout(std140, binding = 0) uniform PerFrameData {
  mat4 view;
  mat4 proj;
  vec4 cameraPos;
  float tessellationScale;
};
```

3. Let's describe the input and output data structures that correspond to each individual vertex. Besides the required vertex position, we store the vec2 texture coordinates:

```glsl
in gl_PerVertex {
  vec4 gl_Position;
} gl_in[];

out gl_PerVertex {
  vec4 gl_Position;
} gl_out[];

struct vertex {
  vec2 uv;
};
layout(location = 0) out vertex Out[];
```

4. The `getTessLevel()` function calculates the desired tessellation level based on the distance of two adjacent vertices from the camera. The hardcoded distance values, which are used to switch the levels, are scaled using the `tessellationScale` uniform coming from the user interface:

```
float getTessLevel(float distance0, float distance1) {
  const float distanceScale1 = 7.0;
  const float distanceScale2 = 10.0;
  const float avgDistance =
    (distance0 + distance1) * 0.5;
  if (avgDistance <=
      distanceScale1 * tessellationScale)
    return 5.0;
  else if (avgDistance <=
           distanceScale2 * tessellationScale)
    return 3.0;
  return 1.0;
}
```

5. The `main()` function is straightforward. It passes the positions and UV coordinates as-is and then calculates the distance from each vertex in the triangle to the camera:

```
void main() {
  gl_out[gl_InvocationID].gl_Position =
    gl_in[gl_InvocationID].gl_Position;
  Out[gl_InvocationID].uv = uv_in[gl_InvocationID];
  vec3 c = cameraPos.xyz;
  float eyeToVertexDistance0 =
    distance(c, worldPos_in[0]);
  float eyeToVertexDistance1 =
    distance(c, worldPos_in[1]);
  float eyeToVertexDistance2 =
    distance(c, worldPos_in[2]);
```

6. Based on these distances, we can calculate the required inner and outer tessellation levels in the following way:

```
  gl_TessLevelOuter[0] = getTessLevel(
    eyeToVertexDistance1, eyeToVertexDistance2);
  gl_TessLevelOuter[1] = getTessLevel(
    eyeToVertexDistance2, eyeToVertexDistance0);
  gl_TessLevelOuter[2] = getTessLevel(
    eyeToVertexDistance0, eyeToVertexDistance1);
  gl_TessLevelInner[0] = gl_TessLevelOuter[2];
};
```

Let's take a look at the data/shaders/chapter05/GL02_duck.tese tessellation evaluation shader:

1. We should specify the triangles as input. The equal_spacing spacing mode tells OpenGL that the n tessellation level should be clamped to a range of 0...64 and rounded to the nearest integer. After that, the corresponding edge should be divided into n equal segments. When the tessellation primitive generator produces triangles, the orientation of the triangles can be specified by an input layout declaration using the cw and ccw identifiers. We use the counter-clockwise orientation:

```glsl
#version 460 core
layout(triangles, equal_spacing, ccw) in;
struct vertex {
  vec2 uv;
};
in gl_PerVertex {
  vec4 gl_Position;
} gl_in[];
layout(location = 0) in vertex In[];
out gl_PerVertex {
  vec4 gl_Position;
};
layout (location=0) out vec2 uv;
```

2. These two helper functions are useful to interpolate between the vec2 and vec4 attribute values at the corners of the original triangle using the barycentric coordinates of the current vertex. The built-in gl_TessCoord variable contains the required barycentric coordinates:

```glsl
vec2 interpolate2(in vec2 v0, in vec2 v1, in vec2 v2){
  return v0 * gl_TessCoord.x +
         v1 * gl_TessCoord.y +
         v2 * gl_TessCoord.z;
}
vec4 interpolate4(in vec4 v0, in vec4 v1, in vec4 v2){
  return v0 * gl_TessCoord.x +
         v1 * gl_TessCoord.y +
         v2 * gl_TessCoord.z;
}
```

3. The actual interpolation code is straightforward and can be written in the following way:

```
void main() {
  gl_Position = interpolate4(gl_in[0].gl_Position,
                             gl_in[1].gl_Position,
                             gl_in[2].gl_Position);
  uv = interpolate2(In[0].uv, In[1].uv, In[2].uv);
};
```

The next stage of our hardware tessellation graphics pipeline is the data/shaders/chapter05/GL02_duck.geom geometry shader. We use it to generate barycentric coordinates for all of the small tessellated triangles. It is used to render a nice antialiased wireframe overlay on top of our colored mesh, as described in *Chapter 2*, *Using Essential Libraries*:

1. The geometry shader consumes triangles that have been generated by the tessellation hardware and outputs triangle strips, each consisting of a single triangle:

```
#version 460 core
layout (triangles) in;
layout (triangle_strip, max_vertices = 3) out;
layout (location=0) in vec2 uv[];
layout (location=0) out vec2 uvs;
layout (location=1) out vec3 barycoords;
void main() {
```

2. Barycentric coordinates are assigned per vertex using these hardcoded constants:

```
const vec3 bc[3] = vec3[] (
  vec3(1.0, 0.0, 0.0),
  vec3(0.0, 1.0, 0.0),
  vec3(0.0, 0.0, 1.0)
);
for ( int i = 0; i < 3; i++ ) {
  gl_Position = gl_in[i].gl_Position;
  uvs = uv[i];
  barycoords = bc[i];
  EmitVertex();
}
EndPrimitive();
}
```

The final stage of this rendering pipeline is the `data\shaders\chapter05\GL02_` `duck.frag` fragment shader:

1. We take in the barycentric coordinates from the geometry shader and use them to calculate a wireframe overlay for our mesh:

```
#version 460 core
layout (location=0) in vec2 uvs;
layout (location=1) in vec3 barycoords;
layout (location=0) out vec4 out_FragColor;
layout (location=0) uniform sampler2D texture0;
```

2. A helper function returns the blending factor based on the distance to the edge and the desired thickness of the wireframe contour:

```
float edgeFactor(float thickness) {
  vec3 a3 = smoothstep(vec3(0.0),
    fwidth(barycoords) * thickness, barycoords);
  return min( min( a3.x, a3.y ), a3.z );
}
```

3. Let's sample the texture using the UV values and call it a day:

```
void main() {
  vec4 color = texture(texture0, uvs);
  out_FragColor =
    mix( color * vec4(0.8), color, edgeFactor(1.0) );
};
```

The GLSL shader part of our OpenGL hardware tessellation pipeline is over. Now it is time to look at the C++ code. The source code is located in the `Chapter5/GL02_` `Tessellation/src/main.cpp` file:

1. The shaders for the tessellated mesh rendering are loaded in the following way:

```
GLShader shaderVertex(
  "data/shaders/chapter05/GL02_duck.vert");
GLShader shaderTessControl(
  "data/shaders/chapter05/GL02_duck.tesc");
GLShader shaderTessEval(
  "data/shaders/chapter05/GL02_duck.tese");
GLShader shaderGeometry(
  "data/shaders/chapter05/GL02_duck.geom");
GLShader shaderFragment(
  "data/shaders/chapter05/GL02_duck.frag");
```

2. Now we can use our helper class to link everything inside an OpenGL shader program:

```
GLProgram program(shaderVertex, shaderTessControl,
    shaderTessEval,shaderGeometry, shaderFragment);
```

The data/rubber_duck/scene.gltf mesh loading code is identical to that of the previous chapter, so we will skip it here. What's more important is how we render the ImGui widget to control the tessellation scale factor:

1. First, we define an ImGuiGLRenderer object, which will take care of all the ImGui rendering functionality, as described in the *Rendering a basic UI with Dear ImGui* recipe from *Chapter 2*, *Using Essential Libraries*. The minimalist implementation we provide can be found in the shared/glFramework/UtilsGLImGui.h file:

```
ImGuiGLRenderer rendererUI;
```

2. Inside our frame rendering loop, we can access all the ImGui rendering functionality as usual. Here, we just render a single slider containing a floating-point value for the tessellation scale factor:

```
io.DisplaySize = ImVec2((float)width, (float)height);
ImGui::NewFrame();
ImGui::SliderFloat("Tessellation scale",
    &tessellationScale, 1.0f, 2.0f, "%.1f");
ImGui::Render();
```

3. After we have issued all the ImGui drawing commands, we can render the resulting user interface using a single call to ImGuiGLRenderer::render(). The implementation will take care of all the necessary OpenGL render states to draw the ImGui data:

```
rendererUI.render(
    width, height, ImGui::GetDrawData() );
```

Here is a screenshot of the running demo application:

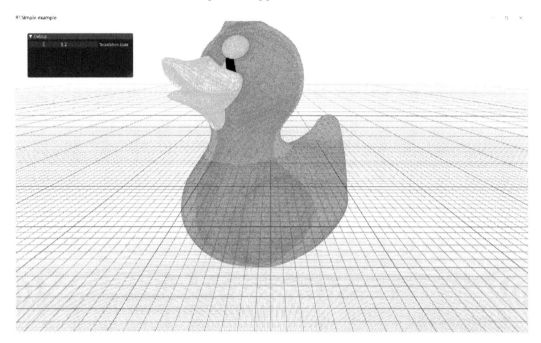

Figure 5.3 – A tessellated duck

Note how the different tessellation levels vary based on the distance to the camera. Try playing with the control slider to emphasize the effect.

There's more...

This recipe can be used as a cornerstone to hardware mesh tessellation techniques in your OpenGL applications. One natural step forward would be to apply a displacement map to the fine-grained tessellated vertices using the direction of normal vectors. Please refer to https://www.geeks3d.com/20100804/test-opengl-4-tessellation-with-displacement-mapping for inspiration. If you want to go serious on the adaptive tessellation of subdivision surfaces, there is a chapter in the *GPU Gems 2* book, which covers this advanced topic in more detail.

6

Physically Based Rendering Using the glTF2 Shading Model

This chapter will cover the integration of **Physically Based Rendering** (PBR) into your graphics pipeline. We use the **Graphics Language Transmission Format 2.0** (glTF 2.0) shading model as an example. PBR is not a single specific technique but rather a set of concepts, like using measured surface values and realistic shading models, to accurately represent real-world materials. Adding PBR to your graphics application or retrofitting an existing rendering engine with PBR might be challenging because it requires multiple big steps to be completed and work simultaneously before a correct image can be rendered.

Our goal here is to show how to implement all these steps from scratch. Some of these steps, such as precomputing irradiance maps or **bidirectional reflectance distribution function (BRDF) lookup tables (LUTs)**, require additional tools to be written. We are not going to use any third-party tools here and will show how to implement the entire skeleton of a PBR pipeline from the ground up. Some pre-calculations can be done using **general-purpose graphics processing unit (GPGPU)** techniques and compute shaders, which will be covered here as well. We assume our readers have some basic understanding of PBR. For those who wish to acquire this knowledge, make sure you read the free book *Physically Based Rendering: From Theory To Implementation* by Matt Pharr, Wenzel Jakob, and Greg Humphreys, available online at `http://www.pbr-book.org/`.

In this chapter, we will learn the following recipes:

- Simplifying Vulkan initialization and frame composition
- Initializing compute shaders in Vulkan
- Using descriptor indexing and texture arrays in Vulkan
- Using descriptor indexing in Vulkan to render an ImGui **user interface (UI)**
- Generating textures in Vulkan using compute shaders
- Implementing computed meshes in Vulkan
- Precomputing BRDF LUTs
- Precomputing irradiance maps and diffuse convolution
- Implementing the glTF2 shading model

Technical requirements

Here is what it takes to run the code from this chapter on your Linux or Windows PC. You will need a **graphics processing unit (GPU)** with recent drivers supporting OpenGL 4.6 and Vulkan 1.2. The source code can be downloaded from `https://github.com/PacktPublishing/3D-Graphics-Rendering-Cookbook`. To run the demo applications from this chapter, you are advised to download and unpack the entire Amazon Lumberyard Bistro dataset from the *McGuire Computer Graphics Archive*, at `http://casual-effects.com/data/index.html`. Of course, you can use smaller meshes if you cannot download the 2.4 **gigabyte (GB)** package.

Simplifying Vulkan initialization and frame composition

Before jumping into this chapter, let's learn how to generalize Vulkan application initialization for all of our remaining demos and how to extract common parts of the frame composition code.

How to do it...

The **Graphics Library Framework** (**GLFW**) window creation and Vulkan rendering surface initialization are performed in the `initVulkanApp` function. Let's take a closer look:

1. A `Resolution` structure can be passed as an optional parameter:

    ```
    struct Resolution {
      uint32_t width  = 0;
      uint32_t height = 0;
    };
    GLFWwindow* initVulkanApp(
      int width, int height,
      Resolution* outResolution = nullptr)
    {
    ```

2. In our examples, we always use the `glslang` compiler and the **Vector-Optimized Library of Kernels** (**VOLK**) library. If anything goes wrong with initialization, we terminate the application:

    ```
    glslang_initialize_process();
    volkInitialize();
    if (!glfwInit() || !glfwVulkanSupported())
      exit(EXIT_FAILURE);
    ```

3. As in *Chapter 3*, *Getting Started with OpenGL and Vulkan*, we tell GLFW we do not need any graphics **application programming interface** (**API**) context:

    ```
    glfwWindowHint(GLFW_CLIENT_API, GLFW_NO_API);
    glfwWindowHint(GLFW_RESIZABLE, GL_FALSE);
    ```

4. If the `outResolution` argument is not `null`, we store the detected window
    resolution in there for further use. The `detectResolution()` function is shown
    in the following code snippet. The `width` and `height` parameters are passed as
    a reference. If these values are negative, we consider them as percentages of the
    screen's width and height:

```
if (resolution) {
  *resolution = detectResolution(width, height);
  width  = resolution->width;
  height = resolution->height;
}
```

5. Once we have the detected window resolution, we create a GLFW window. If an
    application requires a different window title, this is the place to set it. If the window
    creation fails, we terminate the GLFW library and application:

```
GLFWwindow* result = glfwCreateWindow(
    width, height, "VulkanApp", nullptr, nullptr);
if (!result) {
  glfwTerminate();
  exit(EXIT_FAILURE);
}
return result;
}
```

Let's take a look at the `detectResolution()` function. The actual resolution detection
happens in `glfwGetVideoMode()`. For our purposes, we get the parameters of the
"primary" monitor. In multi-display configurations, we should properly determine which
monitor displays our application; however, this goes beyond the scope of this book. The
video-mode information for the selected monitor provides us screen dimensions in pixels.
If the provided width or height values are positive, they are used directly. Negative values
are treated as a percentage of the screen:

```
Resolution detectResolution(int width, int height) {
  GLFWmonitor* monitor = glfwGetPrimaryMonitor();
  if (glfwGetError(nullptr)) exit(EXIT_FAILURE);
  const GLFWvidmode* info = glfwGetVideoMode(monitor);
  const uint32_t W = width  >= 0 ?
    width  : (uint32_t)(info->width * width / -100);
```

```
  const uint32_t H = height >= 0 ?
    height : (uint32_t)(info->height * height / -100);
  return Resolution{ .width = W, .height = H };
}
```

To render and present a single frame on the screen, we implement the `drawFrame()` function, which contains the common frame-composition code refactored from the previous chapters.

1. Two `std::function` callbacks, `updateBuffersFunc()` and `composeFrameFunc()`, are used to encapsulate all application-specific rendering code. The `drawFrame()` function is used in all the remaining Vulkan demos as the main frame composer:

```
bool drawFrame(VulkanRenderDevice& vkDev,
  const std::function<void(uint32_t)>&
    updateBuffersFunc,
  const std::function<void(VkCommandBuffer,
    uint32_t)>& composeFrameFunc)
{
```

2. Before we can render anything on the screen, we should acquire a framebuffer image from the swapchain. When the next image in the swapchain is not ready to be rendered, we return `false`. This is not a fatal error but an indication that no frame has been rendered yet. The calling code decides what to do with the result. One example of such a reaction can be skipping the **frames-per-second** (**FPS**) counter update:

```
uint32_t imageIndex = 0;
VkResult result = vkAcquireNextImageKHR(
  vkDev.device, vkDev.swapchain, 0,
  vkDev.semaphore, VK_NULL_HANDLE, &imageIndex);
if (result != VK_SUCCESS) return false;
```

3. The global command pool is reset to allow the filling of the command buffers anew:

```
VK_CHECK( vkResetCommandPool(
  vkDev.device, vkDev.commandPool, 0) );
```

4. The `updateBuffersFunc()` callback is invoked to update all the internal buffers for different renderers. Revisit the *Organizing Vulkan frame rendering code* recipe from *Chapter 4, Adding User Interaction and Productivity Tools* for a discussion of frame composition. This can be done in a more effective way—for example, by using a dedicated transfer queue and without waiting for all the GPU transfers to complete. For the purpose of this book, we deliberately choose code simplicity over performance. A command buffer, corresponding to the selected swapchain image, is acquired:

```
updateBuffersFunc(imageIndex);
VkCommandBuffer commandBuffer =
  vkDev.commandBuffers[imageIndex];
const VkCommandBufferBeginInfo bi = {
  .sType =
    VK_STRUCTURE_TYPE_COMMAND_BUFFER_BEGIN_INFO,
  .pNext = nullptr,
  .flags =
    VK_COMMAND_BUFFER_USAGE_SIMULTANEOUS_USE_BIT,
  .pInheritanceInfo = nullptr
};
VK_CHECK(vkBeginCommandBuffer(commandBuffer, &bi));
```

5. After we have started recording to the command buffer, the `composeFrameFunc()` callback is invoked to write the command buffer's contents from different renderers. There is a large potential for optimizations here because Vulkan provides a primary-secondary command buffer separation, which can be used to record secondary buffers from multiple **central processing unit (CPU)** threads. Once all the renderers have contributed to the command buffer, we stop recording:

```
composeFrameFunc(commandBuffer, imageIndex);
VK_CHECK(vkEndCommandBuffer(commandBuffer));
```

Next comes the submission of the recorded command buffer to a GPU graphics queue. The code is identical to that in *Chapter 3, Getting Started with OpenGL and Vulkan*:

```
const VkPipelineStageFlags waitStages[] = {
  VK_PIPELINE_STAGE_COLOR_ATTACHMENT_OUTPUT_BIT
};
const VkSubmitInfo si = {
  .sType = VK_STRUCTURE_TYPE_SUBMIT_INFO,
  .pNext = nullptr,
  .waitSemaphoreCount = 1,
```

```
    .pWaitSemaphores = &vkDev.semaphore,
    .pWaitDstStageMask = waitStages,
    .commandBufferCount = 1,
    .pCommandBuffers =
      &vkDev.commandBuffers[imageIndex],
    .signalSemaphoreCount = 1,
    .pSignalSemaphores = &vkDev.renderSemaphore
  };
  VK_CHECK(vkQueueSubmit(
    vkDev.graphicsQueue, 1, &si, nullptr));
```

6. After submitting the command buffer to the graphics queue, the swapchain is presented to the screen:

```
const VkPresentInfoKHR pi = {
  .sType = VK_STRUCTURE_TYPE_PRESENT_INFO_KHR,
  .pNext = nullptr,
  .waitSemaphoreCount = 1,
  .pWaitSemaphores = &vkDev.renderSemaphore,
  .swapchainCount = 1,
  .pSwapchains = &vkDev.swapchain,
  .pImageIndices = &imageIndex
};
VK_CHECK(vkQueuePresentKHR(
  vkDev.graphicsQueue, &pi));
```

7. The final call to vkDeviceWaitIdle() ensures we have no frame tearing:

```
VK_CHECK(vkDeviceWaitIdle(vkDev.device));
return true;
}
```

More sophisticated synchronization schemes with multiple in-flight frames can help to gain performance. However, those are beyond the scope of this book.

Initializing compute shaders in Vulkan

Up until now, we used only graphics-capable command queues on a Vulkan device. This time, we have to find device queues that are also capable of **GPGPU** computations. In Vulkan, such queues allow execution of compute shaders, which can read from and write to buffers used in the graphics rendering pipeline. For example, in *Chapter 10*, *Advanced Rendering Techniques and Optimizations*, we will show how to implement a GPU frustum culling technique by modifying the indirect rendering buffer introduced in the *Indirect rendering in Vulkan* recipe from *Chapter 5*, *Working with Geometry Data*.

Getting ready

The first thing we need to do to start using compute shaders is to revisit the render device initialization covered in *Chapter 3, Getting Started with OpenGL and Vulkan*. Check out the *Initializing Vulkan instances and graphical device* recipe before moving forward.

How to do it...

We add the code to search for a compute-capable device queue and to create a separate command buffer for compute shader workloads. Since the graphics hardware may not provide a separate command queue for arbitrary computations, our device and queue initialization logic must somehow remember if the graphics and compute queues are the same.

> **Note**
>
> On the other hand, using separate Vulkan queues for graphics and compute tasks enables the underlying Vulkan implementation to reduce the amount of work done on the GPU, by making decisions on the device about what sort of work is generated and how this is generated. This is especially important when dealing with GPU-generated commands. Check out the post *New: Vulkan Device Generated Commands* by Christoph Kubisch from NVIDIA, at `https://developer.nvidia.com/blog/new-vulkan-device-generated-commands/`.

Let's learn how to do it.

1. As a starter, we declare new GPGPU-related fields in the `VulkanRenderDevice` class. The first one is a flag that signals whether this device supports compute shaders. Although the compute shader support is guaranteed to be true by the Vulkan specification if the device is capable of graphics operations, we show how to use this flag in our code:

    ```
    bool useCompute = false;
    ```

2. The next two fields hold the index and handle of an internal queue for compute shaders' execution. If the device does not support a dedicated compute queue, the values of the `computeFamily` and the `graphicsFamily` fields are equal:

    ```
    uint32_t computeFamily;
    VkQueue computeQueue;
    ```

Since we may want to use more than one device queue, we have to store indices and handles for each of those. This is needed because `VkBuffer` objects are bound to the device queue at creation time. For example, to use a vertex buffer generated by a compute shader in a graphics pipeline, we have to allocate this `VkBuffer` object explicitly, specifying the list of queues from which this buffer may be accessed. Later in this recipe, we introduce the `createSharedBuffer()` routine that explicitly uses these stored queue indices.

> **Note**
>
> Buffers are created with a sharing mode, controlling how they can be accessed from queues. Buffers created using `VK_SHARING_MODE_EXCLUSIVE` must only be accessed by queues in the queue family that has ownership of the resource. Buffers created using `VK_SHARING_MODE_CONCURRENT` must only be accessed by queues from the queue families specified through the `queueFamilyIndexCount` and `pQueueFamilyIndices` members of the corresponding `...CreateInfo` structures. Concurrent sharing mode may result in lower performance compared to exclusive mode. Refer to the Vulkan specifications for more details, at `https://www.khronos.org/registry/vulkan/specs/1.2-extensions/man/html/VkSharingMode.html`.

3. The lists of initialized queue indices and appropriate queue handles are stored in two dynamic arrays:

```
std::vector<uint32_t> deviceQueueIndices;
std::vector<VkQueue> deviceQueues;
```

4. Finally, we need a command buffer and a command buffer pool to create and run compute shader instances:

```
VkCommandBuffer computeCommandBuffer;
VkCommandPool computeCommandPool;
```

Now, let's learn how to initialize a rendering device capable of running compute shaders.

1. To avoid breaking previous demos, we proceed step by step and introduce the new `initVulkanRenderDeviceWithCompute()` routine:

```
bool initVulkanRenderDeviceWithCompute(
    VulkanInstance& vk,
    VulkanRenderDevice& vkDev,
    uint32_t width, uint32_t height,
    VkPhysicalDeviceFeatures deviceFeatures)
```

```
{
    vkDev.framebufferWidth = width;
    vkDev.framebufferHeight = height;
```

2. After finding the physical device and graphics queue, we also search for the compute-capable queue. This code will find a combined graphics plus compute queue even on devices that support a separate compute queue, as the combined queue tends to have a lower index. For simplicity, we use this approach throughout the book:

```
VK_CHECK(findSuitablePhysicalDevice(
    vk.instance, &isDeviceSuitable,
    &vkDev.physicalDevice));
vkDev.graphicsFamily = findQueueFamilies(
    vkDev.physicalDevice, VK_QUEUE_GRAPHICS_BIT);
vkDev.computeFamily = findQueueFamilies(
    vkDev.physicalDevice, VK_QUEUE_COMPUTE_BIT);
```

3. To initialize both queues, or a single one if these queues are the same, we call a new function, createDeviceWithCompute(), as illustrated in the following code snippet:

```
VK_CHECK(createDeviceWithCompute(
    vkDev.physicalDevice, deviceFeatures,
    vkDev.graphicsFamily, vkDev.computeFamily,
    &vkDev.device));
```

4. Next, we save unique queue indices for later use in the createSharedBuffer() routine:

```
vkDev.deviceQueueIndices.push_back(
    vkDev.graphicsFamily);
if (vkDev.graphicsFamily != vkDev.computeFamily)
    vkDev.deviceQueueIndices.push_back(
        vkDev.computeFamily);
```

5. After saving queue indices, we acquire the graphics and compute queue handles:

```
vkGetDeviceQueue(vkDev.device, vkDev.graphicsFamily,
    0, &vkDev.graphicsQueue);
if (!vkDev.graphicsQueue) exit(EXIT_FAILURE);
vkGetDeviceQueue(vkDev.device, vkDev.computeFamily,
    0, &vkDev.computeQueue);
if (!vkDev.computeQueue) exit(EXIT_FAILURE);
```

6. After initializing the queues, we create everything related to the swapchain. A few lines of the following code snippet are also identical to those in the rendering device initialization procedure described earlier in the *Initializing Vulkan instances and graphical devices* recipe in *Chapter 3, Getting Started with OpenGL and Vulkan*:

```
VkBool32 presentSupported = 0;
vkGetPhysicalDeviceSurfaceSupportKHR(
  vkDev.physicalDevice, vkDev.graphicsFamily,
  vk.surface, &presentSupported);
if (!presentSupported) exit(EXIT_FAILURE);
VK_CHECK(createSwapchain(vkDev.device,
  vkDev.physicalDevice, vk.surface,
  vkDev.graphicsFamily,
  width, height, vkDev.swapchain));
const size_t imageCount = createSwapchainImages(
  vkDev.device, vkDev.swapchain,
  vkDev.swapchainImages,
  vkDev.swapchainImageViews);
vkDev.commandBuffers.resize(imageCount);
```

7. The rendering synchronization primitives and a command buffer with a command pool are also created the same way as in the *Indirect rendering in Vulkan* recipe of *Chapter 5, Working with Geometry Data*:

```
VK_CHECK(createSemaphore(
  vkDev.device, &vkDev.semaphore));
VK_CHECK(createSemaphore(
  vkDev.device, &vkDev.renderSemaphore));
```

8. For each swapchain image, we create a separate command queue, just as in the `initVulkanRenderDevice()` function:

```
const VkCommandPoolCreateInfo cpi1 = {
  .sType =
    VK_STRUCTURE_TYPE_COMMAND_POOL_CREATE_INFO,
  .flags = 0,
  .queueFamilyIndex = vkDev.graphicsFamily
};
VK_CHECK(vkCreateCommandPool(vkDev.device, &cpi1,
  nullptr, &vkDev.commandPool));
const VkCommandBufferAllocateInfo ai1 = {
  .sType =
    VK_STRUCTURE_TYPE_COMMAND_BUFFER_ALLOCATE_INFO,
  .pNext = nullptr,
  .commandPool = vkDev.commandPool,
```

```
    .level = VK_COMMAND_BUFFER_LEVEL_PRIMARY,
    .commandBufferCount = static_cast<uint32_t>(
      vkDev.swapchainImages.size())
  };
  VK_CHECK(vkAllocateCommandBuffers(
    vkDev.device, &ai1, &vkDev.commandBuffers[0]));
```

9. Next, we create a single command pool for the compute queue:

```
  const VkCommandPoolCreateInfo cpi2 = {
    .sType =
      VK_STRUCTURE_TYPE_COMMAND_POOL_CREATE_INFO,
    .pNext = nullptr,
    .flags =
      VK_COMMAND_POOL_CREATE_RESET_COMMAND_BUFFER_BIT,
    .queueFamilyIndex = vkDev.computeFamily
  };
  VK_CHECK(vkCreateCommandPool(vkDev.device, &cpi2,
    nullptr, &vkDev.computeCommandPool));
```

10. Using the created command pool, we allocate the command buffer for
    compute shaders:

```
  const VkCommandBufferAllocateInfo ai2 = {
    .sType =
      VK_STRUCTURE_TYPE_COMMAND_BUFFER_ALLOCATE_INFO,
    .pNext = nullptr,
    .commandPool = vkDev.computeCommandPool,
    .level = VK_COMMAND_BUFFER_LEVEL_PRIMARY,
    .commandBufferCount = 1,
  };
  VK_CHECK(vkAllocateCommandBuffers(
    vkDev.device, &ai2, &vkDev.computeCommandBuffer));
```

11. At the end, we raise a flag saying that we support the command buffer execution:

```
  vkDev.useCompute = true;
  return true;
}
```

The initVulkanRenderDeviceWithCompute() routine written in the preceding
code uses the createDeviceWithCompute() helper function to create a compatible
Vulkan device. Let's see how this can be implemented.

1. The function takes in the graphics and compute queue indices we want to use:

```
VkResult createDeviceWithCompute(
  VkPhysicalDevice physicalDevice,
  VkPhysicalDeviceFeatures deviceFeatures,
  uint32_t graphicsFamily,
  uint32_t computeFamily,
  VkDevice* device)
{
  const std::vector<const char*> extensions = {
    VK_KHR_SWAPCHAIN_EXTENSION_NAME
  };
```

2. If we use a single queue, we can call the old device initialization routine:

```
if (graphicsFamily == computeFamily)
  return createDevice(physicalDevice,
    deviceFeatures, graphicsFamily, device);
```

3. For a case of two distinct queues, we fill in two individual
VkDeviceQueueCreateInfo structures. Each of these queues has a default
execution priority:

```
const float queuePriorities[2] = { 0.f, 0.f };
```

4. The graphics queue creation structure refers to the graphics queue family index:

```
const VkDeviceQueueCreateInfo qciGfx = {
  .sType =
    VK_STRUCTURE_TYPE_DEVICE_QUEUE_CREATE_INFO,
  .pNext = nullptr,
  .flags = 0,
  .queueFamilyIndex = graphicsFamily,
  .queueCount = 1,
  .pQueuePriorities = &queuePriorities[0]
};
```

5. The compute queue creation structure is similar and uses the compute queue family index:

```
const VkDeviceQueueCreateInfo qciComp = {
  .sType =
    VK_STRUCTURE_TYPE_DEVICE_QUEUE_CREATE_INFO,
  .pNext = nullptr,
  .flags = 0,
  .queueFamilyIndex = computeFamily,
  .queueCount = 1,
  .pQueuePriorities = &queuePriorities[1]
};
```

6. Both queue creation structures should be stored in an array for further use:

```
const VkDeviceQueueCreateInfo qci[] =
  { qciGfx, qciComp };
```

7. The device creation structure now uses two references to the graphics and compute queues:

```
const VkDeviceCreateInfo ci = {
  .sType = VK_STRUCTURE_TYPE_DEVICE_CREATE_INFO,
  .pNext = nullptr,
  .flags = 0,
  .queueCreateInfoCount = 2,
  .pQueueCreateInfos = qci,
  .enabledLayerCount = 0,
  .ppEnabledLayerNames = nullptr,
  .enabledExtensionCount =
    uint32_t(extensions.size()),
  .ppEnabledExtensionNames = extensions.data(),
  .pEnabledFeatures = &deviceFeatures
};
return vkCreateDevice(
  physicalDevice, &ci, nullptr, device);
}
```

To read the results of compute shaders and store them, we need to create shared VkBuffer instances using the following steps:

1. The createSharedBuffer() routine is analogous to createBuffer() but it explicitly enumerates the command queues:

```
bool createSharedBuffer(
  VulkanRenderDevice& vkDev, VkDeviceSize size,
  VkBufferUsageFlags usage,
```

```
    VkMemoryPropertyFlags properties,
    VkBuffer& buffer, VkDeviceMemory& bufferMemory)
{
```

2. If we have a single queue for graphics and compute, we delegate all the work to our old `createBuffer()` routine:

```
const size_t familyCount =
  vkDev.deviceQueueIndices.size();
if (familyCount < 2u)
  return createBuffer(vkDev.device,
    vkDev.physicalDevice, size,
    usage, properties, buffer, bufferMemory);
```

3. Inside the buffer creation structure, we should designate this buffer as being accessible from multiple command queues and pass a list of all the respective queue indices:

```
const VkBufferCreateInfo bufferInfo = {
  .sType = VK_STRUCTURE_TYPE_BUFFER_CREATE_INFO,
  .pNext = nullptr,
  .flags = 0,
  .size = size,
  .usage = usage,
  .sharingMode = (familyCount > 1u) ?
    VK_SHARING_MODE_CONCURRENT :
    VK_SHARING_MODE_EXCLUSIVE,
  .queueFamilyIndexCount =
    static_cast<uint32_t>(familyCount),
  .pQueueFamilyIndices = (familyCount > 1u) ?
    vkDev.deviceQueueIndices.data() : nullptr
};
```

4. The buffer itself is created, but no memory is associated with it yet:

```
VK_CHECK(vkCreateBuffer(
  vkDev.device, &bufferInfo, nullptr, &buffer));
```

5. The rest of the code allocates memory with specified parameters, just as in the `createBuffer()` routine. To do this, we ask the Vulkan implementation which memory-block properties we should use for this buffer:

```
VkMemoryRequirements memRequirements;
vkGetBufferMemoryRequirements(
  vkDev.device, buffer, &memRequirements);
```

6. In the allocation structure, we specify the physical buffer size and the exact memory heap type:

```
const VkMemoryAllocateInfo allocInfo = {
   .sType = VK_STRUCTURE_TYPE_MEMORY_ALLOCATE_INFO,
   .pNext = nullptr,
   .allocationSize = memRequirements.size,
   .memoryTypeIndex = findMemoryType(
     vkDev.physicalDevice,
     memRequirements.memoryTypeBits, properties)
};
```

7. Memory allocation and buffer binding conclude this routine:

```
VK_CHECK(vkAllocateMemory(vkDev.device, &allocInfo,
   nullptr, &bufferMemory));
vkBindBufferMemory(
   vkDev.device, buffer, bufferMemory, 0);
return true;
}
```

To execute compute shaders, we require a pipeline object, just as in the case with the graphics rendering. Let's write a function to create a Vulkan compute pipeline object.

1. As usual, we fill in the Vulkan creation structure for the pipeline. The compute pipeline contains a VK_SHADER_STAGE_COMPUTE_BIT single shader stage and an attached Vulkan shader module:

```
VkResult createComputePipeline(
   VkDevice device,
   VkShaderModule computeShader,
   VkPipelineLayout pipelineLayout,
   VkPipeline* pipeline)
{
   VkComputePipelineCreateInfo
     computePipelineCreateInfo = {
     .sType =
       VK_STRUCTURE_TYPE_COMPUTE_PIPELINE_CREATE_INFO,
     .pNext = nullptr,
     .flags = 0,
     .stage = {
       .sType = VK_STRUCTURE_TYPE_PIPELINE_SHADER
                _STAGE_CREATE_INFO,
       .pNext = nullptr,
       .flags = 0,
       .stage = VK_SHADER_STAGE_COMPUTE_BIT,
       .module = computeShader,
```

2. For the purpose of simplicity, all our compute shaders must have `main()` as their entry point:

```
.pName = "main",
.pSpecializationInfo = nullptr
},
```

3. Most of the parameters are set to default and zero values. The only required field is the pipeline layout object:

```
.layout = pipelineLayout,
.basePipelineHandle = 0,
.basePipelineIndex   = 0
};
return vkCreateComputePipelines(device, 0, 1,
    &computePipelineCreateInfo, nullptr, pipeline);
}
```

The pipeline layout is created using the same function as for the graphics part. It is worth mentioning that the compute shader compilation process is the same as for other shader stages.

We can now begin using the shaders after device initialization. The descriptor set creation process is the same as with the graphics-related descriptor sets, but the execution of compute shaders requires the insertion of new commands into the command buffer.

1. The function that we now implement shows how to execute a compute shader workload given the prepared pipeline and descriptor set objects. The `xSize`, `ySize`, and `zSize` parameters are the numbers of local workgroups to dispatch in the X, Y, and Z dimensions:

```
bool executeComputeShader(
   VulkanRenderDevice& vkDev,
   VkPipeline pipeline,
   VkPipelineLayout pipelineLayout,
   VkDescriptorSet ds,
   uint32_t xSize, uint32_t ySize, uint32_t zSize)
{
```

2. As with the graphics work items, we begin filling the command buffer:

```
VkCommandBuffer commandBuffer =
   vkDev.computeCommandBuffer;

VkCommandBufferBeginInfo commandBufferBeginInfo = {
   VK_STRUCTURE_TYPE_COMMAND_BUFFER_BEGIN_INFO,
   0, VK_COMMAND_BUFFER_USAGE_ONE_TIME_SUBMIT_BIT, 0
```

```
    };
    VK_CHECK(vkBeginCommandBuffer(
        commandBuffer, &commandBufferBeginInfo));
```

3. To execute a compute shader, we should first bind the pipeline and the descriptor set object, and then emit the vkCmdDispatch() command with the required execution range:

```
    vkCmdBindPipeline(commandBuffer,
        VK_PIPELINE_BIND_POINT_COMPUTE, pipeline);
    vkCmdBindDescriptorSets(commandBuffer,
        VK_PIPELINE_BIND_POINT_COMPUTE, pipelineLayout,
        0, 1, &ds, 0, 0);
    vkCmdDispatch(commandBuffer, xSize, ySize, zSize);
```

4. Before the CPU can read back data written to a buffer by a compute shader, we have to insert a memory barrier. More Vulkan synchronization details can be found in this tutorial: https://github.com/KhronosGroup/Vulkan-Docs/wiki/Synchronization-Examples. The code is illustrated here:

```
    VkMemoryBarrier readoutBarrier = {
        .sType = VK_STRUCTURE_TYPE_MEMORY_BARRIER,
        .pNext = nullptr,
        .srcAccessMask = VK_ACCESS_SHADER_WRITE_BIT,
        .dstAccessMask = VK_ACCESS_HOST_READ_BIT
    };
    vkCmdPipelineBarrier(commandBuffer,
        VK_PIPELINE_STAGE_COMPUTE_SHADER_BIT,
        VK_PIPELINE_STAGE_HOST_BIT, 0, 1, &readoutBarrier,
        0, nullptr, 0, nullptr);
```

5. After adding all the commands, we complete the recording of the command buffer:

```
    VK_CHECK(vkEndCommandBuffer(commandBuffer));
```

6. We immediately submit this command buffer to the queue:

```
    VkSubmitInfo submitInfo = {
        VK_STRUCTURE_TYPE_SUBMIT_INFO,
        0, 0, 0, 0, 1, &commandBuffer, 0, 0
    };
    VK_CHECK(vkQueueSubmit(
        vkDev.computeQueue, 1, &submitInfo, 0));
```

7. To synchronize buffers between computations and rendering, we should wait for
    the compute shader completion. Here, let's do it in a simple blocking way, just by
    waiting until the GPU finishes its work:

```
VK_CHECK(vkQueueWaitIdle(vkDev.computeQueue));
return true;
}
```

We omit the descriptor set creation process here because it depends on what kind of data we
want to access in the compute shader. The next recipe shows how to write compute shaders to
generate images and vertex buffer contents, which is where a descriptor set will be required.

There's more...

We are going to use the Vulkan compute shaders functionality later in this chapter in the
following recipes: *Implementing computed meshes in Vulkan*, *Generating textures in Vulkan
using compute shaders*, *Precomputing BRDF LUTs*, and *Precomputing irradiance maps and
diffuse convolution*.

Using descriptor indexing and texture arrays in Vulkan

Before we dive deep into the glTF and PBR implementation code, let's look at some lower-
level functionality that will be required to minimize the number of Vulkan descriptor sets
in applications that use lots of materials with multiple textures. Descriptor indexing is an
extremely useful feature recently added to Vulkan 1.2 and, at the time of writing this book,
is already supported on some devices. It allows us to create unbounded descriptor sets and
use non-uniform dynamic indexing to access textures inside them. This way, materials can
be stored in shader storage buffers and each one can reference all the required textures
using integer **identifiers (IDs)**. These IDs can be fetched from a **shader storage buffer
object (SSBO)** and are directly used to index into an appropriate descriptor set that
contains all the textures required by our application. Vulkan descriptor indexing is rather
similar to the OpenGL bindless textures mechanism and significantly simplifies managing
descriptor sets in Vulkan. Let's check out how to use this feature.

Getting ready

The source code for this recipe can be found in Chapter6/VK02_
DescriptorIndexing. All the textures we used are stored in the data/explosion
folder.

How to do it...

Before we can use the descriptor indexing feature in Vulkan, we need to enable it during the Vulkan device initialization. This process is a little bit verbose, but we will go through it once to show the basic principles. Let's take a look at new fragments of the `initVulkan()` function to see how it is done.

1. After the window surface is created, we should construct an instance of the `VkPhysicalDeviceDescriptorIndexingFeaturesEXT` structure to enable non-uniform image array indexing and a variable descriptor set count:

```
VkPhysicalDeviceDescriptorIndexingFeaturesEXT
  physicalDeviceDescriptorIndexingFeatures = {
  .sType = VK_STRUCTURE_TYPE_PHYSICAL_DEVICE
        _DESCRIPTOR_INDEXING_FEATURES_EXT,
  .shaderSampledImageArrayNonUniformIndexing =
     VK_TRUE,
  .descriptorBindingVariableDescriptorCount = VK_TRUE,
  .runtimeDescriptorArray = VK_TRUE,
};
```

2. The required feature should be enabled using `VkPhysicalDeviceFeatures`:

```
const VkPhysicalDeviceFeatures deviceFeatures = {
  .shaderSampledImageArrayDynamicIndexing = VK_TRUE
};
```

3. After that, both structures can be used to construct `VkPhysicalDeviceFeatures2`:

```
const VkPhysicalDeviceFeatures2 deviceFeatures2 = {
  .sType =
    VK_STRUCTURE_TYPE_PHYSICAL_DEVICE_FEATURES_2,
  .pNext = &physicalDeviceDescriptorIndexingFeatures,
  .features = deviceFeatures
};
```

4. The `VkPhysicalDeviceFeatures2` instance should be passed into our `initVulkanRenderDevice2()` Vulkan initialization helper implemented in `shared/UtilsVulkan.cpp`:

```
if (!initVulkanRenderDevice2(vk, vkDev,
      kScreenWidth, kScreenHeight,
      isDeviceSuitable, deviceFeatures2))
  exit(EXIT_FAILURE);
```

The initialization process for this extension is similar to how we initialized the Vulkan indirect rendering extension in the *Indirect rendering in Vulkan* recipe from *Chapter 5, Working with Geometry Data*. The only difference here is that the descriptor indexing feature was added into Vulkan 1.2, hence the different `VkPhysicalDeviceFeatures2` structure and a separate initialization function.

Once we have a proper Vulkan device initialized, we can implement a simple flipbook animation using descriptor indexing. Our example application uses three different explosion animations released by Unity Technologies under the liberal **Creative Commons (CC0)** license (`https://blogs.unity3d.com/2016/11/28/free-vfx-image-sequences-flipbooks`). Let's look at the steps.

1. First, let's get prepared to load three different explosions. Each explosion is stored as a separate flipbook and contains 100 frames defined as `kNumFlipbookFrames`:

```
std::vector<std::string> textureFiles;
for (uint32_t j = 0; j < 3; j++) {
  for (uint32_t i = 0; i != kNumFlipbookFrames; i++) {
    char fname[1024];
    snprintf(fname, sizeof(fname),
      "data/explosion/explosion%02u-frame%03u.tga",
      j, i+1);
    textureFiles.push_back(fname);
  }
}
```

2. We implemented a `VulkanQuadRenderer` helper class to render textured quads using Vulkan. We should construct it the following way using the texture filenames. To avoid having to deal with any kind of synchronization, we fill a separate SSBO with data for each swapchain image. It is far from being a silver bullet, but makes this entire book so much simpler:

```
quadRenderer =
  std::make_unique<VulkanQuadRenderer>(
    vkDev, textureFiles);
for (size_t i = 0; i < vkDev.swapchainImages.size();
    i++)
  fillQuadsBuffer(vkDev, *quadRenderer.get(), i);
```

3. Before we finish the initialization process, we should construct our rendering layers—one for clearing the screen and another to present the rendered image. If you forget how our Vulkan frame composition works, check out the *Organizing Vulkan frame rendering code* recipe from *Chapter 4, Adding User Interaction and Productivity Tools*:

```
VulkanImage nullTexture = {
  .image = VK_NULL_HANDLE,
  .imageView = VK_NULL_HANDLE
};
clear = std::make_unique<VulkanClear>(
  vkDev, nullTexture);
finish = std::make_unique<VulkanFinish>(
  vkDev, nullTexture);
```

For all the implementation details of `VulkanQuadRenderer`, check out the `shared/vkRenderers/VulkanQuadRenderer.cpp` file, which contains mostly Vulkan descriptors initialization and texture-loading code—all its parts were extensively covered in the previous chapters. We will skip it here in the book text and focus on the actual demo application logic and **OpenGL Shading Language** (**GLSL**) shaders.

The `Chapter6/VK02_DescriptorIndexing` application renders an animated explosion every time a user clicks somewhere in the window. Multiple explosions, each using a different flipbook, can be rendered simultaneously. Let's see how to implement them using the following steps.

1. First, we need a data structure to store the state of a single flipbook animation. Here, `position` defines the position of an animation in the window, `startTime` marks the timestamp when this animation was started, `textureIndex` is the index of the current texture inside the flipbook, and `flipbookOffset` points to the beginning of the current flipbook in the big array of textures we loaded earlier. We are going to store all active animations in a collection:

```
struct AnimationState {
  vec2 position = vec2(0);
  double startTime = 0;
  uint32_t textureIndex = 0;
  uint32_t flipbookOffset = 0;
};
std::vector<AnimationState> animations;
```

2. Here's the animation update logic put into a separate function. The current texture index is updated for each animation based on its start time. As we go through all animations, we can safely remove finished ones. Instead of using a swap-and-pop pattern here to remove an element from the container, which will create ugly Z-fighting where animations suddenly pop in front of each other, we use a straightforward naive removal via `erase()`:

```cpp
void updateAnimations() {
  for (size_t i = 0; i < animations.size();) {
    const auto& anim = animations[i];
    anim.textureIndex = anim.flipbookOffset +
      (uint32_t)(kAnimationFPS *
        ((glfwGetTime() - anim.startTime)));
    if (anim.textureIndex - anim.flipbookOffset >
        kNumFlipbookFrames)
      animations.erase(animations.begin() + i);
    else i++;
  }
}
```

3. The final touch to the C++ part of our application is the mouse click handling callback that spawns a new animated explosion at the cursor position. The flipbook starting offset is selected randomly for each explosion:

```cpp
glfwSetMouseButtonCallback(window, [](GLFWwindow*
  window, int button, int action, int mods) {
    if (button == GLFW_MOUSE_BUTTON_LEFT &&
        action == GLFW_PRESS) {
      float mx =
        (mouseX/vkDev.framebufferWidth )*2.0f - 1.0f;
      float my =
        (mouseY/vkDev.framebufferHeight)*2.0f - 1.0f;
      animations.push_back(AnimationState{
        .position = vec2(mx, my),
        .startTime = glfwGetTime(),
        .textureIndex = 0,
        .flipbookOffset =
          kNumFlipbookFrames * (uint32_t)(rand() % 3)
      });
    }
  });
```

The `chapter06/VK02_texture_array.vert` vertex shader to render our textured rectangles is presented next.

1. The `programmable-vertex-fetch` technique takes care of the vertices stored as `ImDrawVert` structures inside the SSBO:

```
layout(location = 0) out vec2 out_uv;
layout(location = 1) flat out uint out_texIndex;
struct ImDrawVert {
  float x, y, z, u, v;
};
layout(binding = 1) readonly buffer SBO {
  ImDrawVert data[];
} sbo;
```

2. The geometry buffer is constant for all rendered rectangles, so we pass a `vec2` position to shift the origin of our quad on the screen. The `textureIndex` field corresponds to the same field in `AnimationState`. It is easy to pass this information as a Vulkan push constant:

```
layout(push_constant) uniform uPushConstant {
  vec2 position;
  uint textureIndex;
} pc;
```

3. Fetch the data from the buffers, apply the position to calculate the resulting value of `gl_Position`, and we are done here:

```
void main() {
  uint idx = gl_VertexIndex;
  ImDrawVert v = sbo.data[idx];
  out_uv = vec2(v.u, v.v);
  out_texIndex = pc.textureIndex;
  gl_Position =
    vec4(vec2(v.x, v.y) + pc.position, 0.0, 1.0);
}
```

The chapter06/VK02_texture_array.frag fragment shader is trivial and uses the non-uniform descriptor indexing feature. Let's take a look.

1. First, we have to enable the GL_EXT_nonuniform_qualifier extension to be able to use the texture index value. Note the unbounded array of textures:

```
#version 460
#extension GL_EXT_nonuniform_qualifier : require
layout (binding = 2) uniform sampler2D textures[];
layout (location = 0) in vec2 in_uv;
layout (location = 1) flat in uint in_texIndex;
layout (location = 0) out vec4 outFragColor;
```

2. The nonuniformEXT type qualifier can be used to assert that a variable or expression is not dynamically uniform:

```
void main() {
  outFragColor = texture(
    textures[nonuniformEXT(in_texIndex)], in_uv);
}
```

We can now run our application. Click a few times in the window to see something similar to this:

Figure 6.1 – Animated explosions using descriptor indexing and texture arrays in Vulkan

There's more...

While this example passes a texture index into a shader as a push constant, making it uniform, with the GL_EXT_nonuniform_qualifier extension it is possible to store texture indices inside Vulkan buffers in a completely dynamic way. In *Chapter 7, Graphics Rendering Pipeline*, we will build a material system based around this Vulkan extension, similar to how the bindless textures mechanism in OpenGL is deployed.

In the next recipe, we will show one more useful application of texture arrays.

Using descriptor indexing in Vulkan to render an ImGui

Another extremely useful application of descriptor indexing is the ability to trivially render multiple textures in ImGui. Up until now, our ImGui renderer was able to use only one single font texture and there was no possibility to render any static images in our UI. To allow backward compatibility with *Chapter 4, Adding User Interaction and Productivity Tools*, and *Chapter 5, Working with Geometry Data*, we add a new constructor to the ImGuiRenderer class and modify the addImGuiItem() method in the shared/vkRenderers/VulkanImGui.cpp file. We provide a thorough discussion of the required changes here because, to the best of our knowledge, there is no small down-to-earth tutorial on using multiple textures in the Vulkan ImGui renderer.

Getting ready

Check the previous *Using descriptor indexing and texture arrays in Vulkan* recipe, to learn how to initialize the descriptor indexing feature.

How to do it...

Let's start with the description of source code changes.

1. First, we declare a list of used external textures as a field in the ImGuiRenderer structure:

    ```
    std::vector<VulkanTexture> extTextures_;
    ```

2. The new constructor of the ImGuiRenderer class takes a list of Vulkan texture handles as a parameter:

    ```
    ImGuiRenderer::ImGuiRenderer(
       VulkanRenderDevice& vkDev,
       const std::vector<VulkanTexture>& textures)
    ```

```
: RendererBase(vkDev, VulkanImage())
, extTextures_(textures)
```

3. The only parts of the constructor that are different is the descriptor set and pipeline layout initialization. The render pass, framebuffers, and uniform buffers are created in a standard way:

```
if (!createColorAndDepthRenderPass(vkDev, false,
    &renderPass_, RenderPassCreateInfo()) ||
  !createColorAndDepthFramebuffers(vkDev,
    renderPass_, VK_NULL_HANDLE,
    swapchainFramebuffers_) ||
  !createUniformBuffers(vkDev, sizeof(mat4)) ||
```

4. The descriptor pool now has to accommodate the font and all the external textures:

```
!createDescriptorPool(
  vkDev, 1, 2, 1 + textures.size(),
  &descriptorPool_) ||
```

5. To create a descriptor set, we use the following new function:

```
!createMultiDescriptorSet(vkDev) ||
```

6. The pipeline for our renewed ImGui renderer must allow a single push constant that we use to pass the texture index of a rendered element:

```
!createPipelineLayoutWithConstants(vkDev.device,
  descriptorSetLayout_, &pipelineLayout_, 0,
  sizeof(uint32_t)) ||
```

7. The graphics pipeline uses the vertex shader from *Chapter 4, Adding User Interaction and Productivity Tools*, and the new fragment shader is described here:

```
!createGraphicsPipeline(vkDev, renderPass_,
  pipelineLayout_,
  { "data/shaders/chapter04/imgui.vert",
    "data/shaders/chapter06/imgui_multi.frag" },
  &graphicsPipeline_,
  VK_PRIMITIVE_TOPOLOGY_TRIANGLE_LIST,
  true, true, true))
```

8. If we fail to create any of the Vulkan objects, we display a small error message.
    Further diagnostics are displayed in the validation layer's output:

```
{
  printf(
    "ImGuiRenderer: pipeline creation failed\n");
  exit(EXIT_FAILURE);
}
```

This concludes our list of changes to the constructor code. The descriptor set creation code
is similar to that of the `VulkanQuadRenderer::createDescriptorSet()` function,
but since we skipped the implementation details at the beginning of this recipe, we describe
the complete `ImGuiRenderer::createMultiDesriptorSet()` method here.

1. The method starts with a description of buffer bindings. The difference here is that
    we might have more than one texture, so we specify this explicitly by asking for the
    `extTextures_` array size:

```
bool ImGuiRenderer::createMultiDescriptorSet(
  VulkanRenderDevice& vkDev)
{
  const std::array<VkDescriptorSetLayoutBinding, 4>
    bindings = {
    descriptorSetLayoutBinding(0,
      VK_DESCRIPTOR_TYPE_UNIFORM_BUFFER,
      VK_SHADER_STAGE_VERTEX_BIT),
    descriptorSetLayoutBinding(1,
      VK_DESCRIPTOR_TYPE_STORAGE_BUFFER,
      VK_SHADER_STAGE_VERTEX_BIT),
    descriptorSetLayoutBinding(2,
      VK_DESCRIPTOR_TYPE_STORAGE_BUFFER,
      VK_SHADER_STAGE_VERTEX_BIT),
    descriptorSetLayoutBinding(3,
      VK_DESCRIPTOR_TYPE_COMBINED_IMAGE_SAMPLER,
      VK_SHADER_STAGE_FRAGMENT_BIT,
      1 + extTextures_.size())
  };
```

2. To create the descriptor set layout, we need the creation structure, which contains a
    reference to our binding flags:

```
const VkDescriptorSetLayoutCreateInfo layoutInfo = {
  .sType = VK_STRUCTURE_TYPE_DESCRIPTOR_SET
           _LAYOUT_CREATE_INFO,
```

```
  .pNext = nullptr,
  .flags = 0,
  .bindingCount =
    static_cast<uint32_t>(bindings.size()),
  .pBindings = bindings.data()
};
VK_CHECK(vkCreateDescriptorSetLayout(vkDev.device,
  &layoutInfo, nullptr, &descriptorSetLayout_));
```

3. As usual, we allocate descriptor sets for each of the swapchain images:

```
std::vector<VkDescriptorSetLayout> layouts(
  vkDev.swapchainImages.size(),
  descriptorSetLayout_);
const VkDescriptorSetAllocateInfo allocInfo = {
  .sType =
    VK_STRUCTURE_TYPE_DESCRIPTOR_SET_ALLOCATE_INFO,
  .pNext = nullptr,
  .descriptorPool = descriptorPool_,
  .descriptorSetCount = static_cast<uint32_t>(
    vkDev.swapchainImages.size()),
  .pSetLayouts = layouts.data()
};
descriptorSets_.resize(
  vkDev.swapchainImages.size());
VK_CHECK(vkAllocateDescriptorSets(vkDev.device,
  &allocInfo, descriptorSets_.data()));
```

4. Now, we should create image information structures for all of the used textures. The first texture is the ImGui font loaded in the constructor:

```
std::vector<VkDescriptorImageInfo>
  textureDescriptors = {
    { fontSampler_, font_.imageView,
      VK_IMAGE_LAYOUT_SHADER_READ_ONLY_OPTIMAL }
};
```

5. For each of the external textures, we create an image information structure. For simplicity, we assume all of our textures are in the shader-optimal layout:

```
for (size_t i = 0; i < extTextures_.size(); i++)
  textureDescriptors.push_back({
    .sampler = extTextures_[i].sampler,
    .imageView = extTextures_[i].image.imageView,
    .imageLayout =
      VK_IMAGE_LAYOUT_SHADER_READ_ONLY_OPTIMAL
  });
```

6. Now, we should proceed to updating each of the created descriptor sets:

```
for (size_t i = 0; i < vkDev.swapchainImages.size();
   i++) {
  VkDescriptorSet ds = descriptorSets_[i];
```

7. The three buffers with uniform data, item indices, and vertices are the same as in the `createDescriptorSet()` function:

```
const VkDescriptorBufferInfo bufferInfo1 =
  { uniformBuffers_[i], 0, sizeof(mat4) };
const VkDescriptorBufferInfo bufferInfo2 =
  { storageBuffer_[i], 0, ImGuiVtxBufferSize };
const VkDescriptorBufferInfo bufferInfo3 =
  { storageBuffer_[i], ImGuiVtxBufferSize,
    ImGuiIdxBufferSize };
```

8. The parameters to `vkUpdateDescriptorSets()` include the buffer information structures at the beginning:

```
const std::array<VkWriteDescriptorSet, 4>
  descriptorWrites = {
  bufferWriteDescriptorSet(ds, &bufferInfo1,  0,
    VK_DESCRIPTOR_TYPE_UNIFORM_BUFFER),
  bufferWriteDescriptorSet(ds, &bufferInfo2, 1,
    VK_DESCRIPTOR_TYPE_STORAGE_BUFFER),
  bufferWriteDescriptorSet(ds, &bufferInfo3, 2,
    VK_DESCRIPTOR_TYPE_STORAGE_BUFFER),
```

9. The last binding in our descriptor sets is the indexed texture array. We explicitly state that this binding is indexed and refers to an array of texture handles in the `textureDescriptors` variable:

```
VkWriteDescriptorSet {
  .sType =
    VK_STRUCTURE_TYPE_WRITE_DESCRIPTOR_SET,
  .dstSet = descriptorSets_[i],
  .dstBinding = 3,
  .dstArrayElement = 0,
  .descriptorCount = static_cast<uint32_t>(
    1 + extTextures_.size()),
  .descriptorType =
    VK_DESCRIPTOR_TYPE_COMBINED_IMAGE_SAMPLER,
  .pImageInfo = textureDescriptors.data()
  },
};
```

10. After updating each descriptor set, the function quietly returns:

```
    vkUpdateDescriptorSets(vkDev.device,
        static_cast<uint32_t>(descriptorWrites.size()),
        descriptorWrites.data(), 0, nullptr);
  }
  return true;
}
```

11. The only thing we modify in `ImGuiRenderer::addImGuiItem()` is the passing of the texture index. We should insert the following snippet between the `vkCmdSetScissor()` and `vkCmdDraw()` calls. If our external textures array is not empty, we extract the texture ID and pass it to our fragment shader using the push constants mechanism:

```
  if (textures.size()) {
    uint32_t texture =
        (uint32_t)(intptr_t)pcmd->TextureId;
    vkCmdPushConstants(commandBuffer,
        pipelineLayout, VK_SHADER_STAGE_FRAGMENT_BIT,
        0, sizeof(uint32_t), (const void*)&texture);
  }
```

Finally, we implement a new fragment shader in `data/shaders/chapter06/imgui_multi.frag`, because the vertex shader remains the same.

1. The fragment shader takes the UV texture coordinates and an optional item color as input. The only output is the fragment color:

```
#version 460
#extension GL_EXT_nonuniform_qualifier : require
layout(location = 0) in vec2 uv;
layout(location = 1) in vec4 color;
layout(location = 0) out vec4 outColor;
layout(binding = 3) uniform sampler2D textures[];
```

2. Since we are rendering different UI elements using the same shader, we pass the texture index as a push constant:

```
layout(push_constant) uniform pushBlock
  { uint index; } pushConsts;
```

3. The `main()` function is slightly more complicated than the one in *Chapter 4,*
    Adding User Interaction and Productivity Tools. Here, we "decode" the passed texture
    index and decide how to interpret this texture's contents before outputting the
    fragment color. The higher 16 bits of the texture index indicate whether the fetched
    texture value should be interpreted as a color or as the depth buffer value:

```
void main() {
  const uint kDepthTextureMask = 0xFFFF;
  uint texType =
    (pushConsts.index >> 16) & kDepthTextureMask;
```

4. The actual texture index in the `textures` array is stored in the lower 16 bits. After
    selecting the texture index, we sample the texture:

```
  uint tex = pushConsts.index & kDepthTextureMask;
  vec4 value = texture(
    textures[nonuniformEXT(tex)], uv);
```

5. If the texture type is a standard font texture or a **red-green-blue** (**RGB**) image, we
    multiply by the color and return. Otherwise, if the texture contains depth values, we
    output a grayscale value:

```
  outColor = (texType == 0) ?
    (color * value) : vec4(value.rrr, 1.0);
}
```

Let's look at the C++ counterpart of the code. The hypothetical usage of this new
ImGui renderer's functionality can be wrapped in the following helper function.
It accepts a window title and a texture ID, which is simply the index in the
`ImGuiRenderer::extTextures_` array passed to the constructor at creation time.

1. The function creates a default window and fills the entire window with the texture's
    content. We get the minimum and maximum boundaries:

```
void imguiTextureWindow(
  const char* Title, uint32_t texId)
{
  ImGui::Begin(Title, nullptr);
  ImVec2 vMin = ImGui::GetWindowContentRegionMin();
  ImVec2 vMax = ImGui::GetWindowContentRegionMax();
```

2. The `ImGui::Image()` call creates a rectangular texture item, which is added to the draw list:

```
ImGui::Image( (void*)(intptr_t)texId,
   ImVec2(vMax.x - vMin.x, vMax.y - vMin.y));
ImGui::End();
}
```

3. If we need to display the contents of a color buffer, we use the call with a texture index. If the texture contains depth data, we set the higher 16 bits to the texture index:

```
imguiTextureWindow("Some title", textureID);
imguiTextureWindow("Some depth buffer",
   textureID | 0xFFFF);
```

In the subsequent chapters, we will show how to use this ability to display intermediate buffers for debugging purposes.

Generating textures in Vulkan using compute shaders

Now that we can initialize and use compute shaders, it is time to give a few examples of how to use these. Let's start with some basic procedural texture generation. In this recipe, we implement a small program to display animated textures whose pixel values are calculated in real time inside our custom compute shader. To add even more value to this recipe, we will port a GLSL shader from `https://www.shadertoy.com` to our Vulkan compute shader.

Getting ready

The compute pipeline creation code and Vulkan application initialization are the same as in the *Initializing compute shaders in Vulkan* recipe. Make sure you read this before proceeding further. To use and display the generated texture, we need a textured quad renderer. Its complete source code can be found in `shared/vkRenderers/VulkanSingleQuad.cpp`. We will not focus on its internals here because, at this point, it should be easy for you to implement such a renderer on your own using the material of the previous chapters. One of the simplest ways to do so would be to modify the `ModelRenderer` class from `shared/vkRenderers/VulkanModelRenderer.cpp` and fill the appropriate index and vertex buffers in the class constructor.

The original **Industrial Complex** shader that we are going to use here to generate a Vulkan texture was created by Gary "Shane" Warne (`https://www.shadertoy.com/user/Shane`) and can be downloaded from *ShaderToy* at `https://www.shadertoy.com/view/MtdSWS`.

How to do it...

Let's start by discussing the process of writing a texture-generating GLSL compute shader. The simplest shader to generate a **red-green-blue-alpha** (**RGBA**) image without using any input data outputs an image by using the `gl_GlobalInvocationID` built-in variable to know which pixel to output. This maps directly to how *ShaderToy* shaders operate, thus we can transform them into a compute shader just by adding some **input and output** (**I/O**) parameters and layout modifiers specific to compute shaders and Vulkan. Let's take a look at a minimalistic compute shader that creates a red-green gradient texture.

1. As in all other compute shaders, one mandatory line at the beginning tells the driver how to distribute the workload on the GPU. In our case, we are processing tiles of 16x16 pixels:

```
layout (local_size_x = 16, local_size_y = 16) in;
```

2. The only buffer binding that we need to specify is the output image. This is the first time we have used the `image2D` image type in this book. Here, it means that the `result` variable is a **two-dimensional** (**2D**) array whose elements are nothing else but pixels of an image. The `writeonly` layout qualifier instructs the compiler to assume we will not read from this image in the shader:

```
layout (binding = 0, rgba8) uniform
    writeonly image2D result;
```

3. The GLSL compute shading language provides a set of helper functions to retrieve various image attributes. We use the built-in `imageSize()` function to determine the size of an image in pixels:

```
void main()
{
    ivec2 dim = imageSize(result);
```

4. The `gl_GlobalInvocationID` built-in variable tells us which global element of our compute grid we are processing. To convert this value into 2D image coordinates, we divide it by the image size. As we are dealing with 2D textures, only x and y components matter. The calling code from the C++ side executes the `vkCmdDispatch()` function and passes the output image size as the X and Y numbers of local workgroups:

```
vec2 uv = vec2(gl_GlobalInvocationID.xy) / dim;
```

5. The actual real work we do in this shader is to call the `imageStore()` GLSL function:

```
imageStore(result, ivec2(gl_GlobalInvocationID.xy),
    vec4(uv, 0.0, 1.0));
}
```

Now, the preceding example is rather limited, and all you get is a red-and-green gradient image. Let's change it a little bit to use the actual shader code from *ShaderToy*. The compute shader that renders a Vulkan version of the **Industrial Complex** shader from *ShaderToy*, available via the following **Uniform Resource Locator** (**URL**), https:// shadertoy.com/view/MtdSWS, can be found in the shaders/chapter06/VK03_ compute_texture.comp file.

1. First, let's copy the entire original ShaderToy GLSL code into our new compute shader. There is a function called `mainImage()` in there that is declared as follows:

```
void mainImage(out vec4 fragColor, in vec2 fragCoord)
```

2. We should replace it with a function that returns a `vec4` color instead of storing it in the output parameter:

```
vec4 mainImage(in vec2 fragCoord)
```

Don't forget to add an appropriate `return` statement at the end.

3. Now, let's change the `main()` function of our compute shader to invoke `mainImage()` properly. It is a pretty neat trick:

```
void main()
{
   ivec2 dim = imageSize(result);
   vec2 uv = vec2(gl_GlobalInvocationID.xy) / dim;
   imageStore(result, ivec2(gl_GlobalInvocationID.xy),
      mainImage(uv*dim));
}
```

4. There is still one issue that needs to be resolved before we can run this code. The ShaderToy code uses two custom input variables, iTime for the elapsed time, and iResolution, which contains the size of the resulting image. To avoid any search and replace in the original GLSL code, we mimic these variables, one as a push constant, and the other with a hardcoded value for simplicity:

```
layout(push_constant) uniform uPushConstant {
  float time;
} pc;
vec2 iResolution = vec2( 1280.0, 720.0 );
float iTime = pc.time;
```

> **Important note**
>
> The GLSL imageSize() function can be used to obtain the iResolution value based on the actual size of our texture. We leave this as an exercise for the reader.

5. The C++ code is rather short and consists of invoking the aforementioned compute shader, inserting a Vulkan pipeline barrier, and rendering a texture quad. The pipeline barrier that ensures the compute shader finishes before texture sampling happens can be created in the following way:

```
void insertComputedImageBarrier(
  VkCommandBuffer commandBuffer, VkImage image)
{
  const VkImageMemoryBarrier barrier = {
    .sType = VK_STRUCTURE_TYPE_IMAGE_MEMORY_BARRIER,
    .srcAccessMask = VK_ACCESS_SHADER_WRITE_BIT,
    .dstAccessMask = VK_ACCESS_SHADER_READ_BIT,
    .oldLayout = VK_IMAGE_LAYOUT_GENERAL,
    .newLayout = VK_IMAGE_LAYOUT_GENERAL,
    .image = image,
    .subresourceRange =
      { VK_IMAGE_ASPECT_COLOR_BIT, 0, 1, 0, 1 }
  };
  vkCmdPipelineBarrier(commandBuffer,
    VK_PIPELINE_STAGE_COMPUTE_SHADER_BIT,
    VK_PIPELINE_STAGE_FRAGMENT_SHADER_BIT,
    0, 0, nullptr, 0, nullptr, 1, &barrier);
}
```

The running application should render an image like the one shown in the following screenshot, which is similar to the output of `https://www.shadertoy.com/view/MtdSWS`:

Figure 6.2 – Using compute shaders to generate textures

In the next recipe, we will continue learning the Vulkan compute pipeline and implement a mesh-generation compute shader.

Implementing computed meshes in Vulkan

In the *Initializing compute shaders in Vulkan* recipe, we learned how to initialize the compute pipeline in Vulkan. We are going to need it in this chapter to implement a BRDF precomputation tool for our PBR pipeline. But before that, let's learn a few simple and interesting ways to use compute shaders in Vulkan and combine this feature with mesh geometry generation on the GPU.

We are going to run a compute shader to create triangulated geometry of a **three-dimensional** (**3D**) torus knot shape with different P and Q parameters.

> **Important note**
>
> A torus knot is a special kind of knot that lies on the surface of an unknotted torus in 3D space. Each torus knot is specified by a pair of p and q coprime integers. You can read more on this at `https://en.wikipedia.org/wiki/Torus_knot`.

The data produced by the compute shader is stored in a shader storage buffer and used in a vertex shader in a typical programmable-vertex-fetch way. To make the results more visually pleasing, we will implement real-time morphing between two different torus knots controllable from an ImGui widget. Let's get started.

Getting ready

The source code for this example is located in `Chapter6/VK04_ComputeMesh`.

How to do it...

The application consists of three different parts: the C++ part, which drives the UI and Vulkan commands, the mesh-generation compute shader, and the rendering pipeline with simple vertex and fragment shaders. The C++ part in `Chapter6/VK04_ComputeMesh/src/main.cpp` is rather short, so let's tackle this first.

1. We store a queue of `P-Q` pairs that defines the order of morphing. The queue always has at least two elements that define the current and the next torus knot. We also store a `morphCoef` floating-point value that is the `0...1` morphing factor between these two pairs in the queue. The mesh is regenerated every frame and the morphing coefficient is increased until it reaches `1.0`. At this point, we will either stop morphing or, in case there are more than two elements in the queue, remove the top element from it, reset `morphCoef` back to `0`, and repeat. The `animationSpeed` value defines how fast one torus knot mesh morphs into another:

    ```cpp
    std::deque<std::pair<uint32_t, uint32_t>> morphQueue =
      { { 5, 8 }, { 5, 8 } };
    float morphCoef = 0.0f;
    float animationSpeed = 1.0f;
    ```

2. Two global constants define the tessellation level of a torus knot. Feel free to play around with them:

```
const uint32_t numU = 1024;
const uint32_t numV = 1024;
```

3. Another global declaration is the structure to pass data into the compute shader inside a uniform buffer. Note two sets of P and Q parameters here:

```
struct MeshUniformBuffer {
   float time;
   uint32_t numU;
   uint32_t numV;
   float minU, maxU;
   float minV, maxV;
   uint32_t p1, p2;
   uint32_t q1, q2;
   float morph;
} ubo;
```

4. Regardless of the P and Q parameter values, we have a single order in which we should traverse vertices to produce torus knot triangles. The generateIndices() function prepares index buffer data for this purpose:

```
void generateIndices(uint32_t* indices) {
   for (uint32_t j = 0 ; j < numV - 1 ; j++) {
      for (uint32_t i = 0 ; i < numU - 1 ; i++) {
         uint32_t offset = (j * (numU - 1) + i) * 6;
         uint32_t i1 = (j + 0) * numU + (i + 0);
         uint32_t i2 = (j + 0) * numU + (i + 1);
         uint32_t i3 = (j + 1) * numU + (i + 1);
         uint32_t i4 = (j + 1) * numU + (i + 0);
         indices[offset + 0] = i1;
         indices[offset + 1] = i2;
         indices[offset + 2] = i4;
         indices[offset + 3] = i2;
         indices[offset + 4] = i3;
         indices[offset + 5] = i4;
      }
   }
}
```

Besides that, our C++ initialization part is in the `initMesh()` function. This allocates all the necessary buffers, uploads indices data into the GPU, loads compute shaders for texture and mesh generation, and creates two model renderers, one for a textured mesh and another for a colored one.

1. First, we should allocate storage for our generated indices data. To make things simpler, we do not use triangle strips, so it is always 6 indices for each quad defined by the UV mapping:

```
void initMesh() {
  std::vector<uint32_t> indicesGen(
    (numU - 1) * (numV - 1) * 6);
      generateIndices(indicesGen.data());
```

2. Compute all the necessary sizes for our GPU buffer. 12 floats are necessary to store three `vec4` components per vertex. The actual data structure is defined only in GLSL and can be found in `data/shaders/chapter06/mesh_common.inc`:

```
uint32_t vertexBufferSize =
  12 * sizeof(float) * numU * numV;
uint32_t indexBufferSize =
  6 * sizeof(uint32_t) * (numU-1) * (numV-1);
uint32_t bufferSize =
  vertexBufferSize + indexBufferSize;
```

3. Load both compute shaders. The grid size for texture generation is fixed at 1024x1024. The grid size for the mesh can be tweaked using `numU` and `numV`:

```
imgGen = std::make_unique<ComputedImage>(vkDev,
  "data/shaders/chapter06/VK04_compute_texture.comp",
  1024, 1024, false);
meshGen = std::make_unique<ComputedVertexBuffer>(
  vkDev,
  "data/shaders/chapter06/VK04_compute_mesh.comp",
  indexBufferSize, sizeof(MeshUniformBuffer),
  12 * sizeof(float), numU * numV);
```

4. Use a staging buffer to upload indices data into the GPU memory:

```
VkBuffer stagingBuffer;
VkDeviceMemory stagingBufferMemory;
createBuffer(vkDev.device, vkDev.physicalDevice,
  bufferSize,
  VK_BUFFER_USAGE_TRANSFER_SRC_BIT,
  VK_MEMORY_PROPERTY_HOST_VISIBLE_BIT |
```

```
       VK_MEMORY_PROPERTY_HOST_COHERENT_BIT,
    stagingBuffer, stagingBufferMemory);
  void* data = nullptr;
  vkMapMemory(vkDev.device, stagingBufferMemory, 0,
    bufferSize, 0, &data);
  memcpy((void*)((uint8_t*)data + vertexBufferSize),
    indicesGen.data(), indexBufferSize);
  vkUnmapMemory(vkDev.device, stagingBufferMemory);
  copyBuffer(vkDev, stagingBuffer,
    meshGen->computedBuffer, bufferSize);
```

> **Note**
>
> More examples of staging buffers can be found in the *Using texture data in Vulkan* recipe from *Chapter 3, Getting Started with OpenGL and Vulkan.*

5. Since indices are static, we do not require the staging buffer anymore, so it can be deallocated right here:

```
  vkDestroyBuffer(
    vkDev.device, stagingBuffer, nullptr);
  vkFreeMemory(
    vkDev.device, stagingBufferMemory, nullptr);
```

6. Fill the Vulkan command buffer for our computed mesh generator, submit it for execution, and wait for the results:

```
  meshGen->fillComputeCommandBuffer();
  meshGen->submit();
  vkDeviceWaitIdle(vkDev.device);
```

Last but not least, let's create two model renderers.

1. The first one will draw the generated mesh geometry textured with an image generated by a compute shader. The texture-generation process can be learned in the previous *Generating textures in Vulkan using compute shaders* recipe. The texture comes from a compute shader:

```
  std::vector<const char*> shaders =
    { "data/shaders/chapter06/VK04_render.vert",
      "data/shaders/chapter06/VK04_render.frag" };
  mesh = std::make_unique<ModelRenderer>(vkDev, true,
    meshGen->computedBuffer, meshGen->computedMemory,
    vertexBufferSize, indexBufferSize,
```

```
        imgGen->computed, imgGen->computedImageSampler,
        shaders, (uint32_t)sizeof(mat4), true);
```

2. The second `ModelRenderer` object will apply only a solid color with some simple lighting. The only difference is in the set of shaders:

```
    std::vector<const char*> shadersColor =
      {"data/shaders/chapter06/VK04_render.vert",
        "data/shaders/chapter06/VK04_render_color.frag"};
    meshColor = std::make_unique<ModelRenderer>(vkDev,
      true, meshGen->computedBuffer,
      meshGen->computedMemory,
      vertexBufferSize, indexBufferSize,
      imgGen->computed, imgGen->computedImageSampler,
      shadersColor, (uint32_t)sizeof(mat4),
      true, mesh->getDepthTexture(), false);
}
```

Now, we need our `chapter06/VK04_compute_mesh.comp` mesh-generation compute shader.

1. The compute shader outputs vertex data into the buffer filling the `VertexData` structure per each vertex:

```
#version 440
layout (local_size_x = 2, local_size_y = 1, local_size_z
  = 1) in;
struct VertexData {
  vec4 pos, tc, norm;
};
layout (binding = 0) buffer VertexBuffer {
  VertexData vertices[];
} vbo;
```

2. A bunch of uniforms come from C++. They correspond to the `MeshUniformBuffer` structure mentioned earlier:

```
layout (binding = 1) uniform UniformBuffer {
  float time;
  uint  numU,  numV;
  float minU, maxU, minV, maxV;
  uint P1, P2, Q1, Q2;
  float morph;
} ubo;
```

3. The heart of our mesh-generation algorithm is the `torusKnot()` function, which uses the following parametrization to triangulate a torus knot:

```
x = r * cos(u)
y = r * sin(u)
z = -sin(v)
```

4. The `torusKnot()` function is rather long and is implemented directly from the aforementioned parametrization. Feel free to play with the `baseRadius`, `segmentRadius`, and `tubeRadius` values:

```
VertexData torusKnot(vec2 uv, vec2 pq) {
  const float p = pq.x;
  const float q = pq.y;
  const float baseRadius    = 5.0;
  const float segmentRadius = 3.0;
  const float tubeRadius    = 0.5;
  float ct = cos(uv.x);
  float st = sin(uv.x);
  float qp = q / p;
  float qps = qp * segmentRadius;
  float arg = uv.x * qp;
  float sqp = sin(arg);
  float cqp = cos(arg);
  float BSQP = baseRadius + segmentRadius * cqp;
  float dxdt = -qps * sqp * ct - st * BSQP;
  float dydt = -qps * sqp * st + ct * BSQP;
  float dzdt =  qps * cqp;
  vec3 r =
    vec3(BSQP * ct, BSQP * st, segmentRadius * sqp);
  vec3 drdt = vec3(dxdt, dydt, dzdt);
  vec3 v1 = normalize(cross(r, drdt));
  vec3 v2 = normalize(cross(v1, drdt));
  float cv = cos(uv.y);
  float sv = sin(uv.y);
  VertexData res;
  res.pos = vec4(r+tubeRadius*(v1 * sv + v2 * cv), 1);
  res.norm = vec4(cross(v1 * cv - v2 * sv, drdt ), 0);
  return res;
}
```

5. We are running this compute shader on each frame so, instead of generating a static set of vertices, we can actually pre-transform them to make the mesh look like it is rotating. Here are a couple of helper functions to compute appropriate rotation matrices:

```
mat3 rotY(float angle) {
    float c = cos(angle), s = sin(angle);
    return mat3(c, 0, -s, 0, 1, 0, s, 0, c);
}
mat3 rotZ(float angle) {
    float c = cos(angle), s = sin(angle);
    return mat3(c, -s, 0, s, c, 0, 0, 0, 1);
}
```

Using the aforementioned helpers, the `main()` function of our compute shader is now straightforward, and the only interesting thing worth mentioning here is the real-time morphing that blends two torus knots with different P and Q parameters. This is pretty easy because the total number of vertices always remains the same. Let's take a closer look.

1. First, the two sets of UV coordinates for parametrization need to be computed:

```
void main() {
    uint index = gl_GlobalInvocationID.x;
    vec2 numUV = vec2(ubo.numU, ubo.numV);
    vec2 ij = vec2(float(index / ubo.numU),
                   float(index % ubo.numU));
    const vec2 maxUV1 =
        2.0 * 3.1415926 * vec2(ubo.P1, 1.0);
    vec2 uv1 = ij * maxUV1 / (numUV - vec2(1));
    const vec2 maxUV2 =
        2.0 * 3.1415926 * vec2(ubo.P2, 1.0);
    vec2 uv2 = ij * maxUV2 / (numUV - vec2(1));
```

Note

Refer to the `https://en.wikipedia.org/wiki/Torus_knot` Wikipedia page for additional explanation of the math details.

2. Compute the model matrix for our mesh by combining two rotation matrices:

```
mat3 modelMatrix =
   rotY(0.5 * ubo.time) * rotZ(0.5 * ubo.time);
```

3. Compute two vertex positions for two different torus knots:

```
VertexData v1 =
   torusKnot(uv1, vec2(ubo.P1, ubo.Q1));
VertexData v2 =
   torusKnot(uv2, vec2(ubo.P2, ubo.Q2));
```

4. Do a linear blend between them using the ubo.morph coefficient. We need to blend only the position and the normal vector:

```
vec3 pos = mix(v1.pos.xyz, v2.pos.xyz, ubo.morph);
vec3 norm =
   mix(v1.norm.xyz, v2.norm.xyz, ubo.morph);
```

5. Fill in the resulting VertexData structure and store it in the output buffer:

```
VertexData vtx;
vtx.pos  = vec4(modelMatrix * pos, 1);
vtx.tc   = vec4(ij / numUV, 0, 0);
vtx.norm = vec4(modelMatrix * norm, 0);
vbo.vertices[index] = vtx;
}
```

Both the vertex and fragment shaders used to render this mesh are trivial and can be found in chapter06/VK04_render.vert, chapter06/VK04_render.frag, and chapter06/VK04_render_color.frag. Feel free to take a look yourself, as we are not going to copy and paste them here.

The demo application will produce a variety of torus knots similar to the one shown in the following screenshot. Each time you select a new pair of P-Q parameters from the UI, the morphing animation will kick in and transform one knot into another. Checking the **Use colored mesh** box will apply colors to the mesh instead of a computed texture:

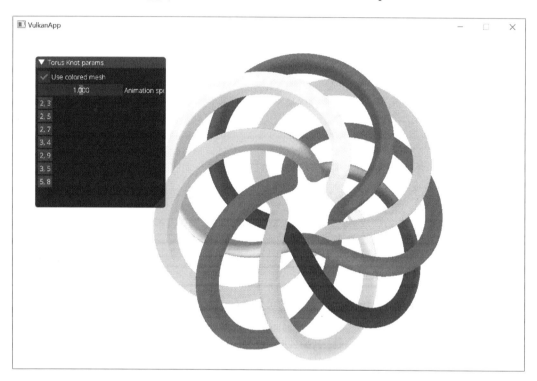

Figure 6.3 – Computed mesh with real-time animation

There's more...

In this recipe, all the synchronization between the mesh-generation process and rendering was done using `vkDeviceWaitIdle()`, essentially making these two processes completely serial and inefficient. While this is acceptable for the purpose of showing a single feature in a standalone demo app, in a real-world application a fine-grained synchronization would be desirable to allow mesh generation and rendering to run—at least partially—in parallel. Check out the guide on Vulkan synchronization from Khronos for useful insights on how to do this: `https://github.com/KhronosGroup/Vulkan-Docs/wiki/Synchronization-Examples`.

Now, let's switch back to the main topic of this chapter and learn how to precompute BRDF LUTs for PBR rendering using compute shaders.

Precomputing BRDF LUTs

In the previous recipes, we learned how to initialize compute pipelines in Vulkan and demonstrated the basic functionality of compute shaders. Let's switch gears back to PBR and learn how to precompute the **Smith GGX** BRDF LUT. To render a PBR image, we have to evaluate the BRDF at each point based on surface properties and viewing direction. This is computationally expensive, and many real-time implementations, including the reference `glTF-Sample-Viewer` implementation from Khronos, use precalculated tables of some sort to find the BRDF value based on surface roughness and viewing direction. A BRDF LUT can be stored as a 2D texture where the x axis corresponds to the dot product between the surface normal vector and the viewing direction, and the y axis corresponds to the $0 \ldots 1$. surface roughness. Each texel stores two 16-bit floating-point values—namely, a scale and bias to `F0`, which is the specular reflectance at normal incidence.

> **Important note**
>
> In this recipe, we focus purely on details of a minimalistic implementation and do not touch on any math behind it. For those interested in the math behind this approach, check out the *Environment BRDF* section from the *Real Shading in Unreal Engine 4* presentation by Brian Karis at `https://cdn2.unrealengine.com/Resources/files/2013SiggraphPresentationsNotes-26915738.pdf`.

We are going to use Vulkan to calculate this texture on the GPU and implement a compute shader to do this.

Getting ready

It would be helpful to revisit the compute pipeline creation from the *Initializing compute shaders in Vulkan* recipe. Our implementation is based on `https://github.com/SaschaWillems/Vulkan-glTF-PBR/blob/master/data/shaders/genbrdflut.frag`, which runs the same computations in a fragment shader. Our compute shader can be found in `data/shaders/chapter06/VK01_BRDF_LUT.comp`.

How to do it...

Before we look into the shader code, let's implement a generic class to process data arrays on the GPU.

To manipulate data buffers on the GPU and use the data, we need three basic operations: upload data from the host memory into a GPU buffer, download data from a GPU buffer to the host memory, and run a compute shader workload on that buffer. The data uploading and downloading process consists of mapping the GPU memory to the host address space and then using `memcpy()` to transfer buffer contents.

1. Our `uploadBufferData()` function uses the `vkMapMemory()` and `vkUnmapMemory()` Vulkan API calls to map and unmap memory:

```
void uploadBufferData(const VulkanRenderDevice& vkDev,
  VkDeviceMemory& bufferMemory,
  VkDeviceSize deviceOffset,
  const void* data, const size_t dataSize)
{
  void* mappedData = nullptr;
  vkMapMemory(vkDev.device, bufferMemory,
    deviceOffset, dataSize, 0, &mappedData);
  memcpy(mappedData, data, dataSize);
  vkUnmapMemory(vkDev.device, bufferMemory);
}
```

2. The `downloadBufferData()` function is quite similar to the preceding code. The only difference is the copying "direction"—we read from the mapped memory and store it on our app's heap:

```
void downloadBufferData(VulkanRenderDevice& vkDev,
  VkDeviceMemory& bufferMemory,
  VkDeviceSize deviceOffset,
  void* outData, const size_t dataSize)
{
  void* mappedData = nullptr;
  vkMapMemory(vkDev.device, bufferMemory,
    deviceOffset, dataSize, 0, &mappedData);
  memcpy(outData, mappedData, dataSize);
  vkUnmapMemory(vkDev.device, bufferMemory);
}
```

> **Note**
>
> The `downloadBufferData()` function should be called only after a corresponding memory barrier was executed in the compute command queue. Make sure to read the *Initializing compute shaders in Vulkan* recipe and the source code of `executeComputeShader()` for more details.

We now have two helper functions to move data around from the CPU to GPU buffers, and vice versa. Recall that in the *Initializing compute shaders in Vulkan* recipe, we implemented the `executeComputeShader()` function, which starts the compute pipeline. Let's focus on data manipulation on the GPU.

1. By using the `executeComputeShader()` function, we can implement the `ComputeBase` class to nicely hide mentions of Vulkan devices, pipelines, and descriptor sets:

```
class ComputeBase {
  void uploadInput(uint32_t offset,
    void* inData, uint32_t byteCount) {
    uploadBufferData(vkDev, inBufferMemory, offset,
      inData, byteCount);
  }
  void downloadOutput(uint32_t offset,
    void* outData, uint32_t byteCount) {
    downloadBufferData(vkDev, outBufferMemory,
      offset, outData, byteCount);
  }
```

2. To immediately execute a GPU compute workload, the `execute()` method is provided:

```
bool execute(uint32_t xSize, uint32_t ySize,
  uint32_t zSize) {
  return executeComputeShader(vkDev, pipeline,
    pipelineLayout, descriptorSet,
    xSize, ySize, zSize);
}
```

3. Early in the constructor, we allocate I/O buffers. Those are shared between the compute and graphics queues:

```
ComputeBase::ComputeBase(VulkanRenderDevice& vkDev,
  const char* shaderName, uint32_t inputSize,
  uint32_t outputSize)
: vkDev(vkDev)
{
  createSharedBuffer(vkDev, inputSize,
    VK_BUFFER_USAGE_STORAGE_BUFFER_BIT,
    VK_MEMORY_PROPERTY_HOST_VISIBLE_BIT |
      VK_MEMORY_PROPERTY_HOST_COHERENT_BIT,
    inBuffer, inBufferMemory);
```

4. To simplify our code, we allocate both buffers as host-visible. If the output buffer is needed only for rendering purposes, host visibility and coherence can be disabled:

```
createSharedBuffer(vkDev, outputSize,
  VK_BUFFER_USAGE_STORAGE_BUFFER_BIT,
  VK_MEMORY_PROPERTY_HOST_VISIBLE_BIT |
    VK_MEMORY_PROPERTY_HOST_COHERENT_BIT,
  outBuffer, outBufferMemory);
```

5. This class uses a single compute shader to process the input buffer and write the output buffer:

```
ShaderModule s;
createShaderModule(vkDev.device, &s, shaderName);
```

6. We use a descriptor set and pipeline creation routines similar to the ones from the previous recipe:

```
createComputeDescriptorSetLayout(
  vkDev.device, &dsLayout);
createPipelineLayout(
  vkDev.device, dsLayout, &pipelineLayout);
createComputePipeline(vkDev.device, s.shaderModule,
  pipelineLayout, &pipeline);
createComputeDescriptorSet(vkDev.device, dsLayout);
```

7. Finally, we dispose of the unused compute shader module:

```
vkDestroyShaderModule(
  vkDev.device, s.shaderModule, nullptr);
}
```

As we might suspect, the longest method is the `createComputeDescriptorSet()` dreaded descriptor set creation function. Let's take a closer look at the steps.

1. Fortunately, we only have two buffers, so the descriptor pool creation is relatively simple:

```
bool ComputeBase::createComputeDescriptorSet(
  VkDevice device,
  VkDescriptorSetLayout descriptorSetLayout)
{
  VkDescriptorPoolSize descriptorPoolSize = {
    VK_DESCRIPTOR_TYPE_STORAGE_BUFFER, 2
  };
```

```
VkDescriptorPoolCreateInfo descriptorPoolCreateInfo = {
  VK_STRUCTURE_TYPE_DESCRIPTOR_POOL_CREATE_INFO,
  0, 0, 1, 1, &descriptorPoolSize
};
VK_CHECK(vkCreateDescriptorPool(device,
  &descriptorPoolCreateInfo, 0, &descriptorPool));
```

2. The descriptor set creation is also straightforward, since we only need one set for
    the computation:

```
VkDescriptorSetAllocateInfo
  descriptorSetAllocateInfo = {
    VK_STRUCTURE_TYPE_DESCRIPTOR_SET_ALLOCATE_INFO,
    0, descriptorPool, 1, &descriptorSetLayout
};
VK_CHECK(vkAllocateDescriptorSets(device,
  &descriptorSetAllocateInfo, &descriptorSet));
```

3. The I/O buffer handles are bound to the descriptor set. The buffer information
    structures are as simple as possible:

```
VkDescriptorBufferInfo inBufferInfo =
  { inBuffer, 0, VK_WHOLE_SIZE };
VkDescriptorBufferInfo outBufferInfo =
  { outBuffer, 0, VK_WHOLE_SIZE };
```

4. The descriptor set update parameters refer to both buffers. After updating descriptor
    sets, we can return successfully:

```
VkWriteDescriptorSet writeDescriptorSet[2] = {
  { VK_STRUCTURE_TYPE_WRITE_DESCRIPTOR_SET, 0,
    descriptorSet, 0, 0, 1,
    VK_DESCRIPTOR_TYPE_STORAGE_BUFFER, 0,
    &inBufferInfo, 0},
  { VK_STRUCTURE_TYPE_WRITE_DESCRIPTOR_SET, 0,
    descriptorSet, 1, 0, 1,
    VK_DESCRIPTOR_TYPE_STORAGE_BUFFER, 0,
    &outBufferInfo, 0}
};
vkUpdateDescriptorSets(
  device, 2, writeDescriptorSet, 0, 0);
return true;
}
```

The preceding `ComputeBase` class is used directly in our `Chapter6/VK01_BRDF_LUT` tool. The entire computational heavy lifting to precalculate a BRDF LUT is done in a compute shader. Let's look inside the `data/chapter06/VK01_BRDF_LUT.comp` GLSL code:

1. To break down our work into smaller pieces, we start from the preamble and the `main()` function of the BRDF LUT calculation shader. The preamble first sets the compute shader dispatching parameters. In our case, a single point of the texture is calculated by one GPU worker. The number of Monte Carlo trials for numeric integration is declared as a constant:

    ```
    layout (local_size_x = 1, local_size_y = 1,
      local_size_z = 1) in;
    layout (constant_id = 0)
      const uint NUM_SAMPLES = 1024u;
    layout (set = 0, binding = 0)
      buffer SRC { float data[]; } src;
    layout (set = 0, binding = 1)
      buffer DST { float data[]; } dst;
    ```

2. We use a fixed width and height for the I/O buffer layouts. Last, but not least, `PI` is the only "physical" constant we use:

    ```
    const uint BRDF_W = 256;
    const uint BRDF_H = 256;
    const float PI = 3.1415926536;
    ```

3. The `main()` function just wraps the BRDF function call. First, we recalculate the worker ID to output array indices:

    ```
    void main() {
      vec2 uv;
      uv.x = float(gl_GlobalInvocationID.x) / float(BRDF_W);
      uv.y = float(gl_GlobalInvocationID.y) / float(BRDF_H);
    ```

4. The `BRDF()` function does all the actual work. The calculated value is put into the 2D array:

```
vec2 v = BRDF(uv.x, 1.0 - uv.y);
uint offset = gl_GlobalInvocationID.y * BRDF_W +
              gl_GlobalInvocationID.x;
dst.data[offset * 2 + 0] = v.x;
dst.data[offset * 2 + 1] = v.y;
}
```

Now that we have described some mandatory compute shader parts, we can see how the BRDF LUT items are calculated. Technically, we calculate the integral value over the hemisphere using the Monte Carlo integration procedure. Let's look at the steps.

1. To generate random directions in the hemisphere, we use so-called Hammersley points calculated by the following function:

```
vec2 hammersley2d(uint i, uint N) {
  uint bits = (i << 16u) | (i >> 16u);
  bits = ((bits&0x55555555u) << 1u) |
         ((bits&0xAAAAAAAAu) >> 1u);
  bits = ((bits&0x33333333u) << 2u) |
         ((bits&0xCCCCCCCCu) >> 2u);
  bits = ((bits&0x0F0F0F0Fu) << 4u) |
         ((bits&0xF0F0F0F0u) >> 4u);
  bits = ((bits&0x00FF00FFu) << 8u) |
         ((bits&0xFF00FF00u) >> 8u);
  float rdi = float(bits) * 2.3283064365386963e-10;
  return vec2(float(i) /float(N), rdi);
}
```

> **Important note**
>
> The code is based on the following post: `http://holger.dammertz.org/stuff/notes_HammersleyOnHemisphere.html`. The bit-shifting magic for this application and many other applications is thoroughly described in Henry J. Warren's book called *Hacker's Delight*. Interested readers may also look up the *Van der Corput sequence* to see why this can be used as random directions on the hemisphere.

2. We also need some kind of a pseudo-random number generator. We use the output array indices as input and pass them through another magic set of formulas:

```
float random(vec2 co) {
  float a = 12.9898;
  float b = 78.233;
  float c = 43758.5453;
  float dt= dot(co.xy ,vec2(a,b));
  float sn= mod(dt, PI);
  return fract(sin(sn) * c);
}
```

> **Note**
>
> Check out this link to find some useful details about this code:
> `http://byteblacksmith.com/improvements-to-the-canonical-one-liner-glsl-rand-for-opengl-es-2-0/`.

3. Let's take a look at how importance sampling is implemented according to the paper *Real Shading in Unreal Engine 4* by Brian Karis. Check out the fourth page of the following document: `https://cdn2.unrealengine.com/Resources/files/2013SiggraphPresentationsNotes-26915738.pdf`. This function maps a 2D point to a hemisphere with spread based on surface roughness:

```
vec3 importanceSample_GGX(
  vec2 Xi, float roughness, vec3 normal)
{
  float alpha = roughness * roughness;
  float phi =
    2.0 * PI * Xi.x + random(normal.xz) * 0.1;
  float cosTheta =
    sqrt((1.0-Xi.y)/(1.0+(alpha*alpha-1.0)*Xi.y));
  float sinTheta = sqrt(1.0 - cosTheta * cosTheta);
  vec3 H = vec3(
    sinTheta*cos(phi), sinTheta*sin(phi), cosTheta);
  vec3 up = abs(normal.z) < 0.999 ?
    vec3(0.0, 0.0, 1.0) : vec3(1.0, 0.0, 0.0);
  vec3 tangentX = normalize(cross(up, normal));
  vec3 tangentY = normalize(cross(normal, tangentX));
  return normalize(
    tangentX*H.x + tangentY*H.y + normal*H.z);
}
```

4. There's one more utility function required to calculate BRDF—the geometric shadowing function:

```
float G_SchlicksmithGGX(
    float dotNL, float dotNV, float roughness)
{
    float k = (roughness * roughness) / 2.0;
    float GL = dotNL / (dotNL * (1.0 - k) + k);
    float GV = dotNV / (dotNV * (1.0 - k) + k);
    return GL * GV;
}
```

5. The value of BRDF is calculated in the following way, using all of the preceding code. The NUM_SAMPLES number of Monte Carlo trials was set earlier to be 1024:

```
vec2 BRDF(float NoV, float roughness)
{
    const vec3 N = vec3(0.0, 0.0, 1.0);
    vec3 V = vec3(sqrt(1.0 - NoV*NoV), 0.0, NoV);
    vec2 LUT = vec2(0.0);
    for(uint i = 0u; i < NUM_SAMPLES; i++) {
        vec2 Xi = hammersley2d(i, NUM_SAMPLES);
        vec3 H = importanceSample_GGX(Xi, roughness, N);
        vec3 L = 2.0 * dot(V, H) * H - V;
        float dotNL = max(dot(N, L), 0.0);
        float dotNV = max(dot(N, V), 0.0);
        float dotVH = max(dot(V, H), 0.0);
        float dotNH = max(dot(H, N), 0.0);
        if (dotNL > 0.0) {
            float G =
                G_SchlicksmithGGX(dotNL, dotNV, roughness);
            float G_Vis = (G * dotVH) / (dotNH * dotNV);
            float Fc = pow(1.0 - dotVH, 5.0);
            LUT += vec2((1.0 - Fc) * G_Vis, Fc * G_Vis);
        }
    }
    return LUT / float(NUM_SAMPLES);
}
```

The C++ part of the project is trivial and just runs the compute shader, saving all the results into the `data/brdfLUT.ktx` file using the **OpenGL Image** (**GLI**) library. You can use Pico Pixel (`https://pixelandpolygon.com`) to view the generated image. It should look like the image shown in the following screenshot:

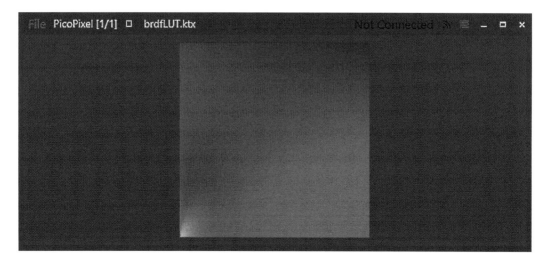

Figure 6.4 – BRDF LUT

This concludes the BRDF LUT tool description. We will need yet another tool to calculate an irradiance cubemap from an environment cube map, which we will cover next.

There's more...

The method described previously can be used to precompute BRDF LUTs using high-quality Monte Carlo integration and store them as textures. Dependent texture fetches can be expensive on some mobile platforms. There is an interesting runtime approximation used in Unreal Engine that does not rely on any precomputation, as described in `https://www.unrealengine.com/en-US/blog/physically-based-shading-on-mobile`. Here is the GLSL source code:

```glsl
vec3 EnvBRDFApprox(
  vec3 specularColor, float roughness, float NoV )
{
  const vec4 c0 = vec4(-1, -0.0275, -0.572, 0.022);
  const vec4 c1 = vec4( 1, 0.0425, 1.04, -0.04);
  vec4 r = roughness * c0 + c1;
  float a004 =
    min( r.x * r.x, exp2(-9.28 * NoV) ) * r.x + r.y;
```

```
    vec2 AB = vec2( -1.04, 1.04 ) * a004 + r.zw;
    return specularColor * AB.x + AB.y;
}
```

Precomputing irradiance maps and diffuse convolution

The second part of the split sum approximation necessary to calculate the glTF2 physically based shading model comes from the irradiance cube map, which is precalculated by convolving the input environment cube map with the **GGX** distribution of our shading model.

Getting ready

Check out the source code for this recipe in `Chapter6/Util01_FilterEnvmap`. If you want to dive deep into the math theory behind these computations, make sure you read Brian Karis's paper at `https://cdn2.unrealengine.com/Resources/files/2013SiggraphPresentationsNotes-26915738.pdf`.

How to do it...

This code is written for simplicity rather than for speed or precision, so it does not use importance sampling and convolves the input cube map using simple Monte Carlo integration and the Hammersley sequence to generate uniformly distributed 2D points on an equirectangular projection of our input cube map.

The source code can be found in the `Chapter6/Util01_FilterEnvmap/src/main.cpp` file. Let's quickly go through the steps to cover the entire process.

1. We need a C++ function to calculate the Van der Corput sequence, as described in Henry J. Warren's *Hacker's Delight*. Similar code was used in the GLSL shader in the previous recipe:

```
float radicalInverse_VdC(uint32_t bits) {
    bits = (bits << 16u) | (bits >> 16u);
    bits = ((bits&0x55555555u) << 1u) |
           ((bits&0xAAAAAAAAu) >> 1u);
    bits = ((bits&0x33333333u) << 2u) |
           ((bits&0xCCCCCCCCu) >> 2u);
    bits = ((bits&0x0F0F0F0Fu) << 4u) |
           ((bits&0xF0F0F0F0u) >> 4u);
```

```
  bits = ((bits&0x00FF00FFu) << 8u) |
         ((bits&0xFF00FF00u) >> 8u);
  return float(bits) * 2.3283064365386963e-10f;
}
```

2. By definition of the Hammersley point set, the `i`-th point can be generated using the following function, as described in `http://holger.dammertz.org/stuff/notes_HammersleyOnHemisphere.html`:

```
vec2 hammersley2d(uint32_t i, uint32_t N) {
  return vec2( float(i)/float(N),
               radicalInverse_VdC(i) );
}
```

Using this random points generator, we can finally convolve the cube map. For simplicity, our code supports only equirectangular projections where the width is twice the height of the image. Here are the steps.

1. First, we resize the input environment cube map into a smaller image sized `dstW x dstH`:

```
void convolveDiffuse(const vec3* data,
  int srcW, int srcH, int dstW, int dstH,
  vec3* output, int numMonteCarloSamples)
{
  assert(srcW == 2 * srcH);
  if (srcW != 2 * srcH) return;
  std::vector<vec3> tmp(dstW * dstH);
  stbir_resize_float_generic(
    reinterpret_cast<const float*>(data), srcW, srcH,
    0,
    reinterpret_cast<float*>(tmp.data()), dstW, dstH,
    0, 3, STBIR_ALPHA_CHANNEL_NONE, 0,
    STBIR_EDGE_CLAMP, STBIR_FILTER_CUBICBSPLINE,
    STBIR_COLORSPACE_LINEAR, nullptr);
  const vec3* scratch = tmp.data();
  srcW = dstW;
  srcH = dstH;
```

2. Then, we iterate over every pixel of the output cube map. We calculate two vectors, `V1` and `V2`. The first vector, `V1`, is the direction to the current pixel of the output cube map. The second one, `V2`, is the direction to a randomly selected pixel of the input cube map:

```
for (int y = 0; y != dstH; y++)
{
  const float theta1 =
    float(y) / float(dstH) * Math::PI;
  for (int x = 0; x != dstW; x++)
  {
    const float phi1 =
      float(x) / float(dstW) * Math::TWOPI;
    const vec3 V1 = vec3(sin(theta1) * cos(phi1),
      sin(theta1) * sin(phi1), cos(theta1));
    vec3 color = vec3(0.0f);
    float weight = 0.0f;
    for (int i = 0; i != numMonteCarloSamples; i++)
    {
      const vec2 h =
        hammersley2d(i, numMonteCarloSamples);
      const int x1 = int(floor(h.x * srcW));
      const int y1 = int(floor(h.y * srcH));
      const float theta2 =
        float(y1) / float(srcH) * Math::PI;
      const float phi2 =
        float(x1) / float(srcW) * Math::TWOPI;
      const vec3 V2 = vec3(sin(theta2) * cos(phi2),
        sin(theta2) * sin(phi2), cos(theta2));
```

3. We use the dot product between `V1` and `V2` to convolve the values of the input cube map. This is done according to the implementation of `PrefilterEnvMap()` from the following paper: `https://cdn2.unrealengine.com/Resources/files/2013SiggraphPresentationsNotes-26915738.pdf`. To speed up our CPU-based implementation, we sacrifice some precision by replacing `NdotL > 0` from the original paper with `0.01f`. The output value is renormalized using the sum of all `NdotL` weights:

```
const float NdotL =
  std::max(0.0f, glm::dot(V1, V2));
if (NdotL > 0.01f) {
```

```
            color += scratch[y1 * srcW + x1] * NdotL;
            weight += NdotL;
        }
    }
    output[y * dstW + x] = color / weight;
    }
  }
}
```

The remaining part of the code is purely mechanical work, such as loading the cube map image from the file, invoking the `convolveDiffuse()` function, and saving the result using the **STB** library. Let's check out the results of prefiltering for the input image shown in the following screenshot:

Figure 6.5 – Environment cube map

The convolved image should look like this:

Figure 6.6 – Prefiltered environment cube map using diffuse convolution

There's one more fly in the ointment of the approximations already mentioned in this recipe. Technically, we should have a separate convolution for each different BRDF. This is, however, not practical in terms of storage, memory, and performance on mobile. It is wrong but good enough.

We now have all supplementary parts in place to render a PBR image. In the next *Implementing the glTF2 shading model* recipe, we are going to put everything together into a simple application to render a physically based glTF2 3D model.

There's more...

Paul Bourke created a set of tools and a great resource explaining how to convert cube maps between different formats. Make sure to check it out at `http://paulbourke.net/panorama/cubemaps/index.html`.

Implementing the glTF2 shading model

This recipe will cover how to integrate a PBR into your graphics pipeline. Since the topic of PBR rendering is vast, we focus on a minimalistic implementation just to guide you and get you started. In the book text right here, we focus on the GLSL shader code for the PBR shading model and use OpenGL to make things simpler. However, the source code bundle for this book contains a relatively small Vulkan implementation that reuses the same GLSL code. Indeed, rendering a physically based image is nothing more than running a fancy pixel shader with a set of textures.

Getting ready

It is recommended to read about glTF 2.0 before you proceed with this recipe. A lightweight introduction to the glTF 2.0 shading model can be found at `https://github.com/KhronosGroup/glTF-Sample-Viewer/tree/glTF-WebGL-PBR`.

The C++ source code for this recipe is in the `Chapter6/GL01_PBR` folder. The GLSL shader code responsible for PBR calculations can be found in `data/shaders/chapter06/PBR.sp`.

How to do it...

Before we dive deep into the GLSL code, we'll look at how the input data is set up from the C++ side. We are going to use the *Damaged Helmet* 3D model provided by Khronos. You can find the glTF file here: `deps/src/glTF-Sample-Models/2.0/DamagedHelmet/glTF/DamagedHelmet.gltf`. Let's get started.

1. After loading the model vertices using `AssImp`, we need to load all the textures corresponding to our 3D model:

```
GLTexture texAO(GL_TEXTURE_2D,
  "DamagedHelmet/glTF/Default_AO.jpg");
GLTexture texEmissive(GL_TEXTURE_2D,
  "DamagedHelmet/glTF/Default_emissive.jpg");
GLTexture texAlbedo(GL_TEXTURE_2D,
  "DamagedHelmet/glTF/Default_albedo.jpg");
GLTexture texMeR(GL_TEXTURE_2D,
  "DamagedHelmet/glTF/Default_metalRoughness.jpg");
GLTexture texNormal(GL_TEXTURE_2D,
  "DamagedHelmet/glTF/Default_normal.jpg");
```

2. Textures are bound to OpenGL binding points, starting from `0`:

```
const GLuint textures[] = { texAO.getHandle(),
  texEmissive.getHandle(), texAlbedo.getHandle(),
  texMeR.getHandle(), texNormal.getHandle() };
glBindTextures(
  0, sizeof(textures)/sizeof(GLuint), textures);
```

3. The environment cube map and convolved irradiance map are loaded and bound to the OpenGL context:

```
GLTexture envMap(GL_TEXTURE_CUBE_MAP,
  "data/piazza_bologni_1k.hdr");
GLTexture envMapIrradiance(GL_TEXTURE_CUBE_MAP,
  "data/piazza_bologni_1k_irradiance.hdr");
const GLuint envMaps[] = {
  envMap.getHandle(), envMapIrradiance.getHandle() };
glBindTextures(5, 2, envMaps);
```

Check the previous *Precomputing irradiance maps and diffuse convolution* recipe for details of where it came from.

4. The BRDF LUT is loaded. Check out the *Precomputing BRDF LUTs* recipe for all the precalculation details:

```
GLTexture brdfLUT(GL_TEXTURE_2D, "data/brdfLUT.ktx");
glBindTextureUnit(7, brdfLUT.getHandle());
```

Everything else is just mesh rendering, similar to how it was done in the previous chapter. Let's skip the rest of the C++ code and focus on the GLSL shaders. There are two shaders used to render our PBR model in OpenGL: `GL01_PBR.vert` and `GL01_PBR.frag`. The vertex shader does nothing interesting. It uses programmable vertex pulling to read vertex data from the SSBO and passes data further down the graphics pipeline. The fragment shader does the real, actual work. Let's take a look.

1. As usual, we require per-frame data from the CPU side using a uniform buffer. Texture coordinates, the normal vector, and the fragment's world position are obtained from the vertex shader:

```
#version 460 core
layout(std140, binding = 0) uniform PerFrameData {
  mat4 view;
  mat4 proj;
```

```
   vec4 cameraPos;
};
layout (location=0) in vec2 tc;
layout (location=1) in vec3 normal;
layout (location=2) in vec3 worldPos;
layout (location=0) out vec4 out_FragColor;
```

2. The five textures we loaded in C++ are bound to the 0 . . . 4 OpenGL binding points:

```
layout (binding = 0) uniform sampler2D texAO;
layout (binding = 1) uniform sampler2D texEmissive;
layout (binding = 2) uniform sampler2D texAlbedo;
layout (binding = 3)
  uniform sampler2D texMetalRoughness;
layout (binding = 4) uniform sampler2D texNormal;
```

3. The environment cube map, the prefiltered cube map, and the BRDF LUT are here:

```
layout (binding = 5) uniform samplerCube texEnvMap;
layout (binding = 6)
  uniform samplerCube texEnvMapIrradiance;
layout (binding = 7) uniform sampler2D texBRDF_LUT;
```

4. Now, we include a GLSL source file containing a set of PBR calculation routines that are shared between our OpenGL and Vulkan implementations. It does all the heavy lifting, and we will come back to this file in a moment:

```
#include <data/shaders/chapter06/PBR.sp>
```

5. The `main()` function starts by fetching all the necessary texture data required for our shading model. Here come ambient occlusion, emissive color, albedo, metallic factor, and roughness. The last two values are packed into a single texture:

```
void main() {
   vec4 Kao = texture(texAO, tc);
   vec4 Ke  = texture(texEmissive, tc);
   vec4 Kd  = texture(texAlbedo, tc);
   vec2 MeR = texture(texMetalRoughness, tc).yz;
```

6. To calculate the proper normal mapping effect according to the normal map, we evaluate the normal vector per pixel. We do this in world space. The `perturbNormal()` function calculates the tangent space per pixel using the derivatives of the texture coordinates, and it is implemented in `chapter06/PBR.sp`. Make sure you check it out. If you want to disable normal mapping and use only per-vertex normals, just comment out the second line here:

```
vec3 n = normalize(normal);
n = perturbNormal(n,
    normalize(cameraPos.xyz - worldPos), tc);
```

7. Let's fill in the `PBRInfo` structure, which encapsulates multiple inputs used by the various functions in the PBR shading equation:

```
PBRInfo pbrInputs;
vec3 color = calculatePBRInputsMetallicRoughness(
    Kd, n, cameraPos.xyz, worldPos, pbrInputs);
```

8. For this demo application, we use only one hardcoded directional light source—`(-1, -1, -1)`. Let's calculate the lighting coming from it:

```
color += calculatePBRLightContribution( pbrInputs,
    normalize(vec3(-1.0, -1.0, -1.0)), vec3(1.0) );
```

9. Now, we should multiply the color by the ambient occlusion factor. Use `1.0` in case there is no ambient occlusion texture available:

```
color = color * ( Kao.r < 0.01 ? 1.0 : Kao.r );
```

10. Add the emissive color contribution. Make sure the input emissive texture is converted into the linear color space before use. Convert the resulting color back into the **standard RGB (sRGB)** color space before writing it into the framebuffer:

```
color = pow(
    SRGBtoLINEAR(Ke).rgb + color, vec3(1.0/2.2) );
out_FragColor = vec4(color, 1.0);
};
```

Let's take a look at the calculations that happen inside `chapter06/PBR.sp`. Our implementation is based on the reference implementation of glTF 2.0 Sample Viewer from Khronos, which you can find at `https://github.com/KhronosGroup/glTF-Sample-Viewer/tree/glTF-WebGL-PBR`.

1. First of all, here is the `PBRInfo` structure that holds various input parameters for our shading model:

```
struct PBRInfo {
  // cos angle between normal and light direction
  float NdotL;
  // cos angle between normal and view direction
  float NdotV;
  // cos angle between normal and half vector
  float NdotH;
  // cos angle between light dir and half vector
  float LdotH;
  // cos angle between view dir and half vector
  float VdotH;
  // roughness value (input to shader)
  float perceptualRoughness;
  // full reflectance color
  vec3 reflectance0;
  // reflectance color at grazing angle
  vec3 reflectance90;
  // remapped linear roughness
  float alphaRoughness;
  // contribution from diffuse lighting
  vec3 diffuseColor;
  // contribution from specular lighting
  vec3 specularColor;
  // normal at surface point
  vec3 n;
  // vector from surface point to camera
  vec3 v;
};
```

2. The sRGB-to-linear color space conversion routine is implemented this way. It is a rough approximation, done for simplicity:

```
vec4 SRGBtoLINEAR(vec4 srgbIn) {
  vec3 linOut = pow(srgbIn.xyz,vec3(2.2));
  return vec4(linOut, srgbIn.a);
}
```

3. Here is the calculation of the lighting contribution from an **image-based lighting (IBL)** source:

```
vec3 getIBLContribution(
  PBRInfo pbrInputs, vec3 n, vec3 reflection)
{

  float mipCount =
    float(textureQueryLevels(texEnvMap));
  float lod =
    pbrInputs.perceptualRoughness * mipCount;
```

4. Retrieve a scale and bias to `F0` from the BRDF LUT:

```
vec2 brdfSamplePoint = clamp(vec2(pbrInputs.NdotV,
  1.0-pbrInputs.perceptualRoughness),
  vec2(0.0), vec2(1.0));
vec3 brdf =
  textureLod(texBRDF_LUT, brdfSamplePoint, 0).rgb;
```

5. This code is reused by both the OpenGL and Vulkan implementations. Convert the cube map coordinates into the Vulkan coordinate space:

```
#ifdef VULKAN
  vec3 cm = vec3(-1.0, -1.0, 1.0);
#else
  vec3 cm = vec3(1.0);
#endif
```

6. Fetch values from the cube maps. No conversion to the linear color space is required since **High Dynamic Range (HDR)** cube maps are already linear. Besides that, we can directly add `diffuse` and `specular` because our precalculated BRDF LUT already takes care of energy conservation:

```
vec3 diffuseLight =
  texture(texEnvMapIrradience, n.xyz * cm).rgb;
vec3 specularLight = textureLod(texEnvMap,
  reflection.xyz * cm, lod).rgb;
```

```
      vec3 diffuse =
        diffuseLight * pbrInputs.diffuseColor;
      vec3 specular = specularLight *
        (pbrInputs.specularColor * brdf.x + brdf.y);
      return diffuse + specular;
    }
```

Now, let's go through all the helper functions that are necessary to calculate different parts of the rendering equation.

1. The `diffuseBurley()` function implements the diffuse term from the *Physically Based Shading at Disney* paper by Brent Burley, found at `http://blog.selfshadow.com/publications/s2012-shading-course/burley/s2012_pbs_disney_brdf_notes_v3.pdf`:

    ```
    vec3 diffuseBurley(PBRInfo pbrInputs) {
        float f90 = 2.0 * pbrInputs.LdotH *
          pbrInputs.LdotH * pbrInputs.alphaRoughness - 0.5;
        return (pbrInputs.diffuseColor / M_PI) *
          (1.0 + f90 * pow((1.0 - pbrInputs.NdotL), 5.0)) *
          (1.0 + f90 * pow((1.0 - pbrInputs.NdotV), 5.0));
    }
    ```

2. The next function models the Fresnel reflectance term of the rendering equation, also known as the `F` term:

    ```
    vec3 specularReflection(PBRInfo pbrInputs) {
      return pbrInputs.reflectance0 +
        (pbrInputs.reflectance90 - pbrInputs.reflectance0)
        * pow(clamp(1.0 - pbrInputs.VdotH, 0.0, 1.0), 5.0);
    }
    ```

3. The `geometricOcclusion()` function calculates the specular geometric attenuation `G`, where materials with a higher roughness will reflect less light back to the viewer:

    ```
    float geometricOcclusion(PBRInfo pbrInputs) {
       float NdotL = pbrInputs.NdotL;
       float NdotV = pbrInputs.NdotV;
       float rSqr =
         pbrInputs.alphaRoughness *
         pbrInputs.alphaRoughness;
       float attenuationL = 2.0 * NdotL /
         (NdotL + sqrt(rSqr + (1.0 - rSqr) *
    ```

```
        (NdotL * NdotL)));
    float attenuationV = 2.0 * NdotV /
      (NdotV + sqrt(rSqr + (1.0 - rSqr) *
        (NdotV * NdotV)));
    return attenuationL * attenuationV;
}
```

4. The following function models the distribution of microfacet normals D across the area being drawn:

```
float microfacetDistribution(PBRInfo pbrInputs) {
    float roughnessSq =
      pbrInputs.alphaRoughness *
      pbrInputs.alphaRoughness;
    float f = (pbrInputs.NdotH * roughnessSq -
      pbrInputs.NdotH) * pbrInputs.NdotH + 1.0;
    return roughnessSq / (M_PI * f * f);
}
```

This implementation is from *Average Irregularity Representation of a Rough Surface for Ray Reflection* by T. S. Trowbridge and K. P. Reitz.

Before we can calculate the light contribution from a light source, we need to fill in the fields of the PBRInfo structure. The following function does this.

1. As it is supposed to be in glTF 2.0, roughness is stored in the green channel, while metallic is stored in the blue channel. This layout intentionally reserves the red channel for optional occlusion map data:

```
vec3 calculatePBRInputsMetallicRoughness(
    vec4 albedo, vec3 normal, vec3 cameraPos,
    vec3 worldPos, out PBRInfo pbrInputs)
{
    float perceptualRoughness = 1.0;
    float metallic = 1.0;
    vec4 mrSample = texture(texMetalRoughness, tc);
    perceptualRoughness =
      mrSample.g * perceptualRoughness;
    metallic = mrSample.b * metallic;
    perceptualRoughness =
      clamp(perceptualRoughness, 0.04, 1.0);
    metallic = clamp(metallic, 0.0, 1.0);
```

2. Roughness is authored as perceptual roughness; by convention, we convert this to material roughness by squaring the perceptual roughness. The albedo may be defined from a base texture or a flat color. Let's compute the specular reflectance in the following way:

```
float alphaRoughness =
  perceptualRoughness * perceptualRoughness;
vec4 baseColor = albedo;
vec3 f0 = vec3(0.04);
vec3 diffuseColor =
  baseColor.rgb * (vec3(1.0) - f0);
diffuseColor *= 1.0 - metallic;
vec3 specularColor =
  mix(f0, baseColor.rgb, metallic);
float reflectance = max(max(specularColor.r,
  specularColor.g), specularColor.b);
```

3. For a typical incident reflectance range between 4% to 100%, we should set the grazing reflectance to 100% for a typical Fresnel effect. For a very low reflectance range on highly diffused objects, below 4%, incrementally reduce the grazing reflectance to 0%:

```
float reflectance90 =
  clamp(reflectance * 25.0, 0.0, 1.0);
vec3 specularEnvironmentR0 = specularColor.rgb;
vec3 specularEnvironmentR90 =
  vec3(1.0, 1.0, 1.0) * reflectance90;
vec3 n = normalize(normal);
vec3 v = normalize(cameraPos - worldPos);
vec3 reflection = -normalize(reflect(v, n));
```

4. Finally, we should fill in the PBRInfo structure with precalculated values. It will be reused to calculate the contribution of each individual light in the scene:

```
pbrInputs.NdotV = clamp(abs(dot(n, v)), 0.001, 1.0);
pbrInputs.perceptualRoughness = perceptualRoughness;
pbrInputs.reflectance0 = specularEnvironmentR0;
pbrInputs.reflectance90 = specularEnvironmentR90;
pbrInputs.alphaRoughness = alphaRoughness;
pbrInputs.diffuseColor = diffuseColor;
pbrInputs.specularColor = specularColor;
```

```
    pbrInputs.n = n;
    pbrInputs.v = v;
```

5. Calculate the lighting contribution from an IBL source using the
   getIBLContribution() function:

```
    vec3 color = getIBLContribution(
       pbrInputs, n, reflection);
    return color;
}
```

The lighting contribution from a single light source can be calculated in the following way
using the precalculated values from PBRInfo.

1. Here, l is the vector from the surface point to the light source, and h is the half
   vector between l and v:

```
vec3 calculatePBRLightContribution(
    inout PBRInfo pbrInputs, vec3 lightDirection,
    vec3 lightColor)
{
    vec3 n = pbrInputs.n;
    vec3 v = pbrInputs.v;
    vec3 l = normalize(lightDirection);
    vec3 h = normalize(l + v);
    float NdotV = pbrInputs.NdotV;
    float NdotL = clamp(dot(n, l), 0.001, 1.0);
    float NdotH = clamp(dot(n, h), 0.0, 1.0);
    float LdotH = clamp(dot(l, h), 0.0, 1.0);
    float VdotH = clamp(dot(v, h), 0.0, 1.0);
    pbrInputs.NdotL = NdotL;
    pbrInputs.NdotH = NdotH;
    pbrInputs.LdotH = LdotH;
    pbrInputs.VdotH = VdotH;
```

2. Calculate the shading terms for the microfacet specular shading model using the
   helper functions described earlier in this recipe:

```
    vec3 F = specularReflection(pbrInputs);
    float G = geometricOcclusion(pbrInputs);
    float D = microfacetDistribution(pbrInputs);
```

3. Here is the calculation of the analytical lighting contribution:

```
vec3 diffuseContrib =
  (1.0 - F) * diffuseBurley(pbrInputs);
vec3 specContrib =
  F * G * D / (4.0 * NdotL * NdotV);
```

4. Obtain the final intensity as reflectance (BRDF) scaled by the energy of the light using the cosine law:

```
vec3 color = NdotL * lightColor *
  (diffuseContrib + specContrib);
return color;
}
```

The resulting demo application should render an image like the one shown in the following screenshot. Try also using different PBR glTF 2.0 models:

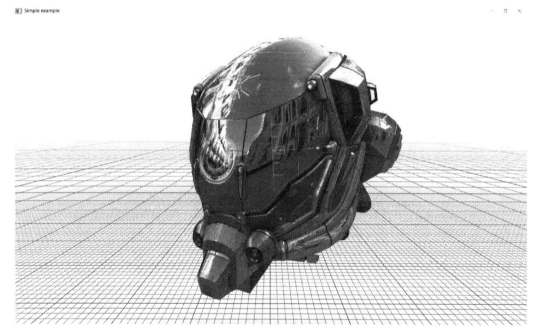

Figure 6.7 – PBR of the Damaged Helmet glTF 2.0 model

There's more...

We've also made a Vulkan version of this app that reuses the same PBR calculation code from `PBR.sp`. This can be found in `Chapter06/VK05_PBR`.

The whole area of PBR is vast, and it is possible only to scratch its surface on these half-a-hundred pages. In real life, much more complicated PBR implementations can be created that are built on the requirements of content production pipelines. For an endless source of inspiration for what can be done, we recommend looking into the Unreal Engine source code, which is available for free on GitHub at `https://github.com/EpicGames/UnrealEngine/tree/release/Engine/Shaders/Private`.

7
Graphics Rendering Pipeline

In this chapter, we will learn how to implement a hierarchical scene representation and corresponding rendering pipeline. This will help us combine the rendering we completed for the geometry and materials we explored in the previous chapters. Instead of implementing a naive object-oriented scene graph where each node is represented by an object that's allocated on the heap, we will learn how to apply the data-oriented design approach to simplify the memory layout of our scene. This will make the modifications we apply to the scene graph significantly faster. This will also act as a basis for learning about data-oriented design principles and applying them in practice. The scene graph and materials representation presented here is compatible with glTF2.

This chapter will cover how to organize the overall rendering process of complex scenes with multiple materials. We will be covering the following recipes:

- How not to create a scene graph
- Using data-oriented design for a scene graph
- Loading and saving a scene graph
- Implementing transformation trees
- Implementing a material system
- Importing materials from Assimp

- Implementing a scene conversion tool

- Managing Vulkan resources

- Refactoring Vulkan initialization and the main loop

- Working with rendering passes

- Unifying descriptor set creation routines

- Putting it all together into a Vulkan application

Technical requirements

To run the recipes in this chapter, you must have a computer with a video card that supports OpenGL 4.6, with `ARB_bindless_texture`, and Vulkan 1.2, with nonuniform indexing for sampled image arrays. Read *Chapter 1, Establishing a Build Environment*, if you want to learn how to build the demo applications shown in this book.

The source code for this chapter can be found on GitHub at `https://github.com/PacktPublishing/3D-Graphics-Rendering-Cookbook`.

How not to do a scene graph

Numerous hobby 3D engines use a straightforward and naive class-based approach to implement a scene graph. It is always tempting to define a structure similar to the following code, but please do not do this:

```
struct SceneNode {
  SceneNode* parent_;
  vector<SceneNode*> children_;
  mat4 localTransform_;
  mat4 globalTransform_;
  Mesh* mesh_;
  Material* material_;
  void Render();
};
```

On top of this structure, you can define numerous recursive traversal methods, such as the dreaded `render()` operation. Let's say we have the following root object:

```
SceneNode* root;
```

Here, rendering a scene graph can be as simple as doing the following:

```
root->render();
```

The rendering routine in this case does multiple things. Most importantly, the `render()` method calculates the global transform for the current node. After that, depending on the rendering API being used, mesh geometry and material information is sent to the rendering pipeline. At the end, a recursive call is made to render all the children:

```
void SceneNode::render() {
  globalTransform_ = parent_ ?
    parent_->globalTransform : mat4(1) * localTransform_;
  … API-specific rendering calls…
  for (auto& c: this->children_)
    c->Render();
}
```

While being a simple and "canonical" object-oriented implementation, it has multiple serious drawbacks:

- Non-locality of data due to the use of pointers, unless a custom memory allocator is used.

- Performance issues due to explicit recursion.

- Potential memory leaks and crashes while using raw pointers, unless you're using smart pointers. This will slow down the performance even further due to atomic operations.

- Difficulties with circular references and the need to employ weak pointers and similar tricks while using smart pointers to solve memory leak problems.

- Cumbersome and error-prone recursive loading and saving of the structure.

- Difficulties with implementing extensions (having to add more and more fields to `SceneNode`).

The 3D engine grows and scene graph requirements become increasingly numerous, new fields, arrays, callbacks, and pointers must be added and handled in the `SceneNode` structure making this approach essentially fragile and hard to maintain.

Let us step back and rethink how to keep the relative scene structure without using large monolithic classes with heavyweight dynamic containers inside.

Using data-oriented design for a scene graph

To represent complex nested visual objects such as robotic arms, planetary systems, or deeply branched animated trees, you can split the object into parts and keep track of the hierarchical relationships between them. A directed graph of parent-child relationships between different objects in a scene is called a scene graph. We are deliberately avoiding using the words "acyclic graph" here because, for convenience, you may decide to use circular references between nodes in a controlled way. Most 3D graphics tutorials aimed at hobbyists lead directly down the simple but non-optimal path we identified in the previous recipe, *How not to do a scene graph*. Let's go a bit deeper into the rabbit hole and learn how to apply data-oriented design to implement a faster scene graph.

In this recipe, we will learn how to get started with a decently performant scene graph design. Our focus will be on scene graphs with fixed hierarchies. In *Chapter 9, Working with Scene Graphs*, we will elaborate on this topic more and explore how to deal with runtime topology changes and other scene graph operations.

Getting ready

The source code for this recipe is split between the scene geometry conversion tool, `Chapter7/Scene Converter/src/main.cpp`, and the rendering code, which can be found in the `Chapter7/GL01_LargeScene` and `Chapter7/VK01_SceneGraph` demos.

How to do it...

It seems logical to store a linear array of individual nodes, and also replace all the "external" pointers such as `Mesh*` and `Material*`, by using suitably sized integer handles, which are just indices to some other arrays. The array of child nodes and references to parent nodes are left outside.

The local and global transforms are also stored in separate arrays and can be easily mapped to a GPU buffer without conversion, making them directly accessible from GLSL shaders. Let's look at the implementation:

1. Here, we have a new simplified scene node declaration. Our new scene is a composite of arrays:

    ```
    struct SceneNode {
      int mesh_;
      int material_;
    };
    struct Scene {
    ```

```
  vector<SceneNode> nodes_;
  vector<mat4> local_;
  vector<mat4> global_;
};
```

One question remains: how can we store the hierarchy? The solution is well-known and is called the **Left Child – Right Sibling** tree representation. Since a scene graph is really a tree, at least in theory, where no optimization-related circular references are introduced, we may convert any tree with more than two children into a binary tree by "tilting" the branches, as shown in the following diagram:

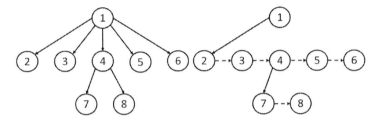

Figure 7.1 – Tree representations

The image on the left-hand side shows a standard tree with a variable number of children for each node, while the image on the right-hand side shows a new structure that only stores a single reference to the first child and another reference to the next "sibling." Here, "being a sibling node" means "to be a child node of the same parent node." This transformation removes the need to store `std::vector` in each scene node. Finally, if we "tilt" the right image, we get a familiar binary tree structure where the left arrows are solid and represent a "first child" reference and the right arrows are dashed and represent the "next sibling" reference:

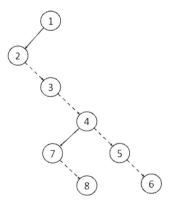

Figure 7.2 – Tilted tree

2. Let's add indices to the `SceneNode` structure to represent the aforementioned storage schema. Along with the mesh and material indices for each node, we will store a reference to the parent, an index for the first child (or a negative value if there are no child nodes), and an index for the next sibling scene node:

```
struct SceneNode {
   int mesh_, material_;
   int parent_;
   int firstChild_;
   int rightSibling_;
};
```

What we have now is a compact linear list of constant sized objects that are plain old data. Yes, the tree traversal and modification routines may seem unusual, but these are just linked list iterations. It would be unfair not to mention a rather serious disadvantage, though: random access to a child node is now slower on average because we must traverse each node in a list. For our purposes, this is not fatal since we will either touch all the children or none of them.

3. Before turning to the implementation, let's perform another unconventional transformation of the new `SceneNode` structure. It contains the indices of the mesh and material, along with hierarchical information, but the local and global transformations are stored outside. This suggests that we may need to define the following structure to store our scene hierarchy:

```
struct Hierarchy {
   int parent_;
   int firstChild_;
   int nextSibling_;
   int level_;
};
```

We have changed "left" to "first" and "right" to "next" since tree node geometry does not matter here. The `level_` field stores the cached depth of the node from the top of the scene graph. The root node is at level zero; all the children have a level that's greater by one with respect to their parents.

Also, the `Mesh` and `Material` objects for each node can be stored in separate arrays. However, if not all the nodes are equipped with a mesh or material, we can use a hash table to store node-to-mesh and node-to-material mappings. Absence of such mappings simply indicates that a node is only being used for transformations or hierarchical relation storage. The hash tables are not as linear as arrays, but they can be trivially converted to and from arrays of {`key, value`} pairs.

4. Finally, we can declare a new `Scene` structure with logical "compartments" that we will later call **components**:

```cpp
struct Scene {
  vector<mat4> localTransforms_;
  vector<mat4> globalTransforms_;
  vector<Hierarchy> hierarchy_;
  // Meshes for nodes (Node -> Mesh)
  unordered_map<uint32_t, uint32_t> meshes_;
  // Materials for nodes (Node -> Material)
  unordered_map<uint32_t, uint32_t> materialForNode_;
```

5. The following components are not strictly necessary, but they help a lot while debugging scene graph manipulation routines or while implementing an interactive scene editor, where the ability to see some human-readable node identifiers is crucial:

```cpp
  // Node names: which name is assigned to the node
  std::unordered_map<uint32_t, uint32_t> nameForNode_;
  // Collection of scene node names
  std::vector<std::string> names_;
  // Collection of debug material names
  std::vector<std::string> materialNames_;
};
```

One thing that is missing is the `SceneNode` structure itself, which is now represented by integer indices in the arrays of the `Scene` structure. It is rather amusing and unusual for an object-oriented mind to speak about `SceneNode` while not needing or having the scene node class itself.

The conversion routine for Assimp's `aiScene` into our format is implemented in the `Chapter7/SceneConverter` project. It is a form of top-down recursive traversal where we create our implicit `SceneNode` objects in the `Scene` structure. Let's go through the steps for traversing a scene stored in the aforementioned format:

1. Traversal starts from some node with a given parent that's passed as a parameter. A new node identifier is returned by the `addNode()` routine shown here. If `aiNode` contains a name, we store it in the `Scene::names_` array:

```
void traverse(const aiScene* sourceScene,
  Scene& scene,
  aiNode* node, int parent, int atLevel)
{
  int newNodeID = addNode(scene, parent, atLevel);
  if (node->mName.C_Str()) {
    uint32_t stringID = (uint32_t)scene.names_.size();
    scene.names_.push_back(
      std::string( node->mName.C_Str()) );
    scene.nameForNode_[newNodeID] = stringID;
  }
}
```

2. If this `aiNode` object has meshes attached to it, we must create one subnode for each of the meshes. For easier debugging, we will add a name for each new mesh subnode:

```
for (size_t i = 0; i < node->mNumMeshes ; i++) {
  int newSubNodeID = addNode(
    scene, newNode, atLevel + 1);
  uint32_t stringID = (uint32_t)scene.names_.size();
  scene.names_.push_back(
    std::string(node->mName.C_Str()) +
    "_Mesh_" + std::to_string(i));
  scene.nameForNode_[newSubNodeID] = stringID;
```

3. Each of the meshes is assigned to the newly created subnode. Assimp ensures that a mesh has a material assigned to it, so we will assign that material to our node:

```
int mesh = (int)node->mMeshes[i];
scene.meshes_[newSubNodeID] = mesh;
scene.materialForNode_[newSubNodeID] =
  sourceScene->mMeshes[mesh]->mMaterialIndex;
```

4. Since we only use subnodes for to attach meshes, we will set the local and global transformations to identity matrices:

```
scene.globalTransform_[newSubNode] =
   glm::mat4(1.0f);
scene.localTransform_[newSubNode] =
   glm::mat4(1.0f);
}
```

5. The global transformation is set to identity at the beginning of node conversion. It will be recalculated at the first frame or if the node is marked as changed. See the *Implementing transformations trees* recipe in this chapter for the implementation details. The local transformation is fetched from `aiNode` and converted into a `glm::mat4` object:

```
scene.globalTransform_[newNode] = glm::mat4(1.0f);
scene.localTransform_[newNode] =
   toMat4(N->mTransformation);
```

6. At the end, we recursively traverse the children of this `aiNode` object:

```
for (unsigned int n = 0 ; n < N->mNumChildren ; n++)
   traverse(sourceScene, scene, N->mChildren[n],
      newNode, atLevel+1);
}
```

7. The `toMat4()` helper function is a per-component conversion of the `aiMatrix4x4` parameter, and is transformed into a GLM matrix:

```
glm::mat4 toMat4(const aiMatrix4x4& m) {
  glm::mat4 mm;
  for (int i = 0; i < 4; i++)
    for (int j = 0; j < 4; j++)
      mm[i][j] = m[i][j];
  return mm;
}
```

The most complex part of the code for dealing with the `Scene` data structure is the `addNode()` routine, which allocates a new scene node and adds it to the scene hierarchy. Let's check out how to implement it:

1. First, the addition process acquires a new node identifier, which is the current size of the hierarchy array. New identity transforms are added to the local and global transform arrays. The hierarchy for the newly added node only consists of the parent reference:

```
int addNode(Scene& scene, int parent, int level)
{
   int node = (int)scene.hierarchy_.size();
   scene.localTransform_.push_back(glm::mat4(1.0f));
   scene.globalTransform_.push_back(glm::mat4(1.0f));
   scene.hierarchy.push_back({ .parent = parent });
```

2. If we have a parent, we must fix its first child reference and, potentially, the next sibling reference of some other node. If a parent node has no children, we must directly set its `firstChild_` field; otherwise, we should run over the siblings of this child to find out where to add the next sibling:

```
if (parent > -1) {
   int s = scene.hierarchy_[parent].firstChild_;
   if (s == -1) {
      scene.hierarchy_[parent].firstChild_ = node;
      scene.hierarchy_[node].lastSibling_ = node;
   } else {
      int dest = scene.hierarchy_[s].lastSibling_;
      if (dest <= -1) {
         // iterate nextSibling_ indices
         for (dest = s;
            scene.hierarchy_[dest].nextSibling_ != -1;
            dest = scene.hierarchy_[dest].nextSibling_);
      }
      scene.hierarchy_[dest].nextSibling_ = node;
      scene.hierarchy_[s].lastSibling_ = node;
   }
}
```

After the for loop, we assign our new node as the next sibling of the last child. Note that this linear run over the siblings is not really necessary if we store the index of the last child node that was added. Later, in the *Implementing transformations* recipe, we will show you how to modify addNode() and remove the preceding loop.

3. The level of this node is stored for correct global transformation updating. To keep the structure valid, we will store the negative indices for the newly added node:

```
    scene.hierarchy[node].level = level;
    scene.hierarchy_[node].nextSibling_ = -1;
    scene.hierarchy_[node].firstChild_  = -1;
    return node;
}
```

Once we have the material system in place, we can use the traverse() routine in our new SceneConvert tool.

There's more...

Data-oriented design (DOD) is a vast domain, and we just used a few techniques from it. We recommend reading the online book *Data-Oriented Design*, by Richard Fabian, to get yourself familiar with more DOD concepts: https://www.dataorienteddesign.com/dodbook.

The Chapter7/VK01_SceneGraph demo application contains some basic scene graph editing capabilities for ImGui. These can help you get started with integrating scene graphs into your productivity tools. Check out shared/vkFramework/GuiRenderer.cpp for more details. The following recursive function, called renderSceneTree(), is responsible for rendering the scene graph tree hierarchy in the UI and selecting a node for editing:

```
int renderSceneTree(const Scene& scene, int node) {
  int selected = -1;
  std::string name = getNodeName(scene, node);
  std::string label = name.empty() ?
    (std::string("Node") + std::to_string(node)) : name;
  int flags = (scene.hierarchy_[node].firstChild_ < 0) ?
    ImGuiTreeNodeFlags_Leaf|ImGuiTreeNodeFlags_Bullet : 0;
  const bool opened = ImGui::TreeNodeEx(
    &scene.hierarchy_[node], flags, "%s", label.c_str());
  ImGui::PushID(node);
  if (ImGui::IsItemClicked(0)) selected = node;
```

```
  if (opened) {
    for (int ch = scene.hierarchy_[node].firstChild_;
         ch != -1; ch = scene.hierarchy_[ch].nextSibling_)
    {
      int subNode = renderSceneTree(scene, ch);
      if (subNode > -1) selected = subNode;
    }
    ImGui::TreePop();
  }
  ImGui::PopID();
  return selected;
}
```

The editNode() function can be used as a basis for building editing functionality for nodes, materials, and other scene graph content.

Loading and saving a scene graph

To quote Frederick Brooks, *"Show me your data structures and I do not need to see your code."* Hopefully, it is already more or less clear how to implement basic operations on a scene graph, but the remaining recipes in this chapter will explicitly describe all the required routines. Here, we will provide an overview of the loading and saving operations for our scene graph structure.

Getting ready

Make sure you have read the previous recipe, *Using data-oriented design for a scene graph*, before proceeding any further.

How to do it...

The loading procedure is a sequence of fread() calls, followed by a pair of loadMap() operations. As usual, we will be omitting any error handling code in this book's text; however, the accompanying source code bundle contains many necessary checks to see if the file was actually opened and so on. Let's get started:

1. After opening the file, we can read the count of stored scene nodes. The data arrays are resized accordingly:

```
void loadScene(const char* fileName, Scene& scene)
{
```

```
FILE* f = fopen(fileName, "rb");
uint32_t sz;
fread(&sz, sizeof(sz), 1, f);
scene.hierarchy.resize(sz);
scene.globalTransform.resize(sz);
scene.localTransform.resize(sz);
```

2. `fread()` reads the transformations and hierarchical data for all the scene nodes:

```
fread(scene.localTransform.data(),
   sizeof(glm::mat4), sz, f);
fread(scene.globalTransform.data(),
   sizeof(glm::mat4), sz, f);
fread(
   scene.hierarchy.data(), sizeof(Hierarchy), sz, f);
```

3. Node-to-material and node-to-mesh mappings are loaded with the calls to the `loadMap()` helper routine:

```
loadMap(f, scene.materialForNode);
loadMap(f, scene.meshes);
```

4. If there is still some data left, we must read the scene node names and material names:

```
if (!feof(f)) {
   loadMap(f, scene.nameForNode_);
   loadStringList(f, scene.names_);
   loadStringList(f, scene.materialNames_);
}
fclose(f);
}
```

Saving the scene reverses the `loadScene()` routine. Let's take a look:

1. At the beginning of the file, we must write the count of scene nodes:

```
void saveScene(const char* fileName,
   const Scene& scene)
{
   FILE* f = fopen(fileName, "wb");
   uint32_t sz = (uint32_t)scene.hierarchy.size();
   fwrite(&sz, sizeof(sz), 1, f);
```

2. Three `fwrite()` calls save the local and global transformations, followed by the hierarchical information:

```
fwrite(scene.localTransform.data(),
    sizeof(glm::mat4), sz, f);
fwrite(scene.globalTransform.data(),
    sizeof(glm::mat4), sz, f);
fwrite(scene.hierarchy.data(), sizeof(Hierarchy),
    sz, f);
```

3. Two `saveMap()` calls store the node-to-materials and node-to-mesh mappings:

```
saveMap(f, scene.materialForNode);
saveMap(f, scene.meshes);
```

If the scene node and material names are not empty, we must also store these maps:

```
if (!scene.names_.empty() &&
    !scene.nameForNode_.empty()) {
  saveMap(f, scene.nameForNode_);
  saveStringList(f, scene.names_);
  saveStringList(f, scene.materialNames_);
}
fclose(f);
}
```

Now, let's briefly describe the helper routines for loading and saving unordered maps. `std::unordered_map` is loaded in three steps:

1. First, the count of {`key, value`} pairs is read from a file:

```
void loadMap(FILE* f,
  std::unordered_map<uint32_t, uint32_t>& map)
{
  std::vector<uint32_t> ms;
  uint32_t sz;
  fread(&sz, 1, sizeof(sz), f);
```

2. Then, all the key-value pairs are loaded with a single `fread` call:

```
ms.resize(sz);
fread(ms.data(), sizeof(int), sz, f);
```

3. Finally, the array is converted into a hash table:

```
for (size_t i = 0; i < (sz / 2) ; i++)
    map[ms[i * 2 + 0]] = ms[i * 2 + 1];
}
```

The saving routine for `std::unordered_map` is created by reversing `loadMap()` line by line:

1. A temporary `{key, value}` pair array is allocated:

```
void saveMap(FILE* f,
    const std::unordered_map<uint32_t, uint32_t>& map)
{
    std::vector<uint32_t> ms;
    ms.reserve(map.size() * 2);
```

2. All the values from `std::unordered_map` are copied to the array:

```
for (const auto& m : map) {
    ms.push_back(m.first);
    ms.push_back(m.second);
}
```

3. The count of `{key, value}` pairs is written to the file:

```
uint32_t sz = ms.size();
fwrite(&sz, sizeof(sz), 1, f);
```

4. Finally, the `{key, value}` pairs are written with one `fwrite()` call:

```
fwrite(ms.data(), sizeof(int), ms.size(), f);
}
```

There's more...

Topology changes for the nodes in our scene graph pose a certain, nevertheless solvable, problem. The corresponding source code is discussed in the *Deleting nodes and merging scene graphs* recipe of *Chapter 9, Working with Scene Graphs*. We just have to keep all the mesh geometries in a single GPU buffer. We will show you how to implement this later in this chapter in `MultiRenderer`, which is a refactoring of the `MultiMeshRenderer` class from `Chapter5/VK01_MultiMeshDraw`.

The material conversion routines will be implemented in the *Implementing a material system* recipe. Together with scene loading and saving, they complete the `SceneConvert` tool.

Implementing transformation trees

A scene graph is typically used to represent spatial relationships. For the purpose of rendering, we must calculate a global affine 3D transformation for each of the scene graph nodes. This recipe will show you how to correctly calculate global transformations from local transformations without making any redundant calculations.

Getting ready

Using the previously defined Scene structure, we will show you how to correctly recalculate global transformations. Please revisit the *Using data-oriented design for a scene graph* recipe before proceeding. To start this recipe, recall that we had the dangerous but tempting idea of using a recursive global transform calculator in the non-existent SceneNode::render() method:

```
SceneNode::Render() {
  mat4 parentTransform = parent ?
    parent->globalTransform : identity();
  this->globalTransform = parentTransform * localTransform;
  ... rendering and recursion
}
```

It is always better to separate operations such as rendering, scene traversal, and transform calculation, while at the same time executing similar operations in large batches. This separation becomes even more important when the number of nodes becomes large.

We have already learned how to render several meshes with a single GPU draw call by using a combination of indirect rendering and programmable vertex pulling. Here, we will show you how to perform the minimum amount of global transform recalculations.

How to do it...

It is always good to avoid unnecessary calculations. In the case of global transformations of the scene nodes, we need a way to mark certain nodes whose transforms have changed in this frame. Since changed nodes may have children, we must also mark those children as changed. Let's take a look:

1. In the Scene structure, we should declare a collection of changedAtLevel_ arrays to quickly add any changed nodes to the appropriate scene graph level:

    ```
    struct Scene {
      ... somewhere in transform component ...
      std::vector<int>
    ```

```
    changedAtThisFrame_[MAX_NODE_LEVEL];
};
```

2. The `markAsChanged()` routine starts with a given node and recursively descends to each and every child node, adding it to the `changedAtLevel_` arrays. First, the node itself is marked as changed:

```
void markAsChanged(Scene& scene, int node) {
  int level = scene.hierarchy_[node].level;
  scene.changedAtThisFrame_[level].push_back(node);
```

3. We start from the first child and advance to next sibling, descending the hierarchy:

```
  for (int s = scene.hierarchy_[node].firstChild_ ;
       s != - 1; s = scene.hierarchy_[s].nextSibling_)
    markAsChanged(scene, s);
}
```

To recalculate all the global transformations for changed nodes, the following function must be implemented. No work is done if no local transformations were updated, and the scene is essentially static. Let's take a look:

1. We start from the root layer of the list of changed scene nodes, supposing we have only one root node. This is because root node global transforms coincide with their local transforms. The changed nodes list is then cleared:

```
void recalculateGlobalTransforms(Scene& scene)
{
  if (!scene.changedAtThisFrame_[0].empty()) {
    int c = scene.changedAtThisFrame_[0][0];
    scene.globalTransform_[c] =
      scene.localTransform_[c];
    scene.changedAtThisFrame_[0].clear();
  }
```

2. For all the lower levels, we must ensure that we have parents so that the loops are linear and there are no conditions inside. We will start from level 1 because the root level is already being handled. The exit condition is the emptiness of the list at the current level. We will also avoid descending deeper than our list allows:

```
  for (int i = 1 ; i < MAX_NODE_LEVEL &&
       !scene.changedAtThisFrame_[i].empty(); i++ )
  {
```

3. Now, we must iterate all the changed nodes at this level. For each of the iterated nodes, we fetch the parent transform and multiply it by the local node transform:

```
for (int c : scene.changedAtThisFrame_[i]) {
  int p = scene.hierarchy_[c].parent;
  scene.globalTransform_[c] =
    scene.globalTransform_[p] *
    scene.localTransform_[c];
}
```

4. At the end of the node iteration process, we should clear the list of changed nodes for this level:

```
    scene.changedAtThisFrame_[i].clear();
  }
}
```

The essence of this implementation is the fact that we do not recalculate any of the global transformations multiple times. Since we start from the root layer of the scene graph tree, all the changed layers below the root acquire a valid global transformation for their parents.

> **Note**
> Depending on how frequently local transformations are updated, it may be more performant to eliminate the list of recently updated nodes and always perform a full update. Profile your real code before making a decision.

There's more...

As an advanced exercise, transfer the computation of changed node transformations to your GPU. This is relatively easy to implement, considering that we have compute shaders and buffer management in place.

Implementing a material system

Chapter 6, Physically Based Rendering Using the glTF2 Shading Model, provided a description of the PBR shading model and presented all the required GLSL shaders for rendering a single 3D object using multiple textures. Here, we will show you how to organize scene rendering with multiple objects with different materials and properties. Our material system is compatible with the glTF2 material format and easily extensible for incorporating many existing glTF2 extensions.

Getting ready

The previous chapters dealt with rendering individual objects and applying a PBR model to lighten them. In the *Using data-oriented design for a scene graph* recipe, we learned the general structure for scene organization and used opaque integers as material handles. Here, we will define a structure for storing material parameters and show you how this structure can be used in GLSL shaders. The routine to convert material parameters from the ones loaded by Assimp will be described later in this chapter, in the *Importing materials with Assimp* recipe.

How to do it...

We need a structure to represent our PBR material, both in CPU memory to load it from a file and in a GPU buffer. Let's get started:

1. The structure contains both the numeric values that define the lighting properties of the material and the set of texture indices. At the beginning of the definition, we use a custom macro, PACKED_STRUCT, that hides the details of structure member alignment. This is necessary to make sure the structure layout in memory matches the corresponding structure declaration in the GLSL shader. The first two fields store the emissive and ambient color constants of our shading model:

```
#ifdef __GNUC__
#  define PACKED_STRUCT \
     __attribute__((packed,aligned(1)))
#else
#  define PACKED_STRUCT
#endif
struct PACKED_STRUCT MaterialDescription final
{
   gpuvec4 emissiveColor_ = { 0.0f, 0.0f, 0.0f, 0.0f};
   gpuvec4 albedoColor_   = { 1.0f, 1.0f, 1.0f, 1.0f };
```

2. The roughness_ field contains the surface's roughness. Two components, .x and .y, can be used to represent anisotropic roughness when necessary:

```
   gpuvec4 roughness_     = { 1.0f, 1.0f, 0.0f, 0.0f };
```

3. We can describe the transparent materials by using a transparency factor, which is used to render with alpha-blended materials, or by using an alpha test threshold, which is used for the simple punch-through transparency rendering we have implemented in the demo applications for this chapter. Besides that, we must store the metallic factor for our PBR rendering:

```
float transparencyFactor_  = 1.0f;
float alphaTest_           = 0.0f;
float metallicFactor_      = 1.0f;
```

4. To customize our rendering pipeline, we may want to use some flags that differ from material to material or from object to object. In the demos for this book, we do not need such flexibility, so will render all the objects with a single shader where only the texture inputs change. However, there is a placeholder for storing these flags:

```
uint32_t flags_  = sMaterialFlags_CastShadow |
                   sMaterialFlags_ReceiveShadow;
```

5. The second part of the structure contains indices into the list of all textures. In Vulkan, the texture is addressed by a 32-bit integer in a big texture array, while in OpenGL, the texture is an opaque 64-bit handle provided by the OpenGL implementation via the ARB_bindless_texture extension. To make sure the same GLSL material declaration can be shared between OpenGL and Vulkan, we will use 64-bit values here. For empty textures, we will use a special guard value. In both cases, this is a 32-bit integer with all its bits set to one:

```
uint64_t ambientOcclusionMap_  = 0xFFFFFFFF;
uint64_t emissiveMap_  = 0xFFFFFFFF;
uint64_t albedoMap_  = 0xFFFFFFFF;
uint64_t metallicRoughnessMap_  = 0xFFFFFFFF;
uint64_t normalMap_  = 0xFFFFFFFF;
```

6. The opacity map is only used during conversion and has only been included because we are using the same structure in our SceneConverter tool:

```
uint64_t opacityMap_  = 0xFFFFFFFF;
};
```

See the *Implementing a scene conversion tool* recipe for further details on how to convert and pack material textures.

7. Each vector value is packed to four floats. The `gpuvec4` structure is tightly packed and occupies exactly 16 bytes. The `PACKED_STRUCT` macro instructs the GCC compiler to pack the structure tightly:

```
struct PACKED_STRUCT gpuvec4 {
  float x, y, z, w;
  gpuvec4() = default;
  gpuvec4(float a, float b, float c, float d)
  : x(a), y(b), z(c), w(d) {}
  gpuvec4(const vec4& v) : x(v.x), y(v.y), z(v.z),
  w(v.w) {}
};
```

Note that we have the data structures in place, let's take a look at the loading and saving code:

1. The following function reads a list of materials from file. The `loadStringList()` function loads the texture file names into the `files` container:

```
void loadMaterials(const char* fileName,
  std::vector<MaterialDescription>& materials,
  std::vector<std::string>& files)
{
  FILE* f = fopen(fileName, "rb");
  if (!f) return;
  uint32_t sz;
  fread(&sz, 1, sizeof(uint32_t), f);
  materials.resize(sz);
  fread(materials.data(), materials.size(),
    sizeof(MaterialDescription), f);
  loadStringList(f, files);
  fclose(f);
}
```

2. Our SceneConverter tool needs the `saveMaterialList()` function, which saves the converted material data in files. The code uses a helper function called `saveStringList()`, which appends a list of strings to an opened binary file:

```
void saveMaterials(const char* fileName,
  const std::vector<MaterialDescription>& materials,
  const std::vector<std::string>& files)
{
```

```
FILE* f = fopen(fileName, "wb");
if (!f) return;
uint32_t sz = (uint32_t)materials.size();
fwrite(&sz, 1, sizeof(uint32_t), f);
fwrite(materials.data(), sz,
   sizeof(MaterialDescription), f);
saveStringList(f, files);
fclose(f);
}
```

At program start, we load the list of materials and all the texture files into GPU textures. Now, we are ready to learn how the `MaterialDescription` structure is used in GLSL shaders:

1. The vertex shader is similar to the GLSL shader from *Chapter 5, Working with Geometry Data*. The output values for each vertex are the texture coordinates uvw, the normal vectors v_worldNormal, and the positions in world space coordinates v_worldPos:

```
layout(location = 0) out vec3 uvw;
layout(location = 1) out vec3 v_worldNormal;
layout(location = 2) out vec4 v_worldPos;
```

2. The matIdx output attribute contains the index of the material that was used in the fragment shader. The flat attribute instructs the GPU to avoid interpolating this value:

```
layout(location = 3) out flat uint matIdx;
```

3. The per-vertex attributes are used in all the subsequent shaders, so they are declared in separate reusable files. The VK01.h file contains the memory layout of the per-vertex attributes in the ImDrawVert structure:

```
#include <data/shaders/chapter07/VK01.h>
struct ImDrawVert {
   float x, y, z; float u, v; float nx, ny, nz;
};
```

4. The `DrawData` structure contains information for rendering a mesh instance with a specific material. The mesh and material indices represent offsets into GPU buffers; these will be discussed shortly. The level of detail the `lod` field indicates the relative offset to the vertex data. The `indexOffset` and `vertexOffset` fields contain byte offsets into the mesh index and geometry buffers. The `transformIndex` field stores the index of the global object-to-world-space transformation that's calculated by scene graph routines. We showed you how transformation data is packed in the previous recipe, *Implementing transformation trees*:

```
struct DrawData {
  uint mesh;
  uint material;
  uint lod;
  uint indexOffset;
  uint vertexOffset;
  uint transformIndex;
};
```

5. After including `VK01.h`, we have another `#include` statement:

```
#include <data/shaders/chapter07/VK01_VertCommon.h>
```

The `VK01_VertCommon.h` file contains all the buffer attachments for the vertex shader. The first buffer contains two per-frame uniforms – the model-view-projection matrix and the camera position in the world space:

```
layout(binding = 0) uniform  UniformBuffer
  { mat4 inMtx; vec4 cameraPos; } ubo;
```

6. As usual, we must employ the programmable vertex pulling technique, so we need the indices and vertices to be in separate buffers:

```
layout(binding = 1) readonly buffer SBO
  { ImDrawVert data[]; } sbo;
layout(binding = 2) readonly buffer IBO
  { uint data[]; } ibo;
layout(binding = 3) readonly buffer DrawBO
  { DrawData data[]; } drawDataBuffer;
layout(binding = 5) readonly buffer XfrmBO
  { mat4 data[]; } transformBuffer;
```

The rest of the `VK01.h` file refers to yet another file, called `data/shaders/ chapter07/MaterialData.h`, that defines a GLSL structure equivalent to `MaterialData`, which was described at the beginning of this recipe.

Now, let's return to the main vertex shader:

1. First, we must fetch the `DrawData` typed buffer. Using the per-instance data and local `gl_VertexIndex`, we will calculate the offset as index data:

```
void main() {
  DrawData dd = drawDataBuffer.data[gl_BaseInstance];
  uint refIdx = dd.indexOffset + gl_VertexIndex;
```

2. The vertex index is calculated by adding the global vertex offset for this mesh to the vertex index fetched from the `ibo` buffer:

```
ImDrawVert v = sbo.data[ibo.data[refIdx] +
dd.vertexOffset];
```

3. The object-to-world transformation is read directly from `transformBuffer` using the instance index:

```
mat4 model = transformBuffer.data[gl_BaseInstance];
```

4. At the end of the vertex shader, we calculate the fragment's world space position and normal vector. Since the code needs to be compatible with our OpenGL demos, we will flip the `y` coordinate to convert OpenGL's coordinates into Vulkan's inverted coordinate system:

```
v_worldPos    = model * vec4(v.x, -v.y, v.z, 1.0);
v_worldNormal = transpose(inverse(mat3(model))) *
  vec3(v.nx, -v.ny, v.nz);
```

5. For rasterization purposes, we will multiply the world space position by the aggregate camera view and projection matrix. This gives us the clip space coordinates of the fragment:

```
gl_Position = ubo.inMtx * v_worldPos;
```

6. The only difference from the shader shown in *Chapter 5, Working with Geometry Data*, is the `matIdx` output value's assignment. This index is used in the fragment shader to read the appropriate material parameters. The texture coordinates are passed into the fragment shader without any conversions needing to take place:

```
matIdx = dd.material;
uvw = vec3(v.u, v.v, 1.0);
}
```

Now, let's take a look at the fragment shader:

1. The fragment shader uses a single buffer that contains the material data we defined previously. Also, a single array of textures is used for all the maps:

```
layout(binding = 4) readonly
   buffer MatBO { MaterialData data[]; } mat_bo;
layout(binding = 9) uniform sampler2D textures[];
```

2. The `main` function looks up the material data using the material index that was passed from the vertex shader. For demonstration purposes, we will read the emissive color value, which is added to the output color later:

```
void main() {
   MaterialData md = mat_bo.data[matIdx];
   vec4 emission = md.emissiveColor_;
```

3. The default values for the ambient color and normal vector are assigned:

```
   vec4 albedo = vec4(1.0, 0.0, 0.0, 1.0);
   vec3 normalSample = vec3(0.0, 0.0, 1.0);
```

4. The albedo color value is read from the appropriate texture by non-uniformly addressing the global texture array:

```
   {
      uint texIdx = uint(md.albedoMap_);
      albedo = texture(
         textures[nonuniformEXT(texIdx)], uvw.xy);
   }
```

5. The normal map is read in the same way:

```
   {
      uint texIdx = uint(md.normalMap_);
      normalSample = texture(
         textures[nonuniformEXT(texIdx)], uvw.xy).xyz;
   }
```

6. Just as we did with the PBR shader from *Chapter 6, Physically Based Rendering Using the glTF2 Shading Model*, an alpha test is performed for objects with transparency masks:

```
   runAlphaTest(albedo.a, md.alphaTest_);
```

To avoid dealing with any kind of scene sorting at this point, alpha transparency is simulated using dithering and punch-through transparency. You can find some useful insights at http://alex-charlton.com/posts/Dithering_on_the_GPU. The following is the final solution:

```
void runAlphaTest(float alpha, float alphaThreshold) {
  if (alphaThreshold == 0.0) return;
  mat4 thresholdMatrix = mat4(
    1.0 /17.0,  9.0/17.0,  3.0/17.0, 11.0/17.0,
    13.0/17.0,  5.0/17.0, 15.0/17.0,  7.0/17.0,
    4.0  17.0, 12.0/17.0,  2.0/17.0, 10.0/17.0,
    16.0/17.0,  8.0/17.0, 14.0/17.0,  6.0/17.0
  );
  int x = int(mod(gl_FragCoord.x, 4.0));
  int y = int(mod(gl_FragCoord.y, 4.0));
  alpha = clamp(
    alpha - 0.5 * thresholdMatrix[x][y], 0.0, 1.0);
  if (alpha < alphaThreshold) discard;
}
```

7. The world normal is normalized to compensate for the interpolation that occurred while rasterizing the triangle:

```
vec3 n = normalize(v_worldNormal);
```

8. If the normal map value is bigger than the threshold that's been set, we must modify the world space normal:

```
if (length(normalSample) > 0.5)
  n = perturbNormal(n,
        normalize(ubo.cameraPos.xyz -
          v_worldPos.xyz),normalSample, uvw.xy);
```

9. The rest of the fragment shader applies a simplified lighting model:

```
vec3 lightDir = normalize(vec3(-1.0, -1.0, 0.1));
float NdotL = clamp( dot(n, lightDir), 0.3, 1.0 );
outColor = vec4(
  albedo.rgb * NdotL + emission.rgb, 1.0 );
}
```

The next recipe will show you how to extract and pack the values from the Assimp library's aiMaterial structure into our MaterialData structure.

Importing materials from Assimp

In *Chapter 5, Working with Geometry Data*, we learned how to define a runtime data storage format for mesh geometry. This recipe will show you how to use the Assimp library to extract material properties from Assimp data structures. Combined with the next recipe, which will cover our `SceneConverter` tool, this concludes the process of describing our data content exporting pipeline.

Getting ready

In the previous recipe, we learned how to render multiple meshes with different materials. Now, it is time to learn how to import the material data from popular 3D asset formats.

How to do it...

Let's take a look at the `convertAIMaterialToDescription()` function that's used in the `SceneConverter` tool. It retrieves all the required parameters from the `aiMaterial` structure and returns a `MaterialDescription` object that can be used with our GLSL shaders. Let's take a look:

1. Each texture is addressed by an integer identifier. We will store a list of texture filenames in the `files` parameter. The `opacityMap` parameter contains a list of textures that need to be combined with transparency maps:

    ```
    MaterialDescription convertAIMaterialToDescription(
      const aiMaterial* M,
      std::vector<std::string>& files,
      std::vector<std::string>& opacityMaps)
    {

      MaterialDescription D;
      aiColor4D Color;
    ```

2. The Assimp API provides **getter** functions to extract individual color parameters. We will use some of these here:

    ```
    if ( aiGetMaterialColor(M, AI_MATKEY_COLOR_AMBIENT,
        &Color) == AI_SUCCESS ) {
      D.emissiveColor_ =
        { Color.r, Color.g, Color.b, Color.a };
      if ( D.emissiveColor_.w > 1.0f )
        D.emissiveColor_.w = 1.0f;
    }
    ```

The first parameter we are trying to extract is the "ambient" color, which is stored in the `emissiveColor_` field of `MaterialDescription`. The alpha value is clamped to `1.0`.

3. In the same way, the diffuse color is stored in the `albedoColor_` field of `MaterialDescription` with a clamped alpha channel:

```
if ( aiGetMaterialColor(M, AI_MATKEY_COLOR_DIFFUSE,
    &Color) == AI_SUCCESS ) {
  D.albedoColor_ =
    { Color.r, Color.g, Color.b, Color.a };
  if ( D.albedoColor_.w > 1.0f )
    D.albedoColor_.w = 1.0f;
}
```

4. If `aiMaterial` contains an emissive color value, we will add it to the `emissiveColor_` property we loaded previously. The per-component color addition is necessary here because this is the only place where we will use color addition. Due to this, we did not define the addition operator for gpuvec4:

```
if (aiGetMaterialColor(M, AI_MATKEY_COLOR_EMISSIVE,
    &Color) == AI_SUCCESS ) {
  D.emissiveColor_.x += Color.r;
  D.emissiveColor_.y += Color.g;
  D.emissiveColor_.z += Color.b;
  D.emissiveColor_.w += Color.a;
  if ( D.emissiveColor_.w > 1.0f )
    D.albedoColor_.w = 1.0f;
}
```

5. The following constant sets the opaqueness threshold value to 5%:

```
const float opaquenessThreshold = 0.05f;
float Opacity = 1.0f;
```

In our conversion routine, we are using one simple optimization trick for transparent materials: anything with an opaqueness of 95% or more is considered opaque and avoids any blending.

6. The material opacity is converted into `transparencyFactor` and then clamped against the threshold value:

```
if ( aiGetMaterialFloat(M, AI_MATKEY_OPACITY,
    &Opacity) == AI_SUCCESS ) {
  D.transparencyFactor_ =
    glm::clamp(1.0f-Opacity, 0.0f, 1.0f);
  if ( D.transparencyFactor_ >=
      1.0f - opaquenessThreshold )
    D.transparencyFactor_ = 0.0f;
}
```

7. If the material contains a transparency factor as an RGB value, we use the maximum component value to calculate our transparency factor. As we did previously, we will clamp the transparency factor against a threshold:

```
if ( aiGetMaterialColor(M,
    AI_MATKEY_COLOR_TRANSPARENT,
    &Color) == AI_SUCCESS ) {
  const float Opacity =
    std::max(std::max(Color.r, Color.g), Color.b);
  D.transparencyFactor_ =
    glm::clamp( Opacity, 0.0f, 1.0f );
  if ( D.transparencyFactor_ >=
      1.0f - opaquenessThreshold )
    D.transparencyFactor_ = 0.0f;
  D.alphaTest_ = 0.5f;
}
```

8. Once we've finished reading the colors and transparency factors, we must fetch scalar properties of the material with the help of the `aiGetMaterialFloat()` function. All the values are loaded into a temporary variable. The PBR metallic and roughness factors are loaded into the appropriate `MaterialDescription` fields:

```
float tmp = 1.0f;
if (aiGetMaterialFloat(M,
    AI_MATKEY_GLTF_PBRMETALLICROUGHNESS
    _METALLIC_FACTOR, &tmp) == AI_SUCCESS)
  D.metallicFactor_ = tmp;
if (aiGetMaterialFloat(M,
    AI_MATKEY_GLTF_PBRMETALLICROUGHNESS
    _ROUGHNESS_FACTOR, &tmp) == AI_SUCCESS)
  D.roughness_ = { tmp, tmp, tmp, tmp };
```

9. All the textures for our materials are stored in external files. The names of these files
    can be extracted by using the `aiGetMaterialTexture()` function:

```
aiString Path;
aiTextureMapping Mapping;
unsigned int UVIndex = 0;
float Blend = 1.0f;
aiTextureOp TextureOp = aiTextureOp_Add;
const aiTextureMapMode TextureMapMode[2] =
  { aiTextureMapMode_Wrap, aiTextureMapMode_Wrap };
unsigned int TextureFlags = 0;
```

This function requires several parameters, most of which we will ignore in our
converter for the sake of simplicity.

10. The first texture is an emissive map. We will use the `addUnique()` function to add
    the texture file to our textures list:

```
if (aiGetMaterialTexture( M, aiTextureType_EMISSIVE,
    0, &Path,&Mapping, &UVIndex, &Blend, &TextureOp,
    TextureMapMode,&TextureFlags ) == AI_SUCCESS)
  D.emissiveMap_ = addUnique(files, Path.C_Str());
```

11. The diffuse map is stored as the `albedoMap_` field in our material structure:

```
if (aiGetMaterialTexture( M, aiTextureType_DIFFUSE,
    0, &Path,&Mapping, &UVIndex, &Blend, &TextureOp,
    TextureMapMode, &TextureFlags ) == AI_SUCCESS)
  D.albedoMap_ = addUnique(files, Path.C_Str());
```

12. The normal map can be extracted from either the `aiTextureType_NORMALS`
    property or `aiTextureType_HEIGHT` in `aiMaterial`. We must check for the
    presence of an `aiTextureType_NORMALS` texture map and store the texture
    index in the `normalMap_` field:

```
if (aiGetMaterialTexture( M, aiTextureType_NORMALS,
    0, &Path,&Mapping, &UVIndex, &Blend, &TextureOp,
    TextureMapMode, &TextureFlags) == AI_SUCCESS)
  D.normalMap_ = addUnique(files, Path.C_Str());
```

13. If there is no classic normal map, we should check if a heightmap texture is present. This can be converted into a normal map at a later stage of the conversion process:

```
if (D.normalMap_ == 0xFFFFFFFF)
  if (aiGetMaterialTexture( M, aiTextureType_HEIGHT,
      0, &Path,&Mapping, &UVIndex, &Blend,
      &TextureOp, TextureMapMode,
      &TextureFlags ) == AI_SUCCESS)
    D.normalMap_ = addUnique(files, Path.C_Str());
```

14. The last map we will be using is the opacity map, which is stored in a separate `opacityMaps` array. We will pack the opacity maps into the alpha channel of our albedo textures:

```
if (aiGetMaterialTexture( M, aiTextureType_OPACITY,
    0, &Path,&Mapping, &UVIndex, &Blend, &TextureOp,
    TextureMapMode, &TextureFlags ) == AI_SUCCESS) {
  D.opacityMap_ =
    addUnique(opacityMaps, Path.C_Str());
  D.alphaTest_ = 0.5f;
}
```

15. The final part of the material conversion routine applies some heuristics for guessing the material's properties, just by looking at the material's name. Here, we are only checking for glass-like materials in our largest test scene, but some common names, such as "gold," "silver," and so on can also be used to assign metallic coefficients and albedo colors. Essentially, this is an easy trick to make our test scene look better. At the end, the `MaterialDescription` instance is returned for further processing:

```
aiString Name;
std::string materialName;
if (aiGetMaterialString(M, AI_MATKEY_NAME, &Name)
    == AI_SUCCESS)
  materialName = Name.C_Str();
if (materialName.find("Glass") != std::string::npos)
  D.alphaTest_ = 0.75f;
if (materialName.find("Bottle") !=
    std::string::npos)
  D.alphaTest_ = 0.54f;
return D;
}
```

16. The only thing we need to mention here is the addUnique() function, which populates the list of texture files. We must check if this filename is already in the collection. If the file is not there, we must add it and return its index. Otherwise, the index of a previously added texture file is returned:

```
int addUnique(std::vector<std::string>& files,
  const std::string& file)
{
  if (file.empty()) return -1;
  auto i = std::find(std::begin(files),
    std::end(files), file);
  if (i != files.end())
    return (int)std::distance(files.begin(), i);
  files.push_back(file);
  return (int)files.size() - 1;
}
```

Before we move on, let's take a look at how to implement all the helper routines necessary for our scene converter tool, which will be described in the next recipe. The convertAndDownscaleAllTextures() function is used to generate the internal filenames for each of the textures and convert the contents of each texture into a GPU-compatible format. Let's take a look:

1. As parameters, this routine accepts a list of material descriptions, an output directory for texture data, and the containers for all the texture files and opacity maps:

```
void convertAndDownscaleAllTextures(
  const std::vector<MaterialDescription>& materials,
  const std::string& basePath,
  std::vector<std::string>& files,
  std::vector<std::string>& opacityMaps)
{
```

2. Each of the opacity maps is combined with the albedo map. To keep the correspondence between the opacity map list and the global texture indices, we will use a standard C++ hash table:

```
std::unordered_map<std::string, uint32_t>
  opacityMapIndices(files.size());
```

3. We must iterate over all the materials and check if they have both an opacity and albedo map. If the opacity and albedo maps are present, we must associate this opacity map with the albedo map:

```
for (const auto& m : materials)
  if (m.opacityMap_ != 0xFFFFFFFF &&
      m.albedoMap_ != 0xFFFFFFFF)
    opacityMapIndices[files[m.albedoMap_]] =
      m.opacityMap_;
```

4. The following lambda takes a source texture filename and returns a modified texture filename. Internally, the texture date is converted here:

```
auto converter = [&](const std::string& s) ->
  std::string {
  return convertTexture(
    s, basePath, opacityMapIndices, opacityMaps);
};
```

5. We use the `std::transform()` algorithm to convert all of the texture files:

```
std::transform(std::execution::par,
  std::begin(files), std::end(files),
  std::begin(files), converter);
}
```

The `std::execution::par` parameter is a C++20 feature that allows us to parallel process the array. Since converting the texture data is a rather lengthy process, this straightforward parallelization reduces our processing time significantly.

A single texture map is converted into our runtime data format with the following routine:

1. All our output textures will have no more than 512x512 pixels:

```
std::string convertTexture(const std::string& file,
  const std::string& basePath,
  std::unordered_map<std::string, uint32_t>&
    opacityMapIndices,
  const std::vector<std::string>& opacityMaps)
{
  const int maxNewWidth = 512;
  const int maxNewHeight = 512;
```

2. A temporary dynamic array will contain a combined albedo and opacity map. To run this on Windows, Linux, and macOS, we should replace all the path separators with the "/" symbol:

```
std::vector<uint8_t> tmpImage(
   maxNewWidth * maxNewHeight * 4);
const auto srcFile =
   replaceAll(basePath + file, "\\",  "/");
```

3. The new filename is a concatenation of a fixed output directory and a source filename, with all path separators replaced by double underscores:

```
const auto newFile =
   std::string("data/out_textures/") +
   lowercaseString(replaceAll(replaceAll(
      srcFile, "..", "__"), "/", "__") +
   std::string("__rescaled")) + std::string(".png");
```

4. Just as we did in the previous chapters, we will use the stb_image library to load the textures. We must force the loaded image to be in RGBA format, even if there is no opacity information. This is a shortcut that we can take here to make our texture handling code significantly simpler:

```
int texWidth, texHeight, texChannels;
stbi_uc* pixels =
   stbi_load(fixTextureFile(srcFile).c_str(),
   &texWidth, &texHeight, &texChannels,
   STBI_rgb_alpha);
uint8_t* src = pixels;
texChannels = STBI_rgb_alpha;
```

Note

The fixTextureFile() function fixes situations where 3D model material data references texture files with inappropriate case in filenames. For example, the .mtl file may contain map_Ka Texture01.png, while the actual filename on the file system is called texture01.png. This way, we can fix naming inconsistencies in the Bistro scene on Linux.

---

5. If the texture failed to load, we must set our temporary array as input data to avoid having to exit here:

```
if (!src) {
  printf("Failed to load [%s] texture\n",
    srcFile.c_str());
  texWidth = maxNewWidth;
  texHeight = maxNewHeight;
  src = tmpImage.data();
}
```

6. If this texture has an associated opacity map stored in the hash table, we must load that opacity map and add its contents to the albedo map. As with the source texture file, we must replace the path separators for cross-platform operations. The opacity map is loaded as a simple grayscale image:

```
if (opacityMapIndices.count(file) > 0) {
  const auto opacityMapFile = replaceAll(basePath +
    opacityMaps[opacityMapIndices[file]], "\\", "/");
  int opacityWidth, opacityHeight;
  stbi_uc* opacityPixels =
    stbi_load(opacityMapFile.c_str(),
    &opacityWidth, &opacityHeight, nullptr, 1);
```

7. After signaling a possible loading error, we must check the loaded image's validity:

```
if (!opacityPixels) {
  printf("Failed to load opacity mask [%s]\n",
    opacityMapFile.c_str());
}
assert(opacityPixels);
assert(texWidth == opacityWidth);
assert(texHeight == opacityHeight);
```

8. After successfully loading the opacity map with the correct dimensions, we must store the opacity values in the alpha component of this albedo texture:

```
for (int y = 0; y != opacityHeight; y++)
  for (int x = 0; x != opacityWidth; x++)
    src[(y * opacityWidth + x) * texChannels + 3]
      = opacityPixels[y * opacityWidth + x];
```

9. The `stb_image` library uses explicit memory management, so we must free the loaded opacity map manually:

```
    stbi_image_free(opacityPixels);
}
```

10. At this point, all the loaded textures have been downscaled. We must allocate a maximum number of bytes to hold the output image. The output texture size isn't bigger than the constants we defined at the start of this function:

```
const uint32_t imgSize =
  texWidth * texHeight * texChannels;
std::vector<uint8_t> mipData(imgSize);
uint8_t* dst = mipData.data();
const int newW = std::min(texWidth, maxNewWidth);
const int newH = std::min(texHeight, maxNewHeight);
```

11. The `stb_image_resize` library provides a simple function for rescaling an image without losing too much quality. Finally, let's write the output texture in PNG format using the `stb_image_write` library:

```
stbir_resize_uint8(src, texWidth, texHeight, 0, dst,
  newW, newH, 0, texChannels);
stbi_write_png(
  newFile.c_str(), newW, newH, texChannels, dst, 0);
```

12. If the source texture was loaded in the first place, we must free it manually. No matter what the result of the conversion is, we must return the new texture's filename:

```
if (pixels) stbi_image_free(pixels);
return newFile;
}
```

This way, we ensure that if the conversion tool has completed without errors, the converted dataset is always valid and requires significantly fewer runtime checks.

There's more...

This relatively long recipe has shown all the necessary routines for retrieving material and texture data from external 3D assets. To learn how these functions are used in real code, let's jump to the next recipe, *Implementing a scene conversion tool*. The previous recipe, *Implementing a material system*, showed you how to use the imported materials with GLSL shaders.

Implementing a scene conversion tool

In *Chapter 5, Working with Geometry Data*, we implemented a geometry conversion tool capable of loading meshes in various formats supported by the Assimp library, such as `.gltf` or `.obj`, and storing them in our runtime format, which is suitable for fast loading and rendering. In this recipe, we will extend this tool into a full scene converter that will handle all our materials and textures. Let's get started and learn how to do this.

Getting ready

The source code for the scene conversion tool described in this chapter can be found in the `Chapter7\SceneConverter` folder. The entire project is covered in this recipe. If you want to start with a simpler version of the tool that only deals with geometry data, take a look at the *Implementing a geometry conversion tool* recipe in *Chapter 5, Working with Geometry Data*.

Before we look at this recipe, make sure you're familiar with the *Implementing a material system* and *Importing materials from Assimp* recipes of this chapter.

Our geometry conversion tool takes its configuration from a `.json` file that, for the Lumberyard Bistro mesh used in this book, looks like this:

```
[{ "input_scene": "deps/src/bistro/Exterior/exterior.obj",
   "output_mesh": "data/meshes/test.meshes",
   "output_scene": "data/meshes/test.scene",
   "output_materials": "data/meshes/test.materials",
   "output_boxes": "data/meshes/test.boxes",
   "scale": 0.01,
   "calculate_LODs": false,
   "merge_instances": true
},
 { "input_scene": "deps/src/bistro/Interior/interior.obj",
   "output_mesh": "data/meshes/test2.meshes",
   "output_scene": "data/meshes/test2.scene",
   "output_materials": "data/meshes/test2.materials",
   "output_boxes": "data/meshes/test2.boxes",
   "scale": 0.01,
   "calculate_LODs": false,
   "merge_instances": true
}]
```

To parse this configuration file, we are going to use the RapidJSON library, which can be found on GitHub at `https://github.com/Tencent/rapidjson`.

How to do it...

First, we should take a look at how to implement the `.json` parsing step:

1. There's a single function we can use for this that returns a container of
    `SceneConfig` structures describing where to load a mesh file from, as well as
    where to save the converted data:

```
struct SceneConfig {
  std::string fileName;
  std::string outputMesh;
  std::string outputScene;
  std::string outputMaterials;
  std::string outputBoxes;
  float scale;
  bool calculateLODs;
  bool mergeInstances;
};
```

2. The JSON parsing code for using RapidJSON is straightforward. We will omit all
    error checking in this book's text, but the actual code in this book's code bundle
    contains some useful asserts:

```
std::vector<SceneConfig> readConfigFile(
    const char* cfgFileName) {
  std::ifstream ifs(cfgFileName);
  rapidjson::IStreamWrapper isw(ifs);
  rapidjson::Document document;
  const rapidjson::ParseResult =
    document.ParseStream(isw);
  std::vector<SceneConfig> configList;
  for (rapidjson::SizeType i = 0; i < document.Size();
      i++) {
    configList.emplace_back(SceneConfig {
      .fileName =
        document[i]["input_scene"].GetString(),
      .outputMesh =
        document[i]["output_mesh"].GetString(),
      .outputScene =
        document[i]["output_scene"].GetString(),
      .outputMaterials =
        document[i]["output_materials"].GetString(),
      .outputBoxes =
        document[i].HasMember("output_boxes") ?
```

```
                document[i]["output_boxes"].GetString() :
                  std::string(),
            .scale =
              (float)document[i]["scale"].GetDouble(),
            .calculateLODs =
              document[i]["calculate_LODs"].GetBool(),
            .mergeInstances =
              document[i]["merge_instances"].GetBool()
        });
    }
    return configList;
}
```

3. Now, let's take a look at the converter's `main()` function. We will read the configuration settings for all the scenes and invoke the conversion process for each one:

```
int main() {
    fs::create_directory("data/out_textures");
    const auto configs =
      readConfigFile("data/sceneconverter.json");
    for (const auto& cfg: configs)
      processScene(cfg);
    return 0;
}
```

The actual heavy lifting is done inside `processScene()`. It loads a single scene file using Assimp and converts all the data into formats suitable for rendering. Let's look deeper to see how this is done:

1. First, we will introduce a global state to simplify our implementation. Other functions, besides `processScene()`, will access this data; we don't want to overcomplicate the design:

```
std::vector<Mesh> g_meshes;
std::vector<BoundingBox> g_boxes;
std::vector<uint32_t> g_indexData;
std::vector<float> g_vertexData;
uint32_t g_indexOffset = 0;
uint32_t g_vertexOffset = 0;
```

2. The processing functions start by clearing all the global mesh data from where it
    was used previously:

```
void processScene(const SceneConfig& cfg) {
  g_meshes.clear();
  g_indexData.clear();
  g_vertexData.clear();
  g_indexOffset = 0;
  g_vertexOffset = 0;
```

3. To load a mesh using Assimp, we must extract the base path from the filename:

```
const size_t pathSeparator =
  cfg.fileName.find_last_of("/\\");
const string basePath =
  (pathSeparator != string::npos) ?
    cfg.fileName.substr(0, pathSeparator + 1) : "";
```

The actual file is in another folder. We are going to need it later, when we deal with
the textures.

4. Import a scene file using the following Assimp flags. We want to apply most of the
    optimizations and convert all the polygons into triangles. Normal vectors should
    be generated for those meshes that do not contain them. Error checking has been
    skipped here so that we can focus on the code's flow:

```
const unsigned int flags = 0 |
  aiProcess_JoinIdenticalVertices |
  aiProcess_Triangulate |
  aiProcess_GenSmoothNormals |
  aiProcess_LimitBoneWeights |
  aiProcess_SplitLargeMeshes |
  aiProcess_ImproveCacheLocality |
  aiProcess_RemoveRedundantMaterials |
  aiProcess_FindDegenerates |
  aiProcess_FindInvalidData |
  aiProcess_GenUVCoords;
const aiScene* scene =
  aiImportFile(cfg.fileName.c_str(), flags);
```

5. Once the mesh file has been loaded, we should convert the Assimp meshes into our representation. We will do this in the same way we did it in the *Implementing a geometry conversion tool* recipe of *Chapter 5, Working with Geometry Data.* Additionally, we will generate a bounding box for each mesh. Bounding boxes will be used in the next chapter to implement frustum culling:

```
g_meshes.reserve(scene->mNumMeshes);
for (unsigned int i = 0; i != scene->mNumMeshes;
        i++) {
  Mesh = convertAIMesh(scene->mMeshes[i], cfg);
  g_meshes.push_back(mesh);
  if (!cfg.outputBoxes.empty()) {
    BoundingBox box = calculateBoundingBox(
      g_vertexData.data()+mesh.vertexOffset,
      mesh.vertexCount);
    g_boxes.push_back(box);
  }
}
saveMeshesToFile(cfg.outputMesh.c_str());
if (!cfg.outputBoxes.empty())
  saveBoundingBoxes(
    cfg.outputBoxes.c_str(), g_boxes);
```

6. The next step of the conversion process is to convert all the Assimp materials that was loaded from file into our runtime material representation, which is suitable for rendering. All the texture filenames will be saved in the `files` container. The opacity maps will be packed into the alpha channels of the corresponding textures:

```
std::vector<MaterialDescription> materials;
std::vector<std::string>& materialNames =
  ourScene.materialNames_;
std::vector<std::string> files;
std::vector<std::string> opacityMaps;
for (unsigned int m = 0; m < scene->mNumMaterials;
    m++) {
  aiMaterial* mm = scene->mMaterials[m];
  materialNames.push_back(
    std::string(mm->GetName().C_Str()));
  MaterialDescription matDescription =
    convertAIMaterialToDescription(
      mm, files, opacityMaps);
```

```
        materials.push_back(matDescription);
    }
```

7. The textures are converted, rescaled, and packed into the output folder. The
    `basePath` folder's name is needed to extract plain filenames:

```
    convertAndDownscaleAllTextures(
        materials, basePath, files, opacityMaps);
    saveMaterials(
        cfg.outputMaterials.c_str(), materials, files);
```

8. Now, the scene is converted into the first-child-next-sibling form and saved:

```
    traverse(scene, ourScene, scene->mRootNode, -1, 0);
    saveScene(cfg.outputScene.c_str(), ourScene);
}
```

At this point, the data is ready for rendering. The output from running the
conversion tool should look as follows:

```
Loading scene from 'deps/src/bistro/Exterior/exterior.
obj'...
Converting meshes 1/22388...
... skipped ...
Loading scene from 'deps/src/bistro/Interior/interior.
obj'...
Converting meshes 1/2381...
... skipped ...
```

If everything works as planned, the tool will output the converted mesh data to `data/meshes` and the packed textures to `data/out_textures`.

There's more...

Our texture conversion code goes through all the textures, downscales them to 512x512
where necessary, and saves them in RGBA `.png` files. In a real-world content pipeline,
this conversion process may include a texture compression phase. We recommend
that you implement this as an exercise using the `ETC2Comp` library described in
Chapter 2, Using Essential Libraries. Adding texture compression code directly to the
`convertTexture()` function in `Chapter7\SceneConverter\src\main.cpp`
should be the easiest way to go about this.

Managing Vulkan resources

In the previous chapters, we implemented individual manual management for Vulkan resources in all our rendering classes. This recipe describes the system that manages all Vulkan-related objects and provides utility functions to create entities such as offscreen framebuffers, render passes, pipelines, textures, and storage buffers. All the functions described here will be used in the subsequent recipes.

Getting ready

The largest part of our resource management scene, which includes creating the descriptor set and update routines, is not included in this recipe. See the *Unifying descriptor set creation routines* recipe for additional implementation details.

How to do it...

The `VulkanResources` class contains a list of all the Vulkan objects. Its private part, along with a reference to `VulkanRenderDevice`, contains various `std::vector` members for storing our whole safari park of Vulkan objects. Let's take a look:

1. First, we must store all the loaded textures:

```
struct VulkanResources {
private:
  VulkanRenderDevice& vkDev;
  std::vector<VulkanTexture> allTextures;
```

2. Vulkan buffers are used for storing geometry, uniform parameters, and indirect draw commands. The *Unifying descriptor set creation routines* recipe contains descriptions of certain helper routines for creating different types of buffers:

```
  std::vector<VulkanBuffer> allBuffers;
```

3. The framebuffers and renderpasses will be created and used in the next recipe, *Refactoring Vulkan initialization and the main loop*. Graphical pipelines are used in all the Vulkan renderers and postprocessors:

```
  std::vector<VkFramebuffer> allFramebuffers;
  std::vector<VkRenderPass> allRenderPasses;
  std::vector<VkPipelineLayout> allPipelineLayouts;
  std::vector<VkPipeline> allPipelines;
```

4. Descriptor set layouts and pools must be created using the routines described in the *Unifying descriptor set creation routines* recipe:

```
std::vector<VkDescriptorSetLayout> allDSLayouts;
std::vector<VkDescriptorPool>      allDPools;
```

5. The class constructor simply stores the reference in an externally passed Vulkan device object:

```
explicit VulkanResources(VulkanRenderDevice& vkDev)
: vkDev(vkDev) {}
```

6. The only place where this destructor gets called implicitly is in the `VulkanRenderContext` class, which will be described in the following recipe. The destructor iterates over all the Vulkan objects and calls the appropriate destruction functions:

```
~VulkanResources() {
  for (auto& t: allTextures)
    destroyVulkanTexture(vkDev.device, t);
  for (auto& b: allBuffers) {
    vkDestroyBuffer(
      vkDev.device, b.buffer, nullptr);
    vkFreeMemory(vkDev.device, b.memory, nullptr);
  }
```

7. The framebuffers and renderpasses from all our renderers are also destroyed here:

```
  for (auto& fb: allFramebuffers)
    vkDestroyFramebuffer(vkDev.device, fb, nullptr);
  for (auto& rp: allRenderPasses)
    vkDestroyRenderPass(vkDev.device, rp, nullptr);
```

8. The descriptor pools and pipelines are destroyed at the end of this process:

```
  for (auto& ds: allDSLayouts)
    vkDestroyDescriptorSetLayout(
      vkDev.device, ds, nullptr);
  for (auto& pl: allPipelineLayouts)
    vkDestroyPipelineLayout(
      vkDev.device, pl, nullptr);
  for (auto& p: allPipelines)
    vkDestroyPipeline(vkDev.device, p, nullptr);
```

```
    for (auto& dpool: allDPools)
      vkDestroyDescriptorPool(
        vkDev.device, dpool, nullptr);
  }
```

9. In the next recipe, the full screen renderpasses and framebuffers are allocated externally and passed to the `VulkanResources` class for deallocation at the end of the runtime. Here are two routines that register framebuffer and renderpass instances for deallocation:

```
    inline void registerFramebuffer(VkFramebuffer fb) {
      allFramebuffers.push_back(fb);
    }
    inline void registerRenderPass(VkRenderPass rp) {
      allRenderPasses.push_back(rp);
    }
```

In our previous examples, we loaded the textures in an ad hoc fashion, as well as created the image and sampler. Here, we will wrap the texture file loading code in a single method:

1. The `createTextureImage()` function, from the *Using texture data in Vulkan* recipe of *Chapter 3, Getting Started with OpenGL and Vulkan*, loads the image:

```
    VulkanTexture loadTexture2D(const char* filename) {
      VulkanTexture tex;
      if (!createTextureImage(vkDev, filename,
          tex.image.image, tex.image.imageMemory)) {
        printf("Cannot load %s 2D texture file\n",
          filename);
        exit(EXIT_FAILURE);
      }
```

2. Let's assume that all the loaded images are in the RGBA 8-bit per-channel format. This is enforced by the scene converter tool described in this chapter. We will be using the `VK_IMAGE_LAYOUT_SHADER_READ_ONLY_OPTIMAL` layout since loaded images are intended to be used as inputs for fragment shaders:

```
    VkFormat format = VK_FORMAT_R8G8B8A8_UNORM;
    transitionImageLayout(vkDev, tex.image.image,
      format,
      VK_IMAGE_LAYOUT_UNDEFINED,
      VK_IMAGE_LAYOUT_SHADER_READ_ONLY_OPTIMAL);
```

3. Here, the image view is created for the new texture. Here, we will use the default layer count parameter for `createImageView()`. A major improvement we could make to this routine would be to calculate the MIP levels for the loaded image:

```
if (!createImageView(vkDev.device, tex.image.image,
    format, VK_IMAGE_ASPECT_COLOR_BIT,
    &tex.image.imageView)) {
  printf("Cannot create image view for 2d texture
    (%s)\n", filename);
  exit(EXIT_FAILURE);
}
```

4. After creating the texture sampler, we must store our newly created `VulkanTexture` instance in the `allTextures` array:

```
createTextureSampler(vkDev.device, &tex.sampler);
allTextures.push_back(tex);
return tex;
}
```

Along with `loadTexture()`, three other loading methods are provided for different types of textures:

```
VulkanTexture loadCubeMap(
  const char* fileName, uint32_t mipLevels);
VulkanTexture loadKTX(const char* fileName);
VulkanTexture createFontTexture(const char* fontFile);
```

The source code for `loadCubeMap()` is located in the `UtilsVulkanPBRModelRenderer.cpp` file. The only difference, as with all the loading routines, is that we are adding the created `VulkanTexture` to our `allTextures` container so that it will be deleted at the end of our program. The `loadKTX()` function is similar to the KTX file loading process that's described in the constructor of `PBRModelRenderer`.

After loading the texture data, we must create an image view in the `VK_FORMAT_R16G16_SFLOAT` format and add the created `VulkanTexture` to our `allTextures` array. The code for the `createFontTexture()` method can be found in the `UtilsVulkanImGui.cpp` file.

Let's look at some other helper functions that will make dealing with Vulkan objects somewhat easier:

1. All the buffers in our renderers are created by calling the `addBuffer()` routine either directly or indirectly:

```
VulkanBuffer addBuffer(VkDeviceSize size,
   VkBufferUsageFlags usage,
   VkMemoryPropertyFlags properties)
{
   VulkanBuffer buffer = {
     .buffer = VK_NULL_HANDLE,
     .size = 0,
     .memory = VK_NULL_HANDLE
   };
```

2. The `createSharedBuffer()` method is called so that we can use the buffer in compute shaders. If successful, the buffer is added to the `allBuffers` container:

```
  if (!createSharedBuffer(vkDev, size, usage,
       properties, buffer.buffer, buffer.memory)) {
    printf("Cannot allocate buffer\n");
    exit(EXIT_FAILURE);
  } else {
    buffer.size = size;
    allBuffers.push_back(buffer);
  }
  return buffer;
}
```

3. We haven't used offscreen rendering in the previous chapters, but pretty much every rendering and composition technique requires offscreen framebuffers. By default, a new texture is the size of the output framebuffer. The new texture contains dimensions and format information that will be passed to the framebuffer creation routine:

```
VulkanTexture addColorTexture(
   int texWidth, int texHeight, VkFormat colorFormat)
{
   const uint32_t w = (texWidth > 0) ?
     texWidth  : vkDev.framebufferWidth;
   const uint32_t h = (texHeight> 0) ?
     texHeight : vkDev.framebufferHeight;
```

```
VulkanTexture res = {
  .width = w,   .height = h,   .depth = 1,
  .format = colorFormat
};
```

4. The `createOffscreenImage()` function sets the appropriate usage flags for the image. Should the creation process fail, we must terminate the program after issuing an error message. An image view and a texture sampler can be created in the standard way, as follows:

```
if (!createOffscreenImage(vkDev,
    res.image.image, res.image.imageMemory,
    w, h, colorFormat, 1, 0)) {
  printf("Cannot create color texture\n");
  exit(EXIT_FAILURE);
}
createImageView(vkDev.device, res.image.image,
  colorFormat, VK_IMAGE_ASPECT_COLOR_BIT,
  &res.image.imageView);
createTextureSampler(vkDev.device, &res.sampler);
```

5. To keep the code size minimal, we will set a fixed layout for our texture at creation time and we won't change the layout each frame. Just like the other textures, we will store this one in the `allTextures` container:

```
transitionImageLayout(vkDev, res.image.image,
  colorFormat, VK_IMAGE_LAYOUT_UNDEFINED,
  VK_IMAGE_LAYOUT_SHADER_READ_ONLY_OPTIMAL);
allTextures.push_back(res);
return res;
}
```

Rendering to an offscreen depth texture is used for shadow mapping and approximating ambient occlusion. The routine is almost the same as `addColorTexture()`, but `depthFormat` and image usage flags must be different. We must also explicitly specify the image layout to avoid performance warnings from validation layers. Let's take a look:

1. Using `findDepthFormat()` from *Chapter 3, Getting Started with OpenGL and Vulkan*, we will set the format of our new texture:

```
VulkanTexture addDepthTexture(int texWidth,
  int texHeight, VkImageLayout layout =
  VK_IMAGE_LAYOUT_DEPTH_STENCIL_ATTACHMENT_OPTIMAL)
{
```

```
const uint32_t w = (texWidth  > 0) ?
  texWidth : vkDev.framebufferWidth;
const uint32_t h = (texHeight > 0) ?
  texHeight : vkDev.framebufferHeight;
const VkFormat depthFormat =
  findDepthFormat(vkDev.physicalDevice);
```

2. After storing the texture dimensions, we must call `createImage()` with the necessary flags:

```
VulkanTexture depth = {
  .width = w,  .height = h,  .depth = 1,  .format =
  depthFormat
};
if (!createImage(vkDev.device, vkDev.physicalDevice,
    w, h, depthFormat, VK_IMAGE_TILING_OPTIMAL,
    VK_IMAGE_USAGE_SAMPLED_BIT |
    VK_IMAGE_USAGE_DEPTH_STENCIL_ATTACHMENT_BIT,
    VK_MEMORY_PROPERTY_DEVICE_LOCAL_BIT,
    depth.image.image, depth.image.imageMemory)) {
  printf("Cannot create depth texture\n");
  exit(EXIT_FAILURE);
}
```

3. An image view is created and its layout is set:

```
createImageView(vkDev.device, depth.image.image,
  depthFormat, VK_IMAGE_ASPECT_DEPTH_BIT,
  &depth.image.imageView);
transitionImageLayout(vkDev, depth.image.image,
  depthFormat, VK_IMAGE_LAYOUT_UNDEFINED, layout);
```

4. The sampler for the depth textures uses different flags, so it is created with a dedicated function:

```
if (!createDepthSampler(
    vkDev.device, &depth.sampler)) {
  printf("Cannot create a depth sampler");
  exit(EXIT_FAILURE);
}
allTextures.push_back(depth);
return depth;
}
```

5. The rest of the resource management is dedicated to framebuffers, renderpasses, and pipelines. Internally, we refer to render passes using the `RenderPass` structure, which holds a Vulkan handle, along with the list of parameters that were used to create this render pass:

```
struct RenderPass {
  RenderPass() = default;
  explicit RenderPass(VulkanRenderDevice& device,
    bool useDepth = true,
    const RenderPassCreateInfo& ci =
      RenderPassCreateInfo()): info(ci)
  {
    if (!createColorAndDepthRenderPass(
        vkDev, useDepth, &handle, ci)) {
      printf("Failed to create render pass\n");
      exit(EXIT_FAILURE);
    }
  }
  RenderPassCreateInfo info;
  VkRenderPass handle = VK_NULL_HANDLE;
};
```

Creating the framebuffer is a frequent operation, so to make our rendering initialization code shorter, we must implement the `addFramebuffer()` function, which takes a render pass object and a list of attachments to create a framebuffer:

1. First, we must extract individual image view objects from a container of `VulkanTexture` objects:

```
VkFramebuffer addFramebuffer(
  RenderPass,
  const std::vector<VulkanTexture>& images)
{
  VkFramebuffer framebuffer;
  std::vector<VkImageView> attachments;
  for (const auto& i: images)
    attachments.push_back(i.image.imageView);
```

2. Just as we did in the *Initializing the Vulkan pipeline* recipe of *Chapter 3, Getting Started with OpenGL and Vulkan*, we will pass a list of attachments to the creation structure. It's assumed that all the images are the same size, so we will use the size of the first one here:

```
VkFramebufferCreateInfo fbInfo = {
  .sType =
    VK_STRUCTURE_TYPE_FRAMEBUFFER_CREATE_INFO,
  .pNext = nullptr,
  .flags = 0,
  .renderPass = renderPass.handle,
  .attachmentCount = (uint32_t)attachments.size(),
  .pAttachments = attachments.data(),
  .width = images[0].width,
  .height = images[0].height,
  .layers = 1
};
```

3. After completing the `vkCreateFramebuffer()` call, we should store the newly created framebuffer in the `allFramebuffers` container:

```
if (vkCreateFramebuffer(
      vkDev.device, &fbInfo, nullptr, &framebuffer)
    != VK_SUCCESS) {
  printf("Unable to create offscreen
    framebuffer\n");
  exit(EXIT_FAILURE);
}
allFramebuffers.push_back(framebuffer);
return framebuffer;
}
```

4. Our renderers from the following samples require different kinds of rendering passes. The most generic `addRenderPass()` function assumes that there is at least one attachment. Render passes with empty attachment lists are not supported:

```
RenderPass addRenderPass(
  const std::vector<VulkanTexture>& outputs,
  const RenderPassCreateInfo ci = {
    .clearColor_ = true, .clearDepth_ = true,
    .flags_ = eRenderPassBit_Offscreen |
              eRenderPassBit_First },
  bool useDepth = true)
{
```

```
VkRenderPass renderPass;
if (outputs.empty()) {
  printf("Empty list of output attachments for
    RenderPass\n");
  exit(EXIT_FAILURE);
}
```

5. A render pass with one color attachment is a special case:

```
if (outputs.size() == 1) {
  if (!createColorOnlyRenderPass(
      vkDev, &renderPass, ci, outputs[0].format)) {
    printf("Unable to create offscreen color-only
      pass\n");
    exit(EXIT_FAILURE);
  }
```

6. For more than one attachment, we should call the general render pass creation routine from the *Initializing the Vulkan pipeline* recipe of *Chapter 3, Getting Started with OpenGL and Vulkan*:

```
} else {
  if (!createColorAndDepthRenderPass(
      vkDev, useDepth && (outputs.size() > 1),
      &renderPass, ci, outputs[0].format)) {
    printf("Unable to create offscreen render
      pass\n");
    exit(EXIT_FAILURE);
  }
}
```

7. Finally, our new render pass should be stored in an appropriate container:

```
allRenderPasses.push_back(renderPass);
RenderPass rp;
rp.info = ci;
rp.handle = renderPass;
return rp;
}
```

8. A depth-only render pass creation, used for shadow mapping, contains less logic and simply redirects to the `createDepthOnlyRenderPass()` function:

```
RenderPass addDepthRenderPass(
  const std::vector<VulkanTexture>& outputs,
  const RenderPassCreateInfo ci = {
    .clearColor_ = false, .clearDepth_ = true,
    .flags_ = eRenderPassBit_Offscreen |
              eRenderPassBit_First
  })
{
  VkRenderPass renderPass;
  if (!createDepthOnlyRenderPass(
      vkDev, &renderPass, ci)) {
    printf("Unable to create offscreen render
      pass\n");
    exit(EXIT_FAILURE);
  }
  allRenderPasses.push_back(renderPass);
  RenderPass rp;
  rp.info = ci;
  rp.handle = renderPass;
  return rp;
}
```

9. Two helper methods allow for shorter initialization periods for swap chains and full screen renderpasses. All the framebuffers associated with a swapchain are added to the framebuffer list:

```
std::vector<VkFramebuffer> addFramebuffers(
  VkRenderPass renderPass,
  VkImageView depthView = VK_NULL_HANDLE)
{
  RenderPass  std::vector<VkFramebuffer>
    framebuffers;
  createColorAndDepthFramebuffers(vkDev,
    renderPass, depthView, framebuffers);
  for (auto f : framebuffers)
    allFramebuffers.push_back(f);
  return framebuffers;
}
```

10. Once it's been created, the render pass is added to our local repository, in the `allRenderPasses` container:

```
RenderPass addFullScreenPass(
  bool useDepth = true,
  const RenderPassCreateInfo& ci =
    RenderPassCreateInfo())
{

  RenderPass result(vkDev, useDepth, ci);

  allRenderPasses.push_back(result.handle);

  return result;

}
```

11. Along with descriptor sets, which refer to individual buffers and textures, pipelines define the rendering process. Pipeline creation parameters are passed around in a structure:

```
struct PipelineInfo {
  uint32_t width  = 0;
  uint32_t height = 0;
  VkPrimitiveTopology topology =
    VK_PRIMITIVE_TOPOLOGY_TRIANGLE_LIST;
  bool useDepth = true;
  bool useBlending = true;
  bool dynamicScissorState = false;
};
```

12. The pipeline layouts are created with a function `createPipelineLayoutWithConstants()`, which is similar to `createPipelineLayout()` from *Chapter 3, Getting Started with OpenGL and Vulkan*, but adds push constants to the Vulkan pipeline. The newly created pipeline layout is stored in a container:

```
VkPipelineLayout addPipelineLayout(
  VkDescriptorSetLayout dsLayout,
  uint32_t vtxConstSize = 0,
  uint32_t fragConstSize = 0)
{

  VkPipelineLayout pipelineLayout;
  if (!createPipelineLayoutWithConstants(
      vkDev.device, dsLayout, &pipelineLayout,
      vtxConstSize, fragConstSize))  {
```

```
      printf("Cannot create pipeline layout\n");
      exit(EXIT_FAILURE);
    }
    allPipelineLayouts.push_back(pipelineLayout);
    return pipelineLayout;
}
```

13. The `addPipeline()` method wraps the `createGraphicsPipeline()` function. Once it's been created, the pipeline is put into yet another container of Vulkan objects:

```
VkPipeline addPipeline(
  VkRenderPass renderPass,
  VkPipelineLayout pipelineLayout,
  const std::vector<const char*>& shaderFiles,
  const PipelineInfo& pipelineParams = PipelineInfo {
    .width = 0, .height = 0,
    .topology = VK_PRIMITIVE_TOPOLOGY_TRIANGLE_LIST,
    .useDepth = true, .useBlending = false,
    .dynamicScissorState = false })
{

  VkPipeline pipeline;
  if (!createGraphicsPipeline(vkDev, renderPass,
      pipelineLayout, shaderFiles, &pipeline,
      ppInfo.topology,ppInfo.useDepth,
      ppInfo.useBlending, ppInfo.dynamicScissorState,
      ppInfo.width, ppInfo.height)) {
    printf("Cannot create graphics pipeline\n");
    exit(EXIT_FAILURE);
  }
  allPipelines.push_back(pipeline);
  return pipeline;
}
```

The only instance of the `VulkanResources` class resides in the `VulkanRenderContext` structure, which will be described in the next recipe. All the resources are deleted strictly the global `VkDevice` object encapsulated in `VulkanRenderDevice` is destroyed.

There's more...

The examples in this chapter heavily rely on indirect rendering, so individual mesh rendering is hidden within our scene graph. However, if you wish to update the sample code from *Chapter 3, Getting Started with OpenGL and Vulkan*, and use it for direct mesh geometry manipulation, the `addVertexBuffer()` method has been provided. The mesh geometry uploading code is similar to the `createTexturedVertexBuffer()` and `createPBRVertexBuffer()` functions we described in previous chapters:

```
VulkanBuffer addVertexBuffer(uint32_t indexBufferSize,
    const void* indexData,
    uint32_t vertexBufferSize,
    const void* vertexData)
{

    VulkanBuffer result;
    result.size = allocateVertexBuffer(vkDev, &result.buffer,
        &result.memory, vertexBufferSize, vertexData,
        indexBufferSize, indexData);
    allBuffers.push_back(result);
    return result;
}
```

The last important issue in terms of resource management is the descriptor set creation routines. This will be covered in the *Unifying descriptor set creation routines* recipe of this chapter.

We typically use `VulkanResources` in the constructors of different `Renderer` classes. The *Putting it all together into a Vulkan application* recipe will show you how our resource management fits the general application code.

Refactoring Vulkan initialization and the main loop

Starting from *Chapter 3, Getting Started with OpenGL and Vulkan*, we introduced an ad hoc rendering loop for each demo application, which resulted in significant code duplication. Let's revisit this topic and learn how to create multiple rendering passes for Vulkan without too much boilerplate code.

Getting ready

Before completing this recipe, make sure to revisit the *Putting it all together into a Vulkan application* recipe of *Chapter 3, Getting Started with OpenGL and Vulkan*, as well as all the related recipes.

How to do it...

The goal of this recipe is to improve the rendering framework to avoid code repetition in renderers, as well as to simplify our rendering setup. In the next recipe, as a useful side effect, we will use a system capable of setting up and composing multiple rendering passes without too much hustle.

The `main` function for all our upcoming demos should consist of just three lines:

```
int main() {
  MyApp app;
  app.mainLoop();
  return 0;
}
```

Let's take a look at how to organize the `MyApp` class for this purpose:

1. The `MyApp` class is derived from our base `VulkanApp`. Its constructor initializes all the resources needed for scene and UI rendering:

   ```
   class MyApp: public VulkanApp {
   public:
     MyApp()
       ... field initializers list ...
       ... rendering sequence setup ...
   ```

   The base class constructor creates a GLFW window and initializes a Vulkan rendering surface, just like we did previously throughout *Chapter 3, Getting Started with OpenGL and Vulkan*, to *Chapter 6, Physically Based Rendering Using the glTF2 Shading Model*.

2. There is no need to override the destructor because all our Vulkan objects are destroyed by the resource management system we discussed in the previous recipe, *Managing Vulkan resources*. The default destructor also takes care of GLFW windows and Vulkan device instances. The rendering method is called once per frame internally, in `VulkanApp::mainLoop()`:

   ```
   void draw3D() override {
       ... whatever render control commands required ...
     }
   ```

3. The `drawUI()` method may contain arbitrary ImGui library calls that are internally converted into a list of Vulkan commands:

```
void drawUI() override {
    ... ImGUI commands ...
}
```

4. The overridden `VulkanApp::update()` method gets called once per fixed time interval. In the *Adding Bullet physics to a graphics application* recipe of *Chapter 9, Working with Scene Graph*, we will initiate the physical world update process. Camera control may also be added here:

```
void update(float deltaSeconds) override {
    ... update whatever needs to be updated ...
}
```

5. The private section contains references to `VulkanTexture`, `VulkanBuffer`, and the renderer classes we discussed earlier:

```
private:
    ... Vulkan buffers, scene geometry, textures etc....
    ... e.g., some texture:  VulkanTexture envMap ...
    ... whatever renderers an app needs ...
    MultiRenderer;
    GuiRenderer imgui;
};
```

Having said this, let's see how the `VulkanApp` class wraps all the initialization and uses the previously defined `VulkanResources`.

The application class relies on previously developed functions and some new items that we must describe before implementing `VulkanApp` itself. In the previous chapters, we used `VulkanRenderDevice` as a simple C structure and called all the initialization routines explicitly in every sample. Following the C++ **resource acquisition is initialization (RAII)** paradigm, we must wrap these calls with the constructors and destructors of the helper class:

1. The `VulkanContextCreator` class holds references to `VulkanInstance` and `VulkanRenderDevice`, which are stored in `VulkanApp`:

```
struct VulkanContextCreator {
  VulkanInstance& instance;
  VulkanRenderDevice& vkDev;
```

2. The constructor of the class performs familiar initialization for Vulkan instances
   and logical devices. If anything fails, we must terminate the program:

```
VulkanContextCreator(VulkanInstance& vk,
   VulkanRenderDevice& dev, void* window,
   int screenWidth, int screenHeight):instance(vk),
   vkDev(dev)
{
   createInstance(&vk.instance);
   if (!setupDebugCallbacks(vk.instance,
         &vk.messenger, vk.reportCallback) ||
      glfwCreateWindowSurface(vk.instance,
      (GLFWwindow *)window, nullptr, &vk.surface) ||
      !initVulkanRenderDevice3(
         vk, dev, screenWidth, screenHeight))
      exit(EXIT_FAILURE);
}
```

3. The destructor performs trivial deinitialization of the Vulkan instance and
   render device:

```
~VulkanContextCreator() {
   destroyVulkanRenderDevice(vkDev);
   destroyVulkanInstance(instance);
}
};
```

The Vulkan instance and device alone are not enough to render anything: we must declare
a basic rendering interface and combine multiple renderers in one frame.

In the previous chapter, we figured out one way to implement a generic interface for a
Vulkan renderer. Let's take a look once more:

1. Here, we will only present the interface, which consists of a function to fill
   command buffers and a function to update all the current auxiliary buffers
   containing uniforms or geometry data. This is because the interface is what matters
   for implementing the application's main loop:

```
struct Renderer {
   Renderer(VulkanRenderContext& c);
   virtual void fillCommandBuffer(
      VkCommandBuffer cmdBuffer,
      size_t currentImage,
      VkFramebuffer fb = VK_NULL_HANDLE,
```

```
          VkRenderPass rp = VK_NULL_HANDLE) = 0;
     virtual void updateBuffers(size_t currentImage) {}
};
```

The details of our implementation are provided in the subsequent recipe, *Working with rendering passes*.

2. Since individual `Renderer` class creation is rather expensive, we must define a wrapper structure that takes a reference to the `Renderer` class. Thanks to C++11's move semantics, an `std::vector` of `RenderItem` instances can be filled with `emplace_back()`, without it triggering copy constructors or reinitialization:

```
struct RenderItem {
  Renderer& renderer_;
  bool enabled_ = true;
  bool useDepth_ = true;
  explicit RenderItem(
    Renderer& r, bool useDepth = true)
  : renderer_(r)
  , useDepth_(useDepth)
  {}
};
```

3. The `VulkanRenderContext` class holds all basic Vulkan objects (instance and device), along with a list of on-screen renderers. This class will be used later in `VulkanApp` to compose a frame. `VulkanContextCreator` helps initialize both the instance and logical Vulkan device. The resource management system described in the previous recipe, *Managing Vulkan resources*, is also initialized here:

```
struct VulkanRenderContext {
  VulkanInstance vk;
  VulkanRenderDevice vkDev;
  VulkanContextCreator ctxCreator;
  VulkanResources resources;
```

4. In essence, this class contains a list of on-screen renderers, declared as a dynamic array. Along with composite subsystems, a list of renderpass and framebuffer handles are declared for use in `Renderer` instances. All framebuffers share a single depth buffer. The render passes for on-screen rendering are also declared here:

```
  std::vector<RenderItem> onScreenRenderers_;
  VulkanTexture depthTexture;
```

```
RenderPass screenRenderPass;
RenderPass screenRenderPass_NoDepth;
```

5. Two special render passes for clearing and finalizing the frame are used, just as in the demo application from *Chapter 5, Working with Geometry Data*, the VulkanClear and VulkanFinish classes. The framebuffers for depth-buffered and 2D rendering are also here, along with any render passes:

```
RenderPass clearRenderPass, finalRenderPass;
std::vector<VkFramebuffer> swapchainFramebuffers;
std::vector<VkFramebuffer>
swapchainFramebuffers_NoDepth;
```

6. The constructor of the class is empty; only the initializers' list sets up all the fields:

```
VulkanRenderContext(void* window,
  uint32_t screenWidth, uint32_t screenHeight)
: ctxCreator(vk, vkDev, window, screenWidth,
    screenHeight)
, resources(vkDev)
, depthTexture(resources.addDepthTexture(0, 0,
    VK_IMAGE_LAYOUT_SHADER_READ_ONLY_OPTIMAL))
, screenRenderPass(resources.addFullScreenPass())
, screenRenderPass_NoDepth(
    resources.addFullScreenPass(false))
```

7. The finalization and screen clearing render passes are initialized with a special set of creation parameters:

```
, finalRenderPass(resources.addFullScreenPass(
    true, RenderPassCreateInfo {
    .clearColor_ = false, .clearDepth_ = false,
    .flags_ = eRenderPassBit_Last  }))
, clearRenderPass(resources.addFullScreenPass(
    true, RenderPassCreateInfo {
    .clearColor_ = true, .clearDepth_ = true,
    .flags_ = eRenderPassBit_First }))
, swapchainFramebuffers(
    resources.addFramebuffers(
      screenRenderPass.handle,
      depthTexture.image.imageView))
, swapchainFramebuffers_NoDepth(
    resources.addFramebuffers(
      screenRenderPass_NoDepth.handle))
{}
```

8. The `updateBuffers()` method iterates over all the enabled renderers and updates their internal buffers:

```
void updateBuffers(uint32_t imageIndex) {
  for (auto& r : onScreenRenderers_)
    if (r.enabled_)
      r.renderer_.updateBuffers(imageIndex);
}
```

9. All the renderers in our framework use custom rendering passes. Starting a new rendering pass can be implemented with the following routine:

```
void beginRenderPass(
  VkCommandBuffer cmdBuffer, VkRenderPass pass,
  size_t currentImage, const VkRect2D area,
  VkFramebuffer fb = VK_NULL_HANDLE,
  uint32_t clearValueCount = 0,
  const VkClearValue* clearValues = nullptr)
{
```

10. As we saw in *Chapter 3, Getting Started with OpenGL and Vulkan*, the `vkCmdBeginRenderPass()` API call takes a structure as its parameter. If an external framebuffer is unspecified, we use our local full screen framebuffer. Optional clearing values are also passed as parameters:

```
  const VkRenderPassBeginInfo renderPassInfo = {
    .sType =
      VK_STRUCTURE_TYPE_RENDER_PASS_BEGIN_INFO,
    .renderPass = pass,
    .framebuffer = (fb != VK_NULL_HANDLE) ?
      fb : swapchainFramebuffers[currentImage],
    .renderArea = area,
    .clearValueCount = clearValueCount,
    .pClearValues = clearValues
  };
  vkCmdBeginRenderPass(
    cmdBuffer, &renderPassInfo,
    VK_SUBPASS_CONTENTS_INLINE);
  }
};
```

Now, let's see how our frame composition works. It is similar to what we did in *Chapter 5, Working with Geometry Data*, where we had multiple renderers. The following code can and should only be considered as a refactoring. The added complexity is due to the offscreen rendering support that we need for the next few remaining chapters:

1. To specify the output region for our renderers, we must declare a rectangle variable:

```
void VulkanRenderContext::composeFrame(
  VkCommandBuffer commandBuffer, uint32_t imageIndex)
{
  const VkRect2D defaultScreenRect {
    .offset = { 0, 0 },
    .extent = { .width  = vkDev.framebufferWidth,
                .height = vkDev.framebufferHeight }
  };
```

2. Clearing the screen requires values for both the color buffer and the depth buffer. If any custom user-specified clearing value is required, this is the place in our framework to add modifications:

```
static const VkClearValue defaultClearValues[]  =  {
  VkClearValue { .color = {1.f, 1.f, 1.f, 1.f} },
  VkClearValue { .depthStencil = {1.f, 0} }
};
```

3. The special screen clearing render pass is executed first:

```
beginRenderPass(commandBuffer,
  clearRenderPass.handle,
  imageIndex, defaultScreenRect, VK_NULL_HANDLE,
  2u, defaultClearValues);
vkCmdEndRenderPass( commandBuffer );
```

4. When the screen is ready, we iterate over the list of renderers and fill the command buffer sequentially. We skip inactive renderers while iterating. This is mostly a debugging feature for manually controlling the output. An appropriate full screen rendering pass is selected for each renderer instance:

```
for (auto& r : onScreenRenderers_)
  if (r.enabled_) {
    RenderPass rp = r.useDepth_ ?
      screenRenderPass : screenRenderPass_NoDepth;
```

5.   The framebuffer is also selected according to the `useDepth` flag in a renderer:

```
VkFramebuffer fb =
    (r.useDepth_ ? swapchainFramebuffers:
     swapchainFramebuffers_NoDepth)[imageIndex];
```

6.   If this renderer outputs to some offscreen buffer with a custom rendering pass, we replace both the `rp` and `fb` pointers accordingly:

```
if (r.renderer_.renderPass_.handle !=
    VK_NULL_HANDLE)
   rp = r.renderer_.renderPass_;
if (r.renderer_.framebuffer_ != VK_NULL_HANDLE)
   fb = r.renderer_.framebuffer_;
```

7.   Finally, we ask the renderer to fill the current command buffer. At the end, the framebuffer is converted into a presentation-optimal format using a special render pass:

```
   r.renderer_.fillCommandBuffer(
       commandBuffer, imageIndex, fb, rp.handle);
   }
beginRenderPass(commandBuffer,
   finalRenderPass.handle, imageIndex,
   defaultScreenRect);
vkCmdEndRenderPass(commandBuffer);
}
```

This concludes the definition of our helper classes for the new frame composition framework. Now, we have everything in place to define the application structure:

1.   The protected section of the class contains the mouse state for GUI handling, the screen resolution for correct aspect ratio calculation, and the GLFW window pointer. We also have our one and only `VulkanRendererContext` instance. To save some typing, we will refer to `ctx_.onScreenRenderers_` by defining a local reference field:

```
class VulkanApp {
protected:
  struct MouseState {
    glm::vec2 pos = glm::vec2(0.0f);
    bool pressedLeft = false;
  } mouseState_;
```

```
Resolution_;
GLFWwindow* window_ = nullptr;
VulkanRenderContext ctx_;
std::vector<RenderItem>& onScreenRenderers_;
```

2. The public section of the class provides initialization, deinitialization, and miscellaneous event handlers:

```
public:
  VulkanApp(int screenWidth, int screenHeight)
  : window_(initVulkanApp(
      screenWidth, screenHeight, &resolution_))
  , ctx_(window_, resolution_.width,
      resolution_.height)
  , onScreenRenderers_(ctx_.onScreenRenderers_)
  {
    glfwSetWindowUserPointer(window_, this);
    assignCallbacks();
  }
```

3. The destructor contains explicit GLSL compiler library deinitialization features, as well as the GLFW termination call:

```
~VulkanApp() {
  glslang_finalize_process();
  glfwTerminate();
}
```

4. As we mentioned at the beginning of this recipe, the user provides two overridden methods for UI and 3D rendering. The update() routine performs whatever actions necessary to calculate the new application state:

```
virtual void drawUI() {}
virtual void draw3D() = 0;
virtual void update(float deltaSeconds) = 0;
```

For example, the CameraApp class, described later in this recipe, calls a 3D camera position update routine, while the physics simulation recipe calls physics simulation routines.

5. The `mainLoop()` method is called from the `main()` function of our application. One thing to note is that the method implementation in the source code bundle for this book include a frames per second counter. It has been omitted here to keep the source code shorter:

```
void mainLoop() {
   double timeStamp = glfwGetTime();
   float deltaSeconds = 0.0f;
   do {
     update(deltaSeconds);
```

6. Usual time counting is performed to calculate `deltaSeconds` for the next frame. Note that here, we are processing the frames as fast as possible, but internally, the overridden `update()` function may quantize time into fixed intervals. This will be used in our physics example in *Chapter 9*:

```
const double newTimeStamp = glfwGetTime();
deltaSeconds = newTimeStamp - timeStamp;
timeStamp = newTimeStamp;
```

7. The `drawFrame()` method from *Chapter 6, Physically Based Rendering Using the glTF2 Shading Model*, takes our new `updateBuffers()` and `VulkanRenderContext::composeFrame()` functions to perform frame composition:

```
drawFrame(ctx_.vkDev,
   [this](uint32_t img)
   { this->updateBuffers(img); },
   [this](uint32_t b, uint32_auto img)
   { ctx_.composeFrame(b, img); }
);
```

8. After polling for system events, we wait for all the graphics operations to complete:

```
   glfwPollEvents();
   vkDeviceWaitIdle(ctx_.vkDev.device);
 } while (!glfwWindowShouldClose(window_));
}
```

The final part of the public interface of `VulkanApp` is related to UI event handling:

1. The `shouldHandleMouse()` function asks if ImGui has already consumed the incoming event; we can handle mouse movements and clicks ourselves. This is used in most of our demos to control the camera in our main view, but only if the user does not interact with UI widgets:

```
inline bool shouldHandleMouse() const
{ return !ImGui::GetIO().WantCaptureMouse; }
```

2. The `handleKey()` method processes incoming key presses. One useful override is done in the `CameraApp` class:

```
virtual void handleKey(int key, bool pressed) = 0;
```

3. `handleMouseClick()` and `handleMouseMove()` just save the parameters of incoming mouse events:

```
virtual void handleMouseClick(
  int button, bool pressed) {
  if (button == GLFW_MOUSE_BUTTON_LEFT)
    mouseState_.pressedLeft = pressed;
}
virtual void handleMouseMove(float mx, float my) {
  mouseState_.pos = glm::vec2(mx, my);
}
```

To complete the description of the new `VulkanApp` class, let's look at its implementation details:

1. The `assignCallbacks()` method uses `glfwSetCursorPosCallback()`, `glfwSetMouseButtonCallback()`, and `glfwSetKeyCallback()` to forward mouse and keyboard events from GLFW to the `handleMouseMove()`, `handleMouseClick()`, and `handleKey()` methods of the `VulkanApp` class, respectively. The event handlers repeat the code from the previous recipes, so only the key press handler is shown here:

```
private:
  void assignCallbacks() {
    … set mouse callbacks (not shown here) …
    glfwSetKeyCallback(window_,
      [](GLFWwindow* window, int key, int scancode,
        int action, int mods) {
```

```
const bool pressed = action != GLFW_RELEASE;
if (key == GLFW_KEY_ESCAPE && pressed)
  glfwSetWindowShouldClose(window, GLFW_TRUE);
```

The only modification we've made to the handler's code is for a custom pointer from GLFW's `window_` to be extracted. The only predefined key is the *Esc* key. When the user presses it, we exit the application.

2. The `initVulkanApp()` function, which is called in the constructor of `VulkanApp`, associates the `this` pointer with GLFW's `window_` object. Here, we are extracting the `this` pointer and, after casting it to `VulkanApp*`, calling the `handleKey()` method to process keypresses:

```
void* ptr = glfwGetWindowUserPointer(window);
reinterpret_cast<VulkanApp*>(
  ptr)->handleKey(key, pressed);
});
}
```

3. The `updateBuffers()` method updates the ImGui display dimensions and resets any internal draw lists. The user-provided `drawUI()` function is called to render the app-specific UI. Then, `draw3D()` updates internal scene descriptions and whatever else is necessary to render the frame:

```
void updateBuffers(uint32_t imageIndex) {
  ImGuiIO& io = ImGui::GetIO();
  io.DisplaySize =
    ImVec2((float)ctx_.vkDev.framebufferWidth,
    (float)ctx_.vkDev.framebufferHeight);
  ImGui::NewFrame();
  drawUI();
  ImGui::Render();
  draw3D();
  ctx_.updateBuffers(imageIndex);
}
};
```

The following recipes contain numerous examples of this function's implementations. The call to the previously described `VulkanRenderContext::updateBuffers()` concludes this function.

Our `VulkanApp` class is now complete, but there are still some pure virtual methods that prevent us from using it directly. A derived `CameraApp` class will be used as a base for all the future examples in this book:

1. The constructor performs the usual `VulkanApp` initialization, along with setting up the 3D camera:

```
struct CameraApp: public VulkanApp {
  CameraApp(int screenWidth, int screenHeight)
  : VulkanApp(screenWidth, screenHeight)
  , positioner(vec3(0.0f, 5.0f, 10.0f)
  , vec3(0.0f, 0.0f, -1.0f), vec3(0.0f, -1.0f, 0.0f))
  , camera(positioner)
  {}
```

2. The overridden `update()` method sends mouse event parameters to the 3D camera positioner:

```
virtual void update(float deltaSeconds) override {
  positioner.update(deltaSeconds, mouseState_.pos,
    shouldHandleMouse() && mouseState_.pressedLeft);
}
```

3. The default camera projection calculator uses the screen aspect ratio:

```
glm::mat4 getDefaultProjection() const {
  const float ratio = ctx_.vkDev.framebufferWidth /
    (float)ctx_.vkDev.framebufferHeight;
  return glm::perspective(
    glm::pi<float>() / 4.0f, ratio, 0.1f, 1000.0f);
}
```

4. The `handleKey()` method redirects key press events to the Boolean fields of the camera positioner:

```
virtual void handleKey(int key, bool pressed)
  override {
  if (key == GLFW_KEY_W)
    positioner.movement_.forward_ = pressed;
  … handle the rest of camera keys similarly …
}
```

All the keys are handled just as in the recipes from *Chapter 3, Getting Started with OpenGL and Vulkan*, through *Chapter 6, Physically Based Rendering Using the glTF2 Shading Model*.

5. The protected section of the class defines the camera positioner and the camera itself. Subclasses may use the current camera position for lighting calculations by passing it to uniform buffers:

```
protected:
    CameraPositioner_FirstPerson positioner;
    Camera;
};
```

The next recipe concentrates on implementing the `Renderer` interface based on the samples from previous chapters.

Working with rendering passes

In *Chapter 4, Adding User Interaction and Productivity Tools*, we introduced our "layered" frame composition, which we will now refine and extend. These modifications will allow us to do offscreen rendering and significantly simplify initialization and Vulkan object management.

This recipe will describe the rendering interface that's used by the `VulkanApp` class. At the end of this recipe, a few concrete classes will be presented that can render quadrilaterals and the UI. Please revisit the previous two recipes to see how the `Renderer` interface fits in the new framework.

Getting ready

Check out the *Putting it all together into a Vulkan application* recipe of *Chapter 4, Adding User Interaction and Productivity Tools*, to refresh your memory on how our "layered" frame composition works.

How to do it...

Each of the frame rendering passes is represented by an instance of the `Renderer` class. The list of references to these instances is stored in `VulkanRenderContext`. The usage of these instances was thoroughly discussed in the previous recipe:

1. The `Renderer` class contains an empty public constructor that stores a reference to `VulkanRenderContext` and the default size of the output framebuffer:

```
struct Renderer {
  Renderer(VulkanRenderContext& c)
  : processingWidth(c.vkDev.framebufferWidth)
  , processingHeight(c.vkDev.framebufferHeight)
  , ctx_(c)
  {}
```

2. To produce anything on the screen, we need to record a command buffer for our graphics queue. A pure virtual `fillCommandBuffer()` method is overridden in subclasses to record rendering commands. Each frame can be rendered to a different framebuffer, so we will pass the image index as a parameter. A frame can be rendered to an onscreen framebuffer. In this case, we pass null handles as the output framebuffer and render pass:

```
virtual void fillCommandBuffer(
   VkCommandBuffer cmdBuffer,
   size_t currentImage,
   VkFramebuffer fb = VK_NULL_HANDLE,
   VkRenderPass rp = VK_NULL_HANDLE) = 0;
```

3. At each frame, we may need to update the contents of some of the buffers. By default, the respective method is empty:

```
virtual void updateBuffers(size_t currentImage) {}
```

4. One frequent operation we must perform is updating the uniform buffer that corresponds to the current frame:

```
inline void updateUniformBuffer(
  uint32_t currentImage,
  const uint32_t offset,
  const uint32_t size, const void* data)
  {
```

```
        uploadBufferData(ctx_.vkDev,
          uniforms_[currentImage].memory, offset, data,
          size);
      }
```

5. Each of our renderers uses a dedicated Vulkan graphics pipeline. This pipeline is determined by the list of used shaders, the sizes of push constant buffers for the vertex and fragment stages, and a `PipelineInfo` structure with additional parameters. The `initPipeline()` function creates a pipeline layout and then immediately uses this layout to create the Vulkan pipeline itself. Just like with any of the Vulkan objects, the pipeline handle is stored in the `ctx_.resources` object, so we do not have to worry about its destruction:

```
      void initPipeline(
        const std::vector<const char*>& shaders,
        const PipelineInfo& pInfo,
        uint32_t vtxConstSize = 0,
        uint32_t fragConstSize = 0)
      {

        pipelineLayout_ =
          ctx_.resources.addPipelineLayout(
            descriptorSetLayout_, vtxConstSize,
            fragConstSize);
        graphicsPipeline_ = ctx_.resources.addPipeline(
          renderPass_.handle, pipelineLayout_, shaders,
          pInfo);
      }
```

6. Each renderer defines a dedicated render pass that is compatible with the set of input textures. The `initRenderPass()` function contains the logic that's used in most of the renderer classes. The input pipeline parameters can be changed if offscreen rendering is performed (non-empty list of output textures). If we pass in a valid `renderPass` object, then it is directly assigned to the internal `renderPass_` field:

```
      PipelineInfo initRenderPass(
        const PipelineInfo& pInfo,
        const std::vector<VulkanTexture>& outputs,
        RenderPass = RenderPass(),
        RenderPass fallbackPass = RenderPass())
      {
```

7. If the output list is empty, which means we are rendering to the screen, and the
    `renderPass` parameter is not valid, then we take `fallbackPass` as the rendering
    pass. Usually, it is taken from one of the class fields of `VulkanRenderContext`
    – `screenRenderPass` or `screenRenderPass_NoDepth` – depending on
    whether we need depth buffering or not. We may need to modify the input pipeline
    description, so we will declare a new `PipelineInfo` variable. If we are rendering
    to an offscreen buffer, we must store the buffer dimensions in the rendering area. The
    output pipeline information structure also contains the actual rendering area's size:

    ```
    PipelineInfo outInfo = pInfo;
    if (!outputs.empty()) {
      processingWidth = outputs[0].width;
      processingHeight = outputs[0].height;
      outInfo.width = processingWidth;
      outInfo.height = processingHeight;
    ```

8. If no external renderpass is provided, we allocate a new one that's compatible with
    the output framebuffer. If we have only one depth attachment, then we must use
    a special rendering pass. The `isDepthFormat()` function is a one-liner that
    compares the `VkFormat` parameter with one of the predefined Vulkan depth
    buffer formats; see the `UtilsVulkan.h` file for details. To render to the screen
    framebuffer, we will use one of the renderpasses from our parameters:

    ```
    bool hasHandle =
      renderPass.handle != VK_NULL_HANDLE;
    bool hasDepth = (outputs.size() == 1)) &&
      isDepthFormat(outputs[0].format);
    renderPass_ = hasHandle ? renderPass :
      ((hasDepth ?
        ctx_.resources.addDepthRenderPass(outputs) :
          ctx_.resources.addRenderPass(outputs));
    framebuffer_ = ctx_.resources.addFramebuffer(
      renderPass_, outputs);
    } else {
      renderPass_ =
        hasHandle ? renderPass : fallbackPass;
    }
    return outInfo;
    }
    ```

The last helper function we need in all our renderers is the `beginRenderPass()`
function, which adds the appropriate commands to start a rendering pass.

9. Just as we did in `VulkanRenderContext::beginRenderPass()`, we will declare some buffer clearing values and the output area:

```
void beginRenderPass(
  VkRenderPass rp, VkFramebuffer fb,
  VkCommandBuffer commandBuffer,
  size_t currentImage)
{
  const VkClearValue clearValues[2] = {
    VkClearValue { .color = {1.f, 1.f, 1.f, 1.f} },
    VkClearValue { .depthStencil = {1.f, 0} }
  };
  const VkRect2D rect {
    .offset = { 0, 0 },
    .extent = { .width  = processingWidth,
                .height = processingHeight }
  };
```

10. To avoid calling the Vulkan API directly, we will pass a complete set of parameters to the `VulkanRenderContext::beginRenderPass()` function we implemented in the previous recipe. Some arithmetic is required to calculate the number of clear values. If we don't need to clear the color, depth, or both buffers, we will change the offset in the `clearValues` array:

```
ctx_.beginRenderPass(
  commandBuffer, rp, currentImage, rect, fb,
  (renderPass_.info.clearColor_ ? 1u : 0u) +
  (renderPass_.info.clearDepth_ ? 1u : 0u),
  renderPass_.info.clearColor_ ? &clearValues[0] :
    (renderPass_.info.clearDepth_ ?
      &clearValues[1] : nullptr));
```

11. After starting a renderpass, we must bind our local graphics pipeline and descriptor set for this frame:

```
vkCmdBindPipeline(commandBuffer,
  VK_PIPELINE_BIND_POINT_GRAPHICS,
  graphicsPipeline_);
vkCmdBindDescriptorSets(commandBuffer,
  VK_PIPELINE_BIND_POINT_GRAPHICS,
  pipelineLayout_, 0, 1,
  &descriptorSets_[currentImage], 0, nullptr);
}
```

12. The public part of the `Renderer` class contains cached instances of the framebuffer and renderpass, as well as the output framebuffer dimensions:

```
VkFramebuffer framebuffer_ = nullptr;
RenderPass_;
uint32_t processingWidth;
uint32_t processingHeight;
```

13. The protected part of the renderer is very similar to our `RendererBase` from *Chapter 4*, *Adding User Interaction and Productivity Tools*, but here, we will use the `VulkanRendererContext` reference to cleanly manage Vulkan objects. Each renderer contains a list of descriptor sets, along with a pool and a layout for all the sets. The pipeline layout and the pipeline itself are also present in every renderer. An array of uniform buffers, one for each of the frames in a swapchain, is the last field of our `Renderer`:

```
protected:
  VulkanRenderContext& ctx_;
  VkDescriptorSetLayout descriptorSetLayout_ =
    nullptr;
  VkDescriptorPool descriptorPool_ = nullptr;
  std::vector<VkDescriptorSet> descriptorSets_;
  VkPipelineLayout pipelineLayout_ = nullptr;
  VkPipeline graphicsPipeline_ = nullptr;
  std::vector<VulkanBuffer> uniforms_;
};
```

With all the components in place, we are now ready to begin implementing renderers.

In the next chapter, we will use offscreen rendering. For debugging, we could output the contents of a texture to some part of the screen. The `QuadRenderer` class, which is derived from the base `Renderer`, provides a way to output textured quads. In *Chapter 8*, *Image-Based Techniques*, we will use this class to output postprocessed frames:

1. The constructor of this class takes a list of textures, which can be mapped to quadrangles later, and an array of output textures. If the list of output textures is empty, this class renders directly to the screen. A render pass that's compatible with the output textures can be passed from the outside context as an optional parameter:

```
struct QuadRenderer: public Renderer {
  QuadRenderer(VulkanRenderContext& ctx,
    const std::vector<VulkanTexture>& textures,
```

```
      const std::vector<VulkanTexture>& outputs = {},
      RenderPass screenRenderPass = RenderPass())
   : Renderer(ctx)
{
```

2. The initialization begins by creating an appropriate framebuffer and a render pass. The `QuadRenderer` class does not use the depth buffer, so a depthless framebuffer is passed as a parameter:

```
const PipelineInfo pInfo = initRenderPass(
    PipelineInfo {}, outputs, screenRenderPass,
    ctx.screenRenderPass_NoDepth);
```

3. The vertex buffer must contain six vertices for each item on the screen since we are using two triangles to represent a single quadrangle. `MAX_QUADS` is just an integer constant containing the largest number of quadrangles in a buffer. The number of geometry buffers and descriptor sets equals the number of swapchain images:

```
uint32_t vertexBufferSize =
    MAX_QUADS * 6 * sizeof(VertexData);
const size_t imgCount =
    ctx.vkDev.swapchainImages.size();
descriptorSets_.resize(imgCount);
storages_.resize(imgCount);
```

4. Each of the descriptor sets for this renderer contains a reference to all the textures and uses a single geometry buffer. Here, we will only fill in a helper structure that is then passed to the construction routine:

```
DescriptorSetInfo dsInfo = {
    .buffers = {
        storageBufferAttachment(VulkanBuffer {}, 0,
        vertexBufferSize, VK_SHADER_STAGE_VERTEX_BIT)
    },
    .textureArrays = {
        fsTextureArrayAttachment(textures)
    }
};
```

For a complete explanation of the descriptor set creation process, see the *Unifying descriptor set creation routines* recipe.

5. Once we have a structure that describes the layout of the descriptor set, we will call the `VulkanResources` object to create Vulkan's descriptor set layout and a descriptor pool:

```
descriptorSetLayout_ =
  ctx.resources.addDescriptorSetLayout(dsInfo);
descriptorPool_ =
  ctx.resources.addDescriptorPool(dsInfo, imgCount);
```

6. For each of the swapchain images, we allocate a GPU geometry buffer and put it in the first slot of the descriptor set:

```
for (size_t i = 0 ; i < imgCount ; i++) {
  storages_[i] = ctx.resources.addStorageBuffer(
    vertexBufferSize);
  dsInfo.buffers[0].buffer = storages_[i];
  descriptorSets_[i] =
    ctx.resources.addDescriptorSet(
      descriptorPool_, descriptorSetLayout_);
  ctx.resources.updateDescriptorSet(
    descriptorSets_[i], dsInfo);
}
```

7. At the end of the constructor, we should create a pipeline using the following shaders:

```
initPipeline({
  "data/shaders/chapter08/VK02_QuadRenderer.vert",
  "data/shaders/chapter08/VK02_QuadRenderer.frag"},
  pInfo);
}
```

8. Filling in the command buffer consists of starting a render pass and issuing a single `vkCmdDraw()` command to render the quadrangles:

```
void fillCommandBuffer(
  VkCommandBuffer cmdBuffer,
  size_t currentImage,
  VkFramebuffer fb = VK_NULL_HANDLE,
  VkRenderPass rp = VK_NULL_HANDLE) override
{
```

9. If the quads list is empty, no commands need to be issued:

```
if (quads_.empty()) return;
bool hasRP = rp != VK_NULL_HANDLE;
bool hasFB = fb != VK_NULL_HANDLE;
beginRenderPass(hasRP ? rp : renderPass_.handle,
  hasFB ? fb : framebuffer_, commandBuffer,
  currentImage);
vkCmdDraw(commandBuffer,
  static_cast<uint32_t>(quads_.size()), 1, 0, 0);
vkCmdEndRenderPass(commandBuffer);
}
```

10. If the quad geometry or amount changes, the quad geometry buffer implicitly reuploads to the GPU using the overridden uploadBuffers() function:

```
void updateBuffers(size_t currentImage) override {
  if (quads_.empty()) return;
  uploadBufferData(ctx_.vkDev,
    storages_[currentImage].memory, 0,
    quads_.data(),
    quads_.size() * sizeof(VertexData));
}
```

11. The main function for us is, of course, the quad routine, which adds a new quadrangle to the buffer. A quadrangle is defined by four corner points whose coordinates are calculated from parameters. Each of the vertices is marked with a texture index that is passed to the fragment shader. Since Vulkan does not support quadrangles as a rendering primitive, we will split the quadrangle into two adjacent triangles. Each triangle is specified by three vertices:

```
void quad(
  float x1, float y1, float x2, float y2, int texIdx)
{
  VertexData v1 { { x1, y1, 0 }, { 0, 0 }, texIdx };
  VertexData v2 { { x2, y1, 0 }, { 1, 0 }, texIdx };
  VertexData v3 { { x2, y2, 0 }, { 1, 1 }, texIdx };
  VertexData v4 { { x1, y2, 0 }, { 0, 1 }, texIdx };
  quads_.push_back(v1);
  quads_.push_back(v2);
  quads_.push_back(v3);
  quads_.push_back(v1);
  quads_.push_back(v3);
  quads_.push_back(v4);
}
```

12. The following method allows us to clear the entire list of quadrangles:

```
void clear() { quads_.clear(); }
```

13. In the `private:` part of the class, we store a structured buffer of vertex data. Note that no index buffer is being used, so there are additional possibilities for optimizations. At the end, we store a list of buffers for storing geometry data on our GPU – one buffer per swapchain image:

```
private:
  struct VertexData {
    glm::vec3 pos;
    glm::vec2 tc;
    int texIdx;
  };
  std::vector<VertexData> quads_;
  std::vector<VulkanBuffer> storages_;
};
```

Now that we have finished the C++ part of the code, let's take a look at the GLSL part, as well as the `VKArrayTextures.vert` and `VKArrayTextures.frag` shaders we mentioned in the constructor of the `QuadRenderer` class:

1. As output, the vertex shader produces interpolated texture coordinates and a constant texture index. We will use a vertex layout similar to the one we used for ImGui widget rendering. The `SBO` buffer, which we will be using as input, contains packed vertex data:

```
layout(location = 0) out vec2 out_uv;
layout(location = 1) flat out uint out_texIndex;
struct DrawVert {
  float x, y, z, u, v;
  uint texIdx;
};
layout(binding = 0)
  readonly buffer SBO { DrawVert data[]; } sbo;
```

2. In the `main()` function, we fetch the vertex data into a local variable. Then, the vertex data is unpacked into output variables. The mandatory `gl_Position` variable is filled from vertex data without any transformations:

```
void main() {
  uint idx = gl_VertexIndex;
  DrawVert v = sbo.data[idx];
  out_uv    = vec2(v.u, v.v);
  out_texIndex = v.texIdx;
  gl_Position = vec4(vec2(v.x, v.y), 0.0, 1.0);
}
```

The fragment shader uses an array of textures to color the pixel:

1. First, we should enable the `GL_EXT_nonuniform_qualifier` extension to address the array using values that have been read from a buffer:

```
#extension GL_EXT_nonuniform_qualifier : require
layout (binding = 1) uniform sampler2D textures[];
```

2. The inputs of the pixel shader are the output of the previous vertex shader. The only output is the pixel's color:

```
layout (location = 0) in vec2 in_uv;
layout (location = 1) flat in uint in_texIndex;
layout (location = 0) out vec4 outFragColor;
```

3. The following constant allows us to mark some textures as containing "depth" values:

```
const uint depthTextureMask = 0xFFFF;
```

4. The following function converts a non-linear depth buffer value into an intensity value:

```
float linearizeDepth(float d, float zNear, float zFar) {
  return zNear * zFar / (zFar + d * (zNear - zFar));
}
```

5. The `main()` function renders the quadrangle's fragments. First, we extract the texture index. Then, we look at the higher bits of the texture index and determine the texture type. The texture value at the given texture coordinates is fetched from an appropriate texture. Depending on the type of the texture, the value is either output directly or linearized and converted into grayscale:

```
void main() {
  uint tex = in_texIndex & depthTextureMask;
  uint texType =
    (in_texIndex >> 16) & depthTextureMask;
  vec4 value = texture(
    textures[nonuniformEXT(tex)], in_uv);
  outFragColor = (texType == 0 ? value : vec4(
    vec3(linearizeDepth(value.r, 0.01, 100.0)), 1.0));
}
```

The next recipe will conclude our review of the new rendering framework by describing the routines for creating the descriptor set.

There's more...

Similar to `QuadRenderer`, the new `LineCanvas` class is (re)implemented by following the code of `VulkanCanvas` from the *Implementing an immediate mode drawing canvas* recipe of *Chapter 4, Adding User Interaction and Productivity Tools*. The only thing that has changed is the simplified constructor code, which is now using the new resource management scheme and descriptor set initialization.

The `GuiRenderer` class also (re)implements `ImGuiRenderer` from the *Rendering the Dear ImGui user interface with Vulkan* recipe of *Chapter 4, Adding User Interaction and Productivity Tools*, and adds support for multiple textures. The usage of this class will be shown in most of the upcoming examples in this book.

Unifying descriptor set creation routines

Before we can complete our material system implementation using the Vulkan API, we must reconsider the descriptor set creation routines in all the previous recipes. The reason we didn't implement the most generic routines right away is simple: as with all the examples, we decided to follow the "natural" evolution of the code instead of provided all the solutions at the beginning. The routines presented in this recipe complete the resource management system for this book.

Getting ready

The source code for this recipe can be found in the `shared/vkFramework/`
`VulkanResources.h` and `shared/vkFramework/VulkanResources.cpp` files.

How to do it...

The *Managing Vulkan resources* recipe from this chapter introduced the
`VulkanResources` class, which contains all our allocated Vulkan objects. The
descriptor sets and descriptor pools are also allocated by the methods of this class. Here is
a list of requirements for descriptor set management:

- There are three types of objects to support: buffers, textures, and arrays of textures
  (or indexed textures). For the purposes of this book, we will not use indexed buffers,
  though they might be useful in general.

- We should be able to specify the layout of a descriptor set.

- Once the descriptor set has been created, we should be able to perform "update"
  operations to fill the descriptor set with concrete resource handles.

Let's construct a system that addresses all these requirements:

1. The first and second requirements immediately tell us to create a structure that we
   can use as input for our descriptor set creation routine:

   ```
   struct DescriptorSetInfo {
     std::vector<BufferAttachment>       buffers;
     std::vector<TextureAttachment>      textures;
     std::vector<TextureArrayAttachment> textureArrays;
   };
   ```

2. Individual attachments are described in a similar fashion. The attachment contains
   a `DescriptorInfo` structure that tells us about the usage type and exact shader
   stages where the attachment is used:

   ```
   struct DescriptorInfo {
     VkDescriptorType type;
     VkShaderStageFlags shaderStageFlags;
   };
   ```

3. A buffer attachment contains a reference to the `VulkanBuffer` structure, which provides a buffer size and an offset to the data. The offset and size fields may seem redundant because the size is already present in the `VulkanBuffer` structure. However, we have frequently used parts of a single buffer as two logical attachments. For example, this is the case with the index and vertex data buffers:

```
struct BufferAttachment {
  DescriptorInfo dInfo;
  VulkanBuffer    buffer;
  uint32_t        offset;
  uint32_t        size;
};
```

4. The texture attachment is similar to `BufferAttachment` and contains a `VulkanTexture` object:

```
struct TextureAttachment {
  DescriptorInfo dInfo;
  VulkanTexture   texture;
};
```

5. The only thing that's different in an attachment of texture arrays is the `std::vector` field, which contains a textures list:

```
struct TextureArrayAttachment {
  DescriptorInfo dInfo;
  std::vector<VulkanTexture> textures;
};
```

6. The `VulkanBuffer` object contains the `VkDeviceMemory` and `VkBuffer` handles, along with information about the buffer size:

```
struct VulkanBuffer {
  VkBuffer        buffer;
  VkDeviceSize    size;
  VkDeviceMemory memory;
};
```

For the purposes of this book, such aggregation is more than enough, but in a multi-GPU configuration, a separate form of device memory and buffer handles may be needed.

Next, let's look at `VulkanTexture`, a helper for aggregating `VulkanImage` and `VkSampler` so that we don't have to pass multiple objects as function parameters:

1. At the start of `VulkanTexture`, we will store the texture dimensions and pixel format. This is because, later in the code, we will deduce rendering pass parameters for offscreen buffers from this data:

    ```
    struct VulkanTexture final {
       uint32_t width;
       uint32_t height;
       uint32_t depth;
       VkFormat format;
    ```

2. `VulkanImage` is an aggregate structure we used in *Chapter 6, Physically Based Rendering Using the glTF2 Shading Model*, to pass texture image data around. As a reminder, it contains the `VkImage` and `VkImageView` handles:

    ```
    VulkanImage image;
    VkSampler sampler;
    ```

3. The last field of `VulkanTexture` keeps track of the layout of this texture at creation time. This is important so that we correctly use the texture as an offscreen buffer or as a texture source for shaders:

    ```
    VkImageLayout desiredLayout;
    };
    ```

A descriptor set needs a layout, so the following steps create `VkDescriptorSetLayout` from our `DescriptorSetInfo` structure. Notice that at this point, we are omitting the actual buffer handles from attachment descriptions:

1. As we described in the *Using descriptor indexing and texture arrays in Vulkan* recipe of *Chapter 6, Physically Based Rendering Using the glTF2 Shading Model*, we need to specify some extra flags for our indexed texture arrays:

    ```
    VkDescriptorSetLayout
      VulkanResources::addDescriptorSetLayout(
        const DescriptorSetInfo& dsInfo)
    {
      VkDescriptorSetLayout descriptorSetLayout;
      std::vector<VkDescriptorBindingFlagsEXT>
        descriptorBindingFlags;
    ```

2. For each type of resource, we collect the appropriate bindings. The loops over our buffers and textures push attachments to the `bindings` array:

```
uint32_t bindingIdx = 0;
std::vector<VkDescriptorSetLayoutBinding> bindings;
for (const auto& b: dsInfo.buffers) {
  descriptorBindingFlags.push_back(0u);
  bindings.push_back(descriptorSetLayoutBinding(
    bindingIdx++, b.dInfo.type,
    b.dInfo.shaderStageFlags));
}
for (const auto& i: dsInfo.textures) {
  descriptorBindingFlags.push_back(0u);
  bindings.push_back(descriptorSetLayoutBinding(
    bindingIdx++, i.dInfo.type,
    i.dInfo.shaderStageFlags));
}
```

3. For the texture array attachments, we must also store the non-zero binding flag:

```
for (const auto& t: dsInfo.textureArrays) {
  bindings.push_back(
    descriptorSetLayoutBinding(bindingIdx++,
    VK_DESCRIPTOR_TYPE_COMBINED_IMAGE_SAMPLER,
    t.dInfo.shaderStageFlags,
    static_cast<uint32_t>(t.textures.size())));
}
```

4. Here, a `VkDevice` object is created with the `shaderSampledImageArrayDynamicIndexing` option enabled, so we must pass the descriptor binding flags to a descriptor layout information structure. As a side note, the `sType` field probably uses the longest constant name in this entire book as its value:

```
const VkDescriptorSetLayoutBindingFlagsCreateInfoEXT
  setLayoutBindingFlags = {
    .sType = VK_STRUCTURE_TYPE_DESCRIPTOR_SET
             _LAYOUT_BINDING_FLAGS_CREATE_INFO_EXT,
    .bindingCount = static_cast<uint32_t>(
      descriptorBindingFlags.size()),
    .pBindingFlags = descriptorBindingFlags.data()
  };
```

5. The usual creation structure for the layout is defined with references to the layout binding flags and binding descriptions:

```
const VkDescriptorSetLayoutCreateInfo layoutInfo = {
  .sType = VK_STRUCTURE_TYPE_DESCRIPTOR
           _SET_LAYOUT_CREATE_INFO,
  .pNext = dsInfo.textureArrays.empty() ?
    nullptr : &setLayoutBindingFlags,
  .flags = 0,
  .bindingCount =
    static_cast<uint32_t>(bindings.size()),
  .pBindings = bindings.size() > 0 ?
    bindings.data() : nullptr
};
```

6. As with all the errors, we exit if anything goes wrong:

```
if (vkCreateDescriptorSetLayout(vkDev.device,
    &layoutInfo, nullptr,
    &descriptorSetLayout) != VK_SUCCESS) {
  printf("Failed to create descriptor set
    layout\n");
  exit(EXIT_FAILURE);
}
```

7. As with the rest of the Vulkan objects, the descriptor set layout is stored in an internal array to be destroyed at the end:

```
allDSLayouts.push_back(descriptorSetLayout);
return descriptorSetLayout;
}
```

To correctly allocate the correct descriptor set, we need a descriptor pool with enough handles for buffers and textures:

1. The following routine creates such a pool. We must count each type of buffer and all the samplers:

```
VkDescriptorPool VulkanResources::addDescriptorPool(
  const DescriptorSetInfo& dsInfo, uint32_t dSetCount)
{
  uint32_t uniformBufferCount = 0;
  uint32_t storageBufferCount = 0;
  uint32_t samplerCount =
    static_cast<uint32_t>(dsInfo.textures.size());
```

2. Each texture array generates a fixed number of textures:

```
for (const auto& ta : dsInfo.textureArrays)
  samplerCount +=
    static_cast<uint32_t>(ta.textures.size());
```

3. The buffers we will use should be of the storage or uniform type:

```
for (const auto& b: dsInfo.buffers) {
  if (b.dInfo.type ==
      VK_DESCRIPTOR_TYPE_UNIFORM_BUFFER)
    uniformBufferCount++;
  if (b.dInfo.type ==
      VK_DESCRIPTOR_TYPE_STORAGE_BUFFER)
    storageBufferCount++;
}
```

4. In our GLSL shaders, we use uniforms, storage buffers, and texture samplers. The `poolSizes` array contains three (or less, if a buffer type is absent) items for each type of buffer:

```
std::vector<VkDescriptorPoolSize> poolSizes;
```

5. For each buffer type, we add an item to `poolSizes`:

```
if (uniformBufferCount)
  poolSizes.push_back(VkDescriptorPoolSize{
    .type = VK_DESCRIPTOR_TYPE_UNIFORM_BUFFER,
    .descriptorCount = dSetCount *
      uniformBufferCount });
```

6. The storage buffer differs by a single constant in the `type` field:

```
if (storageBufferCount)
  poolSizes.push_back( VkDescriptorPoolSize{
    .type = VK_DESCRIPTOR_TYPE_STORAGE_BUFFER,
    .descriptorCount = dSetCount *
      storageBufferCount });
```

7. Texture samplers also generate an item in the `poolSizes` array:

```
if (samplerCount)
  poolSizes.push_back( VkDescriptorPoolSize{
    .type =
      VK_DESCRIPTOR_TYPE_COMBINED_IMAGE_SAMPLER,
    .descriptorCount = dSetCount * samplerCount });
```

8. Having counted everything, we must declare the descriptor pool creation structure:

```cpp
const VkDescriptorPoolCreateInfo poolInfo = {
  .sType =
    VK_STRUCTURE_TYPE_DESCRIPTOR_POOL_CREATE_INFO,
  .pNext = nullptr,
  .flags = 0,
  .maxSets = static_cast<uint32_t>(dSetCount),
  .poolSizeCount =
    static_cast<uint32_t>(poolSizes.size()),
  .pPoolSizes = poolSizes.empty() ?
    nullptr : poolSizes.data()
};
```

9. If Vulkan's `vkCreateDescriptorPool()` function fails, we should exit. The descriptor pool must be destroyed at the end, so we will keep the handle in an array:

```cpp
VkDescriptorPool descriptorPool = VK_NULL_HANDLE;
if (vkCreateDescriptorPool(vkDev.device,
    &poolInfo, nullptr, &descriptorPool) !=
    VK_SUCCESS) {
  printf("Cannot allocate descriptor pool\n");
  exit(EXIT_FAILURE);
}
allDPools.push_back(descriptorPool);
return descriptorPool;
}
```

10. The `addDescriptorSet()` function is nothing more than a wrapper on top of `vkAllocateDescriptorSets()`:

```cpp
VkDescriptorSet
  VulkanResources::addDescriptorSet(
    VkDescriptorPool descriptorPool,
    VkDescriptorSetLayout dsLayout)
{
  VkDescriptorSet descriptorSet;
  const VkDescriptorSetAllocateInfo allocInfo = {
    .sType =
      VK_STRUCTURE_TYPE_DESCRIPTOR_SET_ALLOCATE_INFO,
    .pNext = nullptr,
    .descriptorPool = descriptorPool,
    .descriptorSetCount = 1,
    .pSetLayouts = &dsLayout
  };
```

11. Error checking terminates the program in case of a failure:

```
if (vkAllocateDescriptorSets(
        vkDev.device, &allocInfo, &descriptorSet) !=
    VK_SUCCESS) {
  printf("Cannot allocate descriptor set\n");
  exit(EXIT_FAILURE);
}
return descriptorSet;
}
```

The most important function for us is `updateDescriptorSet()`, which attaches the actual buffers and texture samplers to the descriptor set's logical slots. Let's take a look:

1. This function prepares a list of the descriptor write operations for all the buffers and textures. Note that we do not provide a method to update some specific descriptor set item, but the entire set. Individual buffer and image descriptors are stored in separate arrays:

```
void VulkanResources::updateDescriptorSet(
  VkDescriptorSet ds, const DescriptorSetInfo& dsInfo)
{
  uint32_t bindingIdx = 0;
  std::vector<VkWriteDescriptorSet> descriptorWrites;
  std::vector<VkDescriptorBufferInfo>
    bufferDescriptors(dsInfo.buffers.size());
  std::vector<VkDescriptorImageInfo>
    imageDescriptors(dsInfo.textures.size());
  std::vector<VkDescriptorImageInfo>
    imageArrayDescriptors;
```

2. The first array is used to convert buffer descriptions into `VkDescriptorBufferInfo` structures:

```
for (size_t i = 0 ; i < dsInfo.buffers.size() ; i++)
{
  BufferAttachment b = dsInfo.buffers[i];
  bufferDescriptors[i] = VkDescriptorBufferInfo {
    .buffer = b.buffer.buffer,
    .offset = b.offset,
    .range  = (b.size > 0) ? b.size : VK_WHOLE_SIZE
  };
```

```
descriptorWrites.push_back(
    bufferWriteDescriptorSet(ds,
        &bufferDescriptors[i],
        bindingIdx++, b.dInfo.type));
}
```

3. The second one is used to convert all individual textures into
   `VkDescriptorImageInfo` structures:

```
for(size_t i = 0 ; i < dsInfo.textures.size() ; i++)
{
    VulkanTexture t = dsInfo.textures[i].texture;
    imageDescriptors[i] = VkDescriptorImageInfo {
        .sampler = t.sampler,
        .imageView = t.image.imageView,
        .imageLayout =
            VK_IMAGE_LAYOUT_SHADER_READ_ONLY_OPTIMAL
    };
    descriptorWrites.push_back(
        imageWriteDescriptorSet(ds,
            &imageDescriptors[i], bindingIdx++));
}
```

4. Finally, the trickiest pair of loops is required to process a list of texture arrays. The
   first loop collects all the individual image descriptions in a single array and stores
   the offsets of these images for each individual texture array. To keep track of the
   offset in the global list of textures, we will use the `taOffset` variable:

```
uint32_t taOffset = 0;
std::vector<uint32_t> taOffsets(
    dsInfo.textureArrays.size());
for (size_t ta = 0 ; ta <
        dsInfo.textureArrays.size() ; ta++) {
    taOffsets[ta] = taOffset;
```

5. Inside each texture array, we must convert each texture handle, just as we did with single texture attachments:

```
for (size_t j = 0;
     j<dsInfo.textureArrays[ta].textures.size();
     j++) {
  VulkanTexture t =
    dsInfo.textureArrays[ta].textures[j];
  VkDescriptorImageInfo imageInfo = {
    .sampler = t.sampler,
    .imageView = t.image.imageView,
    .imageLayout =
      VK_IMAGE_LAYOUT_SHADER_READ_ONLY_OPTIMAL
  };
  imageArrayDescriptors.push_back(imageInfo);
}
```

6. The offset of the global texture array is updated with the size of the current texture array:

```
taOffset += static_cast<uint32_t>(
  dsInfo.textureArrays[ta].textures.size());
}
```

7. The second loop over the `textureArrays` field fills Vulkan's write descriptor set operation structure with the appropriate pointers inside the `imageArrayDescriptors` array:

```
for (size_t ta = 0 ; ta <
     dsInfo.textureArrays.size() ; ta++) {
  VkWriteDescriptorSet writeSet = {
    .sType = VK_STRUCTURE_TYPE_WRITE_DESCRIPTOR_SET,
    .dstSet = ds,
    .dstBinding = bindingIdx++,
    .dstArrayElement = 0,
    .descriptorCount =
      static_cast<uint32_t>(
        dsInfo.textureArrays[ta].textures.size()),
    .descriptorType =
      VK_DESCRIPTOR_TYPE_COMBINED_IMAGE_SAMPLER,
    .pImageInfo = imageArrayDescriptors.data() +
      taOffsets[ta]
  };
  descriptorWrites.push_back(writeSet);
}
```

8. Once we have all the descriptor write operations filled and packed, we can pass them to the `vkUpdateDescriptorSets()` routine:

```
vkUpdateDescriptorSets(vkDev.device,
    static_cast<uint32_t>(descriptorWrites.size()),
    descriptorWrites.data(), 0, nullptr);
}
```

In all this book's examples, the descriptor sets are created early at runtime, usually in the constructor of some renderer class. All we need to do is fill the `DescriptorSetInfo` structure with references to our loaded texture and buffer attachments. Check out the `vkFramework/VulkanResources.h` file for multiple examples of how to implement various attachments using this mechanism.

There's more...

Our new set of Vulkan renderers, located in the `shared/vkFramework` folder, uses the unified descriptor set creators we described in this recipe. Make sure you check it out.

Putting it all together into a Vulkan application

Now, let's conclude this chapter by putting all the recipes we have just learned together, into a single demo application. The app will render the Lumberyard Bistro scene using meshes and materials from `.obj` files.

Getting ready

The `Chapter7/VK03_LargeScene` demo application combines the code from all the recipes of this chapter, so it will be helpful to skim through the entire chapter before proceeding.

To correctly execute the demo application, the Scene Converter tool from the *Implementing a scene conversion tool* recipe should be compiled and executed with all the default configuration, prior to running this demo.

How to do it...

Despite being able to render a fairly large scene, the main application, which can be found in the `Chapter7/VK03_LargeScene` folder, is surprisingly simple. All we must do here is define a `MyApp` class containing the scene data, textures, and all the renderer instances. The code is almost purely declarative; the only exception is when we must pass 3D camera parameters in the `draw3D()` function, which can also be wrapped in the `VulkanBuffer` interface. However, this would require some more framework code as we would have to synchronize the camera data and this new GPU buffer. Anyway, let's get started:

1. First, we have two constants with environment map texture filenames:

```
const char* envMapFile = "data/piazza_bologni_1k.hdr";
const char* irrMapFile =
  "data/piazza_bologni_1k_irradience.hdr";
```

2. The initialization part of the `MyApp` class sets up scene rendering and frame composition, which, in this example, consists of rendering two scene parts – the exterior and interior objects of the Bistro dataset. The application is instructed to create a window that takes up 80% of our screen space:

```
struct MyApp: public CameraApp {
  MyApp(): CameraApp(-80, -80)
```

3. Two environment maps are loaded for PBR lighting:

```
, envMap(ctx_.resources.loadCubeMap(envMapFile))
, irrMap(ctx_.resources.loadCubeMap(irrMapFile))
```

4. Two parts of the scene are loaded from the files that were generated by the Scene Converter tool:

```
, sceneData(ctx_, "data/meshes/test.meshes",
    "data/meshes/test.scene",
    "data/meshes/test.materials", envMap, irrMap)
, sceneData2(ctx_, "data/meshes/test2.meshes",
    "data/meshes/test2.scene",
    "data/meshes/test2.materials", envMap, irrMap)
```

5. Each part of the scene is rendered by a dedicated `MultiRenderer` instance. A mandatory ImGui renderer instance is initialized at the end:

```
, multiRenderer(ctx_, sceneData)
, multiRenderer2(ctx_, sceneData2)
, imgui(ctx_)
```

6. Here, the frame composition process is rendering two scene parts directly to the screen's framebuffer:

```
{
    onScreenRenderers_.emplace_back(multiRenderer);
    onScreenRenderers_.emplace_back(multiRenderer2);
}
```

7. The `draw3D()` function passes the current camera parameters to both scene renderers:

```
void draw3D() override {
    const mat4 p = getDefaultProjection();
    const mat4 view =camera.getViewMatrix();
    const mat4 model = glm::rotate(
        mat4(1.f), glm::pi<float>(), vec3(1, 0, 0));
    multiRenderer.setMatrices(p, view, model);
    multiRenderer2.setMatrices(p, view, model);
    multiRenderer.setCameraPosition(
        positioner.getPosition());
    multiRenderer2.setCameraPosition(
        positioner.getPosition());
}
```

8. The private members of the class contain two environment maps for the PBR model and two VKSceneData instances. These contain the interior and exterior geometry of the test scene. Besides that, we must declare two MultiRenderer instances to display two parts of the Lumberyard Bistro scene. Though we will not be directly using the ImGui renderer in this example, we are doing this because its constructor contains the ImGui context initialization routine, which is required in VulkanApp:

```
private:
    VulkanTexture envMap, irrMap;
    VKSceneData sceneData, sceneData2;
    MultiRenderer, multiRenderer2;
    GuiRenderer imgui;
};
```

The main() function contains only three lines, all of which were explained in the *Refactoring Vulkan initialization and the main loop* recipe.

How it works...

The main workhorse for this demo application is the VulkanApp class and two MultiRenderer instances, both of which are responsible for rendering scene objects that are loaded into VKSceneData objects. For a quick recap on the GPU data storage scheme of our application, look at the following diagram:

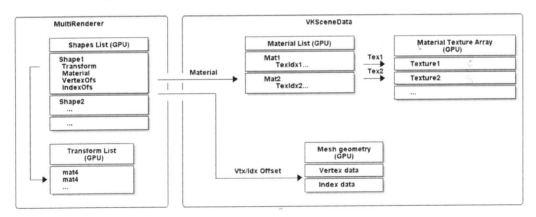

Figure 7.3 – Scene data scheme

The `VKSceneData` class loads the geometry data for all the scene objects, a list of material parameters, and an array of textures, referenced by individual materials. All the loaded data is transferred into the appropriate GPU buffers. The `MultiRenderer` class maintains the Shape and Transform lists in dedicated GPU buffers. Internally, the Shape List points to individual items in the Material and Transform lists, and it also holds offsets to the index and vertex data in the `Mesh` geometry buffer. At each frame, the `VulkanApp` class asks `MultiRenderer` to fill the command buffer with indirect draw commands to render the shapes of the scene. The parameters of the indirect draw command are taken directly from the Shape list. The running demo application should render the Lumberyard Bistro scene with materials, as shown in the following screenshot:

Figure 7.4 – Rendering the Lumberyard Bistro scene with materials

In *Chapter 8, Image-Based Techniques*, we will use the aforementioned `MultiRenderer` class to implement a few screen space effects, while in *Chapter 10, Advanced Rendering Techniques and Optimizations*, we will optimize the internal indirect draw commands by using frustum culling techniques. We will also implement a simple shadow mapping technique in Vulkan for this scene.

There's more...

We have also implemented an OpenGL version of this app. Check out the `Chapter7/GL01_LargeScene` project in the source code's bundle for more information.

8

Image-Based Techniques

In this chapter, we will show how to create a framework for a number of techniques to implement image-based effects via **Open Graphics Library** (**OpenGL**) and Vulkan and integrate them with the rest of our scene-rendering code. Most of these techniques are actually part of the postprocessing pipeline, such as ambient occlusion, **High Dynamic Range** (**HDR**) tone mapping and light adaptation, and temporal antialiasing. The idea is to render a scene and then apply an effect to it, hence the name. Besides that, shadow mapping uses somewhat similar machinery of offscreen framebuffers underneath. We will implement a very basic shadow mapping algorithm here as the first example and then return to the topic of shadow mapping, with more advanced techniques, in the next chapter.

This chapter covers the postprocessing pipeline and has the following recipes:

- Implementing offscreen rendering in OpenGL
- Implementing fullscreen quad rendering
- Implementing shadow maps in OpenGL
- Implementing SSAO in OpenGL

- Implementing HDR rendering and tone mapping

- Implementing HDR light adaptation

- Writing postprocessing effects in Vulkan

- Implementing SSAO in Vulkan

- Implementing HDR rendering in Vulkan

Technical requirements

To run the recipes from this chapter, you will need a computer with a video card supporting OpenGL 4.6 with `ARB_bindless_texture` and Vulkan 1.2. Read *Chapter 1*, *Establishing a Build Environment*, if you want to learn how to build demonstration applications from this book.

This chapter relies on the geometry-loading code explained in the previous chapter, *Chapter 7*, *Graphics Rendering Pipeline*, so make sure you read it before proceeding any further and run the `Chapter7/SceneConverter` tool before running the demos from this chapter.

All Vulkan demos from this chapter require multiple rendering passes and are using multiple **input and output** (**I/O**) textures and framebuffers. To specify these memory dependencies without using Vulkan subpasses, we insert pipeline barriers in between the rendering commands. Inserting barriers into a command buffer is performed in the `shared/vkFramework/Barriers.h` file, which declared a number of helper classes that essentially just emit the appropriate `vkCmdPipelineBarrier()` function. These helper classes are used in the form of `Renderer` from the previous chapters. We declare a variable, initialize that barrier with an appropriate texture handle and flags, and add this variable to the list of renderers. Make sure you read `Barriers.h` before proceeding with this chapter.

Implementing offscreen rendering in OpenGL

Before we can proceed with generic postprocessing effects, let's implement some basic OpenGL machinery for offscreen rendering using framebuffer objects. We will rely on this code throughout the remaining chapters of this book to implement various rendering and postprocessing techniques.

Getting ready

The code for this recipe is located in the `shared/glFramework/GLFramebuffer.h` file. It would be helpful to quickly go through the entire code before reading the rest of this recipe.

How to do it...

Let's implement a simple `GLFramebuffer` class to handle all the underlying OpenGL framebuffer objects' manipulations and attachments:

1. Our framebuffer implementation holds the width and height dimensions of the framebuffer, its OpenGL handle, and two `GLTexture` objects, for color and depth buffers respectively. As we do not need to render into multiple render targets, having just one of each buffer is sufficient for now:

```
class GLFramebuffer {
private:
   int width_, height_;
   GLuint handle_ = 0;
   std::unique_ptr<GLTexture> texColor_;
   std::unique_ptr<GLTexture> texDepth_;
```

2. The constructor takes dimensions of the framebuffer and texture formats for color and depth buffers. Whenever a texture format is set to `0`, no corresponding buffer is created. This is handy when we need color-only framebuffers for fullscreen rendering or depth-only framebuffers for shadow map rendering. Texture wrapping is set to `GL_CLAMP_TO_EDGE` for proper filtering of fullscreen data. Once we have attached all the textures, we should check if our framebuffer is complete. After that, it can be used for rendering:

```
public:
  GLFramebuffer(
     int width, int height,
     GLenum formatColor, GLenum formatDepth)
     : width_(width), height_(height) {
     glCreateFramebuffers(1, &handle_);
     if (formatColor)   {
       texColor_ = std::make_unique<GLTexture>(
          GL_TEXTURE_2D, width, height, formatColor);
       glTextureParameteri(texColor_->getHandle(),
          GL_TEXTURE_WRAP_S, GL_CLAMP_TO_EDGE);
```

```
        glTextureParameteri(texColor_->getHandle(),
          GL_TEXTURE_WRAP_T, GL_CLAMP_TO_EDGE);
        glNamedFramebufferTexture(
          handle_, GL_COLOR_ATTACHMENT0,
          texColor_->getHandle(), 0);
      }
      if (formatDepth) {
        texDepth_ = std::make_unique<GLTexture>(
          GL_TEXTURE_2D, width, height, formatDepth);
        glNamedFramebufferTexture(
          handle_, GL_DEPTH_ATTACHMENT,
          texDepth_->getHandle(), 0);
      }
      const GLenum status =
        glCheckNamedFramebufferStatus(
          handle_, GL_FRAMEBUFFER);
      assert(status == GL_FRAMEBUFFER_COMPLETE);
    }
```

3. The destructor takes care of the framebuffer deletion. The OpenGL specification says that if the currently bound framebuffer is deleted, the binding reverts to 0 automatically:

```
    ~GLFramebuffer() {
      glDeleteFramebuffers(1, &handle_);
    }
```

4. A pair of bind()/unbind() functions are provided for symmetry. The bind() function is a shortcut to use this framebuffer for rendering and set the OpenGL viewport accordingly. The unbind() function reverts to the default framebuffer. To simplify our implementation, we do not restore the viewport parameters after unbinding. However, this might be very handy in a more generic rendering framework. Feel free to implement this as an exercise by adding a respective glViewport() call:

```
    void bind() {
      glBindFramebuffer(GL_FRAMEBUFFER, handle_);
      glViewport(0, 0, width_, height_);
    }
    void unbind() {
      glBindFramebuffer(GL_FRAMEBUFFER, 0);
    }
```

> **Note**
>
> The value of the target parameter to `glBindFramebuffer()` is hardcoded to be `GL_FRAMEBUFFER`, which makes both read and write framebuffers be set to the same framebuffer object. Additional functionality where read and write framebuffers can be separate is not used in this book. However, it might be useful in situations where you want to make OpenGL reading commands such as `glReadPixels()` and rendering commands use different framebuffer objects.

5. Last, but not least, there are a bunch of accessor functions to serve as shortcuts for the OpenGL framebuffer handle and underlying textures:

```
GLuint getHandle() const { return handle_; }
const GLTexture& getTextureColor() const
{ return *texColor_.get(); }
const GLTexture& getTextureDepth() const
{ return *texDepth_.get(); }
};
```

This class is used as a building block for all our offscreen-rendering OpenGL demos. We demonstrate how to use this class later in this chapter, in the *Implementing shadow maps in OpenGL* recipe.

Implementing fullscreen quad rendering

All postprocessing recipes in this chapter require you to render a fullscreen quad using a specific fragment shader for each effect. While the fragment shaders should be very specific to each effect, the vertex shader can be the same. Furthermore, while we can trivially render a quad using a classic vertex buffer object approach, this might be cumbersome to manage in situations where we should mix and match tens or hundreds of shader combinations in different parts of the rendering pipeline. In this recipe, we show a very simple way to generate a quad right in the vertex shader in a similar way to how we generated a cube in *Chapter 3, Getting Started with OpenGL and Vulkan*.

Getting ready

Check out the *Implementing programmable vertex pulling in OpenGL* recipe from *Chapter 3, Getting Started with OpenGL and Vulkan*.

How to do it...

Let's go through the code of our fullscreen quad vertex shader. The shader can be found in the `data\shaders\chapter08\GL02_FullScreenQuad.vert` file:

1. There is no input to the shader except the `gl_VertexID` built-in variable, which we want to go from 0 to 5. Instead of calculating the vertex position in world space, as we implemented in *Chapter 3, Getting Started with OpenGL and Vulkan*, we do it directly in the homogeneous clip-space coordinates consumed by OpenGL. The clip-space coordinates go from `-1.0` to `+1.0` to cover the whole screen. Hence, simple arithmetic involving `gl_VertexID` will do the trick. Our UV texture coordinates go from `0.0` to `1.0`, from top to bottom and from left to right:

```
#version 460 core
layout (location=0) out vec2 uv;
void main() {
   float u = float(((uint(gl_VertexID)+2u) / 3u) % 2u);
   float v = float(((uint(gl_VertexID)+1u) / 3u) % 2u);
   gl_Position = vec4(-1.0+u*2.0, -1.0+v*2.0, 0., 1.);
   uv = vec2(u, v);
}
```

2. To render a fullscreen quad using this vertex shader, the following OpenGL call is required. Make sure to bind the appropriate shader program and an empty dummy vertex array object (or any other vertex array object, for that matter):

```
GLuint dummyVAO;
glCreateVertexArrays(1, &dummyVAO);
glBindVertexArray(dummyVAO);
...
glDrawArrays(GL_TRIANGLES, 0, 6);
```

In the subsequent recipes, we will learn how to combine this vertex shader with different fragment shaders to render different postprocessing effects.

There's more...

While rendering a fullscreen quad seems straightforward and simple, and it is indeed good for educational purposes, rendering a fullscreen triangle might be faster in many real-world scenarios:

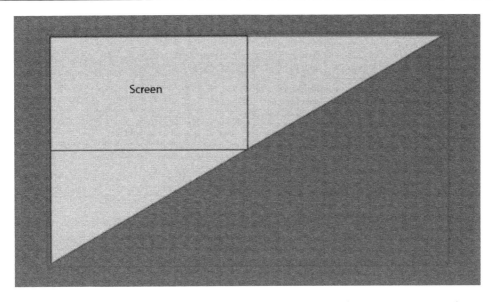

Figure 8.1 – Rendering a fullscreen triangle

These two **OpenGL Shading Language** (**GLSL**) functions will generate the OpenGL position and UV coordinates for a screen-covering triangle using just three values of the vertex index, going from 0 to 2:

```
vec4 fsTrianglePosition(int vtx) {
  float x = -1.0 + float((vtx & 1) << 2);
  float y = -1.0 + float((vtx & 2) << 1);
  return vec4(x, y, 0.0, 1.0);
}
vec2 fsTriangleUV(int vtx) {
  float u = (vtx == 1) ? 2.0 : 0.0;   // 0, 2, 0
  float v = (vtx == 2) ? 2.0 : 0.0;   // 0, 0, 2
  return vec2(u, v);
}
```

As an exercise, feel free to update the code using this code snippet. The triangle shader program should be invoked via `glDrawArrays(GL_TRIANGLES, 0, 3)`.

Implementing shadow maps in OpenGL

As we learned from the previous chapters, we can render complex scenes with varying sets of materials, including **physically based rendering** (**PBR**) materials. While these techniques can produce very nice images, the visual realism of our scenes was severely lacking. Shadow mapping is one of the cornerstones of getting more realistic rendering results. In this recipe, we will give initial guidance on how to approach basic shadow mapping in OpenGL. Considering OpenGL is significantly less verbose compared to Vulkan, this recipe's main focus will be the shadow-mapping algorithm details, while its Vulkan counterpart is focused on the Vulkan **application programming interface** (**API**) details to get you started with shadow mapping.

Getting ready

The `Chapter8/GL01_ShadowMapping` demo application for this recipe implements basic steps for a projective shadow-mapping pipeline. It would be helpful to quickly go through the code before reading this recipe.

How to do it...

The projective shadow-mapping idea is quite straightforward. The scene is rendered from the light's point of view. The objects closest to the light are lit, while everything else is in the shadow. To determine the set of closest objects, a depth buffer can be used. To do that, we require a way to render our scene into an offscreen framebuffer.

The rendering process consists of three phases: calculating the light's projection and view matrices, rendering the entire scene from the light's point of view into an offscreen framebuffer, and rendering the entire scene again using the offscreen framebuffer's depth texture to apply the shadow map. Let's go through the C++ part of the code from `Chapter8/GL01_ShadowMapping/src/main.cpp` to see how this can be done:

1. First, we need some per-frame data for our shaders. The `view` and `proj` matrices here are the standard view and projection matrices we already used earlier. The `light` matrix is the product of the light's view and projection matrices. This is sufficient for now because we are going to use only a single light in this recipe. The `cameraPos` field is a shortcut for the world-space camera position. The `lightAngles` field stores cosines of the light's inner and outer angles:

```
struct PerFrameData {
  mat4 view;
  mat4 proj;
  mat4 light;
```

```
  vec4 cameraPos;
  vec4 lightAngles; // cos(inner), cos(outer)
  vec4 lightPos;
};
```

2. The light's view and projection matrices can be calculated from the following variables. Here, g_LightAngle is going to be the field-of-view angle of our light, g_LightInnerAngle defines the light's inner code, while g_LightXAngle and g_LightYAngle are the rotation angles around the X and Y axis respectively:

```
float g_LightAngle = 60.0f;
float g_LightInnerAngle = 10.0f;
float g_LightNear = 1.0f;
float g_LightFar = 20.0f;
float g_LightDist = 12.0f;
float g_LightXAngle = -1.0f;
float g_LightYAngle = -2.0f;
```

We now have the main() function with our standard GLApp object, which handles all the window-creation and input routines. All the shader programs loading happens right here. There are GL01_grid.* shaders for the grid rendering, GL01_scene.* for the scene rendering, and GL01_shadow.vert shaders for the shadow-map rendering:

```
int main(void) {
  GLApp app;
  GLShader shdGridVert(
    "data/shaders/chapter05/GL01_grid.vert");
  GLShader shdGridFrag(
    "data/shaders/chapter05/GL01_grid.frag");
  GLProgram progGrid(shdGridVert, shdGridFrag);
  GLShader shdModelVert(
    "data/shaders/chapter08/GL01_scene.vert");
  GLShader shdModelFrag(
    "data/shaders/chapter08/GL01_scene.frag");
  GLProgram progModel(shdModelVert, shdModelFrag);
  GLShader shdShadowVert(
    "data/shaders/chapter08/GL01_shadow.vert");
  GLShader shdShadowFrag(
    "data/shaders/chapter08/GL01_shadow.frag");
  GLProgram progShadowMap(
    shdShadowVert, shdShadowFrag);
```

We should create a uniform buffer for our per-frame values and set up some OpenGL state:

```
const GLsizeiptr kUniformBufferSize =
  sizeof(PerFrameData);
GLBuffer perFrameDataBuffer(
  kUniformBufferSize, nullptr,
  GL_DYNAMIC_STORAGE_BIT);
glBindBufferRange(GL_UNIFORM_BUFFER, 0,
  perFrameDataBuffer.getHandle(), 0,
  kUniformBufferSize);
glClearColor(1.0f, 1.0f, 1.0f, 1.0f);
glBlendFunc(GL_SRC_ALPHA, GL_ONE_MINUS_SRC_ALPHA);
```

Now, let's create a couple of meshes for our scene. The first one is our basic `Duck` mesh loaded from `.gltf`. The second one is just a plane that will receive a shadow. The plane is created right from the vertices. The `GLMeshPVP` class is used to store our meshes and feed them into OpenGL using a **programmable-vertex-pulling** (**PVP**) approach:

```
// 1. Duck
GLMeshPVP mesh("data/rubber_duck/scene.gltf");
GLTexture texAlbedoDuck(GL_TEXTURE_2D,
  "data/rubber_duck/textures/Duck_baseColor.png");
// 2. Plane
const std::vector<uint32_t> indices =
  { 0, 1, 2, 2, 3, 0 };
const std::vector<VertexData> vertices = {
  {vec3(-2, -2, 0), vec3(0,0,1), vec2(0,0)},
  {vec3(-2, +2, 0), vec3(0,0,1), vec2(0,1)},
  {vec3(+2, +2, 0), vec3(0,0,1), vec2(1,1)},
  {vec3(+2, -2, 0), vec3(0,0,1), vec2(1,0)},
};
GLMeshPVP plane(indices, vertices.data(),
  uint32_t(sizeof(VertexData) * vertices.size()));
GLTexture texAlbedoPlane(GL_TEXTURE_2D,
  "data/ch2_sample3_STB.jpg");
const std::vector<GLMeshPVP*> meshesToDraw =
  { &mesh, &plane };
```

3. Let's allocate a buffer to store model matrices for our meshes. We need to store only 2 matrices. We'll define our `ImGui` renderer and OpenGL canvas right here as well:

```
const mat4 m(1.0f);
GLBuffer modelMatrices(sizeof(mat4), value_ptr(m),
```

```
      GL_DYNAMIC_STORAGE_BIT);
  glBindBufferBase(GL_SHADER_STORAGE_BUFFER, 2,
    modelMatrices.getHandle());
  ImGuiGLRenderer rendererUI;
  CanvasGL canvas;
```

4. The shadow map is allocated using the GLFramebuffer class we explained previously in the *Implementing offscreen rendering in OpenGL* recipe. For a shadow map, the color buffer is not required per se. However, we set it to GL_RGBA8 to have a nice visualization of what is being rendered into the shadow map. The depth buffer is set to 24 bits and the entire framebuffer is 1024x1024 pixels:

```
  GLFramebuffer shadowMap(1024, 1024, GL_RGBA8,
    GL_DEPTH_COMPONENT24);
```

That was the entire setup process necessary to render our scene. We skipped the keyboard and mouse-handling code because it is identical to all the previous demos. Now, let's take a look at the main loop and how everything is updated:

1. We start by updating the camera positioner, recalculating the current time, and retrieving the actual application window dimensions:

```
  while (!glfwWindowShouldClose(app.getWindow())) {
    positioner.update(deltaSeconds, mouseState.pos,
      mouseState.pressedLeft);
    const double newTimeStamp = glfwGetTime();
    deltaSeconds =
      static_cast<float>(newTimeStamp - timeStamp);
    timeStamp = newTimeStamp;
    int width, height;
    glfwGetFramebufferSize(app.getWindow(),
      &width, &height);
    const float ratio = width / (float)height;
    if (g_RotateModel)
      angle += deltaSeconds;
```

2. Before we can render the scene, we have to update the **shader storage buffer object** (**SSBO**) buffer with model-to-world matrices for each mesh. These are set based on the current rotation angle:

```
  const mat4 scale = glm::scale(
    mat4(1.0f), vec3(3.0f));
  const mat4 rot = glm::rotate(mat4(1.0f),
```

```
    glm::radians(-90.0f), vec3(1.0f, 0.0f, 0.0f));
const mat4 pos = glm::translate(
  mat4(1.0f), vec3(0.0f, 0.0f, +1.0f));
const mat4 m = glm::rotate(scale * rot * pos,
  angle, vec3(0.0f, 0.0f, 1.0f));
glNamedBufferSubData(modelMatrices.getHandle(), 0,
  sizeof(mat4), value_ptr(m));
```

3. Let's calculate the light's view and projection matrices based on the global variables we control directly via ImGui:

```
const glm::mat4 rotY = glm::rotate(
  mat4(1.f), g_LightYAngle, glm::vec3(0, 1, 0));
const glm::mat4 rotX = glm::rotate(
  rotY, g_LightXAngle, glm::vec3(1, 0, 0));
const glm::vec4 lightPos =
  rotX * glm::vec4(0, 0, g_LightDist, 1.0f);
const mat4 lightProj = glm::perspective(
  glm::radians(g_LightAngle), 1.0f,
  g_LightNear, g_LightFar);
const mat4 lightView = glm::lookAt(
  glm::vec3(lightPos), vec3(0), vec3(0, 1, 0));
```

Rendering to the shadow map is similar to an ordinary scene rendering. We update the per-frame data so that our current view and projection matrices are set to represent the light's point of view. Before rendering, we clear the color and depth buffers of the shadow-map framebuffer using OpenGL's direct state access functions. The PerFrameData::light field is not used in the shadow shader, so we can leave this field uninitialized:

```
glEnable(GL_DEPTH_TEST);
glDisable(GL_BLEND);
const PerFrameData = {
  .view = lightView,
  .proj = lightProj,
  .cameraPos =
    glm::vec4(camera.getPosition(), 1.0f)
};
glNamedBufferSubData(
  perFrameDataBuffer.getHandle(), 0,
  kUniformBufferSize, &perFrameData);
shadowMap.bind();
glClearNamedFramebufferfv(shadowMap.getHandle(),
  GL_COLOR, 0,
```

```
          glm::value_ptr(vec4(0.0f, 0.0f, 0.0f, 1.0f)));
      glClearNamedFramebufferfi(shadowMap.getHandle(),
        GL_DEPTH_STENCIL, 0, 1.0f, 0);
      progShadowMap.useProgram();
      for (const auto& m : meshesToDraw)
        m->drawElements();
      shadowMap.unbind();
```

4. Once the shadow map is ready, we should render the scene from an actual camera
    and apply the shadow map. As we mentioned in the *Implementing offscreen
    rendering in OpenGL* recipe, we have to restore the OpenGL viewport ourselves. The
    per-frame data is updated again, now using the data of our actual camera:

```
      glViewport(0, 0, width, height);
      glClear(GL_COLOR_BUFFER_BIT|GL_DEPTH_BUFFER_BIT);
      const mat4 proj = glm::perspective(
        45.0f, ratio, 0.5f, 5000.0f);
      const mat4 view = camera.getViewMatrix();
      const PerFrameData = {
        .view = view,
        .proj = proj,
        .light = lightProj * lightView,
        .cameraPos =
          glm::vec4(camera.getPosition(), 1.0f),
        .lightAngles = vec4(
          cosf(radians(0.5f * g_LightAngle)),
          cosf(radians(0.5f *
            (g_LightAngle-g_LightInnerAngle))),
          1.0f, 1.0f),
        .lightPos = lightPos
      };
      glNamedBufferSubData(
        perFrameDataBuffer.getHandle(), 0,
        kUniformBufferSize, &perFrameData);
```

5. The scene-rendering shader uses two textures, one for the albedo texture and
    another for the shadow map:

```
      const GLuint textures[] =
        { texAlbedoDuck.getHandle(),
          texAlbedoPlane.getHandle() };
      glBindTextureUnit(
        1, shadowMap.getTextureDepth().getHandle());
      progModel.useProgram();
```

```
for (size_t i = 0; i != meshesToDraw.size(); i++)
{
  glBindTextureUnit(0, textures[i]);
  meshesToDraw[i]->drawElements();
}
```

6. Once the main models are rendered, we should render the **three-dimensional** (**3D**) grid from the *Implementing an infinite grid GLSL shader* recipe of *Chapter 5, Working with Geometry Data*. On top of that, we render a debug view of our light's frustum using the `CanvasGL` class declared in `shared/glFramework/ LineCanvasGL.h`:

```
glEnable(GL_BLEND);
progGrid.useProgram();
glDrawArraysInstancedBaseInstance(
  GL_TRIANGLES, 0, 6, 1, 0);
renderCameraFrustumGL(canvas, lightView,
  lightProj, vec4(0.0f, 1.0f, 0.0f, 1.0f));
canvas.flush();
```

7. On top of the 3D scene, we render the ImGui **user interface** (**UI**), where we can change all the parameters of our shadow map. The mechanism was described in the *Rendering a basic UI with Dear ImGui* recipe from *Chapter 2, Using Essential Libraries*. The new functionality here is the calls to the `imguiTextureWindowGL()` function, which is our debug helper, to render the contents of an OpenGL texture in a separate ImGui window:

```
ImGuiIO& io = ImGui::GetIO();
io.DisplaySize =
  ImVec2((float)width, (float)height);
ImGui::NewFrame();
ImGui::Begin("Control", nullptr);
ImGui::Checkbox("Rotate", &g_RotateModel);
ImGui::End();
ImGui::Begin("Light parameters", nullptr);
ImGui::SliderFloat("Proj::Light angle",
  &g_LightAngle, 15.0f, 170.0f);
ImGui::SliderFloat("Proj::Light inner angle",
  &g_LightInnerAngle, 1.0f, 15.0f);
ImGui::SliderFloat("Proj::Near",
  &g_LightNear, 0.1f, 5.0f);
```

```
        ImGui::SliderFloat("Proj::Far",
          &g_LightFar, 0.1f, 100.0f);
        ImGui::SliderFloat("Pos::Dist",
          &g_LightDist, 0.5f, 100.0f);
        ImGui::SliderFloat("Pos::AngleX",
          &g_LightXAngle, -3.15f, +3.15f);
        ImGui::SliderFloat("Pos::AngleY",
          &g_LightYAngle, -3.15f, +3.15f);
        ImGui::End();
        imguiTextureWindowGL("Color",
          shadowMap.getTextureColor().getHandle());
        imguiTextureWindowGL("Depth",
          shadowMap.getTextureDepth().getHandle());
        ImGui::Render();
        rendererUI.render(
          width, height, ImGui::GetDrawData());
        app.swapBuffers();
      }
    return 0;
  }
```

Rendering a texture into a separate ImGui window is very handy for debugging and can be done via the following snippet. Note that our texture coordinates are vertically flipped:

```
void imguiTextureWindowGL(
  const char* title, uint32_t texId)
{
  ImGui::Begin(title, nullptr);
  const ImVec2 vMin = ImGui::GetWindowContentRegionMin();
  const ImVec2 vMax = ImGui::GetWindowContentRegionMax();
  ImGui::Image((void*)(intptr_t)texId,
    ImVec2(vMax.x - vMin.x, vMax.y - vMin.y),
    ImVec2(0.0f, 1.0f), ImVec2(1.0f, 0.0f)
  );
  ImGui::End();
}
```

The demo application should render a shadowed scene, as in the following screenshot:

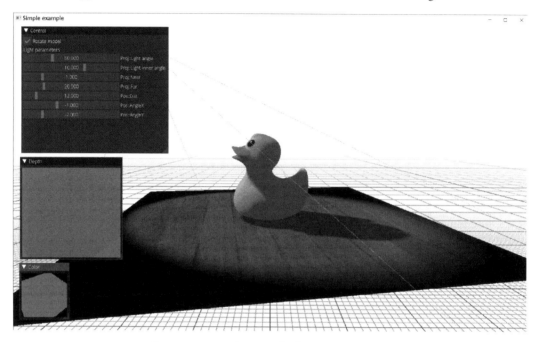

Figure 8.2 – Rendering a shadow-mapped duck

Let's take a look at the GLSL shaders necessary to render the shadow map and apply it to a scene. We have a set of vertex and fragment shaders necessary to render the scene into the shadow map, which can be found in the `data/shaders/chapter08/GL01_shadow.frag` and `data/shaders/chapter08/GL01_shadow.vert` files:

1. The vertex shader reads vertex positions from an SSBO buffer and transforms them using the model matrix and the light's view and projection matrices:

```
#version 460 core
#include
    <data/shaders/chapter04/GLBufferDeclarations.h>
vec3 getPos(int i) {
  return vec3(in_Vertices[i].p[0],
              in_Vertices[i].p[1],
              in_Vertices[i].p[2]);
}
void main() {
  mat4 MVP =
    proj * view * in_ModelMatrices[gl_BaseInstance];
```

```
    gl_Position = MVP * vec4(getPos(gl_VertexID), 1.0);
}
```

2. The fragment shader trivially outputs the red color into the framebuffer. The main thing we care about here is the depth values:

```
#version 460 core
layout (location=0) out vec4 out_FragColor;
void main() {
    out_FragColor = vec4(1.0, 0.0, 0.0, 1.0);
};
```

The resulting shadow map looks like this. Here, the content of the depth buffer is rendered as an R channel:

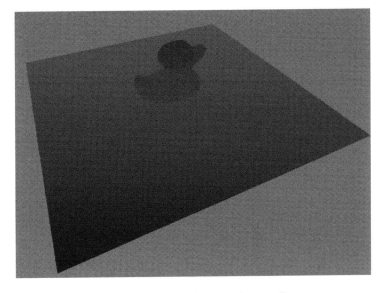

Figure 8.3 – A shadow map (cropped)

The remaining part of the application is a set of shaders used to apply this shadow map to our scene. They can be found in `data/shaders/chapter08/GL01_scene.frag` and `data/shaders/chapter08/GL01_scene.vert`. Let's take a look at the vertex shader:

1. The vertex data retrieval from an SSBO buffer remains almost the same and just adds texture coordinates:

```
#version 460 core
#include
   <data/shaders/chapter08/GLBufferDeclarations.h>
layout(std140, binding = 0) uniform PerFrameData {
  mat4 view;
  mat4 proj;
  mat4 light;
  vec4 cameraPos;
  vec4 lightAngles;
  vec4 lightPos;
};
vec3 getPosition(int i) {
   return vec3(in_Vertices[i].p[0],
              in_Vertices[i].p[1],
              in_Vertices[i].p[2]);
}
vec2 getTexCoord(int i) {
   return vec2(in_Vertices[i].tc[0],
              in_Vertices[i].tc[1]);
}
struct PerVertex {
  vec2 uv;
  vec4 shadowCoord;
  vec3 worldPos;
};
layout (location=0) out PerVertex vtx;
```

2. We now have two sets of matrices. The main camera view and projection matrices are stored in the `view` and `proj` variables. We should use them directly to transform the vertex into the OpenGL clip space. The view and projection matrices representing the light are premultiplied and stored in the `light` variable. This matrix will transform our `model*pos` coordinates into the light's clip-space system. The OpenGL clip-space goes from `-1.0` to `+1.0` in all X, Y, and Z axes, making (`0, 0, 0`) the center point. However, when we sample a texture in OpenGL, the sampling coordinates have a center point at (`0.5, 0.5, 0.5`). To implement this remapping, we have to multiply the clip-space coordinates by `0.5` and translate them by `0.5`. This linear transformation can be done manually, right after the `light*model*pos` multiplication. Instead, we can trivially construct a `scaleBias` matrix that will do everything in one multiplication. Transformed shadow coordinates are passed into the fragment shader:

```
const mat4 scaleBias = mat4(
  0.5, 0.0, 0.0, 0.0,
  0.0, 0.5, 0.0, 0.0,
  0.0, 0.0, 0.5, 0.0,
  0.5, 0.5, 0.5, 1.0);
void main() {
  mat4 model = in_ModelMatrices[gl_BaseInstance];
  mat4 MVP = proj * view * model;
  vec3 pos = getPosition(gl_VertexID);
  gl_Position = MVP * vec4(pos, 1.0);
  vtx.uv = getTexCoord(gl_VertexID);
  vtx.shadowCoord =
    scaleBias * light * model * vec4(pos, 1.0);
  vtx.worldPos = (model * vec4(pos, 1.0)).xyz;
}
```

> **Note**
>
> One interesting remark is that in Vulkan, the clip-space Z axis goes from 0
> to 1, making the scale-bias matrix different. This is a rather common mistake
> when porting existing OpenGL shaders to Vulkan. Another option is to use the
> `ARB_clip_control` extension to change OpenGL clip-space to use the
> `0..1` range and use the same matrix for both OpenGL and Vulkan:
>
> ```
> const mat4 scaleBiasVulkan = mat4(
>       0.5, 0.0, 0.0, 0.0,
>       0.0, 0.5, 0.0, 0.0,
>       0.0, 0.0, 1.0, 0.0,
>       0.5, 0.5, 0.0, 0.1);
> ```

The fragment shader is more interesting. Let's take a look at what is happening there. As
you may have already noticed from *Figure 8.3*, we have a soft shadow effect implemented
using a **percentage-closer filtering** (**PCF**) technique. PCF is a method to reduce the
aliasing of shadow mapping by averaging the results of multiple depth comparisons in the
fragment shader. Here's how to do it:

1. The fragment-shader prologue remains similar to our previous rendering, with the
    exception of an additional texture sampler, `textureShadow`:

```glsl
#version 460 core
layout(std140, binding = 0) uniform PerFrameData {
  mat4 view;
  mat4 proj;
  mat4 light;
  vec4 cameraPos;
  vec4 lightAngles;
  vec4 lightPos;
};
struct PerVertex {
  vec2 uv;
  vec4 shadowCoord;
  vec3 worldPos;
};
layout (location=0) in PerVertex vtx;
layout (location=0) out vec4 out_FragColor;
layout (binding = 0) uniform sampler2D texture0;
layout (binding = 1) uniform sampler2D textureShadow;
```

2. The `PCF()` function performs averaging of multiple depth-comparison operations. The `kernelSize` argument is expected to be an odd number and defines the dimensions in texels of the `kernelSize * kernelSize` averaging square. Note that we average not the results of depth-map sampling at adjacent locations but the results of multiple comparisons of the `depth` value of the current fragment (in the light space) with sampled depth values obtained from the shadow map:

```
float PCF(
   int kernelSize, vec2 shadowCoord, float depth) {
   float size =
      1.0 / float(textureSize(textureShadow, 0).x);
   float shadow = 0.0;
   int range = kernelSize / 2;
   for (int v = -range; v <= range; v++)
     for (int u = -range; u <= range; u++)
       shadow += (depth >= texture(textureShadow,
          shadowCoord+size*vec2(u, v)).r) ? 1.0 : 0.0;
   return shadow / (kernelSize * kernelSize);
}
```

3. The `shadowFactor()` function hides all the shadowing machinery and returns a single shadow factor for the current fragment. The `shadowCoord` value is the position of the current fragment in the light's clip-space, interpolated from the vertex shader. We check if the fragment is within the `-1.0...+1.0` clip-space Z range and call the `PCF()` function to evaluate the result. The depth value of the fragment is adjusted by `depthBias` to reduce shadow-acne artifacts while self-shadowing scene objects, which result from Z-fighting. This parameter is somewhat ad hoc and tricky and requires significant fine-tuning in real-world applications. A more sophisticated approach to fight shadow acne might be to modify bias values according to the slope of the surface. However, we will leave this here as it is, just for the sake of simplicity:

```
float shadowFactor(vec4 shadowCoord) {
   vec4 shadowCoords4 = shadowCoord / shadowCoord.w;
   if (shadowCoords4.z > -1.0 && shadowCoords4.z < 1.0)
   {
      float depthBias = -0.001;
      float shadowSample =
        PCF( 13, shadowCoords4.xy,
          shadowCoords4.z + depthBias );
```

```
        return mix(1.0, 0.3, shadowSample);
    }
    return 1.0;
}
```

4. The lightFactor() function calculates the spot-light shadowing coefficient based on the inner and outer cone angles:

```
float lightFactor(vec3 worldPos) {
  vec3 dirLight = normalize(lightPos.xyz - worldPos);
  // the light is always looking at (0, 0, 0)
  vec3 dirSpot  = normalize(-lightPos.xyz);
  float rho = dot(-dirLight, dirSpot);
  float outerAngle = lightAngles.x;
  float innerAngle = lightAngles.y;
  if (rho > outerAngle)
    return smoothstep(outerAngle, innerAngle, rho);
  return 0.0;
}
```

5. With all the aforementioned helper functions in place, writing the main() function is trivial. We modulate the albedo color of the object with the shadow and spot-light factors:

```
void main() {
  vec3 albedo = texture(texture0, vtx.uv).xyz;
  out_FragColor = vec4(albedo *
    shadowFactor(vtx.shadowCoord) *
    lightFactor(vtx.worldPos), 1.0);
};
```

This concludes our basic OpenGL shadow-mapping example and the first use case of offscreen rendering. Let's switch gears back to the main topic of this chapter and implement some image-based postprocessing effects.

There's more...

The technique used to calculate the light's view and projection matrices described in this recipe is suitable only for spot and—partially —omnidirectional lights. For directional lights, which influence the entire visible scene, the values of view and projection matrices will depend on the geometry of the scene and how it intersects the main camera frustum. We will touch on this topic in *Chapter 10*, *Advanced Rendering Techniques and Optimizations*, and generate an outdoor shadow map for the Bistro scene.

In this recipe, we focused on the basic shadow-mapping math, while the actual OpenGL code was fairly trivial and easy to follow. In the subsequent recipes, we will demonstrate similar functionality via the Vulkan API. We also implemented a Vulkan version of this demo in the `Chapter08/VK01_ShadowMapping` project. Make sure you read the remaining Vulkan-related recipes in this chapter before digging into that source code.

Implementing SSAO in OpenGL

Screen Space Ambient Occlusion (**SSAO**) is an image-based technique to roughly approximate global illumination in real time. Ambient occlusion itself is a very crude approximation of global illumination. It can be thought of as the amount of open "sky" visible from a point on a surface and not occluded by any local adjacent geometry. In its simplest form, we can estimate this amount by sampling several points in the neighborhood of our point of interest and checking their visibility from the central point.

Getting ready

The `Chapter8/GL02_SSAO` demo application for this recipe implements basic steps for SSAO. Check out two previous recipes in this chapter, *Implementing offscreen rendering in OpenGL* and *Implementing fullscreen quad rendering*, before proceeding with this one.

How to do it...

Instead of tracing the depth buffer's height field, we use an even simpler approach where every selected neighborhood point is projected onto the depth buffer. The projected point is used as a potential occluder. The `O(dZ)` occlusion factor for such a point is calculated from the difference (`dZ`)between the projected depth value and the depth of the current fragment based on the following formula:

```
O(dZ)= (dZ > 0) ? 1/(1+dZ^2) : 0
```

These occlusion factors are averaged and used as the SSAO value for the current fragment. Before applying the resulting SSAO to the scene, it is blurred to reduce aliasing artifacts.

The SSAO shader operates purely on the depth buffer without any additional scene data, which makes this implementation a simple drop-in code snippet to start your own exploration of SSAO. Let's go through the C++ part of the code to see how to implement it:

1. First, we need our usual data structure for per-frame data and SSAO parameters. The SSAO parameters are chosen arbitrarily and can be tweaked using the ImGui interface:

```
struct PerFrameData {
  mat4 view;
  mat4 proj;
  vec4 cameraPos;
};
struct SSAOParams {
  float scale_  = 1.0f;
  float bias_   = 0.2f;
  float zNear = 0.1f;
  float zFar = 1000.0f;
  float radius = 0.2f;
  float attScale = 1.0f;
  float distScale = 0.5f;
} g_SSAOParams;
```

2. We reuse a single uniform buffer both for per-frame data for scene rendering and for SSAO parameters in fullscreen-rendering passes. Let's make sure that the size of the uniform buffer allocated for PerFrameData is large enough to store SSAOParams. Two ImGui-modifiable Boolean variables are used to enable the SSAO effect and blur:

```
static_assert(sizeof(SSAOParams) <=
  sizeof(PerFrameData));
bool g_EnableSSAO = true;
bool g_EnableBlur = true;
```

We skip all the keyboard and mouse-handling code because it is similar to the previous demos and jump straight into the main() function:

1. First, we load all the GLSL shaders necessary for our rendering. The GL01_grid.* and GL01_mesh.* shaders are responsible for infinite grid rendering and mesh rendering respectively. They remain unchanged from the previous chapters:

```
int main(void) {
  GLApp app;
```

```
GLShader shdGridVert(
    "data/shaders/chapter05/GL01_grid.vert");
GLShader shdGridFragt(
    "data/shaders/chapter05/GL01_grid.frag");
GLProgram progGrid(shdGridVert, shdGridFrag);
GLShader shaderVert(
    "data/shaders/chapter07/GL01_mesh.vert");
GLShader shaderFrag(
    "data/shaders/chapter07/GL01_mesh.frag");
GLProgram program(shaderVert, shaderFrag);
```

2. The fullscreen quad vertex shader is shared by multiple fragment shaders. This vertex shader was described earlier, in the *Implementing fullscreen quad rendering* recipe. The GL02_SSAO.frag shader implements the SSAO effect itself. The GL02_SSAO_combine.frag shader combines the blurred SSAO buffer with the rendered scene. A pair of GL02_Blur*.frag shaders do a fullscreen separable Gaussian blur:

```
GLShader shdFullScreenQuadVert(
    "data/shaders/chapter08/GL02_FullScreenQuad.vert");
GLShader shdSSAOFrag(
    "data/shaders/chapter08/GL02_SSAO.frag");
GLShader shdCombineSSAOFrag(
    "data/shaders/chapter08/GL02_SSAO_combine.frag");
GLProgram progSSAO(
    shdFullScreenQuadVert, shdSSAOFrag);
GLProgram progCombineSSAO(
    shdFullScreenQuadVert, shdCombineSSAOFrag);
GLShader shdBlurXFrag(
    "data/shaders/chapter08/GL02_BlurX.frag");
GLShader shdBlurYFrag(
    "data/shaders/chapter08/GL02_BlurY.frag");
GLProgram progBlurX(
    shdFullScreenQuadVert, shdBlurXFrag);
GLProgram progBlurY(
    shdFullScreenQuadVerx, shdBlurYFrag);
```

3. Let's allocate a buffer for our per-frame parameters, initialize some OpenGL state, and load a special texture for our SSAO shader and the Bistro scene. This is similar to the Bistro scene rendering from the previous chapter, *Chapter 7, Graphics Rendering Pipeline*. The additional SSAO texture will be created in the following snippet:

```
const GLsizeiptr kUniformBufferSize =
    sizeof(PerFrameData);
```

```
GLBuffer perFrameDataBuffer(kUniformBufferSize,
  nullptr, GL_DYNAMIC_STORAGE_BIT);
glBindBufferRange(GL_UNIFORM_BUFFER,
  kBufferIndex_PerFrameUniforms,
  perFrameDataBuffer.getHandle(), 0,
  kUniformBufferSize);
glClearColor(1.0f, 1.0f, 1.0f, 1.0f);
glBlendFunc(GL_SRC_ALPHA, GL_ONE_MINUS_SRC_ALPHA);
glEnable(GL_DEPTH_TEST);
GLTexture rotationPattern(
  GL_TEXTURE_2D, "data/rot_texture.bmp");
GLSceneData sceneData1("data/meshes/test.meshes",
  "data/meshes/test.scene",
  "data/meshes/test.materials");
GLSceneData sceneData2("data/meshes/test2.meshes",
  "data/meshes/test2.scene",
  "data/meshes/test2.materials");
GLMesh mesh1(sceneData1);
GLMesh mesh2(sceneData2);
ImGuiGLRenderer rendererUI;
positioner.maxSpeed_ = 1.0f;
double timeStamp = glfwGetTime();
float deltaSeconds = 0.0f;
```

4. Before we can jump into the main() function, let's define offscreen render targets. Our scene will be rendered into framebuffer with dimensions equal to the size of our application's window. The SSAO effect goes into a framebuffer with a fixed size of 1024x1024 and no depth buffer. The same applies to the blurred render target. The ssao and blur framebuffers will be used in a ping-ping fashion to do a multipass Gaussian blur:

```
int width, height;
glfwGetFramebufferSize(
  app.getWindow(), &width, &height);
GLFramebuffer framebuffer(
  width, height, GL_RGBA8, GL_DEPTH_COMPONENT24);
GLFramebuffer ssao(1024, 1024, GL_RGBA8, 0);
GLFramebuffer blur(1024, 1024, GL_RGBA8, 0);
```

5. The `main()` loop is quite straightforward. For simplicity, we omit the camera- and time-updating code from this listing. The first thing we do is clear `framebuffer` and update the view and projection matrices for the scene:

```
while (!glfwWindowShouldClose(app.getWindow()))
{
  ... skipped positioner/deltatime updates
  glfwGetFramebufferSize(
    app.getWindow(), &width, &height);
  const float ratio = width / (float)height;
  glClearNamedFramebufferfv(framebuffer.getHandle(),
    GL_COLOR, 0,
    glm::value_ptr(vec4(0.0f, 0.0f, 0.0f, 1.0f)));
  glClearNamedFramebufferfi(framebuffer.getHandle(),
    GL_DEPTH_STENCIL, 0, 1.0f, 0);
  const mat4 proj = glm::perspective(45.0f, ratio,
    g_SSAOParams.zNear, g_SSAOParams.zFar);
  const mat4 view = camera.getViewMatrix();
  const PerFrameData = {
   .view = view,
   .proj = proj,
   .cameraPos =
     glm::vec4(camera.getPosition(), 1.0f)
  };
  glNamedBufferSubData(
    perFrameDataBuffer.getHandle(), 0,
    kUniformBufferSize, &perFrameData);
```

6. Then, we should render the actual scene. We bind the framebuffer and render the `Bistro` meshes together with the infinite grid:

```
glDisable(GL_BLEND);
glEnable(GL_DEPTH_TEST);
framebuffer.bind();
// 1.1 Bistro
program.useProgram();
mesh1.draw(sceneData1);
mesh2.draw(sceneData2);
// 1.2 Grid
```

```
glEnable(GL_BLEND);
progGrid.useProgram();
glDrawArraysInstancedBaseInstance(
  GL_TRIANGLES, 0, 6, 1, 0);
framebuffer.unbind();
```

7. Once the scene is rendered, we can use it to calculate the SSAO effect. The color buffer is cleared, SSAO parameters are uploaded into the uniform buffer object, and the `ssao` framebuffer is bound. We need to pass the depth texture of the main framebuffer into the SSAO shader, as well as a special **two-dimensional (2D)** texture with the rotation pattern. We will look into this in a moment while checking the GLSL code. A fullscreen quad is rendered via `glDrawArrays(GL_TRIANGLES, 0, 6)`:

```
glDisable(GL_DEPTH_TEST);
glClearNamedFramebufferfv(ssao.getHandle(),
  GL_COLOR, 0,
  glm::value_ptr(vec4(0.0f, 0.0f, 0.0f, 1.0f)));
glNamedBufferSubData(
  perFrameDataBuffer.getHandle(), 0,
  sizeof(g_SSAOParams), &g_SSAOParams);
ssao.bind();
progSSAO.useProgram();
glBindTextureUnit(
  0, framebuffer.getTextureDepth().getHandle());
glBindTextureUnit(1, rotationPattern.getHandle());
glDrawArrays(GL_TRIANGLES, 0, 6);
ssao.unbind();
```

After running this fragment, the `ssao` framebuffer will contain something similar to this:

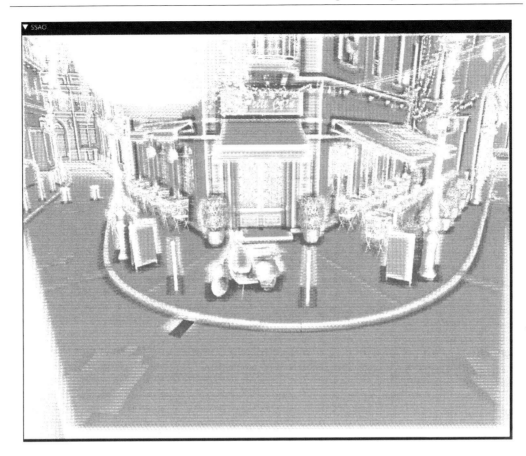

Figure 8.4 – Raw SSAO buffer

8. While the result in *Figure 8.4* is already useful, it can be improved significantly by simple blurring. We run a simple separable Gaussian blur effect in two passes. The first pass blurs in the horizontal direction, and the second one blurs the image vertically. Here, the `blur` and `ssao` render targets are used in a ping-ping fashion. This is handy because if the blur effect is turned off via ImGui, the content of the original `ssao` framebuffer remains intact:

```
if (g_EnableBlur) {
  blur.bind();
  progBlurX.useProgram();
  glBindTextureUnit(
    0, ssao.getTextureColor().getHandle());
  glDrawArrays(GL_TRIANGLES, 0, 6);
  blur.unbind();
  ssao.bind();
```

```
    progBlurY.useProgram();
    glBindTextureUnit(
      0, blur.getTextureColor().getHandle());
    glDrawArrays(GL_TRIANGLES, 0, 6);
    ssao.unbind();
  }
```

The blurred SSAO image should look like this:

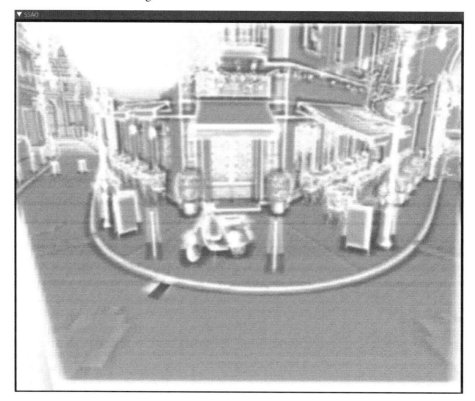

Figure 8.5 – Blurred SSAO buffer

9. All the intermediate steps are now done, and we can combine these auxiliary
    framebuffers into a final image. Let's restore the OpenGL viewport and render the
    final fullscreen pass using color textures from the main offscreen framebuffer and
    ssao. Should SSAO be disabled, we can use the OpenGL 4.5 functionality to blit or
    copy our offscreen framebuffer right into the app's main window:

```
    glViewport(0, 0, width, height);
    if (g_EnableSSAO) {
      progCombineSSAO.useProgram();
```

```
      glBindTextureUnit(
        0, framebuffer.getTextureColor().getHandle());
      glBindTextureUnit(
        1, ssao.getTextureColor().getHandle());
      glDrawArrays(GL_TRIANGLES, 0, 6);
    }
    else {
      glBlitNamedFramebuffer(
        framebuffer.getHandle(), 0, 0, 0,
        width, height, 0, 0, width, height,
        GL_COLOR_BUFFER_BIT, GL_LINEAR);
    }
```

10. To conclude the C++ implementation of the effect, here's the ImGui snippet to control SSAO parameters. Note how some parameters can be disabled in the UI based on the value of `g_EnableSSAO`. More details regarding the ImGui item flags and how to control rendering styles can be found at `https://github.com/ocornut/imgui/issues/1889#issuecomment-398681105`. Debug texture rendering with ImGui was explained in the previous recipe, *Implementing shadow maps in OpenGL*:

```
      ImGuiIO& io = ImGui::GetIO();
      io.DisplaySize =
        ImVec2((float)width, (float)height);
      ImGui::NewFrame();
      ImGui::Begin("Control", nullptr);
      ImGui::Checkbox("Enable SSAO", &g_EnableSSAO);
      ImGui::PushItemFlag(
        ImGuiItemFlags_Disabled, !g_EnableSSAO);
      ImGui::PushStyleVar(ImGuiStyleVar_Alpha,
        ImGui::GetStyle().Alpha * g_EnableSSAO
        ? 1.f : 0.2f);
      ImGui::Checkbox("Enable blur", &g_EnableBlur);
      ImGui::SliderFloat(
        "SSAO scale", &g_SSAOParams.scale_, 0.0f,2.0f);
      ImGui::SliderFloat(
        "SSAO bias",  &g_SSAOParams.bias_, 0.0f, 0.3f);
      ImGui::PopItemFlag();
      ImGui::PopStyleVar();
      ImGui::Separator();
      ImGui::SliderFloat("SSAO radius",
        &g_SSAOParams.radius, 0.05f, 0.5f);
```

```
        ImGui::SliderFloat("SSAO attenuation scale",
          &g_SSAOParams.attScale, 0.5f, 1.5f);
        ImGui::SliderFloat("SSAO distance scale",
          &g_SSAOParams.distScale, 0.0f, 1.0f);
        ImGui::End();
        imguiTextureWindowGL("Color",
          framebuffer.getTextureColor().getHandle());
        imguiTextureWindowGL("Depth",
          framebuffer.getTextureDepth().getHandle());
        imguiTextureWindowGL("SSAO",
          ssao.getTextureColor().getHandle());
        ImGui::Render();
        rendererUI.render(
          width, height, ImGui::GetDrawData());
        app.swapBuffers();
    }
    return 0;
}
```

This demo application should render the following image:

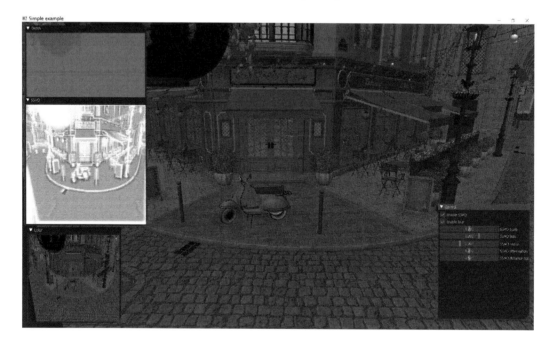

Figure 8.6 – SSAO demo

We have now got an overall feel of the rendering process and can start looking into the GLSL shaders code.

The GL02_SSAO.frag fragment shader takes input as the scene-depth buffer and the rotation vectors texture that contains 16 random vec3 vectors. This technique was proposed by Crytek in the early days of real-time SSAO algorithms:

Figure 8.7 – Random vectors' texture (4x4 pixels)

1. We start by defining a table with offsets to 8 points to sample around the current fragment and all the SSAO parameters we receive from the C++ code:

```
#version 460 core
layout(location = 0) in vec2 uv;
layout(location = 0) out vec4 outColor;
layout(binding = 0) uniform sampler2D texDepth;
layout(binding = 1) uniform sampler2D texRotation;
const vec3 offsets[8] = vec3[8](
   vec3(-0.5,-0.5,-0.5), vec3( 0.5, -0.5,-0.5),
   vec3(-0.5, 0.5,-0.5), vec3( 0.5, 0.5,-0.5),
   vec3(-0.5, -0.5, 0.5), vec3( 0.5,-0.5, 0.5),
   vec3(-0.5, 0.5, 0.5), vec3( 0.5,  0.5, 0.5));
layout(std140, binding = 0) uniform SSAOParams {
   float scale;
   float bias;
   float zNear;
   float zFar;
   float radius;
   float attScale;
   float distScale;
};
```

2. We should retrieve the depth value from `texDepth` and convert it to eye space:

```
void main() {
    float size =
        1.0 / float(textureSize(texDepth, 0).x);
    float Z = (zFar * zNear) /
        (texture(texDepth, uv).x * (zFar-zNear)-zFar);
```

3. Then, we take the aforementioned random rotation's 4x4 texture, tile it across the size of our entire framebuffer, and sample a `vec3` value from it, corresponding to the current fragment. This value becomes a normal vector to a random plane. In the loop, we reflect each of our `vec3` offsets from this plane, producing a new `rSample` sampling point in the neighborhood of our area of interest defined by the `radius` value. The `zSample` depth value corresponding to this point is sampled from the depth texture and immediately converted to eye space. After that, this value is zero-clipped and scaled using an ad hoc `distScale` parameter controllable from ImGui:

```
    vec3 plane = texture(
        texRotation, uv * size / 4.0).xyz - vec3(1.0);
    float att = 0.0;
    for ( int i = 0; i < 8; i++ ) {
        vec3   rSample = reflect(offsets[i], plane);
        float zSample = texture(
            texDepth, uv + radius*rSample.xy / Z ).x;
        zSample = (zFar*zNear) /
            (zSample * (zFar-zNear) - zFar);
        float dist = max(zSample - Z, 0.0) / distScale;
```

4. The `occl` distance difference is scaled by an arbitrarily selected weight. Further averaging is done using quadratic attenuation, according to the $O(dZ) = (dZ > 0) ? 1/(1+dZ^2) : 0$ formula. The final scale factor, `attScale`, is controlled from ImGui:

```
        float occl = 15.0 * max(dist * (2.0 - dist), 0.0);
        att += 1.0 / (1.0 + occl*occl);
    }
    att = clamp(att*att/64. + 0.45, 0., 1.) * attScale;
    outColor = vec4(vec3(att), 1.0);
}
```

While this method does not get close to the best SSAO implementations, it is very simple with regard to its input parameters and can operate just on a naked depth buffer.

Let's quickly look into how to blur the SSAO values. The set of blurring fragment shaders is located in `shaders/chapter08/GL02_BlurX.frag` and `shaders/chapter08/GL02_BlurY.frag`. Their difference is just the direction of the blur, so we can show only one:

1. There is a table containing weights for Gaussian blur. They add up to `1.0`:

```glsl
#version 460 core
layout(location = 0) in  vec2 uv;
layout(location = 0) out vec4 outColor;
layout(binding = 0) uniform sampler2D texSSAO;
const vec2 gaussFilter[11] = vec2[](
  vec2(-5.0,  3.0/133.0), vec2(-4.0,  6.0/133.0),
  vec2(-3.0, 10.0/133.0), vec2(-2.0, 15.0/133.0),
  vec2(-1.0, 20.0/133.0), vec2( 0.0, 25.0/133.0),
  vec2( 1.0, 20.0/133.0), vec2( 2.0, 15.0/133.0),
  vec2( 3.0, 10.0/133.0), vec2( 4.0,  6.0/133.0),
  vec2( 5.0,  3.0/133.0));
```

2. Averaging is trivially done in a `for` loop:

```glsl
void main() {
  vec3 color = vec3(0.0);
  float scale = 1.0 / textureSize(texSSAO, 0).x;
  for ( int i = 0; i < 11; i++ ) {
    vec2 coord = vec2(
      uv.x + gaussFilter[i].x * scale, uv.y);
    color += textureLod(
      texSSAO, coord, 0).rgb * gaussFilter[i].y;
  }
  outColor = vec4(color, 1.0);
}
```

To combine the SSAO effect with the rendered scene, the following GLSL fragment shader should be used: `shaders/chapter08/GL02_SSAO_combine.frag`. The `scale` and `bias` values are controlled from ImGui:

```glsl
#version 460 core
layout(location = 0) in vec2 uv;
layout(location = 0) out vec4 outColor;
layout(binding = 0) uniform sampler2D texScene;
layout(binding = 1) uniform sampler2D texSSAO;
layout(std140, binding = 0) uniform SSAOParams {
  float scale;
```

```
    float bias;
};
void main() {
  vec4 color = texture(texScene, uv);
  float ssao =
    clamp(texture(texSSAO, uv).r + bias, 0.0, 1.0);
  outColor =
    vec4(mix(color, color * ssao, scale).rgb, 1.0);
}
```

With all this knowledge, you should be able to add a similar SSAO effect to your rendering engine.

In the next recipe, we will learn how to implement a more complex postprocessing scheme for HDR rendering and tone mapping.

There's more...

While running the demo, you may have noticed that the SSAO effect behaves somewhat weirdly on transparent surfaces. That is quite understandable since our transparency rendering is done via punch-through transparency whereby a part of transparent surface pixels is discarded proportionally to the transparency value. These holes expose the depth values beneath the transparent surface, hence our SSAO implementation works partially. In a real-world rendering engine, you might want to calculate the SSAO effect after the opaque objects have been fully rendered and before any transparent objects influence the depth buffer.

Implementing HDR rendering and tone mapping

In all our previous examples, the resulting color values in the framebuffer were clamped between 0.0 and 1.0. Furthermore, we used 1 byte per color component, making only 256 shades of brightness possible, which means the ratio between the darkest and the brightest regions in the image cannot be larger than $256:1$. This might seem sufficient for many applications, but what happens if we have a really bright region illuminated by the Sun or multiple lights? Everything will be clamped at 1.0, and any additional information in the higher values of brightness, or luminance, will be lost. These HDR brightness values can be remapped back into a **Low Dynamic Range** (**LDR**) $0..1$ interval using a tone-mapping technique.

Getting ready

The source code for this demo is located in `Chapter8/GL03_HDR/src/main.cpp`.

How to do it...

To implement HDR rendering, we need to store HDR values in framebuffers. This can be done using our existing `GLFramebuffer` framework and providing appropriate OpenGL color texture formats. OpenGL has a `GL_RGBA16F` 16-bit floating-point **red-green-blue** (**RGB**) format that can be used for rendering.

Once the scene is rendered into a floating-point framebuffer, we can calculate the average luminance value of the HDR image and use it to guide the tone-mapping calculation. Furthermore, we can detect high values of luminance in the image and use those areas to simulate the bloom of real-world cameras. See `https://en.wikipedia.org/wiki/Bloom_(shader_effect)` for more on this.

Let's go through the C++ code to understand the entire pipeline:

1. First, we need a data structure for per-frame data and HDR parameters. Similar to the previous recipe, we reuse our uniform buffer for both, so let's make sure its size is sufficiently large:

```
struct PerFrameData {
  mat4 view;
  mat4 proj;
  vec4 cameraPos;
};
struct HDRParams {
  float exposure_ = 0.9f;
  float maxWhite_ = 1.17f;
  float bloomStrength_ = 1.1f;
} g_HDRParams;
static_assert(
  sizeof(HDRParams) <= sizeof(PerFrameData));
```

2. The `main()` function has a typical layout and starts by loading all the necessary shaders. The main scene is rendered via the `GL03_scene_IBL.*` set of shaders, which apply image-space lighting to the Bistro model, similar to how it was done in *Chapter 6, Physically Based Rendering Using the glTF2 Shading Model*, with the exception that we use only the diffuse part of **image-based lighting** (**IBL**) this time. We will look into this when studying the GLSL code:

```
int main(void) {
  GLApp app;
  GLShader shdGridVert(
    "data/shaders/chapter05/GL01_grid.vert");
  GLShader shdGridFrag(
    "data/shaders/chapter05/GL01_grid.frag");
  GLProgram progGrid(shdGridVert, shdGridFra);
  GLShader shdFullScreenQuadVert(
    "data/shaders/chapter08/GL02_FullScreenQuad.vert");
  GLShader shdCombineHDR(
    "data/shaders/chapter08/GL03_HDR.frag");
  GLProgram progCombineHDR(
    shdFullScreenQuadVert, shdCombineHDR);
  GLShader shdBlurX(
    "data/shaders/chapter08/GL02_BlurX.frag");
  GLShader shdBlurY(
    "data/shaders/chapter08/GL02_BlurY.frag");
  GLProgram progBlurX(
    shdFullScreenQuadVertex, shdBlurX);
  GLProgram progBlurY(
    shdFullScreenQuadVertex, shdBlurY);
  GLShader shdToLuminance(
    "data/shaders/chapter08/GL03_ToLuminance.frag");
  GLProgram progToLuminance(
    shdFullScreenQuadVertex, shdToLuminance);
  GLShader shdBrightPass(
    "data/shaders/chapter08/GL03_BrightPass.frag");
  GLProgram progBrightPass(
    shdFullScreenQuadVertex, shdBrightPass);
  GLShader shaderVert(
    "data/shaders/chapter08/GL03_scene_IBL.vert");
  GLShader shaderFrag(
    "data/shaders/chapter08/GL03_scene_IBL.frag");
  GLProgram program(shaderVert, shaderFrag);
```

3. Allocate a uniform buffer object, set up the OpenGL state, and load `Bistro` meshes. Again, the keyboard and mouse-handling code is skipped here:

```
const GLsizeiptr kUniformBufferSize =
  sizeof(PerFrameData);
GLBuffer perFrameDataBuffer(kUniformBufferSize,
  nullptr, GL_DYNAMIC_STORAGE_BIT);
glBindBufferRange(GL_UNIFORM_BUFFER,
  kBufferIndex_PerFrameUniforms,
  perFrameDataBuffer.getHandle(), 0,
  kUniformBufferSize);
glClearColor(1.0f, 1.0f, 1.0f, 1.0f);
glBlendFunc(GL_SRC_ALPHA, GL_ONE_MINUS_SRC_ALPHA);
glEnable(GL_DEPTH_TEST);
GLSceneData sceneData1("data/meshes/test.meshes",
  "data/meshes/test.scene",
  "data/meshes/test.materials");
GLSceneData sceneData2("data/meshes/test2.meshes",
  "data/meshes/test2.scene",
  "data/meshes/test2.materials");
GLMesh mesh1(sceneData1);
GLMesh mesh2(sceneData2);
```

4. Let's create some offscreen framebuffers to store intermediate data. There is a fullscreen framebuffer to store a freshly rendered scene. Note the `GL_RGBA16F` color format here, which can store color values outside the `0..1` range. The `luminance` framebuffer is used to convert the rendered scene into grayscale luminance values, and the `GL_R16F` single-channel format is used for this purpose. Besides that, we create two ping-pong framebuffers for a multipass bloom:

```
int width, height;
glfwGetFramebufferSize(
  app.getWindow(), &width, &height);
GLFramebuffer framebuffer(width, height,
  GL_RGBA16F, GL_DEPTH_COMPONENT24);
GLFramebuffer luminance(64, 64, GL_R16F, 0);
GLFramebuffer brightPass(256, 256, GL_RGBA16F, 0);
GLFramebuffer bloom1(256, 256, GL_RGBA16F, 0);
GLFramebuffer bloom2(256, 256, GL_RGBA16F, 0);
```

5. The `luminance` texture should be downscaled to the size of `1x1` texels before it can be used as an average luminance value. We might do this with multiple subsequent rendering passes into framebuffers of diminishing sizes and a downscaling fragment shader, giving you precise control over filtering. We decided to go a simpler way and use the last automatically generated MIP-level of the `luminance` texture as the final `1x1` average luminance texture. Starting from OpenGL 4.3, there is functionality to create texture views, which allows developers to create references to elements of existing textures. The following snippet creates a view into the last mip-level, `6`, of our `64x64` `luminance` texture. Setting the texture swizzle mode allows us to automatically sample this `GL_R16F` texture as if it were a `GL_RGBA16F` texture, propagating the `R` channel into all `RGBA` values. This trick eases compatibility with our ImGui debug rendering:

```
GLuint luminance1x1;
glGenTextures(1, &luminance1x1);
glTextureView(luminance1x1, GL_TEXTURE_2D,
  luminance.getTextureColor().getHandle(), GL_R16F,
  6, 1, 0, 1);
const GLint Mask[] =
  { GL_RED, GL_RED, GL_RED, GL_RED };
glTextureParameteriv(
  luminance1x1, GL_TEXTURE_SWIZZLE_RGBA, Mask);
```

Because our mesh-rendering shader applies IBL to the scene, let's render this IBL cube map as a sky box. The cube map for this demo was downloaded from `https://hdrihaven.com/hdri/?h=immenstadter_horn`. The irradiance map was generated using our `Util01_FilterEnvmap` tool from *Chapter 6, Physically Based Rendering Using the glTF2 Shading Model*:

```
GLTexture envMap(GL_TEXTURE_CUBE_MAP,
  "data/immenstadter_horn_2k.hdr");
GLTexture envMapIrradiance(GL_TEXTURE_CUBE_MAP,
  "data/immenstadter_horn_2k_irradiance.hdr");
GLShader shdCubeVertex(
  "data/shaders/chapter08/GL03_cube.vert");
GLShader shdCubeFragment(
  "data/shaders/chapter08/GL03_cube.frag");
GLProgram progCube(shdCubeVertex, shdCubeFragment);
GLuint dummyVAO;
glCreateVertexArrays(1, &dummyVAO);
const GLuint pbrTextures[] = {
  envMap.getHandle(), envMapIrradiance.getHandle() };
```

```
glBindTextures(5, 2, pbrTextures);
ImGuiGLRenderer rendererUI;
```

6. After all these preparations, we can enter the main loop. We start by clearing the main framebuffer, updating the view and projection matrices, and refreshing the content of the uniform buffer object:

```
while (!glfwWindowShouldClose(app.getWindow())) {
  ...camera positioner/time update code skipped here
  int width, height;
  glfwGetFramebufferSize(
    app.getWindow(), &width, &height);
  const float ratio = width / (float)height;
  glClearNamedFramebufferfv(framebuffer.getHandle(),
    GL_COLOR, 0,
    glm::value_ptr(vec4(0.0f, 0.0f, 0.0f, 1.0f)));
  glClearNamedFramebufferfi(framebuffer.getHandle(),
    GL_DEPTH_STENCIL, 0, 1.0f, 0);
  const mat4 p = glm::perspective(45.0f, ratio,
    0.1f, 1000.0f);
  const mat4 view = camera.getViewMatrix();
  const PerFrameData = {
    .view = view,
    .proj = p,
    .cameraPos =
      glm::vec4(camera.getPosition(), 1.0f)
  };
  glNamedBufferSubData(
    perFrameDataBuffer.getHandle(), 0,
    kUniformBufferSize, &perFrameData);
```

7. Let's render our sky box, the `Bistro` mesh, and the infinite grid. To simplify dealing with transparency, we render the sky box before everything else:

```
glDisable(GL_BLEND);
glEnable(GL_DEPTH_TEST);
framebuffer.bind();
// 1.0 Cube map
progCube.useProgram();
glBindTextureUnit(1, envMap.getHandle());
glDepthMask(false);
glBindVertexArray(dummyVAO);
glDrawArrays(GL_TRIANGLES, 0, 36);
```

```
glDepthMask(true);
// 1.1 Bistro
program.useProgram();
mesh1.draw(sceneData1);
mesh2.draw(sceneData2);
// 1.2 Grid
glEnable(GL_BLEND);
progGrid.useProgram();
glDrawArraysInstancedBaseInstance(
  GL_TRIANGLES, 0, 6, 1, 0);
framebuffer.unbind();
```

8. After we are done with rendering into the main framebuffer, we can start our postprocessing pipeline. Bright regions are extracted from the rendered image and stored in the `brightPass` framebuffer. The fragment shader used is `chapter08/GL03_BrightPass.frag`:

```
glDisable(GL_BLEND);
glDisable(GL_DEPTH_TEST);
brightPass.bind();
progBrightPass.useProgram();
glBindTextureUnit(
  0, framebuffer.getTextureColor().getHandle());
glDrawArrays(GL_TRIANGLES, 0, 6);
brightPass.unbind();
```

Then, the main framebuffer is downscaled to `64x64` pixels and converted to luminance using the `chapter08/GL03_ToLuminance.frag` shader. After the luminance pass has finished, we automatically update the mipmap chain of the `luminance` framebuffer's color texture. This provides correct data for the `luminance1x1` texture view:

```
luminance.bind();
progToLuminance.useProgram();
glBindTextureUnit(
  0, framebuffer.getTextureColor().getHandle());
glDrawArrays(GL_TRIANGLES, 0, 6);
luminance.unbind();
glGenerateTextureMipmap(
  luminance.getTextureColor().getHandle());
```

9. Let's switch back to the bright areas of the scene and run a multipass separable Gaussian filter to simulate the bloom effect. The bright areas will be heavily blurred and start leaking into the adjacent pixels, producing nice halos. We built the data into the `bloom2` framebuffer and apply 4 passes of horizontal and vertical blur:

```
glBlitNamedFramebuffer(
  brightPass.getHandle(), bloom2.getHandle(),
  0, 0, 256, 256, 0, 0, 256, 256,
  GL_COLOR_BUFFER_BIT, GL_LINEAR);
for (int i = 0; i != 4; i++) {
  // Horizontal blur
  bloom1.bind();
  progBlurX.useProgram();
  glBindTextureUnit(
    0, bloom2.getTextureColor().getHandle());
  glDrawArrays(GL_TRIANGLES, 0, 6);
  bloom1.unbind();
  // Vertical blur
  bloom2.bind();
  progBlurY.useProgram();
  glBindTextureUnit(
    0, bloom1.getTextureColor().getHandle());
  glDrawArrays(GL_TRIANGLES, 0, 6);
  bloom2.unbind();
}
```

10. Now, everything is ready to do tone mapping. Let's restore the viewport, update the uniform buffer, and render a fullscreen quad with our `chapter08/GL03_HDR.frag` tone-mapping shader. The input textures for our shader are the HDR scene, the average luminance value, and the blurred bloom:

```
glViewport(0, 0, width, height);
if (g_EnableHDR) {
  glNamedBufferSubData(
    perFrameDataBuffer.getHandle(), 0,
    sizeof(g_HDRParams), &g_HDRParams);
  progCombineHDR.useProgram();
  glBindTextureUnit(
    0, framebuffer.getTextureColor().getHandle());
  glBindTextureUnit(1, luminance1x1);
  glBindTextureUnit(
    2, bloom2.getTextureColor().getHandle());
```

```
    glDrawArrays(GL_TRIANGLES, 0, 6);
  }
  else {
    glBlitNamedFramebuffer(framebuffer.getHandle(),
      0, 0, 0, width, height, 0, 0, width, height,
      GL_COLOR_BUFFER_BIT, GL_LINEAR);
  }
```

11. Last, but not least, here's the ImGui snippet to control all HDR values we use in this demo. Note how the `luminance` texture is rendered in red because it has the `GL_R16F` color format, while the average 1x1 luminance is rendered as grayscale because of the texture-swizzle mode we set:

```
    ImGui::GetIO().DisplaySize =
      ImVec2((float)width, (float)height);
    ImGui::NewFrame();
    ImGui::Begin("Control", nullptr);
    ImGui::Checkbox("Enable HDR", &g_EnableHDR);
    ImGui::PushItemFlag(ImGuiItemFlags_Disabled,
      !g_EnableHDR);
    ImGui::PushStyleVar(
      ImGuiStyleVar_Alpha,
      ImGui::GetStyle().Alpha * g_EnableHDR
      ? 1.0f : 0.2f);
    ImGui::Separator();
    ImGui::Text("Average luminance:");
    ImGui::Image(
      (void*)(intptr_t)luminance1x1, ImVec2(128, 128),
      ImVec2(0.0f, 1.0f), ImVec2(1.0f, 0.0f));
    ImGui::Separator();
    ImGui::SliderFloat("Exposure",
      &g_HDRParams.exposure_, 0.1f, 2.0f);
    ImGui::SliderFloat("Max White",
      &g_HDRParams.maxWhite_, 0.5f, 2.0f);
    ImGui::SliderFloat("Bloom strength",
      &g_HDRParams.bloomStrength_, 0.0f, 2.0f);
    ImGui::PopItemFlag();
    ImGui::PopStyleVar();
    ImGui::End();
    imguiTextureWindowGL("Color",
      framebuffer.getTextureColor().getHandle());
    imguiTextureWindowGL("Luminance",
```

```
        luminance.getTextureColor().getHandle());
    imguiTextureWindowGL("Bright Pass",
        brightPass.getTextureColor().getHandle());
    imguiTextureWindowGL(
        "Bloom", bloom2.getTextureColor().getHandle());
    ImGui::Render();
    rendererUI.render(
        width, height, ImGui::GetDrawData());
    app.swapBuffers();
  }
```

12. We created the texture view manually. Don't forget to delete it:

```
    glDeleteTextures(1, &luminance1x1);
    return 0;
  }
```

The C++ part was rather short, and the overall pipeline looked quite similar to the previous recipe. Now, let's look into the GLSL shaders code.

Let's quickly recap on the `chapter08/GL03_scene_IBL.frag` mesh rendering shader and check the modifications we used here to apply diffuse IBL to the scene.

1. We start with declaring data structures. The material data format from the previous chapter, *Chapter 7, Graphics Rendering Pipeline*, is reused:

```
#version 460 core
#extension GL_ARB_bindless_texture : require
#extension GL_ARB_gpu_shader_int64 : enable
#include <data/shaders/chapter07/MaterialData.h>
layout(std140, binding = 0) uniform PerFrameData {
  mat4 view;
  mat4 proj;
  vec4 cameraPos;
};
layout(std430, binding = 2)
  restrict readonly buffer Materials {
  MaterialData in_Materials[];
};
layout (location=0) in vec2 v_tc;
layout (location=1) in vec3 v_worldNormal;
layout (location=2) in vec3 v_worldPos;
```

```
layout (location=3) in flat uint matIdx;
layout (location=0) out vec4 out_FragColor;
```

2. We declare two cube map textures and a **bidirectional reflectance distribution function (BRDF) lookup table (LUT)**, similar to our PBR demo from *Chapter 6, Physically Based Rendering Using the glTF2 Shading Model*. However, only the irradiance map is actually required to implement a diffuse IBL. The other two samplers are declared to allow compilation of the included `data/shaders/chapter06/PBR.sp` file, which accesses these samplers:

```
layout (binding = 5) uniform samplerCube texEnvMap;
layout (binding = 6) uniform samplerCube
   texEnvMapIrradiance;
layout (binding = 7) uniform sampler2D   texBRDF_LUT;
#include <data/shaders/chapter07/AlphaTest.h>
#include <data/shaders/chapter06/PBR.sp>
```

3. Material data is fetched from a buffer. The `albedo` texture and a normal map are sampled, if present, and the bump mapping effect is computed. This is similar to how the `Bistro` mesh was rendered in the previous chapter, *Chapter 7, Graphics Rendering Pipeline*:

```
void main() {
  MaterialData mtl = in_Materials[matIdx];
  vec4 albedo = mtl.albedoColor_;
  vec3 normalSample = vec3(0.0, 0.0, 0.0);
  // fetch albedo
  if (mtl.albedoMap_ > 0)
    albedo = texture(sampler2D(
      unpackUint2x32(mtl.albedoMap_)), v_tc);
  if (mtl.normalMap_ > 0)
    normalSample = texture(sampler2D(
      unpackUint2x32(mtl.normalMap_)), v_tc).xyz;
  runAlphaTest(albedo.a, mtl.alphaTest_);
  // world-space normal
  vec3 n = normalize(v_worldNormal);
  // normal mapping: skip missing normal maps
  if (length(normalSample) > 0.5)
    n = perturbNormal(
      n, normalize(cameraPos.xyz - v_worldPos.xyz),
      normalSample, v_tc);
```

4. The main difference happens when it comes to lighting. Instead of computing the `dot(N, L)` diffuse factor, we use the diffuse part of the glTF2 **physically based shading (PBS)** IBL lighting model:

```
vec3 f0 = vec3(0.04);
vec3 diffuseColor = albedo.rgb * (vec3(1.0) - f0);
vec3 diffuse = texture(
   texEnvMapIrradiance, n.xyz).rgb * diffuseColor;
out_FragColor = vec4(diffuse, 1.0);
};
```

This shader renders a fully shaded Bistro scene into the `16`-bit framebuffer. Let's look into how to extract bright areas of the rendered image using the `chapter08/GL03_BrightPass.frag` shader and convert the scene to `luminance` using `chapter08/GL03_ToLuminance.frag`:

1. The `GL03_BrightPass.frag` shader uses a dot product to convert **red-green-blue-alpha (RGBA)** values to `luminance`. Output the values only if the result is brighter than `1.0`:

```
#version 460 core
layout(location = 0) in vec2 uv;
layout(location = 0) out vec4 outColor;
layout(binding = 0) uniform sampler2D texScene;
void main() {
  vec4 color = texture(texScene, uv);
  float luminance =
    dot(color, vec4(0.33, 0.34, 0.33, 0.0));
  outColor =
    luminance >= 1.0 ? color : vec4(vec3(0.0), 1.0);
}
```

2. The `GL03_ToLuminance.frag` shader outputs the result of a similar dot product directly into the framebuffer. Note the different weights used here. This is a very rough approximation that runs pretty well for our demo:

```
#version 460 core
layout(location = 0) in vec2 uv;
layout(location = 0) out vec4 outColor;
layout(binding = 0) uniform sampler2D texScene;
void main() {
  vec4 color = texture(texScene, uv);
```

```
    float luminance =
        dot(color, vec4(0.3, 0.6, 0.1, 0.0));
    outColor = vec4(vec3(luminance), 1.0);
}
```

The tone-mapping process is implemented in the `chapter08/GL03_HDR.frag` shader. Let's go through its GLSL code:

1. Three texture samplers are required—the main framebuffer with the HDR scene, the `1x1` average luminance texture, and the blurred bloom texture. The parameters of the HDR tone-mapping function are controlled by ImGui:

```
#version 460 core
layout(location = 0) in vec2 uv;
layout(location = 0) out vec4 outColor;
layout(binding = 0) uniform sampler2D texScene;
layout(binding = 1) uniform sampler2D texLuminance;
layout(binding = 2) uniform sampler2D texBloom;
layout(std140, binding = 0) uniform HDRParams {
    float exposure;
    float maxWhite;
    float bloomStrength;
};
```

2. The tone mapping is done using the **Extended Reinhard** tone-mapping operator. The `maxWhite` value is tweaked to represent the maximal brightness value in the scene. Everything brighter than this value will be mapped to `1.0`:

```
vec3 Reinhard2(vec3 x) {
    return
    (x * (1.0 + x / (maxWhite * maxWhite))) / (1.0 + x);
}
```

3. This function is applied to the HDR color values in the following way. After the tone mapping is done, the `bloom` texture can be added on top of everything:

```
void main() {
    vec3 color = texture(texScene, uv).rgb;
    vec3 bloom = texture(texBloom, uv).rgb;
    float avgLuminance =
        texture(texLuminance, vec2(0.5, 0.5)).x;
    float midGray = 0.5;
```

```
   color *=
     exposure * midGray / (avgLuminance + 0.001);
   color = Reinhard2(color);
   outColor = vec4(color + bloomStrength * bloom, 1.0);
 }
```

This demo renders the Bistro scene with a sky box, as in the following screenshot. Note where Bloom causes the bright sky color to bleed over the edges of the buildings:

Figure 8.8 – A tone-mapped HDR scene

When you move the camera around, you can see how the scene brightness is adjusted based on the current luminance. If you look at the sky, you will be able to see the details in bright areas, but the rest of the scene will become dark. If you look at the dark corners of the buildings, the sky will go into white. The overall exposure can be manually shifted using the ImGui slider.

One downside of this approach is that changes in exposure happen momentarily. You look at a different area of the scene, and in the next frame, you have the exposure instantly changed. This is not how human vision works in reality. It takes time for our eyes to adapt from bright to dark areas. In the next recipe, we will learn how to extend the HDR postprocessing pipeline and simulate light adaptation.

There's more...

Strictly speaking, applying a tone-mapping operator directly to RGB channel values is very crude. The more correct model would be to tone-map the luminance and then apply it back to RGB values. However, for many practical purposes, this simple approximation is sufficient.

Implementing HDR light adaptation

In the previous recipe, *Implementing HDR rendering and tone mapping*, we learned how to do the basic stages of an HDR pipeline. Let's extend this and add a realistic light-adaptation process to simulate how the human-vision system adapts to bright light.

Getting ready

Make sure you go through the previous recipe, *Implementing HDR rendering and tone mapping*, before taking on this one.

The source code for this demo is located at `Chapter8/GL04_HDR_Adaptation`.

How to do it...

In order to add a light-adaptation step to our previous HDR tone-mapping demo, let's introduce a few additions to the C++ code:

1. First, we need a new parameter to control the light-adaptation speed:

```
struct HDRParams {
  float exposure_  = 0.9f;
  float maxWhite_  = 1.17f;
  float bloomStrength_ = 1.1f;
  float adaptationSpeed_ = 0.1f;
} g_HDRParams;
static_assert(
  sizeof(HDRParams) <= sizeof(PerFrameData));
```

2. The initialization code should load yet another shader. This one is a compute shader that does an adaptation of luminance based on the new average luminance value in the rendered scene and the previous luminance value used for tone mapping:

```
int main(void) {
  GLApp app;
  ...
  GLShader shdAdaptation(
```

```
    "data/shaders/chapter08/GL03_Adaptation.comp");
GLProgram progAdaptation(shdAdaptation);
```

3. In addition to the render targets we already have, let's introduce two more textures, `luminance1` and `luminance2`. Those will be used as ping-pong images in the light-adaptation compute shader. For simplicity, we declare the luminance render targets to be `GL_RGBA16F` and omit any texture-swizzling modes:

```
GLFramebuffer framebuffer(width, height, GL_RGBA16F,
  GL_DEPTH_COMPONENT24);
GLFramebuffer luminance(64, 64, GL_RGBA16F, 0);
GLFramebuffer brightPass(256, 256, GL_RGBA16F, 0);
GLFramebuffer bloom1(256, 256, GL_RGBA16F, 0);
GLFramebuffer bloom2(256, 256, GL_RGBA16F, 0);
GLuint luminance1x1;
glGenTextures(1, &luminance1x1);
glTextureView(luminance1x1, GL_TEXTURE_2D,
  luminance.getTextureColor().getHandle(),
  GL_RGBA16F, 6, 1, 0, 1);
GLTexture luminance1(
  GL_TEXTURE_2D, 1, 1, GL_RGBA16F);
GLTexture luminance2(
  GL_TEXTURE_2D, 1, 1, GL_RGBA16F);
const GLTexture* luminances[] =
  { &luminance1, &luminance2 };
```

4. The first luminance texture is initialized with a really bright value, `50.0`, right from the get-go. This will simulate a situation when our vision is adapting from a bright area to a darker one, giving a nice effect when the application starts:

```
const vec4 brightPixel(vec3(50.0f), 1.0f);
glTextureSubImage2D(luminance1.getHandle(), 0, 0, 0,
  1, 1, GL_RGBA, GL_FLOAT,
  glm::value_ptr(brightPixel));
```

5. In the main loop, we pass our HDR parameters to shaders, downscale the scene, and convert it to luminance, similar to the previous recipe, *Implementing HDR rendering and tone mapping*, and then apply the light-adaptation compute shader:

```
while (!glfwWindowShouldClose(app.getWindow())) {
  ...
  // pass HDR params to shaders
  glNamedBufferSubData(
```

```
    perFrameDataBuffer.getHandle(), 0,
    sizeof(g_HDRParams), &g_HDRParams);
// 2.1 Downscale and convert to luminance
luminance.bind();
progToLuminance.useProgram();
glBindTextureUnit(
    0, framebuffer.getTextureColor().getHandle());
glDrawArrays(GL_TRIANGLES, 0, 6);
luminance.unbind();
glGenerateTextureMipmap(
    luminance.getTextureColor().getHandle());
```

The OpenGL memory model requires the insertion of explicit memory barriers to make sure that a compute shader can access correct data in a texture after it was written by a render pass. More details regarding the OpenGL memory model can be found at `https://www.khronos.org/opengl/wiki/Memory_Model`:

```
glMemoryBarrier(
    GL_SHADER_IMAGE_ACCESS_BARRIER_BIT);
progAdaptation.useProgram();
```

There are two ways to bind our textures to compute shader-image units. Either way is possible but in the first case, all the access modes will be automatically set to GL_READ_WRITE:

```
#if 0
    const GLuint imageTextures[] = {
        luminances[0]->getHandle(),
        luminance1x1,
        luminances[1]->getHandle() };
    glBindImageTextures(0, 3, imageTextures);
#else
    glBindImageTexture(0, luminances[0]->getHandle(),
        0, GL_TRUE, 0, GL_READ_ONLY, GL_RGBA16F);
    glBindImageTexture(1, luminance1x1, 0, GL_TRUE,
        0, GL_READ_ONLY, GL_RGBA16F);
    glBindImageTexture(2, luminances[1]->getHandle(),
        0, GL_TRUE, 0, GL_WRITE_ONLY, GL_RGBA16F);
#endif
```

6. The compute shader is invoked on a single texel. One more memory barrier is
    required to make sure that the subsequent rendering code fetches the texture data
    that has already been properly updated by the compute shader:

```
glDispatchCompute(1, 1, 1);
glMemoryBarrier(GL_TEXTURE_FETCH_BARRIER_BIT);
```

The further C++ workflow remains intact, except for the site where we pass the
average luminance texture into the final tone-mapping shader. Instead of using
`luminance1x1` directly, we should use one of the ping-pong luminance textures
we created earlier:

```
glViewport(0, 0, width, height);
if (g_EnableHDR) {
  progCombineHDR.useProgram();
  glBindTextureUnit(
    0, framebuffer.getTextureColor().getHandle());
  glBindTextureUnit(
    1, luminances[1]->getHandle());
  glBindTextureUnit(
    2, bloom2.getTextureColor().getHandle());
  glDrawArrays(GL_TRIANGLES, 0, 6);
}
else {
  . . .
}
... ImGui code skipped ...
```

7. At the end of the main loop, we only need to swap the ping-pong buffers for the
    current and adapted luminances:

```
  std::swap(luminances[0], luminances[1]);
}
glDeleteTextures(1, &luminance1x1);
return 0;
}
```

Those are all the changes necessary for our previous C++ code. The addition to the GLSL part of our HDR pipeline is the light-adaptation compute shader. This is located in the file `shaders/chapter08/GL03_Adaptation.comp` folder and is described next:

1. The local workgroup size is `(1, 1, 1)`, as we are dealing with just a single texel. The input images correspond to the previous luminance from the `imgLuminancePrev` rendered scene, the `imgLuminanceCurr` current luminance from the first ping-ping luminance texture, and the `imgLuminanceAdapted` output adapted luminance going into the second ping-pong texture:

```glsl
#version 460 core
layout(local_size_x = 1, local_size_y = 1,
  local_size_z = 1) in;
layout(rgba16f, binding=0)
  uniform readonly image2D imgLuminancePrev;
layout(rgba16f, binding=1)
  uniform readonly image2D imgLuminanceCurr;
layout(rgba16f, binding=2)
  uniform writeonly image2D imgLuminanceAdapted;
layout(std140, binding = 0) uniform HDRParams {
  float exposure;
  float maxWhite;
  float bloomStrength;
  float adaptationSpeed;
};
```

2. The `main()` function loads a single texel from each input image and computes the adapted luminance using the `Lavg=Lavg+(L-Lavg) * (1-exp(c*dt*adaptationSpeed))` modified the *8.1.4.3 Adaptation* equation from `https://google.github.io/filament/Filament.md.html#mjx-eqn-adaptation`. Here, `dt=30.0` is the delta time since the previous frame, which we hardcoded for the sake of simplicity, and `adaptationSpeed` is a parameter that controls the light-adaptation rate. A single texel representing the adapted luminance is written to the output texture using `imageStore()`:

```glsl
void main() {
  float lumPrev =
    imageLoad(imgLuminancePrev, ivec2(0, 0)).x;
  float lumCurr =
    imageLoad(imgLuminanceCurr, ivec2(0, 0)).x;
  float newAdaptation = lumPrev + (lumCurr-lumPrev) *
    (1.0 - pow(0.98, 30.0 * adaptationSpeed));
```

```
        imageStore(imgLuminanceAdapted, ivec2(0, 0),
          vec4(vec3(newAdaptation), 1.0));
    }
```

This technique enables a pleasing smooth light-adaptation effect when the scene luminance changes abruptly. Try running the `Chapter8/GL04_HDR_Adaptation` demo application and pointing the camera at bright areas in the sky and dark areas in the corners. The light-adaptation speed can be user-controlled from ImGui, as in the following screenshot:

Figure 8.9 – An HDR tone-mapped scene with light adaptation

Now, let's switch from OpenGL to Vulkan and learn how to deal with postprocessing effects with the more verbose API.

There's more...

HDR rendering is a huge topic, and we barely scratched its surface in this chapter. If you want to learn more advanced state-of-the-art HDR lighting techniques, we recommend watching the **Game Developers Conference (GDC)** 2010 session *Uncharted 2: HDR Lighting* by John Hable: `https://www.gdcvault.com/play/1012351/Uncharted-2-HDR`.

Writing postprocessing effects in Vulkan

In the previous recipes of this chapter, we learned about some popular image-based postprocessing effects and how to implement them in OpenGL. Now, we can focus on the Vulkan API to approach one solution to a similar problem.

In this recipe, we use the `Renderer` class from the *Working with rendering passes* recipe from the previous chapter, *Chapter 7*, *Graphics Rendering Pipeline*, to wrap a sequence of rendering operations in a single composite item. A helper class to perform fullscreen per-pixel image processing is also presented here.

Getting ready...

Make sure you read the previous OpenGL-related recipes in this chapter as they focus on the algorithm flow, and from this point on, we will be focused on the Vulkan API details and how to wrap them in a manageable way.

How to do it...

Most of the effects in this chapter use a number of rendering passes to calculate the output image. The `CompositeRenderer` class is a collection of renderers acting as one renderer:

1. The code follows the composite software design pattern (`https://en.wikipedia.org/wiki/Composite_pattern`). It provides an interface by delegating the operation to each object in a collection of objects implementing the `Renderer` interface:

   ```
   struct CompositeRenderer: public Renderer {
     CompositeRenderer(VulkanRenderContext& c)
     : Renderer(c) {}
   ```

2. The internal loop over the renderers in `fillCommandBuffer()` is the same as in `VulkanApp::composeFrame()`. Individual renderers can have their own render passes and output framebuffers. We delegate all the actual work to these renderers, which is done in `r.renderer.fillCommandBuffer()`:

   ```
   void fillCommandBuffer(VkCommandBuffer cmdBuffer,
     size_t currentImage,
     VkFramebuffer fb1 = VK_NULL_HANDLE,
     VkRenderPass rp1 = VK_NULL_HANDLE) override
   {

     for (auto& r: renderers_) {
       if (!r.enabled_) continue;
   ```

```
VkRenderPass rp = rp1;
VkFramebuffer fb = fb1;
if (r.renderer_.renderPass_.handle !=
    VK_NULL_HANDLE)
  rp = r.renderer_.renderPass_.handle;
if (r.renderer_.framebuffer_ != VK_NULL_HANDLE)
  fb = r.renderer_.framebuffer_;
r.renderer_.fillCommandBuffer(
    cmdBuffer, currentImage, fb, rp);
}
}
```

3. The `updateBuffers()` method also follows the composite design pattern and redirects buffer updates to individual internal renderers. The only field this class has is the list of `Renderer`-derived objects wrapped in the `RenderItem` structure to allow a No-Raw-Pointers implementation. As a reminder, the `RenderItem` structure contains a reference to the `Renderer`-derived class and allows the use of `std::vector::emplace_back()` to fill the list of renderers without triggering copy constructors and without dynamic allocations:

```
void updateBuffers(size_t currentImage) override {
  for (auto& r: renderers_)
    r.renderer_.updateBuffers(currentImage);
}
protected:
  std::vector<RenderItem> renderers_;
};
```

We now have a method to produce a sequence of postprocessing operations, but we have not yet defined a postprocessing operation itself. Let's approach this task step by step.

The postprocessing framework has a single operation as its building block: the fullscreen quadrangle rendered with a shader that takes some textures (possibly, other framebuffers) as an input:

1. First, let's introduce a short helper class, `OffscreenMeshRenderer`, for single mesh rendering into an offscreen framebuffer:

```
struct OffscreenMeshRenderer: public BufferProcessor {
  OffscreenMeshRenderer(
    VulkanRenderContext& ctx,
    VulkanBuffer uniformBuffer,
```

```
      const std::pair<BufferAttachment,
        BufferAttachment>& meshBuffer,
      const std::vector<TextureAttachment>&
        usedTextures,
      const std::vector<VulkanTexture>& outputs,
      const std::vector<const char*>& shaderFiles,
      bool firstPass = false)
    : BufferProcessor(ctx,
      DescriptorSetInfo {
        .buffers = {
          uniformBufferAttachment(uniformBuffer,  0,
          0, VK_SHADER_STAGE_VERTEX_BIT |
            VK_SHADER_STAGE_FRAGMENT_BIT),
          meshBuffer.first,
          meshBuffer.second,
        },
        .textures = usedTextures
      },
      outputs, shaderFiles, meshBuffer.first.size,
      ctx.resources.addRenderPass(outputs,
        RenderPassCreateInfo {
          .clearColor_ = firstPass,
          .clearDepth_ = firstPass,
          .flags_ = (uint8_t)((firstPass ?
          eRenderPassBit_First :
          eRenderPassBit_OffscreenInternal) |
          eRenderPassBit_Offscreen)
        }))
  {}
};
```

2. The `VulkanShaderProcessor` class derived from `Renderer` implements
   a generic `fillCommandBuffer()` method that calls a custom shader. The
   `indexBufferSize` parameter has a default value of `24`, which is the number of
   bytes to store six `32`-bit integers. This is the size of an index array for two triangles
   that form a single quadrangle. The reason this class exposes this parameter to
   the user is simple: rendering a complex 3D mesh instead of a single quadrangle
   is performed in the same way. This class generalizes our approach to mesh
   rendering from *Chapter 3, Getting Started with OpenGL and Vulkan*. In our sample
   application, we use the `OffscreenMeshRenderer` derived class to render a
   single mesh using different effects:

```
struct VulkanShaderProcessor: public Renderer {
  VulkanShaderProcessor(VulkanRenderContext& ctx,
    const PipelineInfo& pInfo,
    const DescriptorSetInfo& dsInfo,
```

```
      const std::vector<const char*>& shaders,
      const std::vector<VulkanTexture>& outputs,
      uint32_t indexBufferSize = 6 * 4,
      RenderPass screenRenderPass = RenderPass())
    : Renderer(ctx)
    , indexBufferSize(indexBufferSize) {
```

3. Fullscreen processors need only a single descriptor set, which is created using the
    dsInfo structure passed via parameters. At the end of initialization, a graphics
    pipeline with a suitable render pass is created:

```
      descriptorSetLayout_ =
        ctx.resources.addDescriptorSetLayout(dsInfo);
      descriptorSets_ = {
        ctx.resources.addDescriptorSet(
          ctx.resources.addDescriptorPool(dsInfo),
          descriptorSetLayout_)
      };
      ctx.resources.updateDescriptorSet(
        descriptorSets_[0], dsInfo);
      initPipeline(shaders, initRenderPass(
        pInfo, outputs, screenRenderPass,
        ctx.screenRenderPass_NoDepth));
    }
```

4. The fillCommandBuffer() method uses the stored size of an index buffer.
    The data part of the class stores the size of the index buffer for the vkCmdDraw()
    command:

```
    void fillCommandBuffer(VkCommandBuffer cmdBuffer,
      size_t currentImage,
      VkFramebuffer fb = VK_NULL_HANDLE,
      VkRenderPass rp = VK_NULL_HANDLE) override
    {
      beginRenderPass((rp != VK_NULL_HANDLE)
        ? rp : renderPass_.handle,
        (fb != VK_NULL_HANDLE)
        ? fb : framebuffer_, cmdBuffer, 0);
      vkCmdDraw(cmdBuffer,
        indexBufferSize / sizeof(uint32_t), 1, 0, 0);
      vkCmdEndRenderPass(cmdBuffer);
    }
  private:
```

```
    uint32_t indexBufferSize;
};
```

Let's check how to render a fullscreen quad using this approach:

1. The `QuadProcessor` class is a helper class that specifies the default shader
    for `VulkanShaderProcessor`. The vertex shader is always the same, but the
    fragment shader specified as a parameter contains custom postprocessing per-pixel
    logic. If there are no offscreen render targets, we use a screen render pass:

```
struct QuadProcessor: public VulkanShaderProcessor {
   QuadProcessor(VulkanRenderContext& ctx,
   const DescriptorSetInfo& dsInfo,
   const std::vector<VulkanTexture>& outputs,
   const char* shaderFile):
   VulkanShaderProcessor(
     ctx, ctx.pipelineParametersForOutputs(outputs),
     dsInfo,
     std::vector<const char*>{
       "data/shaders/chapter08/quad.vert", shaderFile
     },
     outputs, 6 * 4,
     outputs.empty() ?
       ctx.screenRenderPass : RenderPass())
   {}
};
```

2. The vertex shader to render a screen-size quadrangle is similar to the cube shader
    from *Chapter 3, Getting Started with OpenGL and Vulkan*. Since we use PVP, there
    is no need to bind an input vertex array. We get away with declaring indices, vertex
    coordinates, and texture coordinates as shader constants:

```
layout(location = 0) out vec2 texCoord;
int indices[6] = int[] ( 0, 1, 2, 0, 2, 3 );
vec2 positions[4] = vec2[] (
   vec2(1.0, -1.0), vec2(1.0, 1.0),
   vec2(-1.0, 1.0), vec2(-1.0, -1.0)
);
vec2 texcoords[4] = vec2[] (
   vec2(1.0, 1.0), vec2(1.0, 0.0),
   vec2(0.0, 0.0), vec2(0.0, 1.0)
);
```

3. The shader fetches an index and outputs a position along with the interpolated texture coordinate:

```
void main() {
  int idx = indices[gl_VertexIndex];
  gl_Position = vec4(positions[idx], 0.0, 1.0);
  texCoord   = texcoords[idx];
}
```

A postprocessed image can be output to the screen using the `QuadRenderer` class from the previous chapter, *Chapter 7, Graphics Rendering Pipeline*, or the new class `QuadProcessor` described previously.

Implementing SSAO in Vulkan

Earlier in this chapter, we learned how to implement SSAO in OpenGL and went through every detail of our code. This recipe shows how to implement this technique using the Vulkan API.

We will skip the GLSL shaders here because they are almost identical to those for OpenGL, and rather focus on the C++ parts of the code that deal with Vulkan.

Getting ready...

Make sure you read the *Implementing SSAO in OpenGL* recipe to understand the data flow of our SSAO implementation and the previous recipe, *Writing postprocessing effects in Vulkan*, to have a good grasp of the basic classes we use in our Vulkan wrapper.

The source code for this demo can be found in `Chapter08/VK02_SSAO`.

How to do it...

The `SSAOProcessor` class wraps multiple `QuadProcessor` instances into a single streamlined reusable pipeline for SSAO rendering:

1. A set of GLSL shaders for SSAO rendering is passed as arguments to the `QuadProcessor` instances:

```
struct SSAOProcessor: public CompositeRenderer {
  SSAOProcessor(
    VulkanRenderContext&ctx, VulkanTexture colorTex,
    VulkanTexture depthTex, VulkanTexture outputTex)
  : CompositeRenderer(ctx)
```

```
      , rotateTex(ctx.resources.loadTexture2D(
          "data/rot_texture.bmp"))
      , SSAOTex(ctx.resources.addColorTexture(
          SSAOWidth, SSAOHeight))
      , SSAOBlurXTex(ctx.resources.addColorTexture(
          SSAO_W, SSAO_H))
      , SSAOBlurYTex(ctx.resources.addColorTexture(
          SSAO_W, SSAO_H))
      , SSAO(ctx, { .textures = {
          fsTextureAttachment(depthTex),
          fsTextureAttachment(rotateTex) } },
          { SSAOTex },
          "data/shaders/chapter08/SSAO.frag")
      , BlurX(ctx, { .textures = {
          fsTextureAttachment(SSAOTex) } },
          { SSAOBlurXTex },
          "data/shaders/chapter08/SSAOBlurX.frag")
      , BlurY(ctx, { .textures = {
          fsTextureAttachment(SSAOBlurXTex) } },
          { SSAOBlurYTex },
          "data/shaders/chapter08/SSAOBlurY.frag")
      , SSAOFinal(ctx, { .textures = {
          fsTextureAttachment(colorTex),
          fsTextureAttachment(SSAOBlurYTex) } }, {
          outputTex },
          "data/shaders/chapter08/SSAOFinal.frag")
  {
```

2. The only code we need in the constructor fills the `renderers_` container. None of these renderers performs depth buffer writes, so the second parameter, `useDepth`, should be set to `false`:

```
      renderers_.emplace_back(SSAO, false);
      renderers_.emplace_back(BlurX, false);
      renderers_.emplace_back(BlurY, false);
      renderers_.emplace_back(SSAOFinal, false);
  }
```

3. For debugging purposes, we expose access to intermediate textures. The `private:` section declares all the intermediate textures and individual `QuadProcessor` instances. You already know the principle of their operation from the *Implementing SSAO in OpenGL* recipe:

```
  VulkanTexture getSSAO()  const { return SSAOTex; }
  VulkanTexture getBlurX() const
```

```
      { return SSAOBlurXTex; }
    VulkanTexture getBlurY() const
      { return SSAOBlurYTex; }
  private:
    VulkanTexture rotateTex;
    VulkanTexture SSAOTex, SSAOBlurXTex, SSAOBlurYTex;
    QuadProcessor SSAO, BlurX, BlurY, SSAOFinal;
};
```

Here is a snippet from the source code of `Chapter08/VK02_SSAO/src/main.cpp`
that uses the `SSAOProcessor` class presented previously:

1. The data is initialized similarly to the Vulkan recipes from the previous chapter,
    Chapter 7, Graphics Rendering Pipeline:

```
struct MyApp: public CameraApp {
  MyApp()
  : CameraApp(-80, -80)
  , envMap(ctx_.resources.loadCubeMap(envMapFile))
  , irrMap(ctx_.resources.loadCubeMap(irrMapFile))
  , colorTex(ctx_.resources.addColorTexture())
  , depthTex(ctx_.resources.addDepthTexture())
  , finalTex(ctx_.resources.addColorTexture())
  , sceneData(ctx_, "data/meshes/test.meshes",
      "data/meshes/test.scene",
      "data/meshes/test.materials", envMap, irrMap)
  , multiRenderer(ctx_, sceneData,
      "data/shaders/chapter07/VK01.vert",
      "data/shaders/chapter07/VK01.frag",
      { colorTex, depthTex }
  , ctx_.resources.addRenderPass({colorTex, depthTex}
  , RenderPassCreateInfo {
      .clearColor_ = true,
      .clearDepth_ = true,
      .flags_ = eRenderPassBit_First |
                eRenderPassBit_Offscreen }))
  , SSAO(ctx_, colorTex, depthTex, finalTex)
  , quads(ctx_, { colorTex, depthTex, finalTex })
  , imgui(ctx_)
{
  onScreenRenderers_.emplace_back(multiRenderer);
  onScreenRenderers_.emplace_back(SSAO);
```

```
  onScreenRenderers_.emplace_back(quads, false);
  onScreenRenderers_.emplace_back(imgui, false);
}
```

2. The drawing code is straightforward:

```
void draw3D() override {
  const mat4 m1 = glm::rotate(
    mat4(1.f), glm::pi<float>(), vec3(1, 0, 0));
  multiRenderer.setMatrices(getDefaultProjection(),
    camera.getViewMatrix(), m1);
  quads.clear();
  quads.quad(-1.0f, -1.0f, 1.0f, 1.0f, 2);
}
private:
  VulkanTexture envMap, irrMap;
  VulkanTexture colorTex, depthTex, finalTex;
  VKSceneData sceneData;
  MultiRenderer;
  SSAOProcessor SSAO;
  QuadRenderer quads;
  GuiRenderer imgui;
};
```

We can now add the SSAO effect to different Vulkan demos just by moving the instance of `SSAOProcessor`. While this might be pretty neat for learning and demonstration, it is far from the most performant solution and can be difficult to synchronize in postprocessing pipelines that include tens of different effects. We will touch on this topic a bit more in *Chapter 10, Advanced Rendering Techniques and Optimizations.*

Implementing HDR rendering in Vulkan

Just recently, in the previous recipe, we learned how to implement one OpenGL postprocessing effect in Vulkan, and here, we will learn how to implement HDR rendering and tone mapping using the Vulkan API.

Getting ready...

Make sure you read the *Implementing HDR rendering and tone mapping* recipe to understand the HDR rendering pipeline, and the *Writing postprocessing effects in Vulkan* recipe to have a good grasp of the basic classes we use in our Vulkan postprocessors.

The complete source code for this recipe can be found in `Chapter8/VK03_HDR`.

How to do it...

We define an `HDRPostprocessor` class derived from `QuadProcessor` that performs a per-pixel tone-mapping operation on an input framebuffer. The tone-mapping parameter pointers can be tweaked by the application code in the UI window.

One C++-related subtlety must be addressed in the initialization of the `HDRProstprocessor` class:

1. The base class constructor is called before any field initializers, but at this point, we already need to pass the `tonemapUniforms` buffer field as a parameter for the constructor of `QuadProcessor`. To tackle this, we declare a `bufferAllocator()` function, which takes a reference to `VulkanBuffer`, allocates this buffer, and immediately returns the created instance. The code for this function is given after the `HDRPostprocessor` class. The postprocessor requires an input color framebuffer in `16`-bit floating-point format to allow greater-than-one values and a single output texture. The base class constructor is called with a descriptor set that has a pre-initialized uniform buffer with tone-mapping parameters and a single input texture. The output framebuffer and the tone-mapping shader name are passed directly to `QuadProcessor`:

```
struct HDRPostprocessor: public QuadProcessor {
  HDRPostprocessor(VulkanRenderContext& ctx,
    VulkanTexture input,
    VulkanTexture output)
  : QuadProcessor(ctx,
      DescriptorSetInfo {
        .buffers = {
          uniformBufferAttachment(
            bufferAllocator(ctx.resources,
            tonemapUniforms_, sizeof(UniformBuffer)),
            0, 0, VK_SHADER_STAGE_FRAGMENT_BIT)
        },
```

```
        .textures = { fsTextureAttachment(input) }
      }, { output },
      "data/shaders/chapter08/VK_ToneMap.frag")
  {}
```

2. The overridden `updateBuffers()` method uploads the uniform buffer into the **graphics processing unit (GPU)**. As an alternative, a permanent mapping to the `ubo` field can be created in the class constructor:

```
void updateBuffers(size_t currentImage) override {
  uploadBufferData(
    ctx_.vkDev, tonemapUniforms_.memory, 0,
    &ubo, sizeof(ubo));
}
```

3. A pair of getter functions allow modification of the tone-mapping parameters by external code. The data section of the class contains **central processing unit (CPU)** and GPU buffers to store uniform values:

```
inline float* getGammaPtr() { return &ubo.gamma; }
float* getExposurePtr() { return &ubo.exposure; }
private:
  struct UniformBuffer {
    float gamma;
    float exposure;
  } ubo;
  VulkanBuffer tonemapUniforms_;
};
```

4. The `bufferAllocator()` function used in the initialization is a wrapper on top of the `addUniformBuffer()` method from the `VulkanResources` class:

```
VulkanBuffer bufferAllocator(
  VulkanResources& resources,
  VulkanBuffer& buffer, VkDeviceSize size)
{
  return (buffer = resources.addUniformBuffer(size));
}
```

The per-pixel processing is performed by the fragment shader. The descriptor-set layout from the constructor of `HDRPostprocessor` is repeated in the GLSL code.

The `Chapter08/VK03_HDR` sample application loads the exterior part of the Bistro scene, renders this scene into the `HDRLuminance` buffer, and finally uses the `HDRPostprocessor` class to compose the final image. A small UI is provided to modify the tone-mapping parameters:

1. Our intermediate buffer format contains `16`-bit floating-point RGBA values:

```
const VkFormat LuminanceFormat =
   VK_FORMAT_R16G16B16A16_SFLOAT;
```

2. The application class is derived from `CameraApp`, as in all the samples for this chapter. `MultiRenderer` requires two input textures, one for color and one for the depth buffer. A `32`-bit RGBA output texture for the HDR postprocessor is allocated:

```
struct MyApp: public CameraApp {
  MyApp(): CameraApp(-80, -80),
    HDRDepth(ctx_.resources.addDepthTexture()),
    HDRLuminance(
      ctx_.resources.addColorTexture(0, 0,
        LuminanceFormat)),
      hdrTex(ctx_.resources.addColorTexture()),
```

3. The scene data is loaded and then passed to `MultiRenderer`. Two environment-map texture files are the same as in the `Chapter07/VK03_LargeScene` demo application from the previous chapter, *Chapter 7, Graphics Rendering Pipeline*:

```
sceneData(ctx_, "data/meshes/test.meshes",
  "data/meshes/test.scene",
  "data/meshes/test.materials",
  ctx_.resources.loadCubeMap(envMapFile),
  ctx_.resources.loadCubeMap(irrMapFile)),
```

4. The only `MultiRenderer` instance in this application outputs to previously allocated buffers using the same shaders as in *Chapter 7, Graphics Rendering Pipeline*:

```
multiRenderer(ctx_, sceneData,
  "data/shaders/chapter07/VK01.vert",
  "data/shaders/chapter07/VK01.frag",
  { HDRLuminance, HDRDepth },
```

5. A custom offscreen rendering pass compatible with our HDR framebuffers is a required parameter. The constructor body creates a rendering sequence. In order to see anything on the screen, we use the `QuadRenderer` instance. The upper half of the screen shows an intermediate HDR buffer, and the lower part displays the final image:

```
ctx_.resources.addRenderPass(
  { HDRLuminance, HDRDepth },
  RenderPassCreateInfo {
    .clearColor_ = true,
    .clearDepth_ = true,
    .flags_ = eRenderPassBit_Offscreen })
),
hdrPP(ctx_, HDRLuminance, { hdrTex }),
quads(ctx_, { hdrTex, HDRLuminance }),
imgui(ctx_)
{

  onScreenRenderers_.emplace_back(multiRenderer);
  onScreenRenderers_.emplace_back(hdrPP);
  onScreenRenderers_.emplace_back(quads, false);
  onScreenRenderers_.emplace_back(imgui, false);
  quads.clear();
  quads.quad(-1.0f,  0.0f, 1.0f, 1.0f, 0);
  quads.quad(-1.0f, -1.0f, 1.0f, 0.0f, 1);
}
```

6. The `drawUI()` member function creates a window with two sliders for controlling the HDR parameters:

```
void drawUI() override {
 ImGui::Begin("Settings", nullptr);
  ImGui::SliderFloat("Gamma: ",
    hdrPP.getGammaPtr(), 0.1f, 10.0f);
  ImGui::SliderFloat("Exposure: ",
    hdrPP.getExposurePtr(), 0., 10.);
 ImGui::End();
}
```

7. In the `draw3D()` function, we pass camera parameters to a `MultiRenderer` instance, just as we did in the `Chapter07/VK03_LargeScene` sample application from the previous chapter, *Chapter 7, Graphics Rendering Pipeline*. The private section of the class declares intermediate textures and all the renderers for this application:

```
void draw3D() override {
    const mat4 p = getDefaultProjection();
    const mat4 view =camera.getViewMatrix();
    const mat4 m1 = glm::rotate(
        mat4(1.f), glm::pi<float>(), vec3(1, 0, 0));
    multiRenderer.setMatrices(p, view, m1);
}
private:
    VulkanTexture HDRDepth, HDRLuminance;
    VulkanTexture hdrTex;
    VKSceneData sceneData;
    MultiRenderer;
    HDRPostprocessor hdrPP;
    GuiRenderer imgui;
    QuadRenderer quads;
};
```

The application functionality is similar to that of the OpenGL one from the *Implementing HDR rendering and tone mapping* recipe. Implementing light adaptation in Vulkan is left as an exercise to our readers.

There's more...

This `Chapter8/VK03_HDR` Vulkan demo uses an asynchronous texture-loading approach, as described in the *Loading texture assets asynchronously* recipe from *Chapter 10, Advanced Rendering Techniques and Optimizations*. If the calls to the asynchronous texture loader are removed, the demo just loads the textures upfront. As a side note, Vulkan allows the use of dedicated transfer queues for asynchronous uploading of the textures into the GPU, but this requires some more tweaking in the Vulkan device and queue-initialization code. We leave this as an exercise to our readers.

9

Working with Scene Graphs

In this chapter, we add a few more touches to our scene-graph code to allow dynamic scene graphs. Besides that, we show how to handle custom components using an example with a physics simulation library, `Bullet`. Using these techniques, we can extend our scene-graph implementation even further and cover many real-world use cases.

This chapter covers the following recipes:

- Deleting nodes and merging scene graphs
- Finalizing the scene-converter tool
- Implementing lightweight rendering queues in **Open Graphics Library** (**OpenGL**)
- Working with shape lists in Vulkan
- Adding `Bullet` physics to a graphics application

Technical requirements

To run the recipes from this chapter, you will need to use a computer with a video card supporting OpenGL 4.6 with `ARB_bindless_texture` and Vulkan 1.2. Read *Chapter 1, Establishing a Build Environment,* if you want to learn how to build demonstration applications from this book.

This chapter relies on the geometry-loading code explained in *Chapter 7, Graphics Rendering Pipeline*, so make sure you read it before proceeding any further.

You can find the code files present in this chapter on GitHub at `https://github.com/PacktPublishing/3D-Graphics-Rendering-Cookbook/tree/master/Chapter9`.

Deleting nodes and merging scene graphs

Our scene-management routines from *Chapter 7, Graphics Rendering Pipeline,* are incomplete without a few more operations:

- Deleting scene nodes

- Merging multiple scenes into one (in our case, Lumberyard Bistro's exterior and interior objects)

- Merging material and mesh data lists

- Merging multiple static meshes with the same material into a large single mesh

These operations are crucial to the success of our final demo application since, without a combined list of render operations, we cannot easily construct auxiliary draw lists for shadow casters and transparent objects. Frustum culling is significantly easier to do while dealing with a single list of renderable items. Mesh merging is also essential for optimization purposes. The original Lumberyard Bistro scene contains a big tree in the backyard, where small orange and green leaves comprise almost two-thirds of the total draw call count of the entire scene—that is, roughly 18,000 out of 27,000 objects.

This recipe describes `deleteSceneNodes()` and `mergeScene()` routines used for scene-graph manipulations. Together with the next recipe, *Finalizing the scene-converter tool*, these functions complete our scene data-conversion and preprocessing tool, which we started back in *Chapter 7, Graphics Rendering Pipeline*.

Let's recall *Chapter 7, Graphics Rendering Pipeline*, where we packed all the scene data into a continuous array wrapped in `std::vector` for convenience so that the data was directly usable by the **Graphics Processing Unit** (**GPU**). Here, we use **Standard Template Library's** (**STL's**) partitioning algorithms to keep everything tightly packed while deleting and merging scene nodes.

For a starter, let's implement a utility function to delete a collection of items from an array. It may seem superfluous to implement a routine to remove an entire collection of nodes at once, but even in the simplest case of deleting a single node, we also need to remove all of the node's children.

The idea is to move all the nodes marked for deletion to the end of the array using the `std::stable_partition()` algorithm. After moving the nodes, we only need to resize the container. The following diagram clarifies the deletion process:

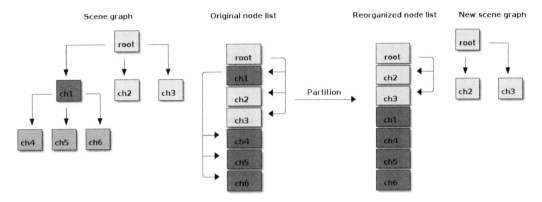

Figure 9.1 – Deleting nodes from a scene graph

On the left, we have an initial scene graph with some nodes marked for deletion (**ch1** and **ch4, ch5, ch6**). In the middle, we have a linear list of nodes, with arrows indicating inter-node references. On the right, we have a reorganized node list and the resulting scene graph.

How to do it...

Let's take a look at how to implement our utility functions.

1. The `eraseSelected()` routine is generic enough to delete any kind of items from an array, so we use template arguments:

```
template <class T, class Index = int>
void eraseSelected(
  std::vector<T>& v,
  const std::vector<Index>& selection) {
  v.resize(std::distance(v.begin(),
    std::stable_partition(v.begin(), v.end(),
      [&selection, &v](const T& item) {
        return !std::binary_search(
          selection.begin(), selection.end(),
          static_cast<Index>(
            static_cast<const T*>(&item) - &v[0]));
      }))
  );
}
```

The function "chops off" the elements moved to the end of the vector by using `vector::resize()`. The exact number of items to retain is calculated as a distance from the start of the array to the iterator returned by the `stable_partition()` function. The `std::stable_partition()` algorithm takes a lambda function that checks whether the element should be moved to the end of the array. In our case, this lambda function checks whether the item is in the `selection` container passed as an argument. The "usual" way to find an item index in the array is to use `std::distance()` and `std::find()`, but we can also resort to good old pointer arithmetic, as the container is tightly packed.

2. Now that we have our workhorse, the `eraseSelected()` routine, we can implement scene-node deletion. When we want to delete one node, all its children must also be marked for deletion. We collect all the nodes to be deleted with the following recursive routine. To do this, we iterate all the children, as we did in *Chapter 7, Graphics Rendering Pipeline*, while traversing a scene graph. Each iterated index is added to the array:

```
void collectNodesToDelete(
  const Scene& scene, int node,
  std::vector<uint32_t>& nodes)
{
  for (int n = scene.hierarchy_[node].firstChild_;
    n != - 1 ; n = scene.hierarchy_[n].nextSibling_)
  {
    addUniqueIdx(nodes, n);
    collectNodesToDelete(scene, n, nodes);
  }
}
```

3. An `addUniqueIndex()` helper routine avoids adding items twice:

```
void addUniqueIdx(std::vector<uint32_t>& v, int index) {
  if (!std::binary_search(v.begin(), v.end(), index))
    v.push_back(index);
}
```

One subtle requirement here is that the array is sorted. When all the children come strictly after their parents, this is not a problem. Otherwise, `std::find()` should be used, which naturally increases the runtime cost of the algorithm.

4. Our `deleteSceneNodes()` deletion routine starts by adding all child nodes to the deleted nodes list. To keep track of moved nodes, we create a `nodes` linear list of indices, starting at 0:

```
void deleteSceneNodes(Scene& scene,
  const std::vector<uint32_t>& nodesToDelete)
{
  auto indicesToDelete = nodesToDelete;
  for (auto i: indicesToDelete)
    collectNodesToDelete(scene, i, indicesToDelete);
  std::vector<uint32_t> nodes(
    scene.hierarchy_.size());
  std::iota(nodes.begin(), nodes.end(), 0);
```

5. Afterward, we remember the source node count and remove all the indices from our linear index list. To fix the child node indices, we create a linear mapping table from old node indices to the new ones:

```
  auto oldSize = nodes.size();
  eraseSelected(nodes, indicesToDelete);
  std::vector<uint32_t> newIndices(oldSize, -1);
  for (uint32_t i = 0; i < nodes.size(); i++)
    newIndices[nodes[i]] = i;
```

6. Before deleting nodes from the hierarchy array, we remap all node indices. The following lambda modifies a single `Hierarchy` item by finding the non-null node in the `newIndices` container:

```
  auto nodeMover = [&scene, &newIndices](Hierarchy& h)
  {
    return Hierarchy {
      .parent_ = (h.parent_ != -1) ?
        newIndices[h.parent_] : -1,
      .firstChild_ = findLastNonDeletedItem(
        scene, newIndices, h.firstChild_),
      .nextSibling_ = findLastNonDeletedItem(
        scene, newIndices, h.nextSibling_),
      .lastSibling_ = findLastNonDeletedItem(
        scene, newIndices, h.lastSibling_)
    };
  };
```

7. The `std::transform()` algorithm modifies all the nodes in the hierarchy. After fixing node indices, we are ready to actually delete data. Three calls to `eraseSelected()` throw away the unused hierarchy and transformation items:

```
std::transform(scene.hierarchy_.begin(),
  scene.hierarchy_.end(), scene.hierarchy_.begin(),
  nodeMover);
eraseSelected(scene.hierarchy_, indicesToDelete);
eraseSelected(
  scene.localTransform_, indicesToDelete);
eraseSelected(
  scene.globalTransform_, indicesToDelete);
```

8. Finally, we need to adjust the indices in mesh, material, and name maps. For this, we use the `shiftMapIndices()` function shown here:

```
shiftMapIndices(scene.meshes_, newIndices);
shiftMapIndices(scene.materialForNode_, newIndices);
shiftMapIndices(scene.nameForNode_, newIndices);
}
```

9. The search for node replacement used during the node-index shifting is implemented recursively. The `findLastNonDeletedItem()` function returns a deleted node replacement index:

```
int findLastNonDeletedItem(const Scene& scene,
  const std::vector<uint32_t>& newIndices, int node)
{
  if (node == -1)
    return -1;
  return (newIndices[node] == -1) ?
    findLastNonDeletedItem(
      scene, newIndices,
      scene.hierarchy_[node].nextSibling_) :
    newIndices[node];
}
```

If the input is empty, no replacement is necessary. If we have no replacement for the node, we recurse to the next sibling of the deleted node.

10. The last function replaces the `pair::second` value in each map's item:

```
void shiftMapIndices(
  std::unordered_map<uint32_t, uint32_t>& items,
  const std::vector<int>& newIndices)
```

```
{
  std::unordered_map<uint32_t, uint32_t> newItems;
  for (const auto& m: items) {
    int newIndex = newIndices[m.first];
    if (newIndex != -1)
      newItems[newIndex] = m.second;
  }
  items = newItems;
}
```

The deleteSceneNodes() routine allows us to compress and optimize a scene graph while merging multiple meshes with the same material. Now, we need a method to combine multiple meshes into one and delete scene nodes referring to merged meshes. The merging of mesh data requires only the index-data modification. Let's look at the steps involved:

1. The mergeScene() function uses two functions, the first one calculating the number of merged indices. We remember the starting vertex offset for all of the meshes. The loop shifts all the indices in individual mesh blocks of the meshData. indexData_ array. Also, for each Mesh object, a new minVtxOffset value is assigned to the vertex-data offset field. The return value is the difference between the original and merged index count. This difference is also the offset to the point where the merged index data starts:

```
static uint32_t shiftMeshIndices(MeshData& meshData,
  const std::vector<uint32_t>& meshesToMerge)
{
  auto minVtxOffset = numeric_limits<uint32_t>::max();
  for (auto i: meshesToMerge)
    minVtxOffset = std::min(
      meshData.meshes_[i].vertexOffset, minVtxOffset);
  uint32_t mergeCount = 0;
  for (auto i: meshesToMerge) {
    auto& m = meshData.meshes_[i];
    const uint32_t delta =
      m.vertexOffset - minVtxOffset;
    const auto idxCount = m.getLODIndicesCount(0);
    for (auto ii = 0u ; ii < idxCount ; ii++)
      meshData.indexData_[m.indexOffset + ii] +=
        delta;
    m.vertexOffset = minVtxOffset;
```

```
      mergeCount += idxCount;
    }
    return meshData.indexData_.size() - mergeCount;
}
```

2. The `mergeIndexArray()` function copies indices for each mesh into the `newIndices` array:

```
static void mergeIndexArray(MeshData& md,
    const std::vector<uint32_t>& meshesToMerge,
    std::map<uint32_t, uint32_t>& oldToNew)
{
    std::vector<uint32_t> newIndices(
        md.indexData_.size());
    uint32_t copyOffset = 0;
    uint32_t mergeOffset =
        shiftMeshIndices(md, meshesToMerge);
```

For each mesh, we decide where to copy its index data. The `copyOffset` value is used for meshes that are not merged, and the `mergeOffset` value starts at the beginning of the merged index data returned by the `shiftMeshIndices()` function.

3. Two variables contain mesh indices of the merged mesh and the copied mesh. We iterate all the meshes to check whether the current one needs to be merged:

```
const auto mergedMeshIndex =
    md.meshes_.size() - meshesToMerge.size();
auto newIndex = 0u;
for (uint32_t midx = 0;
     midx < md.meshes_.size(); midx++)
{
    const bool shouldMerge =
        std::binary_search(meshesToMerge.begin(),
                           meshesToMerge.end(), midx);
```

4. Each index is stored in an old-to-new correspondence map:

```
oldToNew[midx] =
    shouldMerge ? mergedMeshIndex : newIndex;
newIndex += shouldMerge ? 0 : 1;
```

5. The offset of the index block for this mesh is modified, so first calculate the source offset for the index data:

```
auto& mesh = md.meshes_[midx];
```

```
auto idxCount = mesh.getLODIndicesCount(0);
const auto start =
  md.indexData_.begin() + mesh.indexOffset;
mesh.indexOffset = copyOffset;
```

6. We choose between two offsets and copy index data from the original array to the output. The new index array is copied into the mesh data structure:

```
const auto offsetPtr =
  shouldMerge ? &mergeOffset : &copyOffset;
std::copy(start, start + idxCount,
  newIndices.begin() + *offsetPtr);
*offsetPtr += idxCount;
}
md.indexData_ = newIndices;
```

7. One last step in the merge process is the creation of a merged mesh. Copy the first of the merged mesh descriptors and assign new **Lateral Offset Device (LOD)** offsets:

```
Mesh lastMesh = md.meshes_[meshesToMerge[0]];
lastMesh.indexOffset = copyOffset;
lastMesh.lodOffset[0] = copyOffset;
lastMesh.lodOffset[1] = mergeOffset;
lastMesh.lodCount = 1;
md.meshes_.push_back(lastMesh);
}
```

The mergeScene() routine omits a couple of important things. First, we merge only the finest LOD level. For our purpose, this is sufficient because our scene contains a large amount of simple (one to two triangles) meshes with only a single LOD. Second, we assume that the merged meshes have the same transformation. This is also the case for our test scene, but if correct transformation is necessary, all the vertices should be transformed into the global coordinate system and then transformed back to the local coordinates of the node where we place the resulting merged mesh. Let's take a look at the implementation:

1. To avoid string comparisons, convert material names to their indices in the material name array:

```
void mergeScene(Scene& scene, MeshData& meshData,
  const std::string& materialName)
{
  int oldMaterial = (int)std::distance(
    std::begin(scene.materialNames_),
```

```
std::find(std::begin(scene.materialNames_),
    std::end(scene.materialNames_),
  materialName));
```

2. When you have the material index, collect all the scene nodes that will be deleted:

```
std::vector<uint32_t> toDelete;
for (uint32_t i = 0;
      i < scene.hierarchy_.size(); i++) {
  if (scene.meshes_.contains(i) &&
      scene.materialForNode_.contains(i) &&
      (scene.materialForNode_.at(i) == oldMaterial))
      toDelete.push_back(i);
}
```

3. The number of meshes to be merged is the same as the number of deleted scene nodes (in our scene, at least), so convert scene-node indices into mesh indices:

```
std::vector<uint32_t> meshesToMerge(
  toDelete.size());
std::transform(toDelete.begin(), toDelete.end(),
  meshesToMerge.begin(),
    [&scene](auto i) { return scene.meshes_.at(i); });
```

4. An essential part of this code merges index data and assigns changed mesh indices to scene nodes:

```
std::map<uint32_t, uint32_t> oldToNew;
mergeIndexArray(meshData, meshesToMerge, oldToNew);
for (auto& n: scene.meshes_)
  n.second = oldToNew[n.second];
```

5. Finally, cut out all the merged meshes and attach a new node containing the merged meshes to the scene graph:

```
eraseSelected(meshData.meshes_, meshesToMerge);
int newNode = addNode(scene, 0, 1);
scene.meshes_[newNode] = meshData.meshes_.size()-1;
scene.materialForNode_[newNode] =
  (uint32_t)oldMaterial;
deleteSceneNodes(scene, toDelete);
}
```

The `mergeScene()` function is used in the scene-converter tool. Let's jump to the next recipe to learn how to merge multiple meshes in the Lumberyard Bistro scene.

Finalizing the scene-converter tool

While the scene-node deletion routine from the previous recipe is useful for implementing interactive editors, we still need to automatically optimize our Lumberyard Bistro scene geometry. Here, we provide a few helper routines to merge multiple scenes into one. These routines and the code from the previous recipe allow us to complete the scene data-conversion tool that we started in *Chapter 7, Graphics Rendering Pipeline*.

Getting ready

Make sure you read the previous recipe, *Deleting nodes and merging scene graphs*.

The source code for this recipe is part of the `Chapter7/SceneConverter` tool implemented in *Chapter 7, Graphics Rendering Pipeline*. Start exploring from the `mergeBistro()` function and follow this recipe's text.

How to do it...

The first routine we need is the merging of multiple meshes into a single contiguous array. Since each `MeshData` structure contains an array of triangle indices and an interleaved array of vertex attributes, the merging procedure consists of copying input `MeshData` instances to a single array and modifying index-data offsets. Let's look at the steps:

1. The `mergeMeshData()` routine takes a list of `MeshData` instances and creates a new file header while simultaneously copying all the indices and vertices to the output object:

```
MeshFileHeader mergeMeshData(
  MeshData& m, const std::vector<MeshData*> md)
{
  uint32_t totalVertexDataSize = 0;
  uint32_t totalIndexDataSize  = 0;
  uint32_t offs = 0;
  for (const MeshData* i: md) {
    mergeVectors(m.indexData_, i->indexData_);
    mergeVectors(m.vertexData_, i->vertexData_);
    mergeVectors(m.meshes_, i->meshes_);
    mergeVectors(m.boxes_, i->boxes_);
```

2. After merging the index and vertex data along with the auxiliary precalculated bounding boxes, shift each index by the total size of the merged index array:

```
for (size_t j = 0;
     j < (uint32_t)i->meshes_.size(); j++)
  m.meshes_[offs + j].indexOffset +=
    totalIndexDataSize;
```

3. Each index must be shifted by the current size of the m.vertexData_ array. The "magic" number—8—here is the sum of 3 vertex position components, 3 normal vector components, and 2 texture coordinates:

```
uint32_t vtxOffset = totalVertexDataSize / 8;
for(size_t j = 0 ; j < i->indexData_.size() ; j++)
  m.indexData_[totalIndexDataSize + j] +=
    vtxOffset;
```

4. At each iteration, increment global offsets in the mesh, index, and vertex arrays:

```
offs += (uint32_t)i->meshes_.size();
totalIndexDataSize +=
  (uint32_t)i->indexData_.size();
totalVertexDataSize +=
  (uint32_t)i->vertexData_.size();
}
```

5. The resulting mesh file header contains the total size of index and vertex data arrays:

```
return MeshFileHeader {
  .magicValue = 0x12345678,
  .meshCount = offs,
  .dataBlockStartOffset =
    sizeof(MeshFileHeader) + offs * sizeof(Mesh),
  .indexDataSize =
    totalIndexDataSize * sizeof(uint32_t),
  .vertexDataSize =
    totalVertexDataSize * sizeof(float)
  };
}
```

The mergeVectors() function is a templated one-liner that appends the second vector, v2, to the end of the first one, v1:

```
template<typename T> inline void mergeVectors(
  std::vector<T>& v1, const std::vector<T>& v2)
{
```

```
    v1.insert( v1.end(), v2.begin(), v2.end() );
}
```

6. Along with mesh-data merging, you need to create an aggregate material description list from a collection of material lists. The `mergeMaterialLists()` function creates a single texture filenames list and a material description list with correct texture indices:

```
void mergeMaterialLists(
    const std::vector<vector<MaterialDescription>*>&
        oldMaterials,
    const std::vector<vector<string>*>& oldTextures,
    std::vector<MaterialDescription>& allMaterials,
    std::vector<std::string>& newTextures)
{

    std::unordered_map<string, int> newTextureNames;
    std::unordered_map<int, int> materialToTextureList;
```

7. The merge process starts with the creation of a single list of materials. Each material list index is associated with a texture so that later on, we can figure out in which of the lists the texture appears. Since our beloved C++ does not yet have a canonical Python-style iteration of items while keeping track of the item's index, we declare an index variable manually:

```
int midx = 0;
for (vector<MaterialDescription>* ml: oldMaterials){
    for (const MaterialDescription& m: *ml) {
        allMaterials.push_back(m);
        materialToTextureList[allMaterials.size()-1] =
            midx;
    }
    midx++;
}
```

8. The `newTextures` global texture array contains only unique filenames. Indices of texture files are stored in a map to fix the values in material descriptors below them:

```
for (const auto& tl: oldTextures)
    for (const std::string& file: *tl)
        newTextureNames[file] =
            addUnique(newTextures, file);
```

9. The `replaceTexture()` lambda takes a texture index from a local texture array and assigns a global texture index from the `newTextures` array:

```
auto replaceTexture =
  [&materialToTextureList, &oldTextures,
   &newTextureNames] (int m, uint64_t* textureID)
  {
    if (*textureID < INVALID_TEXTURE) {
      auto listIdx = materialToTextureList[m];
      auto texList = oldTextures[listIdx];
      const std::string& texFile =
        (*texList)[*textureID];
      *textureID = newTextureNames[texFile];
    }
  };
```

The final loop goes over all materials and adjusts the texture indices accordingly:

```
for (size_t i = 0 ; i < allMaterials.size() ; i++) {
  auto& m = allMaterials[i];
  replaceTexture(i, &m.ambientOcclusionMap_);
  replaceTexture(i, &m.emissiveMap_);
  replaceTexture(i, &m.albedoMap_);
  replaceTexture(i, &m.metallicRoughnessMap_);
  replaceTexture(i, &m.normalMap_);
}
}
```

To merge interior and exterior object lists, we need one more routine that merges multiple scene hierarchies into one large scene graph. The scene data is specified by the hierarchy item array, local and global transforms, mesh, material, and scene-node associative arrays. Just as with mesh index and vertex data, the merge routine boils down to merging individual arrays and then shifting indices in individual scene nodes:

1. The `shiftNodes()` routine increments individual fields of the `Hierarchy` structure by the given amount:

```
void shiftNodes(Scene& scene,
  int startOffset, int nodeCount, int shiftAmount)
{
  auto shiftNode = [shiftAmount] (Hierarchy& node)  {
    if (node.parent_ > -1)
      node.parent_ += shiftAmount;
```

```
       if (node.firstChild_ > -1)
         node.firstChild_ += shiftAmount;
       if (node.nextSibling_ > -1)
         node.nextSibling_ += shiftAmount;
       if (node.lastSibling_ > -1)
         node.lastSibling_ += shiftAmount;
     };
     for (int i = 0; i < nodeCount; i++)
       shiftNode(scene.hierarchy_[i + startOffset]);
   }
```

2. The `mergeMaps()` helper routine adds the `otherMap` collection to the m output map and shifts item indices by specified amounts:

```
   using ItemMap =
     std::unordered_map<uint32_t, uint32_t>;
   void mergeMaps(ItemMap& m, const ItemMap& otherMap,
     int indexOffset, int itemOffset)
   {
     for (const auto& i: otherMap)
       m[i.first + indexOffset] = i.second + itemOffset;
   }
```

3. The `mergeScenes()` routine creates a new scene node named `"NewRoot"` and adds all the root scene nodes from the list to the new scene as children of the `"NewRoot"` node. In the accompanying source-code bundle, this routine has two more parameters, `mergeMeshes` and `mergeMaterials`, which allow the creation of composite scenes with shared mesh and material data. We omit these non-essential parameters to shorten the description:

```
   void mergeScenes(Scene& scene,
     const std::vector<Scene*>& scenes,
     const std::vector<glm::mat4>& rootTransforms,
     const std::vector<uint32_t>& meshCounts,
     bool mergeMeshes, bool mergeMaterials)
   {
     scene.hierarchy_ = { {
       .parent_ = -1,
       .firstChild_ = 1,
       .nextSibling_ = -1,
       .lastSibling_ = -1,
       .level_ = 0
     } };
```

4. Name and transform arrays initially contain a single element, `"NewRoot"`:

```
scene.nameForNode_[0] = 0;
scene.names_ = { "NewRoot" };
scene.localTransform_.push_back(glm::mat4(1.f));
scene.globalTransform_.push_back(glm::mat4(1.f));
if (scenes.empty()) return;
```

5. While iterating the scenes, we merge and shift all the arrays and maps. The next few variables keep track of item counts in the output scene:

```
int offs = 1;
int meshOffs = 0;
int nameOffs = (int)scene.names_.size();
int materialOfs = 0;
auto meshCount = meshCounts.begin();
if (!mergeMaterials)
  scene.materialNames_ = scenes[0]->materialNames_;
```

6. This implementation is not the best possible one, not least because we risk merging all the scene-graph components in a single routine:

```
for (const Scene* s: scenes) {
  mergeVectors(
    scene.localTransform_, s->localTransform_);
  mergeVectors(
    scene.globalTransform_, s->globalTransform_);
  mergeVectors(scene.hierarchy_, s->hierarchy_);
  mergeVectors(scene.names_, s->names_);
  if (mergeMaterials)
    mergeVectors(
      scene.materialNames_, s->materialNames_);
  int nodeCount = (int)s->hierarchy_.size();
  shiftNodes(scene, offs, nodeCount, offs);
  mergeMaps(scene.meshes_,
    s->meshes_, offs, mergeMeshes ? meshOffs : 0);
  mergeMaps(scene.materialForNode_,
    s->materialForNode_, offs,
    mergeMaterials ? materialOfs : 0);
  mergeMaps(scene.nameForNode_,
    s->nameForNode_, offs, nameOffs);
```

7. At each iteration, we add the sizes of the current arrays to global offsets:

```
offs += nodeCount;
materialOfs += (int)s->materialNames_.size();
nameOffs += (int)s->names_.size();
if (mergeMeshes) {
    meshOffs += *meshCount;
    meshCount++;
}
}
```

8. Logically, the routine is complete, but there is one more step to perform. Each scene node contains a cached index of the last sibling node, which we have to set for the new root nodes. Each root node can now have a new local transform, which we set in the following loop:

```
offs = 1;
int idx = 0;
for (const Scene* s: scenes) {
    int nodeCount = (int)s->hierarchy_.size();
    bool isLast = (idx == scenes.size() - 1);
    int next = isLast ? -1 : offs + nodeCount;
    scene.hierarchy_[offs].nextSibling_ = next;
    scene.hierarchy_[offs].parent_ = 0;
    if (!rootTransforms.empty())
        scene.localTransform_[offs] =
            rootTransforms[idx] *
            scene.localTransform_[offs];
    offs += nodeCount;
    idx++;
}
```

9. At the end of the routine, we should increment all the levels of the scene nodes but leave the "NewRoot" node untouched—hence, +1:

```
for (auto i = scene.hierarchy_.begin() + 1;
     i != scene.hierarchy_.end() ; i++)
    i->level_++;
}
```

Our final addition to the scene-converter tool is a routine that combines interior and exterior objects of the Lumberyard Bistro scene. This routine also merges almost 20,000 leaves and a tree trunk into just three large aggregate meshes. Here are the steps involved:

1. In the beginning, we load two `MeshData` instances, two `Scene` objects, and two `MaterialDescription` containers. All of this data is produced in the `main()` function of `SceneConverter` when it is run with the provided configuration file:

```
void mergeBistro() {
  Scene scene1, scene2;
  std::vector<Scene*> scenes = { &scene1, &scene2 };
  MeshData m1, m2;
  auto header1 = loadMeshData(
    "data/meshes/test.meshes", m1);
  auto header2 = loadMeshData(
    "data/meshes/test2.meshes", m2);
  std::vector<uint32_t> meshCounts =
    { header1.meshCount, header2.meshCount };
  loadScene("data/meshes/test.scene", scene1);
  loadScene("data/meshes/test2.scene", scene2);
  Scene scene;
  mergeScenes(scene, scenes, {}, meshCounts);
  MeshData meshData;
  std::vector<MeshData*> meshDatas = { &m1, &m2 };
```

2. Once we have loaded all the mesh data, we create an aggregate `MeshData` object. Material data is also loaded and merged, similar to the mesh data:

```
MeshFileHeader header =
  mergeMeshData(meshData, meshDatas);
std::vector<MaterialDescription>
  materials1, materials2;
std::vector<std::string>
  textureFiles1, textureFiles2;
loadMaterials("data/meshes/test.materials",
  materials1, textureFiles1);
loadMaterials("data/meshes/test2.materials",
  materials2, textureFiles2);
std::vector<MaterialDescription> allMaterials;
std::vector<std::string> allTextures;
```

3. A global material list is created with the `mergeMaterialLists()` function described previously:

```
mergeMaterialLists(
   { &materials1, &materials2 },
   { &textureFiles1, &textureFiles2 },
   allMaterials, allTextures);
```

4. Our scene contains a leafy tree object in the backyard. Just by inspecting the source mesh files, we can easily find out the names of materials for the meshes to be merged. Green and orange leaves constitute almost two-thirds of the total mesh count in the combined scene, so they are merged into two large meshes. The trunk is almost 1,000 meshes, so we merge it as well:

```
mergeScene(scene, meshData,
   "Foliage_Linde_Tree_Large_Orange_Leaves");
mergeScene(scene, meshData,
   "Foliage_Linde_Tree_Large_Green_Leaves");
mergeScene(scene, meshData,
   "Foliage_Linde_Tree_Large_Trunk");
```

5. Following the modification, we have our bounding-box array broken, so we call the calculation routine. The saving of optimized mesh, material, and scene node lists is done in the same way as in the `processScene()` function described in *Chapter 7, Graphics Rendering Pipeline*:

```
recalculateBoundingBoxes(meshData);
saveMaterials(
   "data/meshes/bistro_all.materials",
   allMaterials, allTextures);
saveMeshData(
   "data/meshes/bistro_all.meshes", meshData);
saveScene("data/meshes/bistro_all.scene", scene);
}
```

Now, we can consider our `SceneConverter` tool fully implemented. Let's switch back to the actual rendering topics and see how convenient it is to work with a single scene graph.

There's more...

While we can call the scene converter complete for the purpose of this book, there are many improvements that are still desirable and easy to implement. We recommend adding texture compression as an exercise for our readers.

Implementing lightweight rendering queues in OpenGL

All our previous rendering examples in this book were built with the assumption that an indirect draw call renders the entire collection of loaded meshes using the currently bound shader program. This functionality is sufficient to implement simple rendering techniques, where all the meshes can be treated the same way—for example, we can take the entire scene geometry and render it using a shadow-mapping shader program. Then, we take exactly the same scene geometry and render it entirely using another shader program to apply texture mapping. As we try to build a more complex rendering engine, this approach immediately breaks because different parts of the scene require different treatment. It can be as simple as different materials or as complex as having opaque and transparent surfaces, which may require completely different rendering code paths.

One naive solution to this problem would be to physically separate the actual geometry into different buffers and use these separate datasets to render different subparts of the scene. Sounds better compared to what we have now, right? What if the scene has overlapping geometry subsets—for example, all opaque objects should be rendered in the Z-prepass while some of these opaque objects have a **physically based rendering (PBR)** shader and others require simple Blinn-Phong shading? Duplicating subsets of objects with specific properties from the original dataset and putting them into distinct GPU buffers would be wasteful in terms of memory. Instead, we can store all the objects with their geometry and materials in one big set of buffers and use multiple OpenGL indirect buffers that specify objects to be rendered in each and every rendering pass. Let's implement this technique and use it in subsequent OpenGL recipes of this chapter.

Getting ready

Before going forward with this recipe, make sure you check out the previous chapter and see how mesh rendering is organized there. The source code of our old OpenGL mesh renderer is in `Chapter8/GLMesh8.h`.

The source code for this recipe is located in the `Chapter9/GLMesh9.h` file.

How to do it...

Our structure describing a single draw command is contained in `DrawElementsIndirectCommand`, which corresponds to a similar structure from OpenGL. Let's take a look once again:

```
struct DrawElementsIndirectCommand {
  GLuint count_;
```

```
  GLuint instanceCount_;
  GLuint firstIndex_;
  GLuint baseVertex_;
  GLuint baseInstance_;
};
```

In the previous chapters, we had a single immutable container of commands that was immediately uploaded into a GL_DRAW_INDIRECT_BUFFER OpenGL buffer. Let's separate indirect buffers from the mesh data. Here are the steps involved:

1. A separate class would be suitable for this task, holding a container with OpenGL draw commands as well as a buffer. The maxDrawCommands parameter defines the maximum number of commands this indirect buffer can store. It can be inferred from the total number of shapes in our scene data:

```
class GLIndirectBuffer final {
  GLBuffer bufferIndirect_;
public:
  std::vector<DrawElementsIndirectCommand>
    drawCommands_;
  explicit GLIndirectBuffer(size_t maxDrawCommands)
  : bufferIndirect_(
      sizeof(DrawElementsIndirectCommand) *
    maxDrawCommands, nullptr,
    GL_DYNAMIC_STORAGE_BIT)
  , drawCommands_(maxDrawCommands)
  {}
  GLuint getHandle() const
  { return bufferIndirect_.getHandle(); }
```

2. The indirect buffer can be dynamically updated for convenience. This is handy for our **central processing unit** (**CPU**) frustum culling code implemented in the next chapter, *Chapter 10, Advanced Rendering Techniques and Optimizations*:

```
void uploadIndirectBuffer() {
  glNamedBufferSubData(bufferIndirect_.getHandle(),
    0, sizeof(DrawElementsIndirectCommand) *
    drawCommands_.size(), drawCommands_.data());
}
```

3. To simplify our work with indirect buffers, let's add one more useful operation. The `selectTo()` method takes another indirect buffer as an output parameter and populates it with draw commands that satisfy a predicate defined by a `pred` lambda. This is very handy for situations when we take one indirect buffer containing the entire scene and select draw commands that only draw meshes with specific properties, such as having transparent materials or requiring any other special handling:

```cpp
void selectTo(GLIndirectBuffer& buf,
  const std::function<bool(
    const DrawElementsIndirectCommand&)>& pred) {
  buf.drawCommands_.clear();
  for (const auto& c : drawCommands_) {
    if (pred(c))
      buf.drawCommands_.push_back(c);
  }
  buf.uploadIndirectBuffer();
}
};
```

This class is very easy to use. Let's see how it can be used with our new GLMesh class, defined here in the `Chapter9/GLMesh9.h` file. In this chapter, we will have demos with order-independent transparency that requires separate handling of opaque and transparent meshes, and a lazy-loading demo that requires a different data type than GLSceneData from *Chapter 7, Graphics Rendering Pipeline*. Let's see how to implement the new mesh class for this chapter:

1. The class is now parametrized with the scene data type. It can be the good old GLSceneData type or the new GLSceneDataLazy type, which will be discussed later in the next chapter, in the *Loading texture assets asynchronously* recipe. The data members contain all the necessary buffers, as in the previous chapter, *Chapter 8, Image-Based Techniques*, plus an instance of GLIndirectBuffer, which contains draw commands to render the entire mesh:

```cpp
template <typename GLSceneDataType>
class GLMesh final {
public:
  GLuint vao_;
  uint32_t numIndices_;
  GLBuffer bufferIndices_;
  GLBuffer bufferVertices_;
```

```
GLBuffer bufferMaterials_;
GLBuffer bufferModelMatrices_;
GLIndirectBuffer bufferIndirect_;
explicit GLMesh(const GLSceneDataType& data)
  : numIndices_(
      data.header_.indexDataSize / sizeof(uint32_t))
  , bufferIndices_(data.header_.indexDataSize,
      data.meshData_.indexData_.data(), 0)
  , bufferVertices_(data.header_.vertexDataSize,
      data.meshData_.vertexData_.data(), 0)
  , bufferMaterials_(sizeof(MaterialDescription) *
      data.materials_.size(),
      data.materials_.data(),
      GL_DYNAMIC_STORAGE_BIT)
  , bufferModelMatrices_(
      sizeof(glm::mat4) * data.shapes_.size(),
      nullptr, GL_DYNAMIC_STORAGE_BIT)
  , bufferIndirect_(data.shapes_.size())
{
  glCreateVertexArrays(1, &vao_);
  glVertexArrayElementBuffer(
    vao_, bufferIndices_.getHandle());
```

2. OpenGL vertex streams' initialization is hardcoded to `vec3` vertices, `vec3` normals, and `vec2` texture coordinates:

```
glVertexArrayVertexBuffer(
  vao_, 0, bufferVertices_.getHandle(), 0,
  sizeof(vec3) + sizeof(vec3) + sizeof(vec2));
// positions
glEnableVertexArrayAttrib(vao_, 0);
glVertexArrayAttribFormat(
  vao_, 0, 3, GL_FLOAT, GL_FALSE, 0);
glVertexArrayAttribBinding(vao_, 0, 0);
// UVs
glEnableVertexArrayAttrib(vao_, 1);
glVertexArrayAttribFormat(
  vao_, 1, 2, GL_FLOAT, GL_FALSE, sizeof(vec3));
glVertexArrayAttribBinding(vao_, 1, 0);
// normals
glEnableVertexArrayAttrib(vao_, 2);
```

```
glVertexArrayAttribFormat(
  vao_, 2, 3, GL_FLOAT, GL_TRUE,
  sizeof(vec3) + sizeof(vec2));
glVertexArrayAttribBinding(vao_, 2, 0);
std::vector<mat4> matrices(data.shapes_.size());
```

The new constructor is virtually identical to the old one, except for one tricky bit we need to mention. In the previous chapter, our bindless rendering mechanism was built around the idea that we have flat buffers of model-to-world mat4 transformations and materials. Buffers with matrices were indexed inside **OpenGL Shading Language** (**GLSL**) shaders using the integer value of gl_InstanceID, which grows monotonically from 0 to the total number of meshes minus 1. Buffers with materials were indexed values from the gl_BaseInstance built-in variable that comes from DrawElementsIndirectCommand. It was, in turn, initialized in the GLMesh constructor, using an appropriate material index for each mesh. This worked pretty well. Now, we have a slightly different situation. Once we pick a part of the draw commands to form another GLIndirectBuffer instance, we cannot use gl_InstanceID as an index because the indices are no longer sequential. There is a very neat and simple approach to overcome this limitation.

3. Let's split the DrawElementsIndirectCommand::

baseInstance 32-bit member field into two 16-bit parts. One can hold the material index while the other can hold the original index of the mesh. Simple bit-shift arithmetic packs the values, and all GLSL shaders are required to unpack them:

```
for (size_t i = 0; i != data.shapes_.size(); i++)
{
  const uint32_t meshIdx =
    data.shapes_[i].meshIndex;
  const uint32_t lod = data.shapes_[i].LOD;
  bufferIndirect_.drawCommands_[i] = {
    .count_ = data.meshData_.meshes_[meshIdx].
      getLODIndicesCount(lod),
    .instanceCount_ = 1,
    .firstIndex_ = data.shapes_[i].indexOffset,
    .baseVertex_ = data.shapes_[i].vertexOffset,
    .baseInstance_ = data.shapes_[i].materialIndex
      + (uint32_t(i) << 16)
  };
  matrices[i] = data.scene_.globalTransform_[
    data.shapes_[i].transformIndex];
}
```

```
    bufferIndirect_.uploadIndirectBuffer();
    glNamedBufferSubData(
      bufferModelMatrices_.getHandle(), 0,
      matrices.size() * sizeof(mat4),
      matrices.data());
  }
```

4. The materials uploading code is now implemented as a separate method:

```
void updateMaterialsBuffer(
  const GLSceneDataType& data)
{
  glNamedBufferSubData(bufferMaterials_.getHandle(),
    0, sizeof(MaterialDescription) *
    data.materials_.size(),
    data.materials_.data());
}
```

This is necessary to implement the *Loading texture assets asynchronously* recipe in the next chapter, where material data is uploaded to the GPU every time a new texture has streamed in from another thread.

5. The mesh-rendering code is similar to the previous chapter, except that now, we can render only a part of the scene. Instead of using the GLIndirectBuffer instance from this class, we can supply our own one, along with the number of drawing commands we want to invoke:

```
void draw(size_t numDrawCommands,
  const GLIndirectBuffer* buffer = nullptr) const
{
  glBindVertexArray(vao_);
  glBindBufferBase(GL_SHADER_STORAGE_BUFFER,
    kBufferIndex_Materials,
    bufferMaterials_.getHandle());
  glBindBufferBase(GL_SHADER_STORAGE_BUFFER,
    kBufferIndex_ModelMatrices,
    bufferModelMatrices_.getHandle());
  glBindBuffer(GL_DRAW_INDIRECT_BUFFER,
    (buffer ? *buffer :
    bufferIndirect_).getHandle());
  glMultiDrawElementsIndirect(
    GL_TRIANGLES, GL_UNSIGNED_INT,
    nullptr, (GLsizei)numDrawCommands, 0);
}
```

6. The cleanup code is straightforward, as is explicit removal of the copy constructor of this class:

```
~GLMesh() {
  glDeleteVertexArrays(1, &vao_);
}
GLMesh(const GLMesh&) = delete;
GLMesh(GLMesh&&) = default;
};
```

We can now have a single storage system for scene data and partially render it using separate indirect buffers, which can be thought of as rendering queues. We will put this class to work in the next chapter and implement CPU frustum culling for the Bistro scene. Now, let's switch to Vulkan and see how to reorganize our mesh-rendering code there.

There's more...

Here, we used `glMultiDrawElementsIndirect()` with the number of draw commands supplied from the CPU side, instead of using `glMultiDrawElementsIndirectCount()`. This might be OK for many situations; however, if we want to implement GPU culling with indirect buffer compaction, the number of draw commands has to be fetched from a GPU buffer. We will leave this as an exercise for our readers.

Working with shape lists in Vulkan

While a scene graph is a useful conceptual representation of a **three-dimensional** (3D) scene, it is not entirely suitable for GPU processing. We have already dealt with the linearization of a scene graph; now, it's time to prepare another list of renderable items, which we call **shapes**. This term coined the *Advanced Scenegraph Rendering Pipeline* presentation by Markus Tavenrath and Christoph Kubisch from NVIDIA. This list only contains references to packed meshes, introduced in *Chapter 5*, *Working with Geometry Data*, and material representation, discussed in the *Implementing a material system* recipe from *Chapter 7*, *Graphics Rendering Pipeline*. This improvement will allow us to use our `MultiRenderer` class with more complex scenes.

Getting ready

The implementation of this recipe describes the `MultiRenderer` class, which is a modification and an upgrade of `MultiMeshRenderer` from *Chapter 5, Working with Geometry Data*. Following our framework structure described in *Chapter 7, Graphics Rendering Pipeline*, in the *Managing Vulkan resources, Unifying descriptor-set creation routines*, and *Working with rendering passes* recipes, we show how to combine the material data, instanced rendering, and hierarchical transforms.

How to do it...

In *Chapter 5, Working with Geometry Data*, all the mesh rendering was performed using indirect draw commands stored in GPU buffers. The necessary GLSL shaders for indirect rendering with per-object materials support are presented in the *Implementing a material system* recipe in *Chapter 7, Graphics Rendering Pipeline*. To separate mesh and material data handling from the `Renderer` interface, which was described in the *Working with rendering passes* recipe, we introduce the `VKSceneData` data container class that stores all meshes, materials, and indirect buffers. A single instance of `VKSceneData` can be shared between multiple renderers to simplify multipass rendering techniques described in the next chapter:

1. The constructor of `VKSceneData` uses our new resources management scheme to load all the scene data. The mesh file contains vertex and index buffers for all geometry in the scene. The details of the format were described in *Chapter 5, Working with Geometry Data*. The input scene contains the linearized scene graph in the format of our scene-converter tool. A linear list of packed material data is stored in a separate file, which is also written by the `SceneConverter` tool. Environment and irradiance maps are passed from an external context because they can be shared with other renderers:

```
struct VKSceneData {
  VKSceneData(VulkanRenderContext& ctx,
    const char* meshFile,
    const char* sceneFile,
    const char* materialFile,
    VulkanTexture envMap,
    VulkanTexture irradienceMap)
    : ctx(ctx)
    , envMapIrradience_(irradienceMap)
    , envMap_(envMap)
  {
```

2. The **bidirectional reflective distribution function (BRDF) lookup table (LUT)**
    required for the PBR shading model is loaded first. After the LUT, we load material
    data and a complete list of texture files used in all materials:

    ```
    brdfLUT_ = ctx.resources.loadKTX(
      "data/brdfLUT.ktx");
    std::vector<std::string> textureFiles;
    loadMaterials(
      materialFile, materials_, textureFiles);
    ```

3. Here, we might have used `std::transform` with the parallel execution policy to
    allow the multithreaded loading of texture data. This would require some locking
    in the `VulkanResources::loadTexture2D()` method and might give a
    considerable speed-up because the majority of the loading code is context-free and
    should easily run in parallel. However, we have not implemented this approach
    because we still have to load all the textures right here. A real-world solution would be
    the deferred loading and asynchronous update of textures as soon as they are loaded:

    ```
    std::vector<VulkanTexture> textures;
    for (const auto& f: textureFiles)
        textures.push_back(
          ctx.resources.loadTexture2D(f.c_str()));
    allMaterialTextures =
      fsTextureArrayAttachment(textures);
    ```

4. Our material data is tightly packed, so after loading it from a file, we create a GPU
    storage buffer and upload the materials list without any conversions:

    ```
    const uint32_t materialsSize = (uint32_t)(
        sizeof(MaterialDescription)*materials_.size());
    material_ = ctx.resources.addStorageBuffer(
        materialsSize);
    uploadBufferData(ctx.vkDev, material_.memory, 0,
        materials_.data(), materialsSize);
    ```

5. At the end of initialization, the scene graph and mesh data is loaded:

    ```
    loadScene(sceneFile);
    loadMeshes(meshFile);
  }
    ```

6. The constructor depends on two private helper methods. The `loadScene()` method in turn uses the global scene loader from the *Loading and saving a scene graph* recipe from *Chapter 7, Graphics Rendering Pipeline*. The bulk of the method converts scene nodes with attached meshes to a list of indirect draw structures. For nodes without meshes or materials, no renderable items are generated:

```
void loadScene(const char* sceneFile) {
  ::loadScene(sceneFile, scene_);
  for (const auto& c : scene_.meshes_) {
    auto material = scene_.materialForNode_.find(
      c.first);
    if (material == scene_.materialForNode_.end())
    continue;
```

7. The shapes list is filled here just as in *Chapter 5, Working with Geometry Data*, but this time, we also store material indices. No LOD calculation is performed yet, so we set LOD to the 0-th level. In the *Implementing transformation trees* recipe from *Chapter 7, Graphics Rendering Pipeline*, we demonstrated how to effectively linearize hierarchical transform calculations. Essentially, the next line binds our scene node's global transform to the GPU-drawable element: a shape. Usage of `transformIndex` is shown in the following code snippet while discussing the `convertGlobalToShapeTransforms()` method implementation:

```
    shapes_.push_back( DrawData{
      .meshIndex = c.second,
      .materialIndex = material->second,
      .LOD = 0,
      .indexOffset = meshes_[c.second].indexOffset,
      .vertexOffset = meshes_[c.second].vertexOffset,
      .transformIndex = c.first
    });
  }
```

8. After the shape list has been created, we allocate a GPU buffer for all global transformations and recalculate all these transformations:

```
    shapeTransforms_.resize(shapes_.size());
    transforms_ = ctx.resources.addStorageBuffer(
      shapes_.size() * sizeof(glm::mat4));
    recalculateAllTransforms();
    uploadGlobalTransforms();
  }
```

9. The second helper method uses `loadMeshData()` from *Chapter 5, Working with Geometry Data,* to load the scene geometry. After loading, vertices and indices are uploaded into a single buffer. The actual code is slightly more involved because Vulkan requires sub-buffer offsets to be a multiple of the minimum alignment value. The omitted alignment code and `vertexData` padding are the same as that described in *Chapter 5, Working with Geometry Data:*

```cpp
void loadMeshes(const char* meshFile) {
  std::vector<uint32_t> indexData;
  std::vector<float> vertexData;
  MeshFileHeader header = loadMeshData(
    meshFile, meshes_, indexData, vertexData);
  uint32_t idxSize = header.indexDataSize;
  uint32_t vtxSize = header.vertexDataSize;
  auto storage = ctx.resources.addStorageBuffer(
    vtxSize + idxSize);
  uploadBufferData(ctx.vkDev, storage.memory, 0,
    vertexData.data(), vtxSize);
  uploadBufferData(ctx.vkDev, storage.memory,
    vtxSize, indexData.data(), idxSize);
}
```

Before we explain the public interface of the `VKSceneData` class, let's take a look at the encapsulated data. The references to GPU items, stored in `VulkanResources`, are cached here for quick access by external classes:

1. Three shared textures come first, which are shared by all the rendering shapes to handle PBR lighting calculations. The list of all textures used in materials is also stored here and used externally by `MultiRenderer`:

```cpp
VulkanTexture envMapIrradience_, envMap_, brdfLUT_;
TextureArrayAttachment allMaterialTextures;
```

2. Shared GPU buffers representing per-object materials and node global transformations are exposed to external classes too:

```cpp
VulkanBuffer material_, transforms_;
```

3. Probably the second largest GPU buffer after the array of textures is the mesh geometry buffer. References to its parts are stored here. An internal reference to the Vulkan context is at the end of the GPU-related fields:

```
BufferAttachment indexBuffer_, vertexBuffer_;
VulkanRenderContext& ctx;
```

To conclude the GPU part of `VKSceneData`, it is important to note that GPU buffer handles for node transformations and shape lists are not stored here because different renderers and additional processors may alter these buffers—for example, a frustum culler may remove some invisible shapes:

1. Right after the GPU buffers and textures, the `VKSceneData` class declares local CPU-accessible scene, material, and mesh data arrays:

```
Scene scene_;
std::vector<MaterialDescription> materials_;
std::vector<Mesh> meshes_;
```

2. The final part of the `VKSceneData` class contains a `shapes` list and global transformations for each shape. This is done because the list of scene nodes does not map one-to-one shapes due to the invisibility of some nodes or due to the absence of attached node geometry:

```
std::vector<glm::mat4> shapeTransforms_;
std::vector<DrawData> shapes_;
```

Let's now implement a couple of methods to handle local and global transformations of scene nodes following our data declarations:

1. This function fetches current global node transformations and assigns them to the appropriate shapes:

```
void convertGlobalToShapeTransforms() {
  size_t i = 0;
  for (const auto& c : shapes_)
    shapeTransforms_[i++] =
      scene_.globalTransform_[c.transformIndex];
}
```

2. The following method recalculates all the global transformations after marking each node as changed:

```
void recalculateAllTransforms() {
  markAsChanged(scene_, 0);
  recalculateGlobalTransforms(scene_);
}
```

The markAsChanged() function performs a recursive descent down the scene graph from the root node. Revisit the *Implementing transformation trees* recipe from *Chapter 7, Graphics Rendering Pipeline,* for its implementation details.

3. The last method of VKSceneData is a utility function that fetches global shape transforms from the node transform list and immediately uploads these transforms to the GPU buffer:

```
void uploadGlobalTransforms() {
  convertGlobalToShapeTransforms();
  uploadBufferData(ctx.vkDev, transforms_.memory, 0,
                   shapeTransforms_.data(),
                   transforms_.size);
}
};
```

We can now proceed to implement the new scene renderer with material support and the hierarchical scene graph.

With all the loading of scenes, meshes, and materials done by the VKSceneData class, it is straightforward to implement the new MultiRenderer class. Arguably, the hardest part is the initialization, which is made somewhat simpler by our new resource management:

1. The private section of the MultiRenderer class starts with a reference to the VKSceneData object. The only GPU data we use in this class is a list of indirect drawing commands and the shapes list, one for each image in the swapchain. The last few fields contain local copies of the camera-related matrices and camera-position vector:

```
class MultiRenderer: public Renderer {
  VKSceneData& sceneData_;
  std::vector<VulkanBuffer> indirect_;
  std::vector<VulkanBuffer> shape_;
  glm::mat4 proj_, model_, view_;
  glm::vec4 cameraPos_;
```

2. The constructor of the class resembles all the renderers in our new framework and takes as input references to `VulkanRenderContext` and `VKSceneData` (the names of the GLSL shaders used for rendering of this scene, which, by default, are the shaders described in the *Implementing a material system* recipe from *Chapter 7, Graphics Rendering Pipeline*) and a list of output textures for offscreen rendering. Custom render passes may be required for depth-only rendering in shadow mapping or for average lighting calculations:

```
MultiRenderer(
    VulkanRenderContext& ctx,
    VKSceneData& sceneData,
    const char* vtxShaderFile =
        DefaultMeshVertexShader,
    const char* fragShaderFile =
        DefaultMeshFragmentShader,
    const std::vector<VulkanTexture>& outputs =
        std::vector<VulkanTexture> {},
    RenderPass screenRenderPass = { .handle =
        VK_NULL_HANDLE })
  : Renderer(ctx), sceneData_(sceneData)
{
```

3. As with all the renderers, we first initialize the rendering pass and frame buffer. The shape and indirect buffers both depend on the shape list element count, but have different item sizes:

```
const PipelineInfo pInfo = initRenderPass(
    PipelineInfo {}, outputs,
    screenRenderPass, ctx.screenRenderPass);
const uint32_t indirectSize =
    sceneData_.shapes_.size() *
    sizeof(VkDrawIndirectCommand);
const uint32_t shapesSize =
    (uint32_t)sceneData_.shapes_.size() *
    sizeof(DrawData);
```

4. All the containers with per-frame GPU buffers and descriptor sets are resized to match the number of images in a swapchain:

```
const size_t imgCount =
    ctx.vkDev.swapchainImages.size();
uniforms_.resize(imgCount);
shape_.resize(imgCount);
indirect_.resize(imgCount);
descriptorSets_.resize(imgCount);
```

5. The uniform buffer layout is somewhat hardcoded here—an interested reader may change the code to pass this value into a constructor's parameter:

```
const uint32_t uniformsSize =
  sizeof(mat4) + sizeof(vec4);
```

6. The shaders use three predefined textures from the VKSceneData class. All the material-related textures reside in a separate texture array:

```
std::vector<TextureAttachment> textures;
```

7. The array is filled with push_back, but the real code also checks for textures to have non-zero width:

```
textures.push_back(
  fsTextureAttachment(sceneData_.envMap_));
textures.push_back(
 fsTextureAttachment(sceneData_.envMapIrradience_));
textures.push_back(
  fsTextureAttachment(sceneData_.brdfLUT_));
DescriptorSetInfo dsInfo = { .buffers = {
    uniformBufferAttachment(VulkanBuffer {}, 0,
      uniformBufferSize,
      VK_SHADER_STAGE_VERTEX_BIT |
      VK_SHADER_STAGE_FRAGMENT_BIT),
    sceneData_.vertexBuffer_,
    sceneData_.indexBuffer_,
    storageBufferAttachment(VulkanBuffer {}, 0,
      shapesSize,
      VK_SHADER_STAGE_VERTEX_BIT),
    storageBufferAttachment(sceneData_.material_, 0,
      sceneData_.material_.size,
      VK_SHADER_STAGE_FRAGMENT_BIT),
    storageBufferAttachment(
      sceneData_.transforms_, 0,
      sceneData_.transforms_.size,
      VK_SHADER_STAGE_VERTEX_BIT),
  },
  .textures = textures,
  .textureArrays =
    { sceneData_.allMaterialTextures }
};
```

8. After allocating the descriptor-set layout and descriptor pool, we create per-frame indirect and uniform buffers:

```
descriptorSetLayout_ = ctx.resources.
  addDescriptorSetLayout(dsInfo);
descriptorPool_ = ctx.resources.
  addDescriptorPool(dsInfo, imgCount);
for (size_t i = 0; i != imgCount; i++) {
  uniforms_[i] =
    ctx.resources.addUniformBuffer(uniformSize);
  indirect_[i] =
    ctx.resources.addIndirectBuffer(indirectSize);
  updateIndirectBuffers(i);
  shape_[i] =
    ctx.resources.addStorageBuffer(shapesSize);
  uploadBufferData(ctx.vkDev, shape_[i].memory, 0,
    sceneData_.shapes_.data(), shapesSize);
  dsInfo.buffers[0].buffer = uniforms_[i];
  dsInfo.buffers[3].buffer = shape_[i];
  descriptorSets_[i] =
    ctx.resources.addDescriptorSet(
      descriptorPool_, descriptorSetLayout_);
  ctx.resources.updateDescriptorSet(
    descriptorSets_[i], dsInfo);
}
```

9. The final step in initialization is pipeline creation with the user-specified shader stages:

```
initPipeline(
  { vertShaderFile, fragShaderFile }, pInfo);
}
```

10. The rendering logic in the `fillCommandBuffer()` method is extremely simple. Believe it or not, the entire loaded scene is rendered while a single indirect draw command is executed on the Vulkan graphics queue:

```
void fillCommandBuffer(VkCommandBuffer cmdBuffer,
  size_t currentImage,
  VkFramebuffer fb = VK_NULL_HANDLE,
  VkRenderPass rp = VK_NULL_HANDLE) override
{
  beginRenderPass(
    (rp != VK_NULL_HANDLE) ?
```

```
            rp : renderPass_.handle,
      (fb != VK_NULL_HANDLE) ? fb : framebuffer_,
          commandBuffer, currentImage);
    vkCmdDrawIndirect(commandBuffer,
      indirect_[currentImage].buffer,
      0, (uint32_t)sceneData_.shapes_.size(),
      sizeof(VkDrawIndirectCommand));
    vkCmdEndRenderPass(commandBuffer);
  }
```

11. The `updateBuffers()` overridden method uploads the current camera transformation and world position:

```
void updateBuffers(size_t currentImage) override {
  updateUniformBuffer((uint32_t)imageIndex, 0,
    sizeof(glm::mat4),
    glm::value_ptr(proj_ * view_ * model_));
  updateUniformBuffer((uint32_t)imageIndex,
    sizeof(glm::mat4), 4 * sizeof(float),
    glm::value_ptr(cameraPos_));
  }
```

The `updateIndirectBuffers()` method is almost identical to the same method from the `MultiMeshRenderer` class in *Chapter 5, Working with Geometry Data*. The only difference is in the usage of the `VKSceneData` object as a container of the `shapes` list. Here are the steps involved:

1. The indirect command buffer is updated using a local memory mapping:

```
void updateIndirectBuffers(
  size_t currentImage, bool* visibility = nullptr)
  {
    VkDrawIndirectCommand* data = nullptr;
    vkMapMemory(ctx_.vkDev.device,
      indirect_[currentImage].memory, 0,
      sizeof(VkDrawIndirectCommand), 0, (void**)&data);
```

2. Each of the shapes in a scene gets its own draw command:

```
const uint32_t size =
  (uint32_t)sceneData_.shapes_.size();
for (uint32_t i = 0; i != size; i++) {
  const uint32_t j =
    sceneData_.shapes_[i].meshIndex;
  const uint32_t lod = sceneData_.shapes_[i].LOD;
```

3. The draw command extracts a vertex count from the LOD information of this shape. If we have CPU-generated visibility information, we may set the instance count to 0. This will be used in the next chapter to implement frustum culling on the CPU:

```
data[i] = {
    .vertexCount =
    sceneData_.meshes_[j].getLODIndicesCount(lod),
    .instanceCount = visibility ?
        (visibility[i] ? 1u : 0u) : 1u,
```

4. Each rendering command here starts with a 0-th vertex. A brief discussion of how we may use individual draw commands for submeshes can be found in the *Doing frustum culling on the GPU with compute shaders* recipe from *Chapter 10, Advanced Rendering Techniques and Optimizations*. The first instance value is set to be the current shape's index, and it is handled in the GLSL shader manually:

```
    .firstVertex = 0,
    .firstInstance = i
    };
}
vkUnmapMemory(ctx_.vkDev.device,
    indirect_[currentImage].memory);
}
```

There are a couple of helper methods in the class, and they both deal with a 3D camera:

1. The `setMatrices()` method stores the camera matrices for later uploading to the GPU uniform buffer:

```
void setMatrices(const glm::mat4& proj,
    const glm::mat4& view, const glm::mat4& model) {
    proj_ = proj; view_ = view; model_ = model;
}
```

2. Another one-liner function stores a local copy of the current camera position for lighting calculations:

```
void setCameraPosition(const glm::vec3& cameraPos) {
    cameraPos_ = glm::vec4(cameraPos, 1.0f);
}
};
```

The MultiRenderer class is used in all of the demo applications for this chapter. *Chapter 8, Image-Based Techniques,* explains how the MultiRenderer class fits into the postprocessing pipeline, and in the next chapter, *Chapter 10, Advanced Rendering Techniques and Optimizations*, we will see how to optimize indirect rendering using CPU and GPU frustum culling.

Adding Bullet physics to a graphics application

Before we conclude the business of this chapter, let's touch on one more topic, which is not a 3D rendering matter but links very closely to our 3D scene implementation. This recipe shows how to animate individual visual objects in our scene graph by using a rigid-body physics simulation library, Bullet (https://github.com/bulletphysics/bullet3).

Getting ready

To compile the Bullet library, we use a custom CMakeLists.txt file, so it is useful to recall the general CMake workflow for third-party libraries covered in *Chapter 2, Using Essential Libraries.*

The demo application for this recipe can be found in the Chapter9/VK01_Physics folder.

How to do it...

1. To simulate a collection of rigid bodies, we implement the Physics class, which calls the appropriate libBullet methods to create, manage, and update physical objects:

```
struct Physics {
  Physics()
  : collisionDispatcher(&collisionConfiguration)
  , dynamicsWorld(&collisionDispatcher, &broadphase,
      &solver, &collisionConfiguration)
  {
    dynamicsWorld.setGravity(
      btVector3( 0.0f, -9.8f, 0.0f ) );
    // add "floor" object - large massless box
    addBox( vec3(100.f, 0.05f, 100.f),
      btQuaternion(0,0,0,1), vec3(0,0,0), 0.0f);
  }
```

```
    void addBox( const vec3& halfSize,
      const btQuaternion& orientation,
      const vec3& position, float mass);
    void update(float deltaSeconds);
    std::vector<mat4> boxTransform;
  private:
    std::vector<std::uninque_ptr<btRigidBody>>
      rigidBodies;
    btDefaultCollisionConfiguration
      collisionConfiguration;
    btCollisionDispatcher collisionDispatcher;
    btDbvtBroadphase broadphase;
    btSequentialImpulseConstraintSolver solver;
    btDiscreteDynamicsWorld dynamicsWorld;
  };
```

The synchronization point with our rendering framework is the update() method.

2. First, we call the stepSimulation() method from the Bullet **application programming interface** (**API**), which calculates new positions and orientations for each rigid body participating in the simulation:

```
void Physics::update(float deltaSeconds)
{
  dynamicsWorld.stepSimulation(
    deltaSeconds, 10, 0.01f);
```

3. The synchronization itself consists of fetching the transformation for each active body and storing that transformation in glm::mat4 format in the boxTransform array. Our rendering application subsequently fetches that array and uploads it into a GPU buffer for rendering:

```
  for (size_t i = 0; i != rigidBodies.size(); i++) {
    if (!rigidBodies[i]->isActive()) continue;
    btTransform trans;
    rigidBodies[i]->
      getMotionState()->getWorldTransform(trans);
    trans.getOpenGLMatrix(
      glm::value_ptr(boxTransform[i]));
  }
}
```

4. A helper routine converts between `Bullet` and `glm` 3D vector representations:

```
static btVector3 Vec3ToBulletVec3( const vec3& v ) {
    return btVector3( v.x, v.y, v.z );
}
```

5. The creation of a single solid box object proceeds as follows. Refer to the `Bullet` documentation for the details of this, as we are focusing on the rendering part only:

```
void Physics::addBox( const glm::vec3& halfSize,
    const btQuaternion& orientation,
    const vec3& position,
    float mass)
{
    boxSizes.push_back(halfSize);
    boxTransform.push_back(glm::mat4(1.0f));
    btCollisionShape* collisionShape =
        new btBoxShape( Vec3ToBulletVec3(halfSize) );
    btDefaultMotionState* motionState =
        new btDefaultMotionState(
            btTransform(orientation,
            Vec3ToBulletVec3(position)) );
    btVector3 localInertia(0, 0, 0);
    collisionShape->calculateLocalInertia(
        mass, localInertia );
    btRigidBody::btRigidBodyConstructionInfo
        rigidBodyCI(mass, motionState,
            collisionShape, localInertia);
    rigidBodyCI.m_friction = 0.1f;
    rigidBodyCI.m_rollingFriction = 0.1f;
```

6. A new `btRigidBody` object is created and stored in the `rigidBodies` array for later use. We register the rigid body in the `dynamicsWorld` simulation object:

```
    rigidBodies.emplace_back(
        std::make_unique<btRigidBody>(rigidBodyCI));
    dynamicsWorld.addRigidBody(
        rigidBodies.back().get());
}
```

To render rigid-body objects simulated with the `Physics` class, we convert global transformations from the `Physics::boxTransform` array into individual node transformations.

Let's look into how the `Physics` class can be used together with our Vulkan scene-rendering code:

1. The application class uses `MultiRenderer` to draw a scene:

```
struct MyApp: public CameraApp {
  MyApp()
  : CameraApp(-90, -90)
  , plane(ctx)
  , sceneData(ctx, "data/meshes/cube.meshes",
      "data/meshes/cube.scene",
      "data/meshes/cube.material", {}, {})
  , multiRenderer(ctx, sceneData,
      "data/shaders/chapter09/VK01_Simple.vert",
      "data/shaders/chapter09/VK01_Simple.frag")
  , imgui(ctx) {
    onScreenRenderers.emplace_back(plane, false);
    onScreenRenderers.emplace_back(multiRenderer);
    onScreenRenderers.emplace_back(imgui, false);
  }
```

2. The `drawUI()` method provides a way to add more objects to the scene:

```
void drawUI() override {
  ImGui::Begin("Settings", nullptr);
  ImGui::Text("FPS: %.2f", getFPS());
  if (ImGui::Button("Add body"))
    if (physics.boxSizes.size() < maxCubes)
      physics.addRandom();
  ImGui::End();
}
```

3. The `draw3D()` method overrides global transformations for simulated nodes. Since, in this demo, all the objects are simulated, we explicitly update each node's global transform:

```
void draw3D() override {
  const mat4 p = getDefaultProjection();
  const mat4 view = camera.getViewMatrix();
  multiRenderer.setMatrices(
    p, view, glm::mat4(1.f));
```

```
multiRenderer.setCameraPosition(
  positioner.getPosition());
plane.setMatrices(p, view, glm::mat4(1.f));
sceneData.scene_.globalTransform_[0] =
  glm::mat4(1.f);
for (size_t i = 1;
     i < physics.boxSizes.size(); i++) {
  sceneData.scene_.globalTransform_[i] =
    physics.boxTransform[i] * glm::scale(
      glm::mat4(1.f), physics.boxSizes[i]);
}
for (size_t i = physics.boxSizes.size();
     i <= maxCubes; i++) {
  sceneData.scene_.globalTransform_[i] =
    glm::mat4(1.f);
}
}
```

4. The `update()` method allows us to call our physics simulator:

```
void update(float deltaSeconds) override {
  CameraApp::update(deltaSeconds);
  physics.update(deltaSeconds);
  sceneData.uploadGlobalTransforms();
}
```

5. The private data contains all the renderers and a `Physics` instance:

```
private:
  InfinitePlaneRenderer plane;
  VKSceneData sceneData;
  MultiRenderer;
  GuiRenderer imgui;
  Physics;
};
```

The running physics demo should render an image like this:

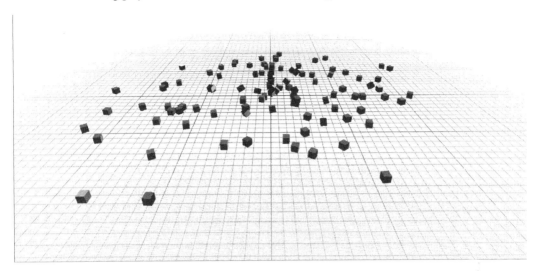

Figure 9.2 – Physics simulation using Bullet

Other components can be added to this scene-graph implementation using the described approach, making it extensible enough to cover many real-world situations.

There's more...

Since `Bullet` provides a set of powerful collision-detection routines, a minor extension to the code may add accelerated mouse-pointer object picking for interactive editing or manipulation of objects in a 3D scene.

10

Advanced Rendering Techniques and Optimizations

In this chapter, we will touch on a few more advanced topics, as well as show you how to integrate multiple effects and techniques into a single graphical application.

This chapter will cover the following recipes:

- Doing frustum culling on the CPU
- Doing frustum culling on the GPU with compute shaders
- Implementing order-independent transparency
- Loading texture assets asynchronously
- Implementing projective shadows for directional lights
- Using GPU atomic counters in Vulkan
- Putting it all together into an OpenGL demo

Technical requirements

To run the recipes in this chapter, you need to use a computer with a video card that supports OpenGL 4.6 with `ARB_bindless_texture` and Vulkan 1.2. Read *Chapter 1, Establishing a Build Environment*, if you want to learn how to build the demo applications shown in this book.

This chapter relies on the geometry loading code that was explained in *Chapter 7, Graphics Rendering Pipeline*, and the lightweight OpenGL rendering queues we described in *Chapter 9, Working with Scene Graphs*. Make sure you read both these chapters before proceeding any further.

You can find the code files present in this chapter on GitHub at `https://github.com/PacktPublishing/3D-Graphics-Rendering-Cookbook/tree/master/Chapter10`.

Doing frustum culling on the CPU

Frustum culling is used to determine whether a part of our scene is visible from a viewing frustum. There are many tutorials on the internet that show how to do this. However, most of them have a significant drawback.

Many frustum culling examples, as was pointed out by Inigo Quilez in his blog `http://www.iquilezles.org/www/articles/frustumcorrect/frustumcorrect.htm`, end up checking if a mesh is outside the viewing frustum by comparing it with six viewing frustum planes. The mesh's **axis-aligned bounding box** (**AABB**) is used for this. Then, anything that lies on the outer side of any of these planes is rejected. This approach will produce false positives when a big enough AABB, which is not visible, intersects some of the frustum planes. The naive approach will accept these AABBs as visible, thereby reducing the culling efficiency. If we are talking about culling individual meshes, taking care of such cases may not be worth it performance-wise. However, if we cull big boxes that are containers of some sort, such as parts of an oct-tree, false positives may become a significant problem. The solution is to add a reversed culling test where eight frustum corner points are tested against six planes of an AABB.

In this recipe, we will show you some self-contained frustum culling code in C++ and teach you how to use it to render the Bistro scene.

Getting ready

Make sure you have checked the *Implementing lightweight rendering queues in OpenGL* recipe in *Chapter 9, Working with Scene Graphs*, so that you know how the new `GLMesh` class operates.

The example source code for this demo can be found in `Chapter10/GL01_CullingCPU`.

How to do it…

To implement both box-in-frustum and frustum-in-box tests, we must extract six frustum planes and eight frustum corner points from our view matrix. Here's the code to do so:

1. By default, GLM uses a right-handed coordinate system. This way, six frustum planes are extracted from the transposed, pre-multiplied view-projection matrix, vp:

```
void getFrustumPlanes(glm::mat4 vp, glm::vec4* planes) {
  using glm::vec4;
  vp = glm::transpose(vp);
  planes[0] = vec4(vp[3] + vp[0]); // left
  planes[1] = vec4(vp[3] - vp[0]); // right
  planes[2] = vec4(vp[3] + vp[1]); // bottom
  planes[3] = vec4(vp[3] - vp[1]); // top
  planes[4] = vec4(vp[3] + vp[2]); // near
  planes[5] = vec4(vp[3] - vp[2]); // far
}
```

2. The eight frustum corner points can be produced by taking a unit cube and transforming it with the inverse of the pre-multiplied view-projection matrix and performing perspective division:

```
void getFrustumCorners(
  glm::mat4 vp, glm::vec4* points)
{
  using glm::vec4;
  const vec4 corners[] = {
    vec4(-1, -1, -1, 1), vec4( 1, -1, -1, 1),
    vec4( 1,  1, -1, 1), vec4(-1,  1, -1, 1),
    vec4(-1, -1,  1, 1), vec4( 1, -1,  1, 1),
    vec4( 1,  1,  1, 1), vec4(-1,  1,  1, 1)
  };
  const glm::mat4 invVP = glm::inverse(vp);
  for (int i = 0; i != 8; i++) {
    const vec4 q = invVP * corners[i];
    points[i] = q / q.w;
  }
}
```

3. Now, the culling code is straightforward. Let's check if a bounding box is fully outside any of the six frustum planes:

```
bool isBoxInFrustum(glm::vec4* frPlanes,
                    glm::vec4* frCorners,
                    const BoundingBox& b)
{
  using glm::dot;
  using glm::vec4;
  for ( int i = 0; i < 6; i++ ) {
    int r = 0;
    r +=(dot(frPlanes[i],
      vec4(b.min_.x,b.min_.y,b.min_.z,1.f))<0) ? 1:0;
    r +=(dot(frPlanes[i],
      vec4(b.max_.x,b.min_.y,b.min_.z,1.f))<0) ? 1:0;
    r +=(dot(frPlanes[i],
      vec4(b.min_.x,b.max_.y,b.min_.z,1.f))<0) ? 1:0;
    r +=(dot(frPlanes[i],
      vec4(b.max_.x,b.max_.y,b.min_.z,1.f))<0) ? 1:0;
    r +=(dot(frPlanes[i],
      vec4(b.min_.x,b.min_.y,b.max_.z,1.f))<0) ? 1:0;
    r +=(dot(frPlanes[i],
      vec4(b.max_.x,b.min_.y,b.max_.z,1.f))<0) ? 1:0;
    r +=(dot(frPlanes[i],
      vec4(b.min_.x,b.max_.y,b.max_.z,1.f))<0) ? 1:0;
    r +=(dot(frPlanes[i],
      vec4(b.max_.x,b.max_.y,b.max_.z,1.f))<0) ? 1:0;
    if (r == 8) return false;
  }
```

> **Note**
>
> Whether something is "inside" or "outside" of a plane is determined by the direction of its normal vector.

4. Then, we can check if the same frustum is inside the box:

```
  int r = 0;
  r = 0; for (int i = 0; i<8; i++)
    r+=((frCorners[i].x>b.max_.x) ? 1:0);
  if (r == 8) return false;
  r = 0; for (int i = 0; i<8; i++)
    r+=((frCorners[i].x<b.min_.x) ? 1:0);
```

```
      if (r == 8) return false;
      r = 0; for (int i = 0; i<8; i++)
        r+=((frCorners[i].y>b.max_.y) ? 1:0);
      if (r == 8) return false;
      r = 0; for (int i = 0; i<8; i++)
        r+=((frCorners[i].y<b.min_.y) ? 1:0);
      if (r == 8) return false;
      r = 0; for (int i = 0; i<8; i++)
        r+=((frCorners[i].z>b.max_.z) ? 1:0);
      if (r == 8) return false;
      r = 0; for (int i = 0; i<8; i++)
        r+=((frCorners[i].z<b.min_.z) ? 1:0);
      if (r == 8) return false;
      return true;
  }
```

Let's take a look at how this culling code can be used in our demos. The main driving code is in the `Chapter10/GL01_CullingCPU/src/main.cpp` file:

1. Our per-frame uniform buffer is unified across all the demos in this chapter because we are using a single set of shaders to render most of the Bistro scene. That's why we have `light` and `cameraPos` here. The GLSL code will check if `light[3][3]` is zero and skip shadow rendering if so:

```
struct PerFrameData {
  mat4 view;
  mat4 proj;
  mat4 light = mat4(0.0f); // unused in this demo
  vec4 cameraPos;
};
```

2. We have a standard camera positioner with a camera, which is used to initialize our view matrix for culling. In this demo, we will allow users to "freeze" a culling frustum and fly around to observe which objects are being culled. All other global variables are used to control the rendering from ImGui:

```
CameraPositioner_FirstPerson positioner(
  vec3(-10.0f, 3.0f, 3.0f), vec3(0.0f, 0.0f, -1.0f),
  vec3(0.0f, 1.0f, 0.0f));
Camera camera(positioner);
mat4 g_CullingView = camera.getViewMatrix();
bool g_FreezeCullingView = false;
```

```
bool g_DrawMeshes = true;
bool g_DrawBoxes = true;
bool g_DrawGrid = true;
```

3. The main() function starts by loading a set of shaders. We will reuse the grid rendering code from the *Implementing an infinite grid GLSL shader* recipe of *Chapter 5, Working with Geometry Data*. The GL01_scene_IBL.vert and GL01_scene_IBL.frag scene rendering shaders are universal for all the demos in this chapter. They are rather similar to the ones we used in the previous chapter, except for the shadow mapping part, which will be discussed later in this chapter, in the *Implementing projective shadows for directional lights* recipe:

```
int main(void) {
  GLApp app;
  GLShader shdGridVert(
    "data/shaders/chapter05/GL01_grid.vert");
  GLShader shdGridFrag(
    "data/shaders/chapter05/GL01_grid.frag");
  GLProgram progGrid(shdGridVert, shdGridFrag);
  GLShader shaderVert(
    "data/shaders/chapter10/GL01_scene_IBL.vert");
  GLShader shaderFrag(
    "data/shaders/chapter10/GL01_scene_IBL.frag");
  GLProgram program(shaderVert, shaderFrag);
```

4. Create a buffer for our per-frame uniforms and configure some global OpenGL states:

```
const GLsizeiptr kUniformBufferSize =
  sizeof(PerFrameData);
GLBuffer perFrameDataBuffer(
  kUniformBufferSize, nullptr,
  GL_DYNAMIC_STORAGE_BIT);
glBindBufferRange(GL_UNIFORM_BUFFER,
  kBufferIndex_PerFrameUniforms,
  perFrameDataBuffer.getHandle(), 0,
  kUniformBufferSize);
glClearColor(1.0f, 1.0f, 1.0f, 1.0f);
glBlendFunc(GL_SRC_ALPHA, GL_ONE_MINUS_SRC_ALPHA);
```

Instead of keeping two separate GLSceneData instances for the external and internal meshes of the Bistro scene, we have merged everything into one big mesh. This is done in the SceneConverter tool, which we covered in *Chapter 7, Graphics Rendering Pipeline*. Furthermore, the original Bistro scene contains a tree with thousands of leaves in it, represented as separate meshes. Our merging code compacts separate meshes for leaves into one single mesh. The code is quite specific for the Bistro scene because it uses explicit names for the materials that the meshes should be merged with. Check the mergeBistro() function in Chapter7/SceneConverter/ src/main.cpp for more details. The GLMesh class here comes from Chapter9/ GLMesh9.h and was discussed in the previous chapter. Check the *Implementing lightweight rendering queues in OpenGL* recipe for more details:

```
GLSceneData sceneData(
    "data/meshes/bistro_all.meshes",
    "data/meshes/bistro_all.scene",
    "data/meshes/bistro_all.materials");
GLMesh mesh(sceneData);
```

5. We will skip the code that sets up glfwSetCursorPosCallback(), glfwSetMouseButtonCallback(), and glfwSetKeyCallback() here and get straight to the rendering-related code. The GLSkyboxRenderer class is declared in Chapter9/GLSkyboxRenderer.h and is used to render the skybox and store light probes for radiance and irradiance, as well as the BRDF LUT texture. The ImGuiGLRenderer class was described in the *Rendering a basic UI with Dear ImGui* recipe of *Chapter 2, Using Essential Libraries*. The minimalist implementation we are providing here can be found in the shared/UtilsGLImGui.h file:

```
GLSkyboxRenderer skybox;
ImGuiGLRenderer rendererUI;
CanvasGL canvas;
```

Now, we have reached the part that's related to frustum culling. We must store bounding boxes for each shape object in our scene data. Considering that the entire scene geometry is static, we can pre-transform all the boxes into world space using the corresponding model-to-world matrices.

6. One big bounding box, called `fullScene`, which encloses the entire scene, will be used to render debug information:

```
for (const auto& c : sceneData.shapes_) {
  mat4 model = sceneData.
    scene_.globalTransform_[c.transformIndex];
  sceneData.meshData_.
    boxes_[c.meshIndex].transform(model);
}
BoundingBox fullScene =
  combineBoxes(sceneData.meshData_.boxes_);
```

7. The main loop goes through the traditional camera position update, sets up the OpenGL viewport, and clears the framebuffer. Once we have all these values, we can fill in the `PerFrameData` structure and upload it to the OpenGL buffer:

```
while (!glfwWindowShouldClose(app.getWindow())) {
    positioner.update(
      app.getDeltaSeconds(), mouseState.pos,
      mouseState.pressedLeft);
    int width, height;
    glfwGetFramebufferSize(
      app.getWindow(), &width, &height);
    const float ratio = width / (float)height;
    glViewport(0, 0, width, height);
    glClearNamedFramebufferfv(0, GL_COLOR, 0,
      glm::value_ptr(vec4(0.0f, 0.0f, 0.0f, 1.0f)));
    glClearNamedFramebufferfi(
      0, GL_DEPTH_STENCIL, 0, 1.0f, 0);
    const mat4 proj = glm::perspective(
      45.0f, ratio, 0.1f, 1000.0f);
    const mat4 view = camera.getViewMatrix();
    const PerFrameData perFrameData = {
      .view = view,
      .proj = proj,
      .light = mat4(0.0f),
      .cameraPos =
        glm::vec4(camera.getPosition(), 1.0f) };
    glNamedBufferSubData(
      perFrameDataBuffer.getHandle(), 0,
      kUniformBufferSize, &perFrameData);
```

8. The culling frustum is separate from our camera's viewing frustum. This is very handy for debugging and pure demonstration. 6 frustum planes and 8 corners are extracted from the pre-multiplied `proj*g_CullingView` matrix:

```
if (!g_FreezeCullingView)
    g_CullingView = camera.getViewMatrix();
vec4 frustumPlanes[6];
getFrustumPlanes(
    proj * g_CullingView, frustumPlanes);
vec4 frustumCorners[8];
getFrustumCorners(
    proj * g_CullingView, frustumCorners);
```

9. Here goes the culling loop. Let's iterate over all the drawing commands in the indirect buffer, get the appropriate bounding box for each one, and check its visibility. Instead of manipulating the order of the draw commands in the buffer, we will set the number of instances to 0 for any object that was culled. Once the new content of the indirect buffer has been uploaded to the GPU, we are ready to render the culled scene:

```
int numVisibleMeshes = 0;
{
    DrawElementsIndirectCommand* cmd =
        mesh.bufferIndirect_.drawCommands_.data();
    for (const auto& c : sceneData.shapes_) {
        cmd->instanceCount_ = isBoxInFrustum(
            frustumPlanes, frustumCorners,
            sceneData.meshData_.
            boxes_[c.meshIndex]) ? 1 : 0;
        numVisibleMeshes += (cmd++)->instanceCount_;
    }
    mesh.bufferIndirect_.uploadIndirectBuffer();
}
```

10. Let's do some debug drawing before we render the actual scene. We will render a red bounding box for every invisible mesh and a green box for visible ones. The `fullScene` box shows the bounds of the entire scene:

```
if (g_DrawBoxes) {
    DrawElementsIndirectCommand* cmd =
        mesh.bufferIndirect_.drawCommands_.data();
    for (const auto& c : sceneData.shapes_)
```

```
        drawBox3dGL(canvas, mat4(1.0f),
          sceneData.meshData_.boxes_[c.meshIndex],
          (cmd++)->instanceCount_ ?
          vec4(0,1,0,1) : vec4(1,0,0,1));
      drawBox3dGL(canvas,
        mat4(1.0f), fullScene, vec4(1,0,0,1));
    }
```

11. The actual scene rendering goes like so. Here, we have a skybox, the Bistro scene, and an optional grid:

```
skybox.draw();
glDisable(GL_BLEND);
glEnable(GL_DEPTH_TEST);
if (g_DrawMeshes) {
  program.useProgram();
  mesh.draw(sceneData.shapes_.size());
}
if (g_DrawGrid) {
  glEnable(GL_BLEND);
  progGrid.useProgram();
  glDrawArraysInstancedBaseInstance(
    GL_TRIANGLES, 0, 6, 1, 0);
}
```

12. If we want to freeze the culling frustum, we must render it with yellow lines. This will help us debug the application and observe how culling behaves in different situations:

```
if (g_FreezeCullingView)
    renderCameraFrustumGL(canvas,
      g_CullingView, proj, vec4(1, 1, 0, 1), 100);
canvas.flush();
```

13. To conclude the main loop and this entire demo, the remaining ImGui code controls the application parameters, as well as displays the number of visible meshes:

```
ImGuiIO& io = ImGui::GetIO();
io.DisplaySize =
  ImVec2((float)width, (float)height);
ImGui::NewFrame();
ImGui::Begin("Control", nullptr);
```

```
        ImGui::Text("Draw:");
        ImGui::Checkbox("Meshes", &g_DrawMeshes);
        ImGui::Checkbox("Boxes",  &g_DrawBoxes);
        ImGui::Checkbox("Grid",   &g_DrawGrid);
        ImGui::Separator();
        ImGui::Checkbox("Freeze culling frustum (P)",
          &g_FreezeCullingView);
        ImGui::Separator();
        ImGui::Text("Visible meshes: %i",
          numVisibleMeshes);
        ImGui::End();
        ImGui::Render();
        rendererUI.render(
          width, height, ImGui::GetDrawData());
        app.swapBuffers();
    }
    return 0;
}
```

Here is a screenshot from the running demo:

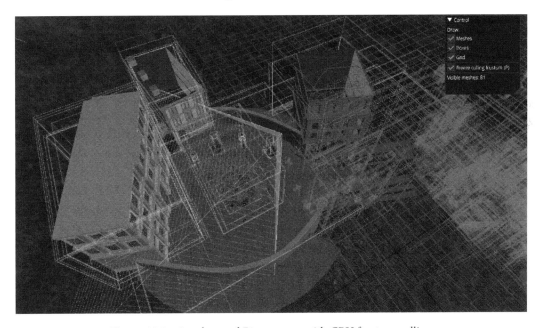

Figure 10.1 – Lumberyard Bistro scene with CPU frustum culling

The culling frustum, rendered with yellow lines, is frozen so that we can observe its orientation. The green boxes highlight visible meshes, while the red boxes are for invisible ones. Each time the *P* key is pressed, the culling frustum is realigned with the view of the camera.

There's more...

You might be thinking that this kind of culling is inefficient because modern GPUs can render small meshes much faster than we can cull them on the CPU. This is mostly true. It does not make sense to cull small things such as bottles or separate leaves this way. However, the CPU culling pipeline still matters if we want to cull big clusters of objects. For example, if we create a 3D grid that covers the entire Bistro scene and has reasonably big cells, we can assign each mesh to cells that intersect it. Now, CPU culling can be applied to each cell instead of individual meshes, completely skipping its entire content. We leave this approach as a moderately complex exercise for you.

Let's try to improve things a bit and move the entire frustum culling pipeline completely to the GPU via compute shaders.

Doing frustum culling on the GPU with compute shaders

In the previous recipe, we learned how to cull invisible meshes on the CPU in a classic and somewhat old-fashioned way. As GPUs grew more and more performant, this CPU-based approach became very inefficient. Let's learn how to utilize compute shaders to implement a frustum culling pipeline on a GPU using OpenGL.

The goal of this recipe is to teach you what you can do on modern GPUs with compute pipelines rather than implementing a very performant culling system. Once we are comfortable with the basics, we will discuss the limitations, as well as further directions for improvements.

Getting ready

Make sure you have read the previous recipe, *Doing frustum culling on the CPU*, so that you're familiar with the frustum culling basics.

The source code for this recipe can be found at `Chapter10/GL02_CullingGPU`.

How to do it...

Let's take a look at how we can port the C++ culling code from the previous recipe to the GLSL compute shaders:

1. The main application starts by declaring per-frame uniform data. Besides the first four fields, which are necessary for our unified GLSL shaders, we will add a few more variables that pass frustum parameters to the GLSL code. Similar to the previous recipe, we need 6 frustum planes and 8 frustum corners. The total number of shapes to cull is passed to the shaders to allow proper bounds checking:

```
struct PerFrameData {
  mat4 view;
  mat4 proj;
  mat4 light = mat4(0.0f); // unused in this demo
  vec4 cameraPos;
  vec4 frustumPlanes[6];
  vec4 frustumCorners[8];
  uint32_t numShapesToCull;
};
```

2. Let's look at some variables that can control the camera and culling parameters. This time, all the culling happens on the GPU side and we do not read back the culling results to render colored bounding boxes. Hence, we have fewer variables here:

```
CameraPositioner_FirstPerson positioner(
  vec3(-10.f, 3.f, 3.f), vec3(0.f, 0.f, -1.f),
  vec3(0.f, 1.f, 0.f));
Camera camera(positioner);
mat4 g_CullingView = camera.getViewMatrix();
bool g_FreezeCullingView = false;
bool g_EnableGPUCulling = true;
```

3. The main() function structure is similar to the one shown in the previous recipe. Besides the grid and scene shaders, we will load a compute shader called GL02_FrustumCulling.comp, which performs culling:

```
int main(void) {
  GLApp app;
  GLShader shdGridVert(
    "data/shaders/chapter05/GL01_grid.vert");
```

```
GLShader shdGridFrag(
  "data/shaders/chapter05/GL01_grid.frag");
GLProgram progGrid(shdGridVert, shdGridFrag);
GLShader shaderVert(
  "data/shaders/chapter10/GL01_scene_IBL.vert");
GLShader shaderFrag(
  "data/shaders/chapter10/GL01_scene_IBL.frag");
GLProgram program(shaderVert, shaderFrag);
GLShader shaderCulling(
  "data/shaders/chapter10/GL02_FrustumCulling.comp");
GLProgram programCulling(shaderCulling);
```

4. To pass the bounding boxes to the culling shader, we need to allocate an OpenGL buffer for them. The culling compute shader uses 3 buffers. Two buffers are used as inputs to read bounding boxes and draw commands. The third one contains a single integer value and is used to read back the number of culled meshes to the CPU side for debugging. The binding points for these buffers go sequentially after `kBufferIndex_PerFrameUniforms`:

```
const GLuintkMaxNumObjects = 128 * 1024;
const GLsizeiptr kUniformBufferSize =
  sizeof(PerFrameData);
const GLsizeiptr kBoundingBoxesBufferSize =
  sizeof(BoundingBox) * kMaxNumObjects;
const GLuint kBufferIndex_BoundingBoxes =
  kBufferIndex_PerFrameUniforms + 1;
const GLuint kBufferIndex_DrawCommands =
  kBufferIndex_PerFrameUniforms + 2;
const GLuint kBufferIndex_NumVisibleMeshes =
  BufferIndex_PerFrameUniforms + 3;
GLBuffer perFrameDataBuffer(kUniformBufferSize,
  nullptr, GL_DYNAMIC_STORAGE_BIT);
glBindBufferRange(GL_UNIFORM_BUFFER,
  kBufferIndex_PerFrameUniforms,
  perFrameDataBuffer.getHandle(), 0,
  kUniformBufferSize);
GLBuffer boundingBoxesBuffer(
  kBoundingBoxesBufferSize, nullptr,
  GL_DYNAMIC_STORAGE_BIT);
```

5. The previous recipe implemented all the culling on the CPU, so it was rather trivial to compute the number of visible meshes. The GPU culling is a bit trickier, though; we need to read a value from the GPU buffer back to the CPU to find out how many meshes are visible. Let's create a buffer with a single integer value and map its content to the CPU memory:

```
GLBuffer numVisibleMeshesBuffer(sizeof(uint32_t),
    nullptr, GL_MAP_READ_BIT | GL_MAP_WRITE_BIT |
    GL_MAP_PERSISTENT_BIT | GL_MAP_COHERENT_BIT);
volatile uint32_t* numVisibleMeshesPtr =
  (uint32_t*)glMapNamedBuffer(
      numVisibleMeshesBuffer.getHandle(),
      GL_READ_WRITE);
assert(numVisibleMeshesPtr);
```

This way, we can access the value using OpenGL synchronization. The integer value that the numVisibleMeshesPtr variable points to is marked as volatile to let the compiler know it is going to be updated from outside the C++ program.

6. Now, let's look at the code for initializing the OpenGL state and loading the Bistro model. The GLFW setup code, identical to what was shown in the previous recipe, will be skipped again here:

```
glClearColor(1.0f, 1.0f, 1.0f, 1.0f);
glBlendFunc(GL_SRC_ALPHA, GL_ONE_MINUS_SRC_ALPHA);
glEnable(GL_DEPTH_TEST);
GLSceneData sceneData(
    "data/meshes/bistro_all.meshes",
    "data/meshes/bistro_all.scene",
    "data/meshes/bistro_all.materials");
GLMesh mesh(sceneData);
GLSkyboxRenderer skybox;
ImGuiGLRenderer rendererUI;
CanvasGL canvas;
bool g_DrawMeshes = true;
bool g_DrawGrid = true;
```

7. Let's pretransform the bounding boxes to world space. The bounding boxes
    are stored non-sequentially inside the `meshData_` container and require an
    indirection to access them. Let's reorder this container sequentially to simplify the
    work for our culling compute shader, which is going to access them later:

```cpp
std::vector<BoundingBox> reorderedBoxes;
reorderedBoxes.reserve(sceneData.shapes_.size());
for (const auto& c : sceneData.shapes_) {
   mat4 model = sceneData.scene_.
     globalTransform_[c.transformIndex];
   reorderedBoxes.push_back(
     sceneData.meshData_.boxes_[c.meshIndex]);
   reorderedBoxes.back().transform(model);
}
glNamedBufferSubData(
   boundingBoxesBuffer.getHandle(), 0,
   reorderedBoxes.size() * sizeof(BoundingBox),
   reorderedBoxes.data());
```

8. The `main()` function starts exactly the same: it updates the camera position, sets
    up the viewport, and clears the framebuffers. Once the frustum planes and corners
    have been retrieved, they are uploaded into the GPU buffer. The actual number of
    shapes to cull goes into the `numShapesToCull` field:

```cpp
while (!glfwWindowShouldClose(app.getWindow())) {
   positioner.update(
     app.getDeltaSeconds(), mouseState.pos,
     mouseState.pressedLeft);
   int width, height;
   glfwGetFramebufferSize(
     app.getWindow(), &width, &height);
   const float ratio = width / (float)height;
   glViewport(0, 0, width, height);
   glClearNamedFramebufferfv(0, GL_COLOR, 0,
     glm::value_ptr(vec4(0.0f, 0.0f, 0.0f, 1.0f)));
   glClearNamedFramebufferfi(
     0, GL_DEPTH_STENCIL, 0, 1.0f, 0);
   if (!g_FreezeCullingView)
     g_CullingView = camera.getViewMatrix();
   const mat4 proj = glm::perspective(
     45.0f, ratio, 0.1f, 1000.0f);
```

```
const mat4 view = camera.getViewMatrix();
PerFrameData perFrameData = {
  .view = view,
  .proj = proj,
  .light = mat4(0.0f),
  .cameraPos = glm::vec4(
    camera.getPosition(), 1.0f),
  .numShapesToCull = g_EnableGPUCulling ?
    (uint32_t)sceneData.shapes_.size() : 0u
};
getFrustumPlanes(proj * g_CullingView,
  perFrameData.frustumPlanes);
getFrustumCorners(proj * g_CullingView,
  perFrameData.frustumCorners);
glNamedBufferSubData(
  perFrameDataBuffer.getHandle(), 0,
  kUniformBufferSize, &perFrameData);
```

9. Here, we should invoke the culling shader program. We will reset the number
    of visible meshes, which is stored in a memory mapped buffer, back to zero. To
    make sure this value is visible on the GPU side, we must insert a GL_BUFFER_
    UPDATE_BARRIER_BIT memory barrier. We need to rebind buffers with
    bounding boxes, draw commands, and the number of visible meshes before we
    call glDispatchCompute(), since the binding points were messed up by the
    GLMesh rendering code in the previous frame. Our compute shader operates on the
    local size of 64, hence the division:

```
*numVisibleMeshesPtr = 0;
programCulling.useProgram();
glMemoryBarrier(GL_BUFFER_UPDATE_BARRIER_BIT);
glBindBufferBase(GL_SHADER_STORAGE_BUFFER,
  kBufferIndex_BoundingBoxes,
  boundingBoxesBuffer.getHandle());
glBindBufferBase(GL_SHADER_STORAGE_BUFFER,
  kBufferIndex_DrawCommands,
  mesh.bufferIndirect_.getHandle());
glBindBufferBase(GL_SHADER_STORAGE_BUFFER,
  kBufferIndex_NumVisibleMeshes,
  numVisibleMeshesBuffer.getHandle());
glDispatchCompute(
  1 + (GLuint)sceneData.shapes_.size()/64, 1, 1);
```

Once the compute shader has been started, we must issue memory barriers to tell OpenGL that it needs to synchronize any further indirect rendering with our compute shader. The GL_COMMAND_BARRIER_BIT flag states that the draw commands are data sourced from buffers by glDraw*Indirect() commands. After this, the barrier will reflect all the data that was written by the shaders prior to the barrier. The buffer objects that are affected by this are derived from the GL_DRAW_INDIRECT_BUFFER binding we use in our rendering code. The GL_SHADER_STORAGE_BARRIER_BIT flag says that access to the shader storage is blocked after the barrier reflects writes prior to the barrier. The second memory barrier and a fence are used to make sure our C++ code can read back the correct number of visible meshes from a memory mapped buffer. The GL_CLIENT_ MAPPED_BUFFER_BARRIER_BIT barrier flag makes sure access from C++ to persistent mapped buffers will reflect any data that was written by the shaders prior to the barrier. The OpenGL specification mentions that this may cause additional synchronization operations. It is only being used here for debugging and demonstration purposes:

```
glMemoryBarrier(
    GL_COMMAND_BARRIER_BIT |
    GL_SHADER_STORAGE_BARRIER_BIT);
glMemoryBarrier(
    GL_CLIENT_MAPPED_BUFFER_BARRIER_BIT);
GLsync fence = glFenceSync(
    GL_SYNC_GPU_COMMANDS_COMPLETE, 0);
```

10. The scene rendering chunk of code follows the same path as in the previous recipe: the skybox, the Bistro mesh, and then the grid. The frozen culling frustum is rendered with yellow lines to help debug the scene:

```
skybox.draw();
glDisable(GL_BLEND);
glEnable(GL_DEPTH_TEST);
if (g_DrawMeshes) {
    program.useProgram();
    mesh.draw(sceneData.shapes_.size());
}
if (g_DrawGrid) {
    glEnable(GL_BLEND);
    progGrid.useProgram();
```

```
      glDrawArraysInstancedBaseInstance(
        GL_TRIANGLES, 0, 6, 1, 0);
    }
    if (g_FreezeCullingView)
      renderCameraFrustumGL(canvas, g_CullingView,
        proj, vec4(1, 1, 0, 1), 100);
    canvas.flush();
```

Before we can display the number of culled meshes using ImGui, we need to ensure the GPU has finished its culling work and that the value has become available.

11. Let's simply wait on the fence we created two steps earlier:

```
    for (;;) {
      GLenum res = glClientWaitSync(
        fence, GL_SYNC_FLUSH_COMMANDS_BIT, 1000);
      if (res == GL_ALREADY_SIGNALED ||
          res == GL_CONDITION_SATISFIED) break;
    }
    glDeleteSync(fence);
```

12. The remaining ImGui code goes like this. After exiting the main loop, do not forget to clean up and unmap the persistent buffer:

```
    ImGuiIO& io = ImGui::GetIO();
    io.DisplaySize =
      ImVec2((float)width, (float)height);
    ImGui::NewFrame();
    ImGui::Begin("Control", nullptr);
    ImGui::Text("Draw:");
    ImGui::Checkbox("Meshes", &g_DrawMeshes);
    ImGui::Checkbox("Grid",   &g_DrawGrid);
    ImGui::Separator();
    ImGui::Checkbox("Enable GPU culling",
      &g_EnableGPUCulling);
    ImGui::Checkbox("Freeze culling frustum (P)",
      &g_FreezeCullingView);
    ImGui::Separator();
    ImGui::Text("Visible meshes: %i",
      *numVisibleMeshesPtr);
    ImGui::End();
```

```
      ImGui::Render();
      rendererUI.render(
          width, height, ImGui::GetDrawData());
        app.swapBuffers();
    }
    glUnmapNamedBuffer(
        numVisibleMeshesBuffer.getHandle());
    return 0;
  }
```

That is all for the C++ part. Now, let's take a look at the GLSL compute shader, which is doing all the heavy lifting:

1. The `PerFrameData` structure should be identical to its C++ counterpart:

```
#version 460 core
layout(local_size_x = 64, local_size_y = 1,
    local_size_z = 1) in;
layout(std140, binding = 0) uniform PerFrameData {
    mat4 view;
    mat4 proj;
    mat4 light;
    vec4 cameraPos;
    vec4 frustumPlanes[6];
    vec4 frustumCorners[8];
    uint numShapesToCull;
};
```

2. The buffer with bounding boxes is declared in the following way. The `BoundingBox` structure on the C++ side contains two `vec3` values, `min` and `max`. Due to the padding requirements of GLSL, we will replace two `vec3` with 6 floats and use preprocessor macros to give them meaningful mnemonic names:

```
struct AABB {
  float pt[6];
};
#define Box_min_x box.pt[0]
#define Box_min_y box.pt[1]
#define Box_min_z box.pt[2]
#define Box_max_x box.pt[3]
```

```
#define Box_max_y box.pt[4]
#define Box_max_z box.pt[5]
layout(std430, binding = 1) buffer BoundingBoxes {
  AABB in_AABBs[];
};
```

3. The buffer is declared in the following way with draw commands:

```
struct DrawCommand {
  uint count;
  uint instanceCount;
  uint firstIndex;
  uint baseVertex;
  uint baseInstance;
};
layout(std430, binding = 2) buffer DrawCommands {
  DrawCommand in_DrawCommands[];
};
layout(std430, binding = 3) buffer NumVisibleMeshes {
  uint numVisibleMeshes;
};
```

The `DrawCommand` structure corresponds to its C++ counterpart. The buffer that specifies the number of visible meshes is optional and is only used for demonstration purposes.

4. Here's the frustum culling function, which has mostly been copy-pasted from its C++ implementation. An identical two-phase approach was used in the previous *Doing frustum culling on the CPU* recipe:

```
bool isAABBinFrustum(AABB box) {
  for (int i = 0; i < 6; i++) {
    int r = 0;
    r += ( dot( frustumPlanes[i],
      vec4(Box_min_x, Box_min_y, Box_min_z, 1.0f) )
      < 0.0 ) ? 1 : 0;
    r += ( dot( frustumPlanes[i],
      vec4(Box_max_x, Box_min_y, Box_min_z, 1.0f) )
      < 0.0 ) ? 1 : 0;
    r += ( dot( frustumPlanes[i],
      vec4(Box_min_x, Box_max_y, Box_min_z, 1.0f) )
      < 0.0 ) ? 1 : 0;
```

```
        r += ( dot( frustumPlanes[i],
          vec4(Box_max_x, Box_max_y, Box_min_z, 1.0f) )
          < 0.0 ) ? 1 : 0;
        r += ( dot( frustumPlanes[i],
          vec4(Box_min_x, Box_min_y, Box_max_z, 1.0f) )
          < 0.0 ) ? 1 : 0;
        r += ( dot( frustumPlanes[i],
          vec4(Box_max_x, Box_min_y, Box_max_z, 1.0f) )
          < 0.0 ) ? 1 : 0;
        r += ( dot( frustumPlanes[i],
          vec4(Box_min_x, Box_max_y, Box_max_z, 1.0f) )
          < 0.0 ) ? 1 : 0;
        r += ( dot( frustumPlanes[i],
          vec4(Box_max_x, Box_max_y, Box_max_z, 1.0f) )
          < 0.0 ) ? 1 : 0;
        if ( r == 8 ) return false;
    }
    int r = 0;
    r = 0; for ( int i = 0; i < 8; i++ )
        r += (frustumCorners[i].x > Box_max_x) ? 1 : 0;
    if ( r == 8 ) return false;
    r = 0; for ( int i = 0; i < 8; i++ )
        r += (frustumCorners[i].x < Box_min_x) ? 1 : 0;
    if ( r == 8 ) return false;
    r = 0; for ( int i = 0; i < 8; i++ )
        r += (frustumCorners[i].y > Box_max_y) ? 1 : 0;
    if ( r == 8 ) return false;
    r = 0; for ( int i = 0; i < 8; i++ )
        r += (frustumCorners[i].y < Box_min_y) ? 1 : 0;
    if ( r == 8 ) return false;
    r = 0; for ( int i = 0; i < 8; i++ )
        r += (frustumCorners[i].z > Box_max_z) ? 1 : 0;
    if ( r == 8 ) return false;
    r = 0; for ( int i = 0; i < 8; i++ )
        r += (frustumCorners[i].z < Box_min_z) ? 1 : 0;
    if ( r == 8 ) return false;
    return true;
}
```

5. Now, the `main()` function of the shader is straightforward. The
    `gl_GlobalInvocationID` value is used to identify which `DrawCommand` we
    are processing now. The lower 16 bits of the `baseInstance` field are used to
    retrieve the index of this mesh in the big collection of meshes, as we explained in
    the previous chapter in the *Implementing lightweight rendering queues in OpenGL*
    recipe. If frustum culling is enabled, we invoke `isAABBinFrustum()` and set
    the number of instances based on its return value, exactly as we did in C++. Don't
    forget to atomically increment the number of visible meshes after that:

```
void main() {
  const uint idx = gl_GlobalInvocationID.x;
  // skip items beyond sceneData.shapes_.size()
  if (idx < numShapesToCull) {
    AABB box = in_AABBs[
      in_DrawCommands[idx].baseInstance >> 16];
    uint numInstances = isAABBinFrustum(box) ? 1 : 0;
    in_DrawCommands[idx].instanceCount =
      numInstances;
    atomicAdd(numVisibleMeshes, numInstances);
  }
  else {
    in_DrawCommands[idx].instanceCount = 1;
  }
}
```

The demo application produces the following image:

Figure 10.2 – Lumberyard Bistro scene with GPU frustum culling

The culling frustum is frozen and only visible geometry is rendered. Try flying around and toggling frustum freezing with the *P* key.

There's more...

It is important to mention that our culling pipeline is based on the assumption that setting the number of instances in `DrawElementsIndirectCommand` to 0 completely eliminates the penalty of rendering a mesh. In reality, this is not true, and you should consider compacting the indirect buffer by completely removing the culled items from it, or constructing a new indirect buffer directly from the compute shader using the atomic value of `numVisibleMeshes` as an index. This is especially important if culling is not done every frame and the buffer is reused across multiple frames.

There is a great presentation called *GPU-Driven Rendering Pipelines*, by Ulrich Haar and Sebastian Aaltonen, that dives deep into GPU culling and using compute functionality in rendering pipelines: `http://advances.realtimerendering.com/s2015/aaltonenhaar_siggraph2015_combined_final_footer_220dpi.pdf`.

Implementing order-independent transparency

So far, we've rendered transparent objects using a very simple punch-through transparency method, as described in the *Implementing a material system* recipe of *Chapter 7, Graphics Rendering Pipeline*. This approach was very limited in terms of quality, but it allowed us to render transparent objects together with opaque objects, which greatly simplified the entire rendering pipeline. Let's push this thing a bit further and implement another approach that allows correctly blended transparent objects.

Alpha blending multiple surfaces is an operation that requires all transparent surfaces to be sorted back to front. There are multiple ways to do this, such as sorting scene objects back to front, using multiple pass depth peeling techniques (`https://matthewwellings.com/blog/depth-peeling-order-independent-transparency-in-vulkan`), making order-independent approximations (`http://casual-effects.blogspot.com/2014/03/weighted-blended-order-independent.html`), and following a more recent work called *Phenomenological Transparency* by Morgan McGuire and Michael Mara (`https://research.nvidia.com/publication/phenomenological-transparency`).

Starting from OpenGL 4.2, it is possible to implement order-independent transparency using per-pixel linked lists via atomic counters and load-store-atomic read-modify-write operations on textures. This method is order-independent, which means it does not require any transparent geometry to be sorted prior to rendering. All necessary sorting happens in a fragment shader at the pixel level, after the actual scene has been rendered. The idea of the algorithm is to construct a linked list of fragments for each pixel of the screen, which helps with storing the color and depth values at each node of the list. Once the per-pixel lists have been constructed, we can sort them and blend them together using a full-screen fragment shader. Essentially, this is a two-pass algorithm. Our implementation is inspired by `https://fr.slideshare.net/hgruen/oit-and-indirect-illumination-using-dx11-linked-lists`. Let's take a look at how it works.

Getting ready

We recommend recapping on the *Implementing a material system* recipe of *Chapter 7, Graphics Rendering Pipeline*, to refresh yourself on the data structures of our material system. This example will use multiple rendering queues, all of which were described in the *Implementing lightweight rendering queues in OpenGL* recipe of the previous chapter.

The source code for this recipe can be found in `Chapter10/GL03_OITransparency`.

How to do it...

Our rendering pipeline for this example goes as follows. First, we will render opaque objects with standard shading, as we did in the previous recipe. Then, we will render transparent objects and add shaded fragments to linked lists instead of rendering them directly into the framebuffer. Finally, we will sort the linked lists and overlay the blended image on top of the opaque framebuffer.

Let's go through the C++ code for implementing this technique:

1. The per-frame data being used here is the same as in the *Doing frustum culling on the CPU* recipe. We will skip the GLFW mouse and keyboard handling code here and focus only on the graphics part. The GLSL shader code is shared between multiple demos, hence the unused `light` field here:

    ```
    struct PerFrameData {
      mat4 view;
      mat4 proj;
      mat4 light = mat4(0.0f); // unused in this demo
      vec4 cameraPos;
    };
    bool g_DrawOpaque = true;
    bool g_DrawTransparent = true;
    bool g_DrawGrid = true;
    ```

    The `main()` function starts by loading the necessary shaders. The grid shader remains the same. The shaders for scene rendering are now split into two sets. The first set, `GL01_scene_IBL.vert` and `GL01_scene_IBL.frag`, is used for opaque objects. The second set, `GL01_scene_IBL.vert` and `GL03_mesh_oit.frag`, is used for transparent ones. A full-screen post-processing pass is handled in `GL03_OIT.frag`. We will look at the shaders right after the C++ code:

    ```
    int main(void) {
      GLApp app;
      GLShader shdGridVert(
        "data/shaders/chapter05/GL01_grid.vert");
      GLShader shdGridFrag(
        "data/shaders/chapter05/GL01_grid.frag");
      GLProgram progGrid(shdGridVert, shdGridFrag);
      GLShader shaderVert(
        "data/shaders/chapter10/GL01_scene_IBL.vert");
      GLShader shaderFrag(
        "data/shaders/chapter10/GL01_scene_IBL.frag");
    ```

```
GLProgram program(shaderVert, shaderFrag);
GLShader shaderFragOIT(
  "data/shaders/chapter10/GL03_mesh_oit.frag");
GLProgram programOIT(shaderVert, shaderFragOIT);
GLShader shdFullScreenQuadVert(
  "data/shaders/chapter08/GL02_FullScreenQuad.vert");
GLShader shdCombineOIT(
  "data/shaders/chapter10/GL03_OIT.frag");
GLProgram progCombineOIT(
  shdFullScreenQuadVert, shdCombineOIT);
```

The per-frame uniforms, OpenGL state, and meshes should be set up the same way as in the previous demos:

```
const GLsizeiptr kUniformBufferSize =
  sizeof(PerFrameData);
GLBuffer perFrameDataBuffer(kUniformBufferSize,
  nullptr, GL_DYNAMIC_STORAGE_BIT);
glBindBufferRange(GL_UNIFORM_BUFFER,
  kBufferIndex_PerFrameUniforms,
  perFrameDataBuffer.getHandle(), 0,
  kUniformBufferSize);
glClearColor(1.0f, 1.0f, 1.0f, 1.0f);
glBlendFunc(GL_SRC_ALPHA, GL_ONE_MINUS_SRC_ALPHA);
glEnable(GL_DEPTH_TEST);
GLSceneData sceneData(
  "data/meshes/bistro_all.meshes",
  "data/meshes/bistro_all.scene",
  "data/meshes/bistro_all.materials");
GLMesh mesh(sceneData);
GLSkyboxRenderer skybox;
ImGuiGLRenderer rendererUI;
```

2. Let's allocate two indirect buffers, as described in *Implementing lightweight rendering queues in OpenGL* – one for opaque meshes and the other for transparent ones. A simple lambda can be used to discriminate draw commands based on the sMaterialFlags_Transparent bit in the material flags that were set up by the SceneConverter tool from *Chapter 7, Graphics Rendering Pipeline*:

```
GLIndirectBuffer meshesOpaque(
  sceneData.shapes_.size());
GLIndirectBuffer meshesTransparent(
  sceneData.shapes_.size());
```

```
auto isTransparent = [&sceneData](
  const DrawElementsIndirectCommand& c) {
  const auto mtlIndex = c.baseInstance_ & 0xffff;
  const auto& mtl = sceneData.materials_[mtlIndex];
  return
    (mtl.flags_ & sMaterialFlags_Transparent) > 0;
};
mesh.bufferIndirect_.selectTo(meshesOpaque,
  [&isTransparent](const
    DrawElementsIndirectCommand& c) -> bool {
      return !isTransparent(c);
    });
mesh.bufferIndirect_.selectTo(meshesTransparent,
  [&isTransparent](const
    DrawElementsIndirectCommand& c) -> bool {
      return isTransparent(c);
    });
```

3. Besides rendering queues, we require a bunch of buffers to store linked lists data. The C++ `TransparentFragment` structure is a replica of the related structure in our GLSL shaders, which stores a single node of a per-pixel linked list. We require a floating-point color value with an alpha channel to accommodate HDR reflections on transparent objects, a depth value, and an index of the next node:

```
struct TransparentFragment {
  float R, G, B, A;
  float depth;
  uint32_t next;
};
```

Note

In real-world applications, 32-bit floats for color channels can be replaced with 16-bit half-floats to save some memory when using the appropriate GLSL extensions. In C++, they can be mimicked using `uint16_t`. We avoid using vendor-specific OpenGL extensions for the sake of simplicity.

---

4. The buffer allocation goes as follows. We allocate storage to allow an overdraw of 16M transparent fragments. Anything beyond that will be clipped by our fragment shader, which performs bounds checking:

```
int width, height;
glfwGetFramebufferSize(
  app.getWindow(), &width, &height);
GLFramebuffer framebuffer(
  width, height, GL_RGBA8, GL_DEPTH_COMPONENT24);
const uint32_t kMaxOITFragments = 16 * 1024 * 1024;
const uint32_t kBufferIndex_TransparencyLists =
  kBufferIndex_Materials + 1;
GLBuffer oitAtomicCounter(sizeof(uint32_t),
  nullptr, GL_DYNAMIC_STORAGE_BIT);
GLBuffer oitTransparencyLists(
  sizeof(TransparentFragment) * kMaxOITFragments,
  nullptr, GL_DYNAMIC_STORAGE_BIT);
GLTexture oitHeads(GL_TEXTURE_2D,
  width, height, GL_R32UI);
glBindImageTexture(0, oitHeads.getHandle(), 0,
  GL_FALSE, 0, GL_READ_WRITE, GL_R32UI);
glBindBufferBase(GL_ATOMIC_COUNTER_BUFFER, 0,
  oitAtomicCounter.getHandle());
glBindBufferBase(GL_SHADER_STORAGE_BUFFER,
  kBufferIndex_TransparencyLists,
  oitTransparencyLists.getHandle());
```

The `oitAtomicCounter` buffer contains the total number of allocated fragments and is used as an atomic counter in a linear memory allocator, which is implemented in the GLSL shader. The `oitTransparencyLists` buffer is an actual pool of memory that's used to store linked lists. `oitHeadsBuffer` contains the integer values of the heads of per-pixel linked lists.

5. Every frame, we should reset the atomic counter back to `0` and clear the heads buffer with the `0xFFFFFFFF` value, which is a guard value to signal that there are no transparent fragments for this pixel of the viewport. Here is a lambda to do so:

```
auto clearTransparencyBuffers =
  [&oitAtomicCounter, &oitHeads]() {
    const uint32_t minusOne = 0xFFFFFFFF;
    const uint32_t zero = 0;
    glClearTexImage(oitHeads.getHandle(), 0,
      GL_RED_INTEGER, GL_UNSIGNED_INT, &minusOne);
```

```
      glNamedBufferSubData(
         oitAtomicCounter.getHandle(),
         0, sizeof(uint32_t), &zero);
   };
```

6. All the preparations are now complete, and we can enter the main loop. Clear the main framebuffer and upload the per-frame uniforms:

```
while (!glfwWindowShouldClose(app.getWindow())) {
   positioner.update(
      app.getDeltaSeconds(), mouseState.pos,
      mouseState.pressedLeft);
   int width, height;
   glfwGetFramebufferSize(
      app.getWindow(), &width, &height);
   const float ratio = width / (float)height;
   glViewport(0, 0, width, height);
   glClearNamedFramebufferfv(
      framebuffer.getHandle(), GL_COLOR, 0,
      glm::value_ptr(vec4(0.0f, 0.0f, 0.0f, 1.0f)));
   glClearNamedFramebufferfi(framebuffer.getHandle(),
      GL_DEPTH_STENCIL, 0, 1.0f, 0);
   const mat4 proj = glm::perspective(
      45.0f, ratio, 0.1f, 1000.0f);
   const mat4 view = camera.getViewMatrix();
   PerFrameData perFrameData = {
      .view = view,
      .proj = proj,
      .light =  mat4(0.0f),
      .cameraPos =
         glm::vec4(camera.getPosition(), 1.0f)
   };
   glNamedBufferSubData(
      perFrameDataBuffer.getHandle(), 0,
      kUniformBufferSize, &perFrameData);
```

7. Scene rendering starts with clearing the transparency buffers and drawing the skybox. Then, we can render the opaque meshes of the Bistro scene using the corresponding rendering queue:

```
clearTransparencyBuffers();
framebuffer.bind();
skybox.draw();
```

```
  glDisable(GL_BLEND);
  glEnable(GL_DEPTH_TEST);
  if (g_DrawOpaque) {
    program.useProgram();
    mesh.draw(meshesOpaque.drawCommands_.size(),
      &meshesOpaque);
  }
```

8. The grid is rendered after all the opaque objects have been rendered. This way, it will be correctly clipped to the opaque geometry and lie under transparent objects:

```
  if (g_DrawGrid) {
    glEnable(GL_BLEND);
    progGrid.useProgram();
    glDrawArraysInstancedBaseInstance(
      GL_TRIANGLES, 0, 6, 1, 0);
    glDisable(GL_BLEND);
  }
```

Transparent meshes are rendered differently, with the depth buffer writes turned off but the depth test enabled. This way, all transparent objects will be correctly clipped against opaque geometry, while not affecting each other. Rendering with `programOIT` should not impact the color buffer either, since all the transparent fragments go into per-pixel linked lists only. Once we have rendered the transparent objects, a flush and a memory barrier called `GL_SHADER_STORAGE_BARRIER_BIT` is required, so that subsequent reads from linked lists stored in an SSBO can correctly access the data written by the `programOIT` shader program:

```
  if (g_DrawTransparent) {
    glDepthMask(GL_FALSE);
    programOIT.useProgram();
    mesh.draw(
      meshesTransparent.drawCommands_.size(),
      &meshesTransparent);
    glFlush();
    glMemoryBarrier(GL_SHADER_STORAGE_BARRIER_BIT);
    glDepthMask(GL_TRUE);
  }
  framebuffer.unbind();
```

9. Now, we should run our full screen pass to blend the fragments stored in the linked lists. The framebuffer is used as input to provide the color "below" the transparent fragments. Don't forget to disable the depth test as well as blending, which is going to be handled manually in the shader:

```
glDisable(GL_DEPTH_TEST);
glDisable(GL_BLEND);
progCombineOIT.useProgram();
glBindTextureUnit(0,
   framebuffer.getTextureColor().getHandle());
glDrawArrays(GL_TRIANGLES, 0, 6);
```

10. The last part of the main loop is the ImGui interface, which controls the rendering process:

```
ImGuiIO& io = ImGui::GetIO();
io.DisplaySize =
   ImVec2((float)width, (float)height);
ImGui::NewFrame();
ImGui::Begin("Control", nullptr);
ImGui::Text("Draw:");
ImGui::Checkbox("Opaque meshes", &g_DrawOpaque);
ImGui::Checkbox("Transparent meshes",
   &g_DrawTransparent);
ImGui::Checkbox("Grid", &g_DrawGrid);
ImGui::End();
ImGui::Render();
rendererUI.render(
   width, height, ImGui::GetDrawData());
app.swapBuffers();
}
   return 0;
}
```

That is all for the C++ part. Now, let's switch to the GLSL code and look at both the new shaders that handle transparent objects.

The first fragment shader, GL03_mesh_oit.frag, takes care of populating the linked lists. Let's go through the entire source code to make things clearer:

1. First, we will declare the required extensions and include our material description header from *Chapter 7, Graphics Rendering Pipeline*:

```
#version 460 core
#extension GL_ARB_bindless_texture : require
#extension GL_ARB_gpu_shader_int64 : enable
#include <data/shaders/chapter07/MaterialData.h>
layout (early_fragment_tests) in;
#include
  <data/shaders/chapter10/GLBufferDeclarations.h>
layout(std430, binding = 2) restrict readonly buffer
 Materials {
  MaterialData in_Materials[];
};
```

The `early_fragment_tests` layout specifier states that we want to prevent this fragment shader from being executed unnecessarily, should the fragment be discarded based on the depth test. This is necessary, as any redundant invocation of this shader will result in messed-up transparency lists.

2. The fragment shader inputs correspond to the GL01_scene_IBL.vert vertex shader, which was described earlier:

```
layout (location=0) in vec2 v_tc;
layout (location=1) in vec3 v_worldNormal;
layout (location=2) in vec3 v_worldPos;
layout (location=3) in flat uint matIdx;
layout (location=0) out vec4 out_FragColor;
layout (binding = 5) uniform samplerCube texEnvMap;
layout (binding = 6) uniform samplerCube
  texEnvMapIrradiance;
layout (binding = 7) uniform sampler2D texBRDF_LUT;
#include <data/shaders/chapter07/AlphaTest.h>
#include <data/shaders/chapter06/PBR.sp>
```

3. The `TransparentFragment` structure here corresponds to the respective C++ structure. The bindings of auxiliary buffers should match those in the C++ code as well:

```
struct TransparentFragment {
  vec4 color;
  float depth;
  uint next;
};
layout (binding = 0, r32ui) uniform uimage2D heads;
layout (binding = 0, offset = 0) uniform atomic_uint
  numFragments;
layout (std430, binding = 3) buffer Lists {
  TransparentFragment Fragments[];
};
```

4. The `main()` function calculates perturbed normals and does simple image-based diffuse lighting using an irradiance map, similar to what we did in *Chapter 7, Graphics Rendering Pipeline.* The diffuse part of the physically-based shading comes from `chapter06/PBR.sp`:

```
void main() {
  MaterialData mtl = in_Materials[matIdx];
  vec4 albedo = mtl.albedoColor_;
  vec3 normalSample = vec3(0.0, 0.0, 0.0);
  if (mtl.albedoMap_ > 0)
    albedo = texture(sampler2D(
      unpackUint2x32(mtl.albedoMap_)), v_tc);
  if (mtl.normalMap_ > 0)
    normalSample = texture(sampler2D(
      unpackUint2x32(mtl.normalMap_)), v_tc).xyz;
  vec3 n = normalize(v_worldNormal);
  if (length(normalSample) > 0.5)
    n = perturbNormal(n,
        normalize(cameraPos.xyz - v_worldPos.xyz),
        normalSample, v_tc);
  vec3 f0 = vec3(0.04);
  vec3 diffuseColor = albedo.rgb * (vec3(1.0) - f0);
  vec3 diffuse = texture(
    texEnvMapIrradiance, n.xyz).rgb * diffuseColor;
```

5. Let's add some ad hoc environment reflections for transparent objects and store the resulting color in `out_FragColor`. This is just a temporary variable, given that color writes were disabled for this shader in the C++ code:

```
vec3 v = normalize(cameraPos.xyz - v_worldPos);
vec3 reflection = reflect(v, n);
vec3 colorRefl = texture(texEnvMap, reflection).rgb;
out_FragColor = vec4(diffuse + colorRefl, 1.0);
```

6. Once we have calculated the color value, we can insert this fragment into the corresponding linked list:

```
float alpha = clamp(albedo.a, 0.0, 1.0) *
              mtl.transparencyFactor_;
bool isTransparent = alpha < 0.99;
if (isTransparent && gl_HelperInvocation == false) {
  if (alpha > 0.01) {
    uint index =
      atomicCounterIncrement(numFragments);
    const uint maxOITfragments = 16*1024*1024;
    if (index < maxOITfragments) {
      uint prevIndex = imageAtomicExchange(
        heads, ivec2(gl_FragCoord.xy), index);
      Fragments[index].color =
        vec4(out_FragColor.rgb, alpha);
      Fragments[index].depth = gl_FragCoord.z;
      Fragments[index].next  = prevIndex;
    }
  }
  discard;
}
};
```

Besides the value of `mtl.transparencyFactor_`, transparency can be controlled by the values in the alpha channel of the albedo texture. The `gl_HelperInvocation` value tells us whether this fragment shader invocation is considered a helper invocation. As the OpenGL specification states, a helper invocation is a fragment shader invocation that is created solely for the purpose of evaluating derivatives for use in non-helper fragment shader invocations. Helper invocations should not disturb our linked lists data. A linear memory allocator is implemented using `imageAtomicExchange()`, which replaces the head of a corresponding linked list with a new value.

> **Note**
>
> While being correct for transparent fragments, the preceding code has a serious limitation when it comes to opaque fragments where the `isTransparent` value is false. Opaque fragments do not contribute to linked lists and end up in the framebuffer. This is seemingly OK at first glance, but it is not correct. With the depth writes disabled, opaque fragments are not Z-sorted properly, resulting in an incorrectly rendered image when the opaque fragments of one transparent surface overlay another transparent surface containing opaque fragments. This can be avoided by adding everything to linked lists, regardless of the `isTransparent` value. Whether you should choose increased memory consumption or visuals is up to you. We are just showing the possibilities of making such optimizations.

Now that we have populated the linked lists, let's learn how to blend and combine them into the resulting image. This can done in a full-screen pass in the `GL03_OIT.frag` shader:

1. Fragment shader inputs contain a `texScene` texture that provides all the opaque objects in rendered format. The `TransparentFragment` structure should match the one from the previous shader. The buffer binding points correspond to the C++ code:

```
#version 460 core
layout(location = 0) in vec2 uv;
layout(location = 0) out vec4 out_FragColor;
layout(binding = 0) uniform sampler2D texScene;
struct TransparentFragment {
  vec4 color;
  float depth;
  uint next;
};
layout (binding = 0, r32ui) uniform uimage2D heads;
layout (std430, binding = 3) buffer Lists {
  TransparentFragment fragments[];
};
```

2. The `main()` function starts by copying the linked list for this pixel into a local array. This is done in a loop until we reach the `0xFFFFFFFF` guard marker or we reach the maximal number of overlapping transparent fragments; that is, `MAX_FRAGMENTS`:

```
void main() {
  #define MAX_FRAGMENTS 64
```

```
TransparentFragment frags[64];
int numFragments = 0;
uint idx = imageLoad(
  heads, ivec2(gl_FragCoord.xy)).r;
while (idx != 0xFFFFFFFF &&
       numFragments < MAX_FRAGMENTS) {
  frags[numFragments] = fragments[idx];
  numFragments++;
  idx = fragments[idx].next;
}
```

3. Let's sort the array by depth by using insertion sort from largest to smallest. This is fast, considering we have a reasonably small number of overlapping fragments:

```
for (int i = 1; i < numFragments; i++) {
  TransparentFragment toInsert = frags[i];
  uint j = i;
  while (j > 0 && toInsert.depth >
         frags[j-1].depth) {
    frags[j] = frags[j-1];
    j--;
  }
  frags[j] = toInsert;
}
```

4. Finally, we can blend the fragments together. Get the color of the closest non-transparent object from the frame buffer and traverse the array blending colors based on their alpha values. Clamping is necessary to prevent any HDR values leaking into the alpha channel:

```
vec4 color = texture(texScene, uv);
for (int i = 0; i < numFragments; i++)
  color = mix(color, vec4(frags[i].color),
    clamp(float(frags[i].color.a), 0.0, 1.0));
out_FragColor = color;
}
```

The demo application should render the following image:

Figure 10.3 – Inside the Lumberyard Bistro bar with order-independent transparency

Make sure you check the bottles and glasses on the tables, windows, and how all these objects overlay each other.

Loading texture assets asynchronously

All our demos up to this point have preloaded all the assets at startup, before anything can be rendered. This is okay for applications where the size of the data is small, and everything can be loaded in an instant. Once our content gets into the territory of gigabytes, a mechanism would be desirable to stream assets as required. Let's extend our demos with some basic lazy-loading functionality to load textures while the application is already rendering a scene. Multithreading will be done using the Taskflow library and standard C++14 capabilities.

Getting ready

We recommend revisiting the *Multithreading with Taskflow* recipe of *Chapter 2, Using Essential Libraries*.

The source code for this recipe can be found in `Chapter10/GL04_LazyLoading`.

How to do it...

To make things simple, the idea behind our approach is to replace the GLSceneData class, which handled all scene loading so far, with another class called GLSceneDataLazy, which is capable of loading textures lazily. As we explained in the *Implementing lightweight rendering queues in OpenGL* recipe in the previous chapter, our new GLMesh class is a template that's been parameterized with GLSceneDataType and can accept both GLSceneData and GLSceneDataLazy. Let's take a look at the declaration of a new scene loading class in the shared/glFramework/GLSceneDataLazy.h file:

1. We will store a dummy texture that will be used as a replacement for any texture that hasn't been loaded yet. In our case, it is a white 1x1 image. The textureFiles_ container stores the filenames of all the textures in the scene and is populated at startup in the class constructor:

```
class GLSceneDataLazy {
public:
  const std::shared_ptr<GLTexture> dummyTexture_ =
    std::make_shared<GLTexture>(
      GL_TEXTURE_2D, "data/const1.bmp");
  std::vector<std::string> textureFiles_;
```

The LoadedImageData structure contains all the information that's required to load an RGBA8 uncompressed texture. The index_ field stores an index of the loaded texture inside allMaterialTextures_. The other members are the width, height, and the actual RGBA8 pixel data. Once the loading thread has finished loading a texture from the file, it creates another instance of LoadedImageData and appends it to the loadedFiles_ container, which is guarded by a loadedFilesMutex_ mutex:

```
struct LoadedImageData {
  int index_ = 0;
  int w_ = 0;
  int h_ = 0;
  const uint8_t* img_ = nullptr;
};
std::vector<LoadedImageData> loadedFiles_;
std::mutex loadedFilesMutex_;
std::vector<std::shared_ptr<GLTexture>>
  allMaterialTextures_;
```

The geometry and scene graph data is stored intact, similar to how it is done in the original GLSceneData class:

```
MeshFileHeader header_;
MeshData meshData_;
Scene scene_;
std::vector<DrawData> shapes_;
```

2. When it comes to materials, we must store two copies:

```
// materials loaded from the scene file
std::vector<MaterialDescription> materialsLoaded_;
// materials uploaded into GPU buffers
std::vector<MaterialDescription> materials_;
```

The reason for this is that our original code in GLSeneData converts the integer texture indices inside MaterialDescription into OpenGL bindless texture handles. Obviously, this transformation is destructive and once we have a bindless handle, we cannot convert it back into a texture index. To simplify our loading code, we must upload an entirely new copy of the materials into the GPU every time a new texture is loaded. Hence, we require the original indices of textures, which are stored intact in the materialsLoaded_ vector.

3. Our code for the Taskflow library needs the Executor and Taskflow objects:

```
tf::Taskflow taskflow_;
tf::Executor executor_;
```

We will store an instance of Executor right here for the sake of simplicity. However, if there are many instances of GLSceneDataLazy, an external Executor shared by all the scene data instances should be preferred.

4. The uploadLoadedTextures() method is polled from the main loop. It uploads any new textures that were loaded since the last frame to the GPU, and then calls updateMaterials() to update material descriptions and replace dummy textures with newly loaded ones:

```
bool uploadLoadedTextures();
GLSceneDataLazy(
  const char* meshFile,
  const char* sceneFile,
  const char* materialFile);
private:
```

```
    void updateMaterials();
    void loadScene(const char* sceneFile);
};
```

The implementation of the GLSceneDataLazy class is located in the shared/
glFramework/GLSceneDataLazy.h file and is pretty straightforward:

1. There is a static helper function getTextureHandleBindless() that is used to
   convert a texture index into an OpenGL bindless texture handle:

```
static uint64_t getTextureHandleBindless(uint64_t idx,
    const std::vector<shared_ptr<GLTexture>>& textures) {
    if (idx == INVALID_TEXTURE) return 0;
    return textures[idx]->getHandleBindless();
}
```

2. The class constructor loads the mesh, scene graph, and materials data exactly as it
   was done earlier in the GLSceneData class:

```
GLSceneDataLazy::GLSceneDataLazy(
  const char* meshFile,
  const char* sceneFile,
  const char* materialFile)
{
  header_ = loadMeshData(meshFile, meshData_);
  loadScene(sceneFile);
  loadMaterials(
    materialFile, materialsLoaded_, textureFiles_);
```

Instead of loading textures from files right here, we will replace each texture with
a dummy and update the materials data using these textures. This way, the entire
scene will be rendered with white textures applied.

3. Let's reserve some space in the loadedFiles_ container to make sure no
   reallocation will be done while we asynchronously append items to it later:

```
  for (const auto& f: textureFiles_)
    allMaterialTextures_.emplace_back(dummyTexture_);
  updateMaterials();
  loadedFiles_.reserve(textureFiles_.size());
```

4. Now, we can initialize the `taskflow_` object using the `for_each_index()` algorithm. It will create an independent asynchronous task for each texture file using the provided lambda. This lambda loads a texture from a file using the STB library and stores the loaded data in `loadedFiles_`. Once the `taskflow_` object has been initialized, we can run it using `Executor`:

```cpp
taskflow_.for_each_index(0u,
  (uint32_t)textureFiles_.size(), 1,
  [this](int idx) {
    int w, h;
    const uint8_t* img = stbi_load(
      this->textureFiles_[idx].c_str(),
      &w, &h, nullptr, STBI_rgb_alpha);
    std::lock_guard lock(loadedFilesMutex_);
    loadedFiles_.emplace_back(
      LoadedImageData{ idx, w, h, img });
  }
);
executor_.run(taskflow_);
}
```

5. The `uploadLoadedTextures()` method is polled every frame from the main loop. It locks the `loadedFilesMutex_` mutex and checks if any new texture was loaded. The explicit scope guard here is used to reduce the amount of work under the locked mutex. Once a new image data has been retrieved, we can create a new OpenGL texture and update the materials accordingly:

```cpp
bool GLSceneDataLazy::uploadLoadedTextures()
{
  LoadedImageData data;
  {
    std::lock_guard lock(loadedFilesMutex_);
    if (loadedFiles_.empty()) return false;
    data = loadedFiles_.back();
    loadedFiles_.pop_back();
  }
  allMaterialTextures_[data.index_] =
    std::make_shared<GLTexture>(
      data.w_, data.h_, data.img_);
  stbi_image_free((void*)data.img_);
```

```
    updateMaterials();
    return true;
}
```

6. The material's updating code is somewhat similar to the GLSceneData
    implementation, with the exception that this variant is non-destructive. It sources
    the material data from materialsLoaded_ and converts all texture indices into
    bindless handles:

```
void GLSceneDataLazy::updateMaterials() {
  const size_t numMaterials = materialsLoaded_.size();
  materials_.resize(numMaterials);
  for (size_t i = 0; i != numMaterials; i++) {
    const auto& in = materialsLoaded_[i];
    auto& out = materials_[i];
    out = in;
    out.ambientOcclusionMap_ =
      getTextureHandleBindless(
        in.ambientOcclusionMap_,
        allMaterialTextures_);
    out.emissiveMap_ = getTextureHandleBindless(
      in.emissiveMap_, allMaterialTextures_);
    out.albedoMap_ = getTextureHandleBindless(
      in.albedoMap_, allMaterialTextures_);
    out.metallicRoughnessMap_ =
      getTextureHandleBindless(
        in.metallicRoughnessMap_,
        allMaterialTextures_);
    out.normalMap_ = getTextureHandleBindless(
      in.normalMap_, allMaterialTextures_);
  }
}
```

7. Last but not least, the loadScene() function loads the scene graph data and
    converts it into a shapes list exactly, as was done in the GLSceneData class:

```
void GLSceneDataLazy::loadScene(const char* sceneFile) {
  ::loadScene(sceneFile, scene_);
  for (const auto& c: scene_.meshes_) {
    auto material = scene_.
      materialForNode_.find(c.first);
```

```
  if (material != scene_.materialForNode_.end())
    shapes_.push_back(DrawData{
      .meshIndex = c.second,
      .materialIndex = material->second,
      .LOD = 0,
      .indexOffset =
        meshData_.meshes_[c.second].indexOffset,
      .vertexOffset =
        meshData_.meshes_[c.second].vertexOffset,
      .transformIndex = c.first});
  }
  markAsChanged(scene_, 0);
  recalculateGlobalTransforms(scene_);
}
```

All the support code is now complete and ready to be tested. Let's take a look at the
Chapter10/GL04_LazyLoading demo application to see how the Bistro scene can be
rendered with lazy-loaded textures.

The application is based on the code in the previous *Implementing order-independent
transparency* recipe, and will render all the transparent objects exactly as in the previous
demo. Here, we will only highlight the differences necessary to introduce lazy-loading:

1. Inside the main() function, we should use the GLSceneDataLazy class instead
    of GLSceneData:

```
int main(void) {
  ...
  GLSceneDataLazy sceneData(
    "data/meshes/bistro_all.meshes",
    "data/meshes/bistro_all.scene",
    "data/meshes/bistro_all.materials");
  GLMesh mesh(sceneData);
  ...
```

2. Inside the main loop, we should poll uploadLoadedTextures() and, in case there are newly loaded textures, upload a new materials buffer into an appropriate OpenGL buffer:

```
while (!glfwWindowShouldClose(app.getWindow()))  {
  if (sceneData.uploadLoadedTextures())
    mesh.updateMaterialsBuffer(sceneData);
  ... do all the rendering here
      exactly as it was done before ...
}
return 0;
}
```

And that is it. Just by changing a few lines of code, our previous demo gains asynchronous texture loading functionality. If you run the demo, the geometry data will be loaded and rendered almost instantly, producing an image that's similar to the following:

Figure 10.4 – Lumberyard Bistro scene rendered with dummy textures before asynchronous loading kicks in

You can navigate the app with a keyboard and mouse while all the textures are streamed in in mere moments. This functionality, while being essential to any serious rendering engine, is very handy for smaller scale applications, where being able to quickly rerun the app improves your debugging capabilities.

There's more...

The approach of asynchronous textures being loaded gives much better responsiveness compared to preloading the entire textures pool at startup. However, a better approach may be to maintain persistent mapped buffers to texture data and load images directly into these memory regions. The best performance can be achieved if the texture data in files has already been compressed into GPU runtime formats. This might be an interesting exercise for you. Texture compression can be added to the `SceneConverter` tool and additional loading code can be accommodated in the `GLSceneDataLazy` class.

Another improvement could occur in the `uploadLoadedTextures()` method. Instead of polling each `GLSceneDataLazy` object, texture updates might become a part of the events system in your rendering engine. One more thing to mention is that instead of loading only one texture on each iteration, a load balancer could be implemented that can upload multiple textures into the GPU; their number is based on texture sizes through some heuristics. We recommend running the scene converter tool to output 1,024x1,024 textures and so that you can experiment with this approach on a much heavier dataset.

Implementing projective shadows for directional lights

In the previous chapter, we learned how to set up a shadow mapping pipeline with OpenGL and Vulkan. Our focus was more on the API rather than on shadow correctness or versatility. In the *Implementing shadow maps in OpenGL* recipe of *Chapter 8, Image-Based Techniques*, we learned how to render shadows from spotlights using perspective projection for our shadow-casting light source. Directional light sources typically simulate sunlight, and a single light source can illuminate the entire scene. In its simplest form, this means we should construct a projection matrix which takes the bounds of the scene into account. Let's take a look at how to implement this basic approach and add some shadows to our Bistro rendering example.

Getting ready

Make sure you revisit the *Implementing shadow maps in OpenGL* recipe of *Chapter 8, Image-Based Techniques*, before you learn about the shadow mapping topic.

The calculations described in this recipe are part of the `Chapter10/GL05_Final` OpenGL demo.

How to do it...

To construct a projection matrix for a directional light, we must calculate the axis-aligned bounding box of the entire scene, transform it into light-space using the light's view matrix, and use the bounds of the transformed box to construct an orthographic frustum that entirely encloses this box.

The scene bounding box can be calculated in two simple steps:

1. First, we should pretransform the bounding boxes of individual meshes into world space. The same code was used earlier for frustum culling in the *Doing frustum culling on the GPU with compute shaders* recipe:

```
for (const auto& c : sceneData.shapes_)         {
  mat4 model = sceneData.scene_.
    globalTransform_[c.transformIndex];
  reorderedBoxes.push_back(
    sceneData.meshData_.boxes_[c.meshIndex]);
  reorderedBoxes.back().transform(model);
}
```

2. Then, we can combine all the transformed bounding boxes into one big box:

```
BoundingBox bigBox = reorderedBoxes.front();
for (const auto& b : reorderedBoxes) {
  bigBox.combinePoint(b.min_);
  bigBox.combinePoint(b.max_);
}
```

Since our scene is static, we can only do these calculations once outside the main loop.

Now, we can construct a projection matrix for our directional light source. To make things more interactive, the light source direction can be controlled from ImGui using two angles, g_LightTheta and g_LightPhi:

1. Let's construct two rotation matrices using these two angles and rotate a vertical top-down light at (0, -1, 0) appropriately. The view matrix for our light is constructed using the resulting light direction vector. As the light covers the entire scene, we do not really care about its origin point, so we can put it at (0, 0, 0):

```
const glm::mat4 rot1 = glm::rotate(mat4(1.f),
  glm::radians(g_LightTheta), vec3(0, 0, 1));
const glm::mat4 rot2 = glm::rotate(
  rot1, glm::radians(g_LightPhi), vec3(1, 0, 0));
const vec3 lightDir = glm::normalize(
  vec3(rot2 * vec4(0.0f, -1.0f, 0.0f, 1.0f)));
const mat4 lightView = glm::lookAt(
  vec3(0), lightDir, vec3(0, 0, 1));
```

2. Now, we can use this light's view matrix to transform the world-space bounding box of the scene into light-space. OpenGL's NDC space has its Z-axis facing forward, away from the camera, so we should negate and swap the Z coordinates here:

```
const BoundingBox box =
  bigBox.getTransformed(lightView);
const mat4 lightProj = glm::ortho(
  box.min_.x, box.max_.x,
  box.min_.y, box.max_.y,
  -box.max_.z, -box.min_.z);
```

3. The light's view and projection matrices are passed into GLSL shaders via our traditional PerFrameData structure:

```
PerFrameData perFrameData = {
  .view = view,
  .proj = proj,
  .light = lightProj * lightView,
  .cameraPos = glm::vec4(camera.getPosition(), 1.0f),
  .enableCulling = g_EnableGPUCulling ? 1u : 0u
};
```

The remaining shadow map rendering logic remains exactly the same as in our previous spotlight example. Here's a screenshot from the running demo showing what the shadow map for the entire scene should look like, with the `g_LightTheta` and `g_LightPhi` angles set to `0`:

Figure 10.5 – A shadow map for top-down directional light

Note how the light's viewing frustum is fit to the scene bounds.

There's more...

This type of projection for directional shadow maps covers the entire scene, which results in significant aliasing. Instead of using this orthographic projection as-is, we can wrap it in such ways that parts of the scene closer to the camera occupy a larger area of the shadow map. One of the first algorithms of this kind was called is **Perspective Shadow Maps** (**PSMs**) and was presented at SIGGRAPH 2002 by Stamminger and Drettakis. It uses post-projective space, where all nearby objects become larger than farther ones. A more recent algorithm is Light Space Perspective Shadow Maps (`https://www.cg.tuwien.ac.at/research/vr/lispsm`).

A more generic technique to reduce shadow maps aliasing is to split one big light frustum into multiple frustums, or cascades, which are at different distances from the camera, render multiple shadow maps, and apply them based on their distance from the viewer. Google the Parallel Split Shadow Maps and Cascaded Shadow Maps algorithms for more information.

Furthermore, PSMs and cascades can be combined into a single shadow mapping pipeline to produce the best results.

Now, we are ready to combine multiple effects and techniques into a single application. But before we do that, let's switch back to Vulkan and learn how to use atomics to visualize the rendering order of fragments.

Using GPU atomic counters in Vulkan

The goal of this recipe is to introduce atomics in Vulkan and demonstrate how to use them to see how the GPU scheduler distributes the fragment shader workload. In a sense, this is the order in which the GPU rasterizes triangles into fragments on the screen. Let's learn how to implement a Vulkan application to visualize the rendering order of fragments in a full-screen quad consisting of two triangles.

Getting ready

The demo from *Implementing order-independent transparency* uses an atomic counter to maintain per-pixel linked lists of transparent fragments. Make sure you read that recipe. Please recall our Vulkan scene data structures by reading the *Working with shapes lists in Vulkan* recipe of *Chapter 9, Working with Scene Graphs*.

The source code for this recipe can be found in `Chapter10/VK01_AtomicsTest`.

How to do it...

The application runs using just two render passes. The first pass renders a full-screen quad and, at each fragment shader's invocation, saves its coordinates by atomically appending them to an SSBO buffer. The second pass takes point coordinates from the list and outputs these points onto the screen. The user can control the percentage of displayed points. The visual randomness of the points reflects the order in which the GPU schedules the fragment workload. It is worth comparing the output of this demo across various GPUs of different vendors.

Let's take a look at the GLSL shaders. The vertex shader to render a full-screen quad was described and used extensively in this book. The real work in the first pass is done in the fragment shader:

1. The fragment shader fills the `value` buffer with fragment coordinates. To keep track of the number of added fragments, we can use the `count` buffer, which holds an integer atomic counter. To enable atomic buffer access instructions, we can set the GLSL version to 4.6. The `value` output buffer contains a fragment index and its screen coordinates. The `ubo` uniform buffer contains the framebuffer dimensions for calculating the number of output pixels:

    ```
    #version 460 core
    layout(set = 0, binding = 0) buffer Atomic
      { uint count; };
    struct node { uint idx; float xx, yy; };
    layout (set = 0, binding = 1) buffer Values
      { node value[]; };
    layout (set = 0, binding = 2) uniform UniformBuffer
      { float width; float height; } ubo;
    layout(location = 0) out vec4 outColor;
    ```

2. The main function calculates the total number of screen pixels and compares our current counter with the number of pixels. The `gl_HelperInvocation` check helps us avoid touching the fragments list for any helper invocations of the fragment shader. If there is still space in the buffer, we increment the counter atomically and write out a new fragment. As we are not actually outputting anything to the frame buffer, we can use `discard` after updating the list:

    ```
    void main() {
      const uint maxPixels =
        uint(ubo.width) * uint(ubo.height);
      if (count < maxPixels &&
          gl_HelperInvocation == false) {
        uint idx = atomicAdd(count, 1);
        // exchange new head index and previous head index
        value[idx].idx = idx;
        value[idx].xx  = gl_FragCoord.x;
        value[idx].yy  = gl_FragCoord.y;
      }
      discard;
    }
    ```

Let's take a look at the C++ part:

1. The application class creates three Renderers – the GUI, the atomic buffer filler and the point list renderer – in the constructor:

```cpp
struct MyApp: public CameraApp {
  MyApp()
  : CameraApp(-80, -80, {
    .vertexPipelineStoresAndAtomics_ = true,
    .fragmentStoresAndAtomics_ = true })
  , sizeBuffer(ctx_.resources.addUniformBuffer(8))
  , atom(ctx_, sizeBuffer)
  , anim(ctx_, atom.getOutputs(), sizeBuffer)
  , imgui(ctx_, std::vector<VulkanTexture>{})
  {
    onScreenRenderers_.emplace_back(atom, false);
    onScreenRenderers_.emplace_back(anim, false);
    onScreenRenderers_.emplace_back(imgui, false);
```

2. The framebuffer dimensions are uploaded to the uniform buffer:

```cpp
struct WH {
    float w, h;
  } wh {
    (float)ctx_.vkDev.framebufferWidth,
    (float)ctx_.vkDev.framebufferHeight
  };
  uploadBufferData(ctx_.vkDev, sizeBuffer.memory,
    0, &wh, sizeof(wh));
}
```

3. The only thing we must do to render the frame is add a Settings window, with the slider configuring the percentage of rendered points:

```cpp
void draw3D() override {}
void drawUI() override {
  ImGui::Begin("Settings", nullptr);
  ImGui::SliderFloat("Percentage",
    &g_Percentage, 0.0f, 1.0f);
  ImGui::End();
}
```

```
private:
  VulkanBuffer sizeBuffer;
  AtomicRenderer atom;
  AnimRenderer anim;
  GuiRenderer imgui;
};
```

The visualization part is handled by another pair of GLSL shaders, `VK01_AtomicVisualize.frag` and `VK01_AtomicVisualize.vert`:

1. The `VK01_AtomicVisualize.vert` vertex shader goes through the list and calculates the position and color of the fragment. Darker colors correspond to the earliest fragments:

```
#version 460 core
struct node { uint idx; float xx, yy; };
layout (set = 0, binding = 0) buffer Values
  { node value[]; };
layout (set = 0, binding = 1) uniform UniformBuffer
  { float width; float height; } ubo;
layout(location = 0) out vec4 color;
void main() {
  node n = value[gl_VertexIndex];
  gl_Position = vec4(2 * (vec2(
    n.xx / ubo.width, n.yy / ubo.height) - vec2(.5)),
    0, 1);
  gl_PointSize = 1;
  color = vec4(
    (float(n.idx)/ubo.width) / ubo.height, 0, 0, 1);
}
```

2. The fragment shader outputs the color to the framebuffer:

```
#version 460 core
layout(location = 0) in vec4 color;
layout(location = 0) out vec4 outColor;
void main() {
  outColor = color;
}
```

Let's run the application. By manually dragging the slider from 0 to 1, we can slowly observe the order in which the GPU rasterizes these two triangles, as shown in the following screenshot:

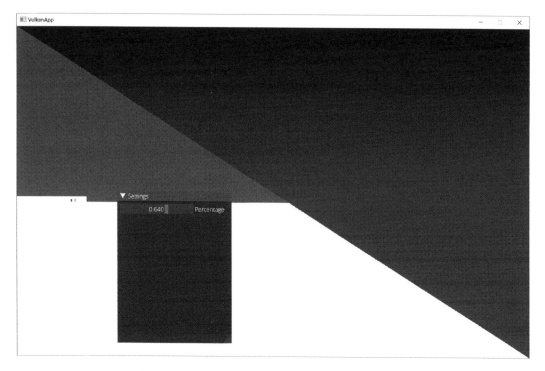

Figure 10.6 – Visualizing the order of fragments and their rasterization using Vulkan atomics

There's more...

Atomics can be used as building blocks for various GPU-based data structures. Order-independent transparency was another example of their use in this book.

This recipe was inspired by the following good old OpenGL demo: `https://www.geeks3d.com/20120309/opengl-4-2-atomic-counter-demo-rendering-order-of-fragments`.

Putting it all together into an OpenGL demo

To conclude our OpenGL rendering engine, let's combine the techniques from *Chapter 8, Image-Based Techniques, Chapter 9, Working with Scene Graphs*, and *Chapter 10, Advanced Rendering Techniques and Optimizations*, into a single application.

Our final OpenGL demo application renders the Lumberyard Bistro scene with the following techniques and effects:

- Screen-space ambient occlusion
- HDR rendering with light adaptation
- Directional shadow mapping with percentage closer filtering
- GPU frustum culling using compute shaders
- Order-independent transparency
- Asynchronously loading textures
- OpenGL bindless textures

Getting ready

Make sure you have a good grasp of all the recipes from this and the previous chapters.

The demo application for this recipe can be found in the `Chapter10/GL05_Final` folder.

How to do it...

We are already familiar with all the rendering techniques that will be used in this recipe, so let's quickly go through the C++ source code and highlight some parts that enable the interoperability of these techniques:

1. The `PerFrameData` structure combines everything we have into one place:

```
struct PerFrameData {
  mat4 view;
  mat4 proj;
  mat4 light;
  vec4 cameraPos;
  vec4 frustumPlanes[6];
  vec4 frustumCorners[8];
  uint32_t enableCulling;
};
```

2. Tweak the SSAO parameters for this specific scene. The structure layout remains the same so that we can work with the original GLSL shaders from the *Implementing SSAO in OpenGL* recipe:

```
struct SSAOParams {
   float scale_ = 1.5f;
   float bias_ = 0.15f;
   float zNear = 0.1f;
   float zFar = 1000.0f;
   float radius = 0.05f;
   float attScale = 1.01f;
   float distScale = 0.6f;
} g_SSAOParams;
static_assert(sizeof(SSAOParams) <=
   sizeof(PerFrameData));
```

3. The same applies to HDR and light adaptation, as described in the *Implementing HDR rendering and tone mapping* and *Implementing HDR light adaptation* recipes of *Chapter 8, Image-Based Techniques*:

```
struct HDRParams {
   float exposure_ = 0.9f;
   float maxWhite_ = 1.17f;
   float bloomStrength_ = 1.1f;
   float adaptationSpeed_ = 0.1f;
} g_HDRParams;
static_assert(
   sizeof(HDRParams) <= sizeof(PerFrameData));
```

4. There are a bunch of values that are controlled by ImGui:

```
mat4 g_CullingView = camera.getViewMatrix();
bool g_EnableGPUCulling = true;
bool g_FreezeCullingView = false;
bool g_DrawOpaque = true;
bool g_DrawTransparent = true;
bool g_DrawGrid = true;
bool g_EnableSSAO = true;
bool g_EnableBlur = true;
bool g_EnableHDR = true;
bool g_DrawBoxes = false;
bool g_EnableShadows = true;
bool g_ShowLightFrustum = false;
float g_LightTheta = 0.0f;
float g_LightPhi = 0.0f;
```

5. The `main()` function starts by loading all the shaders we need:

```
int main(void) {
  GLApp app;
  // grid
  GLShader shdGridVert(
    "data/shaders/chapter05/GL01_grid.vert");
  GLShader shdGridFrag(
    "data/shaders/chapter05/GL01_grid.frag");
  GLProgram progGrid(shdGridVert, shdGridFrag);
  // scene
  GLShader shaderVert(
    "data/shaders/chapter10/GL01_scene_IBL.vert");
  GLShader shaderFrag(
    "data/shaders/chapter10/GL01_scene_IBL.frag");
  GLProgram program(shaderVert, shaderFrag);
  // generic postprocessing
  GLShader shdFullScreenQuadVert(
    "data/shaders/chapter08/GL02_FullScreenQuad.vert");
  // OIT
  GLShader shaderFragOIT(
    "data/shaders/chapter10/GL03_mesh_oit.frag");
  GLProgram programOIT(shaderVert, shaderFragOIT);
  GLShader shdCombineOIT(
    "data/shaders/chapter10/GL03_OIT.frag");
  GLProgram progCombineOIT(
    shdFullScreenQuadVert, shdCombineOIT);
  // GPU culling
  GLShader shaderCulling(
    "data/shaders/chapter10/GL02_FrustumCulling.comp");
  GLProgram programCulling(shaderCulling);
  // SSAO
  GLShader shdSSAOFrag(
    "data/shaders/chapter08/GL02_SSAO.frag");
  GLShader shdCombineSSAOFrag(
    "data/shaders/chapter08/GL02_SSAO_combine.frag");
  GLProgram progSSAO(
    shdFullScreenQuadVert, shdSSAOFrag);
  GLProgram progCombineSSAO(
    shdFullScreenQuadVert, shdCombineSSAOFrag);
  // blur
```

```
GLShader shdBlurXFrag(
  "data/shaders/chapter08/GL02_BlurX.frag");
GLShader shdBlurYFrag(
  "data/shaders/chapter08/GL02_BlurY.frag");
GLProgram progBlurX(
  shdFullScreenQuadVert, shdBlurXFrag);
GLProgram progBlurY(
  shdFullScreenQuadVert, shdBlurYFrag);
// HDR
GLShader shdCombineHDR(
  "data/shaders/chapter08/GL03_HDR.frag");
GLProgram progCombineHDR(
  shdFullScreenQuadVert, shdCombineHDR);
GLShader shdToLuminance(
  "data/shaders/chapter08/GL03_ToLuminance.frag");
GLProgram progToLuminance(
  shdFullScreenQuadVert, shdToLuminance);
GLShader shdBrightPass(
  "data/shaders/chapter08/GL03_BrightPass.frag");
GLProgram progBrightPass(
  shdFullScreenQuadVert, shdBrightPass);
GLShader shdAdaptation(
  "data/shaders/chapter08/GL03_Adaptation.comp");
GLProgram progAdaptation(shdAdaptation);
// shadows
GLShader shdShadowVert(
  "data/shaders/chapter10/GL05_shadow.vert");
GLShader shdShadowFrag(
  "data/shaders/chapter10/GL05_shadow.frag");
GLProgram progShadowMap(
  shdShadowVert, shdShadowFrag);
```

6. To make sure different techniques work together, we should be careful in terms of the binding points for our buffers:

```
const GLsizeiptr kBoundingBoxesBufferSize =
  sizeof(BoundingBox) * kMaxNumObjects;
const GLuint kBufferIndex_BoundingBoxes =
  kBufferIndex_PerFrameUniforms + 1;
const GLuint kBufferIndex_DrawCommands =
  kBufferIndex_PerFrameUniforms + 2;
const GLuint kBufferIndex_NumVisibleMeshes =
  kBufferIndex_PerFrameUniforms + 3;
```

7. The actual buffers' declaration code is skipped for brevity. Now, let's make sure we lazy load the scene data and reuse the skybox, canvas, and UI rendering code. The rotation pattern texture is used for SSAO:

```
GLSceneDataLazy sceneData(
  "data/meshes/bistro_all.meshes",
  "data/meshes/bistro_all.scene",
  "data/meshes/bistro_all.materials");
GLMesh mesh(sceneData);
GLSkyboxRenderer skybox;
ImGuiGLRenderer rendererUI;
CanvasGL canvas;
GLTexture rotationPattern(
  GL_TEXTURE_2D, "data/rot_texture.bmp");
```

8. The OIT setup code is identical to the source code from the *Implementing order-independent transparency* recipe. What we want to do differently here is create two helper functions for ImGui rendering. These lambdas push and pop ImGui flags and styles based on the provided Boolean value so that parts of our UI can be enabled and disabled:

```
auto imGuiPushFlagsAndStyles = [](bool value) {
  ImGui::PushItemFlag(
    ImGuiItemFlags_Disabled, !value);
  ImGui::PushStyleVar(ImGuiStyleVar_Alpha,
    ImGui::GetStyle().Alpha * value ? 1.0f : 0.2f);
};
auto imGuiPopFlagsAndStyles = []() {
  ImGui::PopItemFlag();
  ImGui::PopStyleVar();
};
```

9. To render the shadow map in shades of gray, let's use the OpenGL texture swizzling functionality. This way, a single value from an R8 texture is duplicated into three RGB channels. Compare the shadow map's output in this example to the one from the previous chapter:

```
GLFramebuffer shadowMap(
  8192, 8192, GL_R8, GL_DEPTH_COMPONENT24);
const GLint swizzleMask[] =
  { GL_RED, GL_RED, GL_RED, GL_ONE };
```

```
glTextureParameteriv(
  shadowMap.getTextureColor().getHandle(),
  GL_TEXTURE_SWIZZLE_RGBA, swizzleMask);
glTextureParameteriv(
  shadowMap.getTextureDepth().getHandle(),
  GL_TEXTURE_SWIZZLE_RGBA, swizzleMask);
```

10. Inside the main loop, we will use the FPS counter we implemented in the *Adding a frames-per-second counter* recipe of *Chapter 4, Adding User Interaction and Productivity Tools*:

```
FramesPerSecondCounter fpsCounter(0.5f);
while (!glfwWindowShouldClose(app.getWindow())) {
  fpsCounter.tick(app.getDeltaSeconds());
  if (sceneData.uploadLoadedTextures())
    mesh.updateMaterialsBuffer(sceneData);
  ...
```

11. The following snippet renders a nice ImGUI user interface for our application:

```
const float indentSize = 16.0f;
ImGuiIO& io = ImGui::GetIO();
io.DisplaySize =
  ImVec2((float)width, (float)height);
ImGui::NewFrame();
ImGui::Begin("Control", nullptr);
ImGui::Text("Transparency:");
ImGui::Indent(indentSize);
ImGui::Checkbox("Opaque meshes", &g_DrawOpaque);
ImGui::Checkbox("Transparent meshes",
  &g_DrawTransparent);
ImGui::Unindent(indentSize);
ImGui::Separator();
ImGui::Text("GPU culling:");
ImGui::Indent(indentSize);
ImGui::Checkbox("Enable GPU culling",
  &g_EnableGPUCulling);
imGuiPushFlagsAndStyles(g_EnableGPUCulling);
ImGui::Checkbox("Freeze culling frustum (P)",
  &g_FreezeCullingView);
ImGui::Text("Visible meshes: %i",
  *numVisibleMeshesPtr);
```

```
imGuiPopFlagsAndStyles();
ImGui::Unindent(indentSize);
ImGui::Separator();
ImGui::Text("SSAO:");
ImGui::Indent(indentSize);
ImGui::Checkbox("Enable SSAO", &g_EnableSSAO);
imGuiPushFlagsAndStyles(g_EnableSSAO);
ImGui::Checkbox("Enable SSAO blur",
  &g_EnableBlur);
ImGui::SliderFloat("SSAO scale",
  &g_SSAOParams.scale_, 0.0f, 2.0f);
ImGui::SliderFloat("SSAO bias",
  &g_SSAOParams.bias_, 0.0f, 0.3f);
ImGui::SliderFloat("SSAO radius",
  &g_SSAOParams.radius, 0.02f, 0.2f);
ImGui::SliderFloat("SSAO attenuation scale",
  &g_SSAOParams.attScale, 0.5f, 1.5f);
ImGui::SliderFloat("SSAO distance scale",
  &g_SSAOParams.distScale, 0.0f, 1.0f);
imGuiPopFlagsAndStyles();
ImGui::Unindent(indentSize);
ImGui::Separator();
ImGui::Text("HDR:");
ImGui::Indent(indentSize);
ImGui::Checkbox("Enable HDR", &g_EnableHDR);
imGuiPushFlagsAndStyles(g_EnableHDR);
ImGui::SliderFloat("Exposure",
  &g_HDRParams.exposure_, 0.1f, 2.0f);
ImGui::SliderFloat("Max white",
  &g_HDRParams.maxWhite_, 0.5f, 2.0f);
ImGui::SliderFloat("Bloom strength",
  &g_HDRParams.bloomStrength_, 0.0f, 2.0f);
ImGui::SliderFloat("Adaptation speed",
  &g_HDRParams.adaptationSpeed_, 0.01f, 0.5f);
imGuiPopFlagsAndStyles();
ImGui::Unindent(indentSize);
ImGui::Separator();
ImGui::Text("Shadows:");
ImGui::Indent(indentSize);
```

```
ImGui::Checkbox("Enable shadows",
  &g_EnableShadows);
imGuiPushFlagsAndStyles(g_EnableShadows);
ImGui::Checkbox("Show light's frustum (red) and
  scene AABB (white)",&g_ShowLightFrustum);
ImGui::SliderFloat("Light Theta",
  &g_LightTheta, -85.0f, +85.0f);
ImGui::SliderFloat("Light Phi",
  &g_LightPhi, -85.0f, +85.0f);
imGuiPopFlagsAndStyles();
ImGui::Unindent(indentSize);
ImGui::Separator();
ImGui::Checkbox("Grid", &g_DrawGrid);
ImGui::Checkbox("Bounding boxes (all)",
  &g_DrawBoxes);
ImGui::End();
```

12. Render the debug windows with the SSAO results and the shadow map:

```
if (g_EnableSSAO)
   imguiTextureWindowGL("SSAO",
     ssao.getTextureColor().getHandle());
if (g_EnableShadows)
   imguiTextureWindowGL("Shadow Map",
     shadowMap.getTextureDepth().getHandle());
ImGui::Render();
rendererUI.render(
  width, height, ImGui::GetDrawData());
...
app.swapBuffers();
}
glUnmapNamedBuffer(
  numVisibleMeshesBuffer.getHandle());
glDeleteTextures(1, &luminance1x1);
return 0;
}
```

The demo application should render the Lumberyard Bistro scene like so:

Figure 10.7 – The final OpenGL demo

Try running the demo and playing with the different UI controls.

And with that, we can conclude our OpenGL examples. By the way, we made a similar Vulkan demo in the `Chapter10/VK02_Final` project.

There's more...

The possibilities here are endless. You can use this framework to experiment with more advanced rendering techniques. Adding more complex screen space effects, such as temporal antialiasing or screen-space reflections, should be relatively easy. Integrating texture compression into the final demo can be yet another interesting exercise. Adding multiple light sources can be achieved by storing their parameters in a buffer and iterating over it in a fragment shader. Various optimizations are possible here, such as tile deferred shading or clustered shading: `http://www.cse.chalmers.se/~uffe/clustered_shading_preprint.pdf`.

The easiest way to accommodate shadows from multiple light sources in this demo would be to use separate shadow maps and access them via bindless textures. Going deeper into complex materials rendering might be yet another vast direction in which to explore. A good starting point could be converting the Bistro scene materials into PBR and using the glTF2 rendering code from *Chapter 6, Physically-Based Rendering Using the glTF2 Shading Model*, to render them properly. If you decide to go in this direction and learn more about the practical side of PBR rendering, the documentation for the Filament engine is an awesome source to explore: `https://google.github.io/filament/Filament.html`.

Packt.com

Subscribe to our online digital library for full access to over 7,000 books and videos, as well as industry leading tools to help you plan your personal development and advance your career. For more information, please visit our website.

Why subscribe?

- Spend less time learning and more time coding with practical eBooks and Videos from over 4,000 industry professionals

- Improve your learning with Skill Plans built especially for you

- Get a free eBook or video every month

- Fully searchable for easy access to vital information

- Copy and paste, print, and bookmark content

Did you know that Packt offers eBook versions of every book published, with PDF and ePub files available? You can upgrade to the eBook version at packt.com and as a print book customer, you are entitled to a discount on the eBook copy. Get in touch with us at customercare@packtpub.com for more details.

At www.packt.com, you can also read a collection of free technical articles, sign up for a range of free newsletters, and receive exclusive discounts and offers on Packt books and eBooks.

Other Books You May Enjoy

If you enjoyed this book, you may be interested in these other books by Packt:

OpenGL 4 Shading Language Cookbook

David Wolff

ISBN: 978-1-78934-225-3

- Compile, debug, and communicate with shader programs
- Use compute shaders for physics, animation, and general computing
- Learn about features such as shader storage buffer objects and image load/store
- Utilize noise in shaders and learn how to use shaders in animations
- Use textures for various effects including cube maps for reflection or refraction
- Understand physically based reflection models and the SPIR-V Shader binary
- Learn how to create shadows using shadow maps or shadow volumes
- Create particle systems that simulate smoke, fire, and other effects

Vulkan Cookbook

Pawel Lapinski

ISBN: 978-1-78646-815-4

- Work with Swapchain to present images on screen

- Create, submit, and synchronize operations processed by the hardware

- Create buffers and images, manage their memory, and upload data to them from CPU

- Explore descriptor sets and set up an interface between application and shaders

- Organize drawing operations into a set of render passes and subpasses

- Prepare graphics pipelines to draw 3D scenes and compute pipelines to perform mathematical calculations

- Implement geometry projection and tessellation, texturing, lighting, and post-processing techniques

- Write shaders in GLSL and convert them into SPIR-V assemblies

- Find out about and implement a collection of popular, advanced rendering techniques found in games and benchmarks

Packt is searching for authors like you

If you're interested in becoming an author for Packt, please visit `authors.packtpub.com` and apply today. We have worked with thousands of developers and tech professionals, just like you, to help them share their insight with the global tech community. You can make a general application, apply for a specific hot topic that we are recruiting an author for, or submit your own idea.

Share Your Thoughts

Now you've finished *3D Graphics Rendering Cookbook*, we'd love to hear your thoughts! Scan the QR code below to go straight to the Amazon review page for this book and share your feedback or leave a review on the site that you purchased it from.

`https://packt.link/r/< 1838986197>`

Your review is important to us and the tech community and will help us make sure we're delivering excellent quality content.

Index